# Handbook of International and Intercultural Communication

Editors
**Molefi Kete Asante**
**William B. Gudykunst**

*with the assistance of*
*Eileen Newmark*

**SAGE PUBLICATIONS**
*The International Professional Publishers*
Newbury Park   London   New Delhi

*For information address:*

SAGE Publications, Inc.
2111 West Hillcrest Drive
Newbury Park, California 91320

SAGE Publications Ltd.
28 Banner Street
London EC1Y 8QE
England

SAGE Publications India Pvt. Ltd.
M-32 Market
Greater Kailash I
New Delhi 110 048 India

Printed in the United States of America

Library of Congress Cataloging-in-Publication Data

Main entry under title:

Handbook of international and intercultural communication / edited by
   Molefi Kete Asante and William B. Gudykunst, with the assistance of
   Eileen Newmark.
      p.     cm.
   Includes index.
   ISBN 0-8039-3202-2
      1. Communication, International.     2. Intercultural communication.
   I. Asante, Molefi K., 1942-      II. Gudykunst, William B.
   III. Newmark, Eileen.
   P96.I5H37     1989
   302.2—dc19                                                      88-32672
   SECOND PRINTING, 1990                                            CIP

# Contents

## Part III: Contexts

## Part IV: Research Issues

# Preface

The purpose of this volume is to summarize the state of the art on international, intercultural, and development communication and set the agenda for future research in the three areas. International, intercultural, and development communication have developed as separate, but inter-related areas of research. The tie that binds the three areas of research together is that each is concerned with the interrelationship between communication and culture. While culture and communication are related reciprocally, the focus of the vast majority of the chapters in this volume is on one side of this relationship, the influence of culture on communication. Before discussing the contents of the present volume, a brief historical overview is necessary to place it in context.

The term *intercultural communication* appears to have been first used by Edward T. Hall (1959) in his classic book *The Silent Language*. The appearance of Hall's book stimulated the study of intercultural communication, but it cannot be said that the field began with its publication. Intercultural research that included the examination of communication, but did not focus on it, existed prior to this time. A program of research on intercultural adjustment, for example, was begun in the early 1950s.

If the conception of the field of intercultural communication took place in the 1950s, its birth was in the 1970s. Several distinct, but interrelated, events occurred during this period, making it possible for the serious study of international and intercultural communication to begin. In the early 1970s, the Speech Communication Association created a Commission on International and Intercultural Communication (it became a division in the mid-1980s) and the International Communication Association formed an Intercultural Communication Division (its title was changed to include "Development" in the middle 1980s). Also, the first volume of *The International and Intercultural Communication Annual*, edited by Fred Casmir, appeared in 1974 (see Casmir, 1974-1976; Jain, 1977-1983), and the *International Journal of Intercultural Relations*, edited by Dan Landis, began publication in 1977. Finally, *The Handbook of Intercultural Com-*

7

*munication*, edited by Molefi Asante, Cecil Blake, and Eileen Newmark, was published in 1979.

The field has changed considerably during its adolescence in the 1980s. In 1983, for example, the *International and Intercultural Communication Annual* altered its editorial policy and began focusing on specific topics for each volume. The first thematic volume focused on theory (Gudykunst, 1983; this theme also was the focus of a 1988 volume: Kim & Gudykunst, 1988b) and the second focused on research methods (Gudykunst & Kim, 1984). Other volumes have focused on communication, culture, and organizational processes (Gudykunst, Stewart, & Ting-Toomey, 1985); interethnic communication (Kim, 1986); cross-cultural adaptation (Kim & Gudykunst, 1988a); and communication, language, and culture (Ting-Toomey & Korzenny, in press). A volume on diplomacy and negotiation across cultures (Korzenny & Ting-Toomey, in press) is being prepared at this writing. These volumes focused attention on specific issues related to the development of the field. The first thematic volume on theory, for example, emphasized the need for theorizing and stimulated the development of several theories included in Volume 12 (Kim & Gudykunst, 1988b). The thematic volumes also have attracted contributors from numerous academic disciplines thereby increasing awareness of what scholars in the various disciplines are doing vis-à-vis international and intercultural communication.

In addition to the thematic volumes of the *International and Intercultural Communication Annual*, numerous scholarly books have been published in the last decade (see the chapter references in this volume for specific citations). Extensive theoretically based and methodologically sound research on international and intercultural communication also has been published in *Human Communication Research*, *Communication Monographs*, *Journal of Communication*, *International Journal of Intercultural Relations*, *Journal of Black Studies*, and *Journal of Language and Social Psychology*, among others, in recent years. The theory and research published in recent years has provided the foundation for significant advances in the study of international and intercultural communication.

As the preceding overview indicates, there have been advances in theory and research on international and intercultural communication during the 1980s. At the same time, there also have been extensive changes in the applied arena as well. The earth has become an even smaller place than McLuhan anticipated. The international community is now the local neighborhood for people in many parts of the world and nations have become more and more interdependent over the last decade. This interdependence is, in part, responsible for the debate surrounding the New World Information and Communication Order and the role of communication in national development. Within nations, changes also are occurring with respect to communication between numbers of different cultural/ethnic/racial groups. Racial incidents on university campuses in the United States and interethnic confrontations in other countries (e.g., China, Japan, Yugoslavia, the Soviet Union) have increased in recent years. Scholars interested in international, intercultural, and development communication cannot avoid becoming involved in finding solutions for these critical applied issues.

The present volume is meant to capture some of the intellectual excitement around the theoretical advances that have occurred and the application of these advances to the practical issues confronting scholars in the field. We hope it will help to frame the critical issues facing scholars studying international and intercultural communication, stimulate new theoretical formulations, demonstrate the application of diverse methods of research, and provide the basis for finding solutions for critical issues facing the world.

The contents of this volume clearly indicate that the study of culture and communication is not one unified field of inquiry. Figure P.1 presents two dimensions that differentiate the various areas of inquiry: interactive-comparative and mediated-interpersonal. Quadrant I represents intercultural communication research; that is, interpersonal communication between members of different cultures, races, or ethnic groups. Quadrant II represents cross-cultural communication or a comparison of patterns of interpersonal communication across cultures. Quadrants III and IV differ from Quadrants I and II in that the channel of communication is mediated, not interpersonal. Research in Quadrant III focuses on mediated communication from one culture to another, research typically labeled international communication. Quadrant IV, in contrast, involves comparisons of media systems across cultures (i.e., comparative mass communication).

The areas of inquiry outlined in Figure P.1 are relatively inclusive, but some areas of research are not readily incorporated. Research on the effects of television on minorities, for example, has objectives similar to research in international communication, but the research generally occurs within one culture. Because areas of research overlap the four quadrants, we have not used them as an organizing schema for the volume. Rather, we have organized the volume into four parts: Overviews (I), Processes and Effects (II), Contexts (III), and Research Issues (IV).

The first part contains overviews of the major theoretical and applied issues in the study of international and intercultural communication. Gudykunst and Nishida (Chapter 1) examine the major theoretical perspectives used to explain intercultural communication. McPhail (Chapter 2) and Rogers (Chapter 3) overview the major issues involved in studying international and development communication, respectively. This part concludes with Nordenstreng and Kleinwächter's (Chapter 4) history of

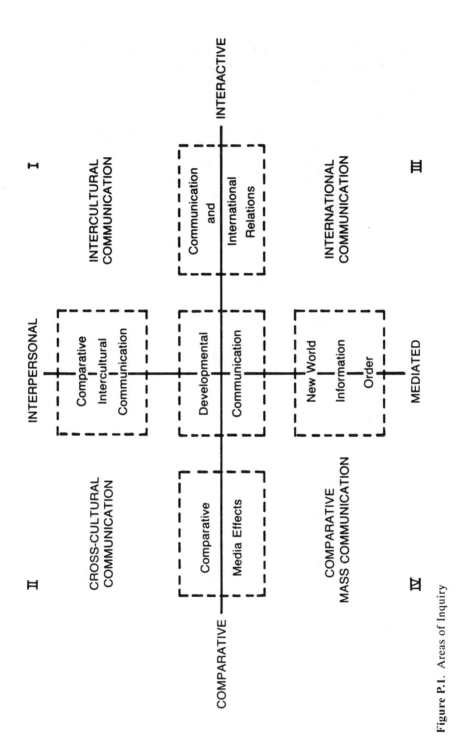

**Figure P.1.** Areas of Inquiry

10

the issues involved in the New International Information and Communication Order debate.

Part II comprises chapters that address processes and effects in international and intercultural communication. The first three chapters focus on channels of communication. Giles and Franklyn-Stokes (Chapter 5) examine characteristics of communicators that affect intercultural communication, including the characteristic of language spoken. Gudykunst, Ting-Toomey, Hall, and Schmidt's (Chapter 6) essay on language and intergroup communication also focuses on language. There is some overlap between the research reviewed in this chapter and in the Giles and Franklyn-Stokes's chapter, but the emphasis is different (though complementary): Giles and Franklyn-Stokes emphasize language spoken as an independent variable, while Gudykunst and his associates focus on language issues as dependent variables. In the third chapter in this part, Hecht, Andersen, and Ribeau (Chapter 7) examine the cultural dimensions of nonverbal communication.

The next group of chapters in Part II examine basic processes. Weimann (Chapter 8) reviews research on social networks and communication and lays out a model for studying cross-level networks. Social cognitive and emotional aspects of intercultural communication are examined in Chapters 9 (Gudykunst and Gumbs) and 10 (Matsumoto, Wallbott, and Scherer), respectively. Hammer (Chapter 11) discusses the process of becoming competent in intercultural communication, while Pennington (Chapter 12) assesses the role of interpersonal power and the influence process on intercultural communication.

The final chapters in Part II are devoted to effects or outcomes. In Chapter 13, Kim summarizes research and theory on intercultural adaptation. The effects of media across cultures and across ethnic groups within a culture are examined in Chapters 14 (Yaple and Korzenny) and 15 (Gandy and Matabane), respectively.

Part III is devoted to the contexts of international and intercultural communication. Ting-Toomey (Chapter 16) focuses on intercultural communication in the context of interpersonal bonds. The interracial workplace and international marketplace are examined in Chapters 17 (Asante and Davis) and Chapter 18 (Shuter), respectively. Fisher (Chapter 19) looks at the diplomatic context, while Awa (Chapter 20) examines the development context. This part concludes with Brislin's (Chapter 21) assessment of intercultural communication training.

Part IV focuses on issues of conducting research on culture, language, and communication. Johnson and Tuttle (Chapter 22) examine the research process in toto, while Gonzalez (Chapter 23) focuses on the issue of translation.

Taken together, the chapters in this volume reveal that significant progress has been made in understanding international and intercultural communication in recent years. Much of this progress is due to the formation of bi- or multicultural research teams that have begun lines of research examining variations in mediated and interpersonal communication across cultures (comparative mass communication and cross-cultural communication, respectively), as well as communication between members of different cultures using interpersonal and mediated channels (intercultural and international communication, respectively). While progress has been made in recent years, much remains to be done. If the present volume stimulates future theorizing and/or research on international and intercultural communication, it will have been successful.

Before concluding, we want to take this opportunity to thank those who have assisted in the preparation of this volume. To begin, we want to express our appreciation to the staff at Sage Publications for bringing us together to edit this volume and Everett Rogers for assisting us in finalizing the original outline. We also want to thank colleagues and students in the Department of African American Studies at Temple University and the Department of Communication at Arizona State University for providing supportive environments in which to work. Our greatest debt of gratitude, however, is to the authors of the chapters; without them this volume would not have been possible. While some were late (we won't mention any names), all came through in time for their work to be included. Finally, Molefi wants to thank Nadia Kravchenko for her assistance in preparing the volume and Bill wants to thank Sandy for helping him to keep the volume in perspective and remember that it is not a big deal if it is a little late.

—Molefi Kete Asante
—William B. Gudykunst

## REFERENCES

Asante, M. K., Blake, C., & Newmark, E. (Eds.). (1979). *Handbook of intercultural communication*. Beverly Hills, CA: Sage.

Casmir, F. (Ed.). (1974-1976). *International and intercultural communication annual* (Vols. 1-3). Annandale, VA: Speech Communication Association.

Gudykunst, W. B. (Ed.). (1983). *Intercultural communication theory*. Beverly Hills, CA: Sage.

Gudykunst, W. B. (1987). Cross-cultural comparisons. In C. Berger & S. Schaffee (Eds.), *Handbook of communication science*. Newbury Park, CA: Sage.

Gudykunst, W. B., & Kim, Y. Y. (Eds.). (1984). *Methods for intercultural communication research*. Beverly Hills, CA: Sage.

Gudykunst, W. B., Stewart, L., & Ting-Toomey, S. (Eds.). (1985). *Communication, culture, and organizational processes*. Beverly Hills, CA: Sage.

Hall, E. T. (1959). *The silent language*. New York: Doubleday.

Jain, N. (Ed.). (1977-1983). *International and intercultural communication annual* (Vols. 4-6). Annandale, VA: Speech Communication Association.

Kim, Y. Y. (Ed.). (1986). *Interethnic communication*. Beverly Hills, CA: Sage.

Kim, Y. Y., & Gudykunst, W. B. (Eds.). (1988a). *Cross-cultural adaptation*. Newbury Park, CA: Sage.

Kim, Y. Y., & Gudykunst, W. B. (Eds.). (1988b). *Theories in intercultural communication*. Newbury Park, CA: Sage.

Korzenny, F., & Ting-Toomey, S. (Eds.). (in press). *Communication for peace*. Newbury Park, CA: Sage.

Ting-Toomey, S., & Korzenny, F. (Eds.). (in press). *Language, culture, and communication*. Newbury Park, CA: Sage.

# Part I

Overviews

# 1 Theoretical Perspectives for Studying Intercultural Communication

### William B. Gudykunst
### Tsukasa Nishida

> Theories are nets: only he [or she] who casts will catch.
> —*Novalis*

> A good theory is one that holds together long enough
> to get you to a better one.
> —*Anonymous*

The purpose of this chapter is to overview the major theoretical perspectives used to study cross-cultural and intercultural communication. Formulating theories of communication between members of different cultures and/or theories of the influence of culture on communication is a relatively recent phenomenon. The recent emergence of theories in intercultural communication, however, should not be taken to imply that there are only a few theories or that these theories lack sophistication. A plethora of well-developed theoretical perspectives has emerged in the last decade.

Popper (1968, p. 59) argues that theories "are nets cast to catch what we call 'the world': to rationalize, to explain, to master it. We endeavor to make the mesh ever finer and finer." Theories, therefore, help us to understand and to predict the phenomena we are studying (Dubin, 1969). Dubin contends that prediction is concerned with outcomes and understanding involves relationships between variables/concepts.[1] All theoretical perspectives used to explain intercultural communication or the

AUTHORS' NOTE: We want to thank Stella Ting-Toomey for her comments on an earlier version of this chapter.

17

relationship between culture and communication strive for understanding, but proponents of the various approaches often disagree over what constitutes understanding (e.g., they state their theories in different forms, have different goals, and/or focus on different levels of analysis). There also is disagreement among the advocates of the major perspectives over the possibility and/or desirability of prediction as a goal in theory construction. To clarify the differences in the perspectives, we begin by presenting a taxonomy of the approaches used to theorize about intercultural communication.

## A TAXONOMY OF PERSPECTIVES

We use two orthogonal dimensions (assumptions about the nature of social science—"subjectivist" versus "objectivist"—and the origin of the theory—adapted from a communication theory, borrowed from another discipline, or "invented" specifically to deal with intercultural phenomena) to develop a taxonomy of perspectives used to study intercultural communication. The assumptions theorists make regarding social science are a function of the paradigms they use. Kuhn (1970, p. 10) contends that paradigms exist when "accepted examples of actual scientific practice— examples which include law, theory, application, and instrumentation together—provide models from which spring particular coherent traditions of scientific research." He goes on to argue that a paradigm is necessary for researchers to engage in "normal science."

Burrell and Morgan (1979) use the term *paradigm* more broadly than Kuhn to refer to a set of metatheoretical assumptions regarding the nature of science and society. They isolate two contrasting sets of assumptions regarding the nature of social science: the subjectivist (or interpretivist) and the objectivist (for alternative distinctions, see Cronen & Davis, 1978; Cushman & Pearce, 1977; also see the contributions in Fiske & Shweder, 1986; Kruskal, 1982; Secord, 1982).[2] "Subjectivists" take a nonrealist position regarding ontology and an antipositivist position on epistemology, they see human nature as voluntaristic, and they use idiographic methodology (see Table 1.1 for descriptions of these positions). "Objectivists," in contrast, take a realist position regarding ontology and a positivist position on epistemology, they see human nature as deterministic, and they use nomothetic methodology.

The assumptions presented in Table 1.1 are extreme statements of the positions. While Burrell and Morgan (1979) present the two positions on the four issues as dichotomies, we believe it is more useful to view them as the end points of continuums. Further, it should be noted that few, if any, communication scholars take an extreme position on any of the issues.

**TABLE 1.1** Assumptions About the Nature of Social Science

| *Subjectivist Approach* | *Objectivist Approach* |
| --- | --- |
| Ontology: | |
| *Nominalism:* There is no "real" world external to individual; "names," "concepts," and "labels" are artificial and used to construct reality. | *Realism:* There is a "real" world external to the individual; things exist, even if they are not perceived and labeled. |
| Epistemology: | |
| *Antipositivism:* Communication can only be understood from the perspective of the individual communicators; no search for underlying regularities. | *Positivism:* Attempts to explain and predict patterns of communication by looking for regularities and/or causal relationships. |
| Human Nature: | |
| *Voluntarism:* Communicators are completely "autonomous" and have "free-will." | *Determinism:* Communication is "determined" by the "situation" or "environment" in which it occurs. |
| Methodology: | |
| *Ideographic:* To understand communication, "firsthand knowledge" must be attained; analysis of subjective accounts. | *Nomothetic:* Research should be based on systematic protocols and scientific rigor. |

NOTE: These are "extreme" statements of the assumptions drawn from Burrell and Morgan (1979, pp. 3-7).

To our knowledge, for example, there is no objective communication theory that assumes the extreme deterministic position; all theories allow for some degree of voluntarism. Similarly, no subjective theorist assumes an extreme position vis-à-vis antipositivism; such a position would not allow for coordinated action or culture to exist.

Objectivists argue that the goal of social science is to develop "universal generalizations." Nagel (1961), for example, maintains that it is possible to discover "social laws" that are valid across cultures and time periods. Subjectivists, in contrast, contend that universal generalizations are not the sine qua non of science. To illustrate, Geertz (1973) suggests that the goal of social science should be to provide "thick descriptions"; that is, social scientists should understand specific cases and not generalize across cases.

When the objective and subjective approaches to theory are contrasted with approaches to cross-cultural research, the objective approach often appears to be equated with "etic" cross-cultural research and the subjective approach, with "emic" research. The distinction between the emic and etic approaches to cross-cultural research can be traced to Pike's (1966) discussion of phonetics (vocal utterances that are universal) and phonemics (culturally specific vocal utterances). Brislin (1983), however, argues that in current usage the distinction is employed as a metaphor for differences between the culture-specific (emic, single culture) and culture-general (etic, universal) approaches to research. Berry (1980, pp. 11-12) presented a succinct summary of the distinction:

| Emic | Etic |
|---|---|
| studies behavior from within the system | studies behavior for a position outside the system |
| examines only one culture | examines many cultures, comparing them |
| structure discovered by the analyst | structure created by the analyst |
| criteria are relative to internal characteristics | criteria are considered absolute or universal (pp. 11-12) |

While emic research generally is subjective in nature, there is a tendency for recent cultural analyses to be more objective than earlier work (see Wuthnow, 1987; Wuthnow, Hunter, Bergesen, & Kurzweil, 1984). Further, research that appears totally emic, such as the ethnography of communication, has an etic component (i.e., the categories the ethnographer uses for observation; Philipsen, 1988). It also should be noted that while most people view the emic and etic approaches as opposite ends of a continuum, attempts have been made to integrate the two approaches. Triandis (1972), for example, recommends that when studying subjective culture researchers should utilize combined emic and etic measures. Specifically, attributes of concepts under study should be elicited in all cultures studied and both unique (emic) and common (etic) attributes should be included.

The objective and subjective approaches tend to be treated as opposing paradigms, but they are not incompatible. When objective and subjective theories are compared at the same level of analysis, their assumptions appear to be inconsistent. When the different levels of analysis are taken into consideration, however, the assumptions may not be incompatible. Further, subjective methods can be used to test objective theories. Triandis and his associates (1984), for example, used an idiographic methodology to test objective predictions. Objective and subjective approaches can and should be integrated (we discuss this issue in the conclusion). The distinction between the two approaches, however, is useful in differentiating among the major theoretical perspectives used to study intercultural communication and, therefore, we use it in developing our typology.

The second dimension we use to generate our taxonomy of perspectives for the study of intercultural communication is the origin of the theory. There are at least three sources for generating theory in intercultural communication. First, theory can be developed by extending communication theories designed to explain *intra*cultural communication. Second, explanations of intercultural communication can be generated utilizing theories developed in other disciplines involving isomorphic social processes. At times, the first two approaches are difficult to separate because many theories of communication are borrowed from other disciplines. Finally, theory can be developed anew based upon research conducted specifically on intercultural communication.

The combination of the objective versus subjective approaches and the origins of the theory (i.e., from communication, from another discipline, or developed anew) yields a taxonomy of six approaches to developing theory in intercultural communication. The major perspectives for the study of intercultural communication will be overviewed using the taxonomy. First, each perspective is classified as to whether the theory uses an objective or subjective approach. Next, perspectives that are extensions of a communication theory, borrowed from another discipline, or developed anew are identified within these general approaches. An exemplar of a theory in each category is presented and summarized (see Tables 1.2 through 1.7 below).[3]

## OBJECTIVE PERSPECTIVES

Objective studies of cross-cultural variations in communication traditionally have compared specific cultures. When integrating culture with a theory of communication, however, this leads to treating culture as an "atheoretical" concept. Foschi and Hales (1979, pp. 246-247) describe the theoretical and atheoretical approaches to treating culture as a variable:

> In the first, or theoretical use, a culture X and culture Y serve to operationally define a characteristic *a*, which the two cultures exhibit to different degrees, and which is usually the independent variable in the study. The second, or atheoretical use, can be described as follows: the fact that the subjects are from culture X constitutes an experimental limitation, and the researcher is attempting to explore its effect on the dependent variable by also doing the experiment with subjects from culture Y.

Specific cultural differences, therefore, are not of interest in theory construction. Rather, using cultural differences as operationalizations of dimensions of cultural variability (e.g., individualism versus collectivism) is necessary to treat culture theoretically.

Several dimensions of cultural variability can be used in constructing theories. Hofstede (1980), for example, empirically derived four dimensions: individualism-collectivism, power distance, uncertainty avoidance, and masculinity-femininity. Individualistic cultures emphasize the individual's goals, while collectivistic cultures stress that group goals have precedence over individual goals. High power-distance cultures value inequality, with everyone having a "rightful place," and the hierarchy reflects existential inequality. Low power-distance cultures, in contrast, value equality. Uncertainty avoidance involves the lack of tolerance for uncertainty and ambiguity. Cultures high in uncertainty avoidance have high levels of anxiety, a great need for formal rules, and a low tolerance for groups that behave in a deviant manner. Masculinity, according to Hofstede, involves valuing things, money, assertiveness, and unequal sex roles. Cultures where people, quality of life, nurturance, and equal sex roles prevail, on the other hand, are feminine.

While Hofstede's (1980) dimensions of cultural variability were developed in the West (from data collected in over 50 countries), they do appear to be cross-culturally generalizable. Individualism-collectivism, for example, also has been isolated as a dimension of cultural variability by scholars in many Asian cultures, including China (Hsu, 1981; Yang, 1981), Japan (Lebra, 1976; Nakane, 1970), and Korea (Yum, 1987). Further, dimensions of cultural variability were assessed by the Chinese Culture Connection (1987). Their analysis from a Chinese methodological bias revealed dimensions consistent with individualism-collectivism, masculinity-femininity, and power distance. A unique Chinese dimension, Confucian work dynamism, however, also emerged. While Hofstede's dimensions appear to be "imposed etic" categories, a set of combined emic-etic dimensions appear to exist.

In addition to being included as variables in an objective theory, cultural variations also can serve as scope, boundary, or modifying conditions for theoretical statements. Reynolds (1971, p. 92) points out that all theories should include "a set of existence statements that describe the situation in which the theory can be applied." If a theory or hypothesis is tested initially in one culture (e.g., the individualistic culture in the United States), it may or may not be applicable in other cultures (e.g., the collectivistic culture in China). In initial tests, scope conditions should be stated narrowly and then relaxed in future tests until conditions are found where the hypothesis or theory is invalid. This procedure allows researchers to determine the generality of hypotheses or theories and the importance of the scope conditions, thereby increasing robustness.

In order to integrate culture in the study of intercultural communication, cultural variability per se is not of specific interest. Rather, the degree of cultural similarity is the major issue. Cultural similarity can be incorporated using the dimensions of cultural variability. The degree of similarity in individualism-collectivism, for example, might be posited to affect communication between members of different cultures. It also should be noted that there is an emerging tendency to treat intercultural communication as a special case of intergroup communication and, therefore, focus on group similarities in general rather than on cultural similarities in particular (e.g., see the contributions in Gudykunst, 1986a).

Early scholars studying intercultural communication viewed its underlying process as different from intracultural communication. This position, however, is called into question by several theorists (e.g., Ellingsworth, 1977; Gudykunst & Kim, 1984; Sarbaugh, 1979). As Sarbaugh (1979, p. 5) points out:

> There appears to be a temptation among scholars and practitioners of communication to approach intercultural communication as though it were a different process than intracultural communication. As one begins to identify the variables that operate in the communication being studied, however, it becomes apparent that they are the same for both intercultural and intracultural settings.

Given this position, the major task for the scholar interested in explaining intercultural communication is to extend an existing communication theory to explain intercultural interactions. If similarity is included in the communication theory, for example, the scope of the concept can be expanded to include ethnic/cultural similarity in particular or group similarity more generally. Alternatively, if self-concept is included in the theory, it can be elaborated by differentiating personal and social (which subsumes ethnic/cultural identity) identities. This approach, therefore, involves extending the scope and removing boundary conditions of the original theory.

It appears that uncertainty reduction theory (Berger & Calabrese, 1975) has generated the most research and theoretical extensions to intercultural and cross-cultural settings. Uncertainty reduction involves the creation of proactive predictions and retroactive explanations about others' attitudes, beliefs, feelings, and behavior. Berger and Calabrese's (1975) initial formulation of the theory posited 7 axioms and 21 theorems specifying the interrelations among uncertainty, amount of communication, nonverbal affiliative expressiveness, information seeking, intimacy level of communication content, reciprocity, similarity, and liking. Cross-cultural studies suggest the theory generalizes to initial interactions in individualistic and collectivistic cultures (e.g., Gudykunst & Nishida, 1984), as well as to acquaintance, friend, and dating relationships across cultures (Gudykunst, Yang, & Nishida, 1985). Recent research (Gudykunst & Hammer, 1987) also reveals that the theory can account for Black-White differences in initial interactions in the United States. Intercultural research further indicates that uncertainty reduction theory is useful in explaining communication between people from different cultures (e.g., Gudykunst, Chua, & Gray, 1987; Gudykunst, Nishida, & Chua, 1986) and interethnic communication in the United States (Gudykunst, 1986b).

The most recent explication of an uncertainty-reduction-based theory designed to explain intercultural communication is Gudykunst (1988; this is a more general statement of Gudykunst & Hammer's 1988 theory, which was designed to explain intercultural adaptation). The theory attempts to explain interpersonal and intergroup communication, with intercultural communication being viewed as a special case of intergroup communication. Gudykunst also integrates cultural variability, thereby attempting to explain cross-cultural variations in communication and intercultural communication in the same theory (see Table 1.2).

Gudykunst (1988) argues that the focus should be on explaining when interpersonal and intergroup factors are salient in reducing uncertainty (a cognitive process) and anxiety (an affective process). He contends that ethnolinguistic identity, expectations, group similarity, shared networks, interpersonal salience, second-language competence (or more generally communication competence), and personality factors (i.e., self-monitoring, cognitive complexity, and tolerance for ambiguity) affect the reduction of uncertainty and anxiety. Reducing uncertainty and anxiety, in turn, influences interpersonal/intergroup adaptation and effectiveness. The majority of the axioms in the theory are concerned with explaining interpersonal/intergroup communication, but Gudykunst also incorporates two axioms designed to explain cross-cultural variability in uncertainty and anxiety reduction.

Another communication theory extended to intercultural encounters is convergence theory. Rogers and Kincaid (1981) utilized convergence theory in their examination of communication networks across cultures, while Barnett and Kincaid (1983) developed a mathematical theory of cultural convergence. From this perspective, "the main purpose of intercultural communication theory should be to describe, to explain, and to predict changes in cultural differences—the degree and direction of cultural convergence—that occur over time as a result of communication among different cultural groups" (Barnett & Kincaid, 1983, p. 173). Kincaid, Yum, Woelfel, and Barnett's (1983) research supported Barnett and Kincaid's theory. Kincaid (1988) updated the theory.

The second approach to theorizing in intercultural communication is to borrow theories from other disciplines. Based upon a theory of contraculture developed from the prison literature, for example, Gudykunst and Halsall (1980) organized diverse research findings on sojourners' adjustment to foreign cultures. Given the isomorphic nature of the two social processes, they argue that this is a viable approach to theory construction.

By far the most widely used theory from other disciplines adapted to explain intercultural communication is attribution theory. Numerous writers apply this theory to intercultural interactions (e.g., Detweiler, 1975; Ehrenhaus, 1983; Hewstone & Jaspers, 1982; Jaspers & Hewstone,

**Table 1.2** A Summary of Gudykunst's (1988) Theory

___

Assumptions

    1. At least one participant in an intergroup encounter is a stranger vis-à-vis the ingroup being approached.

    2. Strangers' initial experiences with a new ingroup are experienced as a series of crises; that is, strangers are not cognitively sure of how to behave (i.e., cognitive uncertainty) and they experience the feeling of a lack of security (i.e., anxiety).

    3. Uncertainty and anxiety are independent dimensions of intergroup communication.

    4. Strangers' behavior takes place at high levels of awareness.

    5. Both intergroup and interpersonal factors influence all communication.

    6. Strangers overestimate the influence of group membership in explaining members of the other group's behavior.

Axioms

    1. An increase in the strength of strangers' ethnolinguistic identities will produce an increase in their attributional confidence regarding members of the other group's behavior and an increase in the anxiety they experience when interacting with members of other groups. This axiom holds *only* when members of the outgroup are perceived as "typical" and when ethnic status is activated.

    2. An increase in strangers' positive expectations will produce an increase in their attributional confidence regarding members of the other group's behavior and a decrease in the anxiety they experience when interacting with members of other groups.

    3. An increase in the similarity between strangers' ingroups and other groups will produce an increase in their attributional confidence regarding members of those groups' behavior and a decrease in the anxiety strangers experience when interacting with members of other groups.

    4. An increase in the networks strangers share with members of other groups will produce an increase in their attributional confidence regarding members of those groups' behavior and a decrease in the anxiety strangers experience when interacting with members of other groups.

    5. An increase in the interpersonal salience of the relationships strangers form with members of other groups moderates the effect of group dissimilarities and will produce an increase in their attributional confidence regarding members of those groups' behavior.

    6. An increase in strangers' second-language competence will produce an increase in their attributional confidence regarding members of the other group's behavior and a decrease in the anxiety experienced when interacting with members of other groups.

    7. An increase in strangers' self-monitoring will produce an increase in their attributional confidence regarding members of the other group's behavior and a decrease in the anxiety experienced when interacting with members of other groups.

    8. An increase in strangers' cognitive complexity will produce an increase in their attributional confidence regarding members of the other group's behavior and a decrease in the anxiety experienced when interacting with members of other groups.

    9. An increase in strangers' tolerance for ambiguity will produce an increase in their attributional confidence regarding members of the other group's behavior and a decrease in the anxiety experienced when interacting with members of other groups.

___

*(continued)*

**TABLE 1.2.** *(continued)*

10. An increase in strangers' attributional confidence regarding members of other group's behavior will produce an increase in their intergroup adaptation and effectiveness.

11. A decrease in the anxiety strangers experience when interacting with members of other groups will produce an increase in their intergroup adaptation and effectiveness.

12. An increase in collectivism will produce an increase in the differences in attributional confidence between ingroup and outgroup communication.

13. An increase in uncertainty avoidance will produce an increase in the anxiety strangers experience when interacting with members of other groups.

1982). Detweiler, for example, contends that the nature of attributions people make in intercultural settings is influenced by their "category width"; the narrower the width of their categories, the more likely the attributions are based upon their own cultural standards. Ehrenhaus (1983) draws upon Detweiler (1975) and Hall (1976), suggesting that the attributions people make vary depending upon whether they come from high- or low-context cultures. Hewstone and Jaspers's (1982) and Jaspers and Hewstone's (1982) theory of "social attribution" integrates research on attributions with findings on ethnic stereotypes and intergroup relations.

While attribution theory has been used most widely, we believe that Giles and his associates' work in the social psychology of language on ethnolinguistic identity theory (e.g., Giles & Johnson, 1987) and communication accommodation theory (Giles, Mulac, Bradac, & Johnson, 1987) is vital to understanding intercultural communication and, therefore, we use this theory as an exemplar of this approach. Giles and Johnson (1981) isolated interethnic comparisons, perceived ethnolinguistic vitality, perception of ingroup boundaries, identification with other groups, perceived overlap in social categories, and perceived status as important factors in determining whether or not individuals define interactions as intergroup. Giles and his associates (1987) reformulated speech accommodation theory specifying the antecedents and consequences of convergence and divergence. More recently, Gallois, Franklyn-Stokes, Giles, and Coupland (1988) integrated Giles and Johnson's (1987) ethnolinguistic identity theory with Giles et al.'s (1987) theory of communication accommodation processes (see Table 1.3).

Gallois et al.'s (1988) theory of communication accommodation takes into consideration interpersonal and intergroup factors. The intercultural aspects of the theory are subsumed under the intergroup rubric. This theory differentiates the nature of communication accommodation that occurs in encounters where the participants have either high or low dependence on their ingroup and either high or low identification with their ingroup.

**TABLE 1.3** A Summary of Gallois, Franklyn-Stokes, Giles, and Coupland's (1988) Theory

Propositions

1. Members of a subordinate group which has language and speech as important dimensions of its identity, and who
    (a) belong to few other social categories,
    (b) identify strongly with their ethnic ingroup,
    (c) feel that their group situation is threatened,
    (d) perceive threat to their ethnic ingroup resulting from soft and open boundaries *or* low vitality . . .
    are likely to be initially oriented in intergroup encounters to
    (1) defining the situation as having high intergroup salience . . .
    (2) not attuning . . . to . . . features of the outgroup;
    (3) not attuning . . . to outgroup members interpersonally.

2. Members of a subordinate group which has language and speech as important dimensions of its identity, and who
    (a) belong to some other social categories . . .
    (b) identify moderately or weakly with their ethnic ingroup . . .
    (c) feel that their ethnic ingroup situation is threatened . . .
    (d) perceive their ethnic ingroup boundaries to be hard and closed and their group to have high vitality . . .
    are likely to be initially oriented in intergroup encounters to
    (1) defining the situation as having moderate or low intergroup salience and high interpersonal salience . . .
    (2) not attuning . . . the outgroup . . .
    (3) attuning strongly to outgroup members interpersonally.

3. Members of a subordinate group who
    (a) belong to many other social categories . . .
    (b) identify strongly with their ethnic ingroup . . .
    (c) do not feel their group is threatened by change . . .
    (d) do not perceive their ethnic ingroup to be threatened by soft and open boundaries or by low vitality . . .
    are likely to be initially oriented in intergroup encounters to
    (1) defining the situation as high in intergroup and interpersonal salience;
    (2) attuning strongly to . . . features of the outgroup . . .
    (3) attuning strongly to outgroup members interpersonally.

4. Members of a subordinate group who
    (a) belong to many other social categories . . .
    (b) identify moderately or weakly with their ethnic ingroup . . .
    (c) do not feel that their ethnic ingroup is threatened . . .
    (d) see their group as having soft and open boundaries and low vitality . . .
    are likely to be initially oriented in intergroup encounters to
    (1) defining the situation as low in intergroup salience and high in interpersonal salience;
    (2) attuning strongly to . . . features of the outgroup . . .
    (3) attuning strongly to outgroup members interpersonally.

5. Members of majority or dominant groups in this category can be characterized like members of subordinate groups in category 1 above, except that they
    (d) perceive their group's boundaries to be soft and open, but perceive their group to have high vitality
    and their initial orientation is like that of people in category 1.

*(continued)*

**TABLE 1.3.** *(continued)*

6. Members of majority or dominant groups in this category can be characterized like members of category 2 above, and their initial orientation is the same.

7. Members of majority or dominant groups in this type can be characterized in many ways like members of category 3 above, *except* for the fact that the absence of threat and ingroup allegiance would orient them to *maintaining* their distinctive dominant group style.

8. Members of majority or dominant groups in this category can be characterized like members of category 4 above, except that they do not perceive that their group has low vitality, and their initial orientation is the same.

9. In the intergroup situations when they
    (a) are not strongly committed in general to an attitude position on which an outgroup interactant opposes them . . .
    (b) do not perceive the situation . . . to be competitive . . . or
    (c) perceive . . . the situation to emphasize status-stressing dimensions;
    *few* people are likely to define the situation in intergroup terms . . . or to interpret the behavior of others in intergroup terms.

10. In intergroup situations when they
    (a) are strongly committed in general to an attitude position on which an outgroup member opposes them or they perceive the topic to be central to their social identity . . .
    (b) perceive the situation . . . to be competitive . . . or
    (c) perceive few features of the situation to emphasize status-stressing dimensions;
    *many* people are likely to define the situation in intergroup terms . . . and to interpret the behavior of others in intergroup terms.

11. When speakers in an intercultural encounter
    (a) desire recipients' social approval . . .
    (b) desire a high level of communication clarity and comprehension . . .
    (c) desire to meet the perceived communication needs of recipients . . .
    (d) desire a self-presentation shared by recipients . . . and/or
    (e) desire equal-status role relations with recipients . . .
    they attempt to attune positively . . . to the communicative characteristics they *believe* to belong to their message recipients . . .

12. When speakers in an intercultural encounter
    (a) desire to communicate a contrastive self- or group-image . . .
    (b) desire to dissociate personally from the recipients . . .
    (c) desire to signal differences in . . . and/or
    (d) desire to achieve or maintain a high-status role . . .
    they attempt to counter-attune or not to attune to the perceived communicative characteristics of their message recipients . . .

13. When interpersonal concerns are salient in an intergroup encounter, people attempt to attune their behavior . . . using primarily
    (a) *approximation* strategies involving behaviors relevant to idiolectal . . . or ongoing stylistic features . . .
    (b) *discourse management* strategies involving behaviors relevant to the immediate conversation . . .
    (c) *interpersonal control* strategies . . .
    (d) *interpretability strategies* . . .

*(continued)*

**TABLE 1.3.** *(continued)*

whereas when intergroup concerns are salient, people attempt to attune their behavior to or away from their recipients using

- (e) *approximation* strategies involving behaviors relevant to dialectal features . . .
- (f) *interpersonal control* strategies involving behaviors relevant to group and role relations . . .
- (g) *interpretability* strategies involving behaviors relevant to group differences. . . .

14. The degree of attuning depends upon
   - (a) the extent of speakers' repertoires . . .
   - (b) norms about the minimal and maximal limits of conversational attuning in the speech community . . .
   - (c) the magnitude of individual, social, and contextual factors that may increase the level of intergroup salience, interpersonal salience, or both . . . and
   - (d) the extent to which the recipients' actual communication in the situation matches the beliefs that speakers have about it.

15. When recipients perceive message senders' behavior to be well- attuned . . . the recipients explain the sender's behavior positively . . .

16. When recipients perceive message sender's behavior to be badly attuned . . . the recipients explain the sender's behavior negatively.

NOTE: Given the length of Gallois et al.'s propositions, we have edited them to conserve space. While we have tried not to distort the propositions, anyone interested in the theory should consult the original.

Differences between how members of subordinate and dominant groups react are specified and situational constraints on accommodation are isolated. Specific behaviors of "speakers" and "receivers" in intercultural encounters also are identified in the theory.

Alternative attempts to explain intercultural communication using objective theories from other disciplines also exist. Yum (1988), for example, develops a theory designed to explain communication networks between individuals from different cultures. Further, Forgas (1988) extends his work on episode representations to present a cognitive-cultural conceptualization of intercultural communication. Finally, there is Triandis's (e.g., 1972, 1977, 1987) work. His early work on subjective culture (1972) is related directly to the study of intercultural communication. Triandis's (1977) model of behavior forms the basis for Gudykunst's (1987) and Gudykunst and Ting-Toomey's (1988) theoretical model for cross-cultural differences in communication. His recent work on individualism-collectivism (e.g., 1987) provides the foundation for numerous cross-cultural studies of communication.

The final approach to generating theory is to develop it anew from research conducted specifically on intercultural communication. One area where extensive work exists is the communication acculturation of immigrants (e.g., Kim, 1988). While this line of theorizing examines a problem studied in other disciplines, it presents "new" conceptualizations from communication perspectives. Theorizing on communication acculturation utilizes an objective approach to theory. Kim's (1988) theory, for example, is based on systems theory assumptions. This line of theorizing focuses on the intercultural processes that take place when individuals from one culture relocate to another culture.

There is an alternative approach to integrating culture and communication theoretically that has not been illustrated in the previous theories examined; namely, developing a theory to explain cross-cultural variations in specific communication processes. One example of this approach is Ting-Toomey's (1988) theory of culture and face-negotiation (summarized in Table 1.4). Ting-Toomey links individualism-collectivism (Hofstede, 1980) to the face-negotiation process (Brown & Levinson, 1978). She refers to face as the projected image of one's self in a relational situation and notes that it is conjointly defined by the participants in a setting. Ting-Toomey differentiates concern for self-face and other-face, positive-face and negative-face, and direct and indirect face-negotiation strategies. She argues that members of individualistic cultures are concerned with self-face and negative-face and use direct face-negotiation strategies more than members of collectivistic cultures, while people in collectivistic cultures are concerned with other-face and positive-face and use indirect face-negotiation strategies more than people in individualistic cultures.

Attempts to develop objective theory anew also have occurred in the area of conflict. Ting-Toomey (1985), for example, presents the rudiments of a theory of conflict and culture in her examination of the roots of conflict and its management in low- and high-context cultures. Gudykunst (1985) analyzes the potential for conflict in nine different types of stranger-ingroup (intergroup) relationships. Finally, Tafoya (1983) examines the roots of conflict in intracultural and intercultural settings, and offers a typology of conflict and its management.

Two other objective theories can be included in this category (Ellingsworth, 1983, 1988; Szalay, 1981). Szalay (1981) contends that in intercultural communication there is a need for people to adapt their communication content to the frame of reference of their audience, especially the audience's cultural meanings. He goes on to argue that the focus of theory in intercultural communication should be upon the adaptations necessary for effective communication. Ellingsworth, like Szalay, focuses upon the adaptations necessary for effective intercultural communication in task-oriented settings. His theory begins to specify when and under what conditions adaptations are necessary.

**TABLE 1.4** A Summary of Ting-Toomey's (1988) Theory

Propositions

1. Members of individualistic cultures tend to express a greater degree of self-face maintenance in a conflict situation than members of collectivistic cultures.

2. Members of collectivistic cultures tend to express a greater degree of mutual-face or other-face maintenance than members of individualistic cultures.

3. Members of individualistic cultures would tend to use more autonomy-preserving strategies (negative-face need) in managing conflict than members of collectivistic cultures.

4. Members of collectivistic cultures would tend to use more approval-seeking strategies (positive-face need) in managing conflict than members of individualistic cultures.

5. Members of individualistic cultures would tend to use more self-concern positive-face and self-concern negative-face suprastrategies than members of collectivistic cultures.

6. Members of collectivistic cultures would tend to use more other-concern positive-face and other-concern negative-face suprastrategies than members of individualistic cultures.

7. Members of individualistic cultures tend to use a greater degree of direct face-negotiation strategies than members of collectivistic cultures.

8. Members of collectivist cultures tend to use a greater degree of indirect face-negotiation strategies than members of individualistic cultures.

9. Members of individualistic cultures tend to use more dominating or controlling strategies to manage conflict than members of collectivistic cultures.

10. Members of collectivistic cultures tend to use more obliging or smoothing strategies to manage conflict than members of individualistic cultures.

11. Members of individualistic cultures would use a greater degree of solution-oriented conflict style than members of collectivistic cultures.

12. Members of collectivistic cultures would use a greater degree of avoidance-oriented conflict style than members of individualistic cultures.

## SUBJECTIVE PERSPECTIVES

Subjective perspectives on intercultural communication do not treat culture as a "variable." Most subjectivists make assumptions about culture similar to Geertz (1966, pp. 66-67), who uses the octopus as a metaphor for culture:

The problem of cultural analysis is as much a matter of determining independencies as interconnection, gulfs as well as bridges. The appropriate image, if one must have images, of cultural organization, is neither the spider web nor the pile of sand. It is rather more the octopus, whose tentacles are in large part separately integrated, neurally quite poorly connected with one another and with what in the octopus passes for a brain, and yet who nonetheless manages to get around and to preserve himself [or herself], for a while anyway, as a viable, if somewhat ungainly entity.

As indicated earlier, Geertz (1973) contends that social scientists should provide "thick descriptions" of the phenomena they observe and not generalize across cases.

The search for universal generalizations is criticized by most subjective theorists. Gergen (1982, p. 34), for example, points out that there is "little justification for the immense effort devoted to the empirical substantiation of fundamental laws of human conduct. There would seem to be few patterns of human action, regardless of the durability to date, that are not subject to significant alteration." The lack of correspondence between "scientific" and "ordinary" language also is a major concern of subjective theorists (see Harre & Secord, 1972). Given these concerns, subjective analysts focus on "practice, praxis, action, interaction, activity, experience, [or] performance" (Ortner, 1984, p. 144). A concern with these issues leads theorists/researchers to focus on how culture is produced and how it changes. Practice theorists, according to Ortner (1984, p. 149), seek to explain "the genesis, reproduction, and change of form and meaning of a given social/cultural whole." The reference point for understanding communication processes is the individual. Culture, in this view, is a part of the self (see Shweder & LeVine, 1984). We begin our examination of the subjective perspectives by looking at theories that have their roots in communication.

The coordinated management of meaning (Pearce & Cronen, 1981) has generated the most work with respect to culture and extensions of subjective communication theories. This approach to culture and communication follows the trend in cultural anthropology to study culture as a set of practices that are grounded historically (Ortner, 1984). The proponents of this theory reject a "static" conceptualization of culture and communication. In addition to focusing on practice, advocates of the coordinated management of meaning perspective view culture as polyphonic (e.g., there are many aspects of culture that are related to communication; see Curtis, 1978).

There have been several comparisons of communication across cultures using the coordinated management of meaning theory. Alexander, Cronen, Kang, Tsou, and Banks (1986), for example, compared topic sequencing and information gain in relationship development in China and the United States. Wolfson and Pearce (1983) examined the implications of self-disclosure for subsequent conversation among Chinese and North Americans, while Wolfson and Norden (1984) looked at responses to interpersonal conflict in China and the United States, and Nakanishi (1986) studied perceptions of self-disclosure in initial interactions in Japan. In addition, Pearce, Stanback, and Kang (1984) examined the

'·⁻ between culture and communication using this
:al level, Pearce and Lannamann (1978)
en communication competence and inter-
:n and Shuter (1983) applied the coor-
g to the formation of intercultural relation-
) examined reticence across cultures, and
lated the relationship between acculturation
nce. The most recent theoretical statement
nanagement of meaning's approach to com-
rovided by Cronen, Chen, and Pearce (1988;
⌐ ).

⌐ Pearce's (1988) theory is grounded in a pragmatist
⌐ such, it is not purely subjective. Cronen et al.'s theory fits
⌐is rubric better than it fits under the objective approaches, how-
⌐.⌐r, because the focus of the theory is on how individuals construct
meanings. They contend that the focus of study should be on the persons
communicating, that communicators must be looked at as physical beings
who exist at a particular point in time, and that both the idiosyncratic and
the social aspects of communication must be studied. Cronen and his
associates further argue that action and meaning cannot be separated, that
people's reflections on experience provide the basis for their actions, and
that "communication cannot be perfect." They also point out that culture
must be treated as polyphonic. Cronen et al. point out that the coordinated
management of meaning is a critical theory that not only encourages, but
requires, moral judgments.

In addition to the work on the coordinated management of meaning,
there are other applications of rules theory to intercultural communication.
Pearce and Wiseman (1983), for example, discuss three approaches to
rules theory (rule following, rule governed, and rule using) and examine
the application of each to intercultural settings. They contend that a
rule-using perspective is the most useful for explaining intercultural communication. Cushman and his associates (e.g., Cushman & Nishida, 1983)
apply his rules-based theory of mate selection (Cushman, Valentinsen, &
Dietrich, 1982) in cultures other than the United States.

Another communication-based subjective approach to the study of intercultural communication is rhetoric. While much of the early work in
intercultural communication used a rhetorical approach (e.g., Prosser,
1973), there has been little recent work in this area. Koester and Holmberg
(1983), however, argue that returning to a rhetorical approach would not
limit the topics of inquiry in the study of intercultural communication as
other approaches do. They, nevertheless, suggest that the focus of a
rhetorical approach should be on the communication strategies used in
intercultural encounters. Koester and Holmberg (1983, p. 120) contend

**TABLE 1.5** A Summary of Cronen, Chen, and Pearce's (1988) Theory

Propositions

1. Persons communicating constitute the smallest unit of social analysis.
2. Communicating persons are physical beings that endure in real space-time.
3. All human communication is both idiosyncratic and social.
4. Communication entails a reflexive relationship between structure and action.
5. Punctuated historicity is endemic to human communication.
6. Human communication is inherently imperfect.
7. Moral orders emerge as aspects of communication.
8. Communication is the process by which the dual modes of liberation may be materialized.
9. Diversity is essential to elaboration and transformation through communication.

Corollaries

1. Cultures are patterns of coevolving structures and actions.
2. Cultures are polyphonic.
3. Research activity is part of social practice.

that the rhetorical approach can provide "a unique and wide-ranging understanding of intercultural communication."

There is one other subjective perspective on culture and communication that is not an extension of a communication theory per se, but an approach that is designed specifically to examine the relationship between culture and communication. Philipsen's (e.g., 1975, 1982) work on cultural communication focuses on "the use of communication to affirm, negotiate, and test the relationship of individuals to their societies, in particular cases" (Philipsen, 1982, p. 4). He focuses on three forms of cultural communication: ritual, myth, and social drama. This line of research is related closely to Hymes' (1974) sociolinguistic analyses, and extensive work has been conducted using this perspective in recent years (e.g., Carbaugh, 1986; Katriel, 1986).

The major subjective approach to theory borrowed from other disciplines that has been extended to account for culture is constructivism (Kelly, 1955). Applegate and Sypher (1983) provided an initial extension of this theory and they (1988) recently updated the theory (summarized in Table 1.6). Like Cronen et al. (1988), Applegate and Sypher (1988) assume that the study of communication should be embedded historically and that value judgments should be made. They differ, however, in the specifics of the theory. Applegate and Sypher see communication as goal-driven. They further contend that culture defines the logic of communication and that cultures differ in the communication goals they value, as well as in the

**TABLE 1.6** A Summary of Applegate and Sypher's (1988) Theory

Assumptions

1. A theory of communication that focuses on the impact of historically emergent forms of group life on everyday communication is necessary.
2. The theory should be interpretive.
3. Dense and detailed accounts of everyday interactions of cultural participants are needed.
4. The focus of study should be the relationship between culture and communication.
5. Value arguments should be made.
6. Theory and training should be linked closely.

Propositions

1. Communication is goal-driven, but actors are not always aware of their goals.
2. Strategic communicative behavior is indexed hierarchically to reflect increasing complexity in behavior.
3. Person-centered communication reflects an integration of process-oriented communication competencies.
4. The influence of culture on communication is most evident in situations where conventional goals and plans are "given" to actors, but because conventions are implicit and routine, intercultural communicators oftenm are unaware of the differences distorting communication.
5. Cultural communication theories are learned through socialization.
6. Cultural prescriptions are used rather than followed.
7. Culture defines the logic of communication.
8. Cultures differentially value communication goals and alternative strategies for reaching these goals.
9. Cultural communication theories specify how to place and organize events within larger contexts of meaning and elaboration.
10. Intercultural training should focus on developing flexible and integrative strategic means for accomplishing goals.

value attached to strategies for reaching specific goals. This perspective focuses on situated communication and the interpretations of the communicators.

There also are other applications of subjective theoretical approaches from other disciplines. Cooley (1983), for example, argues for the use of linguistic theory in the analysis of intercultural communication, with a focus upon codes. Pilotta (1983), in contrast, suggests phenomenology as a fruitful perspective for the study of intercultural communication, while Blackman (1983) contends that a grounded theory approach from sociology provides a productive method to develop theory. In addition, work in sociolinguistics (e.g., Gumperz, 1982) can be adapted to explain intercultural communication, but it has not been used widely to date.

There are relatively few subjective theories developed specifically to explain some aspect of intercultural communication. One example is Fitchen's (1979) transactional conceptualization of intercultural communication. He argues that the focus of study should be on the mutual experience between communicators from different cultures, rather than on the communicators. Fitchen's model, however, was not based upon specific research and it has not been tested.

There is only one subjective theory that was developed specifically to deal with intercultural communication of which we are aware based on extensive research (e.g., Collier, 1986; Collier, Ribeau, & Hecht, 1986); namely, Collier and Thomas's (1988) rules theory, which focuses upon cultural identity (see Table 1.7). Collier and Thomas argue that cultural identity should not be treated as an independent variable in research, rather it should be viewed as one of many identities that are formed and managed when people from different cultures communicate. They contend that communication is intercultural when cultural interpretations emerge in discourse and that intercultural competence is a function of negotiating mutual meanings, rules, and outcomes that are "positive." Further, the more one communicator's attributed cultural identity for the partner matches the partner's avowed cultural identity, the greater the intercultural competence. Like the other subjective approaches, Collier and Thomas maintain that their perspective offers a viable way to improve human contact.

## CONCLUSION

We have summarized the major perspectives used to study intercultural communication, but we have not evaluated the theories presented. Each perspective must be evaluated on its own merit, rather than one perspective being compared with another. Does the perspective hold together logically (e.g., are the assumptions, propositions or axioms, and theorems logically consistent)? Is the perspective useful in explaining the phenomena under study (e.g., does it help us to better understand the process of intercultural communication)? Each individual must answer these questions for her- or himself when she or he selects a theoretical perspective to explain the relationship between culture and communication.

The distinction between the objective and subjective approaches is artificial, but it is a distinction that is actualized in the writings of social scientists (see, for example, the contributions in Fiske & Shweder, 1986) and in the work of scholars studying intercultural communication. There is a tendency to view these two approaches as opposing paradigms. We contend, however, that this should *not* be the case. Giddens (1979) argues

**TABLE 1.7.** A Summary of Collier and Thomas's (1988) Theory

Assumptions

1. Persons negotiate multiple identities in discourse.

2. Communication is rendered intercultural by the discursive ascription and avowal of differing cultural identities.

3. Intracultural communication competence involves the coherent management of meanings and competencies—appropriate (rule-following) and effective (positive-outcome-producing) conduct.

4. Intercultural competence is created by the negotiation of mutual meaning rules and positive outcomes.

5. Intercultural competence is a process in which cultural identities are validated.

6. Cultural identity varies along three central, interdependent dimensions: scope, salience and intensity.

Axioms

1. The more that norms and meaning differ in discourse, the more intercultural the contact.

2. The higher the degree of intercultural competence, the higher the likelihood that the relationship will be developed or maintained.

3. The more that cultural identities differ in the discourse, the more intercultural the contact.

4. The more the consistency in each individual's ascription of the other's cultural identity matches the other's avowed cultural identity, the higher the intercultural competence.

5. Linguistic references to cultural identity systematically covary with sociocontextual features such as participants, type of episode and topic.

Theorem

1. The more intensity with which cultural identities are avowed in discourse, the higher the salience of those particular identities relative to others.

that the study of practice (e.g., a subjective approach) should not be viewed as an antagonistic alternative to the study of structures or systems (e.g., an objective approach). Rather, he maintains, and we agree, that each approach is a necessary complement to the other.

Theoretical pluralism (i.e., accepting the existence of multiple theoretical perspectives) in the study of intercultural communication is necessary, but the eventual goal must be to integrate research findings and theoretical ideas from objective and subjective perspectives. Theoretical integration is necessary and desirable for at least three reasons. First, "subjective" and "objective" realities interact. While reality is constructed socially (à la Berger & Luckmann, 1967), individuals are not "creative" all of the time and tend to construct the same reality over and over, especially at the macro level. Second, meanings and messages are integral parts of human communication systems. Studying one without the other is incomplete.

Third, participants' interpretations of communication and external observations of their communications are both legitimate foci of inquiry.

Some initial integration of the objective and subjective approaches
already has occurred. Some objective theories, for example, are based on
subjective observations. To illustrate, Ting-Toomey's (1988) theory of
face-negotiation is based, at least in part, on her participation in and
subjective observations of the Chinese and North American cultures.
Objective theories also have been supported by studies using subjective
methods. Sudweeks, Gudykunst, Ting-Toomey, and Nishida's (1988) research illustrates this approach. They conducted open-ended interviews
with members of Japanese-North American dyads and analyzed the tran-
scripts for themes of relationship development. The themes that emerged
in Sudweeks et al.'s study are consistent with many of the axioms and
theorems in Gudykunst's (1988) theory. Further, some subjective theories
have been tested using objective methods (e.g., Alexander et al.'s, 1986,
test of coordinated management of meaning across cultures). Complete
integration of the objective and subjective approaches will not be easy,
however, because we tend to be socialized into either the "objective" or
the "subjective" "culture" and there are few "bicultural" theorists. Research teams with objectivist and subjectivist members, therefore, are
necessary in order to develop an integrated theory.

There are at least two issues that must be addressed to achieve theoretical integration. The first issue involves the internal coherence of an
integrated theory. If the extreme positions of the objectiveist and subjec-
tiveist positions (see Table 1.1) are treated as dichotomies, such coherence is impossible. If, on the other hand, they are treated as endpoints of
continuums, theoretical integration is possible; that is, theories with assumptions toward the center of the various continuums could be integrated
to provide a logically coherent theory. The second issue is methodological.
To develop and test integrated theories, methodological pluralism is not
sufficient. Rather, integrated theories must be developed and tested using
methods that are integrated and triangulated; that is, to study the same
phenomena using observational, interview, survey, and/or laboratory techniques.

One way theoretical integration may be possible is through the development of research programs (Lakatos, 1970). Berger, Conner, and Fisek
(1974) refer to a theoretical research program as a set of interrelated
theories, including theoretically based research designed to test them, as
well as action research that applies the theories to specific cases and uses
the theories for the purpose of social change. Such an approach would not
require a complete integration of objective and subjective theories, but
would allow them to coexist side by side in the same theoretical research
program (assuming their metatheoretical assumptions are consistent). One

example of a productive theoretical research program in the social sciences that is directly applicable to the study of intercultural communication is Berger and his associates' (e.g., Berger & Zelditch, 1985) work on expectation states theory, which includes a number of distinct theories (e.g., expectation states theory, status characteristic theory, among others).

Our summary, out of necessity, has been limited to approaches to the study of intercultural communication used in English-speaking, Western countries. We do not mean to imply that there are not alternative non-English, non-Western perspectives available for the study of intercultural communication. Nishida (1984), for example, developed a model of Japanese-North American communication. Further, the East-West Center sponsored two seminars on "Communication Theory from Eastern and Western Perspectives," one in Honolulu in 1980 (resulting in Kincaid, 1987) and one in Yokohama, Japan, in 1982 (resulting in Tsujimura, in press), which focused on East-West differences in explaining communication. In addition, Asante (1987) outlined an Afrocentric approach to studying communication. With the exception of Nishida's analysis, however, the implications of the different cultural approaches to communication theory have not been extended to intercultural encounters. Such extensions must be made if ethnocentric theories are to be avoided.

One issue with which theorists will have to come to terms in order to develop a nonethnocentric theory is the role of ideology in communication theory. Hall (in press) argues that communication must be "understood in relation to the wider social, political, and economic structures and to developments within the social formation as a whole." He further contends that "ideology" is inherent in any communication theory and that it should be recognized. The inclusion of ideology as an aspect of theory appears to vary as a function of the academic traditions in the country in which the theory is developed (e.g., scholars in some countries are expected to include ideology in their theories and scholars in other countries are expected to develop ideology-free theories). Ideology, therefore, must be addressed in future theoretical developments in dealing with culture and communication. The challenge is to develop theories that are acceptable to scholars who expect ideology to be part of the theory and, at the same time, are also acceptable to scholars who expect theories to be ideology-free.

A related concern that often is not recognized in the development of communication theories involves the gender of the theorists. Most of the theories used to explain communication have been developed by men. Research (e.g., Gilligan, 1982) clearly indicates, however, that the theorist's/researcher's gender affects how he or she approaches the phenomena under study. It is important that future theoretical advances in intercultural communication not be gender-biased, and, therefore, research teams consisting of males and females are needed.

A few of the theories discussed are based on the work of multicultural research teams (e.g., Cronen et al.'s, 1988, theory is based on research conducted with Chinese and Korean colleagues; Gudykunst's, 1988, theory is based on research conducted with Australian, English, Japanese, and Korean colleagues). Further, some of the theories were developed by women or had women on the research team (e.g., Collier & Thomas, 1988; Cronen et al., 1988; Gallois et al., 1988; Ting-Toomey, 1988). These trends are to be applauded. More integration of communication theories from other cultural perspectives and the inclusion of feminine perspectives, nevertheless, are needed if the ethnocentric and gender-based biases in developing theories to explain intercultural communication are to be avoided. These challenges must not go unmet.

In order to meet the challenges made here, a critical mass of scholars developing theory in intercultural communication is needed. As Campbell (1986, p. 127) points out, "there are sociological requirements that must be met for sustaining communities of truth-seeking belief exchanges. A critical mass and the appearance of progress (collective success experiences) are among them." At the present time, there does *not* appear to be a critical mass of multicultural research teams (especially teams with advocates of the objective *and* subjective approaches and with male *and* female members), but there is some "appearance of progress" (e.g., cross-cultural and intercultural research published in the major journals in the field; major reviews of the field; the appearance of this volume). We must not, however, let the "appearance of progress" stop us from making a concerted effort to develop nonethnocentric and non-gender-biased theoretical research programs that integrate subjective and objective perspectives.

Those involved in developing theoretical research programs in intercultural communication would be well-advised to keep Pettigrew's (1986, p. 179) critique of social psychological theories in mind:

1. they are more often loose frameworks than testable theories;
2. they have centered on cold cognition to the relative exclusion of affective considerations;
3. they stress similarities (mechanical solidarity) to the virtual exclusion of differences (organic solidarity) as social bonds;
4. they focus largely on isolated, non-cumulative effects;
5. they too glibly assume universality across time, situations and cultures;
6. they are narrow- to middle-range in scope with bold generic theory that links various levels of analysis conspicuous by its absence.

Addressing each of these issues is important, but linking the various levels of analysis (item 6, above) is critical in developing a theory of culture and communication. The intrapersonal, interpersonal, intergroup, and cultural levels of analysis must be "articulated" to develop a comprehensive, integrated theory (Doise, 1986).

The above criticisms should not be taken as an indictment of the state of theorizing about intercultural communication. Progress in the five years between the first (Gudykunst, 1983) and the most recent (Kim & Gudykunst, 1988) volumes on theory in intercultural communication was enormous. Some of the theories contained in the most recent volume are based on extensive research, while some are generated logically. They all, however, have clear implications for future research and direct applications in practice. Continued theoretical analysis is necessary not only to increase our understanding of intercultural communication but also to improve our ability to help members of one culture communicate effectively with members of other cultures. As Kurt Lewin often is quoted as saying, "There is nothing so practical as a good theory."

## NOTES

1. The "objective" and "subjective" theories isolated in this chapter clearly illustrate that there is little agreement on the form or nature of theoretical statements (e.g., compare the positions in Gallois et al.'s, 1988, theory in Table 1.3 with Cronen et al.'s, 1988, theory in Table 1.5). Given the differences in the form of theoretical statements, there obviously are differences in how the various theorists would define the term *theory* itself. Rather than try to resolve this issue in the space allocated, we will let the "theories" speak for themselves.

2. Burrell and Morgan (1979) also isolate two basic positions with respect to the assumptions about the nature of society: order versus conflict. The order view of society assumes that the basic processes in society are "stability," "integration," "functional coordination," and "consensus." The conflict view of society, in contrast, assumes that "change," "conflict," "disintegration," and "coercion" are basic processes. Drawing a distinction between order and conflict assumptions regarding society is not compatible with theorists who contend that the two processes are interrelated (e.g., Cohen, 1968). Given that no current theory in intercultural communication clearly stems from conflict assumptions and our view that the two processes are interdependent, we do not utilize this distinction in classifying the perspectives used to study intercultural communication.

3. Summarizing the theories in a table "distorts" all of the theories to some extent. Space limitations, however, do not allow us to present complete overviews of all of the theories (or even the examples we use). Readers, therefore, are encouraged to consult the theories in their original form.

## REFERENCES

Alexander, A. F., Cronen, V. E., Kang, K.-W., Tsou, B., & Banks, J. (1986). Patterns of topic sequencing and information gain: A comparative analysis of relationship development in Chinese and American cultures. *Communication Quarterly, 34,* 66-78.

Applegate, J. L., & Sypher, H. E. (1983). A constructivist outline. In W. B. Gudykunst (Ed.), *Intercultural communication theory*. Beverly Hills, CA: Sage.

Applegate, J. L., & Sypher, H. E. (1988). A constructivist theory of communication and culture. In Y. Y. Kim & W. B. Gudykunst (Eds.), *Theories in intercultural communication*. Newbury Park, CA: Sage.

Asante, M. K. (1987). *The Afrocentric idea*. Philadelphia: Temple University Press.

Barnett, G. A., & Kincaid, D. L. (1983). Cultural convergence. In W. B. Gudykunst (Ed.), *Intercultural communication theory*. Beverly Hills, CA: Sage.

Berger, C. R., & Calabrese, R. J. (1975). Some explorations in initial interactions and beyond. *Human Communication Research, 1*, 99-112.

Berger, J., Conner, T., & Fisek, M. (Eds.). (1974). *Expectation states: A theoretical research program*. Cambridge, MA: Winthrop.

Berger, J., & Zelditch, M. (Eds.). (1985). *Status, rewards, and influence*. San Francisco: Jossey-Bass.

Berger, P., & Luckmann, T. (1967). *The social construction of reality*. New York: Doubleday.

Berry, J. (1980). Introduction to methodology. In H. Triandis & J. Berry (Eds.), *Handbook of cross-cultural psychology* (Vol. 2). Boston: Allyn & Bacon.

Blackman, B. I. (1983). Toward a grounded theory. In W. B. Gudykunst (Ed.), *Intercultural communication theory*. Beverly Hills, CA: Sage.

Brislin, R. (1983). Cross-cultural research in psychology. *Annual Review of Psychology, 34*, 363-400.

Brown, P., & Levinson, S. (1978). Universals in language usage: Politeness phenomenon. In E. Goody (Ed.), *Questions and politeness*. Cambridge: Cambridge University Press.

Burrell, G., & Morgan, G. (1979). *Sociological paradigms and organizational analysis*. London: Heinemann.

Campbell, D. T. (1986). Science's social system of validity-enhancing collective belief change and the problems of social science. In D. W. Fiske & R. A. Shweder (Eds.), *Metatheory in social science*. Chicago: University of Chicago Press.

Carbaugh, D. (1986). Some thoughts on organizing as cultural communication. In L. T. Thayer (Ed.), *Organizational communication: Emerging perspectives I*. Norwood, NJ: Ablex.

Chinese Culture Connection. (1987). Chinese values and the search for culture-free dimensions of culture. *Journal of Cross-Cultural Psychology, 18*, 143-164.

Cohen, P. (1968). *Modern social theory*. New York: Basic Books.

Collier, M. J. (1986). Culture and gender: Effects on assertive behavior and communication competence. In M. McLaughlin (Ed.), *Communication yearbook* (Vol. 9). Beverly Hills, CA: Sage.

Collier, M. J., Ribeau, S., & Hecht, M. (1986). Intracultural communication rules and outcomes within three domestic cultures. *International Journal of Intercultural Relations, 10*, 439-457.

Collier, M. J., & Thomas, M. (1988). Cultural identity. In Y. Y. Kim & W. B. Gudykunst (Eds.), *Theories in intercultural communication*. Newbury Park, CA: Sage.

Cooley, R. E. (1983). Codes and context. In W. B. Gudykunst (Ed.), *Intercultural communication theory*. Beverly Hills, CA: Sage.

Cronen, V. E., Chen, V., & Pearce, W. B. (1988). Coordinated management of meaning. In Y. Y. Kim & W. B. Gudykunst (Eds.), *Theories in intercultural communication*. Newbury Park, CA: Sage.

Cronen, V. E., & Davis, L. K. (1978). Alternative approaches for the communication theorists. *Human Communication Research, 4*, 120-128.

Cronen, V. E., & Shuter, R. (1983). Forming intercultural bonds. In W. B. Gudykunst (Ed.), *Intercultural communication theory*. Beverly Hills, CA: Sage.

Curtis, J. (1978). *Culture as polyphony*. Columbia: University of Missouri Press.

Cushman, D. P., & Nishida, T. (1983). *Mate selection in Japan and the United States.* Unpublished paper, State University of New York, Albany.

Cushman, D. P., & Pearce, W. B. (1977). Generality and necessity in three types of theory about human communication, with special attention to rules theory. *Human Communication Research, 3*, 344-353.

Cushman, D. P., Valentinsen, B., & Dietrich, D. (1982). A rules theory of interpersonal relationships. In F. Dance (Ed.), *Human communication theory.* New York: Harper & Row.

Detweiler, R. A. (1975). On inferring the intentions of a person from another culture. *Journal of Personality, 43*, 591-611.

Doise, W. (1986). *Levels of explanation in social psychology.* Cambridge: Cambridge University Press.

Dubin, R. (1969). *Theory building.* New York: Free Press.

Ehrenhaus, P. (1983). Culture and the attribution process. In W. B. Gudykunst (Ed.), *Intercultural communication theory.* Beverly Hills, CA: Sage.

Ellingsworth, H. W. (1977). Conceptualizing intercultural communication. In B. Ruben (Ed.), *Communication yearbook* (Vol. 1). New Brunswick, NJ: Transaction.

Ellingsworth, H. W. (1983). Adaptive intercultural communication. In W. B. Gudykunst (Ed.), *Intercultural communication theory.* Beverly Hills, CA: Sage.

Ellingsworth, H. W. (1988). A theory of adaptation in intercultural dyads. In Y. Y. Kim & W. B. Gudykunst (Eds.), *Theories in intercultural communication.* Newbury Park, CA: Sage.

Fiske, D. W., & Shweder, R. A. (Eds.). (1986). *Metatheory in social science: Pluralisms and subjectivities.* Chicago: University of Chicago Press.

Fitchen, R. (1979). Observing intercultural communication. *International Journal of Intercultural Relations, 3*, 163-174.

Forgas, J. P. (1988). Episode representations in intercultural communication. In Y. Y. Kim & W. B. Gudykunst (Eds.), *Theories in intercultural communication.* Newbury Park, CA: Sage.

Foschi, M., & Hales, W. (1979). The theoretical role of cross-cultural comparisons in experimental social psychology. In L. Eckensberger, W. Lonner, & Y. Poortinga (Eds.), *Cross-cultural contributions to psychology.* Lisse, the Netherlands: Swets and Zeitlinger.

Gallois, C., Franklyn-Stokes, A., Giles, H., & Coupland, N. (1988). Communication accommodation in intercultural encounters. In Y. Y. Kim & W. B. Gudykunst (Eds.), *Theories in intercultural communication.* Newbury Park, CA: Sage.

Geertz, C. (1966). *Person, time, and conduct in Bali: An essay in cultural analysis.* New Haven, CT: Yale University, Southeast Asia Program.

Geertz, C. (1973). *Interpretation of cultures.* New York: Basic Books.

Gergen, K. J. (1982). *Toward transformations in social knowledge.* New York: Springer-Verlag.

Giddens, A. (1979). *Central problems in social theory.* Cambridge: Cambridge University Press.

Giles, H., & Johnson, P. (1981). The role of language in ethnic group relations. In J. Turner & H. Giles (Eds.), *Intergroup behavior.* Chicago: University of Chicago Press.

Giles, H., & Johnson, P. (1987). Ethnolinguistic identity theory: A social psychological approach to language maintenance. *International Journal of the Sociology Language, 68*, 69-99.

Giles, H., Mulac, A., Bradac, J., & Johnson, P. (1987). Speech accommodation theory. In M. McLaughlin (Ed.), *Communication yearbook* (Vol. 10). Newbury Park, CA: Sage.

Gilligan, C. (1982). *In a different voice.* Cambridge, MA: Harvard University Press.

Gudykunst, W. B. (Ed.). (1983). *Intercultural communication theory: Current perspectives.* Beverly Hills, CA: Sage.

Gudykunst, W. B. (1985). Normative power and conflict potential in intergroup relationships. In W. Gudykunst, L. Stewart, & S. Ting-Toomey (Eds.), *Communication, culture, and organizational processes*. Beverly Hills, CA: Sage.

Gudykunst, W. B. (Ed.). (1986a). *Intergroup communication*. London: Edward Arnold.

Gudykunst, W. B. (1986b). Intraethnic and interethnic uncertainty reduction processes. In Y. Y. Kim (Ed.), *Interethnic communication*. Beverly Hills, CA: Sage.

Gudykunst, W. B. (1987). Cross-cultural comparisons. In C. Berger & S. Chaffee (Eds.), *Handbook of communication science*. Newbury Park, CA: Sage.

Gudykunst, W. B. (1988). Uncertainty and anxiety. In Y. Y. Kim & W. B. Gudykunst (Eds.), *Theories in intercultural communication*. Newbury Park, CA: Sage.

Gudykunst, W. B., Chua, E., & Gray, A. (1987). Cultural dissimilarities and uncertainty reduction processes. In M. McLaughlin (Ed.), *Communication yearbook* (Vol. 10). Beverly Hills, CA: Sage.

Gudykunst, W. B., & Halsall, S. J. (1980). The application of a theory of contraculture to intercultural communication. In D. Nimins (Ed.), *Communication yearbook* (Vol. 4). New Brunswick, NJ: Transaction.

Gudykunst, W. B., & Hammer, M. R. (1987). The effects of ethnicity, gender, and dyadic composition on uncertainty reduction in initial interactions. *Journal of Black Studies, 18*, 191-214.

Gudykunst, W. B., & Hammer, M. R. (1988). Strangers and hosts. In Y. Y. Kim & W. B. Gudykunst (Eds.), *Cross-cultural adaptation*. Newbury Park, CA: Sage.

Gudykunst, W. B., & Kim, Y. Y. (1984). *Communicating with strangers: An approach to intercultural communication*. Reading, MA: Addison-Wesley.

Gudykunst, W. B., & Nishida, T. (1984). Individual and cultural influences on uncertainty reduction. *Communication Monographs, 51*, 23-36.

Gudykunst, W. B., Nishida, T., & Chua, E. (1986). Uncertainty reduction in Japanese-North American dyads. *Communication Research Reports, 3*, 39-46.

Gudykunst, W. B., & Ting-Toomey, S., with Chua, E. (1988). *Culture and interpersonal communication*. Newbury Park, CA: Sage.

Gudykunst, W. B., Yang, S. M., & Nishida, T. (1985). A cross-cultural test of uncertainty reduction theory. *Human Communication Research, 11*, 407-454.

Gumperz, J. J. (1982). *Discourse strategies*. Cambridge: Cambridge University Press.

Hall, E. T. (1976). *Beyond culture*. New York: Doubleday.

Hall, S. (in press). Ideology and communication theory. In B. Dervin, L. Grossberg, B. O'Keefe, & E. Wartella (Eds.), *Rethinking communication* (Vol. 1). Newbury Park, CA: Sage.

Harre, R., & Secord, P. F. (1972). *The explanation of social behavior*. Oxford: Basil Blackwell.

Hewstone, M., & Jaspers, J. (1982). Intergroup relations and attributional processes. In H. Tajfel (Ed.), *Social identity and intergroup relations*. Cambridge: Cambridge University Press.

Hofstede, G. (1980). *Culture consequences*. Beverly Hills, CA: Sage.

Hsu, F. (1981). *Americans and Chinese* (3rd ed.). Honolulu: University of Hawaii Press.

Hymes, D. (1974). *Foundations in sociolinguistics*. Philadelphia: University of Pennsylvania Press.

Jaspers, J., & Hewstone, M. (1982). Cross-cultural interaction, social attribution, and intergroup relations. In S. Bochner (Ed.), *Cultures in contact*. Elmsford, NY: Pergamon.

Kang, K.-W., & Pearce, W. B. (1984). The place of transcultural concepts in communication theory and research, with a case study of reticence. *Communication, 9*, 79-96.

Katriel, T. (1986). *Talking straight: Dugri speech in Israeli Sabra culture*. Cambridge: Cambridge University Press.

Kelly, G. A. (1955). *The psychology of personal constructs*. New York: Norton.

Kim, Y. Y. (1988). *Communication and cross-cultural adaptation.* Clevendon, England: Multilingual Matters.

Kim, Y. Y., & Gudykunst, W. B. (Eds.). (1988). *Theories in intercultural communication.* Newbury Park, CA: Sage.

Kincaid, D. L. (Ed.). (1987). *Communication theory from Eastern and Western perspectives.* New York: Academic Press.

Kincaid, D. L. (1988). The convergence theory and intercultural communication. In Y. Y. Kim & W. B. Gudykunst (Eds.), *Theories in intercultural communication.* Newbury Park, CA: Sage.

Kincaid, D. L., Yum, J. O., Woelfel, J., & Barnett, G. A. (1983). The cultural convergence of Korean immigrants in Hawaii. *Quality and Quantity, 15,* 59-78.

Koester, J., & Holmberg, C. B. (1983). Returning to rhetoric. In W. B. Gudykunst (Ed.), *Intercultural communication theory.* Beverly Hills, CA: Sage.

Kruskal, W. H. (Ed.). (1982). *The social sciences: Their nature and uses.* Chicago: University of Chicago Press.

Kuhn, T. S. (1970). *The structure of scientific revolutions* (rev. ed.). Chicago: University of Chicago Press.

Lakatos, I. (1970). Falsification and the methodology of scientific research programs. In I. Lakatos & A. Musgrave (Eds.), *Criticism and the growth of knowledge.* Cambridge: Cambridge University Press.

Lebra, T. (1976). *Japanese patterns of behavior.* Honolulu: University of Hawaii Press.

Nagel, E. (1961). *The structure of science.* New York: Harcourt, Brace and World.

Nakane, C. (1970). *Japanese society.* Berkeley: University of California Press.

Nakanishi, M. (1986). Perceptions of self-disclosure in initial interaction. *Human Communication Research, 13,* 167-190.

Nishida, T. (1984). A method for the analysis of Japanese-American communication. *Nihon University Research Annual, 32,* 93-101.

Ortner, S. B. (1984). Theory in anthropology since the sixties. *Society for Comparative Study of Society and History, 26,* 126-166.

Pearce, W. B., & Cronen, V. E. (1981). *Communication, action, and meaning.* New York: Praeger.

Pearce, W. B., & Kang, K.-W. (1987). Acculturation and communication competence. In D. L. Kincaid (Ed.), *Communication theory from Eastern and Western Perspective.* New York: Academic Press.

Pearce, W. B., & Lannamann, J. W. (1978). Modernity makes immigrants of us all. *Journal of Asian-Pacific and World Perspectives, 6,* 27-34.

Pearce, W. B., Stanback, M., & Kang, K.-W. (1984). Cross-cultural studies of the reciprocal causal relation between communication and culture. In S. Thomas (Ed.), *Studies in communication theory and interpersonal interaction.* Norwood, NJ: Ablex.

Pearce, W. B., & Wiseman, R. L. (1983). Rules theories. In W. B. Gudykunst (Ed.), *Intercultural communication theory.* Beverly Hills, CA: Sage.

Pettigrew, T. F. (1986). The intergroup contact hypothesis reconsidered. In M. Hewstone & R. Brown (Eds.), *Contact and conflict in intergroup encounters.* Oxford: Basil Blackwell.

Philipsen, G. F. (1975). Speaking "like a man" in Teamsterville. *Quarterly Journal of Speech, 61,* 13-22.

Philipsen, G. F. (1982, September). *Communication in contemporary culture.* Paper presented at Fullbright Conference on Communication, Society, and Culture, Dubrovnick, Yugoslavia.

Philipsen, G. F. (1988, April 4). [Comments at the "Culture and Communication Theory" conference held at Arizona State University, Tempe].

Pike, K. (1966). *Language in relation to a unified theory of the structure of human behavior.* The Hague, the Netherlands: Mouton.

Pilotta, J. J. (1983). The phenomenological approach. In W. B. Gudykunst (Ed.), *Intercultural communication theory*. Beverly Hills, CA: Sage.

Popper, K. R. (1968). *The logic of scientific discovery*. New York: Science Editions.

Prosser, M. H. (Ed.). (1973). *Intercommunication among nations and peoples*. New York: Harper & Row.

Reynolds, P. (1971). *A primer in theory construction*. Indianapolis, IN: Bobbs-Merrill.

Rogers, E. M., & Kincaid, D. L. (1981). *Communication networks*. New York: Free Press.

Sarbaugh, L. E. (1979). *Intercultural communication*. Rochelle Park, NJ: Hayden.

Secord, P. F. (Ed.). (1982). *Explaining human behavior: Consciousness, human action, and social structure*. Beverly Hills, CA: Sage.

Shweder, R. A., & LeVine, R. A. (Eds.). (1984). *Culture theory: Essays on mind, self, and emotion*. Cambridge: Cambridge University Press.

Sudweeks, S., Gudykunst, W. B., Ting-Toomey, S., & Nishida, T. (1988, July). *Developmental themes in Japanese-North American interpersonal relationships*. Paper presented at the Fourth International Conference on Personal Relationships, Vancouver, Canada.

Szalay, L. B. (1981). Intercultural communication—A process model. *International Journal of Intercultural Relations, 5*, 133-146.

Tafoya, D. W. (1983). The roots of conflict. In W. B. Gudykunst (Ed.), *Intercultural communication theory*. Beverly Hills, CA: Sage.

Ting-Toomey, S. (1985). Toward a theory of conflict and culture. In W. Gudykunst, L. Stewart, & S. Ting-Toomey (Eds.), *Communication, culture, and organizational processes*. Beverly Hills, CA: Sage.

Ting-Toomey, S. (1988). Intercultural conflict styles: A face-negotiation theory. In Y. Y. Kim & W. B. Gudykunst (Eds.), *Theories in intercultural communication*. Newbury Park, CA: Sage.

Triandis, H. C. (1972). *The analysis of subjective culture*. New York: John Wiley.

Triandis, H. C. (1977). *Interpersonal behavior*. Monterey, CA: Brooks/Cole.

Triandis, H. C. (1987). Collectivism vs. individualism. In C. Bagley & G. Verna (Eds.), *Personality, cognition, and values: Cross-cultural perspectives on childhood and adolescence*. London: Macmillan.

Triandis, H. C., Hui, C. H., Albert, R. D., Leung, S. M., Lisansky, J., Diaz-Loving, R., Plascencia, L., Marin, G., Betancourt, H., & Loyola-Cintron, L. (1984). Individual models of behavior. *Journal of Personality and Social Psychology, 46*, 1389-1404.

Tsujimura, A. (in press). *Communication theory in the East and West* [tentative title; to be published in Japanese].

Wolfson, K., & Norden, M. (1984). A rules approach to measuring responses to interpersonal conflict. In W. B. Gudykunst & Y. Y. Kim (Eds.), *Methods for intercultural communication research*. Beverly Hills, CA: Sage.

Wolfson, K., & Pearce, W. B. (1983). A cross-cultural comparison of the implications of self-disclosure on conversational logics. *Communication Quarterly, 31*, 249-256.

Wuthnow, R. (1987). *Meaning and moral order: Explorations in cultural analysis*. Berkeley: University of California Press.

Wuthnow, R., Hunter, J., Bergesen, A., & Kurzweil, E. (1984). *Cultural analysis*. London: Routledge & Kegan Paul.

Yang, K. (1981). The formation and change of Chinese personality. *Journal of Social Psychology, 113*, 159-170.

Yum, J. O. (1987). Korean philosophy and communication. In D. Kincaid (Ed.), *Communication theory from Eastern and Western perspectives*. New York: Academic Press.

Yum, J. O. (1988). Network theory in intercultural communication. In Y. Y. Kim & W. B. Gudykunst (Eds.), *Theories in intercultural communication*. Newbury Park, CA: Sage.

# 2 Inquiry in International Communication

## Thomas L. McPhail

Traditionally, international communication has been dominated by media concerns ranging initially from the print press to more recent concerns over transnational broadcasting. In particular, the debate has centered on the domestic impact of imported software and the regulatory or legal control options available to limit its impact. During the past two decades, theorists, researchers, and political decision makers alike focused their attention on the New World Information and Communication Order (NWICO).

NWICO derived intellectual support from the large body of scholarly research that revealed the gross inequities in the international flow of information from the developed to the developing countries of the world. Growing evidence of the problem reinforced the position of the developing countries. They claimed that the current system reflected the imperialist bias of the developed countries and demanded a restructuring of international media priorities. This gave rise to NWICO:

> An evolutionary process seeking a more just and equitable balance in the flow and content of information, a right to national self-determination of domestic communication policies, and, finally, at the international level, a two-way information flow reflecting more accurately the aspirations and activities of the less developed countries. (McPhail, 1987, p. 12)

Subsequent research further delineated these inequities, reexamined the concept of "development," provided numerous case studies, and identified and described the practice of development journalism. For the most part, the research concentrated on mass-media-related issues that fostered "electronic colonialism":

> The dependency relationship established by the importation of communication hardware, foreign-produced software, along with engineers, technicians, and related information protocols, that vicariously establish a set of foreign

48

norms, values and expectations which, in varying degrees, may alter the domestic cultures and socialization processes. (McPhail, 1987, p. 18)

During the 1970s, UNESCO became the major forum in which NWICO was debated. In fact, the intensity of the debate threatened to destroy the agency when first the United States and then Great Britain withdrew in response to what they described as critical threats to freedom of the press. Moreover, the inability of UNESCO to resolve the contentious issue led, to a large extent, to the downfall of the former Director-General, Amadou Mahtar M'Bow.

Having just returned from the 24th General Conference of UNESCO, where I was a member of the Working Group on Communication, I am fairly confident in saying that, for all practical purposes, NWICO, as a major international policy debate, is dead. Moreover, given its often bitter and hostile history, it is unlikely that the new Director-General, Fredico Mayor of Spain, will try to revive it. Having said that, however, I do not wish to give the impression that communication and related research traditions are no longer of vital importance to the international community of nations. They most certainly are! Even the concerns initially expressed as part of NWICO still have relevance. The major focus of the debate, however, is shifting to a different research and policy agenda.

Most developing countries are confident that the world has been alerted to the inequities of their situations. The international communication literature clearly has demonstrated the Western bias for reporting "coups and earthquakes," the existence and impact of different news values, the domination of the field by the five major international news agencies, the impact of foreign media software on indigenous cultures, and even the inconsistencies in the definition and practice of press freedom by its most ardent supporters. They recognize, however, that this awareness alone cannot improve the conditions under which they now exist.

The developing countries are beginning to focus on the more constructive international communication theory and research that addresses the issue of how communication and its related technologies can foster development without adversely affecting the domestic social and cultural environment. They, like the more developed countries, increasingly are concentrating on those issues related to the global shift to the Information Society exemplified by the rising importance of the International Telecommunication Union (ITU) as an international forum. Moreover, this shift was reinforced by the findings of the Independent Commission for Worldwide Telecommunications Development (1984), the Maitland Commission, which identified the global need for a basic telecommunications infrastructure before countries can effectively deal with the concerns of media imperialism.

This change in the international communications agenda was prompted by the rapid and exponential nature of technological innovation that has blurred the traditional media boundaries and the borders of sovereign nation-states. Two major telecommunications developments, in particular, are responsible for this transition or revolution, as it so frequently is called. The first is the expansion of satellite-delivered traffic of all types, including voice, video, and data. The second is the development of the sophisticated Integrated Services Digital Network (ISDN).[1] These developments mean that issues such as transborder data flows (TDF), informatics, direct broadcast satellites (DBS), the information economy and a host of related activities now fall under the purview of international communications.

Whereas earlier research focused on the transnational aspects of exporting Hollywood software, new concerns range from electronic banking and electronic mail to the globalization of the information economy. As such, this chapter will discuss international communication within the context of this broader definition, without ignoring the original concerns, in order to establish the theoretical and research agendas in international communication to the year 2000.

## THE PARADOX OF
## INTERNATIONAL COMMUNICATION

Ironically, the international communication arena is complicated by a perplexing phenomenon I term the "McPhail Paradox of International Communication." The ramifications of this paradox are far-reaching, influencing domestic, foreign, and international communication agendas. To date, while the research has identified these disparate trends and identified potential issues, it has not fully examined the resulting impacts.

On the one hand, current technological innovations are creating a global infrastructure much more sophisticated in scope and technical quality than previously imagined. Fostered by satellite delivery and ISDN, this infrastructure makes the concepts of global television, global films, and global information systems of all sorts present realities rather than future dreams. Moreover, isolated policy decisions, national initiatives, and transnational agreements are encouraging the global focus in international communication.

On the other hand, however, technological innovation has also functioned to fracture or fragment the mass audience. The advent of diverse, individualized telecommunications and media systems—from competing media outlets to pay-television, specialty channels, and pay-per-view options, to videocassette recorders, to expanding cable systems and satellite-delivered broadcast signals—threaten to render the concept of mass

national or international systems obsolete. Individuals in the developed
countries, at least, now have a plethora of media products from which to
choose compared with the limited and restricted selection of the past. The
net result is the demise of the mass audience in favor of the narrowcasting
concept of the future; a concept that offers much opportunity for developed
and developing countries alike.

This paradox can be illustrated with examples from all facets of the
communication enterprise. The daily newspaper, once a local product
designed to inform and entertain its subscribers, was among the first
communication media to respond to these technological and economic
imperatives. Today, not only are local newspapers linked to the major wire
services via sophisticated and cost-efficient telecommunications hardware, but the production aspects of the industry also have undergone major
changes in response to these same imperatives. Newspaper ownership is
concentrated in the hands of a few large conglomerates, many of which
are involved in a multitude of communication- or information-related
activities. Some newspapers have enlarged their subscriber base to one
that is global in scope. Satellite delivery has occasioned the development
of national and even international newspapers like *USA Today*, the *Wall
Street Journal, Financial Times*, and the *International Herald Tribune*.
This development has heightened concern about the importation of foreign
news and foreign news values and bears further consideration.

Despite the internationalization of news and newspapers, however,
the technology also brings with it the opportunity to develop more specialized and localized news services. Reduced costs in the news-gathering
and production sectors of the industry have fostered the development of
smaller newsmagazines and newspapers designed to cater to specialized
audiences. Moreover, the development of videotex, a system that is capable of electronically transmitting data of all sorts to individual receiving
sets, is forcing a rethinking of the original newspaper delivery patterns.
If data (i.e., information) can be collected electronically, it also can be
delivered electronically. The electronic newspaper of the not-so-distant
future means that subscribers can access information in their own homes
or offices in a more individualized and specialized manner, thus al-
tering the concept of mass communication to one of mini- or micro-
communication.

In the broadcasting sector, the trend to direct broadcast satellite distribution of television programming exemplifies the global nature of
present communication systems. By transmitting a single signal to a few
satellite transponders, the entire world can receive the same television
program simultaneously. While global television may still be in its in-
fancy, the technology already exists and numerous examples of the trend
are evident. Sky King, an English-language satellite-to-cable-delivered

European television network, tripled its audience in one year and expects continued gains in the future. Like other similar systems, it faces problems with respect to geostationary orbit and spectrum allocation issues, and domestic regulations and restrictions; but it clearly represents the media of the future.

While television-without-borders has the potential to unite the world in McLuhan's "global village," where truth, cooperation, and goodwill are the order of the day, even the most naive observer recognizes the dual potential of the enterprise. The extremely intrusive nature of this technological advance provides, at one and the same time, both a means for fostering international peace and understanding through global communication and a vehicle for the cultural domination of one nation through a phenomenon that has come to be known as the "Dallasization" of the world.

The overwhelming success of the U.S. television broadcasting industry with respect to the production of programming that entertains the world threatens to undermine the indigenous cultures and values of other nations.[2] Even the Soviet Bloc countries, which have protected their citizens from the onslaught of American media fare, appear to be relenting. Television-receive-only (TVRO) satellite dishes, videocassette recorders, and basic off-air television antennae are reinforcing the invasion of foreign broadcast programming. The problem is most acute in East Germany, where television programming from West Germany is watched routinely. In fact, the East German government is considering the installation of cable television in Dresden because its low-lying geographical position makes for poor television reception and, under the current conditions, few East Germans, particularly professionals, are willing to relocate there.

This domination of broadcast systems by one nation is particularly disconcerting for those who view television as a tool to foster nation-building and indigenous development. The values espoused by Americans are not universally acceptable; nor is their preoccupation with television as an entertainment medium. National attempts to restrict foreign media offerings will become more and more ineffective, however, as the technology continues to progress. Those concerned about the future of international communication must continue to address these issues, but they must shift their focus from merely documenting media imperialism to identifying constructive methods of adapting to the present realities. Ironically, some of these alternatives may be found in the "flip side" of the broadcasting paradox.

Along with the globalization of television, the increasing number of broadcast options available serves to fragment the mass broadcast audience and promotes the development of specialized broadcast services. This trend is illustrated by recent developments in the U.S. market. Where once the three national networks, ABC, CBS, and NBC, competed among themselves for the large and lucrative American audience, recent rating trends show them losing ground each month against the independent stations or specialized channels, like Ted Turner's Cable News Network (CNN), which are delivered in a variety of different ways including off-air, cable, and satellite.

As more choices become available, the audience for each option becomes smaller and more specialized. This trend offers a number of opportunities for program producers. As the number of channels or options increases, so does the number of available broadcast hours. No one nation's production industry can realistically expect to produce sufficient high-quality material to fill it all. That means that the opportunities for international producers will increase. Undoubtedly, they may choose to emulate Hollywood's production values and produce poor imitations, but they may also find that by creating programming that reflects their own values and cultures they can entice, entertain, and even educate international audiences. While this avenue offers potential rewards for program producers, it is also an exceedingly rich one for researchers. What is the state of the industry in individual nations? What options and opportunities are available? How can national governments and international agencies best assist in the creation of a new and varied broadcast menu? What is the potential for utilizing this avenue as a means of countering media imperialism? These questions beg answers and only empirical research and careful analysis of the issues can provide them.

A timely example of the global nature of international marketing and advertising is the current International Olympic Committee (IOC) program for Olympic sponsors on a worldwide basis. The worldwide marketing rights of the Olympics and Olympic-related symbols is being handled by ISL Marketing AG. This organization is selling the international marketing rights to the Olympics in the future. Major corporations are signing up and paying handsomely for the privilege. Such companies as Eastman-Kodak, Coca-Cola, 3-M, Visa, Phillips, and Federal Express are some of the early sponsors that have already committed in excess of $125 million for the international marketing rights in order to be associated with future Olympic Games and activities. In terms of advertising, Saatchi & Saatchi is a pertinent example. Saatchi & Saatchi is not only the world's largest advertising agency with more than $6 billion in billings, but it also has in excess of 14,000 employees working in more than 80 nations.

The basic point is that just as satellites no longer respect international boundaries in terms of their broadcasting footprints, so also transnational firms view business expansion with little regard to national borders, but rather view disposable income available from individuals, particularly the rising middle class, notable in many LDCs.

The telecommunications industry, too, is subject to this globalization versus individualization paradox. In fact, it is telecommunications that is the driving force behind the entire change in the communication agenda. The technology is operating to create global information pathways, ones that can supply vast amounts of data at hitherto unbelievable speeds and costs. The single network concept permitted by the adoption of the ISDN protocols fosters the development of a global, border-free communication system. The standardization of the technology enhances the demand for the standardization of laws, regulations, and tariffs, which calls into question the whole concept of national sovereignty. This, too, requires future attention.

To exacerbate the situation further, the same frantic "merger mania" that is sweeping all other major economic sectors has hit the telecommunications industry.[3] This "bigger is better" ideology is visible in almost all aspects of the telecommunications sector and failure to respond brings warnings of impending danger. For example, when the long-awaited merger between Fiat's Telettra telecommunications subsidiary and Italy's state-owned switcher-maker Italtel fell through in November 1987, it was characterized as a disaster for Italy; one that could dash its expectations of becoming a major player in the world telecommunications environment.

While mergers, takeovers, and technology all enhance the push toward large global networks, they also function to increase the options for individualized telecommunications services. Specifically designed systems that minimize costs and maximize efficiency are the order of the day as telecom users demand the most from their communication expenditures. In response, a number of small, specialized telecom service suppliers and manufacturers are appearing to service the needs of these consumers; needs that are not being met by the large multinational conglomerates. This presents another paradox, which if explored may serve to enhance the position of many of the players in the "Information Economy Sweepstakes." If you cannot compete with the giants, don't try to; find your own niche in the marketplace and make it work to your advantage.

Perhaps the most contentious issue facing international communications in the future is the question of transborder data flows (TDF), which has been exacerbated by the development of global information networks. TDF issues, however, focus on the software rather than the hardware. While it may be difficult to separate the two, the issue of information must be examined apart from the questions related to the infrastructures created to transmit it. It has been estimated that by the year 2000 most information, perhaps as much as 90%, will be transmitted by machines. Most of this information will be of a personal or strategically important nature and a large proportion of it will routinely cross national boundaries. Questions of privacy, national security, information ownership or copyright, and many others must be examined.

Scholars and policymakers, alike, are aware of the inadequacies of the current regulatory approaches and the international agencies that may serve to resolve these issues. While many claims have been made about the benefits of eased information flows, these have been of a general nature and have not been adequately documented. Without precise data concerning the types of information available, the channels used to transmit it, the purpose for which it is to be used, and the provisions made for its protection, it will be exceedingly difficult to establish any sort of international cooperation.

While several nations have acknowledged the necessity of establishing a legal right to communicate across national boundaries, independent of national authority, the establishment of a binding legal agreement that will guarantee that right is still a future dream. How to ensure that data networks operate in an unrestricted environment that still serves to protect the interests of individuals, corporations, or nation-states is still an unresolved issue. The degree to which national self-interest should be considered is still undetermined, as is the degree to which these concerns should be dealt with at the regional or international levels.[4] Rationales, guidelines, and regulations need to be developed on the basis of accurate data and realistic expectations. It is incumbent upon those who investigate the field of international communication to provide that data and the accompanying research that identifies, and supports or denies, the myriad options available.

To summarize, this global versus individual paradox has limitless repercussions for the international communication environment in terms of both its theoretical underpinnings and its future research agenda. Some theoreticians and researchers will focus on the globalization of international communication, while others will find ample data and intellectual support for pursuing investigations of fragmented and localized communications. The key here is that both trends, and the manner in which they interact or overlap, must be documented, examined, analyzed, and considered from both a commercial and a public policy perspective in preparation for the world of the twenty-first century.


## BORDERS AND DEFINITIONS DEFY BOUNDARIES

The second major theme in international communication that affects the research agenda is the tendency of technology to defy definition. As the telecommunications infrastructure develops, it inevitably overlaps or encroaches upon the territory once clearly defined as media related. This blurring of traditional boundaries means that a rethinking of the communications agenda is in order. For example, it has been argued that "because of the difficulty of separating broadcasting from telecommunications, the tendency to deregulate has serious consequences for all communication policy decisions, international, national and local" (Cantor & Cantor, 1986, p. 92). As a result, it is increasingly necessary for scholars and policymakers to acknowledge this blurring of once distinct boundaries and to examine its implications for both domestic and international communication.

To date, much of the research has focused on either telecommunications or the media, particularly broadcasting. It has revealed the gross inequities between the developed and developing countries and among the developing countries themselves. The literature has also examined the methods by which telecommunications and/or media services can be utilized to foster development. And finally, the tendency of the developed countries to dominate the less developed nations through the exportation of hardware, software, and technical expertise has been documented.

Future research, however, must be extended to include the more complicated scenario of the Information Society, which is characterized by an exponential increase in the volume of information flows as a result of the increased efficiency and complexity of information systems. These new systems, made possible by the convergence of computers and telecommunication, mean that time and distance restraints on information are virtually removed. Informatics will increase the world's dependence on information and communication services, force abrupt changes in our perception of our environment, and create an interdependence among previously autonomous institutions and nations.

According to Fobes (1987, pp. 172-174), this shift to an information-based society will be "auto-accelerating" and will provide both advantages and disadvantages. It will foster the creation of wealth and enable us to do more with less, but it will also increase uncertainty and alter our cultural environments. The speed with which information can be transmitted may even create an atmosphere of perpetual crisis. As information becomes central to all economic and social activities, it will force a restructuring of economies, alter employment patterns, and heighten competition. In addition, the advent of the Information Society threatens to affect current power structures, blurring the lines between the public and private sectors, service and manufacturing industries, work and leisure, and sovereign nation-states. The technology will affect every facet of life.

It has been estimated that, by the year 2000, information will be routinely treated as a resource, meaning that the shift to the Information Society will involve not only questions of technology, but of infrastructure and software management as well. Because information is power and economic information is economic power, the techniques employed to integrate and use information will be as important as the information itself.

In order to enjoy the benefits of the Information Society, every nation must have a diversity of communication systems that allows for fuller participation and hampers the imposition of arbitrary restrictions. The existence of gross inequities has been well documented, however. For example, while many individuals are still awaiting the arrival of their first telephone or radio services, others are anticipating the benefits of high-definition television (HDTV), which will be delivered to "smart homes"[5] via fiber optics or TVROs. The movement to HDTV will provide sharp, clear picture quality, rendering other television sets and protocols archaic.

At present, the United States and Japan are recognized as world leaders in the shift to the Information Society; they clearly acknowledge that economic or industrial strategies must be applied to information. Both countries have liberalized regulatory restrictions, promoted research and development, and encouraged economic competitiveness in the telecommunications and information sectors. While the European countries lag behind, they have undertaken steps to improve their position by the year 2000. But what of the other developed countries? And what opportunities exist for those countries that are only beginning to establish the minimum telecom infrastructures?

Given their current situation and their past experiences, it is not un-reasonable for the developing countries to fear the arrival of the Information Age. For many of them, universal basic telephone service is still a distant dream. To establish the kind of infrastructure required to handle the information flows of the new era is simply not possible without extensive assistance. Not only do these countries lack the financial resources, but there is also an absence of well-trained, knowledgeable individuals to plan, develop, or operate the high-tech systems required. Moreover, for people who have never operated a telephone, the mysteries of the computer appear overwhelming, so cultural acceptance becomes another problem. For many developing countries and some developed ones as well, there is a real fear that the benefits of the Information Society will pass them by. They face not only increased cultural imperialism, but also the very real possibility of economic and political dependency as information forever flows outward. When others know more about you than you know yourself, their power to dominate is enhanced significantly.

The potential consequences of the Information Age are enormous. In order to enhance the possibility of achieving equitable advantages, there must be full and effective participation of all sovereign states in the critical decision-making processes. Each nation's concerns need to be addressed and development must be geared to the needs of indigenous populations. For one or two nations to dominate the strategy planning in isolation necessarily reduces the autonomy of all others. Informatics knows no national boundaries and, therefore, a cross-national analysis of the relevant issues is desperately required.

The role of research related to this endeavor is not an easy one. The development of neutral and equitable strategies, guidelines, and regulations is an onerous task, but future research must address these issues. In the first place, it must assess the situation in both general and specific terms. In order to do this, we need to be able to make valid comparisons based upon consistent models or methodologies, and reliable and valid empirical measures. Only then can policymakers begin to address the question of "catch-up" plans and costs in a realistic fashion.

In addition, international communication research should investigate the possible cultural strategies that could reduce the negative impacts of the upcoming changes or, at least, prepare society for those changes by addressing the question of how people can best adapt to them. To do that requires that researchers examine the differential impacts on societies, classes, and individuals to determine how the technology can improve social conditions. By providing an agenda for future impacts, research can help to set social and cultural priorities that may serve to mediate the technological imperatives, thereby increasing the possibility that informatics and the Information Age will improve the quality of life and not dehumanize it.

At the present time, most decision making in this sector is ad hoc, defensive, and reactive in nature. These strategies are insufficient; only innovative and proactive planning can hope to achieve the desired results with respect to how to control the distribution and use of the new information technologies. Many factors make this a particularly arduous policy arena, among them the speed with which data may be transmitted and the multinational nature of the enterprise. Information gathered in one country may be transferred to, processed, or stored in many others. Research must address these questions and dilemmas in order to ensure the development of an unfragmented communication system, regulated in fair manner to ensure access and equity. Past research has indicated that telecommunications and information can assist countries in overcoming barriers to development. The key point for future research is to uncover those strategies that can increase efficiency, effectiveness, and equity. While funding considerations are not inconsequential, international commitment to balance national and global benefits is even more crucial. Research should strive to identify the value of democratized control and equitability for all players in the game.

## INFORMATION: MARKET COMMODITY OR
## SOCIAL GOOD?

Business in an information society involves the acquisition, transfer, and utilization of information. Undoubtedly, the telecommunications technology and infrastructure are necessary tools, but information is the key commodity. The shift to an international information economy has a number of ramifications including increased global interdependence and the blurring of once distinct boundaries. One area in which the distinctions between sectors is eroding is in the definition of goods and services. In most industrialized economies, services such as advertising, banking, insurance, accounting, and other financial services are now rivaling manufacturing and the production of goods for the lion's share of domestic GNP. This has resulted in the recognition of communication and information as trade goods. While information has always been an important aspect of any business enterprise, information flows have become critical to the success of many industries, and there is a growing tendency to establish trade policies that seek to promote and facilitate these flows. The debate with respect to whether information is primarily a marketable commodity or social good, however, is still unresolved.

The move to treat information as a marketable good, subject to the same sorts of policies as other trading goods, is fostered primarily by two other factors. The first is the increasing size and power of the large transnational corporations (TNCs). Telecommunications and information flows are central to the operation of all TNCs. Their objective is to develop strategies that enhance global freedom in terms of both markets and information flows. This undoubtedly brings them into conflict with the political power structures that seek to promote sovereignty and domestic control. According to Herbert Schiller (1986, p. 24), TNCs are anathema to political sovereignty because of "the longstanding insistence of capital to what it will, with no accountability whatsoever."

It has been estimated that twenty or fewer transnational corporations will dominate the field of communications, and hence culture, by 2000. It is no surprise, therefore, that many domestic governments fear the large and powerful TNCs, like IBM, which have been described as "omnipotent." Their ability to control telecom infrastructures and information data bases severely inhibits the ability of the state to control their activities or power. This calls into question the distinction between the public and private sectors, and raises concerns about the possible options for equitable participation in the Information Age.

The high cost of gathering and producing information is the second factor that has fostered the notion of information as a trade or market commodity. This trend is visible in all aspects of the communication enterprise. The rapid development of telecommunications including satellites, fiber optics, and computerized digital switching has created a world market, not only for telecommunications, but for broadcasting services as well. In addition, the trend toward the internationalization of broadcasting markets is fostered by deregulation and the privatization of media outlets. This has expanded the communication channel capacity and created a need for more software; software that is costly to produce and that must be marketed globally in order to recoup costs.

The United States is the current leader in the broadcast area with a domestic advertising-supported base sufficient to produce major shows with international appeal, such as *Dynasty* and *Dallas*. Many other countries, however, are now seeking to produce world-class programming in order to capture a share of this large market. Given that the financial success of a movie or television series is dependent upon acceptance in the English-language market, some non-Anglophone producers now produce their movies in English and then dub them for their domestic markets. As American producers find more and larger markets for their products, it raises further questions about cultural issues and the American domination of the industry. Some nations claim that their acceptance of U.S. programming is a trade-motivated action. If they buy American, the United States must reciprocate by buying the indigenous productions of other nations. (In reality, however, the United States is one of the most tightly closed broadcasting markets in the world and this is unlikely to change without some effective pressure.) But regulation, in the form of restrictions on advertising, quotas, standardized formats, and reduced "on-air" hours, has failed to stem the tide of foreign domination. The secret appears to be in achieving some degree of reciprocity with the broadcast markets of other nations. Not only would this promote the development of indigenous production by helping to defray large production costs, but it would also contribute to the weakening of the American stranglehold on the industry and perhaps encourage Americans to look at the productions of other nations. Once again this is an area that requires further research.

Another example that further illuminates the idea of information as a market good involves the film industry, which is dominated by American vertically integrated companies that control both production and distribution. Power to determine content, release patterns, ticket prices, and access and total control over retailing efforts and box office receipts maximizes their profits and greatly reduces the chances for independent producers to exhibit their films. In this way, the major production houses are guaranteed a better return on their investments.

Given that we accept the notion that information and communication are increasingly acknowledged as trade items that constitute an ever larger proportion of a nation's balance of trade, a number of issues become problematic. The present ad hoc arrangements concerning information and communication have been ineffective in promoting cultural sovereignty or in fostering the development of equitable global infrastructures, regulations, or laws. To counter this problem, the United States has put services, including information and communication services, on an equal footing with manufactured goods. Moreover, it is prepared to negotiate international agreements in order to remove barriers and restrictions.

The General Agreement on Tariffs and Trade (GATT) has become an attractive forum for pursuing this debate (Sauvant, 1986, pp. 258-259): the industrialized countries have a great deal of influence; the body has an inherent predisposition to free trade; and trade-offs between goods and services could be worked out in umbrella agreements. For precisely these same reasons, however, the developing countries are vulnerable. In order to ensure equity, reciprocal arrangements that balance the information flows in and out of any one country are necessary. There is no evidence that these complex arrangements can be achieved by GATT.

In addition, the whole issue of information as a trading good raises questions about deregulation. According to Nicole Dewandre (1986, p. 137), those who support deregulation are "the market oriented people who believe that there is nothing better than the market to take care of communications"; while those who favor the status quo believe that monopoly control "is the only way to guarantee good service and public service." This debate cannot be settled by trade negotiations. Moreover, what is right for one nation at one stage of development may not be suitable for another. To accept one standard may mean that deregulation and privatization shape markets before governments and domestic industries have the opportunity to develop protective cultural, educational, or information policies (Manet, 1986, p. 17.)

International communication research needs to examine the idea of information as a trade issue and to identify and analyze the public policy questions it raises. These include regulation and deregulation, public and private roles, the state and development of national systems, the degree of standardization and interconnectivity, the functional restrictions on information flows, the legal ramifications, and the various means that might be used to coordinate use and resolve disputes. The development of a model that is nondiscriminatory, fosters technical innovation, permits domestic sovereignty, and promotes international equity is the ideal. It will give the international community a goal that it can strive to attain.

## INTERNATIONAL COMMUNICATION:
## A MULTIDISCIPLINARY APPROACH

International communication research requires a multidisciplinary approach in the future. Communication, in its broadest form, now involves so many aspects that no one discipline can possibly understand or solve the problems. Included in the research should be an investigation of technology and technological diffusion, the current state and future development of infrastructures, the range of services that are necessary and/or possible, the source, purpose, and impact of software and the potential for domestic software production, the manner in which information is handled in terms of the legal or regulatory requirements, and the potential impact of information and communication services on the receiving countries. The compartmentalization of knowledge and research is no longer functional or even viable.

A multidisciplinary approach to the question of underdevelopment is also necessary. It is no longer sufficient to examine only those economic factors that are easily identifiable and easily quantified. Using those unidimensional criteria biases both the research and the evaluation. Development in the Information Age requires much more, including a commitment to ensure that the new is blended with the old in such a way as to cushion the radical changes that the information revolution can bring. Moreover, research must look again at the impediments to development from a varied perspective to ensure that innovation does not overcome one problem while reinforcing another. The lack of coherence in development policy, which Sonaike (1987, p. 91) identifies as "perhaps the most serious impediment in the way of effective use of communication for development," can be just as damaging as the total absence of any policy.

In order for international communication to achieve its objectives, there needs to be a comprehensive statement that identifies the relevant issues, suggests research needs, and proposes policy options for consideration. While there is no consensus of objectives, there are a number of issue areas that consistently resurface. These include questions of equity, free flow, public/private control, international/domestic priorities, and competitive/cooperative strategies. Such a statement would be functionally useful. It would identify the commitment of the world to the democratization of the technology without which the Information Age may make serfs of us all.

The potential for social change through mass media and telecommunications is great; required now are strategies that foster appropriate, fair, and equitable policies. Among these are the need to provide low-cost communications that will assist developing countries in adapting to and, eventually, participating in the Information Age. In addition, research needs to sharpen its empirical measures. If it is to provide reliable and valid data, it must have adequate, consistent, reliable, and valid yardsticks;

ones that can be used to compare the various stages of development and identify what remains to be done.

Not only will the agenda for international communication research shift in the balance of this century, but so too will the nature of research teams. In the past, the majority of international communications research was undertaken by academic-based scholars, working on their own or within scholarly research institutes.[6] These institutes recognized the multidisciplinary nature of the enterprise and frequently included specialists in diverse fields including sociology, economics, political science, engineering, communication, and law. They also began to recognize the substantial task involved in mounting major investigations in international communication. There is currently another significant research group entering the field: the consultants and specialists who are linked to major "think tanks." These think tanks not only provide interdisciplinary teams, but also have the capacity to attract the substantial external funding to mount the long-term and in-depth investigations in international communication that are increasingly necessary.

As a result, individual university-based researchers may find themselves increasingly outside the mainstream of international communication research because of their limited funding opportunities. Moreover, it is unlikely that the leading-edge research will continue to be reported regularly in the scholarly journals. Instead, these think tanks are more likely to publish substantial and expensive research reports. The trend toward consulting or non-university-based research houses will increase because of both the nature and the expense of investigating international and transborder communication phenomena in either the telecommunications or the broadcasting fields. The individual researcher simply does not have access to the level of financial support necessary to undertake investigations on the scale required in the future because the issues now spread across several disciplines, issue areas, and continents. To produce even a modest monograph on a single issue will require considerable time, travel, assistance, and other expenses, most of which are beyond the capacity of the individual university professor.

## THE FUTURE INTERNATIONAL
## COMMUNICATION RESEARCH AGENDA

To summarize, four major developments in international communication will direct the future research agenda. The first is the paradox of international communication, which simultaneously permits greater diversity in communication systems and content while at the same time promoting a uniformity or conformity. Research needs to examine this paradox, its potential for increased cultural and economic imperialism, the possibilities for international cooperation, and the options available to individual states for adapting to present realities.

The second theme involves the tendency of international communication and its related research traditions to defy established definitions. The blurring boundaries of the Information Society and their implications should be examined in order to identify the needs, opportunities, and potential impacts so that social, cultural, economic, and technological priorities can be realistically proposed and evaluated.

The concept of information also deserves reexamination. Is information a market commodity or a social good? What are the implications of this definition in terms of public policy? Will transnational codes of conduct work in service sector areas?

Finally, the multidisciplinary nature of the research enterprise needs to be acknowledged. International communication involves broadly based and diverse interests, which require thorough and balanced research. Future efforts need to be comprehensive in scope so as to provide a complete analysis. While there may still be opportunities to examine individual issues or individual cases, the imperative will be to relate these to the overall situation.

Some specific future research topics may include direct broadcast satellites; global television; the electronic newspaper; telecommunications: technology, regulation, tariffs, standardization; transborder data flows; the Information Society; information: goods or services; information, communication, and trade; deregulation and public policy; and the democratization of communication. This is merely a partial list of potential topic areas, but the areas do include a number of issues highlighted within this chapter.

The final point is that the research agenda in international communications in the twenty-first century will be totally different from that which confronted research scholars even at the midpoint of the twentieth century. In addition, the research strategy or approach—a team-based approach using interdisciplinary resources—will become the norm rather than the exception in this particularly important research area.

## NOTES

1. ISDN is a telecommunications network that can transmit speech, data, and images simultaneously, at improved speeds. It connects all terminals to a single type of socket that permits intercommunication of hitherto incompatible equipments, thereby allowing the development of new telecom services.

2. This refers to a particularly important concept and it is referred to again later in this chapter. U.S. television is not only a major force on many national television systems, but with the expansion of television networks and stations, particularly in Europe, U.S. program-

ming is enjoying an even greater exposure. U.S. programming enjoys two distinct international advantages; first, because many of their shows survive beyond three years, this provides the stockpile of sufficient episodes to be used in syndication. Many other shows produced elsewhere seldom survive for more than a year or two and thus are not available for international syndication. The second reason is even more important. Essentially it deals with economic imperative of purchasing U.S. programming. U.S. prime-time shows currently can reach budgets of $500,000. The average syndication rights for each episode is $50,000 or less. For Europeans, or any other nation, to compete directly with Hollywood would require a massive outlay of funds. In addition, many of these nations lack the domestic population even to pay a substantial portion of such astronomical costs. This has left the United States, by default, with 80% of the world's film and television export market. With the rapid expansion of satellite-delivered broadcasting channels, this percentage is likely to increase during the next decade. This illustrates the U.S. domination of the world's television and theater screens by the fact that U.S. producers still only produce for their domestic market and do not directly develop either themes or series that have an international appeal or audience. It is only by accident, in fact, that such shows ranging from *Dallas* to *The Cosby Show* have reached international syndication success because they are produced for the American market and the international market is only a supplement.

3. Although the bulk of the activities in terms of mergers and takeovers has appeared in the telecommunication sector, there have also been activities in both the broadcasting and the print media areas that have caused some concerns. For example, the British company, Pearson PLC, purchased a French financial daily and this occurred shortly after the purchase by the *Wall Street Journal* of a 14% interest in another French financial daily. The French press is lamenting that Anglo-Saxon interests are now making inroads in the French press and that such a trend may continue, perhaps even at a rapid rate, given the relatively weak financial structure of many of France's private press outlets.

4. Concerns about one's role in the international telecommunication sweepstakes is not limited to LDCs by any means. In fact, even the European communities are quite concerned about the massive challenge being presented by both Japanese and American firms in the high-technology sector. Realizing that telecommunication is the central nervous system of the evolving Information Economy, the European communities recently commissioned a "green paper" titled "Towards a Dynamic European Economy: Green Paper on the Development of the Common Market for Telecommunications Services and Equipment" (Commission of the European Communities, 1987); it represents a rather modest set of suggestions in their attempt to modernize and make competitive European telecommunications and information manufacturing and services.

5. *Smart homes* merely refers to new homes that are built with much of the electronic equipment already built in with appropriate wiring, particularly fiber optics, that will allow for a significant number of broadcasting and information services to be delivered directly to the home.

6. This change will result in the demise of the "Lone Ranger Scholar." No longer will individual scholars be able to have a substantial impact in the field of international communication as compared with their predecessors in the 1950s or 1960s. During that era it was possible for an individual scholar to carve out for him- or herself an area within a university department known as international communication. They then were able, by virtue of their own travels and resources, to compile a significant publication record in the field. In the future that is going to be a very rare case given both the multidisciplinarity of the phenomena under investigation and the costs associated with mounting a substantial study in the international communication area.

# REFERENCES

Aines, A. A. (1987). Support global competitiveness. *Transnational Data Report, 10*(9), 8.

Ansah, P. A. V. (1986). The struggle for rights and values in communications. In M. Trober (Ed.), *The myth of the information revolution: Social and ethical implications of communication technology* (pp. 64-83). London: Sage.

Branscomb, A. (Ed.). (1986). *Toward a law of global communication networks.* New York: Longman.

Brown, L. (1987, November). Starring on the world stage. *Channels,* p. 18.

Commission of the European Communities. (1987, June). *Towards a dynamic European economy: Green paper on the development of the common market for telecommunications services and equipment.* Brussels: Author.

de la Garde, R. (1987). Is there a market for foreign cultures? *Media, Culture and Society, 9,* 189-207.

Desousa, M. A. (1982). The cultural impact of American TV abroad: An overview of criticisms and research. *International and Intercultural Communication Annual, 6,* 13-26.

Dewandre, N. (1986). Europe and new communication technologies. In M. Ferguson (Ed.), *The new communications technology and the public interest: Comparative perspectives on policy and research* (pp. 137-149). London: Sage.

Fair, J. (1987). The regulation of transborder data flows: An international perspective. *Gazette, International Journal for Mass Communication Studies, 40*(1), 21-38.

Feketekuty, G., & Hauser, K. (1984). A trade perspective of international telecommunications issues. *Telematics and Informatics, 1,* 359-369.

Ferguson, M. (1986). *The new communications technology and the public interest: Comparative perspectives on policy and research.* London: Sage.

Fobes, J. (1987). An overview of informatics and development. *Telematics and Informatics, 4,* 165-194.

Guback, T. (1987). The evolution of the motion picture theatre business in the 1980s. *Journal of Communication, 37*(2), 60-78.

Hamelink, C. J. (1986). Is there life after the information revolution? In M. Trober (Ed.), *The myth of the information revolution: Social and ethical implications of communication technology* (pp. 7-20). London: Sage.

Hudson, H. (1987). Barriers and incentives to telecommunications investment in developing countries. *Telematics and Informatics, 4,* 99-108.

Independent Commission for World Wide Telecommunications Development. (1984). *The missing link.* Geneva: International Telecommunication Union.

Jussawalla, M., & Cheah, C. C. (1987). *The calculus of international communications: A study in the political economy of transborder data flows.* Littleton, CO: Libraries Unlimited.

Kobayashi, K. (1986). *Computers and communications: A vision of C & C.* Cambridge: MIT Press.

Krommenacker, R. K. (1987). Uruguay round service negotiations. *Transnational Data and Communications Report, 10*(9), 11-17.

Leeson, K. W. (1981). *International communication: Blueprint for policy.* Amsterdam: Elsevier.

Mackintosh, I. (1986). *Sunrise Europe: The dynamics of information technology.* Oxford: Basil Blackwell.

Manet, G. (1986). New media: Cultural Trojan horse. *Transnational Data and Communications Report, 9*(3), 17.

Mansell, R. (1987). Information sector policy analysis: Conceptual framework and Canadian illustration. *Gazette, International Journal for Mass Communication Studies, 39*(3), 195-210.

Marbut, B., Temple, L., Harvey Steorts, N., Perryman, M. R., & Reinhold, R. (1987). Economical, political and educational perspectives on the New Texas. In F. Williams (Ed.), *The New Texas* (pp. 15-50). Austin: University of Texas.

Martin, J. (1978). *Telematic society: A challenge for tomorrow*. Englewood Cliffs, NJ: Prentice-Hall.

Mattelart, A., & Stourdze, Y. (1985). *Technology, culture and communication: A report to the French Ministry of Research and Industry*. Amsterdam: Elsevier.

McPhail, T. L. (1987). *Electronic colonialism: The future of international broadcasting and communication* (2nd rev. ed). Newbury Park, CA: Sage.

Mosco, V. (1982). *Pushbutton fantasies, critical perspectives on videotex and information technology*. Norwood, NJ: Ablex.

Moses, J., & Dertoozos, M. (Eds.). (1979). *The computer age: A twenty year view*. Cambridge: MIT Press.

Nora, S., & Minc, A. (1978). *The computerization of society*. Cambridge: MIT Press.

Oliverira, O. S. (1986). Satellite TV and dependency: An empirical approach. *Gazette, International Journal for Mass Communication Studies, 38*(2), 127-145.

Reddi, U. V. (1986). Leapfrogging the industrial revolution. In M. Trober (Ed.), *The myth of the information revolution: Social and ethical implications of communication technology* (pp. 84-98). London: Sage.

Reese, S. D., Shoemaker, D. J., & Danielson, W. A. (1987). Social correlates of public attitudes toward new communications technologies. *Journalism Quarterly, 63*, 675-682.

Renaud, J. (1984). A revised agenda for the new world information order. *Gazette, International Journal for Mass Communication Studies, 34*, 117-135.

Sauvant, K. P. (1986). *International transactions in services: The politics of transborder data flows*. Boulder, CO: Westview.

Schiller, H. (1986). The erosion of national sovereignty by the world business system. In M. Trober (Ed.), *The myth of the information revolution: Social and ethical implications of communication technology* (pp. 21-34). London: Sage.

Sitati, R. N. (1987). Deregulation: Consequences for developing countries. *Transnational Data and Communications Report, 10*(12), 19-21.

Sonaike, S. A. (1987). Going back to basics: Some ideas on the future direction of Third World communication research. *Gazette, International Journal for Mass Communication Studies, 40*(2), 79-99.

Stevenson, R. L. (1986). Radio and TV growth in the Third World, 1960-1985. *Gazette, International Journal for Mass Communication Studies, 38*(2), 115-125.

Williams, F. (1987). Texas as an information society. In F. Williams (Ed.), *The New Texas* (pp. 51-63). Austin: University of Texas.

# 3 Inquiry in Development Communication

## Everett M. Rogers

The purpose of this chapter is to present an up-to-date report on the progress and scope of scholarly research in the field of development communication. We trace the historical background of this field, and stress the potential of new communication technologies like satellites and microcomputers in future development communication.

Development communication is the application of communication with the goal of furthering socioeconomic development (we define development later in this chapter). Thus development communication is a type of planned social change, oftentimes of major concern in the Third World nations of Latin America, Africa, and Asia. Because furthering development is such a priority concern of Third World governments, communication scholars interested in Third World settings share a scholarly interest in development communication. Just as development also occurs in industrialized nations (for instance, the majority of people living in my city, Los Angeles, were born in Third World nations and continue their original culture while living in Southern California), many communication scholars in Euro-America are interested in development. In an increasingly interrelated world, development problems in Third World countries affect everyone.

The field of development communication is often classed with its close intellectual relatives: intercultural communication and international communication. All three deal centrally with the special difficulties related to communication between two or more people who are extremely different from each other in culture, formal education, technical expertise, and so on. So development communication is heterophilous communication, and hence difficult.

AUTHOR'S NOTE: The present chapter is a revision of a paper presented at the Seminar "Communication and Change: An Agenda for the New Age of Communication," East-West Center, Honolulu, July 20-August 1, 1987.

Perhaps no other field of communication research than development communication has been subjected to such a thorough review and synthesis as is represented by three seminars, held in 1964, 1975, and 1987 in Honolulu and sponsored by the East-West Center (and, in the case of the third seminar, cosponsored with the University of Hawaii). The first two seminars on development communication were led by Wilbur Schramm and Daniel Lerner, and the 1987 seminar was organized by Joung-Im Kim and Godwin C. Chu. Each of the three seminars included from twenty to forty specialists in development communication from Asia and Euro-America meeting to discuss the performance, problems, and prospects of this field. Development communication experiences from Latin America and Africa were less directly represented at the three seminars, although not ignored, as examples and experiences from Latin America and Africa were brought into the discussions. Influential books (Lerner & Schramm, 1967; Schramm & Lerner, 1976) came out of the first two seminars, helping define the meaning of development communication as it has changed from decade to decade. In the present chapter, I shall use the three Hawaii seminars as a frame for organizing the nature of inquiry on development communication.

## BACKGROUND OF DEVELOPMENT COMMUNICATION

The mood and tone of the 1964, 1975, and 1987 Hawaii seminars differed in important ways (I was not a participant of the first seminar, but have read the ensuing book and talked to many of the 1964 participants):

- A general *optimism* about development communication was evident in 1964 (Lerner & Schramm, 1967).
- A *questioning stance* about the field characterized the 1975 seminar (Schramm & Lerner, 1976).
- The 1987 seminar was pervaded by a viewpoint of *pluralism*, a willingness to recognize that many different ideas or approaches may be valid, which was an academic stance that did not mask the important differences and disagreements about the nature of development communication.

The former consensus about development communication (the so-called dominant paradigm[1] had broken up by the 1975 seminar, or at least many of us thought so at the time (Rogers, 1976; Schramm & Lerner, 1976). Certain alternatives to the main elements in the dominant paradigm of development communication are today evident in many Third World nations. For example, instead of seeing development communication as mainly a one-way, mass-media-centered process from government to people, stressing capital-intensive technological innovations that often lead to industrialization and urbanization, contemporary development communication approaches are more likely to emphasize equality, the "little media," and people-participation. The dominant paradigm, however, lives on (a) in certain Third World countries, and (b) for certain kinds of development programs. For example, the "Green Revolution" campaigns for diffusing high-yielding rice and wheat varieties in many Third World nations in the late 1960s and 1970s rather closely followed the dominant paradigm of development communication. These were top-down campaigns that pushed a technology package of seeds, fertilizers, and pesticides. And, as Leonard Chu pointed out at the 1987 seminar, the People's Republic of China in the 1980s is emphasizing economic growth (through the "economic responsibility" system) at the expense of socioeconomic equality. So is India today, in efforts to boost its high-tech microelectronics industry through the activities of a new class of Silicon Valley-type entrepreneurs (Singhal & Rogers, in press-a).

So while the dominant paradigm of development communication no longer is pursued by most Third World countries—as it was in the period from the end of World War II to around 1970—certainly this paradigm lives on, even though it is no longer dominant in the way that it once was. The paradigm has changed in its contemporary form, by, for instance, becoming less Western in its cultural assumptions. Most important, a variety of alternative paradigms are now pursued in various Third World nations (Table 3.1).

Perhaps a key question is this: When is the dominant paradigm of development communication appropriate, and when is another theory more appropriate (a) in a particular setting, (b) for a particular development program, or (c) because of certain conceptual factors?

## THE CONTEMPORARY DIVERSITY OF
## DEVELOPMENT COMMUNICATION

Today there are many more scholars interested in development communication than in 1964, and they are much more likely to be from other than Euro-American backgrounds. The national identities of the participants in the 1964, 1975, and 1987 seminars show this trend. When scholars from Third World nations also became major contributors to this field, some of the cultural assumptions that restricted its earlier vision were shed.

Almost all of the early scholars of development communication were North Americans who shared an empirical, positivistic approach. Wilbur Schramm was then a faculty member in the Institute for Communication Research at Stanford University, and Daniel Lerner was a professor at

**TABLE 3.1.** A Shift from the Dominant Paradigm of Development Communication to Alternative Paradigms Occurred in the Early 1970s

---

I. The Dominant Paradigm of Development Communication

   1. One-way in nature, from government-to-people

   2. Mass-media-centered, especially featuring such big media as television

   3. Creating a "climate for development" through the mass media

II. Alternative Paradigms of Development

   1. Participation, knowledge-sharing, and empowerment to the people

   2. More attention so such little media as radio

   3. Equality achieved by focusing development programs on the weaker sections of a
      national population, including the poor, women, villagers

---

MIT. During the 1950s and early 1960s, the main research methods were (a) surveys (for example, Lerner's 1958 survey of individual modernization in six Middle Eastern nations), and (b) field experiments, in which development information was introduced via such electronic media as radio and (later) television to peasant audiences, who were surveyed before and after the experimental intervention in order to measure its effects. The paths not taken by such early research represent certain deficiencies in the 1950's and 1960's understandings of development communication. For example, the electronic media, particularly privately owned radio systems, mainly featured content that was urban-oriented entertainment and advertising. It is not surprising that exposure of individuals to such media content did little to further development, and may have retarded it. But until the nature of development communication research changed to focus also on content analysis techniques and on investigating the impacts of media ownership, the antidevelopment effects of radio and television exposure on audiences in Third World nations could not be very fully understood.

Significantly, the first such content analysis/media ownership studies were carried out by communication scholars in Latin America, during the second era of development communication research (in the 1960s). Early Latin American scholars of development communication like Juan Diaz Bordenave of Paraguay— who worked in Brazil—and Luis Ramiro Beltran of Bolivia—who worked in Ecuador, then Colombia, and finally in much of Latin America—received their postgraduate degrees at the University of Wisconsin and at Michigan State University. But in spite of such outstanding Latin America researchers, U.S. communication scholars were dominant in conducting research in the second era of the 1960s and early 1970s, and in fact are probably still most widely represented in development communication research today. Nevertheless, during the past several decades, a considerable broadening has occurred in the nationality of development communication scholars, and in the range of research methods and theoretic perspectives that were utilized. A wider perspective has thus been given to the development communication field, and it has been freed of many of its limiting assumptions and biases. Also benefited was the parent discipline of communication science, which, through more solid intellectual work in development communication, also shed some of its made-in-America cultural biases.

*There is much less consensus, and much more criticism, in the academic field of development communication today than in 1964.*

Partly this breakup of intellectual agreement results from the decline of the dominant paradigm. The increasing cultural and intellectual heterogeneity of development communication scholars led to a wider diversity of development communication models. Critical scholars like Herbert Schiller at the University of California at San Diego, Cees Mamelink at the Institute for Social Studies (the Hague) and the University of Amsterdam, and Armand Mattelart at the University of Paris have contributed to scholarly thinking about development communication, often asking such important questions as "Who owns and controls the communication systems that are involved?" "Who gains and who loses?" "What is the role of communication technology?" The pluralistic ferment of the 1980s has replaced the unity consensus of 1964 about development communication. The present academic state of development communication represents better scholarship and more useful ideas in application, and it is more intellectually exciting.

A basic reason for the greater diversity of academic thinking about development communication in the 1980s can be traced to the broad questioning of quantitative empirical positivism as the basic approach to social science. August Comte originally labeled his approach to sociology "positivism" because he was positive that scientific methods borrowed from the physical sciences of chemistry and physics could be useful in investigating human behavior to find solutions to social problems. Communication research, a relative latecomer to the family of social sciences, inherited the positivistic assumptions to science and theory-testing characteristic of sociology, social psychology, and political science in the 1940s, the period when communication research was organizing as a social science specialty field (Rogers, 1986). The positivistic approach was carried over in the early study of development communication.

As Tom Jacobson of the State University of New York at Buffalo said at the 1987 Hawaii seminar, the dominant dependence on empirical verification of a theory is "clearly a thing of the past." Some social scientists, including certain development communication scholars, are today disappointed with a strictly quantitative approach to positivism, because it does not inform them about everything that they want to know. As Syed Rahim of the East-West Center noted at the 1987 Hawaii conference, positivism need not be antagonistic to the use of qualitative data, to an interpretive theoretical approach, or to critical theory. Many development communication scholars today prefer to use a triangulation strategy in their choice of theory and of research methods, rather than being completely loyal to any one methodology, either quantitative or qualitative, or to any one theoretical perspective, whether positivism, dependency theory, or other alternatives. So the contemporary questioning by some social scientists of quantitative research conducted in a positivistic approach has led, in the field of development communication, to a wider diversity of theory and method—and to less intellectual agreement.

## WHAT IS DEVELOPMENT COMMUNICATION?
## AND DEVELOPMENT?

Any definition of development communication must rest ultimately on a definition of development. In the early 1970s, the approach to development being followed by most Third World nations changed in a rather fundamental way (Rogers, 1976). Less emphasis was placed upon centralized development planning (such as by a national planning commission) and on capital-intensive heavy industrialization based on energy-driven, imported technologies. Accomplishments with this old type of development paradigm were mostly measured at the national, aggregate level in terms of economic growth (for example, in terms of per capita income and the gross national product).

Questioning of this development model in the early 1970s led to more stress upon achieving greater equality in the socioeconomic benefits of development and upon the social as well as the economic dimensions of development, and to stressing decentralized participation by the people affected by a development program. *Development* today is still more or less defined as a type of directed social change that provides individuals with increased control over nature. The exact behavior changes that today are the goal of development programs in various nations range from the one-child family in China, to decreased pesticide use in the Philippines, to creating a national "computer culture" in Singapore, to combating infant diarrhea with oral rehydration therapy (ORT) in Africa and Latin America, and to preventing AIDS (acquired immune deficiency syndrome) in Mexico, Brazil, and in East Africa. Development in any particular nation may consist of a variety of such development programs and projects. Development is still the top-priority goal of almost every Third World national government. But development today means something rather different to each nation.

So much for the meaning of development. Now for the definition of development communication. Obviously, when the dominant paradigm of development changed in the early 1970s, the dominant model of development communication also changed, as alternatives began to be considered. As mentioned earlier, *development communication* is the application of communication to the goal of furthering development. Such application may be (a) to further development generally, such as by increasing mass media exposure by the population of a nation in order to strengthen the "climate for development," or (b) to support a specific development program or project (this later type of development communication is often called "development support communication," or DSC).

It is difficult for anyone to oppose the purposes of development communication. Who could argue against utilizing communication to decrease the number of infant deaths in a country, to improve the health and nutrition of a nation's population, to prevent AIDS, to produce more food so as to decrease famine, and to overcome the limitations of illiteracy? So the *goals* of this type of directed social change (that we call development) are fairly well agreed on. What is controversial is *how* to utilize development communication to reach these socially acceptable goals. Here there is diversity among development communication specialists.

The first criticisms of the dominant paradigm came particularly from Latin American scholars like the Brazilian Paolo Friere, Luis Ramiro Beltran, and Juan Diaz Bondenave. European/critical and American/empirical traditions coexist in Latin America to a greater degree than in Asia and Africa. Latin American scholars, especially social scientists, also took the lead in the 1960s in proposing dependency theory (the basic idea that underdevelopment may be due to the dependence of Third World nations on Euro-America, rather than due to resistances to development lying *within* a Third World nation). So once Third World scholars became involved in research and in scholarly writing about Third World development, theory and methods began to change.

## THE ACADEMIC FIELD OF
## DEVELOPMENT COMMUNICATION TODAY

At the time of the 1964 Hawaii seminar, the academic field of development communication was barely getting under way. Daniel Lerner's (1958) book, *The Passing of Traditional Society: Modernizing the Middle East*, had appeared, along with Wilbur Schramm's (1964) important volume, *Mass Media and National Development*. But as far as I know, no university courses were being taught on this topic, nor was it then recognized as an academic specialty for professors or graduate students in communication. In other words, the intellectual field of development communication was not yet launched.

The Schramm (1964) book gave visibility to the field and provided a useful textbook. In about 1966, the late Wilbur Schramm launched a course on development communication at Stanford University, and courses began at about the same time at Michigan State University and at the University of Wisconsin, and then at many other universities in the United States and in other nations. Soon centers of excellence in research and education in development communication arose at

* Agricultural University at Wageningen (the Netherlands)
* Cornell University
* Florida State University
* Institute for Social Studies (the Hague) and University of Amsterdam
* Leuven University (Belgium)
* University of Hawaii and the East-West Institute of Culture
  and Communication
* University of Iowa
* University of Leicester
* University of Pennsylvania
* University of the Philippines (both at Silliman and at Los Banos)
* University of Texas
* University of Southern California
* University of Sussex

There are many others. At some of these universities, only one (or a very few) scholars represent the specialty of development communication, so it is actually a "one-person show." At some centers of academic excellence, however, several courses on development communication are offered, and a master's degree or a Ph.D. specialty can be earned. Here there are often several faculty specializing in development communication.

It is surprising that no major textbook on development communication has appeared to replace the 1964 Schramm volume. I hope that such a textbook would be integrative across the lessons learned from such development communication activities as those in agriculture, health, family planning, literacy, and nutrition. Perhaps the fast-moving and incoherent nature of the development communication field has prevented such a consensus document from being written. There are many useful books about development communication, however, and a large and growing number of journal articles and research reports, but *the* textbook that defines the field does not exist today.

This field gained increased recognition in the International Communication Association (ICA) in 1982 when the Division of Intercultural Communication became the Division of Intercultural and Development Communication. The International Association for Mass Communication Research (IAMCR) puts a heavy emphasis upon development communication at its every-other-year meetings. And the annual conferences of the Association for Education in Journalism and Mass Communication (AEJMC) also feature many papers on development communication. But there is no single, specialized association where only scholars of development communication gather.

## RESEARCH ON
## COMMUNICATION AND DEVELOPMENT

What does research indicate are the effects of communication for development in Third World nations? This question is very difficult to answer because mass and interpersonal communication are often so pervasive that their unique contribution to development is almost impossible to partition from the effects of technological, political, and economic changes. Communication research conducted in an empirical, quantitative, and positivistic epistemology has struggled in the decades since Daniel Lerner's 1958 Middle East survey to assess the effects of communication for development. Lerner (1958) operationalized the concept of mass media exposure as a factor in individual modernization. But he paid little attention to the content of the mass media, other than to assume that they were "modern" in nature. Very few development surveys of modernization (like Lerner's) are conducted today.

Another empirical research approach to the communication-effects-on-development question has been to investigate the role of communication in a particular development activity like a national family planning campaign, an oral rehydration therapy program, or an Integrated Pest Management (IPM) campaign in a nation, or in some part of a nation. Here the type of communication involved is much more specific than the general mass media exposure studied by Daniel Lerner. When such development support communication is investigated, rather than the general content of the mass media (much of which is entertainment), more specific answers to the effects question can be obtained. When the communication content is more specified, its effects on development are easier to assess.

In the past decade, certain communication scholars attempted to sharpen their approach to identifying communication's effects on development by investigating the impacts of a new communication technology. Examples are the introduction of satellite television broadcasting in India and Indonesia, and rural telephony in Peru. In this approach, communication's effects on development are somewhat more facile to trace because a new communication capability (e.g., television or telephony) is introduced where it did not previously exist. A pre-post field experimental design is often followed, usually without a control group (we will discuss contemporary research on communication technology in development later in this chapter).

Looking back over the past several decades of communication research on development, we see considerable progress (a) in gaining greater control over possibly intervening variables through more sophisticated research designs (and also through the use of computer-based multivariate statistical analysis), and (b) in specifying the media content whose effects are being investigated. The result of these methodological advances is a more precise, data-based understanding of communication's effects on development.

Much room for improvement exists, however, in the further sharpening of communication development research, and in broadening both the range of research methods that are utilized and the theoretical approaches that are followed.

## THE IMPORTANCE OF COMMUNICATION IN DEVELOPMENT, BY PROGRAM

Diversity exists in the nature of development programs and among Third World nations, and hence the role of communication in development varies considerably. Some development programs consist only (or at least mainly) of information, with little other input, and here communication essentially equals development. One example is ORT, a program in which infants with diarrhea are given an electrolyte mixture of eight parts sugar, one part salt, and water. This ORT mixture (essentially Gatorade without the green color) was discovered by a young medical doctor in Bangladesh in the 1970s. Today ORT programs are under way in many Third World nations, as dehydration due to diarrhea is a main cause of infant mortality. Communication scholars at Stanford University (Foote et al., 1985; Snyder, 1986) and at the University of Pennsylvania (Hornik et al., 1987) have played a key role in designing and evaluating ORT campaigns. While the proper mixing of the ORT solution must usually be demonstrated to people (for example, it can be dangerous if eight parts of *salt* and one part of *sugar* are mixed with the water), the ingredients are cheap and easily available in almost every Third World household. Needless to say, the life-saving effects of ORT programs make them very popular with the people (and with their governments).

In contrast, certain government-sponsored development programs are generally unpopular with the people, and here the role of communication is to be persuasive (and sometimes even coercive) and usually is of relatively modest importance in achieving development objectives. An example is family planning programs, which are popular today with many national governments in the Third World, but not with the target audience of married couples of reproductive age. The government of a country whose population is doubling every twenty years or so cannot build enough schools, create an adequate number of jobs, and provide housing rapidly enough to keep pace with population growth. But parents in these high-population-growth nations generally wish to fulfill an ideal family size norm of five or six children per completed family. So they ignore communication messages from a government family planning program to have a two-child (or a one-child) family.

In such nations as the People's Republic of China, Hong Kong, Korea, Singapore, and Taiwan, however, relatively strong governments have utilized various incentives and disincentives to achieve a sharply reduced rate of population growth as the result of the widespread adoption of family planning methods (by about 70% of fertile-aged married couples, almost the same as in the United States). Indonesia, another Asian nation with a strong, stable government, has achieved an adoption rate of about 40%. Key to the success of such national family planning programs is often some kind of organized local group in which national fertility goals are reduced to the village and neighborhood levels, resulting in one couple being told "You can have your baby this year" and another couple being told "You wait." Examples of such local groups are the *banjars* in the province of Bali in Indonesia (Piet & Piet, 1978), and the group planning of births in the People's Republic of China (Chen, 1976).

But in other Third World countries where national governments are less strong, particularly in their ability to reach down to the village level, family planning programs have been relatively unsuccessful in reaching their demographic goals. An example is India, the first nation in the world to state an official population policy (in 1950). In the four decades since, India has only achieved about 35% adoption of family planning methods, mainly on the part of the more educated, urban couples. Why has India's family planning program not been more successful? Certainly not because the role of communication has been underemphasized. Probably no other nation has stressed family planning communication so heavily as has India. The essential reason for India's ineffective family planning program lies in the unpopularity of the program. Most Indian couples do not want to have just one or two children, and their government has not been able to persuade them otherwise. The case is similar in such other nations as Pakistan, Bangladesh, Nigeria, and Egypt. Prime Minister Indira Gandhi's government proclaimed martial law in the late 1970s, and launched a nationwide vasectomy campaign (which included a certain degree of coercion). The result was that, after several years, Mrs. Gandhi was voted out of office for her unpopular family planning program (Gwatkin, 1979), although she eventually was returned to office.

*The success of development programs that are unpopular with the people rest mainly on a strong government authority, rather than on the role of communication.*

Communication is the main component in certain development programs (like ORT), and communication is almost irrelevant in the success or failure of unpopular development programs in nations without strong governments (for example, family planning in India). In other development programs in other Third World nations, communication is one key component among several others, but it would be a mistake to overestimate its importance (Hornik, 1980). We now realize that development is a "systems" problem, consisting of several interdependent components, each of which must accompany the others if success is to be achieved. Usually, communication is just one component in development.

An illustration is the Green Revolution of the 1960s and 1970s, in which high-yielding varieties of rice and wheat, accompanied by chemical fertilizers, pesticides, irrigation, and improved farm management techniques, were widely diffused by agricultural extension services in many Third World nations. The result has been a tremendous increase in food production, worldwide, with many nations that were food-deficit now becoming food exporters. Famine and hunger today occur because of political, economic, and logistic reasons, but not because of absolute food shortages worldwide. The Green Revolution is one of the brightest development success stories,[2] and communication played an important role in it, along with a powerfully effective technological package.

## DEVELOPMENT COMMUNICATION AND DEMOCRACY

In the 1950s and 1960s, it was assumed that, as development was furthered, one result would be more participatory forms of government in Third World countries. Many Third World nations in Asia and Africa had just gained their independence from European colonial rulers after World War II. Their first priority after independence was development. The audiences of certain mass media, especially radio, were expanding rapidly in the early 1960s, thus increasing citizen levels of political knowledge and feelings of nationhood. Under these conditions, it seemed logical to extend the notion of Jeffersonian democracy, based on a politically informed citizenry, to Third World nations. In fact, this faith in development leading to democratic governments was a basic reason why the people of the United States and several European nations were willing to support international development assistance programs. They thought they were "saving the Third World from communism, and for popular democratic forms of government."

During the 1960s, military dictatorships became a common form of government in Latin America, Africa, and Asia. Often these dictatorships placed a higher priority on law and order (as had the European colonial governments previously) than on development. Public expenditures for arms purchases and for the support of a huge military establishment often outweighed government investments in development programs. Dictatorships are not always antidevelopment, however, as several authoritarian governments have launched successful development programs.

Important questions about development and democracy are these: (1) Does increased development lead toward participatory democracy? (2) Does a participatory democracy facilitate or retard development in a Third World nation?

## EXPANDING TELEVISION
## AUDIENCES AND ENTER-EDUCATION

The potential role of the mass media in development is much greater today than ever before, at least in the sense of much-expanded media audiences. Radio is everywhere. During the 1980s, television's audiences rapidly expanded in Mexico, Brazil, China, India, and in several other Third World nations. A recent survey in the Beijing metropolitan area (including peasant villages surrounding the city) found that over 90% of adults regularly viewed television (Rogers et al., 1984), and this figure is estimated nationally at about 50%. So there are 550 million people in the television audience in China. India's television audience has doubled in the past two or three years, to 10% of the total population (about 70 million TV viewers).

These many millions of new television viewers in Third World countries provide a potential for development communication that is not utilized very fully. Most TV content is entertainment, rather than being educational and prodevelopment. It is possible to convey subtle development themes embedded in entertainment programs, however. Mexico's private television company, Televisa, pioneered prodevelopment TV soap operas in 1976, and has broadcast several series promoting adult literacy, family planning, female equality, national history, and improved family relations.

India, Kenya, Brazil, Nigeria, and several other nations are presently broadcasting family planning TV soap operas (Singhal & Rogers, in press-b). Somewhat similarly, a rock 'n' roll song by two young singers, Tatiana and Johnny, advocating sexual abstinence for teenagers climbed to the top of the hit parade in Mexico in 1986 and elsewhere in Latin American in 1987. Its effects on contraceptive adoption by teenagers were evaluated by communication researchers (Televisa's Institute for Communication Research, 1987).

It is not surprising that most individuals prefer television entertainment programs to educational programs, which are relatively dull. Examples of the ability of entertainment to crowd out instructional messages are provided by

- American Samoa, where an instructional TV system introduced in 1967 has now become mainly a means of broadcasting U.S. entertainment programs (Schramm, Nelson, & Betham, 1981).
- Kheda District in India, where a local transmitter broadcast locally produced television programs on such topics as the exploitation of the poor and other social problems from 1977 to 1985, when the Ahmedabad TV station began broadcasting national programming (mostly entertainment) into Kheda District. Much of the Kheda District audience switched to viewing the national entertainment programming, and the local transmitter was closed down (Singhal & Rogers, in press-a).

A main force behind the emphasis on entertainment programs in television broadcasting is the desire for a large audience, which is motivated in turn by commercial advertising. There is a general trend toward the commercialization of television systems in many European countries and in many Third World nations. The commercialization of TV means that the emphasis on entertainment programming will certainly not go away. Thus prodevelopment TV soap operas, which combine lots of entertainment with a little education, may have an important potential for development communication. Evaluation researchers of the effects of such enter-education media communication suggest a promising potential.

## A COMMUNICATION DEVELOPMENT
## PROJECT AS A "SOMETIMES THING"

A cautionary point is that most development communication projects do not last forever, at least without changing in very major ways. Examples of the "sometimes" nature of development communication projects are:

- Radio forums, launched with the assistance of UNESCO in a pilot project at Pune, India in 1960, then spread to numerous Asian and African nations. Today, few radio forum programs are active in the Third World.
- Instructional television projects in Colombia, El Salvador, Samoa, and the Ivory Coast, launched in the 1960s and 1970s, as Wilbur Schramm noted at the 1987 Hawaii conference, do not continue today, and even the Hagerstown (Maryland) instructional television project, which was the model for its overseas counterparts, is gone.
- "Training and Visit" (T & V) extension systems, promoted by the World Bank during the 1970s in about 75 Third World nations, have been gradually absorbed into national ministries of agriculture and extension services, and are losing their distinctive qualities (and even their identification as "T & V" systems).
- Social marketing of condoms and contraceptive pills by family planning programs in India, Kenya, Sri Lanka, Bangladesh, Jamaica, and other Third World nations was enthusiastically carried out in the 1970s. Today many of these social marketing programs have ended (although social marketing projects for family planning are going strong in Indonesia and a couple of other nations).

These development communication projects are not necessarily failures. Rather, most of these approaches played a useful role in their day, but their day just passed. In some cases, initial enthusiasm for a particular approach was not matched by the results of evaluation studies carried out by communication scholars. In other cases, a communication development project or approach achieved measurable results, but the continued commitment of a government development agency to the approach was lacking, or the original champion for a development communication project passed on and was not replaced.

Perhaps the "sometimes" nature of development communication approaches need not be a historical inevitability. Maybe effective approaches can be kept around longer. As Wilbur Schramm stated in his paper at the 1987 Hawaii conference, an important issue is "how communication can be used in such a way as to maintain the bloom on its development flowers for a long time."

## COMMUNICATION TECHNOLOGY AND DEVELOPMENT

A major cause of optimism about development communication today is communication technology. The issue of communication technology was not considered very directly in the 1964 Hawaii seminar on development communication (although the transistor radio revolution was under way, as was noted at the time), nor did communication technology get very much attention at the 1975 Hawaii seminar (although the Indian Satellite Instructional Television Experiment was then about to begin). Today, it would be impossible to ignore the many applications of such communication technologies as satellite-based long-distance telephony and television broadcasting, video, microcomputers, and videocassette recorders (VCRs). For example, the 1987 Hawaii seminar included reports on the effects of satellite television in Indonesia, satellite-based rural telephones in San Martin, Peru, and the use of video in Nepal and India as a means of conveying villagers' needs and to provide feedback to development officials.

Will the development promise of the newly introduced communication technologies be fulfilled? Many of the technologies are at an early stage of introduction and trial, and what we know about their effects is based only on small pilot projects instead of nationwide applications. In the past, many communication technology projects have failed, as Bella Mody (1985) points out, because they were First World technologies introduced in Third World contexts. Too often in the past, the importance of the social, organizational, economic, and logistical context of a communication technology has not been fully appreciated, and thus another communication technology project failed. An example is the electrical power surges that often occur in certain Third World settings, which play havoc with microcomputer use.

### Feeding the Rhinoceros

Often the crucial decision to adopt and implement some item of communication technology hardware (a communication satellite, for example, or a color television broadcasting system) is made by national political leaders, who often justify their decisions on the basis of potential development benefits. Ultimately, most development decisions are *political* decisions, sometimes also influenced by the results of development communication research. One of the important accomplishments of development communication research in recent decades has been (a) to make such national communication technology policy decisions more informed (and perhaps less "political"), and (b) to facilitate the implementation of these communication technology decisions in a more effective way. Few major development communication projects in the Third World today are carried out without a summative evaluation study conducted by communication researchers. This accomplishment of the development communication field represents an important change from the situation in 1964, when evaluation research was just beginning and when it only rarely affected policy decisions.

Once a major item of hardware communication technology like a communication satellite becomes available in a nation, many related elements of the communication technology system, like the software, social, organizational, and contextual aspects, must necessarily follow if the hardware is to operate effectively. Thus the "rhinoceros" has to be fed, as was pointed out at the 1987 Hawaii seminar. For example, once a national television broadcasting system is launched in a Third World country, a tremendous appetite for many hours of television programming per day is created. Due to cost limitations for domestic television production, the hungry rhinoceros is usually fed with imported television series like *Dallas, Dynasty,* and *Different Strokes.* The result is not much prodevelopment impact of the national television system, and certain antidevelopment consequences (like consumerism and overurbanization) may occur.

But the rhinoceros problem is not inevitable. With awareness of this problem, it can be avoided, or at least minimized. An example is Indonesia, where a national satellite-based television broadcasting system was launched in the mid-1970s. In 1981, after a communication research study (Chu, Alfian, & Schramm, in press) illuminated the antidevelopment impacts of television, the Indonesian government (a) stopped television advertising, and (b) replaced part of the imported television series with domestic productions.

In India, the government-controlled, satellite-based television system now broadcasts relatively few imported entertainment programs, instead depending mainly on Bombay-produced television soap operas. The increasing stress on commercial advertising on Indian television, however, has set off a communication policy debate in New Delhi about the proper role of television in Indian society (Singhal & Rogers, in press-b). At the heart of this debate, I believe, is the hungry rhinoceros. The principle thus illustrated is that appropriate software technology must accompany hardware technology, or else that technology will fail.

### Rural Telephony

The telephone was perceived as a consumer luxury in 1964 (when the first Hawaii seminar was held), and the improvement and expansion of telephone services were given very low priority by most Third World governments. Today, telephone service is perceived by most Third World national governments as an essential spur to business activity, and thus it receives a much higher national priority. Some nations have recently launched R&D centers to create improved telecommunications technologies. An illustration is the Center for the Development of Telematics (C-DOT) in New Delhi, which has developed a rural automated telephone exchange including "hardened" equipment that can operate at the village level in India (where humidity and high temperatures pose a problem for the usual telephone equipment when they are not operated in air-conditioned situations). When the new rural automated exchange was installed in a pilot project in Karnataka State in South India (where rural telephone service had not existed previously), telephone use increased rapidly, along with local business activity (Singhal & Rogers, in press-a).

Similarly, in San Martin, Peru, Professor John Mayo of Florida State University reported in a paper at the 1987 Hawaii seminar that within six weeks of the introduction of a satellite-based rural telephone system the service was being used to capacity. Many of the telephone calls were long distance to Lima, the capital city, and tended to be of an instrumental (rather than a personal-social) nature. The average call, however, cost about 75 cents, an important expense for poor people in Peru.

While telephones are not a new technology in an absolute sense, they are indeed a new communication service to those individuals in rural areas of Third World nations that have not previously had telephone service. Communication research projects typically seek to determine (a) the adoption and use of telephones, and (b) the impacts of telephones on development.

### Video

Today, video equipment is relatively low cost, portable, and easy to learn to use. It fits with the predominately oral tradition of villagers in many Third World nations. Video provides a means to overcome the literacy barrier. Also, video often can uniquely provide a way for rural people and urban poor to *participate* in development programs, by expressing (a) their needs for solutions to certain problems (for example, drinking water, exploitation, etc.) and (b) their feedback on the results of development activities. Because of the unique role that video can play in development communication, it is currently being utilized and evaluated in several Third World sites. Video projects in India and in Nepal were described at the 1987 Hawaii conference.

### The Information Society

The new communication technologies can become something much more than just a delivery system for development messages. They also represent, at least potentially, a new type of industry, one that some enthusiastic observers claim can allow certain Third World nations to leapfrog the industrial era, in order to become information societies.

What is an information society? An *information society* is a nation in which a majority of the labor force is composed of information workers, and in which information is the most important element (Rogers, 1986, p. 10). Information workers are individuals whose main work activity is producing, processing, or distributing information, and producing information technology. Typical information worker occupations are scientists, mass media employees, computer programmers, office workers, teachers, and managers.

The majority of the labor force in most Third World nations works in agriculture, and the next most numerous occupational category is industrial workers. So one might think that Third World countries are unlikely candidates to become information societies. A couple of nations in Latin America, Africa, and Asia, however, are pursuing national policies intended to move them rapidly to becoming information societies. An example is Singapore, where a computer programming software industry is flourishing. Other nations moving toward becoming information societies are South Korea, Hong Kong, and Taiwan.

In an information society, elite status is given to R&D workers and to scientists, as research to create and develop technological innovations is highly valued. The research university or the R&D institute represent a central institution for the information society, much as the factory did for the industrial society. The computer may be the key technology of the information society, much as the steam-powered engine was in the industrial society.

## CONCLUSIONS

We have argued that if the dominant paradigm of development has not passed (as had been thought in 1975), it is certainly much less dominant. Instead, contemporary development communication programs put a main emphasis (a) upon achieving equality in the distribution of development benefits, and (b) upon people-participation.

During the 1980s, the issue of communication technology has become much more important in the Third World, especially the use of communication satellites for television broadcasting and for telephony. A major expansion of television audiences has occurred in several Third World nations, with entertainment featured as the main television content. Thus one of the main issues for development communication in the years ahead may be to explore how television can be utilized more effectively for development goals.

## NOTES

1. A *paradigm* is a scientific approach to some phenomena that provides model problems and solutions to a community of scholars (Rogers, 1986, p. 114).

2. The Green Revolution was successful in terms of the rapid diffusion of technological innovations and the resulting increase in grain yields, but it also led to problems of socioeconomic inequality in some nations.

86 OVERVIEWSOVERVIEWS

# REFERENCES

Chen, P.-C. (1976). *Population and health policy in the People's Republic of China* (Occasional Monograph 9). Washington, DC: Smithsonian Institution, Interdisciplinary Communication Program.

Chu, G. C., Alfian, & Schramm, W. (in press). *Satellite television comes to Indonesian villages: A study of social impact.* Honolulu: University Press of Hawaii.

Foote, D., Matorell, R., McDivitt, J. A., Snyder, L., Spain, P., Stone, S. M., & Storey, J. D. (1985). *The mass media and health practices evaluation in The Gambia: A report of the major findings* (Report to the U.S. Agency for International Development). Menlo Park, CA: Applied Communication Technologies.

Gwatkin, D. R. (1979). Political will and family planning: The implications of India's emergency experience. *Population and Development Review, 5,* 29-59.

Hornik, R. (1980). Communication as complement in development. *Journal of Communication, 30,* 10-24.

Hornik, R. (1988). *Development communication: Information, agriculture, and nutrition in the Third World.* New York: Longman.

Hornik, R. et al. (1987). *Evaluation of ORT campaigns.* Philadelphia: University of Pennsylvania, Annenberg School of Communications.

Lerner, D. (1958). *The passing of traditional society: Modernizing the Middle East.* New York: Free Press.

Lerner, D., & Schramm, W. (Eds.). (1967). *Communication and change in the developing countries.* Honolulu: University Press of Hawaii.

Mody, B. (1985). First World communication technologies in Third World contexts. In E. M. Rogers & F. Balle (Eds.), *The media revolution in America and in Western Europe.* Norwood, NJ: Ablex.

Piet, D., & Piet, N. (1978). *Family planning and the Banjars of Bali.* New York: Cycle.

Rogers, E. M. (1976). Communication and development: The passing of the dominant paradigm. *Communication Research, 3,* 121-133.

Rogers, E. M. (1986). *Communication technology: The new media in society.* New York: Free Press.

Rogers, E. M., Zhao, X., Pan, X., Chen, M., and the Beijing Journalists Association. (1984). The Beijing Audience Survey. *Communication Research, 12,* 179-208.

Schramm, W. (1964). *Mass media and national development: The role of information in the developing nations.* Stanford, CA: Stanford University Press.

Schramm, W., & Lerner, D. (Eds.). (1976). *Communication and change: The last ten years—and the next.* Honolulu: University Press of Hawaii.

Schramm, W., Nelson, L. M., & Betham, M. T. (1981). *Bold experiment: The story of educational television in American Samoa.* Stanford, CA: Stanford University Press.

Singhal, A., & Rogers, E. M. (in press-a). *India's information revolution.* Newbury Park, CA: Sage.

Singhal, A., & Rogers, E. M. (in press-b). Pro-social television for development. In R. E. Rice & C. Atkin (Eds.), *Public communication campaigns* (2nd ed.). Newbury Park, CA: Sage.

Snyder, L. B. (1986). *Learning and acting in a health communication campaign: Teaching rural women to prevent infant dehydration through diarrheal disease control in The Gambia, West Africa.* Unpublished doctoral dissertation, Stanford University.

Televisa's Institute for Communication Research. (1987), *Evaluation of communication for Young People Project* (Report to Johns Hopkins University/Population Communication Services). Mexico City.

# 4 The New International Information and Communication Order

**Kaarle Nordenstreng**
**Wolfgang Kleinwächter**

Information and communication are becoming global problems of mankind. The satellite- and cable-based integrated services digital networks (ISDN) will cover the whole globe in the next century. Developed, as well as developing, countries and socialist, as well as capitalist, states are likewise affected by satellite television (DBS) and transborder data flows (TDF). The signals sent out by high communication technology do not know the frontiers of time and space. The development of new communication technology has far reaching political, economic, social, and cultural consequences for the development of each nation, as well as for the organization of the relationship among the states at the international level. It is no exaggeration to state that the development of communication technology is linked closely to the security and to the well-being of a nation and is inseparable from the global problems of peace and development.

Communication technology, like every technology, is an instrument that can be used or misused. The more the global character of this technology becomes visible, the deeper the nations are concerned. At the international level, communication technology can become an instrument to stabilize international security, to promote understanding among nations, and to initiate development. International information and communication can and must contribute to the creation of a climate of confidence in our interdependent world. But communication technology also can be misused as an instrument to create mistrust, to deepen conflicts, or to dominate and exploit other nations.

EDITORS' NOTE: The references cited in this chapter are clearer using the style the authors choose rather than APA reference style, the format used in the other chapters. The references, therefore, have not been changed to APA.

Indeed, the means of communication are today one of the most important vehicles to accelerate the process of internationalization of life and to deepen the interdependence between the states. The introduction and the use of highly sophisticated communication technology affect the interests of almost all nations. The development of global networks is an unprecedented challenge for all nations regarding the establishment of an international framework for the transborder flow of information and communication.

But the challenges do not come from the future only. They come likewise from the past. One of the most burdening vestiges of colonialism in our century, which has far-reaching consequences up to present time, is the underdevelopment of communication in the developing world. The present technological revolution takes place against the background of a deep gap between developed and developing countries. There are widening disparities in the spreading of the means of communication and there are growing imbalances in the flow of information.

Although more than three-quarters of the world population is living in the developing countries, less than one-quarter of the newspapers and journals, the radio and television receivers and transmitters, the telephones, and the information processing capacities in the world are available in these more than 100 countries (see Table 4.1). Although it is today recognized worldwide that communication is an essential component in the process of development, three-quarters of the world still can be described as underdeveloped in the field of information and communication. Although it is recognized worldwide that the rights to information and communication (i.e., the right to inform and to be informed, to have access to information, and to participate in the national as well as in the international flow of information) are fundamental human rights, more than 70% of the world's population are not able to enjoy this human right embodied in the Universal Declaration and the International Covenants on Human Rights.

Many developing countries have neither a comprehensive national communication policy nor a sufficient national-level framework for information activities. This vacuum does not remain empty, it is being filled by external activities, in particular by actions of the communications-rich countries in the West. They transport millions of newspapers and journals daily to the South. News agencies like UPI, AP, and AFP dominate even the information flow between the developing countries. Radio stations in the North are working around the clock for the millions of receivers in the underdeveloped world. And the big TV networks, in particular in the United States, flood the Asian, African, and Latin American countries with a never-ending flow of films, series, commercials, news, and so on.

**TABLE 4.1.** The Distribution of Newspapers, Radio, and Television Receivers per 1,000 Habitants in Developed and Developing Countries (1983)

|  | *Newspapers* | *Radio Receivers* | *Television Receivers* |
|---|---|---|---|
| Developed Countries | 319 | 835 | 437 |
| Developing Countries | 33 | 113 | 26 |

SOURCE: *UNESCO Statistical Yearbook 1986* (Paris 1987, pp. VI-13 ff.).

Developing countries are confronted with a double challenge in the information age: Internal underinformation as a result of national underdevelopment is combined with external overinformation as a result of global technological progress. Developing countries are using the information and communication resources that they need, and they are overrun with unwanted information, which very often is seen as disturbing national development. Because self-determination in the field of information and communication is interwoven with political, social, economic, and cultural self-determination, the national sovereignty, the national economy, the cultural identity, and even the national security of the developing countries are threatened.

### NEW INTERNATIONAL INFORMATION AND COMMUNICATION ORDER AND THE NONALIGNED MOVEMENT

The concept of the New International Information and Communication Order (NIICO) originally was developed by the more than 100 members of the Non-Aligned Movement. The "discovering of the information and communication gap" in the early 1970s led to a discussion of mass-media-related problems during the 4th summit conference of the movement in Algiers, August 1973. In the "Action Programme for Economic Cooperation" of the 4th summit meeting, a special paragraph was incorporated in which the developing countries were encouraged to "take concerted action in the field of mass communication" in order "to promote a greater interchange of ideas among themselves."[1]

Two years later, the Conference of the Ministers of Foreign Affairs of the Non-Aligned Countries adopted at their conference in Lima, Peru, a special resolution, "Cooperation in the Field of Diffusion of Information and Mass Communications Media." In the resolution the initiative of the Yugoslav news agency TANJUG to create a pool of news agencies of the developing countries was supported and the convening of an international seminar of experts to discuss all information-related problems was proposed.[2] This symposium was held in Tunis in March 1976 and can be seen as the factual starting point for the process of the establishment of a new information and communication order.

This report of the symposium stated that "the peoples of developing countries are the victims of domination in information and this domination is a blow to their most authentic cultural values."[3] The report continues: "Domination in Information has many subtle and varied forms, in the manipulation and control of the biggest part of information by the powerful transnationals such as the big international press agencies and in the technological control of the information media in the hands of the most powerful nations. This is the case, for example, of the communications by satellite whose use by developing countries is subject to the will of those who possess the advanced technology and by it, can decisively influence the economic, political and social reality of the developing countries."[4] And the report concludes: "The emancipation of information in the non-aligned countries and in all the developing countries reflects the fundamental interests of the peoples of those countries in their economic and political liberation and is a basic element in the activities of the countries fighting for independence, equality, progress and cooperation between all the peoples of the world in a framework of respect for the national sovereignty of each country and non-intervention. Every developing country has the right to exercise their full sovereignty over information, as much over information about their daily realities as that diffused to their people, equally they have a right to be informed objectively about external events and the right to publicize widely their national reality."[5]

It was at this symposium that the phrase "New International Information Order" was used for the first time. Paragraph 27 of the report stated: "Since information in the world shows a disequilibrium favoring some and ignoring others, it is the duty of the non-aligned countries and the other developing countries to change this situation and obtain the decolonization of information and initiate a new international order in information."[6]

The symposium adopted 26 recommendations that were presented to the Ministerial Conference of Non-Aligned Countries on Decolonization of Information, which took place in New Delhi, July 1976. The "New Delhi Declaration" based on these recommendations, noted that

1. The present global information flows are marked by a serious inadequacy and imbalance. The means of communication of information are concentrated in a few countries. The great majority of countries are reduced to being passive recipients of information which is disseminated from a few centers.

2. This situation perpetuates the colonial era of dependence and domination. It confines judgments and decisions on what should be known.

3. The dissemination of information rests at present in the hands of a few agencies located in a few developed countries and the rest of the peoples of the world are forced to see each other and even themselves through the medium of these agencies.

4. Just as political and economic dependence are legacies of the era of colonialism so is the case of dependence in the field of information which in turn retards the achievements of political and economic growth.

5. In a situation where the means of information are dominated and monopolized by a few, freedom of information really comes to mean the freedom of these few to propagate information in the manner of their choosing and the virtual denial to the rest of the right to inform and to be informed objectively and accurately.

6. Non-aligned countries have, in particular, been the victims of this phenomenon. Their endeavors, individual or collective, for world peace, justice and for the establishment of an equitable international economic order, have been underplayed or misrepresented by international news media. Their unity has been sought to be eroded. Their efforts to safeguard their political and economic independence and stability have even been denigrated.

7. Non-aligned countries have few means, in the present situation, to know about each other, except through the channel of the existing news media and news centers, their own news media being mainly underdeveloped or undeveloped for want of required resources."[7]

This description of the state of the art and the proposed concept was adopted one month later by the highest body of the nonaligned movement, the summit conference. The Political Declaration of the 5th Summit Conference (Colombo, August 1976) concludes that "a new international order in the fields of information and mass communications is as vital as a new international economic order."[8]

The Political Declaration of the Colombo Summit Conference added three lengthy paragraphs:

161. Non-Aligned Countries noted with concern the vast and ever growing gap between communication capacities in non-aligned countries and in the advanced countries which is a legacy of their colonial past. This has created a situation of dependence and domination in which the majority of countries are reduced to being passive recipients of biased, inadequate and distorted information. The fuller identification and affirmation of their national and cultural identity thus required them to rectify this serious imbalance and to take urgent steps to provide greater momentum in this new area of mutual cooperation.

162. The emancipation and development of national information media is an integral part of the overall struggle for political, economic and social independence for a large majority of the peoples of the world who should not be denied the right to inform and to be informed objectively and correctly. Self-reliance in source of information is as important as technological self-reliance since dependence in the field of information in turn retards the very achievement of political and economic growth.

163. Non-Aligned countries must achieve these objectives through their own efforts as well as by more active cooperation on a bi-lateral, regional as well as inter-regional basis and by coordinating their activities in the United Nations and other international forums. It is particularly necessary for non-aligned countries to strengthen their existing infrastructure and to take full advantage of the scientific and technological break-through already made in this field. This would facilitate more complete dissemination of objective information amongst their own public as well as the world at large about developments in non-aligned countries in the social, economic, cultural and other fields and their growing role in the international community.[9]

The summit meeting endorsed the "New Delhi Declaration" and authorized the establishment of an institutionalized mechanism for the implementation of the new international information and communication order, which included

- the Intergovernmental Council for the Coordination of Information among Non-Aligned Countries (IGC)
- the Coordination Committee of the Non-Aligned News-Agencies-Pool (NANAP)
- the Coordination Committee of the Broadcasting Organizations of the Non-Aligned Countries (BONAC)

The summit decided to introduce the NIICO idea into the global negotiation process within the United Nations system.

All of the decisions of the Colombo Summit were of a strategic nature. The whole international debate around information and communication questions in the following years was influenced mainly by the recommendations of this conference, and all the actions undertaken by the members of the Non-Aligned Movement at the universal, regional, or subregional levels were inspired by the spirit of Colombo. With the Colombo Summit Meeting, the idea of the NIICO was authorized as a topic of high priority in the general strategy of the movement toward decolonization and democratization of international relations.

Practically, the Non-Aligned Movement after Colombo worked in two directions: The first direction was practical and aimed at the strengthening of the information and communication capacities of the developing countries. They started with concrete actions to develop national information systems, to strengthen national communication infrastructures, and to develop capacities for the production of hard- and software in the information field, for the collection, processing, and dissemination of information at the national and international levels, for the training of journalists and technicians, and for different research activities.

The second direction was political and aimed at the democratization of international information and communication relations. This included the elaboration of comprehensive national communication policies, the definition of basic democratic principles and norms that should give guidance for the behavior of the actors in the field of international information and communication, and the start of global negotiations within UN, UNESCO, ITU, and other multilateral organizations with the aim to improve the concrete situation for the developing countries and to reorder the disparities and imbalances by common international actions.

Both activities are interrelated, although sometimes either the practical or the conceptual work was more dominate. In the first year after Colombo, the elaboration of the concept and the drafting of the aims and principles had high priority. Within less than five years, the relevant organs of the movement, and in particular the IGC, elaborated the conceptual framework of the NIICO, defined the aims and principles for the NIICO as well as for bi- and multilateral cooperation in the field of information and communication, and drafted a comprehensive strategy in the form of a Programme of Action.

Later, especially in the 1980s, practical actions toward the strengthening of the information and communication capacities of the developing countries got first priority. The development of news agencies, radio and television networks, and training and research institutions was in the center of the relevant work of the Movement.

The 6th Summit Meeting in Havana, September 1979, took note "with gratification of the fact that non-aligned and other developing countries have made notable progress along the path of emancipation and development of national information media and stresses that the cooperation in the field of information is an integral part of the struggle of non-aligned and other developing countries for the creation of new international relations in general, and a new international information order in particular."[10]

In the Political Declaration of the 7th Summit Meeting in New Delhi, March 1983, the heads of state "expressed their profound sense of satisfaction at the progress recorded by the various agencies that have been established to promote cooperation among non-aligned countries in the field of information and mass media, which is an integral part of their national development process. In particular they commended the work undertaken by NANAP and BONAC and urged these agencies to earnestly implement their respective Programmes of Action so as to further develop and diversify the signal contribution they are making to the decolonization of information and in countering tendentious reporting and mass media campaigns against non-aligned countries and national liberation movements."[11]

And in the Political Declaration of the 8th Summit in Harare, September 1987, the heads of state "reaffirmed the need further to intensify cooperation among non-aligned and other developing countries in the field of information and the mass media so as to establish the New International Information and Communication Order on the basis of the free and balanced flow of information and speedily to remove disparities in communication capabilities which in the era of rapid technological advances create new imbalances and place new and complex obstacles to democratization of global information and communication process. They noted with satisfaction the progress achieved in this field and in particular the significant contribution made by the Non-Aligned New Agencies Pool established among non-aligned countries towards the decolonization of information and towards countering tendentious reporting and mass media campaigns against non-aligned countries and national liberation movements."[12]

At the 2nd Conference of the Ministers of Information (COMINAC II), which took place in Harare one year after the 8th summit, the general strategy of the movement toward the establishment of the NIICO was also outlined in detail. In the "Harare Declaration," the Ministers "insisted that the rights to communicate and to be heard were fundamental human and social rights and that information was a crucial resource for ensuring national independence and national development as well as the exercise of political, economic and cultural power."[13]

The ministers "expressed their continuing concern at the corporate concentration of resources on the mass media, the multi-sectoral integration and global reach of the corporations and the transnational control over new telecommunication technologies and data processing which in recent years have aggravated the general imbalance in the international system of communication and information flow. This situation demands a more active and wider exchange of technology in the field of information, the adoption of convenient ways of sharing knowledge and experience in the new methods of information and communication, and cooperation among the mass media and information services of the non-aligned and other developing countries."[14]

And the ministers considered "that the new phenomena of technological changes affect the nature and volume of the information flow and the interpretation of news to the disadvantage of the developing countries. The microelectronic technologies and their growing monopolization should not be allowed, however, to become a new vehicle for information colonization. To this end, the Ministers reiterated their resolve to make progress towards the decolonization of information and the establishment of the New International Information and Communication Order."[15]

What are the results of this 15-year effort toward the establishment of the NIICO since the 4th Summit Conference in Algiers in 1973? Have the developing countries reached their original aims? The answer to this question is discordant. On the one hand, there is a tendency for an improvement of the situation of the developing countries. On the other hand, a countertendency of growing dependence and widening gaps exists as well.

As positive for the developing countries, one can summarize the following five achievements: First, there is an acceleration in the development of national information systems. In the last 15 years, the number of daily newspapers and radio and television receivers in the developing countries has more than doubled. Today there is almost no developing country without a national news agency and a national radio and TV network. The national telecommunication infrastructure, and in particular the connections between urban and rural areas within the country and among the developing countries, has been improved. Table 4.2 gives an impression of this progress.

Second, there is a new quality of practical interregional and regional cooperation among the developing countries. The main results of the NIICO efforts are undoubtedly NANAP and BONAC. The New Agencies Pool established in 1975 has become an important complementary element in the international news flow. The pool distributed nearly 100,000 words daily in four languages in the middle of the 1980s. It started with a special economic service called Eco-Pool, which has established a well-functioning global system for the collection, processing, and dissemination of information via satellite bridges and regional distribution centers. The Pool has also started an efficient training program for journalists and technicians.

Complementary to the interregional pool, regional networks have been developed. In the early 1980s, the Pan-African News Agency (PANA) in Africa, the Asian News Network (ANN) in Asia, and ALASEI in Latin America started as joint ventures of the developing countries. Subregional services like CANA in the Arab region have also been developed. They provide authentic information about the developing world, correcting, to a certain degree, the one-sided information of other transnational news agencies.

A similar process took place in the field of radio and television broadcasting. BONAC, as the interregional organization of the Non-Aligned

**TABLE 4.2.** Changes from 1970 to 1983

| Year | Radio | | Television | |
|------|-------|-------|------|-------|
| | Receivers | Transmitters | Receivers | Transmitters |
| 1970 | 112 million | 5,900 | 23 million | 800 |
| 1983 | 394 million | 8,370 | 92 million | 3,570 |

SOURCE: *UNESCO Statistical Yearbook 1986* (Paris 1987, pp. VI-19 ff.).

Movement, has developed methods similar to NANAP; that is, it has a coordination committee and regional cooperation is encouraged. The Asian-Pacific Broadcasting Union (ASBU), the Arab Broadcasting Union (ABU), the Union of Radio and Television Networks in Africa (URTNA), and the Latin-American Broadcasting Union (ULCRA) have made progress for the developing countries in this field. The launching of ARAB-SAT, the first communication satellite of the Arab Countries, is similar to the organization of TV Festivals and the establishment of a program bank; it is a concrete result of the efforts of the developing countries in the field of radio and television broadcasting.

Third, there is a political mechanism for the promotion of the process of the establishment of the NIICO within the Non-Aligned Movement. The fact that since 1973 the topic NIICO has been a separate point on the agenda of the summit conferences is of special importance. Together with the established mechanisms, it guarantees the continuance of this process.

The 1976 Intergovernmental Council for the Coordination of Information of the Non-Aligned Countries (IGC)—with annual meetings in New Delhi (1976), Havana (1977), Rome (1979), Baghdad (1980), Georgetown (1981), and La Valetta (1982)—was reorganized at the 7th Summit in New Delhi in 1983. The summit decided to improve the political coordination and establish a new and higher body, the "Conference of the Ministers of Information of the Non-Aligned Countries" (COMINAC). The New Delhi Summit decided "that Ministers of Information meet in general conference within a period of six months following every Conference of Heads of State or Government with a view to consolidating and developing mutual cooperation among non-aligned countries in conformity with the objectives and principles of the New International Information and Communication Order, and to assess the impact of technological developments in this field."[16] COMINAC I took place in Jakarta, January 1984. COMINAC II was hosted by Zimbabwe in Harare, July 1987. COMINAC III will be organized in Havana in 1990.

Now a clear structure for political as well as for practical decision making exists: The highest body is the Conference of the Ministers of Information, which has to report to the summit meetings. The IGC acts between the Conferences of the Ministers as the coordination organ and cooperates with the coordination committees of NANAP and BONAC, which have to report annually to the IGC meetings. The chairman of the IGC is the minister of information of the hosting country of the last COMINAC (from 1987 to 1990, the IGC Chairman is the Minister of Information, Posts and Telecommunication of Zimbabwe, Nathan Shamuyarira).

Fourth, there are defined aims, principles, and concepts for the process of the establishment of the NIICO. The conceptualization of the NIICO is a permanent and evolving process. It started practically with the Algiers summit and continues. The main landmarks in this conceptualization process are

(1) the "New Delhi Declaration" of 1976, where a platform was formulated for further actions and reflections;

(2) the "Baghdad-Resolution" (see Annex I) of the 4th IGC meeting of 1980, where the aims and principles of the NIICO have been defined;

(3) the "Jakarta Declaration" of 1984 (COMINAC I), where a comprehensive Programme of Action was adopted; and

(4) the "Harare Declaration" of 1987 (COMINAC II), where the long-term strategy for the 1990s was elaborated.

The development of the NIICO concept shows a unity between continuity and change. The aims—decolonization and democratization—and the principles—self-determination, sovereignty, noninterference, and cooperation—remained unchanged. Developments concerning the relationship between national and international efforts and the interlinkage of the NIICO with other global problems became visible.

In the late 1970s, many developing countries took the position that the NIICO process should start with the adoption of a universal declaration that obliges all members of the international community to promote the NIICO. In the 1980s, a majority of developing countries realized that there will be no New International Information and Communication Order. The development of a national information and communication system and the elaboration of relevant political behavior is now viewed as a prerequisite for international actions toward the democratization of the transborder flow of information.

The majority of the developing countries were thinking in terms of a new International "Mass Media" Order when they called for the NIICO. In the 1980s, more and more members of the Non-Aligned Movement recognized that the NIICO should include not only mass communication, but also tele- and data communication. They realized that the challenge of the new information and communication technology goes far beyond the mass media and their intellectual and cultural activities. They realized that information questions are strategic questions that are closely related to national security and economic development. So the concept shifted partly from the "software" to the "hardware."

At the Colombo Summit in 1976, the heads of state still argued that the NIICO "is as vital"[17] as a New International Economic Order (NIEO). The Harare Declaration of COMINAC II in 1987 states that the establishment of the NIICO "is an integral component"[18] of the struggle for the NIEO.

Fifth, there are new international mechanisms and instruments, established and adopted within the UN systems, which promote the process of the establishment of a NIICO. The introduction of the NIICO question in the agenda of global negotiations within the UN system resulted in concrete practical and political measures. The International Programme for the Development of Communication (IPDC) was established in 1980 within UNESCO. In the first seven years of its existence, the IPDC has promoted more than 200 communication projects worth about 20 million dollars in the developing countries. The Centre for Telecommunication Development was established in 1986 within the ITU.

On the theoretical level, UNESCO and ITU have established independent commissions that analyzed the realities and future perspectives of the information and communication development in the world. The UNESCO MacBride Commission (1980) and the ITU Maitland Commission (1984) presented comprehensive reports with numerous recommendations.

On the political level, the developing countries initiated or influenced the elaboration of international instruments and the convening of international conferences. The Mass Media Declaration of UNESCO in 1978, the NIICO Resolution of UNESCO in 1980, the UN Resolution on Satellite Television in 1982, the ITU Convention in 1982, the UN Resolution on Remote-Sensing in 1986, and the agendas of the multilateral conferences on the use of the geostationary orbit or on digitized telephone and telegraph services are results in favor of the developing countries and their struggle toward the establishment of the NIICO.

This tendency toward the improvement of the situation of the developing countries in the field of information and communication is on the other hand confronted with a countertendency of stagnation or even steps back in at least three ways. First, the gap between developed and developing countries in the field of information and communication has been widened. Although there was some progress in the development of national information capacities, the speed of the progress in the developing countries is slower than in the developed countries, in particular in the field of radio and TV, as Tables 4.3 and 4.4 show.

Second, there are new imbalances within the developing countries. There are some developing countries that already have reached a more or

**TABLE 4.3.** The Gap Between Developed and Developing Countries in the Field of Radio Broadcasting

| | *Radio Broadcasting* | | | |
| | *Transmitters* | | *Receivers* | |
| | *1970* | *1983* | *1970* | *1983* |
|---|---|---|---|---|
| Developed countries | 16,200 | 21,640 | 572 million | 996 million |
| Developing countries | 5,990 | 8,370 | 112 million | 394 million |
| Difference | 10,300 | 13,270 | 460 million | 602 million |

SOURCE: *UNESCO Statistical Yearbook 1986* (Paris, 1987, pp. VI-19 ff.).

less sufficient level, while others have not reached the minimum of five newspapers, five radio receivers, and two TV receivers per 100 inhabitants, a minimum that was the aim for 1970. Even as of 1985, the following countries have not reached this minimum: for radio receivers, 21 countries; for TV receivers, 43; and for newspapers, 60.

One consequence of this "imbalanced underdevelopment" is that there are some strong members that dominate the others within the institutions of the Non-Aligned-Movement such as NANAP and BONAC. Only one-quarter of the 100 members of the News Agencies Pool participate regularly in its work. A similar situation can be observed concerning PANA. There are some PANA members that do not have the technical, personnel, or financial capability to receive or to send the news service of this All-African Network.

Another consequence is that the introduction of high communication technology in areas of "unbalanced underdevelopment" has the effect of widening the gaps instead of narrowing them. The launching of ARAB-SAT, for instance, created new imbalances in the flow of television and radio programs in the Arab world, creating an enormous overcapacity. The danger that the practical instruments that have been created by the movement—with the aims of strengthening independence, creating self-reliance, and correcting existing imbalances in the flow of information—can be turned into counterproductive mechanisms that again come under the control of the transnational agencies is very evident. The free capacities of ARABSAT can be used quickly by the big transnational networks.

Third, there is a watering down of support from the UN system for the establishment of the NIICO. Western countries, and in particular the United States, have identified the movement toward the NIICO as a threat for their freedom to collect, process, and distribute information worldwide. Organizations like the Heritage Foundation, the World Press Free-

**TABLE 4.4.** The Gap Between Developed and Developing Countries in the Field of Television Broadcasting

| | Television Broadcasting | | | |
| | Transmitters | | Receivers | |
| | 1970 | 1983 | 1970 | 1983 |
|---|---|---|---|---|
| Developed countries | 16,900 | 41,800 | 255 million | 521 million |
| Developing countries | 800 | 3,570 | 23 million | 92 million |
| Difference | 16,100 | 38,230 | 232 million | 429 million |

SOURCE: *UNESCO Statistical Yearbook 1986* (Paris 1987, pp. VI-19 ff.).

dom Committee, the Inter-American Publisher Association, the International Federation of Publishers, and others have started a real "war" against the process of the establishment of the NIICO. As a result of this confrontation, the developing countries could not achieve a full endorsement of their initiatives to overcome the state of underdevelopment in the field of information and to decolonize and democratize the international flow of information. The withdrawal of the United States and United Kingdom from UNESCO, the financial blockade of the majority of Western countries in the IPDC, the slowing down of the process of studying and discussing of the concept of the NIICO within UNESCO and UN, the voting against UN resolutions on information questions, and the like have lead to a growing gap between the objective potential and the real activities of the multilateral organizations of the UN system to contribute effectively in the establishment of the NIICO.

The developing countries have recognized this standstill. In the "Declaration of Harare" (COMINAC II), the Ministers of Information therefore called upon the nonaligned countries "to redouble their efforts to advance their own infrastructures and to establish coherent policies in the field of communication, education and culture." And they added: "This is essential for the establishment of the New International Information and Communication Order."[19]

## NIICO AND THE UNITED NATIONS

The process of the establishment of the NIICO is an item on the agenda of the global multilateral negotiations within the United Nations system. The idea of introducing the NIICO into these negotiations was born during the Tunis Symposium. Paragraph 35 "invites the non-aligned countries to join in a common action for the adoption of the United Nations' system of information and communication . . . and stresses the obligation of the international organizations to assist the non-aligned countries towards the emancipation and development of their national information systems. The non-aligned countries must take actions within these specialized bodies."[20]

A more precise direction of these proposed "actions" within the international organizations was given by the "New Delhi Declaration." The ministers of information decided in New Delhi "to emphasize that non-aligned countries should coordinate their activities in the United Nations and other international forums to enable the adoption at an early date of a proper declaration of fundamental principles of the role of mass media in strengthening peace, promoting international understanding and cooperation contributing to the early establishment of an international economic and social order based on equality and justice and in combating racism, racial discrimination, apartheid, zionism, neo-colonialism and all other forms of oppression. Non-aligned countries should ensure that such declaration could also be an effective instrument for reducing their dependence in the information field in keeping with the objectives incorporated in this declaration."[21] With the endorsement of this decision by the Colombo Summit, the developing countries tabled the idea of the establishment of the NIICO in the form of draft resolutions to the 31st General Assembly of the United Nations and the 19th General Conference of UNESCO, which took place two months after the Colombo Summit in Nairobi, Kenya.

In the UN, the five Asian members—Indonesia, Malaysia, the Philippines, Singapore, and Thailand—asked in a draft resolution for more assistance to the developing countries in the field of information and communication. The UN resolution (31/139) was adopted unanimously on December 16, 1976. The General Assembly decided to ask UNESCO—a specialized agency dealing with communication questions since its foundation in 1946—to prepare a report and to include the item again in the agenda of the 33rd General Assembly. Resolution 31/139 did not mention the term *NIICO*, but nevertheless it became the starting point for the NIICO debate within UN as well as for the creation of the UN Committee on Information, which was established in 1979 with the mandate inter alia "to promote the establishment of a new, more just and effective world information and communication order."[22]

The term *NIICO* also did not appear in the resolutions of the Nairobi General Conference of UNESCO. But like in the United Nations, the idea was adopted. Resolution 4.141 of the General Conference stated "that UNESCO may be regarded as one of the United Nations agencies capable of assisting in liberating the developing countries from the state of dependence." The Director General of UNESCO was invited "to pay very special attention" to "the recommendations relating to information and communication" of the Tunis Symposium, the New Delhi Conference, and the Colombo Summit and "to give priority to such regular program activities as are consistent with these recommendations."[23] Additionally, the DG was invited to establish an international commission for the study of the totality of communication problems in the present world and to redraft the Mass Media Declaration—under discussion within UNESCO as a controversial East-West problem on the role of the mass media in international relations since 1972—by taking into account "the various decisions of the 19th General Conference on achieving a balanced international dissemination of information and the necessity of providing assistance to developing countries in this field."[24]

Practically, the resolutions aimed in three directions: First, the promotion of the development of national information and communication systems in the developing countries (*the practical aspect*). Second, the elaboration of guiding principles for the work of the mass media in the international relations (*the political aspect*). Third, the studying of the complexity of the information and communication problems (*the theoretical aspect*).

What are the landmarks in the NIICO discussion of the 1980s within the UN and UNESCO, and what are the prospects for further debates in the 1990s? UNESCO was undoubtedly the main platform for the NIICO negotiations. In all the general conferences after Nairobi, information and communication questions have been among the most debated issues.

The 20th General Conference (Paris, 1978) adopted a compromise version of the Mass Media Declaration. In the Declaration, the member states of UNESCO expressed their consciousness "of the aspiration of the developing countries for the establishment of a new, more just and more effective world information and communication order."[25] Article IV stated: "For the establishment of a new equilibrium and greater reciprocity in the flow of information, which will be conducive to the institution of a just and lasting peace and to the economic and political independence of the developing countries, it is necessary to correct the inequalities in the flow of information to and from developing countries, and between those countries. To this end, it is essential that their mass media should have conditions and resources enabling them to gain strength and expand, and to cooperate both among themselves and with the mass media in developed countries."[26]

The 21st General Conference (Belgrade, 1980) discussed the Report of the International Commission for the Study of Communication Problems (MacBride Commission) and adopted a lengthy resolution with concrete recommendations for the promotion of the establishment of the NIICO (see Annex II). In Part VI the resolution outlined 11 principles of the NIICO and stated that "this new world information and communication order should be based on the fundamental principles of international law, as laid down in the Charter of the United Nations."[27]

The same General Conference adopted a resolution that established within UNESCO an "International Program for the Development of Communication" (IPDC). The establishment of IPDC was recommended by an Intergovernmental Conference, which took place in Paris, April 1980.

In the Recommendation on the IPDC, the member states of UNESCO noted "the deplorable situations of dependence and the significant inequalities of a technological, professional, material and financial nature which exist between developed countries and developing countries in most fields of communication and further noting calls for a larger participation in, and democratization of international relations in the field of information and for the overcoming of vestiges of colonialism."[28] They underlined "the need to establish a new international information and communication order" and considered "that assistance to developing countries should not be politically tied and that favorable conditions should be enhanced to facilitate better access to modern communication technology for developing countries."[29]

Two years later, at the 4th Extraordinary General Conference, the 2nd UNESCO Six-Year Medium-Term Plan for the period 1984 to 1989 was adopted. The second Medium-Term Plan included a Major Program with the title "Communication in the Service of Man." This Main Program III was seen as "a framework for strengthening the bases upon which a new world information and communication order conducive to a free flow and wider and better balanced dissemination of information might be established."[30] The Main Program III was subdivided into three Programs— "Studies on Communication," "Free Flow and Wider and Better Balanced Dissemination of Information," and "Development of Communication"— and reflected the three lateral structures of the Nairobi decisions.

All of these decisions—the Mass Media Declaration, the NIICO Resolution on the MacBride Report, the establishment of an IPDC, and the adoption of the Medium-Term Plan—were adopted unanimously. They were a carefully negotiated balance of interests. No decisions were directed against the legitimate interests of other members of UNESCO.

Nevertheless, some Western groups started a big campaign in the early 1980s against UNESCO and especially against its information- and communication-related programs. The NIICO became a controversial issue in the UN and UNESCO. It was not seen as a universal problem that called for common action in the name of development, peace, and understanding, but as a threat to the freedom of the Western mass media. The withdrawal of the United States and United Kingdom from UNESCO in 1985 and 1986

was explained as "overpolitization of the communication debate." Both
countries, assisted by some other members of the Western group, urged to
exclude the NIICO item again from the agenda of UNESCO's general
conferences.

A compromise was reached during the 23rd General Conference in
Sofia, 1985. At this conference, the member states of UNESCO agreed
(without the United States, at this time not a member of UNESCO, but
with the United Kingdom, which was still a member of UNESCO) to see
the establishment of a NIICO "as a continuous and evolving process"[31]
and not as a simple set of norms defined in a legally binding instrument.
Despite the consensus on this formula, Western countries continued to
work toward the elimination of the NIICO from the programs of UNESCO.

Concerning the *political level*, the idea to draft a NIICO declaration—as
recommended by the 21st General Conference in Belgrade 1980—was
killed. Even the idea to develop a NIICO concept in an informal way
through high-level roundtable discussions, which started in Innsbruck in
1983, has been watered down. The 2nd roundtable was postponed from
1984 to 1986. And a third roundtable, which was planned for 1987, never
took place.

Concerning the *practical level*, the IPDC did not get sufficient material
to implement its goals as stated in the Belgrade Resolution. Although the
IPDC did a good job and often was quoted as an exciting example and
experience (which demonstrates that even in times of confrontation a
fruitful cooperation in such a delicate field like information and communication is possible), the IPDC in general was not able to "change the
state of dependency of developing countries in the field of information and
communication"—as envisaged in its basic documents[32]—in the first
decade of its existence.

Finally, concerning the *theoretical level*, the study projects of the Main
Program III were cut drastically and restructured. The 23rd General Conference in Sofia 1985 decided to ensure "that an appropriate balance is
maintained"[33] as far as the NIICO was concerned and "to broaden the study
base, where necessary."[34] The *24th General Conference* in Paris in 1987,
however, reduced the budget for studies on communication to less than 8%
of the whole communication program, the lowest level since 1946.

A similar development occurred within the *General Assembly of the
United Nations*. The initiatives of the developing countries, supported by
the socialist states, led, until 1980, to some concrete results. The *33rd
General Assembly in 1978,* which discussed the UNESCO report on the
international cooperation in the field of information and communication,
affirmed in resolution 233/115 B "the need to establish a new, more
just and more effective world information and communication order, intended to strengthen peace and international understanding and based on

the free circulation and wider and better balanced dissemination of information."[35] The *34th General Assembly in 1979* established a special "United Nations Committee on Information" and gave the committee the mandate, inter alia, to promote the establishment of the NIICO, as mentioned above. Of special importance was the clarification of the relationship between the UN and UNESCO in the promotion of the NIICO. Resolution 34/182 affirmed "the primary role which the General Assembly is to play in elaborating, coordinating and harmonizing United Nations policies and activities in the field of information" and recognized "the center and important role of the UNESCO in the field of information and communication."[36]

The United Nations Committee on Information (UNCI), composed of about 70 member states of the UN, developed a fruitful mechanism for work with annual meetings, which elaborated numerous concrete recommendations to the Special Political Committee of the General Assembly. On the basis of these recommendations, the General Assembly adopted each year since 1979 a lengthy resolution on "Questions on Information."[37] Among others, the committee contributed to the development of the concept, to the practical assistance to the developing countries, and to the theoretical discussions by convening roundtables and seminars of experts. In other words, the committee worked in the same three directions—the political, practical, and theoretical ones—as UNESCO.

A major contribution of the committee to the conceptualization of the NIICO is the so-called NIICO definition. The paragraph, reaffirmed by all UN Resolutions since 1983, reads as follows: The General Assembly is conscious "of the need for all countries, the United Nations system as a whole and all other concerned, to collaborate in the establishment of a new world information and communication order based, inter alia, on the free circulation and wider and better balanced dissemination of information, guaranteeing diversity of sources of information and free access to information, and, in particular, the urgent need to change the dependent status of the developing countries in the field of information and communication, as the principle of sovereign equality among nations extends also to this field, and intended also to strengthen peace and international understanding, enabling all persons to participate effectively in political, economic, social and cultural life and promoting understanding and friendship among all nations and human rights."[38]

The committee determined the place of the NIICO to be "linked to the new international economic order" and "an integral part of the international development process."[39] It emphasized "the role that public information plays in promoting support for universal disarmament and increasing awareness of the relationship between disarmament and development."[40] And it encouraged UNESCO to contribute "to the clarification, elaboration and application of the concept of a new world information and communication order."[41]

But like in UNESCO, the UNCI was blocked by the controversial discussion on the NIICO. The consensus of the late 1970s was broken. The United States has voted against every information resolution since the early 1980s and some other countries, including Israel and a group of Western states, have joined the United States in voting against the resolution. One of the most debated issues is the question of whether or not the NIICO should be seen as a "continuous and evolving process." The majority of the developing countries argue that this formula includes the danger of a postponement of concrete activities in favor of the development of their communication infrastructure to the next century. They insist on immediate actions toward the NIICO. The Western countries insist on the "process formula."

A thoughtful analysis of this conflict, however, reveals that the confrontation around this point is an artificial one. Nobody can expect that the NIICO could be established overnight. The establishment of the NIICO is a process. But, on the other hand, it should be clear that this process is an irreversible, progressive, continuous, and evolving process and not a "revolving process."

On the basis of this understanding, the *41st General Assembly* incorporated the "continuous and evolving process-formula" into the Information Resolution and the majority of Western countries came back to voting in favor.[42]

What conclusion can be drawn from the first decade of the NIICO debate within the UN and UNESCO? First, the idea and the legitimacy of the need of the establishment of the NIICO is accepted worldwide. Information and communication have been identified as global problems of mankind, interlinked with the global problems of peace and development.

Second, a conceptual framework of the NIICO has been elaborated. The Mass Media Declaration of 1978, the Recommendation on the IPDC, the Resolution on the MacBride Report (and the report itself), the UN resolutions on "Questions on information," the Final Reports of the two high-level UN/UNESCO Round Tables on the NIICO, and other documents have constituted a representation of the aims of the NIICO and the principles on which it could and should be based. Although all of these instruments are not binding under international law, they have political importance that cannot be underestimated.

Third, a mechanism for negotiations has been established. The NIICO is included as an element in the agendas of both the General Conference of UNESCO and the General Assembly of the UN. The Intergovernmental Council of the IPDC meets annually to negotiate concrete communication projects for the Third World. The UNCI meets annually to negotiate recommendations for further actions in this field. But in which direction will these negotiations go in the 1990s? The present revolution in information and communication technology has changed the understanding of information and communication over the last 15 years. It would be a mistake to reduce global information and communication negotiations only to mass media problems. The perspective of an ISDN makes the discussion of the problems of mass communication isolated from the problems of tele- and data communication obsolete. And the global character of the coming satellite- and cable-based networks makes the discussion of information and communication problems as North-South or East-West issues obsolete. A broader and more complex approach is needed.

## PERSPECTIVES FOR
## INTERNATIONAL NIICO NEGOTIATIONS

The establishment of an international policy framework for the transborder flow of information and communication of all kinds includes the definition of general principles and legal norms. If the coming global networks can be compared with highways on which the resource "information" is transported electronically around the globe with high speed, the question can be framed in terms of the regulation of this traffic. "Electronic highways need rules of the road."[43] This very frequently repeated quotation from James Grant signals the need for clarifying the rights and responsibilities of the participants in the electronic traffic. This traffic touches the interests of all countries, irrespective of their strength and system, of their state of development, or their cultural traditions, but the interests of the states differ. Communication-rich countries have other interests than communication-poor countries, socialist countries have other interests than Western countries, but all are participating in the same global information and communication process.

The attempt of a nation to realize its own interests against the interests of others leads to harmful conflicts that are dangerous for the peaceful coexistence of the peoples of the world. Because we live in an interdependent world, a regulated balance of interests—on the basis of the sovereign equality of states—and the readiness for global cooperation—on the basis of mutual advantage, equality, justice, and the principles of international law—are needed to stabilize peace and international security and to promote development and wealth in the world.

The question of future regulations of international information and communication can be answered only by analyzing the already existing legal framework. The situation in this field is very complex, unsystematized, and disordered. There are a great variety of instruments that have different legal status and that regulate different but quite interrelated things. In spite of all differences, however, one must first of all state that processes of international information and communication are in any case activities that are part of the general international relations. Thus the general norms of international relations consequently are also valid for the transborder flow of data and information. This means that the seven basic principles of international law—sovereign equality, self-determination of peoples, prohibition of the use of force, nonintervention, peaceful settling of disputes, international cooperation, and respect for that are embodied in the United Nations Charter and that have *jus cogens* character, constitute the general legal basis. Agreements on international information and communication must not be contradictory to these basic principles. In this context, Article 52 of the Vienna Convention on the Law of Treaties clearly says that a treaty is null and void if it is "contradictory to a jus cogens norm of the general international law."[44] Therefore, an agreement on freedom of communication can never ignore the jus cogens principle of the sovereign equality of states.

The concrete international regulation of information and communication can be analyzed in a different way. It can be divided as follows: (a) concerning the subject of regulation, into the regulation of international mass communication, international telecommunication, and international data communication, and (b) concerning the nature of the norms, into legal norms in the form of multilateral conventions and agreements binding under international law, political norms in form of declarations and resolutions not legally binding, and ethical norms in form of codes of conduct.

The International Telecommunication Convention of 1982, the Human Rights Convention of 1966, and the Geneva Broadcasting Convention of 1936 are legally binding instruments. Political norms are formulated in the UNESCO Mass Media Declaration of 1978, in the UN Resolution on DBS of 1982, and in the Resolution on the Report of the MacBride Commission adopted by the UNESCO General Conference in 1980. Ethical norms can be found in the "International Principles of Professional Ethics in Journalism" formulated by international professional organizations in 1983. A comparative analysis of the existing regulation shows that international information and communication is already highly regulated, and the rights and duties of the "actors" in this field are defined in a more or less concrete way.

Regardless of some differences, the respective regulations generally follow the above-mentioned twin concepts of the freedom of communication, on one hand, and the protection of the national interests and the sovereign rights of nations, on the other. Additionally, peace, understanding, development, and cooperation are formulated as general aims. A good example of this construction is the International Telecommunication Convention of 1982. On one hand, the ITU members agree in Article 4 "to maintain and extend international cooperation . . . for the improvement and rational use of telecommunications of all kinds." On the other hand, in Article 19, they reserve their right to stop all forms of telecommunications that "may appear dangerous to the security of the state or contrary to their laws, to public order or to decency." And in the Preamble, they recognize "the sovereign right of each country to regulate its telecommunication" as well as "the growing importance of telecommunication for the preservation of peace and the social and economic development of all countries."[45]

The promotion of peace through communication, the guaranteeing of the freedom of information, and the protection of the interests and the sovereign rights of development of nations constitute a triangle in which each "angle" has its own meaning but has to be seen in its relationship with the two other "angles." This is relevant not only for tele- but also for mass and data communication. Summarizing, one can thus speak of the existence of comprehensive international legal instruments that give stability to the international information and communication relations in the sense of peaceful coexistence. But at the same time, a comparison shows that some norms are formulated only in a very general sense. There are divergences, different levels of regulation, and even contradictions that create confusion. International telecommunication, for instance, is regulated in a very detailed form by legally binding multilateral conventions. International mass communication is regulated only partly by a mixture of legal, political, and ethical norms. The regulation of international data communication is still in the developmental stage and scientific and technical progress creates new areas that necessitate international regulation.

It is a very broad challenge. Practically, the question can be asked whether we need an integrated juridical solution if we will have an Integrated Services Digital Network. Is there a need for a "package solution" in the form of an International Law of Communication Convention comparable to the International Law of the Sea Convention? The answer to this question is rather difficult. On one hand, the traditional frontiers between mass, tele-, and data communication begin to disappear and it seems impossible to divide legally a fiber optic cable or a communication satellite into three parts. On the other hand, it is a gigantic and nearly utopian task to regulate all communication problems within one single legally binding international instrument.

Which way the international community will go to draft the "rules of the road" for the electronic highway remains open for discussion. But do we have time enough for discussion? The reality is that technological development today is faster than the diplomatic procedures for finding an integrated solution. But what will happen if, in the absence of "rules of the road," the "law of the stronger" regulates the traffic on the electronic highways? If there is not regulation for international communication that balances the interests of the different participants in the electronic traffic, deep international conflicts can arise that could have unforeseeable consequences for the functioning of the overall system of international relations and the peaceful living together of peoples.

This danger is seen by more and more experts not only in the East and in the South, but also in the West. The last Council of Europe Conference of the Ministers of Information recommended the elaboration of a Western European Mass Media Convention. Within the OECD, a Declaration of TDF was adopted. And some Western experts predict that the wave of "deregulation," which was introduced by the Reagan administration, will be followed by a new wave of "re-regulation" because they realize that, in the absence of the protecting function of international law, the national cultures, national industries, and even national security not only of the developing countries are at stake.

But the problems of the new communication technology are not regional ones. They are global problems concerning all of mankind. And they cannot be solved by separate regional agreements. A global approach is necessary. The role of the United Nations system in the global information and communication negotiations is growing. The UN system is the only universal institution where really all members of the international community are represented and are able to participate on an equal basis.

Practically, there is no information problem that is not under discussion within the UN system. But this diversified dealing with communication questions creates some problems too. Trade in Services, under discussion in UNCTAD and GATT, is linked closely with international telecommunication, which is being discussed in the ITU. The use of the geostationary orbit, under discussion in the ITU, is linked closely to the international satellite television, which is being discussed in the Outer Space Committee in the UN. And the UN Committee on Information, like UNESCO, has the mandate to promote the establishment of the New International Information and Communication Order.

During the 1st UN/UNESCO Round Table on the NIICO in 1983, this overlapping led Costa Rica's Minister of Information, Armando Varga, to propose the creation of a new specialized agency in the UN family that covers all information questions.[46] Certainly there are some doubts whether the founding of a new organization would be helpful. But there is undoubtedly a challenge for more effective coordination among the members of the UN family. The convening of a World Conference on Information and Communication Problems (WORLDCOM) could possibly be a fruitful step forward. Such a conference could

(1) develop a general political framework for international information and communication to promote peace and international understanding;

(2) identify areas of priority for international cooperation and regulation; and

(3) coordinate the different efforts of numerous UN bodies in the field of information and communication.

The NIICO will evolve and continue toward a complex international framework for information in communication. In spite of the growing need for an integrated approach, there are concrete questions waiting for an immediate solution. The new possibilities for the dissemination of information by DBS and for the access to information by TDF are obviously the most important challenges for international regulation in the years to come. DBS and TDF penetrate frontiers. They concern fundamental political, economic, and cultural interests of all states. They are international phenomena and call for multilateral cooperation.

Although there is an objective need to conclude agreements, it is difficult to reach a consensus as the negotiations on the NIICO and DBS within UNESCO and the UN in the last ten years have shown. By referring to their interpretation of the freedom of information, some Western representatives have declared that there is nothing to compromise. Certainly, if it is true that fundamental contradictions exist, it would be an illusion to mix different ideologies by compromising philosophical values. These ideological conflicts will continue to exist. They do not disappear by the construction of electronic highways. But they should not be a barrier for fruitful cooperation on the governmental or nongovernmental levels.

In our interdependent world, where the question of peace and war is a question of the survival of humankind in general, it would be more than dangerous to fight the ideological struggle like medieval fanatics. Such a war of words would sooner or later lead to a war of weapons, and the different ideological positions would disappear together with the peoples. There would be no winners, only losers.

Agreements both for DBS and TDF are possible, regardless of the well-known ideological conflicts concerning the interpretation of the freedom of information and communication. To agree upon the sovereign equality of states; upon cooperation on the basis of justice, equality, mutual benefit, and the principles of international law; and upon the mutual respect for the legitimate interests in the field of international information and communication does not mean agreement upon ideological positions or giving up basic philosophical values. But it would contribute to the development of dialogue and cooperation, to the strengthening of a peaceful world and a better understanding, and to a climate of confidence in the international relations.

## NOTES

1. "Action Program for Economic Cooperation," para. XIII (Algiers, 9 September 1973), in *New International Information and Communication Order—A Sourcebook*, K. Nordenstreng, E. Gonzales-Manet, and W. Kleinwächter (Prague, 1986), p. 275.

2. Resolution VI: Cooperation in the Field of Diffusions of Information and the Mass Media (Lima, 31st August 1975), in V. Bulatovic, *Non-Alignment and Information* (Belgrade, 1978), p. 72

3. "Report on the Non-Aligned Symposium on Information" (Tunis, 30 March 1978), in *New International Information and Communication Order*, p. 281, para. 6.

4. Ibid., para. 7.

5. Ibid., para. 11-12.

6. Ibid., para. 27.

7. "Declaration of the Ministerial Conference of Non-Aligned Countries on Decolonization of Information" (New Delhi, 13 July 1976), in ibid., p. 285, pt. A.

8. "Political Declaration of the 5th Summit Conference of the Non-Aligned Movement" (Colombo, 19 August 1986), in ibid, p. 288, para. 160.

9. Ibid.

10. "Political Declaration of the 6th Summit Conference of the Non-Aligned Movement" (Havana, 9 September 1979), in ibid., p. 296, para. 262.

11. "Political Declaration of the 7th Summit Conference of the Non-Aligned Movement" (New Delhi, 9 March 1983), in ibid., p. 305, para. 173a.

12. *Political Declaration of the 8th Summit Conference of the Non-Aligned Movement* (Harare, 3 September 1986) (mimeo) NAM-Doc. PC/CRP 84, para. 262.

13. *Final Document of the 2nd Conference of the Ministers of Information of the Non-Aligned Countries* (Harare, 12 June 1987), NAM-Doc. COMINAC 2/24, para. 10.

14. Ibid., para. 11.

15. Ibid., para. 12.

16. "Political Declaration of the 7th Summit Conference of the Non-Aligned Movement," in *New International Information and Communication Order*, p. 305, para. 173c.

17. "Political Declaration of the 5th Summit Conference of the Non-Aligned Movement," in *New International Information and Communication Order*, p. 288, para. 160.

18. "Final document of the 2nd Conference of the Ministers," para. 14.

19. Ibid., para. 11.

20. "Report on the Non-Aligned Symposium on Information," p. 283, para. 35.

21. "Declaration of the Ministerial Conference of Non-Aligned Countries," p. 287, pt. D, para. 3.

22. UN Resolution 34/182, 18 December 1979, pt. I, para. 2c.

23. UNESCO Resolution 19 C/4.141, 29 November 1976, para. a, b.

24. UNESCO Resolution 19 C/4.143, 29 November 1976, preamble, para. 5.

25. "Declaration on Fundamental Principles Concerning the Contribution of the Mass Media to Strengthening Peace and International Understanding, to the promotion of Human Rights and to Countering Racialism, Apartheid and Incitement to War," in *New International Information and Communication Order*, p. 227, preamble, para. 16.

26. Ibid., p. 228, Art. VI.

27. UNESCO Resolution 21 C/4.19, 21 October 1980, pt. VI, para. 14b (for full text, see Annex II).

28. "Recommendation on the IPDC" (Paris, 21 April 1980), in *New International Information and Communication Order*, p. 235, preamble, para. 3.

29. Ibid., p. 235, preamble, para. 9.

30. UNESCO Resolution 4 XC/2.03, Paris, 3 December 1982, in *New International Information and Communication Order*, p. 252, para. 4.

31. UNESCO Resolution 23 C/2.3, 8 November 1985, para. 1.

32. "Recommendation on the IPDC," p. 235, preamble, para. 5.

33. UNESCO Resolution 23 C/2.3, 8 November 1985, para. 4.

34. Ibid., para. 5a, ii.

35. UN Resolution 33/115, 18 December 1978, pt. B, para. 1.

36. UN Resolution 34/182, 18 December 1979, pt. I, para. 4.

37. UN Resolutions 33/115 (1978), 34/181 (1979), 35/201 (1980), 36/149 (1981), 37/94 (1982), 38/82 (1983), 39/89 (1984), 40/164 (1985), 41/68 (1986) and 42/ (1987).

38. See, inter alia, UN Resolution 40/164, in *New International Information and Communication Order*, p. 196, pt. A, preamble, para. 9.

39. Ibid., para. 11.

40. Ibid., para. 12.

41. Ibid., p. 201, pt. B, preamble, para. 8.

42. UN Resolution 41/68.

43. James Grant, "Traded Computer Services and the Developing Countries," in *Proceedings of the 2nd World Conference on Transborder Data Flow Policies* (Rome, 27 June 1984), TDF 260, p. 55

44. "Vienna Convention on the Law of Treaties," in *New International Information and Communication Order*.

45. "International Telecommunication Convention" (Nairobi, 6 November 1982), in *New International Information and Communication Order*, p. 257 ff., preamble, Art. 4, 19.

46. Statement of His Excellency Armando Varga, Minister of Communication of the Republic of Costa Rica at the 1st UN/UNESCO Round Table on the NIICO, Innsbruck, 18 September 1982 (mimeo).

Annex I: Baghdad-Resolution on the Aims and Principles of the NIICO, 4th Meeting of the IGC of the NAM, 7 June 1980 (Part I).

Annex II: UNESCO Resolution 21 C/4.19 on the NIICO-Principles, 21 October 1980 (Part VI).

# Part II

Processes and Effects

# 5 Communicator Characteristics

## Howard Giles
## Arlene Franklyn-Stokes

The study of *communicator characteristics* in intercultural settings has been as diverse as it has been voluminous. Scholars have explored an array of issues in fragmentary fashion (for the most part) across a vast array of not only intercultural contexts but subgroups within them. Given the heterogeneity of variables that can differentiate between interethnic encounters (including their *changing* histories, demographies, and political systems), and the wealth of communicative and language variables studied (e.g., nonverbal expressiveness, dialect forms, and discourse patterns), the overall picture that emerges is one of enormous complexity and conceptual confusion. This, of course, is predictable when the different disciplines and individual researchers involved have all had their own local (empirical and theoretical) proclivities. This chapter then is an attempt to provide some conceptual order to this immense field as well as indicate some lacunae with a view to proposing a blueprint for further systematic research.

The issues raised in the chapter can be stated parsimoniously as, first, how do background characteristics determine communication patterns in intercultural settings, and second, what are their outcomes? More specifically, we are concerned with exploring the ways in which cultural background variables, psychological states, needs and experiences, and immediate contextual factors affect communicative beliefs, intentions, tactics, and language patterns. In addition, we shall examine how such communicative consequences may influence both senders and receivers and feed back into reshaping the very cultural contexts out of which they emerged. Given the dialectical relationship between our two major questions above, it will be impossible—as the discussion below will attest—not

AUTHORS' NOTE: We gratefully acknowledge the comments of Michael H. Bond, Richard Y. Bourhis, Nik Coupland, John R. Edwards, William B. Gudykunst, and Miles Hewstone on a previous draft of this chapter.

to refer to aspects of one without incorporating occasional data and theoretical ideas from the other. Of necessity, the review of the literatures attending this challenging brief cannot in any sense be exhaustive, yet it is intended to be representative of the kinds of intriguing findings that emerge within the framework outlined. At the end of the day, we shall see that such concerns can not only have significant effects on the immediacy of particular interethnic interactions themselves, but can also have profound implications for the changing historical relations between and within cultures so represented.

## MACRO FACTORS AFFECTING
## COMMUNICATORS' CHARACTERISTICS

### Minority Language Use and
### Ethnic Maintenance

Arguably the most overt characteristic of communicators is the language(s) they use (Bourhis, 1979). Much has been written about the factors that determine the extent to which minority languages survive or decay in the context of more prestigious languages (e.g., Dow, 1987; Fishman, 1966) as well as pressures of acculturation placed on immigrant groups (Kim, 1988; Kim & Gudykunst, 1988). Indeed, when ethnic groups have low political, social, and economic status and low demographic representation relative to other groups in the community, and where institutional support for the mother tongue is poor (what Giles, Bourhis, & Taylor, 1977, termed a profile of low ethnolinguistic vitality), then the pressures on individuals to assimilate the outgroup language and lose their own are intense. It is also the case that perceiving dire losses in ingroup ethnolinguistic vitality may, for certain communicators, be a mobilizing spur for them to take (sociolinguistic) supportive action on behalf of their beleaguered languages. This can be accomplished in a number of ways, not least of which is refusing to accommodate to the language of the dominant group when speaking to its members and to differentiate from them by maintaining the ethnic tongue (Giles & Johnson, 1987). Indeed, some scholars have argued that the link between ethnic identity and language is so strong that loss of the ethnic language can lead to cultural suicide (Fishman, 1977; Ross, 1979). A number of studies across an array of cultures, using multidimensional scaling procedures, have shown that language can be a core aspect of cultural identity (e.g., Giles, Taylor, & Bourhis, 1977; Leclézio, Louw-Potgieter, & Souchon, 1986). Related to this, Banks (1987), by means of a case study, has shown the ways in which some Hispanic managers can face pressures to deethnicize their discourse before higher-power positions in an Anglo-American organization are available to them, and how, consequentially, this can have an adverse effect on their feelings of Mexican identity. Building no small part on these kinds of data, Giles and Byrne (1982) have argued, in terms of their "intergroup" model of second-language acquisition, that certain ethnic minorities' supposed "failures" to become proficient in a dominant group's language can be due not so much to poor pedagogical techniques or learning deficiencies, but rather to a desire not to manifest (or to be seen to manifest) the distasteful characteristics of the alien outgroup (see Gardner, 1985; Lambert, 1974).

In some settings, the instrumental needs of economic survival dictate that the ingroup language decays in relevance in many formal and public settings. Indeed, in a series of studies, Giles and Bourhis (1976) showed that about 80% of second- and third-generation West Indians in Cardiff (Britain) had assimilated to such an extent that tape recordings of their speech were labeled as "White." Yet, the maintenance of identity can be achieved in many different ways as exemplified in Garner and Rubin's (1986) study of southern attorneys' differential (and diglossic) use of Standard and Black English in work and home settings. Indeed, communicators have immense resources for sociolinguistic creativity when their identity is at issue. This can be seen by minority groups in their mixture of the two target languages as in the case of Cantonese-English mixing among Hong students (Gibbons, 1983; see also, Chana & Romaine, 1984), as in "Punglish" (or Punjabi and English mixing), or as in the establishment of "Singlish" (a so-called creoloid), which is a particular evolving variety of English incorporating a number of Malay, Tamil, and Chinese features as a *lingua franca* in Singapore (Platt, 1977).

It should be stated that such mixings and creativity do not always receive consensual validation by insiders or outsiders as is noted in Bentahila's (1983) study on Moroccan-French mixing. That notwithstanding, a similar kind of mechanism can be observed in the emergence of a distinctive accent in the outgroup language (as with the "Hong Kong" accent of English, see Bolton & Kwok, in press), and Giles (1979) has reviewed the rich ways in which communicators can ethnically mark their speech in the outgroup language phonologically, grammatically, prosodically, and lexically; further, von Raffler Engel (1980) and Tannen (1982) have shown how this can come about nonverbally and in discourse, too. In other words, the need to attenuate group differences at the level of language choice can often give rise to their accentuation at other levels of intralingual analysis. Language characteristics in terms of "ethnic speech markers" (Giles, 1979) can provide an insight into the complex processes of how cultural identity can affect a communicator. It should be mentioned, however, that language changes are not inevitably in the direction of the dominant power group as shown elegantly in Hewitt's (1986) study

of White adolescents's use of Jamaican creole features in mu'
South London.

Others, however, such as Edwards (1985), have been vc
questioning this fundamental association between language
claiming that loss of the former does not inevitably lead to ?
the latter. Indeed, Sawaie (1986) has shown how ethnicity
by side with the disappearance of ethnic language maintena
is a socioeconomic need to learn the majority language, as with Arabs in
the United States. Similarly, San Antonio (1987), in an ethnographic study
of the use of English and associated communicative norms in an American
corporation in Japan, argues that the acquisition of English is a prerequisite
for improving one's status in the organization that need *not* involve a
commensurate loss in Japanese identity. Pak, Dion, and Dion (1985), in
like fashion, found among Chinese students in Toronto that self-rated
confidence in English did not necessarily constitute any corresponding
loss to their cultural identity. Edwards (in press) himself has also shown
evidence of Scottish cultural continuity in Nova Scotia, where Gaelic
language loyalty is not very much in evidence. And in another Canadian
study, Edwards and Doucette (1987) have shown that, even when reported
ethnic salience is low, minority groups nevertheless acknowledge the
importance of *symbolic ethnic groupness* (see Gans, 1979) by means of
such features as ceremonies and ethnic food. Other groups having low
ethnolinguistic vitality (as above) have been shown to adopt more socially
creative strategies for maintaining their group identities (see Giles &
Johnson, 1981; Tajfel & Turner, 1979). In studying the Valdotans (a
French-speaking community in Northern Italy), Saint-Blancat (1985,
p. 22) found that they try to achieve socioeconomic parity with the dominant group by speaking Italian, yet still "perpetuate traditional values by
maintaining family land property and securing its survival by handing on
religious belief and a sense of work and duty." Finally in this respect,
Edwards and Shearn (1987, p. 147), in their study of ethnolinguistic
relations in Brussels, make the salutary point that "language issues can be
manipulated for *political* ends, and need not always imply grassroot
priorities" (emphasis added).

In sum then, communicators' characteristics in terms of their ethnic
speech markers are not inevitably associated with a diminution of cultural
identity and the complexities of the identity-language relationship have
still to be modeled theoretically. Yet the staunch, empirically grounded
approach taken by Edwards and others over the years, which can be
ideologically aggravating to many of those wedded to the ideals of minority language maintenance, is a valued approach moving us toward such an
important theoretical goal.

It should also be recognized that in some parts of the world, particularly where decolonialization or social revolution has occurred, communicators' use of *prestige* or elite languages and dialects can also dissipate. Wherritt (1985) has studied the decline of Portuguese in Goa, India, in the 25 years since the end of colonial rule. She reports that a shift is taking place from Portuguese to English and Konkani (an indigenous Indo-Aryan language) for predictable socioeconomic reasons. This shift, however, is mediated by the variables of religion, sex, and age, and the author posits a social hierarchy in the use of Portuguese in Goa. This language is maintained more by Catholics, especially women and the older generation, because these groups tend to be more home-based and Portuguese has been traditionally spoken at home by Catholics. Hindus, men, and particularly the younger generation now have little incentive to speak Portuguese because outside the home the main languages of commerce are English and Konkani. Young women are now working, which they never did under colonial rule, so they too have little use for Portuguese. The important point here is that individuals' communicative patterns are not only undergoing change in response to changing large-scale social conditions but also that linguistic norms may be nonuniform across all members of the speech community (see also, Scotton & Wanjin, 1984).

## Beliefs About Talk in Cultural Context

One feature that has not been explored much hitherto has been communicators' *beliefs about talk and silence*, which seems a fundamental dimension potentially mediating actual language patterns. Wiemann, Chen, and Giles (1986) devised a reliable measure of beliefs about talk and administered their instrument to Caucasian Americans, Chinese American immigrants born in the United States, and Chinese foreign students who would be returning to their homelands. A factor analysis of the data revealed four dimensions: affiliation/assertiveness, control, tolerance of small talk, and tolerance of silence. The three cultural groups were found to be located differently on these dimensions as predicted on the basis of previous ethnographic and anecdotal work conducted in Western and Eastern cultures. For instance, Caucasian Americans saw talk as more important and enjoyable and reported themselves to initiate conversation and to take advantage of opportunities more than their Chinese counterparts. Chinese Americans were also significantly more likely to behave in this manner than were the native Chinese. Consistent with the cultural stereotype, Caucasians saw talk as more of a means of social control whereas the Chinese groups appear to use silence more in these terms and are certainly more tolerant of it.

The theoretically important point emerging from this study (which is presently being replicated with many diverse cultural groups across the world) is that the distinction tapped by the above-mentioned instrument is not due to culture per se, but to belief dimensions on which cultures vary. This claim is similar to, but not as strong as, Hofstede's (1983), who identified four dimensions on which work values varied in over 50 cultures (see also, Chinese Culture Connection, 1987). The Wiemann et al. findings parallel Hofstede's in that Caucasian Americans compared to native Chinese self-reported themselves to be verbally more assertive and more willing to take risks by engaging strangers in conversation. Similarly, Hofstede characterized U.S. culture as more "masculine" (i.e., showing a preference for assertiveness, heroism, and so on as opposed to "feminine" or preferring modesty, caring, and so on) and lower in "uncertainty avoidance" (i.e., less likely to support beliefs promising certainty or to support institutions and practices that protect certainty) than Taiwanese culture. The similarity of findings lead Wiemann et al. to speculate that at least some of the belief characteristics discussed by Hofstede's framework are not limited to the domain of work only and could be fruitfully considered as a conceptual backdrop for communicative research.

### Individualism-Collectivism and Communicative Intent

Remaining on the more cognitive level and mirroring a concern for West-East differences, a specific dimension of the macro context that has been shown empirically to influence communicator *expectations* is that which draws upon Triandis et al.'s (1988) notion of individualism-collectivism. Individualism characterizes cultures where the goals of the individual take precedence over the goals of the group, and collectivism emphasizes the cultural opposite. Gudykunst, Yoon, and Nishida (1987) examined perceptions of communication with strangers (an outgroup) and classmates (an ingroup) among students in a highly individualistic culture (the United States), a moderately individualistic one (Japan), and a highly collectivist culture (South Korea). Among other hypotheses, they proposed (and subsequently supported) that the greater the degree of collectivism, the more ingroup communication would be perceived to be personalized (i.e., more intimacy and self-disclosures). The findings were more complex on other dimensions investigated and the authors called rightly for future studies to explore more fully *participants'* knowledge of the extent and type of their individualism and collectivism.

This recommendation to explore both seemingly objective *and* subjective dimensions of cultural context in examining communicator characteristics is one that has significance for the previous discussion as well. For instance, Giles, Rosenthal, and Young (1985), in an Australian study among Anglo- and Greek Australians in Melbourne, demonstrated that aspects of vitality have psychological reality. In other words, communicators have corresponding images or social representations (see Farr & Moscovici, 1983) of how their group fares in comparison with others and in ways that belie the objective sociostructural indices measured. For instance, Young, Giles, and Pierson (1986) examined the vitality *perceptions* of Hong Kong students before and after the signing of the British Sino-Treaty, which will result in the colony's becoming part of the People's Republic of China in 1997. Over the 18-month period in which the investigation was conducted, no real changes in objective indices occurred, yet Chinese subjective vitality increased while Western vitality on some measures diminished in parallel fashion. The social structure, therefore, must not be regarded as a static given owing to the fact that large-scale elements of it can be sociopsychological constructions for those involved. Perceptions of it are different depending on social category membership and can also change as a function of the sociopolitical climate. This sentiment accords well with Garza and Gallegos (1985, p. 374), who claim that "even identical cultural, socialization and situational factors may lead to totally different social behaviours, depending on individual *perceptions* of influences" (emphasis added; see also, Giles & Hewstone, 1982).

## Future Priorities

It seems essential in future work then to complement apparently objective measures of background vitality (and also high-low context cultures, see below) with subjective indices (Allard & Landry, 1986) if we are ever to cope with interpreting across piecemeal studies in widely differing intercultural settings (and the subgroups inherent within them). Many other dimensions seem important to incorporate innovatively into a rigorous framework for intercultural work. We need to specify—as evident from the earlier discussion—some measure of the multilinguality/bidialectism of all groups (comparatively relevant) in a given cultural context. Giles (1978) introduced such a model, which allowed both dominant and subordinate groups to be located in two-dimensional space regarding their fluencies in the two contrasting codes. Of relevance, in addition, would be some measure of communicators' views as to the degree of *standardization* of their ingroup variety (see Ryan, Giles, & Sebastian, 1982) because its construal as noncodified could be a contributing factor leading to a diminution of its use in certain formal contexts. Moving to other spheres, it would also seem important to locate cultural groups in terms of Berry's (1984) model of group maintenance and development. This locates individuals and groups in terms of their *beliefs* as to whether they consider it to be of value to maintain or not maintain

(a) their own cultural group characteristics, and (b) positive relationships between their own and other groups in society. Such considerations led Berry to suggest that individuals thereby can be located into quadrants of *assimilation, separation, segregation* and *deculturation.* Finally, Taylor and McKirnan's (1984) developmental theory of intergroup relations also articulates where groups are psychologically in terms of social conflict and change. Indeed, multidimensional perceptions of power, change, and threat, as well as individuals' evaluations and attributions of them, seem crucial to our understanding of background characteristics that influence communicative patterns (see Dube-Simard, 1983); empirical work along these lines is sorely needed. For although some experimental laboratory studies have shown less discrimination from majority than minority groups (e.g., Espinoza & Garza, 1985), it is inevitably the case that all participants in a social conflict feel some degree of insecurity on certain dimensions and in some contexts (Edwards & Shearn, 1987).

## MICRO FACTORS AFFECTING
## COMMUNICATOR CHARACTERISTICS

### Immediate Contextual Concerns

Moving now to the more micro level, studies have also investigated directly the effect of ethnic group membership on communicators' characteristics. This has usually not been the sole aim of these studies that have also examined, variously and in tandem, covariates such as other social group memberships held, interlocutor characteristics and participant relationship, and immediate social context. For instance, Welkowitz, Bond, and Feldstein (1984) showed that temporal patterns of 8-year-old Caucasian and Japanese Hawaiians' speech were a complex function of both their own ethnicity and gender and that of their interlocutors. Gudykunst and colleagues in an independent but related series of studies have also investigated the variables of ethnicity and gender in a variety of communicative contexts. In one of these, and using uncertainty reduction theory as their guiding framework (Berger & Calabrese, 1975), Gudykunst and Hammer (1987) presented 485 middle-class American students with a scenario that involved them imagining being introduced to a person of the same ethnic background as themselves, either the same sex or the opposite sex, and then completing a questionnaire about their behavioral intentions toward interacting with the target other. Although there was an overall influence of ethnicity, the only dependent variable to reach significance was the intent to display nonverbal affiliative expressiveness; Blacks reported less intent here than Whites overall. There were no main effects for gender but there were differences on each of the measures relating to the proposed dyadic composition such that, for example, females reported intent to disclose more in same-sex dyads. The authors concluded the ethnicity may provide boundary conditions for some axioms of uncertainty reduction theory in that Blacks may not place as much importance on uncertainty reduction as Whites.

Giles and Johnson (1981), in line with social identity theory (Tajfel & Turner, 1979) and in accord with the foregoing discussion, noted that the vast majority of work in this area relied on locating communicators according to objective indices of their ethnic group membership. Little attention had been paid to participants' own *subjective* definitions of their social identities nor to the kinds of interethnic comparisons that participants might be making at the time. From this perspective, it is likely that interethnic interactions for those involved who did not identify strongly with their group memberships would define communication with an outgroup more in *interpersonal* terms than *intergroup* ones. In other words, ethnicity would not be salient and they would react to each other in terms of their individual personalities, temperaments, moods, attitudes, and so forth. In addition, construals of the situation in terms of its task-relatedness, formality, and the like might be rendered of more communicative importance (see Furnham, 1986; Giles & Hewstone, 1982). Moreover, given that ethnicity is a variable construct, ethnic salience and evaluations may well change according to fluctuating demands of the situation, including the content of the dialogue and the inferences deriving from it (see Bourhis, Giles, Leyens, & Tajfel, 1979) as well as the perceived prototypicality of in- and outgroup participants (see Marques, Yzerbyt, & Leyens, 1988; Quattrone, 1986; Turner, 1986). It is interesting to note that Kirkland, Greenberg, and Pyszczynski (1987) showed that overhearing a derogatory label levied against a minority target person had the effect not only of devaluing the latter's perceived competence even further when she or he performed poorly but also affected others associated socially with them, even if they were supposed members of the judges' own group. This situational effect on ethnic reactions is all the more interesting given that the authors report informal evidence suggesting that the overhearers appeared to be overtly annoyed by the verbal intrusion of these labels.

In line with this backdrop, Gudykunst and Hammer (in press) examined, in a complex design, the influence of social identity and the intimacy of relationships on uncertainty reduction processes in interethnic relationships. It was found in two separate samples of Hispanics in the Midwest of the United States and Caucasians in the Southwest that the more positive the interethnic comparison when the target other was prototypical, the greater the intent to self-disclose, interrogate, and to be nonverbally affiliative. It is interesting that also found was the higher (or perhaps more secure) the communicators' ingroup identification, the more confidence they had in attributing qualities to the proposed outgroup interactant. Caution obviously has to be taken with the link between fabricated vignette-elicited intentions and actual outcomes in real settings, as well exemplified in Bourhis's (1984) work on French- and English-Canadian communications.

## Subjective and Objective Parameters of Intercultural Communication

Nevertheless, such studies once again open the door for examining subjective and objective indices of communicators' characteristics in a manner that is theoretically more compelling than manipulating gross ethnic group membership. For, as Louw-Potgieter and Giles (1987) have shown in a study of the linguistic strategies of South African dissidents, it is not always the case that we feel we are members of a group to which others would define us as belonging; some individuals want "in" when the majority define them "out" while others want to be seen "out" when they are otherwise defined "in." It is encouraging that Gudykunst in the above study and elsewhere (1985a; Gudykunst & Hammer, in press; Gudykunst, Sodetani, & Sonoda, 1987) is attempting to articulate how the complex web of intrapersonal, relational, and intergroup *processes* operates. There is, as always, still much to be accomplished when we consider more closely the *dimensions* of communicators' identity characteristics and the varying degrees of intercultural effectiveness (e.g., being able to manage psychological stress; see Stephan & Stephan's, 1985, model of intergroup anxiety) that interactants bring to an encounter (Hammer, 1987; see Gudykunst & Kim, 1984, for a review of other personality and individual differences). Hence, not only do different ethnic groups attach varying social meanings to their cultural categories (see Brown & Williams, 1984), but they also attach different values to them in terms of importance, emotion, and stability (Garza & Herringer, 1987; Ting-Toomey, 1985), to name but a few. In addition, the emotive climate associated with interacting with different target ethnic groups can also be of crucial importance. In this regard, Dijker (1987) has shown that different emotional dimensions, such as positive mood, anxiety, and irritation, are associated in some indigenous Dutch's minds with various immigrant groups in the Netherlands and can affect communicative outcomes differentially. Obviously, many subjective characteristics of how communicators see their status within the ingroup (Sachdev & Bourhis, 1987) and the perceived justice of their past dealings with the outgroup (Taylor, Moghaddam, Gamble, & Zellerer, 1987) affect communicative outcomes and should be afforded due theoretical as well as empirical consideration in future studies.

## Ethnic Talk and the Dialectics
## Among Language, Values, and Identity

The discussion thus far has examined the ways in which communicators' identity characteristics mediate outcomes. The process is, of course, far more bidirectional to the extent that communicative outcomes can also reshape cognitions (Kraut & Higgins, 1984) and feelings of social identification (Hewstone & Giles, 1986). There are many studies showing that "forcing" bilinguals to complete a test in their second language can often mean that they will express the values stereotypically associated with that outgroup tongue. For instance, Ervin (1964) showed that when French American bilinguals were administered a projective test (the Thematic Apperception Test) in both languages their narratives were far more romantic and emotional in French than English. Yang and Bond (1980), however, have shown that the converse process can operate (called "ethnic affirmation") with respondents who strongly identify with their cultural group. Hence, when students in Hong Kong were asked to complete a values test in either English or Cantonese they expressed more traditional Chinese values under the former linguistic conditions than the latter. The sociopsychological implications of emotionally charged language use are also well shown in an Israeli study where Arab and Jewish students both differentiated ingroup from outgroup values more when tested in Hebrew than when tested in English (John, Young, Giles, & Hofman, 1985; see also, Bond, 1983) and in Wales where the use of Welsh or English had a dramatic effect on how Welsh bilinguals construed the values of a "typical" English peer (Johnson & Giles, 1982). More immediate to interactive demands, Segalowitz (1976) showed that being induced to use a language variety with which you were not totally proficient was likely to produce negative attributions from the other interactant.

The dialectical processes operating between communicators' social and linguistic characteristics are ones that are rarely, if ever, explored in studies on intercultural communication owing to the fact that investigations are freeze-dried in their sole attention to one side of the equation (e.g., linguistic indices/intentions) or the other (e.g., values). Moreover, attention now ought to be expended in developing research beyond what is expected to happen and how something is said, to which meanings are actually conveyed by participants in intercultural communication. In other words, we have little data on what is said in interethnic communication. Van Dijk (1987), however, provides a refreshing and seminal account from his impressive corpus of interviews in the Netherlands and California on "racist discourse" (see also, Smitherman-Donaldson & van Dijk, 1988). He has analyzed in considerable detail the ways people talk about ethnic minorities and examined the inherent racism in their story-telling, argumentation, and style of discourse and located some of the resource material for their prejudiced talk in the language of the media and allied institutions (see also, Husband, 1977; Wilson & Gutierrez, 1985). A particularly fascinating feature of the study is the way in which interviewees attempt to maintain positive face by producing socially desirable remarks but at the same time expressing a derogatory account of outgroup ethnic communities. Indeed, the emerging literatures on accounting, deception, and tactical communication in the "interpersonal" literatures are fruitful fodder for more elaborate forays into one of the most fundamental characteristics of communicators, namely, discourse style; for an *intergroup* perspective on deception, as an example, see Bradac, Friedman, and Giles (1986). Furthermore, current trends also suggest that the rapprochement between interpersonal and mass media communication scholars (Hawkins, Wiemann, & Pingree, 1988) could be usefully elaborated in the intercultural sphere as well.

## EVALUATIONS OF
## COMMUNICATORS' CHARACTERISTICS

Other communicators' characteristics in intercultural settings are, of course, themselves evaluated, attributed, and acted upon. Indeed, processing such data is part and parcel of the incoming data used by interlocutors in determining their own communicative characteristics. Biases in such decoding can appear even at the *perceptual* level as shown in a study in which a Black child was seen talking on a video screen but at such an angle the mouth movements could not be reliably detected (Williams, 1976). In one condition of the experiment, a middle-class White child's speech patterns were superimposed onto the tape and observers asked a number of questions about her. Despite the objective fact that she sounded "White," she was nevertheless heard by the observers as using nonstandard "Black" (see also Street & Hopper, 1982). In a related way, atypical combinations of the ethnic characteristics of target others (such as physiognomy and voice) are afforded differential weightings in determining our reactions to them (see Hewstone, 1988). In this regard, Beebe (1981) found that when Chinese-Thai bilingual children were interviewed by a Thai standard speaker but ethnic Chinese (looking) adult, they used more Chinese phonological variants than when being questioned by a similarly sounding but Thai-looking interviewer. Differentiating the voice component between what is said and how it is said, Giles and Johnson (1986) found that when ethnically involved respondents are confronted with a member of their ingroup or the outgroup (by means of accent) who is heard either to threaten or to support a central aspect of their identity, then the content of the message is the factor that determines the recipients' anticipated linguistic strategies toward this speaker. To us, this is a crucial study as it tempers at least some of the social significance of the studies to be outlined below in that they have all controlled out ethnicity involving messages and opted more for evaluatively neutral content.

## Evoking Stereotyped Judgments

There is a large literature on ethnic language attitudes that is concerned, in the main, with people's evaluative judgments toward supposedly different people heard on tape using the same content but utilizing different ethnic language characteristics (see Ryan & Giles, 1982). The findings underscore the fact that social inferences about a cultural group can be very swiftly uncovered after hearing short representative exemplars of their language varieties (Lambert, Hodgson, Gardner, & Fillenbaum, 1960) and in a fashion that appears to have universal relevance (e.g., Bond, 1985; Mgbo-Elue, 1987). In a comprehensive review of the area, Giles, Hewstone, Ryan, and Johnson (1987) pointed out that evaluations of different language varieties tend mainly to reflect the social conventions within speech communities and concern the status and prestige associated with the speakers of the different varieties. In general, the language characteristics of the dominant ethnic group imply greater competence than those of ethnic subordinate groups (Sebastian & Ryan, 1985). At the same time, research has shown (albeit less regularly than the previous phenomena) that speakers are rated lower on dimensions such as solidarity, integrity, and social attractiveness. The findings that emerge are often quite complex when other covariates are added into the design. For instance, Foon (1986) presented passages that manipulated the variables of accent, class, and ethnicity. She found that speakers' class affected judgments of competence and social attractiveness and ethnicity was related to judgments of social attractiveness and personal integrity. But, in addition, there was an interaction between class and ethnicity for ratings of personal integrity such that speakers of low ethnic status and high social class were rated more favorably than speakers of low ethnic status and low social class (see also, Gallois, Callan, & Johnstone, 1984, with respect to gender, ethnicity, and context interactions).

Studies demonstrate that significant social advantages are associated with speaking the dominant group's code in many important applied settings such as in the classroom and gaining a job (Kalin, 1982). In this vein, Seggie, Smith, and Hodgins (1986) elicited evaluations of employment suitability based on ethnic accent in Australia. Two groups of subjects of European descent—owners of small businesses and female shoppers—were asked to decide whether a speaker they were to hear on tape was suitable for a low- or high-status job training program; all the speakers had identical backgrounds and qualifications. The owners of small businesses heard Asian-, German-, and two (standard and broad) Anglo-Australian voices; the female shoppers heard Asian- and two Anglo-Australian voices. It is interesting that the businessmen did *not* differentiate between the two Anglo voices whereas the shoppers regarded the standard speaker as being unsuitable for low-status job training. The businessmen rated the Asian voice equally with the standard Anglo voice while the shoppers rated it with the broad Anglo voice. Seggie et al. offer an explanation of these results in terms of the differing cognitive schema of the two groups of subjects. In other words, the businessmen have knowledge of the success of Asian business in Australia whereas the female shoppers are more likely to think of Asians as restaurant workers; different evaluative profiles are thought to emerge as a result of these cognitive structures. It is interesting that in this research area, more than the previous ones discussed, the notion of class as a significant communicator characteristic assumes importance. Hofman and Cais (1984) in this vein examined the manner in which Hebrew fought its way to being a national language in Israel. They argued that, now that Hebrew had a dominant status, people might return to their ethnolinguistic roots. Their study concluded that maintenance of the mother tongue was closely related to the motives of "sentiment" and "habit," but was also contingent on the usefulness of prestige of the particular mother tongue. The results also showed that blue-collar workers tended to shift toward Hebrew as the language most helpful to upward mobility whereas white-collar workers were able to enjoy the luxury of maintaining their own ingroup language.

**The Subjective Specter**

Although the vast majority of listener-judges in these studies were once again classified according to their ethnic group by objective criteria, promising signs of *subjective* and more *macro-contextual* appraisal are also emerging in this research domain as well (McKirnan & Hamayan, 1984). Perhaps the first of these was conducted some years ago by Flores and Hopper (1975) in a study concerned with the evaluation of Mexican and Anglo-American dialects. It was found that those respondents who utilized the self-appellation "Chicano" were more favorably disposed toward the members of their ingroup represented on audiotape (see Hecht & Ribeau, in press). Similarly, Bourhis, Giles, and Tajfel (1973) argued that, when ethnic groups were undergoing a positive redefinition of their identity, the typical pattern of conceding perceived competence to speakers characterized with the dominant ethnic code would be broken. These authors' data showed that, at a time when the Welsh arguably were exuding more pride in their cultural and linguistic heritage, standard English speakers on tape were upgraded relative to Welsh-accented and Welsh-language-speaking targets only on the traits of snobbishness, conservatism, and arrogance.

In an attempt to make this area more theory-oriented and as a means of delimiting the plethora of descriptive (virtually replicative) studies accumulating in culture after culture, Ryan, Hewstone, and Giles (1984) formulated a model that explored different language attitude profiles and the functions they might display at different phases in the changing relations between groups as construed by the individual members themselves (see also, Giles & Johnson, 1987). In this vein, Abrams and Hogg (1987) showed in Scotland how *self*-categorization processes mediate language attitudes while Bourhis and Sachdev (1984) have accomplished the same ends in their Italian-Canadian study for the mediating role of group vitalities. It is interesting that Ros, Cano, and Huici (1987), in their ambitious study of the Spanish attitudes toward Castilian, Catalan, Basque, Valencian, and Galician language characteristics found that *subtractive identity* (i.e., the difference between the identity associated with a specific ethnolinguistic group and that accorded to Spain) was a better predictor than ingroup identification alone. This measure, together with many of the macro-contextual variables mentioned earlier in the chapter, should be ones worthwhile exploring more generally and with respect to the encoding studies outlined above (for further critiques and proposals for future research on ethnic language attitudes, see Giles, Hewstone, & Ball, 1983; Giles & Ryan, 1982; Giles et al., 1987).

As mentioned throughout this chapter, communicator language characteristics are not static, they change over time and, also, due to the demands of the immediate context. A number of studies in the context of "communication accommodation theory" (see Coupland, Coupland, Giles, & Henwood, 1988; Gallois, Franklyn-Stokes, Giles, & Coupland, 1988) have shown that communicators' accommodating to the language features and interpretive competence of an outgroup other in intercultural communication are favorably evaluated. The factors mediating the motive to accommodate (Genesee & Bourhis, 1982) and its consequences, however, depend on a complex number of factors including in the latter case the reduction of sociolinguistic distance at an optimal level and the recipients' attributions being positive (for a review, see Giles, Mulac, Bradac, & Johnson, 1987). Indeed, interpersonally converging in this fashion could sometimes give rise to a loss of identity for the communicator and conceivably be seen by ingroup third parties as a cultural betrayal.

## THE MISINTERPRETATION OF
## COMMUNICATOR CHARACTERISTICS

In sum, the language characteristics of one's interlocutors can have a profound affect on evaluations of them as well as attributions of their intent. By means of a variety of intriguing methods, the latter is well documented in the large literature on cross-cultural miscommunication and illustrates the enormity of the potential for interethnic misunderstanding and the virtual entrenchment of negative stereotypes that follow (Chick, 1985; Liberman, 1984). Interestingly enough, similar *cultural* analyses (more or less stated in these terms) have been made with respect to communication between cancer victims and their families (Dunkel-Schetter & Wortman, 1982), the bereaved and their relatives (Lehrman, Ellard, & Wortman, 1986), the able-bodied and the physically handicapped (Emry & Wiseman, 1987), and the sexes (Maltz & Borker, 1982), and would doubtless pertain to other intergroup contexts involving "cultural" components such as the elderly (see Coupland, Coupland, Giles, & Henwood, 1988). In all these cases, and as pointed out by Varonis and Gass (1985) with respect to native and nonnative speaker interactions, the lack of shared sociolinguistic backgrounds including different beliefs about talk and silence (Giles, 1988), communicative satisfaction (Hecht & Ribeau, 1984), and communicative rule systems (Collier, 1988) does increase the probability that any misunderstanding would go unrecognized and, therefore, be difficult to resolve.

In this paradigm, McNabb (1986) studied the differences in communication between Eskimos and non-Eskimos. Eskimo verbal and nonverbal communicative patterns are very sensitive to social context and have many variations that can lead to attributions of inconsistency and unpredictability by non-Eskimos. Such attributions both generate and reinforce stereotypes leading to miscommunication. For example, the conventional gesture of "taciturn" reserve (i.e., remaining quietly noncommittal) is used by Eskimos while awaiting further information, but may be interpreted by non-Eskimos as apathy or animosity.

Albert (1986), investigating the differing importance of the use of "shame" between Hispanics and Anglo-Americans, required informants to consider various vignettes and attribute causes for behavior depicted in them. For example, one such vignette was "Antonia didn't speak up in front of her classmates because . . ." The attributions from which respondents were asked to chose were because she was (a) ashamed, (b) shy, (c) afraid her classmates will make fun of her, and (c) taught that girls do not speak in front of a group. Overall in these vignettes, Hispanics chose the "shame" attributions more often than the Anglos and, as Albert argues (as does Kochman, 1986, with respect to Black-White differences in verbal insults), this can have important implications in intercultural communication and especially so in educational settings. In a related way, Rubin (1986) has shown the likelihood of ambiguities in classroom questioning. Typically, Anglo teachers use quasi-questions that hint at the information required and the Anglo child knows that it is a test of his or her knowledge and understanding. This kind of questioning is totally unfamiliar to Black cultures and a direct request may be needed to elicit the correct information. Where this is not understood by teachers, Rubin describes how ethnic minority children come to be seen as unresponsive and lacking in understanding and, as a result, they tend to underachieve. Add to all this the plethora of nonverbal differences (e.g., eye contact, interpersonal space) and discourse differences that are part and parcel of communicator characteristics and we have the fodder for cultural misunderstandings.

Miscommunication is not, of course, restricted to the educational sphere (for the business domain, see McCreary, 1986, and, more generally, Coupland, Giles, & Wiemann, in press). Pedersen (1983, p. 405) discusses the problems faced by Americans in counseling Chinese students in that "even when the words in Chinese and English were the same, the contexts in which the words were interpreted were completely different. Some of the more common counseling words such as *concern* (I am *concerned* about you) simply do not exist in Chinese." Pedersen then provides an insightful analysis of how Chinese pictographs can allow one access into the semantic and cultural differences inherent in Chinese words vis-à-vis English. For example, *good* is represented as the combination of the figures of a woman and children, indicating that familial issues constitute much of what is cared for and good. Staying in this cultural context, Cheung and New (1984) give a fascinating historical account of the miscommunications apparent when Canadian Protestant missionaries attempted to provide Western medical services to Chinese people in the early part of this century. Based on analyses of the correspondence and reports mailed from China to the home church, these authors were able to pinpoint how the Chinese medico-culture and its practices, on one hand, and Western medicine, on the other, were mutually misunderstood by both parties, leading to a lack of the communicative empathy necessary for truly effective treatment to be accepted.

In another absorbing study, Cohen (1987) has proposed, on the basis of an analysis of statespersons' autobiographical accounts, that much of the crises (including that of Suez) that arose in American-Egyptian relations in the 1950s could be attributable, at least in part, to the communicative misunderstandings of diplomats on both sides. Adopting Ting-Toomey's (1985) theory of culture and conflict, Cohen locates many of the diplomatic communicational problems as deriving from the fact that the United States and Egypt represent "low- and high-context" cultures. In the simplest of terms, in low-context cultures, meaning is conveyed directly in the message without much of it being implicit in the context, whereas the opposite is the case in high-context cultures in that implicit meaning, nonverbal nuances, and context are paramount in fully understanding the real message. From this framework, Cohen argues that many communicator characteristics will differ radically between the two cultures (including directness-indirectness and exaggeration-understatement) and he provides compelling, concrete examples showing that many important diplomatic statements issued were misinterpreted and acted upon misguidedly by the other nation as a consequence of these dimensions.

Miscommunication notwithstanding, an interesting series of studies by Taylor and Simard (1975) in Canada and the Philippines showed that objective similarities in intercultural communication can still lead to psychological discomfort and misattribution. For instance, they showed that, in their structured and unstructured tasks, dyadic communication within groups was just as efficient (as measured along a host of dependent measures) as between ethnic groups. Nevertheless, subjects reported after the event much less satisfaction and efficiency with inter- than intraethnic communication. Hence, Hewstone and Giles (1986), in their model of intergroup communication breakdown, assign a central role to stereotypes in terms of their *functions* as well as their contents. They point also to the need for a detailed analysis of *types* of breakdown and a conceptualization of it (as occurs in the study of relational dissolution) more in terms of a *process* with many trajectories and underlying dimensions than as a static event. In any case, it is obvious that knowledge of communicators' different characteristics, interpersonal accommodation, and contact are not sufficient for promoting intercultural harmony (see Hewstone & Brown, 1986) and particularly so when social prejudice is rabid (Singh, Lele, & Martohartdjono, 1988).

## EPILOGUE

Research on communicator characteristics has been conducted by scholars in a range of cultural settings, with different subgroups and methodologies, and from different theoretical and ideological stances. As mentioned at the outset, we have not in this short chapter attempted to be exhaustive in our review nor have we been able to critique individual studies or theories along the way. Rather, we have looked for common themes and pinpointed lacunae with a view to providing a conceptual framework for these highly diverse studies as a benchmark for future work in this area. A communicator's characteristics are based on a whole range of macro- and micro-contextual identity profiles and needs that are monitored not only by the communicator him- or herself but also evaluated, attributed, and acted upon in reciprocal fashion by others present (and even subsequently by significant others in the network absent at the time). As we have seen, particular studies have looked at modest numbers and isolated sets of independent and dependent variables, some with attention to beliefs and expectations, others to particular limited sets of communicative behaviors.

We recognize the value in conducting one-off studies with a manageable number of variables, particularly in cultures and settings that have hitherto not been examined. Yet we also see the danger in *only* continuing and proliferating work in this area in a patchwork quilt fashion. We do need, as argued on occasion elsewhere, systematic and programmatic research in some settings that at the very least are cognizant of all the likely micro and macro and dialectical processes operating. On the basis of the foregoing, Table 5.1 is a summary blueprint of the different kinds of characteristics that may, mindfully and or mindlessly (see Langer & Piper, 1987), influence communicators or are used by them as data sources in the process of intercultural communication, and, as such, many more of them should be recognized in our theoretical frameworks (see Giles & Johnson, 1987; Gudykunst, 1985b). Once again, these are not meant to be exhaustive nor ordered in terms of salience (see alongside Table 5.1, Giles & Street, 1985, p. 240). Our point, however, is that many of these important dimensions are empirically and theoretically absent in research examining the roles of communicator characteristics in intercultural communication.

Let us return finally to the two questions posed at the outset of this chapter. First, what determines our communicator characteristics? We have seen that the nature of, and values inherent in, the intercultural settings to which we belong can influence considerably the significance and functions talk and silence are afforded, as well our communicative intent toward certain other groups we encounter. Whether we are members of dominant or subordinate cultural groups and the changing relations that operate between them have been shown to influence the language characteristics we adopt (form and content) in different settings and the effect that has, in feedback fashion, on our own sense of cultural identity, intergroup perceptions, and values. Communicator characteristics can shift fundamentally (in terms of language, dialect, phonological features, and discourse, to name but a few) to accommodate different contextual demands including the characteristics of others whom we are addressing and the cultural stereotypes that mediate our encountering them. And this they do in ways oftentimes unrecognized by those involved, and in the community at large. It is important that we have seen how creative groups and individuals can be in their strategies to maintain their sense of identity under considerable sociopolitical and economic pressure.

**TABLE 5.1.** Language Attitudes, Communicative Intentions, Attributions, Acts, and Breakdowns: A Function of Communicator Characteristics

---

Communicator characteristics:

   High-low absorption of language of the mass media and other institutions, regarding intercultural affairs

   Membership of/knowledge about high-low context cultures

   High-low relative perceived group vitality including familial, kinship, and other network cultural supports

   Intergroup bilinguality: high-low fluency in all relevant others' languages

   Membership of/values for individualistic-collectivistic culture

   Perceived historical relations operating between groups including dimensions of power, conflict, justice, threat, and change

   Frequency and quality of communication with outgroup members

   Membership/knowledge of group defined in terms of assimilation, separation, segregation, and deculturation

   Perceived immediate contextual dimensions, norms, and goals including cues triggering high-low ethnic salience

   Characteristics of those present, including numbers, prototypicality, and social attractiveness

   Cultural premises explicit-implicit in the message/conversation including threat and control involved

   Emotional associations of outgroup community

   High-low identification with ingroup and the multidemensional social meanings of group membership

   Perceived relational history with participants including uncertainty, similarity, and intimacy

   Personality, temperament and mood including intercultural effectiveness

---

Second, what are the social meanings attending communicator characteristics? We have seen how communicators' language is sometimes not seen as perceived by others as intended by the speakers and it is open to cognitive bias. Indeed, the complex social judgments made of linguistic characteristics in terms of perceived competence and social attractiveness are, depending on the context and the status and power of their users in society, a significant factor in forming impressions of others and in mediating important social decisions in applied contexts. Finally, the sociolinguistic characteristics of communicators are, as above, vastly different depending on the macro context from which they derive. In this sense, they are a potential for misattribution of intent and meaning in ways that can seriously detract from the harmony of an interpersonal as well as an international relationship.

Communicators' characteristics then are subtle, manifold, and changing, and we are only just beginning to understand their social influence. Yet, if we can get more of a handle on the grander schema implied in Table 5.1 in the design and interpretation of our encoding *and* decoding studies as well as be more open-minded in an eclectic use of methods, the next *Handbook* may show a quantum leap forward in the study of communicator characteristics as well as provide some weightings regarding their salience for determining differentially the large number of communicative outcomes possible; we ourselves are currently working toward this end theoretically. Of course, to achieve this goal, we need to embrace the literatures and probably the collaborative skills of scholars from other disciplines in an interdisciplinary fashion that is far from common currently.

Finally, we hope to alert readers to the fact that the collective linguistic activities and policies of some groups are not as perverse and destructive as they would seem to some. They are often tactics of maintaining a valued identity. Moreover, the sometimes confusing and irritating use of language by members of other cultural groups we encounter, together with their surprising interpretations of our own actions, are not always based on attributed "deficiencies" and/or devilment. Again, they may be premised on different cultural values and habits that have been hitherto camouflaged by ignorance, prejudice, and so-called tolerance, and would probably not be evident had it not been for rigorous academic studies being conducted (and sometimes modestly disseminated to the wider community). It would, of course, be imprudent to offer panaceas for a healthy advancement of the interculturalism (see Garza & Gallegos, 1985) as evidenced in the complexities apparent in this chapter. Yet, a mere sensitivity to them is a good starting point in this direction.

## REFERENCES

Abrams, D., & Hogg, M. A. (1987). Language attitudes, frame of reference, and social identity: A Scottish dimension. *Journal of Language and Social Psychology, 6*.

Albert, R. D. (1986). Communication and attributional differences between Hispanics and Anglo-Americans. In Y. Y. Kim (Ed.), *Interethnic communication: Recent research* (pp. 42-58). Newbury Park, CA: Sage.

Allard, R., & Landry, R. (1986). Subjective ethnolinguistic vitality viewed as a belief system. *Journal of Multilingual and Multicultural Development, 7*, 1-12.

Banks, S. P. (1987). Achieving "unmarkedness" in organizational discourse: A praxis perspective on ethnolinguistic identity. *Journal of Language and Social Psychology, 6*, 171-190.

Beebe, L. M. (1981). Social and situational factors affecting the strategy of dialect code-switching. *International Journal of the Sociology of Language, 32*, 139-149.

Bentahila, A. (1983). *Language attitudes among Arabic-French bilinguals in Morocco.* Clevendon, England: Multilingual Matters.

Berger, C. R., & Calabrese, R. (1975). Some explorations in initial interactions and beyond: Toward a developmental theory of interpersonal communication. *Human Communication Research, 1*, 99-112.

Berry, J. W. (1984). Multicultural policy in Canada: A social psychological analysis. *Canadian Journal of Behavioral Science, 16*, 353-370.

Bolton, K., & Kwok, H. (in press). The dynamics of the Hong Kong accent: Social identity and sociolinguistic description. *Journal of Pacific Rim Communication, 1*.

Bond, M. H. (1983). How language variation affects inter-cultural differentiation of values by Hong Kong bilinguals. *Journal of Language and Social Psychology, 2*, 57-66.

Bond, M. H. (1985). Language as a carrier of ethnic stereotypes in Hong Kong. *Journal of Social Psychology, 125*, 53-62.

Bourhis, R. Y. (1979). Language in ethnic interaction. In H. Giles & B. Saint-Jacques (Eds.), *Language and ethnic relations* (pp. 117-142). Oxford: Pergamon.

Bourhis, R. Y. (1984). Cross-cultural communication in Montreal: Two field studies since the Charter of the French language. *International Journal of the Sociology of Language, 46*, 33-47.

Bourhis, R. Y., Giles, H., Leyens, J.-P., & Tajfel, H. (1979). Psycholinguistic distinctiveness: Language divergence in Belgium. In H. Giles & R. N. St. Clair (Eds.), *Language and social psychology* (pp. 158-185). Oxford: Basil Blackwell.

Bourhis, R. Y., Giles, H., & Tajfel, H. (1973). Language as a determinant of Welsh identity. *European Journal of Social Psychology, 3*, 447-460.

Bourhis, R. Y., & Sachdev, I. (1984). Vitality perceptions and language attitudes: Some Canadian data. *Journal of Language and Social Psychology, 3*, 97-126.

Bradac, J. J., Friedman, E., & Giles, H. (1986). A social approach to proposition communication: Speakers lie to hearers. In G. McGregor (Ed.), *Language for hearers* (pp. 127-151). Oxford: Pergamon.

Brown, R., & Williams, J. (1984). Group identification: The same thing to all people? *Human Relations, 37*, 547-564.

Chana, U., & Romaine, S. (1984). Evaluative reactions to Punjabi/English code-switching. *Journal of Multilingual and Multicultural Development, 5*, 447-473.

Cheung, Y.-W., & New, P. K.-M. (1984). The magic of the "foreign devils": The missionary doctor-Chinese patient relationship in early twentieth century China. *Proceedings of the 6th International Symposium on Asian Studies* (pp. 95-108). Hong Kong: Asian Research Service.

Chick, J. K. (1985). The interactional accomplishment of discrimination in South Africa. *Language in Society, 14*, 299-326.

Chinese Culture Connection. (1987). Chinese values and the search for culture-free dimensions of culture. *Journal of Cross-Cultural Psychology, 18*, 143-164.

Cohen, R. (1987). Problems of intercultural communication in Egyptian-American diplomatic relations. *International Journal of Intercultural Relations, 11*, 29-47.

Collier, M. J. (1988). A comparison of conversations among and between domestic culture groups: How intra- and intercultural competencies vary. *Communication Quarterly, 36*, 122-144.

Coupland, N., Coupland, J., Giles, H., & Henwood, K. (1988). Accommodating the elderly: Invoking and extending a theory. *Language in Society, 17*, 1-41.

Coupland, N., Giles, H., & Wiemann, J. (Eds.). (in press). *The handbook of miscommunication and problematic talk*. Clevendon, England: Multilingual Matters.

Dijker, A. J. M. (1987). Emotional reactions to ethnic minorities. *European Journal of Social Psychology, 17*, 305-325.

Dow, J. R. (1987). New perspectives on language maintenance and language shift: I. *International Journal of the Sociology of Language, 68*.

Dube-Simard, L. (1983). Genesis of social categorization, threat to identity, and perceptions of social justice: Their role in intergroup communication. *Journal of Language and Social Psychology, 2*, 183-206.

Dunkel-Schetter, C., & Wortman, C. B. (1982). The interpersonal dynamics of cancer: Problems in social relationships and their impact on the patient. In H. S. Friedman & M. R. DiMatteo (Eds.), *Interpersonal issues in health care*. New York: Academic Press.

Edwards, J. R. (1985). *Language, society, and identity*. Oxford: Basil Blackwell.

Edwards, J. R. (in press). Gaelic in Nova Scotia. In C. H. Williams (Ed.), *Geolinguistic essays*. Clevendon, England: Multilingual Matters.

Edwards, J. R., & Doucette, L. (1987). Ethnic salience, identity and symbolic ethnicity. *Canadian Ethnic Studies, 19*, 52-62.

Edwards, J. R., & Shearn, C. (1987). Language and identity in Belgium: Perceptions of French and Flemish students. *Ethnic and Racial Studies, 10*, 135-148.

Emry, R., & Wiseman, R. L. (1987). An intercultural understanding of ablebodied and disabled persons' communication. *International Journal of Intercultural Relations, 11*, 7-27.

Ervin, S. M. (1964). Language and TAT content in bilinguals. *Journal of Abnormal and Social Psychology, 68*, 500-567.

Espinoza, J. A., & Garza, R. T. (1985). Social group salience and interethnic cooperation. *Journal of Experimental Social Psychology, 21*, 380-392.

Farr, R., & Moscovici, S. (Eds.). (1983). *Social representations*. Cambridge: Cambridge University Press.

Fishman, J. A. (1966). *Language loyalty in the United States*. The Hague, the Netherlands: Mouton.

Fishman, J. A. (1977). Language and ethnicity. In H. Giles (Ed.), *Language, ethnicity and intergroup relations* (pp. 15-58). London: Academic Press.

Flores, N., & Hopper, R. (1975). Mexican Americans' evaluation of spoken Spanish and English. *Speech Monographs, 42*, 91-98.

Foon, A. E. (1986). A social structural approach to speech evaluation. *Journal of Social Psychology, 126*, 521-530.

Furnham, A. (1986). Situational determinants of intergroup communication. In W. B. Gudykunst (Ed.), *Intergroup communication* (pp. 96-113). London: Edward Arnold.

Gallois, C., Callan, V. J., & Johnstone, M. (1984). Personality judgments of Australian Aborigine and White speakers: Ethnicity, sex, and context. *Journal of Language and Social Psychology, 3*, 39-58.

Gallois, C., Franklyn-Stokes, A., Giles, H., & Coupland, N. (1988). Communication accommodation in intercultural encounters. In Y. Y. Kim & W. B. Gudykunst (Eds.), *Theories in intercultural communication*. Newbury Park, CA: Sage.

Gans, H. (1979). Symbolic ethnicity: The future of ethnic groups and cultures in America. *Ethnic and Racial Studies, 2*, 1-20.

Gardner, R. C. (1985). *Social psychology and second language learning*. London: Edward Arnold.

Garner, T., & Rubin, D. L. (1986). Middle class Black's perceptions of dialect and style shifting: The case of southern attorneys. *Journal of Language and Social Psychology, 5*, 33-48.

Garza, R. T., & Gallegos, P. I. (1985). Environmental influences and personal choice: A humanistic perspective on acculturation. *Hispanic Journal of Behavioral Sciences, 7*, 365-379.

Garza, R. T., & Herringer, L. G. (1987). Social identity: A multidimensional approach. *Journal of Social Psychology, 127*, 299-308.

Genesee, F., & Bourhis, R. Y. (1982). The social and psychological significance of code-switching in cross-cultural communication. *Journal of Language and Social Psychology, 1,* 1-27.

Gibbons, J. (1983). Attitudes towards languages and code-switching in Hong Kong. *Journal of Multilingual and Multicultural Development, 4,* 129-148.

Giles, H. (1978). Linguistic differentiation between ethnic groups. In H. Tajfel (Ed.), *Differentiation between social groups* (pp. 361-393). London: Academic Press.

Giles, H. (1979). Ethnicity markers in speech. In K. R. Scherer & H. Giles (Eds.), *Social markers in speech* (pp. 251-289). Cambridge: Cambridge University Press.

Giles, H. (1988, April). *"Talk is cheap . . ." but "my word is my bond": Beliefs about talk.* Invited paper delivered at the First Hong Kong Conference on Language and Society.

Giles, H., & Bourhis, R. Y. (1976). Voice and racial categorization in Britain. *Communication Monographs, 43,* 108-114.

Giles, H., Bourhis, R. Y., & Taylor, D. M. (1977). Towards a theory of language in ethnic group relations. In H. Giles (Ed.), *Language, ethnicity, and intergroup relations* (pp. 307-348). London: Academic Press.

Giles, H., & Byrne, J. L. (1982). An intergroup approach to second language acquisition. *Journal of Multilingual and Multicultural Development, 3,* 17-40.

Giles, H., & Hewstone, M. (1982). Cognitive structures, speech and social situations: Two integrative models. *Language Sciences, 4,* 187-219.

Giles, H., Hewstone, M., & Ball, P. (1983). Language attitudes in multilingual settings: Prologue and priorities. *Journal of Multilingual and Multicultural Development, 4,* 81-100.

Giles, H., Hewstone, M., Ryan, E. B., & Johnson, P. (1987). Research on language attitudes. In U. Ammon, N. Dittmar, & K. J. Mattheier (Eds.), *Sociolinguistics: An interdisciplinary handbook of the science of language* (pp. 1068-1081). Berlin: de Gruyter.

Giles, H., & Johnson, P. (1981). The role of language in ethnic group relations. In J. C. Turner & H. Giles (Eds.), *Intergroup behavior* (pp. 199-243). Chicago: Chicago University Press.

Giles, H., & Johnson, P. (1986). Perceived threat, ethnic commitment, and interethnic language behavior. In Y. Y. Kim (Ed.), *Interethnic communication: Recent research* (pp. 91-116). Newbury Park, CA: Sage.

Giles, H., & Johnson, P. (1987). Ethnolinguistic identity theory: A social psychological approach to language maintenance. *International Journal of the Sociology of Language, 68,* 69-99.

Giles, H., Mulac, A., Bradac, J. J., & Johnson, P. (1987). Speech accommodation theory: The next decade and beyond. In M. McLaughlin (Ed.), *Communication yearbook* (Vol. 10, pp. 13-48). Newbury Park, CA: Sage.

Giles, H., Rosenthal, D., & Young, L. (1985). Perceived ethnolinguistic vitality: The Anglo- and Greek-Australian setting. *Journal of Multilingual and Multicultural Development, 6,* 253-269.

Giles, H., & Ryan, E. B. (1982). Proglemena for developing a social psychological theory for language attitudes. In E. B. Ryan & H. Giles (Eds.), *Attitudes toward language variation: Social and applied contexts* (pp. 208-223). London: Edward Arnold.

Giles, H., & Street, R. L., Jr. (1985). Communicator characteristics and behavior: A review, generalizations, and model. In M. Knapp, & G. Miller (Eds.), *The handbook of interpersonal communication* (pp. 205-262). Beverly Hills, CA: Sage.

Giles, H., Taylor, D. M., & Bourhis, R. Y. (1977). Dimensions of Welsh identity. *European Journal of Social Psychology, 7,* 29-39.

Gudykunst, W. B. (1985a). The influence of cultural similarity and type of relationship on uncertainty reduction processes. *Communication Monographs, 52,* 203-217.

Gudykunst, W. B. (1985b). A model of uncertainty reduction in intercultural encounters. *Journal of Language and Social Psychology, 4,* 1-20.

Gudykunst, W. B. (1988). Uncertainty and anxiety. In Y. Y. Kim & W. B. Gudykunst (Eds.), *Theories in intercultural communication*. Newbury Park, CA: Sage.

Gudykunst, W. B., & Hammer, M. R. (1987). The effects of ethnicity, gender, and dyadic composition on uncertainty reduction in initial interactions. *Journal of Black Studies, 18*, 191-214.

Gudykunst, W. B., & Hammer, M. R. (in press). The influence of social identity and intimacy of interethnic relationships on uncertainty reduction processes. *Human Communication Research*.

Gudykunst, W. B., & Kim, Y. Y. (1984). *Communicating with strangers: An approach to intercultural communication*. New York: Random House.

Gudykunst, W. B., Sodetani, L. L., & Sonoda, K. T. (1987). Uncertainty reduction in Japanese/American/Caucasian relationships in Hawaii. *Western Journal of Speech Communication, 51*, 256-278.

Gudykunst, W. B., Yoon, Y.-C., & Nishida, T. (1987). The influence of individualism-collectivism on perception of communication in ingroup and outgroup relationships. *Communication Monographs, 54*, 295-306.

Hammer, M. R. (1986). The influence of ethnic and attitude similarity on initial social penetration. In Y. Y. Kim (Ed.), *Interethnic communication: Recent research* (pp. 225-237). Newbury Park, CA: Sage.

Hammer, M. R. (1987). Behavioral dimensions of intercultural effectiveness: A replication and extension. *International Journal of Intercultural Relations, 11*, 65-88.

Hammer, M. R., & Gudykunst, W. B. (in press). The influence of ethnicity and sex on social penetration in close friendships. *Journal of Black Studies*.

Hawkins, R. P., Wiemann, J. M., & Pingree, S. (1988) *Advancing Communication Science: Merging Mass and Interpersonal Processes*. Newbury Park, CA: Sage.

Hecht, M. L., & Ribeau, S. (1984). Ethnic communication: A comparative analysis of satisfying communication. *International Journal of Intercultural Relations, 8*, 135-151.

Hecht, M., & Ribeau, S. (in press). Afro-American identity labels and communicative effectiveness. *Journal of Language and Social Psychology, 6*.

Hewitt, R. (1986). *White talk Black talk: Inter-racial friendship and communication amongst adolescents*. Cambridge: Cambridge University Press.

Hewstone, M. (1988). Attributional bases of intergroup conflict. In W. Streocbe, A. W. Kruglanski, D. Bar-Tal, & M. Hewstone (Eds.), *The social psychology of intergroup conflict* (pp. 47-72). New York: Springer-Verlag.

Hewstone, M., & Brown, R. P. (Eds.). (1986). *Intergroup contact*. Oxford: Basil Blackwell.

Hewstone, M., & Giles, H. (1986). Social groups and social stereotypes in intergroup communication: Review and model of intergroup communication breakdown. In W. B. Gudykunst (Ed.), *Intergroup communication* (pp. 10-26). London: Edward Arnold.

Hofman, J. E., & Cais, J. (1984). Children's attitudes to language maintenance and shift. *International Journal of the Sociology of Language, 50*, 147-153.

Hofstede, G. (1983). Dimensions of national cultures in fifty countries and three regions. In J. B. Deregowski, S. Dziurawiec, & R. C. Annis (Eds.), *Expiscations in cross-cultural psychology*. Lisse: Swets & Zeitlinger.

Husband, C. (1977). News media, language and race relations: A case study in identity maintenance. In H. Giles (Ed.), *Language, ethnicity and intergroup relations* (pp. 211-240). London: Academic Press.

John, C., Young, L., Giles, H., & Hofman, J. E. (1985). Language, values, and intercultural differentiation in Israel. *Journal of Social Psychology, 125*, 527-529.

Johnson, P., & Giles, H. (1982). Values, language and intercultural differentiation: The Welsh-English context. *Journal of Multilingual and Multicultural Development, 3*, 103-116.

Kalin, R. (1982). The social significance of speech in medical, legal and occupational settings. In E. B. Ryan & H. Giles (Eds.), *Attitudes toward language variation: Social and applied contexts* (pp. 148-163). London: Edward Arnold.

Kim, Y. Y. (1988). *Communication and cross-cultural adaptation: An interdisciplinary approach.* Clevendon, England: Multilingual Matters.

Kim, Y. Y., & Gudykunst, W. B. (Eds.). (1988). *Theories in intercultural communication.* Newbury Park, CA: Sage.

Kirkland, S. L., Greenberg, J., & Pyszczynski, T. (1987). Further evidence of the deleterious effects of overhead derogatory ethnic labels: Derogation beyond the target. *Personality and Social Psychology Bulletin, 13*, 216-227.

Kochman, T. (1986). Black verbal dualing strategies in interethnic communication. In Y. Y. Kim (Ed.), *Interethnic communication: Recent research* (pp. 136-157). Newbury Park, CA: Sage.

Kraut, R. E., & Higgins, E. T. (1984). Communication and social cognition. In R. S. Wyer & T. K. Srull (Eds.), *Handbook of social cognition* (Vol. 3, pp. 87-129). Hillsdale, NJ: Lawrence Erlbaum.

Lambert, W. E. (1974). Culture and language as factors in learning and education. In F. E. Aboud & R. D. Meade (Eds.), *Cultural factors in learning and education.* Bellingham: Western Washington College Press.

Lambert, W. E., Hodgson, R., Gardner, R. C., & Fillenbaum, S. (1960). Evaluational reactions to spoken languages. *Journal of Abnormal and Social Psychology, 60*, 44-51.

Langer, E. J., & Piper, A. I. (1987). The prevention of mindlessness. *Journal of Personality and Social Psychology, 53*, 280-287.

Leclézio, M. K., Louw-Potgieter, J., & Souchon, M. B. S. (1986). The social identity of Mauritian immigrants in South Africa. *Journal of Social Psychology, 126*, 61-69.

Lehrman, D. R., Ellard, J. H., & Wortman, C. B. (1986). Social support for the bereaved: Recipients' and providers' perspectives on what is helpful. *Journal of Counseling and Clinical Psychology, 54*, 438-446.

Liberman, K. B. (1984). Hermeneutics of intercultural communication. *Anthropological Linguistics, 26*, 53-83.

Louw-Potgieter, J., & Giles, H. (1987). Imposed identity and linguistic strategies. *Journal of Language and Social Psychology, 6;, 258-284.*

McCreary, D. R. (1986). Vygotskyan sociolinguistic theory applied to negotiation in Japanese society. *Language Sciences, 8*, 141-151.

McKirnan, D. J., & Hamayan, E. V. (1984). Speech norms and attitudes towards outgroup members: A test of a model in a bicultural context. *Journal of Language and Social Psychology, 3*, 21-38.

McNabb, S. L. (1986). Stereotypes and interaction conventions of Eskimos and non-Eskimos. In Y. Y. Kim (Ed.), *Interethnic communication: Recent research* (pp. 21-41). Newbury Park, CA: Sage.

Maltz, D. N., & Borker, R. (1982). A cultural approach to male-female communication. In J. J. Gumperz (Ed.), *Language and social identity* (pp. 195-216). Cambridge: Cambridge University Press.

Marques, J. M., Yzerbyt, V. Y., & Leyens, J.-P. (1988). The black sheep effect: Extremity of judgments towards ingroup members as a function of group identification. *European Journal of Social Psychology, 18*, 1-16.

Mgbo-Elue, C. N. (1987). Social psychological and linguistic impediments to the acquisition of a second Nigerian language among Yoruba and Ibo. *Journal of Language and Social Psychology, 6*, 309-319.

Pak, A., Dion, K. L., & Dion, K. K. (1985). Correlates of self-confidence with English among Chinese students in Toronto. *Canadian Journal of Behavioral Science, 17*, 369-378.

Pedersen, P. (1983). Learning about the Chinese culture through the Chinese language. *Communication and Cognition, 16*, 403-412.

Platt, J. (1977). A model for polyglossia and multilingualism. *Language in Society, 6*, 361-378.

Quattrone, G. A. (1986). On the perception of a group's variability. In S. Worchel & W. G. Austin (Eds.), *Psychology of intergroup relations* (2nd ed., pp. 25-48). Chicago: Nelson-Hall.

Ros, M., Cano, I. J., & Huici, C. (1987). Language and intergroup perception in Spain. *Journal of Language and Social Psychology, 6*, 243-258.

Ross, J. (1979). Language and the mobilization of ethnic identity. In H. Giles & B. Saint-Jacques (Eds.), *Language and ethnic relations* (pp. 1-14). Oxford: Pergamon.

Rubin, D. L. (1986). "Nobody play by the rule he know": Ethnic interference in classroom questioning events. In Y. Y. Kim (Ed.), *Interethnic communication: Recent research* (pp. 158-175). Newbury Park, CA: Sage.

Ryan, E. B., & Giles, H. (Eds.). (1982). *Attitudes toward language variation: Social and applied contexts.* London: Edward Arnold.

Ryan, E. B., Giles, H., & Sebastian, R. J. (1982). An integrative perspective for the study of attitudes towards language variation. In E. B. Ryan & H. Giles (Eds.), *Attitudes toward language: Social and applied contexts* (pp. 1-19). London: Academic Press.

Ryan, E. B., Hewstone, M., & Giles, H. (1984). Language and intergroup attitudes. In J. R. Eiser (Ed.), *Attitudinal judgment* (pp. 135-160). New York: Springer-Verlag.

Sachdev, I., & Bourhis, R. Y. (1987). Status differentials and intergroup behavior. *European Journal of Social Psychology, 17*, 277-293.

Saint-Blancat, C. (1985). The effect of minority group vitality upon its sociopsychological behavior and strategies. *Journal of Multilingual and Multicultural Development, 6*, 31-44.

San Antonio, P. M. (1987). Social mobility and language use in an American company in Japan. *Journal of Language and Social Psychology, 6*, 191-200.

Sawaie, M. (1986). The present and future status of a minority language: The case of Arabic in the United States. *Journal of Multilingual and Multicultural Development, 7*, 31-40.

Scotton, C. M., & Wanjin, Z. (1984). The multiple meanings of shi.fu: A language change in progress. *Anthropological Linguistics, 76*, 326-344.

Sebastian, R. J., & Ryan, E. B. (1985). Speech cues and social evaluation: Markers of ethnicity, social class and age. In H. Giles & R. N. St. Clair (Eds.), *Recent advances in language, communication and social psychology* (pp. 112-143). London: Lawrence Erlbaum.

Segalowitz, N. (1976). Communicative competence and unfluent bilingualism. *Canadian Journal of Behavioral Science, 8*, 122-131.

Seggie, I., Smith, N., & Hodgins, P. (1986). Evaluations of employment suitability based on accent alone: An Australian case study. *Language Sciences, 8*, 129-140.

Singh, R., Lele, J., & Martohartdjono, G. (1988). Communication in a multilingual society: Some missed opportunities. *Language in Society, 17*, 43-60.

Smitherman-Donaldson, G., & van Dijk, T. A. (Eds.). (1988). *Discourse and discrimination.* Detroit: Wayne State University Press.

Stephan, W. G., & Stephan, C. W. (1985). Intergroup anxiety. *Journal of Social Issues, 41*, 157-176.

Street, R. L., Jr., & Hopper, R. (1982). A model of speech style evaluation. In E. B. Ryan & H. Giles (Eds.), *Attitudes toward language variation: Social and applied contexts* (pp. 175-188). London: Edward Arnold.

Tajfel, H., & Turner, J. C. (1979). An integrative theory of intergroup conflict. In W. C. Austin & S. Worchel (Eds.), *The social psychology of intergroup relations* (pp. 33-53). Monterey: Brooks/Cole.

Tannen, D. (1982). Ethnic style in male-female conversation. In J. J. Gumperz (Ed.), *Language and social identity* (pp. 217-213). Cambridge: Cambridge University Press.

Taylor, D. M., & McKirnan, D. J. (1984). A five-stage theory of intergroup behavior. *British Journal of Social Psychology, 23*, 291-300.

Taylor, D. M., Moghaddam, F. M., Gamble, I., & Zellerer, E. (1987). Disadvantaged group responses to perceived inequality: From passive acceptance to collective action. *Journal of Social Psychology, 127*, 259-272.

Taylor, D. M., & Simard, L. (1975). Social interaction in a bilingual setting. *Canadian Psychological Review, 16*, 240-254.

Ting-Toomey, S. (1985). Toward a theory of conflict and culture. *International and Intercultural Communication Annual, 9*, 71-86.

Triandis, H. C., Bontempo, R., & Villareal, M. J. (1988). Individualism-collectivism: Cross-cultural perspectives on self-group relationships. *Journal of Personality and Social Psychology, 54*, 323-338.

Turner, J. C. (1986). *Rediscovering the social group: A self-categorization theory.* Oxford: Basil Blackwell.

van Dijk, T. A. (1987). *Communicating racism.* Newbury Park, CA: Sage.

Varonis, E. M., & Gass, S. M. (1985). Miscommunication in native/nonative conversation. *Language in Society, 14*, 327-343.

von Raffler Engel, W. (1980). The unconscious element in intercultural communication. In R. N. St. Clair & H. Giles (Eds.), *The social and psychological contexts of language* (pp. 101-130). Hillsdale, NJ: Lawrence Erlbaum.

Welkowitz, J., Bond, R. N., & Feldstein, S. (1984). Conversational time patterns of Hawaiian children as a function of ethnicity and gender. *Language and Speech, 17*, 173-191.

Wherritt, I. (1985). Portugese language use in Goa, India. *Anthropological Linguistics, 27*, 437-451.

Wiemann, J., Chen, V., & Giles, H. (1986, November). *Beliefs about talk and silence in cultural context.* "Top 3" paper presented at the Intercultural Communication Section of the annual conference of the Speech Communication Association, Boston.

Williams, F. (1976). *The exploration of the linguistic attitudes of teachers.* Rowley, MA: Newbury House.

Wilson, C. C., II, & Gutierrez, F. (1985). *Minorities and media.* Beverly Hills, CA: Sage.

Yang, K. S., & Bond, M. H. (1980). Ethnic affirmation by Chinese bilinguals. *Journal of Cross-Cultural Psychology, 2*, 411-425.

Young, L., Giles, H., & Pierson, H. (1986). Sociopolitical change and perceived vitality. *International Journal of Intercultural Relations, 10*, 459-469.

# 6 Language and Intergroup Communication

**William B. Gudykunst**
**Stella Ting-Toomey**
**Bradford J. Hall**
**Karen L. Schmidt**

In *Pygmalion*, Henry Higgins claimed that while "you can spot an Irishman or a Yorkshireman by his brogue, I can place any man within six miles. I can place him within two miles in London. Sometimes within two streets" (Shaw, 1946). Although most people are not able to identify the background of others on the basis of speech as well as Henry Higgins, they know almost immediately whether another person is a member of their ingroup or an outgroup. Research indicates that ethnic group members identity more closely with those who share their language than with those who share their cultural background (Giles, Taylor, & Bourhis, 1973). Individuals also evaluate speakers perceived as ingroup members more favorably than those perceived as outgroup members (Hogg, Joyce, & Abrams, 1984). The recognition of belonging to a particular group and the categorization of others into ingroups and outgroups is a basic social process (Tajfel, 1978). Language is one of the major factors used in social categorization (Giles & Johnson, 1981).

*Language* often is used synonymously with *speech* and communication. There are, however, important differences. Language is an abstract system of rules (phonological, syntactic, semantic, and pragmatic). As such, it is a medium of communication. The abstract rules are translated into a channel (spoken, written, or sign language) in order to create messages. When the channel is the spoken word, speech is involved. "Communi-

AUTHORS'/EDITORS' NOTE: Originally another author was scheduled to write the language chapter for this volume. She was unable to complete the chapter, however, due to an accident. This chapter was drafted for another purpose, but modified for this volume so that a specific chapter on language could be included. Readers also should consult Giles and Franklyn-Stokes chapter in this volume for coverage of language spoken as a communicator characteristic.

cation is a more general concept involving the exchange of messages which may not be spoken and linguistic in form" (Berger & Bradac, 1982, p. 52). Because it is the spoken aspects of language that often provide markers of membership in social categories, "ethnic speech style" (Giles, Bourhis, & Taylor, 1977) must be included in any analysis of language and intergroup communication.

Extensive research on various aspects of language and intergroup communication (e.g., language attitudes, second-language acquisition, code-switching, speech norms, stereotypes, speech accommodation, ethnolinguistic identity; and language also has been examined as a characteristic of the communicators—see the Giles and Franklyn-Stokes chapter in this volume) has been conducted in recent years using a variety of theoretical and methodological perspectives. The purpose of this chapter is to overview the major lines of research. Our focus is on research from a social psychology of language perspective. We have organized the research under two headings: "social psychological factors" and "sociolinguistic factors" (the focus in this section is on research on sociolinguistic factors that has been conducted from a social psychological perspective). Social psychological factors include social/ethnolinguistic identity, language attitudes, stereotypes, and communication accommodation. Sociolinguistic factors involve second-language competence, group vitality, speech norms, and code-switching. We have focused on research conducted from a social psychology of language perspective for two reasons: readers of this *Handbook* are probably familiar with research from a sociolinguistic perspective and recent reviews of sociolinguistic research are available elsewhere (e.g., Gumperz, 1982a, 1982b; Schieffelin & Ochs, 1986).

## SOCIAL PSYCHOLOGICAL FACTORS

### Ethnolinguistic Identity

One of the major cognitive tools individuals use to define themselves vis-à-vis the world in which they live is social categorization, "the ordering of social environment in terms of groupings of persons in a manner which makes sense to the individual" (Tajfel, 1978, p. 61); for example, men and women, Blacks and Whites. Individuals perceive themselves as belonging to social groups and recognition of membership in these groups carries with it a knowledge of the values, positive and negative, attached to these groups. A social group is "two or more individuals who share a common social identification of themselves or . . . perceive themselves to be members of the same social category" (Turner, 1982, p. 15). Once individuals become aware of belonging to social groups, their social identities begin to form. Social identity, according to Tajfel (1978, p. 63), is "that *part* of an individual's self-concept which derives from his [or her] knowledge of his [or her] membership in a social group (or groups) together with the value and emotional significance attached to that membership." Language use facilitates the development of social identities (Eastman, 1985).

Giles and Johnson (1981) argue that language is a vital aspect of any group's, but particularly an ethnic group's, identity. This claim is supported by extensive research (e.g., Bond, 1983; Leclézio, Louw-Potgieter, & Souchon, 1986). Leclézio et al., for example, found that language is the most important aspect of the social identity of Mauritian immigrants in South Africa. Drawing together research on ethnoliguistic vitality, group boundaries, interethnic comparisons, status, and social identity, Giles and Johnson (1981) argued that people tend to adopt positive linguistic distinctiveness strategies with members of outgroups when they (a) identify with an ingroup that considers its language important; (b) make insecure comparisons with other ethnic groups; (c) perceive their group's ethnolinguistic vitality to be high; (d) perceive boundaries between their group and other groups to be closed and hard; (e) do not identify strongly with other social categories; (f) perceive little category membership overlaps with the person with whom they are interacting; (g) do not derive a strong social identity from other social category memberships; and (h) perceive their status to be higher in their ethnic group than in other social category memberships. These conclusions formed the basis for the initial statement of ethnolinguistic identity theory (Beebe & Giles, 1984, however, were the first to use this label for the theory). More recently, Giles and Johnson (1987) elaborated the theory linking it to the attitudes/motivations of members of dominant and subordinate groups and Gallois, Franklyn-Stokes, Giles, and Coupland (1988) articulated the theory with speech accommodation theory (e.g., Giles, Mulac, Bradac, & Johnson, 1986; this theory is discussed briefly below).

Several recent studies support and/or extend Tajfel's (1978) social identity theory to language usage or draw upon Giles and Johnson's (1981, 1987) ethnolinguistic identity theory. Abrams and Hogg's (1987) research, for example, revealed that Tajfel's research on ingroup favoritism can be extended to evaluations of speaker's status, likely employment, and solidarity. Their study also indicated that, while ingroup favoritism correlates positively with social identity, language attitudes vary considerably depending on the degree of self-categorization (Turner, 1987) salient to the speaker.

McNamara's (1987) study of Israelis living in Australia also supports social identity theory. His research demonstrated that social identity influences language attitudes, as well as language maintenance and shift of the immigrant group. Specifically, he found that changes in social identity are accompanied by changes in language attitudes favoring English over Hebrew and a shift to the use of English among the immigrants' children.

Ros, Cano, and Huici's (1987) research extends social identity theory. Their study revealed that social identity and perceived ethnolinguistic vitality affect intergroup relations and attitudes toward the major languages (Castilian, Catalan, Basque, Valencian, and Galacian) in Spain. They found that subtractive identity (i.e., the difference between identification with a specific linguistic ingroup and identification with Spain) is a better predictor of specific intergroup relations than identification with ingroup alone.

Finally, Louw-Potgieter and Giles (1987) examined language and social categorization from a different angle. They studied the linguistic strategies used to deal with imposed identities of high-status group members in South Africa. Their research revealed that when there is an incongruity between members of one group's self-definition and the identity imposed on them by members of another group, they attempt to escape the imposed identity by changing the criteria for group membership and by differentiating themselves from the group with which they are associated. Both of these processes involve specific language usage strategies, but the specific strategies vary depending upon the groups and the relations between them.

## Stereotypes

Inherent in any social categorization is stereotyping. Tajfel (1981b, pp. 146-147) argues that

> "stereotypes" are certain generalizations reached by individuals. They derive in large measure from, or are an instance of, the general cognitive process of categorizing. The main function of the process is to simplify or systematize, for purposes of cognitive and behavioral adaptation, the abundance and complexity of the information received from its environment by the human organism. . . . But such stereotypes can become *social* only when they are shared by large numbers of people within social groups.

Hewstone and Giles (1986) point out that stereotypes provide the context of social categories. Based on their analysis, at least four generalizations are warranted: (a) Stereotyping is the result of cognitive biases stemming from illusory correlations between group membership and psychological attributes; (b) stereotypes influence the way information is processed, that is, more favorable information is remembered about ingroups and more unfavorable information is remembered about outgroups; (c) stereotypes create expectancies (hypotheses) about others and individuals try to confirm those expectancies; and (d) stereotypes constrain others' patterns of communication and engender stereotype-confirming communication, that is, they create self-fulfilling prophecies.

Language cues the activation of stereotypes. Bond (1983), for example, found that language has a significant effect on activating different auto-stereotypes (Chinese) and heterostereotypes (Westerners) of Chinese bilinguals in Hong Kong. This finding is consistent with studies that demonstrate that the language of questionnaires used in research can affect the responses to items dealing with ethnicity (Bond & Yang, 1982; Marin, Triandis, Betancourt, & Kashima, 1983; Punetha, Giles, & Young, 1987). Other research demonstrates that language's effect on stereotypes is different from that of ethnicity. Specifically, Bond (1983) found that language influences Chinese bilinguals' judgments of the likability, Westernization, and benevolence of Chinese and British speakers, while ethnicity influences the speakers' ethnic-group preference.

Stereotypes also influence language choice. Beebe (1981), for example, found that when Chinese-Thai bilingual children are interviewed by a person who looks Chinese, but speaks standard Thai, they use Chinese phonological variants. Similarly, Bell (1982) discovered that stereotypes of listeners influence how New Zealand broadcasters read scripts.

More recently, Mgbo-Elue (1987) examined the stereotypes Yorubas and Ibos in Nigeria hold regarding the other group and the effect these stereotypes have on individuals' desire to learn the outgroup language. She found a positive association between attitudes toward the outgroup and its language and desire to learn the outgroup language. Her research also revealed that positive stereotypes of the outgroup increase the likelihood that individuals will learn the outgroup language.

Hewstone and Giles (1986) developed a stereotype-based model of intergroup communication breakdown that focuses upon sociolinguistic stereotypes and language production/reception strategies. They argue that in intergroup situations sociolinguistic stereotypes are activated. The stereotypes activated and the speech pattern used are a function of the individuals' ethnolinguistic identities that are relevant in the particular context, and the relations between the groups, in turn, influence the communicative distance established between the groups (e.g., Lukens's, 1979, distances of "indifferences," "avoidance," and "disparagement" and Gudykunst and Kim's, 1984, distances of "sensitivity" and "equality"). The ethonolinguistic stereotypes are used to explain difficulties in intergroup communication and to make biased attributions about members of the outgroup (see Hewstone & Jaspers, 1982). In addition, language production and reception strategies feed back and reinforce ethnolinguistic stereotypes and, in combination with the context, can lead to breakdowns in or dissolutions of intergroup communication.

## Language Attitudes

Extensive research has been conducted on language attitudes. Research from Britain (e.g., Cheyne, 1970) and Canada (e.g., Ryan & Carranza, 1977), for example, indicates that nonstandard language usage receives lower evaluations on factors such as intelligence and confidence. Further, research indicates that fine distinctions are made regarding degree of accent (e.g., Ryan Carranza, & Moffie, 1977), that there are differences in attitudes due to convergence/divergence (e.g., Bourhis, Giles, & Lambert, 1975; also see the discussion of speech accommodation below), and that language attitudes are influenced by ethnic stereotypes (e.g., Lambert, 1967), social class (Giles & Powesland, 1975), as well as the situations in which the language is used (e.g., Giles, 1979).

Standardization of the language and language vitality are two major determinants of language attitudes (Ryan, Giles, & Sebastian, 1982), but these do not sufficiently explain the process. Consistent with ethno-linguistic identity theory, Giles and Ryan (1982) explained language attitudes of group members as a function of the situation in which the language is used. Two specific dimensions (status-stressing/solidarity-stressing and person-centered/group-centered) are used to evaluate the situation and language choice. In those situations where the solidarity-stressing or group-centered dimensions are dominant, individuals are likely to diverge linguistically from members of the outgroup. When the status-stressing and person-centered dimensions are most salient, individuals tend to converge linguistically with the members of the outgroup.

Ryan, Hewstone, and Giles (1984) extended Giles and Ryan's (1982) analysis to take into account intergroup dynamics, social attributional processes, and cognitive representatives of forces operating in the general society. They argue that evaluation of speakers is a function of the socio-structural context (i.e., the standardization and vitality of the languages), the immediate social situation (e.g., its domain and degree of formality), the language speakers themselves (i.e., the linguistic/paralinguistic features of the language, the individual/group attributes, and the content of messages), the judges (especially their individual and group attributes), and cognitive processes (both individual and collective). Their intergroup model of language attitudes further distinguishes four patterns, or "language-preference profiles": (a) Profile A involves a preference within both groups for the dominant group—this profile is subdivided into [1a] subordinate group for dominant group is due to "self-hate" and [1b] subordinate group attributing their status to their "negatively valued" group membership—(b) Profile B involves a preference for the dominant group in terms of status, but a preference for the ingroup in terms of solidarity; (c) Profile C involves situations where there is equal status between the groups with an ingroup preference; and (d) Profile D involves a preference for the dominant group in terms of status, but a solidarity preference for the subordinate group. Each of these patterns leads to different language attitudes and occurs under different conditions (e.g., vitality, standardization, and cognitive processes vary across profiles).

## Communication Accommodation

There is a tendency for members of ingroups to react favorably to outgroup members who linguistically converge toward them (Bourhis & Giles, 1976; Giles & Smith, 1979). This, however, is not always the case. Giles and Byrne (1982) point out that as an outgroup's members begin to learn the speech style of the ingroup, ingroup members will diverge in some way so as to maintain linguistic distinctiveness. Reaction to speech convergence of outgroup members depends upon the intent attributed to the speaker (Bourhis, 1984a; Genesee & Bourhis, 1982; Simard, Taylor, & Giles, 1976). Speech divergence and/or speech maintenance can be used to assert a positive group identity (Bourhis, 1984a; Bourhis & Giles, 1977; Giles, Bourhis, & Taylor, 1977).

Cultural/ethnic values influence the nature of the accommodation that occurs. Bond and Yang's (1982) research, for example, revealed that the more importance Chinese in Hong Kong place on Chinese values, the more they display ethnic affirmation and the less they display interethnic accommodation. Context also affects accommodation. Research in Taiwan (van den Berg, 1986) indicated that salespeople accommodate to the language customers use, while customers in banks accommodate to the clerk's language usage. The language itself also influences accommodation. John, Young, Giles, and Hofman (1984) found that Arabs and Jews in Israel differentiate ingroup values from outgroup values more when tested in Hebrew than when tested in English.

In related research, Genesee and Bourhis (1982) studied the influence of situational norms, sociocultural status, ingroup favoritism, and interpersonal accommodation of evaluations of code-switching. Their findings indicated that social categories and situational norms interact to influence evaluations of language choice and that this interaction also affects the role of ingroup favoritism. They argue that one group's evaluation of code-switching by members of another language choice initially is based on situational norms, but it is based on interpersonal language accommodation later in conversations. One plausible explanation is that individuals begin to view the other person less in terms of being a member of a social category and more as a distinct individual.

Bourhis (1985) extended Genesee and Bourhis's (1982) analysis in an attempt to integrate sociolinguistic and speech accommodation approaches to code-switching. He examined customer-clerk communication between Quebec Anglophones and Francophones. His research revealed that listeners' evaluation of dialogues depends "on a dynamic interaction of factors including situational norms, language status, interpersonal accommodation and ingroup favoritism" (Bourhis, 1985, p. 130). Bourhis's data indicated that following situation norms is the safest strategy in the initial states of hostile intergroup encounters, but normative strategies are adopted in later stages depending upon the communicators' goals, desire to assert group identity, and their affective responses to each other. The initial choices, however, influence the choices made later in conversations. Bourhis (in press) outlined research to extend this line of work to superior-subordinate language use within the Canadian government.

Giles, Mulac, Bradac, and Johnson (1986) expanded speech accommodation theory applying it to communication more generally (for a recent review of research and a statement of speech accommodation theory in proposition form, see Street & Giles, 1982; Thakerar, Giles, & Cheshire, 1982; also see Gallois, Franklin-Stokes, Giles, & Coupland, 1988, for an integration of communication accommodation theory and ethnolinguistic identity theory; note: Gallois et al.'s theory is summarized in Gudykunst & Nishida's chapter in this volume). Giles and his associates (1986) argue that communication convergence is a function of a speaker's desire for social approval, for high communication efficiency, for a shared self- or group presentation, and for an appropriate identity definition. The preconditions for communication convergence also require a match between the speaker's view of the recipient's speech style and the actual speech being used, that speech is valued in the situation, and that the specific speech style being used is appropriate for both the speaker and the recipient. Divergence, in contrast, is a function of the speaker's desire for a "contrastive" self-image, to dissociate from the recipient, to change the recipient's speech behavior, and to define the encounter in intergroup terms. Divergence further occurs when recipients use a speech style that deviates from a norm that is valued and consistent with the speaker's expectations regarding the recipient's performance.

## SOCIOLINGUISTIC FACTORS

### Group Vitality

The concept of "group vitality" was introduced by Giles, Bourhis, and Taylor (1977). They argued that ethnolinguistic vitality influences the degree to which group members will act as a group when interacting with individuals from outgroups. Two types of group vitality, objective and subjective, were distinguished in their model. Subjective group vitality refers to a group's societal position as *perceived* by its members, while objective group vitality refers to the group's position as indicated by available data on group membership and activities. They proposed that the more vitality an ethnolinguistic group has, the more likely the group will survive as a distinctive linguistic group in a multilingual setting.

Giles, Bourhis, and Taylor (1977) isolated three categories of variables influencing ethnolinguistic vitality: status, demographic, and institutional support. The status variables are those that influence the prestige of a language group (e.g., economic, social, and language status). Giles and his associates contend that the greater a linguistic group's status, the more vitality it has. Demographic factors involve the group's size and its distribution within regions and a country as a whole. The more favorable the demographic situation, the more vitality the group has. Finally, institutional support is related to the representation of the language use in societal institutions (e.g., churches, businesses, government agencies) and the greater the institutional support for a language group, the greater its vitality.

Several studies have been conducted that compare different ethnic groups' perceptions of their ethnolinguistic vitality. Giles, Rosenthal, and Young (1985), for example, studied perceptions of Greek- and Anglo-Australians' ethnolinguistic vitality, finding that the two groups agreed that Anglos' vitality was higher on certain status and institutional support items, but that they disagreed about each other's sociostructural positions. Bourhis and Sachdev (1984) studied Italian and English Canadians in both an equal setting and a majority setting. Their research indicated that both groups had more realistic perceptions in a majority setting than in an equal setting. English Canadians, however, were biased more against the Italian language in the equal setting than in the majority setting. In a study of ethnic Chinese and non-Chinese in Hong Kong, Young, Giles, and Pierson (1986) found that ingroup vitality perceptions are associated with the amount of exposure to the outgroup language. Recent research (Allard & Landry, 1986) also indicates that perceived ethnolinguistic vitality is related to self-reports of assimilative linguistic behavior.

Sachdev, Bourhis, Phang, and D'Eye's (1987) extended research on ethnolinguistic vitality to Chinese immigrants in Canada. Their study revealed that perceived vitality is consistent with objective vitality estimates of high English Canadian and low Chinese Canadian vitality on status, demographic, and institutional support factors. Sachdev and his associates also discovered that Canadian-born Chinese exaggerated the perceived vitality of Cantonese more than first-generation Chinese Canadians; Canadian-born Chinese further perceived Cantonese to be used less in the home and church than first-generation Chinese Canadians.

## Speech Norms

Speech accommodation practices with different groups are a function of norms (McKirnan & Hamayan, 1984a, 1984b). Ingroups have norms that dictate appropriate speech behavior within the confines of any given situation. While norms are often manifest by only subtle markers in speech style, they affect the process of social categorization (e.g., Scherer & Giles, 1979).

McKirnan and Hamayan (1984b) proposed a general social psychological model of social norms. The factors in their model include the "content" of the speech norm, the "clarity" of the expectancies associated with it, and the "evaluative" (positive or negative) strength of the norms. They argue that the content of speech norms varies from situation to situation, but deviation from or adherence to the norms conveys important information about the actor. Scotton (1980), for example, contends that individuals can "negotiate" specific "personal identities" by choosing to violate speech norms in a particular situation. Further, individuals and groups differ with respect to their ability to judge specific behavior, and whether or not it reflects that following an outgroup norm is just deviant vis-à-vis the ingroup. The assumptions that individuals make regarding the distinctiveness of others' norms, particularly language norms, influences how they are categorized and behave toward them. McKirnan and Hamayan (1984b, p. 174) also suggest that "the intergroup distinctiveness of speech (or other) norms is a direct product of the degree of contact and, more importantly, the potential social conflict between social groups."

McKirnan and Hamayan (1984a) empirically examined their model in a bicultural context. They found that ethnocentric people had less contact with the outgroup and had more negative attitudes toward the outgroup and toward speakers using the outgroup language than individuals who were not ethnocentric. The relationship between ethnocentrism and intergroup contact and outgroup attitudes, however, was mediated by speech norms. McKirnan and Hamayan, therefore, concluded that individual differences in speech norms must be taken into account in order to explain the effect of speech on intergroup attitudes.

Research on the situational factors that affect the choice of communication strategies also indirectly supports McKirnan and Hamayan's (1984b) model. Furnham (1986), for example, contends that individuals have definite ideas about how specific messages are perceived by others in specific situations. Clear expectations could not exist without situation-specific speech norms.

## Second-Language Competence

There are numerous models of second-language learning (see Gardner, 1985, for reviews of the major models), but only the intergroup model (Giles & Byrne, 1982) deals in depth with the effects of intergroup relations on second-language acquisition. Giles and Byrne (1982, pp. 34-35) derived five propositions regarding the role of the social milieu in second-language learning:

> Subordinate group members will most likely acquire native-like proficiency in the dominant group's language when:
>
> (1a) ingroup identification is weak and/or L1 [native language] is not a salient dimension of ethnic group membership;
>
> (2a) quiescent inter-ethnic comparisons exist (e.g., awareness of cognitive alternatives to inferiority);
>
> (3a) perceived ingroup vitality is low;
>
> (4a) perceived ingroup boundaries are soft and open;
>
> (5a) strong identification exists with many other social categories, each of which provides adequate group identities and a satisfactory intragroup status.

Giles and Byrne noted that these propositions "provide an integrative orientation" and, therefore, an "additive" situation (Lambert, 1974) for the individual. When the propositions are reversed, second-language learning is impeded.

When the two "primary" determinants of second-language acquisition motivation, perceived vitality and perceived hardness of boundaries between groups, are correlated inversely with motivation, an "intermediate" situation exists (Beebe & Giles, 1984). Ball, Giles, and Hewstone (1984) extended the theory to account for these situations using a cusp catastrophe. This extension allows the theory to account for conflicting motives that are based on speakers' perceptions of the relations between their own and other linguistic groups.

One recent study (Hall & Gudykunst, 1986) tested Giles and Byrne's (1982) original model of second-language acquisition. Hall and Gudykunst's data generally support the model for international students studying in the United States. Their results, however, indicated that the stronger the ingroup identification, the greater the perceived competence in the outgroup language. While incompatible with the original statement of the intergroup theory, this finding is compatible with Lambert, Mermigis, and Taylor's (1986) study, which suggests that the more secure and positive members of a group feel about their identity, the more tolerant they are of members of other groups. Similar observations emerge from other studies (e.g., Bond & King, 1985; Pak, Dion, & Dion, 1985). While incompatible with Giles and Byrne's original formulation, Hall and Gudykunst's (1986) findings are compatible with Garrett, Giles, and Coupland's (in press) suggested revision of the intergroup theory of second-language acquisition.

Hall and Gudykunst (1986) also found that the influence of ingroup identification, interethnic comparisons, perceived vitality, perceived group boundaries, and identification with other groups on second-language competence is not mediated by integrativeness as suggested by Clèment and Kruidenier (1983) or Gardner (1985). Support for the intergroup theory also emerges from Giles and Johnson's (1987) study of Welsh speakers in Britain.

### Code-Switching

There is extensive evidence that sociolinguistic factors influence code-switching in encounters with members of the same and other groups (see Dittmar, 1976; Giles & Powesland, 1975; Gumperz, 1982a, 1982b; Gumperz & Hymes, 1972, for reviews). Studies of immigrants in the United States, for example, indicate that English is used in public formal settings, while native language is used in informal, nonpublic settings (e.g., Edelman, Cooper, & Fishman, 1968; Kimble, Copper, & Fishman, 1969; Ryan & Carranza, 1977). Data from the Philippines (Sechrest, Flores, & Arellano, 1968), Paraguay (Rubin, 1968), Israel (Herman, 1961), and Nigeria (Mgbo-Elue, 1987) support this conclusion. Similarly, the topic of the conversation affects the code used. Native language tends to be used when discussing stressful or exciting topics (e.g., Brook, 1973; Herman, 1961) and when discussing life in the native country (e.g., Ervin-Tripp, 1968).

Recent research has linked code-switching to ethnolinguistic identity. Banks (1987), for example, extended traditional discourse analytic work to examine the influence of language-in-use on changing ethnolinguistic identities. He argues that the boundary between marked and unmarked discourse (see Scherer & Giles, 1979) is soft and permeable, while the boundary between low- and high-power positions is hard and less permeable. Banks presents evidence from the discourse of an ethnolinguistic minority sales manager to support four general propositions: (a) members of ethnolinguistic minority groups must cross the soft boundary from marked to unmarked ethnic discourse before crossing boundary from low- to high-power positions; (b) crossing the boundary from marked to unmarked ethnic discourse is a function of the individual's strategies to maximize rewards, as well as the norms, values, and discourse routines in the organization; (c) there is an implicit promise from the organization that if members of ethnolinguistic minorities cross the boundary from marked to unmarked ethnic discourse, they will have the opportunity to cross the low to high boundary; and (d) individuals who cross the boundary from marked to unmarked ethnic discourse "subtract from" their ethnolinguistic identity (see Giles, 1979).

San Antonio (1987) also examined language-in-use as an ethnolinguistic identity marker in her study of intergroup communication in a United States corporation in Japan. She argues that speaking Japanese is linked closely with Japanese ethnolinguistic identity. In the company that she observed, the explicit language policy, however, is that only English is to be spoken. The English ability of the Japanese employees varied from almost no ability to speak the language to almost native fluency. San Antonio's ethnographic observations indicated that the use of English by Japanese employees in a range of situations (e.g., meetings, interacting with visitors) is a marker for the claimed identity of being a Japanese with whom the North Americans could work. North American managers interpreted the use of English and following American communication norms (e.g., first names, joking) positively and not using English negatively (e.g., Japanese were evasive). English directly influences Japanese employees' status and role within the organization. The employees who are fluent in English "protect" employees who do not speak English well in meetings by speaking up and answering North American's questions. Further, according to San Antonio's observations, employees who do not speak English well are grateful for the help of those who speak it better. The use of English in this particular setting, therefore, does not necessarily "subtract" from the Japanese's ethnolinguistic identity.

## CONCLUSION

Language is a critical aspect of the study of intergroup communication in general and intercultural communication in particular. Extensive research has been conducted on social psychological factors, such as ethnolinguistic identity, language and stereotypes, language attitudes, speech accommodation, as well as on sociolinguistic factors such as group vitality, speech norms, second-language competence, and code-switching. Unfortunately, not much of this work has been incorporated in research on intercultural communication.

Research on social psychological and sociolinguistic factors affecting language usage must be incorporated into theories in intercultural communication if we are to explain communication between members of different cultures/ethnic groups adequately. Language has been incorporated into some intergroup theories (e.g., Gallois et al., 1988), but it is ignored more than it is addressed in current theories (see the theories reviewed in Gudykunst & Nishida's chapter in this volume). Saint-Jacques and Giles (preface to Giles & Saint-Jacques, 1979) point out, "language is not merely a medium of communication—however important that medium is—but the unifying factor of a particular culture and often a prerequisite for its survival. No other factor is as powerful as language in maintaining *by itself* the genuine and lasting distinctiveness of an ethnic group." For our understanding of intercultural communication to advance, language, therefore, must be given a central role in future theorizing and research.

## REFERENCES

Abrams, D., & Hogg, M. A. (1987). Language attitudes, frames of references and social identity: A Scottish dimension. *Journal of Language and Social Psychology, 6.*

Allard, R., & Landry, R. (1986). Subjective ethnolinguistic vitality viewed as a belief system. *Journal of Multilingual and Multicultural Development, 7,* 1-12.

Ball, P., Giles, H., & Hewstone, M. (1984). The intergroup theory of second language acquisition with catastrophic dimension. In H. Tajfel (Ed.), *The social dimension* (Vol. 2). Cambridge: Cambridge University Press.

Ball, P., Giles, H., & Hewstone, M. (1985). Interpersonal accommodation and situation construals: An integrative formulation. In H. Giles & R. St. Clair (Eds.), *Recent advances in language, communication, and social psychology.* Hillsdale, NJ: Lawrence Erlbaum.

Banks, S. P. (1987). Achieving "unmarkedness" in organizational discourse: A praxis perspective on ethnolinguistic identity. *Journal of Language and Social Psychology, 6,* 171-190.

Beebe, L. M. (1981). Social and situational factors affecting the strategy of dialect code-switching. *International Journal of the Sociology of Language, 32,* 139-149.

Beebe, L. M., & Giles, H. (1984). Speech accommodation theories: A discussion in terms of second-language acquisition. *International Journal of the Sociology of Language, 46,* 5-32.

Bell, A. (1982). Radio: The style of news language. *Journal of Communication, 32,* 150-164.

Berger, C. R., & Bradac, J. (1982). *Language and social knowledge: Uncertainty in interpersonal relations.* London: Edward Arnold.

Bond, M. H. (1983). How language variation affects inter-cultural differentiation of values by Hong Kong bilinguals. *Journal of Language and Social Psychology, 2,* 57-66.

Bond, M. H., & King, A. Y. C. (1985). Coping with the threat of Westernization in Hong Kong. *International Journal of Intercultural Relations, 9,* 351-376.

Bond, M. H., & Yang, K. S. (1982). Ethnic affirmation versus cross-cultural adaptation: The variable impact of questionnaire language on Chinese bilinguals in Hong Kong. *Journal of Cross-Cultural Psychology, 13,* 169-185.

Bourhis, R. Y. (1979). Language in ethnic interaction. In H. Giles & R. Saint-Jacques (Eds.), *Language and ethnic relations.* Elmsford, NY: Pergamon.

Bourhis, R. Y. (Ed.). (1984a). *Conflict and language planning in Quebec.* Clevendon, England: Multilingual Matters.

Bourhis, R. Y. (1984b). Cross-cultural communication in Montreal: Two field studies since the Charter of the French language. *International Journal of the Sociology of Language, 46,* 33-47.

Bourhis, R. Y. (1985). The sequential nature of language choice. In R. Street & J. Capella (Eds.), *Sequence and pattern in communicative behavior.* London: Edward Arnold.

Bourhis, R. Y. (in press). Linguistic work environments and language usage in bilingual settings. In S. Ting-Toomey & F. Korzenny (Eds.), *Communication, language, and culture*. Newbury Park, CA: Sage.

Bourhis, R. Y., & Giles, H. (1976). The language of co-operation in Wales. *Language Sciences, 42*, 13-16.

Bourhis, R. Y., & Giles, H. (1977). The language of intergroup distinctiveness. In H. Giles (Ed.), *Language, ethnicity and intergroup relations*. London: Academic Press.

Bourhis, R. Y., Giles, H., & Lambert, W. E. (1975). Social consequences of accommodating one's style of speech: A cross-national investigation. *International Journal of the Sociology of Language, 6*, 53-71.

Bourhis, R. Y., Giles, H., & Rosenthal, D. (1981). Notes on the construction of a "subjective vitality questionnaire" for ethnolinguistic groups. *Journal of Multilingual and Multicultural Development, 2*, 145-155.

Bourhis, R. Y., & Sachdev, I. (1984). Vitality perceptions and language attitudes: Some Canadian data. *Journal of Language and Social Psychology, 3*, 97-126.

Brook, G. L. (1973). *Varieties of English*. London: Macmillan.

Cheyne, W. (1970). Stereotyped reactions to speakers with Scottish and English regional accents. *British Journal of Social and Clinical Psychology, 9*, 77-79.

Clément, R., & Kruidenier, B. G. (1983). Orientations in second language acquisition. *Language Learning, 33*, 273-291.

Dittmar, N. (1976). *Sociolinguistics*. London: Edward Arnold.

Eastman, C. M. (1985). Establishing social identity through language use. *Journal of Language and Social Psychology, 4*, 1-26.

Edelman, M., Cooper, R. L., & Fishman, J. A. (1968). The contextualization of school-children's bilingualism. *Irish Journal of Education, 2*, 106-111.

Ervin-Tripp, S. M. (1968). An analysis of the interaction of language, topic and listener. In J. Fishman (Ed.), *Readings in the sociology of language*. The Hague, the Netherlands: Mouton.

Furnham, A. (1986). Situational determinants of intergroup communication. In W. Gudykunst (Ed.), *Intergroup communication*. London: Edward Arnold.

Gallois, C., Franklyn-Stokes, A., Giles, H., & Coupland, N. (1988). Communication accommodation in intercultural encounters. In Y. Y. Kim & W. B. Gudykunst (Eds.), *Theories in intercultural communication*. Newbury Park, CA: Sage.

Gardner, R. C. (1985). *Social psychology and second language learning*. London: Edward Arnold.

Garrett, P., Giles, H., & Coupland, N. (in press). The contexts of language: Extending the intergroup model of second language. In S. Ting-Toomey & F. Korzenny (Eds.), *Communication, language and culture*. Newbury Park, CA: Sage.

Genesee, F., & Bourhis, R. Y. (1982). The social psychological significance of code-switching in cross-cultural communication. *Journal of Language and Social Psychology, 1*, 1-27.

Giles, H. (Ed.). (1977). *Language, ethnicity, and intergroup relations*. London: Academic Press.

Giles, H. (1979). Ethnicity markers in speech. In K. R. Scherer & H. Giles (Eds.), *Social markers in speech*. Cambridge: Cambridge University Press.

Giles, H., Bourhis, R., & Taylor, D. M. (1977). Towards a theory of language in ethnic group relations. In H. Giles (Ed.), *Language, ethnicity and intergroup relations*. London: Academic Press.

Giles, H., & Byrne, J. (1982). An intergroup approach to second language acquisition. *Journal of Multilingual and Multicultural Development, 3*, 17-40.

Giles, H., & Johnson, P. (1981). The role of language in ethnic group relations. In J. Turner & H. Giles (Eds.), *Intergroup behavior*. Chicago: University of Chicago Press.

Giles, H., & Johnson, P. (1987). Ethnolinguistic identity theory: A social psychological approach to language maintenance. *International Journal of the Sociology of Language, 68,* 69-99.

Giles, H., Mulac, A., Bradac, J. J., & Johnson, P. (1986). Speech accommodation theory: The next decade and beyond. In M. McLaughlin (Ed.), *Communication yearbook* (Vol. 10). Beverly Hills, CA: Sage.

Giles, H., & Powesland, P. F. (Eds.). (1975). *Speech style and social evaluation.* London: Academic Press.

Giles, H., Rosenthal, D., & Young, L. (1985). Perceived ethnolinguistic vitality: The Anglo- and Greek-Australian setting. *Journal of Multilingual and Multicultural Development, 6,* 253-269.

Giles, H., & Ryan, E. (1982). Prolegomena for developing a social psychological theory of language attitudes. In E. Ryan & H. Giles (Eds.), *Attitudes toward language variation.* London: Edward Arnold.

Giles, H., & Saint-Jacques, B. (Eds.). (1979). *Language and ethnic relations.* Oxford: Pergamon.

Giles, H., & Smith, P. M. (1979). Accommodation theory: Optimal levels of convergence. In H. Giles & R. St. Clair (Eds.), *Language and social psychology.* Oxford: Basil Blackwell.

Giles, H., Taylor, D. M., & Bourhis, R. Y. (1973). Toward a theory of interpersonal accommodation through speech: Some Canadian data. *Language in Society, 2,* 177-192.

Gudykunst, W., & Kim, Y. Y. (1984). *Communicating with strangers.* Reading, MA: Addison-Wesley.

Gudykunst, W. B., & Lim, T. S. (1986). A perspective for the study of intergroup communication. In W. Gudykunst (Ed.), *Intergroup communication.* London: Edward Arnold.

Gumperz, J. (1982a). *Discourse strategies.* Cambridge: Cambridge University Press.

Gumperz, J. (Ed.). (1982b). *Language and social identity.* Cambridge: Cambridge University Press.

Gumperz, J., & Hymes, D. (Eds.). (1972). *Directions in sociolinguistics.* New York: Holt, Rinehart & Winston.

Hall, B. J., & Gudykunst, W. B. (1986). The intergroup theory of second language ability. *Journal of Language and Social Psychology, 5,* 291-302.

Herman, S. (1961). Explorations in the social psychology of language choice. *Human Relations, 4,* 149-164.

Hewstone, M., & Giles, H. (1986). Stereotypes and intergroup communications. In W. Gudykunst (Ed.), *Intergroup communication.* London: Edward Arnold.

Hewstone, M., & Jaspers, J. (1982). Intergroup relations and attributional processes. In H. Tajfel (Ed.), *Social identity and intergroup relations.* Cambridge: Cambridge University Press.

Hogg, M. A., Joyce, N., & Abrams, D. (1984). Diglossia in Switzerland? A social identity analysis of speaker evaluations. *Journal of Language and Social Psychology, 3,* 185-196.

Hopper, R. (1986). Speech evaluation of intergroup dialect differences. In W. B. Gudykunst (Ed.), *Intergroup communication.* London: Edward Arnold.

John, C., Young, L., Giles, H., & Hofman, J. E. (1984). Language, values, and intercultural differentiation in Israel. *Journal of Social Psychology, 125,* 527-529.

Kimble, J., Cooper, R. L., & Fishman, J. A. (1969). Language switching and the interpretation of conversations. *Lingua, 23,* 127-134.

Labrie, N., & Clement, R. (1986). Ethnolinguistic vitality, self-confidence and second language proficiency: An investigation. *Journal of Multilingual and Multicultural Development, 7,* 269-282.

Lambert, W. (1967). The social psychology of bilingualism. *Journal of Social Issues, 23,* 91-109.

Lambert, W. E. (1974). Culture and language as factors in learning and education. In F. E. Aboud & R. D. Meade (Eds.), Cultural factors in learning and education. Bellingham: Fifth Western Washington Symposium on Learning.

Lambert, W. E., Mermigis, L., & Taylor, D. M. (1986). Greek Canadian's attitudes toward own group and other Canadian ethnic groups: A test of the multiculturalism hypotheses. *Canadian Journal of Behavioral Sciences, 18*, 35-51.

Leclézio, M., Louw-Potgieter, J., & Souchon, M. (1986). The social identity of Mauritian immigrants in South Africa. *Journal of Social Psychology, 126*, 61-69.

Louw-Potgieter, J., & Giles, H. (1987). Imposed identity and linguistic strategies. *Journal of Language and Social Psychology, 6*, 258-284.

Lukens, J. (1979). Interethnic conflict and communicative distance. In H. Giles & R. Saint-Jacques (Eds.), *Language and ethnic relations*. Elmsford, NY: Pergamon.

Marin, G., Triandis, H. C., Betancourt, H., & Kashima, Y. (1983). Ethnic affirmation versus social desirability: Explaining discrepancies in bilinguals' responses to a questionnaire. *Journal of Cross-Cultural Psychology, 14*, 173-186.

McKirnan, D. J., & Hamayan, E. (1984a). Speech norms and attitudes toward out-group members. *Journal of Language and Social Psychology, 3*, 21-30.

McKirnan, D. J., & Hamayan, E. (1984b). Speech norms and perceptions of ethnolinguistic group differences. *European Journal of Social Psychology, 14*, 151-168.

McNamara, T. F. (1987). Language and social identity: Israelis abroad. *Journal of Language and Social Psychology, 6*, 202-226.

McNamara, T. F. (in press). Language and social identity: Some Australian studies. *Australian Review of Applied Linguistics*.

Mgbo-Elue, C. N. (1987). Social psychological and linguistic impediments to the acquisition of a second Nigerian language among Yoruba and Ibo. *Journal of Language and Social Psychology, 6*, 309-319.

Pak, A., Dion, K. L., & Dion, K. K. (1985). Correlates of self-confidence with English among Chinese students in Toronto. *Canadian Journal of Behavioral Sciences, 17*, 369-378.

Punetha, D., Giles, H., & Young, L. (1987). Ethnicity and immigrant values: Religion and language choice. *Journal of Language and Social Psychology, 6*, 229-242.

Ros, M., Cano, J. I., & Huici, C. (1987). Language and intergroup perception in Spain. *Journal of Language and Social Psychology, 6*, 243-258.

Rubin, J. (1968). *National bilingualism in Paraguay*. The Hague, the Netherlands: Mouton.

Ryan, E. B., & Carranza, M. A. (1977). Ingroup and outgroup reactions to Mexican-American language varieties. In H. Giles (Ed.), *Language, ethnicity and intergroup relations*. London: Academic Press.

Ryan, E. B., Carranza, M. A., & Moffie, R. W. (1977). Reactions toward varying degrees of accentedness in the speech of Spanish-English bilinguals. *Language and Speech, 20*, 267-273.

Ryan, E., Giles, H., & Sebastian, R. (1982). An integrative perspective for the study of attitudes toward language. In E. Ryan & H. Giles (Eds.), *Attitudes toward language variation*. London: Edward Arnold.

Ryan, E., Hewstone, M., & Giles, H. (1984). Language and intergroup attitudes. In J. Eiser (Ed.), *Attitudinal judgment*. New York: Springer-Verlag.

Sachdev, I., Bourhis, R., Phang, S., & D'Eye, J. (1987). Language attitudes and vitality perceptions: Intergenerational effects amongst Chinese Canadian communities. *Journal of Language and Social Psychology, 6*.

San Antonio, P. M. (1987). Social mobility and language usage in an American company in Japan. *Journal of Language and Social Psychology, 6*, 191-200.

Scherer, K. R., & Giles, H. (Eds.). (1979). *Social markers in speech*. Cambridge: Cambridge University Press.

Schieffelin, B., & Ochs, E. (Eds.). (1986). *Language socialization across cultures.* Cambridge: Cambridge University Press.

Scotton, C. (1980). Explaining linguistic choices as identity negotiations. In H. Giles, P. Robinson, & P. Smith (Eds.), *Language: Social psychological perspectives.* Oxford: Pergamon.

Sechrest, L., Flores, L., & Arellano, L. (1968). Language and social interaction in a bilingual culture. *Journal of Social Psychology, 76,* 155-161.

Shaw, G. B. (1946). *Pygmalion, a romance in five acts.* Harmondsworth, England: Penguin.

Simard, L., Taylor, D., & Giles, H. (1976). Attributional processes and interpersonal accommodation in a bilingual setting. *Language and Speech, 19,* 374-387.

Street, R., & Giles, H. (1982). Speech accommodation theory. In M. Roloff & C. Berger (Eds.), *Social cognition and communication.* Beverly Hills, CA: Sage.

Tajfel, H. (1978). Social categorization, social identity, and social comparison. In H. Tajfel (Ed.), *Differentiation between social groups.* London: Academic Press.

Tajfel, H. (1981a). *Human categories and social groups.* Cambridge: Cambridge University Press.

Tajfel, H. (1981b). Social stereotypes and social groups. In J. Turner & H. Giles (Eds.), *Intergroup behavior.* Chicago: University of Chicago Press.

Tajfel, H., & Turner, J. (1979). An integrative theory of intergroup conflict. In W. Austin & S. Worchel (Eds.), *The social psychology of intergroup relations.* Monterey, CA: Brooks/Cole.

Taylor, D. M., & McKirnan, D. (1984). A five-stage model of intergroup relations. *British Journal of Social Psychology, 23,* 291-300.

Thakerar, J. N., Giles, H., & Cheshire, J. (1982). Psychological and linguistic parameters of speech accommodation theory. In C. Fraser & K. Scherer (Eds.), *Advances in the social psychology of language.* Cambridge: Cambridge University Press.

Turner, J. (1982). Towards a cognitive redefinition of the social group. In H. Tajfel (Ed.), *Social identity and intergroup relations.* Cambridge: Cambridge University Press.

Turner, J. (1987). *Rediscovering the social group.* London: Basil Blackwell.

van den Berg, M. E. (1986). Language planning and language use in Taiwan: Social identity, language accommodation, and language choice behavior. *International Journal of the Sociology of Language, 59,* 97-115.

Young, L., Giles, H., & Pierson, H. (1986). Sociopolitical change and perceived vitality. *International Journal of Intercultural Relations, 10,* 459-460.

# 7 The Cultural Dimensions of Nonverbal Communication

**Michael L. Hecht**
**Peter A. Andersen**
**Sidney A. Ribeau**

This chapter deals with nonverbal communication and culture. Because this is a book concerned with culture, we will emphasize that construct drawing on nonverbal communication as one of its manifestations. In other words, culture will be taken as the primary focus or grounding, and a cultural approach applied to nonverbal communication. This ordering is not straightforward, however, for communication and culture are inseparable (Hecht, Ribeau, & Sedano, in press; Wolfson & Pearce, 1983).

The nonverbal study of culture has its roots in the work of Edward T. Hall (1959, 1966), who defined culture as "the way of life of a people" (1959, p. 31). Synthesizing from the work of Hall and others (Condon & Yousef, 1983; Prosser, 1978; Singer, 1987), we offer the following definition: Culture is the manifold ways of perceiving and organizing the world that are held in common by a group of people and passed on interpersonally and intergenerationally. As Hall (1966) notes, culture affects the sensory processing of phenomena, penetrating to the entire root of the nervous system. Culture has both material and symbolic manifestations, including a common code or language, heritage, history, social organization, norms, knowledge, attitudes, values, beliefs, objects, and patterns of perceptions that are accepted and expected by an identity group. Further, culture is expressed in verbal and nonverbal interaction styles, proverbs, institutions, ceremonies, stories, religion, and politics.

Much useful work dealing with nonverbal communication between or within cultures is descriptive and/or atheoretical. Such descriptive and anecdotal research provides a basis for study by describing the nonverbal patterns that typify various cultural groups and comparing these patterns across groups, often with the goal of understanding if nonverbal communication is universal or culture-specific. An example of such work is

Kochman's (1981) identification of verbal and nonverbal style among Black Americans and summaries of this approach are provided by Burgoon (1985), Poyatos (1983), Ramsey (1979, 1984), Wiemann and Harrison (1983), and Wolfgang (1984).

While useful for articulating categories and typologies, such work does not go far toward building theories of nonverbal behavior in cultures because it describes typical nonverbal behavior but does not *explain* the observed phenomena. Existing research specifies the behaviors that appear most frequently, but not the behaviors that are effective and ineffective. Communication theories should explain what works and what does not work in various situations, and because behavior that is typical may not be effective (Hecht, 1984) it is difficult to build a theoretical understanding of nonverbal behavior in cultures without examining effectiveness.

Further, without referencing some outcome and looking at the range of nonverbal behavior we have what is referred to in research methodology as a "restricted range" problem. When examining any empirical relationship, what is true for one segment of the distribution may not be true throughout the distribution. If two variables such as age and nonverbal communication are nonlinearly related (Hamilton, 1973), then by examining different parts of the distribution one may observe positive (ages 0 through 20), negative (ages 30 through 90), or no relationship (ages 20 through 30) between the variables (age and ability).

In order to provide an organizational framework for understanding nonverbal behavior in cultures, it is necessary to go outside the research and impose a structure. Such structures organize the research by identifying dimensions, categories, or principles to guide research and theorizing. Four such structures are suggested in the literature: nonverbal codes, nonverbal meanings, nonverbal functions, and cultural dimensions. These are examined in the next section.

## NONVERBAL DIMENSIONS

### Nonverbal Codes

Most discussions of nonverbal behavior in cultures are organized around nonverbal codes. These codes are defined in terms of the source of the message. In other words, nonverbal behavior is categorized by the means of expression. Several different, but overlapping systems have been proposed. Knapp (1978), for example, identified kinesic behavior, physical characteristics (appearance), touch (haptics), paralanguage, proxemics (space), artifacts, and environmental factors. A researcher might use this approach to observe how a type of nonverbal behavior (e.g., proxemics) differs among cultures (for summaries of this work, see Gudykunst & Kim, 1984; Hall, 1959, 1976).

A major problem with this approach is the reductionism that implies that there are separate message systems for each code. No evidence has been provided to support this assumption. Andersen (1985) has shown that both encoders and decoders process nonverbal cues as a conceptual multichanneled gestalt. Thus the codes provide useful descriptors of the types of available messages, but not a theoretically grounded system for understanding nonverbal behavior.

## Meanings and Functions

Nonverbal meanings and functions are differentiated by the unit of analysis. Meanings refer to the interpretation of messages, while functions refer to the goals and outcomes of interactions. Each provides a useful system for understanding nonverbal behavior because they are potentially grounded in theoretical explanations of nonverbal communication such as systems theory, interactionism, and cognitivism.

The primary system for classifying nonverbal meaning is derived from the work of Mehrabian (1971) and includes the dimensions of immediacy, status, and responsiveness. Immediacy is an evaluative dimension that includes judgments such as good/bad, positive/negative, and close/far. Based on the immediacy principle, Mehrabian argues that people approach persons and things they like, and avoid or move away from negatively valanced stimuli. Status involves power and dominance. People have power to the degree they can control the events around them. The final dimension is responsiveness which describes the ways people react to the things, people, and events in their environment. Responsiveness is indexed by change and activity level.

These dimensions seem analogous to those derived for verbal meaning by Osgood, Suci, and Tannenbaum (1957): evaluation, potency, and activity. These same three dimensions were verified interculturally as primary dimensions of affective meaning by Osgood, May, and Minon (1975). Because the verbal dimensions appear to be cross-culturally valid, and the same dimensions appear for both verbal and nonverbal meaning, we may call these dimensions of meaning. Research utilizing these dimensions would address the question: How does culture influence the nonverbal expression of meaning?

A third approach to nonverbal behavior focuses on functions. Again, similar systems are offered by a variety of authors. One system consists of providing information, regulating interaction, expressing intimacy, exercising social control, and facilitating service or task goals (Patterson, 1983). It is not known if these functions differ with culture.

While these approaches provide useful frameworks for the study of nonverbal behavior, they are not derived from a cultural framework. This is not to say that the systems will inhibit the study of nonverbal behavior in cultures, but rather that our perspective leads us to an approach more heavily grounded in the construct of culture itself.

## CULTURAL DIMENSIONS

The final set of systems involves the dimensions of culture. These provide a culturally grounded perspective from which to examine nonverbal behavior in cultures. Here we will review two approaches, those of Hofstede (1984) and Hall (1976, 1984).

Hofstede provides a list of four dimensions of cultural values that have cross-cultural support: power distance, individualism, masculinity, and uncertainty. *Power distance* refers to the degree to which power, prestige, and wealth are equally distributed in a culture. *Individualism* denotes a culture's emphasis on personal identity or collectivism, and is similar to Altman and Gauvain's (1981) dimension of identity-communality. *Masculinity* describes a culture's emphasis on traditionally male attributes such as strength, assertiveness, and competitiveness; and *uncertainty* concerns cultural values regarding risk.

These dimensions provide a useful starting point for the study of nonverbal behavior in cultures. In fact, several of the dimensions parallel the meanings and functions identified above. Power distance is comparable to the meaning dimension of status and the functions dealing with the regulation of conversations and self-presentations. Uncertainty is similar to the responsiveness meaning dimension, and the function of expressing emotions is involved with creating and resolving uncertainty. Individualism seems related to the exchange of rituals function. Only masculinity seems totally distinctive to this system.

While Hofstede's (1984) dimensions have much to recommend them, it is curious that a dimension dealing with immediacy or approach is excluded from the analyses. These concepts are represented in most meaning and functional systems, and are identified in Altman and Gauvain's (1981) view of accessibility-inaccessibility as a primary dimension of all relationships. Perhaps this omission is due to Hofstede's sample, which consisted of people in organizations. While salient to organizations, the approach metaphor is more directly relevant to interpersonal relationships (Andersen, 1985). For the present analysis, we will add immediacy as a dimension. Second, we change the label "masculinity," which we feel is sexually biased, to "gender." With this modification, the dimension refers to the rigidity of gender roles as well as the culture's emphasis on task

orientation, assertiveness, competitiveness, social relationships, concilia-
tion, and emotionality as feminine qualities.

Another approach to classifying culture is offered by Hall (1976, 1984),
who differentiates high- and low-context cultures. High-context cultures
place greater emphasis on the environment and relationship in interpreting messages, while those in low-context cultures rely more heavily
on the explicit message. This approach can be seen as complementary to
Hofstede's as the construct of "contextuality" provides a vehicle for
understanding how a member of a culture interprets the cultural values.

The analysis that follows seeks to provide an explanatory system by
organizing nonverbal behavior into six dimensions; the four dimensions
of Hofstede, and immediacy and context. We feel this analysis best promotes an answer to the questions: How does nonverbal behavior express
culture? In what ways are cultures different or similar in their nonverbal
behavior? In this discussion it will not be our goal to provide comprehensive reviews of the construct, rather to demonstrate how these categories
can be used to study nonverbal behavior in cultures.

One note of caution must be presented before proceeding to this discussion. Research shows that even when cross-cultural similarities in the
underlying dimensions of meaning are present, the cultures still differ in
the exemplars or indicants of those dimensions (Herrmann & Raybeck,
1981). In other words, what is power to one culture may not be power to
another. So, even though we may attach the same label to a dimension
across cultures, we cannot assume that a particular behavior actually
represents the same dimension in the eyes of all cultures. The labels, then,
become a convention for organizing research, but must not be reified.

## THE CULTURAL DIMENSIONS OF
## NONVERBAL COMMUNICATION

### Immediacy

The immediacy dimension is anchored on one extreme by actions that
simultaneously communicate closeness, approach, accessibility, and at the
other extreme by behaviors expressing avoidance and distance (Andersen,
1985). Highly immediate behaviors in United States culture include smiling, touching, eye contact, open body positions, closer distances, and more
vocal animation. Some scholars have called this set of behaviors nonverbal
involvement, intimacy, or expressiveness (Patterson, 1983). Others have
focused on the accessibility aspect of immediacy and examined privacy
regulation (Altman, 1975; Petronio, 1988). Research shows that in positive relationships individuals tend to reciprocate immediate behaviors
(Andersen & Andersen, 1984). A bibliography of immediacy studies that

reference culture as a variable is provided by Patterson, Reidhead, Gooch, and Stopka (1984).

Cultures that display considerable interpersonal closeness or immediacy have been labeled "high-contact cultures" because people in these countries stand closer and touch more (Hall, 1966). People in low-contact cultures tend to stand apart and touch less. According to Patterson (1983) these patterns permeate all aspects of everyday life and affect relationships.

Contact cultures also differ in the degree of sensory stimulation they favor. High-contact cultures (e.g., those of South Americans, Southern and Eastern Europeans, and Arabs) create immediacy by increasing sensory input, while low-contact cultures (e.g., those of Asians, North Americans, and Northern Europeans) prefer less sensory involvement (Sussman & Rosenfeld, 1982).

These contrasting styles are exemplified during interaction between Arabs and North Americans. The "distant" style of the North American will often result in perceptions of sensory deprivation and alienation for the Arab interactant, while the North American may feel anxious and imposed upon by the Arab's spatial closeness (Almaney & Alwan, 1982; Cohen, 1987). The distance preferred by North Americans may leave the Arab suspicious of intentions due to the lack of olfactory contact (Almaney & Alwan, 1982). Similar differences are reported for the tactile behavior of people from Latin America and the United States (Shuter, 1976).

Interestingly, high-contact cultures generally are located in warmer countries and low-contact cultures in cooler climates. Research has shown that high-contact cultures include most Arab countries, the Mediterranean region, Eastern Europe, Russia, and Indonesia (Condon & Yousef, 1983; Mehrabian, 1971; Patterson, 1983; Scheflen, 1972). Australians are moderate in their cultural contact level as are North Americans, though North Americans tend toward low contact (Patterson, 1983). Low-contact cultures include most of Northern Europe and Japan (Andersen, Andersen, & Lustig, 1987; Mehrabian, 1971; Patterson, 1983; Scheflen, 1972).

Explanations for these latitudinal variations have included energy level, climate, and metabolism (Andersen, Lustig, & Andersen, 1987b). Evidently, cultures in cooler climates tend to be more task oriented and interpersonally "cool," whereas cultures in warmer climates tend to be more interpersonally oriented and interpersonally "warm." The harshness of northern climates may explain this difference because survival during the long winter requires a high degree of task orientation, cooperation, and tolerance of uncertainty. Cultures closer to the equator may have less need for planning for winter but more need to conserve energy during the heat of summer. Even within the United States, the warmer latitudes tend to be higher-contact cultures (Andersen, Lustig, & Andersen, 1987b).

Other studies show how nonverbal behavior communicates immediacy differently across cultures. For example, Cline and Puhl (1984) report that seating positions function differently in Taiwanese and U.S. cultures. Where Taiwanese generally prefer side-by-side seating to connect same-sex partners, people from the United States generally prefer corner seating for intimate matters and use seating to connect opposite-sex partners and separate same-sex partners. Ickes (1984) found that in interracial (Black-White) conversations in the United States, Whites displayed more cues of interactional involvement and felt more stress than Blacks. A recent study by Booth-Butterfield and Jordan (1987) indicates that gender may moderate this effect, with Black women manifesting more positive cues when conversing with White women than vice versa.

A second group of cultural studies deals primarily with verbal and nonverbal strategies for controlling accessibility to self or group. The strength of privacy needs is signalled by the bulk and height of barriers. Examples of high privacy need levels are signalled by closed doors in the United States and soundproof, double doors in Germany (Hall, 1966), large doors in Norway and trees at property lines in England and Canada (Altman & Gauvin, 1981). In contrast, paper walls in Japan denote a different view of privacy (Geertz, 1973).

## Individualism

Among the most basic cultural dimensions is individualism versus collectivism. Collectivistic cultures emphasize community, shared interests, harmony, tradition, the public good, and maintaining face.

> Individualism is a mature and calm feeling, which disposes each member of the community to sever himself [or herself] from the mass of his [or her] fellows and to draw apart with his [or her] family and friends, so that he [or she] has thus formed a little circle of his [or her] own, he [or she] willingly leaves society at large to itself. (Tocqueville, 1945, p. 104)

The degree of individualism-collectivism in a culture determines how people live together (alone, in families, or tribes), their values, and their reasons for communicating (Andersen, 1985). Individualism is inextricably entwined with the accessibility aspect of immediacy and the use of space. Extreme emphasis on owning space is based on individualism (Altman, 1975). Inevitably, such ownership distances people, limits sensory stimulation, and regulates access and privacy.

Individualism is emphasized particularly in the United States (Bellah et al., 1985). Indeed, the best and worst in U.S. culture can be attributed to individualism. Advocates of individualism have argued that it is the basis of freedom, creativity, and economic incentive. Tocqueville reported

that the majority of Americans believe "that a man [or woman] by following his [or her] own interest, rightly understood, will be led to do what is
just and good" (Tocqueville, 1945, p. 409). Conversely, Bateson (1972)
maintained that individual consciousness may pull humans out of their
ecological niche and disrupt the systemic nature of life on earth. Individualism has been blamed for alienation, loneliness, and materialism.
The extreme individualism in the United States makes it difficult for its
citizens to interact with those from less individualistic cultures (Condon
& Yousef, 1983).

There is little doubt that Western cultures are individualistic, so people
rely on personal judgments. Eastern cultures emphasize harmony among
people, and between people and nature, and value collective judgments.
Tomkins (1984) demonstrated that an individual's psychological makeup
is the result of this cultural dimension. He suggested human beings, in
Western Civilization, have tended toward self-celebration, positive or
negative. In Oriental thought another alternative is represented, that of
harmony between man and nature.

This idea has received empirical support in the landmark work of
Hofstede (1984) on individualism in forty noncommunist countries. The
nine most individualistic (respectively) were the United States, Australia,
Great Britain, Canada, Netherlands, New Zealand, Italy, Belgium, and
Denmark, all of which are Western or European cultures. The ten least
individualistic (respectively) were Venezuela, Colombia, Pakistan, Peru,
Taiwan, Thailand, Singapore, Chile, and Hong Kong—all Oriental or
South American cultures.

Even though the United States is the most individualistic country (Hof-
stede, 1984), specific ethnic groups and geographic regions of the United
States vary in their degree of individualism. Blacks place a great deal of
emphasis on individualism (Collier, Ribeau, & Hecht, 1986; Hecht &
Ribeau, 1984; Kochman, 1981), while Mexican Americans place greater
emphasis on relational solidarity (Hecht & Ribeau, 1984; Hecht, Ribeau,
& Sedeno, in press). But this is all relative and by world standards even
Whites in Alabama constitute an individualistic culture.

A culture's degree of individualism/collectivism affects the nonverbal
behavior in a variety of ways. People from individualistic cultures are
more remote and distant proximally. Collectivistic cultures are interdependent and as a result they work, play, live and sleep in close proximity
to one another. Kinesic behavior tends to be more synchronized in collectivistic cultures. In urban individualistic cultures, family members
often do their "own thing" on different schedules. People in individualistic cultures smile more than in normatively oriented cultures (Tomkins,
1984), probably because individualists are responsible for their relationships and their own happiness, whereas normatively or collectively

oriented people regard compliance with norms as a primary value, and personal or interpersonal happiness is secondary. People in collectivist cultures may suppress emotional displays that are contrary to the mood of the group, because maintaining group affect is a primary value (Andersen, 1988). People in individualistic cultures are encouraged to express emotions because individual freedom is a paramount value.

Individualistic cultures are reportedly more nonverbally affiliative (Andersen, 1988). On the verbal level, members of individualistic cultures signal this accessibility to one another by disclosing more private information during initial encounters than collectivist cultures (Won-Doornink, 1985). Because relationships are not determined socially in individualistic cultures, individuals must provide intimacy cues (Hofstede, 1984). In the United States and other individualistic countries, affiliativeness, dating, flirting, small talk, and initial acquaintance are more important than in collectivist countries, where the social network is more fixed and less reliant on individual initiative. Bellah, et al. (1985) maintain that for centuries in the individualistic and mobile U.S. society, people could meet more easily and their communication was more open. Their relationships, however, were usually more casual and transient.

Individualistic and collectivistic cultures also use time differently. Hall (1984) distinguished between monochronistic patterns of individualistic cultures in which one thing is done at a time and polychronistic patterns of collectivistic cultures in which multiple events are scheduled simultaneously. These time differences highlight the task and time orientation of individualistic cultures in contrast to the relational and socioemotional orientation of collectivist cultures.

Evidence exists that personal individualism may transcend cultural differences for certain variables. Schmidt (1983) compared the effects of crowding on people from an individualistic culture (the United States) and a collectivist culture (Singapore). The study examined the relationships among personal control, crowding annoyance, and stress, reporting similar findings for both cultures.

## Gender

While numerous studies have focused on gender as an individual characteristic, gender has been neglected as a cultural dimension. As conceptualized here this dimension refers to the rigidity and definition of gender roles. More rigid cultures exert influence on members to behave within a narrow range of gender-related behaviors and stress traditional gender role identification. Within such a worldview masculine traits are typically attributes such as strength, assertiveness, competitiveness, and ambitiousness, whereas feminine traits are attributes such as affection, compassion, nurturance, and emotionality (Hofstede, 1984). In general, female communicators are more adaptive because they are more attentive to the silent, nonverbal cues, and cross-cultural research shows that young girls are expected to be more nurturant than boys though there is considerable variation from country to country (Hall, 1984). Hofstede (1984) has measured the degree to which people of both sexes in a culture endorse primarily masculine or feminine goals. Masculine cultures regard competition and assertiveness as important whereas feminine cultures place more importance on nurturance and compassion (Andersen, 1988). It is not surprising that the masculinity of a culture is negatively correlated with the percentage of women in technical and professional jobs and positively correlated with segregation of the sexes in higher education (Hofstede, 1984).

The nine countries with the highest masculinity index scores, respectively, are Japan, Australia, Venezuela, Italy, Switzerland, Mexico, Ireland, Great Britain, and Germany (Hofstede, 1984). These countries lie in Central Europe and the Caribbean, with the exception of Japan. The eight countries highest in feminine values, respectively, are Sweden, Norway, the Netherlands, Denmark, Finland, Chile, Portugal, and Thailand, all Scandinavian or South American cultures with the exception of Thailand. Why would South American cultures not manifest the typical Latin pattern of machismo? Hofstede (1984) suggests that machismo is present in the Caribbean region but not particularly evident in the remainder of South America.

Considerable research suggests that androgynous patterns of behavior (combinations of both feminine and masculine) result in more self-esteem, social competence, success, and intellectual development for both males and females. Buck (1984) has shown that males may harm their health by internalizing emotions rather than externalizing them as women usually do. It is probably not coincidental that more masculine countries display higher levels of stress (Hofstede, 1984). In egalitarian countries where women are economically important and where sexual standards for women are permissive, more relaxed vocal patterns are evident, and there is less tension between the sexes (Lomax, 1968).

## Power Distance

A fourth basic dimension of intercultural communication is power distance, the degree to which power, prestige, and wealth are unequally distributed in a culture. Power distance has been measured in a number of cultures using Hofstede's (1984) Power Distance Index (PDI). Cultures with high PDI scores have control and influence concentrated in the hands of a few rather than more equally distributed. Condon and Yousef (1983) distinguish among three cultural patterns, democratic, authority centered, and authoritarian. The PDI is highly correlated (.80) with authoritarianism (as measured by the F-Scale) (Hofstede, 1984).

Countries highest in PDI are (respectively) the Philippines, Mexico, Venezuela, India, Singapore, Brazil, Hong Kong, France, and Colombia (Hofstede, 1984), all of which are South Asian or Caribbean countries that lie within the tropics, close to the equator (with the exception of France). Gudykunst and Kim (1984) report that both African and Asian cultures generally maintain hierarchical role relationships. The lowest PDI countries (respectively) are Austria, Israel, Denmark, New Zealand, Ireland, Sweden, Norway, Finland, and Switzerland (Hofstede, 1984), all of which are European, middle-class democracies located at very high latitudes. The United States is slightly lower than the median in power distance.

A fundamental determinant of power distance is the latitude of a country. Hofstede (1984) claims that latitude and climate are two of the major forces shaping a culture because in colder climates technology is needed for survival. This produces a chain of events in which children are less dependent on authority and learn from people other than authority figures. In a study conducted at forty universities throughout the United States, Andersen, Lustig, and Andersen (1987b) report a -.47 ecological correlation between latitude and intolerance for ambiguity, and a -.45 ecological correlation between latitude and authoritarianism. This suggests that residents of the northern United States are less authoritarian and more tolerant of ambiguity, perhaps to ensure cooperation needed to survive in harsher climates.

It is obvious that power distance would affect the nonverbal behavior of a culture. High PDI cultures (e.g., India) may severely limit interaction. High PDI countries often prohibit free interclass dating, marriage, and contact, which are taken for granted in low PDI countries. Weitz (1974) suggests that oppressed people must become more skilled at decoding nonverbal behavior.

Social systems with large power discrepancies produce different kinesic behavior. According to Andersen and Bowman (1985) in power-discrepant circumstances subordinates show more bodily tension and smile more in an effort to appease superiors and appear polite. The continuous smiles of many Orientals may be an effort to appease superiors or to produce smooth social relations, a product of being reared in a high PDI culture. Finally, Bizman, Schwarzwald, and Zidon (1984) found that aggressive behavior toward minorities decreased when the minority was seen as having the power to retaliate. Ability to retaliate may be one factor decreasing power distance.

Paralinguistic or vocalic cues are also affected by the power distance in a culture. Residents of low PDI cultures are generally less aware that vocal loudness may be offensive to others (Andersen, 1988). North American vocal tones often are perceived as noisy, exaggerated, and childlike (Condon & Yousef, 1983).

Studies show that cultures differ in the signs of power. In the United States, downcast eyes and a body position below that of another would probably be seen as subordinate. In Japanese culture, however, downcast eyes are signs of attentiveness and agreement (Cambra & Klopf, 1979) and *teishisei* (or low position) signals acceptance and respect and may be perceived as signs that a person is trustworthy, loving, and accepting (Ishii, 1973). Burgoon, Dillard, Doran, and Miller (1982) reported differences in the types of message strategies used in Asian and North American cultures, and American Indian children often feel that their White teachers are mean merely because their voices are louder than those in their own culture (Key, 1975).

Cultural differences in nonverbal behaviors with power implications in one or both cultural groups can contribute to misunderstandings. Eye gaze is a power cue in mainstream U.S. culture, and differences in patterns between Black and White American communicators may lead to interactional difficulties. LaFrance and Mayo (1976, 1978)[1] report that Black speakers look at their conversational partner less while listening than while speaking. The pattern for White communicators is the opposite (Kendon, 1967). In a Black-White conversation, a Black listener will look less than a White speaker expects. This may lead the White interactant to assume disinterest on the part of the Black listener. Conversely, when the Black interactant is talking, both parties will be looking more than each expects. Such overly long, mutual gazes are often interpreted as hostility. In this example, interpretations of disinterest and hostility may be produced by cultural patterning in power-related nonverbal cues. In addition, Blacks decrease gaze while in the presence of powerful people, while Whites increase the amount of gaze in these situations, and the two ethnic groups differ in their interpretations of conversational regulators such as rising and falling inflections (Halberstadt, 1985).

Other power-related predictions, however, have not received support. Booth-Butterfield and Jordan (1987) predicted that Black women, representing a minority group, would have less power and, therefore, adapt more than White females in interethnic conversations. This prediction was not supported. Brown (1981), on the other hand, found that shoppers at a mall are more likely to walk through a Black dyad than a White dyad, supporting the power differential assumption of Booth-Butterfield and Jordan. Researchers have to be careful not to equate societal positions with personal power, particularly in dyadic contexts and within cultures low on power distance (e.g., the United States) or that encourage individual rather than cultural judgments of power.

### Uncertainty

Uncertainty refers to the value placed on risk and ambiguity in a culture. The literature on interpersonal communication contains many references to this construct, many evolving from Berger's uncertainty reduction hypothesis (Berger & Calabrese, 1975). Gudykunst and colleagues (Gudykunst, 1985; Gudykunst & Nishida, 1984, 1986) extended this theory to the intercultural context.

Countries vary greatly in the extent to which they avoid or tolerate uncertainty. In some cultures freedom leads to uncertainty, which leads to stress and anxiety. These cultures may seek to avoid such uncertainty by increasing rules of behavior. Other cultures seem better able to tolerate freedom and diversity without excess stress or anxiety. Hofstede (1984) believed that tendencies toward intolerance of ambiguity, rigidity, and dogmatism are primarily a function of the uncertainty avoidance dimension rather than the power distance dimension. The countries most likely to avoid uncertainty and to be intolerant of ambiguity are Greece, Portugal, Belgium, Japan, Peru, France, Chile, Spain, and Argentina, respectively (Hofstede, 1984). This list is dominated by Southern European and South American countries. The countries lowest in uncertainty avoidance and most tolerant of ambiguity are Singapore, Denmark, Sweden, Hong Kong, Ireland, Great Britain, India, the Philippines, and the United States. This list comprises countries with Northern European cultures or South Asian cultures.

Hofstede (1984) reports that a country's neuroticism or anxiety scores are strongly correlated with uncertainty avoidance, and high uncertainty avoidance is negatively correlated with risk-taking and positively correlated with fear of failure. Hofstede (1984) also has reported that countries higher in uncertainty avoidance tend to be Catholic while countries lower in uncertainty avoidance tend to be Protestant, Hindu, or Buddhist. Eastern religions and Protestantism tend to be less "absolute" while Catholicism tends to be an "absolute" religion. Finally, Hofstede (1984) suggests that countries high in uncertainty avoidance tend to show more emotions than countries low in uncertainty avoidance.

Little else is known about nonverbal behavior and uncertainty. What are the nonverbal cues of uncertainty and how do these differ across cultures? What nonverbal cues create uncertainty? Gudykunst and Nishida (1984) conclude that cultural similarity reduces uncertainty. While Koestar and Olebe (1987) failed to validate this finding, important questions remain. Do nonverbal cues of dissimilarity increase uncertainty? In conversations between culturally similar individuals, do cultural markers increase uncertainty? What is the general relationship among indicants of culture group membership, perceived cultural similarity, and uncertainty? Ducci, Arcuri, W/Georgis, and Sineshaw (1982) reported that familiarity with a culture aids in interpreting nonverbal expressions of emotion. Does the amount of previous interaction with members of a dissimilar culture mediate the relationship between uncertainty and similarity? Answers to these questions would contribute to our understanding of uncertainty and culture.

## High and Low Context

A final important communication dimension is context. Hall (1976, 1984) has described high- and low-context cultures in considerable detail. High-context (HC) communication relies mainly on the physical context or the relationship for information, with little explicitly encoded (Hall, 1976). Lifelong friends often use HC or implicit messages that are nearly impossible for an outsider to understand. In these HC situations, the culture's information integrated from the environment, the context, the situation, and nonverbal cues gives the message meaning unavailable from explicit verbal utterances.

Low-context (LC) messages, in contrast to HC messages, provide most of the information in the explicit code itself (Hall, 1976). LC messages require clear description, unambiguous communication, and a high degree of specificity. Unlike personal relationships that are relatively high-context message systems, institutions such as courts of law and formal systems such as mathematics or computer language require explicit, LC systems because nothing can be taken for granted (Hall, 1984).

Cultures display variation in the degree of context used in communication. The lowest-context cultures are probably Swiss, German, North American (including the United States), and Scandinavian (Hall, 1976, 1984; Gudykunst & Kim, 1984). These cultures are preoccupied with specifics, details, and precise time schedules at the expense of context. They utilize behavior systems built around Aristotelian logic and linear thinking (Hall, 1984). Cultures that have some characteristics of both HC and LC systems would include the French, English, and Italian (Gudykunst & Kim, 1984), which are somewhat less explicit than Northern European cultures.

The highest-context cultures are found in the Orient (Elliott, Scott, Jensen, & McDonough, 1982; Hall, 1976, 1984). Even the Chinese language is an implicit high-context system. To use a Chinese dictionary one must understand thousands of characters that change meaning in combination with other characters. Americans frequently complain that the Japanese never "get to the point" but fail to recognize that HC cultures must provide a context and setting, and let the point evolve (Hall, 1984). American Indian cultures with ancestral, migratory roots in East Asia are remarkably like contemporary Oriental culture in several ways, especially in their need for high context (Hall, 1984). It is not surprising that most Latin American cultures, a fusion of Iberian (Portuguese-Spanish) and

Indian traditions, are also high-context cultures. Southern and Eastern Mediterranean people such as Greeks, Turks, and Arabs tend to have HC cultures as well.

Communication is quite different in high- and low-context cultures. First, verbal communication and other explicit codes are more prevalent in low-context cultures such as the United States and Northern Europe. People from LC cultures are often perceived as excessively talkative, belaboring the obvious and redundant, while people from HC cultures may be perceived as nondisclosing, sneaky, and mysterious (Andersen, 1988). Second, HC and LC cultures do not place the same emphasis on verbal communication. Elliott, et al. (1982) found that more verbal people were perceived as more attractive by people in the United States, but less verbal people were perceived as more attractive in Korea, a HC culture. Third, HC cultures are more reliant on and tuned in to nonverbal communication. LC cultures, particularly men in LC cultures, fail to perceive as much nonverbal communication as members of HC cultures. Nonverbal communication provides the context for all communication (Watzlawick, Beavin, & Jackson, 1967) but people from HC cultures are particularly affected by these contextual cues. Thus facial expressions, tensions, movements, speed of interaction, location of the interaction, and other subtle "vibes" are likely to be perceived by and have more meaning for people from high-context cultures. Finally, people in HC cultures expect more than interactants in LC cultures (Hall, 1976). People in HC cultures expect communicators to understand unarticulated moods, subtle gestures, and environmental clues that people from low-context cultures simply do not process. Worse, both cultural extremes fail to recognize these basic differences in behavior, communication, and context, and are quick to misattribute the causes for their behavior.

## CONCLUSION

This chapter has attempted to articulate a cultural approach to the study of nonverbal communication. An organizational framework was applied to nonverbal research in order to provide a basis for future research. Six dimensions of culture are hypothesized: immediacy, individualism, gender, power distance, uncertainty, and context. The typological system, developed from the work of Hofstede, Hall, and others, suggests a number of directions for future research.

First, the dimensions do not exist in isolation and separately, and, therefore, must be considered in combination. For example, if immediacy and power distance are considered together and each is placed along a separate axis, we can examine relationships in each of the four quadrants.

Assume, for example, a culture in which there is a high degree of power distance and that values immediacy. We can expect more ritualized expressions of affection between members of different power groups, with very strong bonding and free expression of emotion within group relationships. Moving to the next quadrant in which there is a large power distance and a low value on immediacy, one can expect few expressions of intense emotion.

Second, nonverbal research must begin to move beyond descriptions of specific behaviors and examine how such behaviors express meaning, accomplish functions, and achieve outcomes. An "effectiveness" approach (Collier, Ribeau, & Hecht, 1986; Hecht, 1978, 1984; Hecht & Ribeau, 1984, 1987), in which behaviors are juxtaposed with their consequences, is needed in order to create a theoretically grounded approach to nonverbal behavior in cultures. By linking nonverbal messages to meanings, functions, and outcomes, the researcher identifies a range of behavior, provides a means of assessing utility, and develops explanations as well as descriptions of cultural patterns and differences. Grounding research in effectiveness provides the basis for theory-building as well as practice.

Third, researchers need to make finer distinctions when dealing with cultural systems. In the United States, for example, cultural diversity is the rule. Even the mainstream culture manifests regional differences (Andersen, Lustig, & Andersen, 1987a, 1987b). When ethnicity is considered, one is left with the conclusion that many U.S. cultures exist. In fact, even within ethnic groups, diversity exists. Among Black cultures, for example, a number of different ethnic identities—ways of being Black—have been identified (Hecht & Ribeau, in press, 1987).

Fourth, the descriptions summarized in this chapter are of cultural tendencies, not of people. When research describes Arab preference for close distances it does not predict the behavior of any individual. Instead, it describes a cultural tendency. While this conclusion has obvious implications for practice, it also suggests a research style.

Often researchers use cultural categories to differentiate groups without measuring individuals on the cultural variable(s). For example, individualistic and collectivistic cultures are selected, although participants' individualism/collectivism is not assessed. This may be problematic. Robinson (1950), labeling the phenomenon the *ecological fallacy*, criticized the practice of correlating two cultural-level variables and deriving conclusions regarding individual behavior. Other designs are also of concern. For example, we may be interested in testing the relationship between ethnic identity and communication competence. We may hypothesize that a strong correlation will be observed in collectivist cultures due to their emphasis on group membership with a zero correlation in individualistic cultures. Individualism and collectivism would be operationalized by two cultures (e.g., the United States and Japan). Because individualism describes the cultural tendency and not the individual, and the researcher is examining individual-level variables (ethnic identity and competence), it is important to measure the individual's level of individualism in addition to the cultural level. Otherwise, even if there are no differences between conforming participants from the individualistic United States and from collectivist Japanese, nonconforming participants (collectivist people from the United States and individualist Japanese) may produce correlations that support the hypothesis. This is even more problematic when a single culture is used to operationalize a level of a variable.

Fifth, having said this, it is also useful for cultural comparisons to operationalize cultural variables. If two or more cultures are being compared, then we learn more if each represents a cultural category such as those suggested in this chapter. Too many intercultural studies compare cultures with no theoretical frame to explain how they differ.

Sixth, the effects of culture are not always direct. Research by Zatz (1987) and Pettigrew (1985) suggests that the effects of ethnicity are often indirect or in interaction with other variables. For example, Lizotte (1978) reports that in trials in the United States, a defendant's ethnicity does not directly affect sentence length. Instead, ethnicity is found to affect bail status which, in turn, affects sentencing. Another example is provided by Pettigrew (1985), who describes "symbolic racism" as attaching negative perceptions to ostensibly nonethnic objects (e.g., affirmative action, hiring quotas). Such forms of stereotyping have replaced the more obvious ethnic stereotypes, while maintaining discrimination.

A second type of indirect effect is called cumulative disadvantage (Zatz, 1987). Ethnicity has small, maybe even statistically nonsignificant effects on court decision making at any one stage (e.g., arrest, prosecution, conviction, sentencing, probation, parole). The cumulative effect of these small disparities, however, can make a larger difference in the final outcome. Similarly, when evaluating the economic position of Blacks in the United States, researchers must take into account background differences as well as total income. Blacks are less likely to obtain the type of background necessary for economic success and if one examines the economic position of a Black person with a typically "White" background profile, discrimination appears even more extreme (Farley, 1977).

An application of this perspective to the current topic would examine how culture influences nonverbal messages that achieve outcomes, or how cultural differences at various stages of development lead to differing styles or outcomes. For example, in cultures that value immediacy, establishing closer distances will be effective. A second example is provided by cultures that emphasize traditionally masculine gender values. People in this culture who adopt aggressive nonverbal styles will be more effective due to an accumulation effect. These cultures reinforce aggressive play behaviors at early ages. Later in school, the more aggressive children may be encouraged to enter academic tracks, while less aggressive children are pushed toward technical training or home economics. Ultimately, those engendering the masculine styles would achieve more prestige and wealth.

Culture also has been found to interact with other variables. For example, in the United States, race, age, and occupational status interact to affect judicial sentencing (Burke & Turk, 1975). In addition, ethnicity interacts with the number of other minorities in the group to influence evaluations of performance (Kantor, 1977), and interacts with the locus of attribution (the person or the situation) or the characteristics of the perceiver (conservative versus liberal) to influence perception (Pettigrew, 1979).

Zatz (1987) suggests two statistical techniques for dealing with such interaction. First, the researcher can multiply the variables together in regression models. This allows for selected variables to interact with culture. Second, separate regression models can be examined for each cultural group (e.g., Japanese and Arab cultures) and the interaction effects for all variables compared. In addition, analysis of variance models may be used where appropriate. The principle can be applied to the system outlined in the beginning of this chapter, with cultural categories seen as interacting with nonverbal codes, meanings, or functions to influence outcomes and relationships. In addition, culture can interact with other variables (e.g., relationship type) to influence nonverbal behavior.

The interaction between nonverbal codes and culture is the topic of most descriptive nonverbal research. These studies identify cultural patterns and/or differences in typical nonverbal behavior. In setting up a matrix of cultural variables by codes, however, other hypotheses are available. For example, research reviewed in this chapter suggests that time is a code that collectivist cultures emphasize more than individualistic cultures. Does this mean that people in individualist cultures are more likely than those in collectivistic cultures to use time as a means to an end? And do cultures differ in their emphases on the use of other codes? In this manner, researchers can link codes to culture and develop explanatory systems.

Culture should also interact with nonverbal meanings. A matrix of cultural dimensions by meaning dimensions would be informative. One might predict that immediacy behaviors between members of different power/status groups would produce different outcomes depending on the power distance in the culture. A member of a high-power group who manifests an immediacy behavior toward a subordinate may be seen as friendly, while an immediacy behavior from a low-power person to superiors may be seen as being ingratiating. Similarly, one might predict different perceptions of office romances in these two cultures. One may also add the variable of gender, differentiating cultures based on gender role separation.

Another interaction might be between culture and nonverbal functions. The same expression of emotion in cultures differing in their value for immediacy is likely to produce different effects. Similarly, interruptions will vary in effect depending on power distance value and actual power distances. Finally, culture can also be seen as interacting with structural variables (e.g., relational type, topic, setting) to influence nonverbal meanings. One can predict, for example, a stronger interaction between culture and relationship intimacy level in cultures emphasizing immediacy values. Similarly, aggressive styles and individualist versus collectivist values should interact to effect perceived power. One might hypothesize that relational level and immediacy value interact such that friends in a highly immediate culture express affection differently than those in less immediate cultures.

## NOTE

1. LaFrance and Mayo's 1978 article appears to be a reprint of the first of two studies reported in LaFrance and Mayo in 1976. Further, Halberstadt (1985) cites three unpublished studies that contradict this result.

## REFERENCES

Almaney, A., & Alwan, A. (1982). *Communicating with the Arabs*. Prospect Heights, IL: Waveland.

Altman, I. (1975). *The environment and social behavior*. Monterey, CA: Brooks/Cole.

Altman, I., & Gauvain, M. (1981). A cross-cultural dialective analysis of homes. In L. Liben, A. Patterson, & N. Newcombe (Eds.), *Spatial representation and behavior across the life span*. New York: Academic Press.

Andersen, J. F., Andersen, P. A., & Lustig, M. W. (1987). Opposite sex touch avoidance: A national replication and extension. *Journal of Nonverbal Behavior, 11*, 89-109.

Andersen, P. A. (1985). Nonverbal immediacy in interpersonal communication. In A. W. Siegman & S. Feldstein (Eds.), *Multichannel integrations of nonverbal behavior*. Hillsdale, NJ: Lawrence Erlbaum.

Andersen, P. A. (1988). Explaining intercultural differences in nonverbal communication. In L. A. Samovar & R. E. Porter (Eds.), *Intercultural communication: A reader*. Belmont, CA: Wadsworth.

Andersen, P. A., & Andersen, J. F. (1984). The exchange of nonverbal intimacy: A critical review of dyadic models. *Journal of Nonverbal Behavior, 8*, 327-349.

Andersen, P. A., & Bowman, L. (1985). *Positions of power: Nonverbal cues of status and dominance in organizational communication*. Paper presented at the annual convention of the International Communication Association, Honolulu, HI.

Andersen, P. A., Lustig, M. W., & Andersen, J. F. (1987a). Regional patterns of communication in the United States: A theoretical perspective. *Communication Monographs, 54,* 128-144.

Andersen, P. A., Lustig, M. W., & Andersen, J. F. (1987b). *Changes in latitude, changes in attitude: The relationship between climate and interpersonal communication.* Paper presented at the annual convention of the Speech Communication Association, Boston.

Bateson, G. (1972). *Steps to an ecology of mind.* New York: Ballantine.

Bellah, R. N., Madsen, R., Sullivan, W. M., Swidler, A., & Tipton, S. (1985). *Habits of the heart: Individualism and commitment in American life.* New York: Harper & Row.

Berger, C., & Calabrese, R. (1975). Some explorations in initial interactions and beyond: Toward a developmental theory of interpersonal communication. *Human Communication Research, 1,* 99-112.

Bizman, A., Schwarzwald, J., & Zidon, A. (1984). Effects of the power to retaliate on physical aggression directed toward Middle-Eastern Jews, Western Jews, and Israeli-Arabs. *Journal of Cross-Cultural Psychology, 15,* 65-78.

Booth-Butterfield, M., & Jordan, F. (1987). *Verbal and nonverbal adaptation among racially homogeneous and heterogeneous groups.* Paper presented at the annual convention of the Speech Communication Association, Boston.

Brown, C. E. (1981). Shared space invasion. *Personality and Social Psychology Bulletin, 7,* 103-108.

Buck, R. (1984). *The communication of emotion.* New York: Guilford.

Burgoon, J. (1985). Nonverbal signals. In M. Knapp & G. Miller (Eds.), *Handbook of interpersonal communication.* Beverly Hills, CA: Sage.

Burgoon, M., Dillard, J. P., Doran, N. E., & Miller, M. D. (1982). Cultural and situational influences on the process of persuasive strategy selection. *International Journal of Intercultural Relations, 6,* 85-100.

Burke, P. J., & Turk, A. T. (1975). Factors affecting postarrest dispositions: A model for analysis. *Social Problems, 22,* 313-332.

Cambra, R. E., & Klopf, D. W. (1979). *A cross-cultural analysis of interpersonal needs.* Paper presented at the Speech Association Intercultural Communication Conference, Honolulu, HI.

Cline, R. J., & Puhl, C. A. (1984). Gender, culture, and geography: A comparison of seating arrangements in the United States and Taiwan. *International Journal of Intercultural Relations, 8,* 199-219.

Cohen, R. (1987). Problems of intercultural communication in Egyptian-American diplomatic relations. *International Journal of Intercultural Relations, 11,* 29-47.

Collier, M. J., Ribeau, S. A., & Hecht, M. L. (1986). Intracultural rules and outcomes within three domestic cultures. *International Journal of Intercultural Relations, 10,* 439-457.

Condon, J. C., & Yousef, F. (1983). *An introduction to intercultural communication.* Indianapolis, IN: Bobbs-Merrill.

Ducci, L., Arcuri, L., W/Georgis, T., & Sineshaw, D. (1982). Emotion recognition in Ethiopia: The effect of familiarity with Western culture on accuracy of recognition. *Journal of Cross-Cultural Psychology, 13,* 340-351.

Elliot, S., Scott, M. D., Jensen, A. D., & McDonough, M. (1982). Perceptions of reticence: A cross-cultural investigation. In M. Burgoon (Ed.), *Communication yearbook* (Vol. 5). New Brunswick, NJ: Transaction.

Farley, R. (1977). Trends in racial inequalities: Have the gains of the 1960s disappeared in the 1970s? *American Sociological Review, 42,* 189-208.

Geertz, C. (1973). *The interpretation of cultures.* New York: Basic Books.

Gudykunst, W. B. (1985). The influence of cultural similarity, type of relationship, and self-monitoring on uncertainty reduction processes. *Communication Monographs, 52,* 206-216.

Gudykunst, W. B., & Kim, Y. Y. (1984). *Communicating with strangers: An approach to intercultural communication.* New York: Random House.

Gudykunst, W. B., & Nishida, T. (1984). Individual and cultural influences on uncertainty reduction. *Communication Monographs, 51,* 23-36.

Gudykunst, W. B., & Nishida, T. (1986). Attributional confidence in low- and high-context cultures. *Human Communication Research, 12,* 525-549.

Halberstadt, A. G. (1985). Race, socioeconomic status, and nonverbal behavior. In A. W. Siegman & S. Feldstein (Eds.), *Multichannel integrations of nonverbal behavior.* Hillsdale, NJ: Lawrence Erlbaum.

Hall, E. T. (1959). *The silent language.* New York: Doubleday.

Hall, E. T. (1966). *The hidden dimension.* Garden City, NY: Doubleday.

Hall, E. T. (1976). *Beyond culture.* Garden City, NY: Anchor.

Hall, E. T. (1979). Cultural models in transcultural communication. In A. Wolfgang (Ed.), *Nonverbal behavior: Applications and cultural implications.* New York: Academic Books.

Hall, E. T. (1984). *The dance of life: The other dimension of time.* Garden City, NY: Anchor.

Hamilton, M. L. (1973). Imitative behavior and expressive ability in facial expressions of emotions. *Developmental Psychology, 8,* 138.

Hecht, M. L. (1978). The conceptualization and measurement of interpersonal communication satisfaction. *Human Communication Research, 4,* 253-264.

Hecht, M. L. (1984). Satisfying communication and relationship labels: Intimacy and length of relationship as perceptual frames of naturalistic conversations. *Western Journal of Speech Communication, 48,* 201-216.

Hecht, M. L., & Ribeau, S. A. (1984). Ethnic communication: A comparative analysis of satisfying communication. *International Journal of Intercultural Relations, 8,* 135-151.

Hecht, M. L., & Ribeau, S. A. (1987). Afro-American identity labels and communication effectiveness. *Journal of Language and Social Psychology, 6,* 319-326.

Hecht, M. L., & Ribeau, S. A. (in press-b). Socio-cultural roots of ethnic identity: A look at Black America. *Journal of Black Studies.*

Hecht, M. L., Ribeau, S. A., & Sedeno, M. V. (in press). A Mexican American perspective on interethnic communication. *International Journal of Intercultural Relations.*

Herrmann, D. J., & Raybeck, D. (1981). Similarities and differences in meaning in six cultures. *Journal of Cross-Cultural Psychology, 12,* 194-206.

Hofstede, G. (1984). *Culture's consequences.* Beverly Hills, CA: Sage.

Ickes, W. (1984). Compositions in black and white: Determinants of interaction in inter-racial dyads. *Journal of Personality and Social Psychology, 47,* 330-341.

Ishii, S. (1973). Characteristics of Japanese nonverbal communication behavior. *Communication, 2,* 163-180.

Kantor, R. M. (1977). *Men and women of the corporation.* New York: Basic Books.

Kendon, A. (1967). Some functions of gaze direction in social interaction. *Acta Psychologica, 71,* 359-372.

Key, M. R. (1975). *Paralinguistics and kinesics.* Metuchen, NJ: Scarecrow.

Knapp, M. L. (1978). *Nonverbal communication in human interaction.* New York: Holt, Rinehart & Winston.

Kochman, T. (1981). *Black and White: Styles in conflict.* Chicago: University of Chicago Press.

Koester, J., & Oleba, M. (1987). *The relationship of cultural similarity, communication effectiveness and uncertainty reduction.* Paper presented at the annual convention of the Speech Communication Association, Boston.

LaFrance, M., & Mayo, C. (1976). Racial differences in gaze behavior during conversations: Two systematic observational studies. *Journal of Personality and Social Psychology, 33,* 547-552.

LaFrance, M., & Mayo, C. (1978). Gaze direction in interracial dyadic communication. *Ethnicity, 5*, 167-173.

Lizotte, A. J. (1978). Extra-legal factors in Chicago's criminal courts: Testing the conflict model of criminal justice. *Social Problems, 25*, 564-580.

Lomax, A. (1968). *Folk song style and culture*. New Brunswick, NJ: Transaction.

Mehrabian, A. (1971). *Silent messages*. Belmont, CA: Wadsworth.

Osgood, C. E., May, W. H., & Minon, M. S. (1975). *Cross-cultural universals of affective meaning*. Urbana: University of Illinois Press.

Osgood, C. E., Suci, G. T., & Tannenbaum, P. H. (1957). *The measurement of meaning*. Chicago: University of Illinois Press.

Patterson, M. L. (1983). *Nonverbal behavior: A functional perspective*. New York: Springer-Verlag.

Patterson, M. L., Reidhead, S. M., Gooch, M. V., & Stopka, S. J. (1984). A content-classified bibliography of research on the immediacy behaviors: 1965-1982. *Journal of Nonverbal Behavior, 8*, 360-393.

Petronio, S. (1988). *Communicative management of privacy: Process of negotiation between marital couples*. Paper presented at the annual convention of the Western Speech Communication Association, San Diego, CA.

Pettigrew, T. F. (1979). The ultimate attribution error: Extending Allport's cognitive analysis of prejudice. *Personality and Social Psychology Bulletin, 5*, 464-476.

Pettigrew, T. F. (1985). New Black-White patterns: How best to conceptualize them? *Annual Review of Sociology, 11*, 329-346.

Poyatos, F. (1983). *New perspectives on nonverbal communication*. Oxford: Pergamon.

Prosser, M. H. (1978). *The cultural dialogue: An introduction to intercultural communication*. Boston: Houghton Mifflin.

Ramsey, S. (1979). Nonverbal behavior: An intercultural perspective. In M. Asante, E. Newmark, & C. Blake (Eds.), *Handbook of intercultural communication*. Beverly Hills, CA: Sage.

Ramsey, S. (1984). Double vision: Nonverbal behavior East and West. In A. Wolfgang (Ed.), *Nonverbal behavior: Perspectives, applications, intercultural insights*. Lewiston, NY: C. J. Hogrefe.

Ribeau, S., Hecht, M. L., & Sedeno, M. V. (1985, May). *A Mexican American perspective on interethnic communication*. Paper presented at the annual convention of the International Communication Association, Honolulu, HI.

Robinson, W. S. (1950). Ecological correlations and the behavior of individuals. *American Sociological Review, 15*, 351-357.

Scheflen, A. E. (1972). *Body language and the social order*. Englewood Cliffs, NJ: Prentice-Hall.

Schmidt, D. E. (1983). Personal control and crowding stress: A test of similarity in two cultures. *Journal of Cross-Cultural Psychology, 14*, 221-239.

Shuter, P. (1976). Proxemics and tactility in Latin America. *Journal of Communication, 26*, 45-52.

Singer, M. K. (1987). *Intercultural communication: A perceptual approach*. Englewood Cliffs, NJ: Prentice-Hall.

Sussman, N. M., & Rosenfeld, H. M. (1982). Influence of culture, language, and sex on conversational distance. *Journal of Personality and Social Psychology, 42*, 66-74.

Tocqueville, A. D. (1945). *Democracy in America* (Vol. 1, P. Bradley, Trans.). New York: Random House.

Tomkins, S. S. (1984). Affect theory. In K. R. Scherer & P. Ekman (Eds.), *Approaches to emotion*. Hillsdale, NJ: Lawrence Erlbaum.

Watzlawick, P., Beavin, J., & Jackson, D. (1967). *Pragmatics of human communication*. New York: Norton.

Weitz, S. (Ed.). (1974). *Nonverbal communication: Readings with commentary.* New York: Oxford University Press.

Wiemann, J., & Harrison, R. (Eds.). (1983). *Nonverbal interaction.* Beverly Hills, CA: Sage.

Wolfgang, A. (Ed.). (1984). *Nonverbal behavior: Perspectives, applications, intercultural insights.* Lewiston, NY: C. J. Hogrefe.

Wolfson, K., & Pearce, W. B. (1983). A cross-cultural comparison of the implications of self-disclosure on conversational logics. *Communication Quarterly, 31,* 249-256.

Won-Doornink, M. (1985). Self-disclosure and reciprocity in conversation: A cross-national study. *Social Psychology Quarterly, 48,* 97-107.

Zatz, M. S. (1987). The changing forms of racial ethnic biases in sentencing. *Journal of Research in Crime and Delinquency, 24,* 69-92.

# 8 Social Networks and Communication

## Gabriel Weimann

Recent decades have witnessed a growing interest in the study of social networks. One of the reasons for this interest is the applicability of the concept of networks to many disciplines ranging from anthropology and sociology to organizational management and intercultural communication. The notion of social network analysis is not very new, however. As Laumann (1979, p. 391) argues, "close examination reveals that network analysis is, at least in part, some rather old ideas that have been refurbished and made more attractive by being combined with sophisticated mathematical and quantitative tools." In fact, most of the analytical procedures and terminology used by modern network analysis can be traced back to early sociometric research dating from the early 1930s. Moreno's (1934) sociometric measures and techniques provided the foundations for much of modern, advanced, and sophisticated network analysis. Moreno's work, however, was limited to the study and analysis of small groups (that is, networks with a maximum size of 80 to 100 individuals). Moreover, the main data analysis technique was drawing sociometric maps (i.e., sociograms) that enabled the use of rather simple measures of structure and relationships.

Modern network analysis owes its prosperity mainly to the use of modern technologies of data processing, namely, computerized analysis. The use of computers facilitated the analysis of very large networks and the application of advanced statistical measures. The development of special network analysis programs was another breakthrough, especially as it was accompanied by the use of sophisticated mathematics. Graph theory, topology, and matrix algebra provided better measures of network attributes and characteristics. Wolfe (1978, p. 59), after reviewing the development of modern network analysis, concludes: "Without this kind of advance in mathematics we could not hope to get far in the development of social network models."

It was not only technology and improved methodology that led to the present revival of network analysis. As Alba and Kadushin (1976) noted, this revival is attributable not only to technological innovation, ultimately attainable to high-speed computers, but also to an increasing recognition of the importance of networks in bridging the conceptual gap between micro and macro structure. Network analysis may be used to relate small group interaction to macro-scale phenomenon such as the formation of public opinion or the flow of intercultural communication.

Intercultural communication, that is, the flow of communication across racial, ethnic, cultural, or national boundaries, may benefit from the theory and methodology of network analysis. This chapter will clarify the various dimensions of network analysis and their applicability to the study of intercultural communication. Once the levels of analysis have been presented, the reader will realize the need for cross-level analysis, combining various dimensions of network analysis together with the need for a theoretical framework to guide the choice of one cross-level hypothesis out of thousands of possible combinations.

## NETWORKS AND COMMUNICATION

One of the early definitions of a social network referred to "a specific set of linkages among a defined set of persons, with the additional property that the characteristics of these linkages as a whole may be used to interpret the social behavior of the persons involved" (Mitchell, 1969, p. 2). Yet, as Laumann (1979) argued, this definition would not permit a network analysis of social systems of any appreciable size unless two critical aspects were modified. The first concerns the "nodes" (or persons in Mitchell's definition). Entities other than "real persons" (e.g., corporate actors, like business firms or directorates, or aggregates of persons sharing a particular attribute like ethnic, national, or class groups) can act as nodes in a social network. This modification, naturally, is required for any attempt to relate social network analysis to intercultural communication or to the study of large and complex systems.

The second modification relates to Mitchell's "linkage." Once nodes are not only individuals but social groups as well, then the linkages are not merely unidimensional. They may involve a rich variety of relationships—friendship, business, family, work, or a combination of these dimensions. Thus the notion of links is broadened to include the relative presence (or strength) of various relationships between nodes.

Network analysis is meant to explain or predict various aspects of group and intergroup processes. One of the related areas is that of communication. The flow of communication between individuals, groups, organizations, or cultures becomes patterned over time and, as a result, a communication network emerges, one that is relatively stable and predictive of behavior. Intercultural communication should be of special interest for network analysts: Kim (1986) argues that individuals are "embedded" in social milieus (including their ethnic, racial, or cultural groups) that function as "structural contingencies" presenting individuals with possibilities or limitations in their communicative behavior.

Communication network analysis is suggested by Rogers and Kincaid (1981) as consisting of one or more of the following research procedures: (a) identifying certain communication roles in the network such as "liaisons," "bridges," and "isolates"; (b) identifying cliques within the network and determining how these structural subgroupings affect communication behavior in the system; and (c) measuring various communication structural indices (like density, openness, or connectedness) for individuals (or nodes), dyads, cliques, or the entire system. Accordingly, the study of communication networks may be classified by the dimension of analysis into the following categories:

(1) *nodes* as units of analysis: focusing on roles or positions and their communicative functions;

(2) *links* as units of analysis: focusing on the ties between nodes and the characteristics of the ties as affecting their functioning as communication channels;

(3) *cliques* as units of analysis: focusing on subgroups within the networks and the way the division into cliques and their structure is related to communication flow; and

(4) *networks* as units of analysis: focusing on the entire network and studying the relationship between the system's characteristics (e.g., size or structure) and measures of communication flow.

## DIMENSIONS OF ANALYSIS

The various studies of communication networks may be categorized according to the level of analysis. Some focus on the actors, others on the links between them or the groups (cliques) formed within the network. The following division according to dimension of analysis, however, is done for the sake of clarity rather than in order to represent a real conceptual division. Moreover, as this discussion will illustrate, there is a need to cross the boundaries between levels of analysis, because only cross-level analysis can truly represent the complex nature of social networks especially when intercultural communication is concerned.

### Individual-Level Analysis

Many network studies focus on individuals in the network. Naturally, most of the early interest was devoted to *centrality,* or to central positions. The concept of "opinion leadership" (originated by Lazarsfeld et al., 1948; Katz & Lazarsfeld, 1955) was a typical example of such analysis. The researchers mapped the communication flow within a group or community and focused on those who were most often mentioned as the sources of information and influence in various decision-making areas. Rogers and Shoemaker (1971) list several hundred opinion leadership studies that focused on the personal and social characteristics of opinion leaders, the overlap between their areas of influence, and their own sources of information. Thus opinion leadership (operationalized as the number of sociometric choices received by each individual when the flow of communication is mapped) was the first individual-level measure based on network analysis. The analysis of communication sociomatrices, however, revealed the crucial functions of other network positions. Such positions were "liaisons" (who link two or more cliques without being a member of these cliques), "bridges" (who are members of one clique and link it to another clique), "cosmopolites" (who link the system to other systems), and "isolates" (who are totally isolated by lacking any contact or link).

The communication importance of positions other than central ones may be illustrated by the study of the importance of marginals. In a study of the flow of information in a large network, Weimann (1982) focused on marginally positioned individuals (defined by very few choices in the sociomatrices of their groups) and highlighted their "bridging function" in the flow between cliques. His findings reveal a "division of labor" between different network positions: While the intergroup flow of communication (i.e., between groups) is carried out mainly by "marginals" who use the links between them as bridges between cliques, the intragroup flow is activated mainly by the centrally positioned person. This portrays a new version of the multistep flow of communication. The "marginals" serve as the "importers" of new information while the dissemination of information within the group is done by the "centrals," or the opinion leaders.

Another way of relating network positions to communicative functioning is proposed by the notion of *structural interest.* This refers to the perceived utility of the communication act as dependent upon the individual's position in the network. Thus Bart (1980) demonstrates how network position may affect innovation adoption and diffusion. The decision to adopt or recommend an innovation may rely not only on the concrete aspects of the innovation but also on the structural advantages to the individual. Coleman, Katz, and Menzel (1966) studied the diffusion of a new drug among physicians and found that individuals with different

190

network positions react differently to the same innovation, partly as a result of the way they perceive the social risks or benefits of its adoption.

Additional measures on the individual level of analysis are based on studying *personal networks*. These personal communication networks are formed by the interconnected individuals who are linked to a focal individual by a patterned flow of communication. These networks (also called "egocentric networks") are anchored on a specific individual (or a node that may be an organization, a culture, or any social entity). One of the basic measures of such a network is the *integration of personal network*, that is, the degree to which the members of an individual's personal network are linked to each other, computed by the number of actual, activated links, divided by the total number of possible links. Rogers and Kincaid (1981, pp. 136-138) present examples of the relationships between level of integration of personal networks and communication flows on topics such as the search for an abortionist by North American women (Lee, 1969), voting, consumption, and medical problems (see Laumann, 1973). Personal networks are considered to "form a social environment from and through which pressure is exerted to influence behavior" (Boissevain, 1974, p. 27). Burstein (1976), for example, found that such personal network factors are important in explaining patterns of voting in the Israeli national elections. About one-third of the variance in voting behavior was explained by the inclusion of network variables such as the party preference of one's best friends or the dominant choice in one's personal network.

The personal network can also be measured by the homogeneity or heterogeneity of its members, or the *individual diversity*. This is the degree to which the members of an individual's personal network are heterogeneous in some variable (e.g., age, social status, prestige). This concept is evaluated using the standard deviation of some variable that is measured for each member of the focal individual's personal network (Rogers & Kincaid, 1981).

Finally, any node (or individual) may be studied by its integration within the entire system or network. This is the *individual connectedness*, or the degree to which a focal node is linked to other nodes in the system. The concepts of centrality and connectedness are very similar, but not entirely identical: Centrality is usually measured by distance or the average number of steps to every other node in the network (Freeman, 1979) while connectedness is based on the actual number of links that an individual has within a given system.

## Link-Level Analysis

Instead of focusing on the nodes in the network, one may study the links (or ties) that connect the nodes. Various measures have been applied to characterize the links and relate them to measures of communication flow. One of the first and basic measures was the *level of homophily*, that is, the degree to which the link is connecting individuals who are similar in certain attributes, such as sociodemographic characteristics, beliefs, and values. The lack of such homophily is regarded as a heterophilous link. The relationship of this measure to communication flow is complex. As Rogers and Kincaid (1981, p. 128) argue, "more effective communication occurs when the transceivers are homophilous." This is the result of sharing a set of similar interests, common meaning, and a mutual value position. Such homophily, however, may block the flow of new information: The diffusion of innovation, for example, may require the activation of heterophilous links that bridge people from different groups and background. This is related to the notion of the "strength of weak ties."

*The strength of ties*, another measure on the link level, is usually defined by a combination of the amount of time, the emotional intensity, the intimacy, and the reciprocal services that characterize the tie. Most models of network deal, implicitly, with strong ties, whereas Granovetter (1973) points to the "strength of weak ties." He argues that the overlap of two individual networks varies directly with the strength of their tie, thus enabling only weak ties to serve as "bridges" between groups, clusters, or cliques. The argument of the strength of weak ties has been useful in clarifying and explaining a variety of phenomena (for reviews, see Granovetter, 1983; Weimann, 1983).

A somewhat different measure related to links in networks is *multiplexity*. Most scholars of social networks have adopted Gluckman's (1967, pp. 19-20) term "multiplex ties" to refer to links between individuals that serve a multiplicity of interests, as, for instance, when A is simultaneously neighbor, workmate, and friend of B. The notion of multiplexity may be related to various structural features of social networks. Thus Mitchell (1979) argues that multiplex social relationships tend to become dense over time, so that we would expect social networks to polarize between single-stranded space networks on the one hand and many-stranded networks on the other. Laumann, who studied urban networks, found that "interlocking networks are exceptionally likely to be composed of members who are similar to one another in ethno-religious group memberships, occupational activities and political party preferences, while radial preferences are likely to be more heterogeneous in these respects" (Laumann, 1973, p. 124). Multiplexity too may be related to communication flow and to the relative "strength of work ties." Weimann (1983b, p. 263) argues that high multiplexity is assumed to be a communicative advantage, as several forms of interaction can serve the flow of communication; however, "high multiplexity creates communication barriers because it limits the 'expansiveness' of inter-group relations and creates segregation."

Moreover, the main type of interaction that occurs through ties with low multiplexity is communication. Those who do not share a lot of interactions together may have more "news" to one another than those whose relationships are multiplex. This is partly as a result of the overlap between their information sources and acquaintances. This overlap serves as an additional measure of links in networks, referred to as "proximity." *Proximity* is conceptualized as the degree to which two individuals in a network have personal networks that overlap. Thus any link between two persons in the network may be characterized by the amount of overlap in other links related to those two persons. This proximity is considered to affect the communication potential of the link. Rogers and Kincaid propose (1981, p. 131) that "the degree of proximity in communication dyads is negatively related to their information-exchange potential." Granovetter, in his study on job mobility, found the reverse relationship between proximity and communication potential or efficiency (Granovetter, 1974). The reason for his negative relationship between proximity and communication potential is that proximity is related to close relationships and thus to the division of the network into unconnected cliques or segmentation. This segmentation limits the flow of communication and the potential for an individual to get new information.

## Clique-Level Analysis

One of the common procedures of many network analyses is to identify the cliques within the network. A clique is a subsystem or a group within a network whose members interact with each other relatively more frequently than with other members of the network. Identifying the cliques is based on the mapping of the entire network, and analyzing the map or the sociomatrix. Rogers and Kincaid (1981, chap. 4) describe and illustrate various methods of matrix manipulation methods that serve to identify the cliques. A commonly used procedure is based on computer programs designed explicitly for this purpose. These programs use the who-to-whom communication matrix for a sequential reordering of the matrix according to the ties between each two nodes until, after several reorderings, the cliques are revealed.

Once the cliques are identified, several measures can be used to characterize the cliques; the first is their size and number. These may have important effects on the flow of communication: Is the network divided into many small cliques or are there only few large cliques? Second, there is the measure of *clique connectedness*, defined as the degree to which the average member of a given clique is linked to other individuals in his or her clique. This variable, found to be inversely related to clique size, may affect the within-the-clique flow of communication. The between-the-cliques flow of communication, however, may be affected by another measure, *clique integration*. This is the degree to which the cliques in a network are linked to each other. A highly split network will comprise cliques with a low level of clique integration. Another way of looking at the links between cliques is the use of *clique openness*, or the degree to which members of a clique are linked to others from other cliques. The higher the rate of such external links, the more "open" the clique is to other cliques.

The identification of cliques may expose the amount of overlap between cliques, that is, the rate of participation in several cliques at the same time (a position that is an ideal "bridge" between cliques). The greater the overlap, the more proximate are the members of these cliques. This led to a very specific interest in the analysis of "interlocking directorates." This approach (for a review, see Fennema & Schijf, 1979) examines the number of common directors between any two (or more) corporations. The basic notion and methodology of interlocking directorates can be extended to political leadership or any form of membership of various social organizations. Thus common organizational membership may serve as a measure of groups' proximity and predict the efficiency of the intergroup flow of communication.

Finally, one can characterize the clique by the *attributes of the clique's members*. What are the personal variables that form the division into cliques? Is the clique system based on age, sex, occupation, education, kinship, social status, residence, or any combination of these and other variables? The characterization of the cliques' members by these variables may reveal the social mechanisms that shape the social structure of a group or a social system. Moreover, based on this characterization, the measure of *clique diversity* may be computed. This measures the degree to which the members of the cliques are heterogeneous or homogeneous in their personal background.

A different way of looking at cliques and their attributes is provided by a distinctive method of network analysis called "blockmodeling." The procedure, developed by Harrison White and his colleagues, divides the network into "blocks" that are not the cliques as defined earlier. Rather the blocks consist of individuals who have similar communication links and nonlinks. Any two individuals in a block are linked to the same sets of other individuals but they may not be linked to each other. Thus, according to the blockmodeling procedure, the basis for grouping individuals in a network is *structural equivalence*. This procedure is useful for the study of communication flow, not only by identifying the "blocks," but also by revealing the "holes" or "gaps" in a network, thus providing a structural explanation for the nature of personal communication.

## Network-Level Analysis

The total network may serve as a unit of analysis. Several measures have been developed to characterize various attributes of the networks. Most of them are potentially important to the understanding of the communication flow. Obviously, the study of entire networks demanded the use of computer-aided manipulations and computations. Such computerized programs enable the mapping of large networks, translating them into sociomatrices and computing various structural measures based on the matrix data.

One of the frequently used measures was *density*. Density is defined as the ratio of the number of links between the nodes in the networks to the maximum links possible, that is, the number of links that would be present if every node in the network was connected to all the other nodes. This simple measure can be applied to all types of links in the network, or to only a specific type of link, but it can be further refined by using weights, that is, giving each link a weight (according to strength or multiplexity) and calculating a "weighted density" (see Barnes, 1979).

Various measures are related to the *structuredness* of a network. Structuredness may be defined in many ways that lead to different empirical measures. One may refer to structure by its shape or form. Thus Leavitt (1951) studied the effects of various structural patterns on the flow of information within a group. These studies, later refined by others, revealed the importance of the network's structure. There are other ways of looking at structuredness, however. One of them is *connectedness*, that is, the degree to which the average member of a network is linked to the other individuals in the network. The level of connectedness is argued to be influenced by the tendency of a network to be structured, to be clustered. Pool and Kochen (1978) contend that a network that is clustered into many distinct cliques is highly structured and so the level of connectedness in the network is rather limited. Thus one may refer to structure as the relative appearance of *clustering*. The absence of clustering means the absence of cliques—and thus no structure—while any clustering leads to subgrouping and structuredness: "The more cliquisheness there is, the more structure there is" (Pool & Kochen, 1978, p. 15).

Structuredness is related highly to another measure, that of *transitivity*. Holland and Leinhardt (1977) argue that the various models for the structure of personal networks may all be viewed as special cases of a single model, namely, a transitive graph. They propose to adopt transitivity as the key structural concept in the analysis of sociometric data (1977, pp. 49-50).

The notion of transitivity is rooted in the concept of cognitive balance as formulated by Heider (1958) and especially by Newcomb (1961). While Heider was more concerned with cognitive balance regarding personal attitudes and sentiments, he noted its relevance to balance in interpersonal relations as a special case of balanced personal relations. Thus in an A-B-C personal triad, if strong A-B and A-C ties exist, then the B-C link will emerge in order to avoid psychological strain and to create a balanced set of relations. Some evidence supports the assumed rarity of the "forbidden triads" (where the B-C link is missing). Davis (1963, pp. 444-462) found that, in 90% of 651 sociograms, triads consisting of two mutual choices and one nonchoice occurred less often than expected. But, as Granovetter (1973, p. 1362) claims, the tendency toward balanced relations, or transitivity, is less crucial when the ties are weak (see also Homans, 1950, p. 255, and Davis, 1963, p. 448). This tendency toward transitivity should be regarded as a communication barrier where intergroup flow is concerned. Granovetter (1973, pp. 1364-1365) argues that the tendency of strong tie networks to be transitive prevents, or at least limits, the functioning of strong tie networks as bridges (if A is linked to both B and C by strong tie networks, then there is a high probability that the B-C link will also occur, preventing any ties from serving as a "bridge"). It can be argued that the tendency toward transitivity limits the flow of communication by eliminating the existence of bridges, thus limiting the intergroup flow and lengthening the chains linking any pair or persons (Pool & Kochen, 1978, p. 15).

Holland and Leinhardt (1971, 1972, 1977) examine transitivity by analyzing all the possible triads in a given sociomatrix. In order to determine whether or not the network is transitive, they set up a hypothesis-testing apparatus that contrasts the actual occurrence of intransitive triads with those expected under a theoretical random distribution (Holland & Leinhardt, 1970, 1972). If, in a given sociogram, there are about as many intransitive triads (exhibiting at least one intransitivity) as expected by chance, then there is little evidence that this network tends to be transitive.

The transitivity tendency may be used to explain the amount and form of structuredness in a network. A highly transitive network implies a highly dense, intraconnected network, while intransitivity results in a loosely built, open network, divided into cliques that are linked by "bridges." This has a significant impact on the flow of communication, as demonstrated by Weimann's (1982, 1983) relating of structural measures such as transitivity to measures of communicative efficiency.

Finally, the network as a whole may be characterized by its *openness*, that is, the degree to which its members are linked to others external to the network. This measure of openness may indicate whether the network is exposed to the flow of innovations from its environment, and may reveal the internetwork bridges that are so essential for the flow of intercultural communication, diffusion of innovation, and the formation of public opinion.

## NETWORK ANALYSIS AND
## INTERCULTURAL COMMUNICATION

The applicability of network analysis to the study of intercultural communication was noted only recently. Kim (1986) attempted to demonstrate the potential of relating personal network variables to "outgroup communication competence," namely, the overall capacities to communicate with individuals of social cultural membership different from one's own. In fact, several studies revealed the impact of cultural, ethnic, and racial divisions on the flow of communication in social networks. The most frequently used technique was the Small World method. This method, devised by Milgram and his collaborators (Korte & Milgram, 1970; Milgram, 1967; Travers & Milgram, 1969), is a procedure aimed at tracing acquaintance networks. In brief, it consists of asking respondents to forward a message to an assigned target person via any acquaintances who the respondents think are likely to know the target person. By keeping track of the persons who send and receive the message until it either successfully reaches the target or terminates, it becomes possible to map the communication flow and to characterize the intermediaries. This method is useful to study cross-cultural networks by selecting a target person from a different social group than the starting persons (for a review, see Bernard & Killworth, 1978). Thus Korte and Milgram (1970) studied cross-racial communication networks: They used White and Black target persons and compared the different chains used by White starting persons to forward a message. They concluded that "the importance of target race in determining the success of acquaintance chains points to the need for recognizing the role of social structure in our model of the small world. Friendship networks are not laid down in a random fashion, but reflect the social cleavages and divisions that characterize our society" (Korte and Milgram, 1970, p. 108). Indeed, several small world studies have documented the effect of various social divisions on communication networks (e.g., Bochner et al., 1976; Lin et al., 1978; Lundberg, 1975). This procedure was also applied to the study of cross-ethnic networks. In a study of acquaintance networks in Israel, Weimann (1983) used the small world method to focus on interethnic networks. The findings point to a clear tendency toward selective activation of personal networks according to ethnic similarity. The ethnic composition of the network was found to affect both rate of completion and length of chain. "Homogeneous" chains were more successful and shorter than chains involving crossing ethnic boundaries. Most of the participants preferred to forward the message to a person from the same ethnic group as their own, and when crossing the ethnic boundary is required (different ethnicities of starting and target persons), it was delayed by the participants to the last steps of the chain until it was unavoidable. The study examined the links and individuals activated, revealing the "gatekeepers," the individuals who serve as bridges of contact between the ethnic groups and the links used to serve the crossing.

These studies illustrate the applicability of various levels of network analysis to the study of intercultural communication. They highlight the relationships between attributes of individuals, links, groups, and social systems to the form and efficiency of intercultural communication. A large body of research exists that indicates the existence and significance of these relationships (e.g., Blau & Schwartz, 1984; Gudykunst & Kim, 1984; Sarbaugh, 1979; Simard, 1981) and demonstrates the viability of network analysis to the study of intercultural communication. This potential is somewhat hindered, however, by the current state of network analysis. The study of networks and communication so far has not reached the stage of providing the analytical bridge between micro and macro levels of analysis. This is, partly, the result of two factors that should serve as challenges for future research in this area: the need for cross-level network analysis, and the theory gap in network analysis.

## FUTURE CHALLENGES

### Challenge 1: Cross-Level Analysis

Most of the studies that applied network analysis to determine the flow of communication—between individuals, groups, cultures, or societies— have used network measures based on one level. That is, they focused on characteristics of individuals, or of links, or of cliques, or of the entire network as the independent variable. This differentiation, however, is not only artificial but also wrong. In reality, people act as individuals linked to each other by various links, creating various grouping and network structures. Only by applying a cross-level analysis can one reflect the complex combination of factors that, together, form the social environment called a social network. Only by cross-level analysis may a host of difficulties and problems inherent in data that is dependent on one-level analysis be surmounted, and a true presentation of the functioning of a social network be achieved.

Figure 8.1 presents a suggested model for an integrated cross-level network analysis. It attempts to illustrate how a cross-level analysis can be applied to studying the flow of communication and its effects.

It should be noted that the various facets and their categories are used only to illustrate the model and not to represent the full volume of relevant aspects. (Thus, for example, the type of information item or time—long term, short term—could easily be integrated as additional facets.) The scheme, consisting of nine facets taken together, yields 136,080 possible

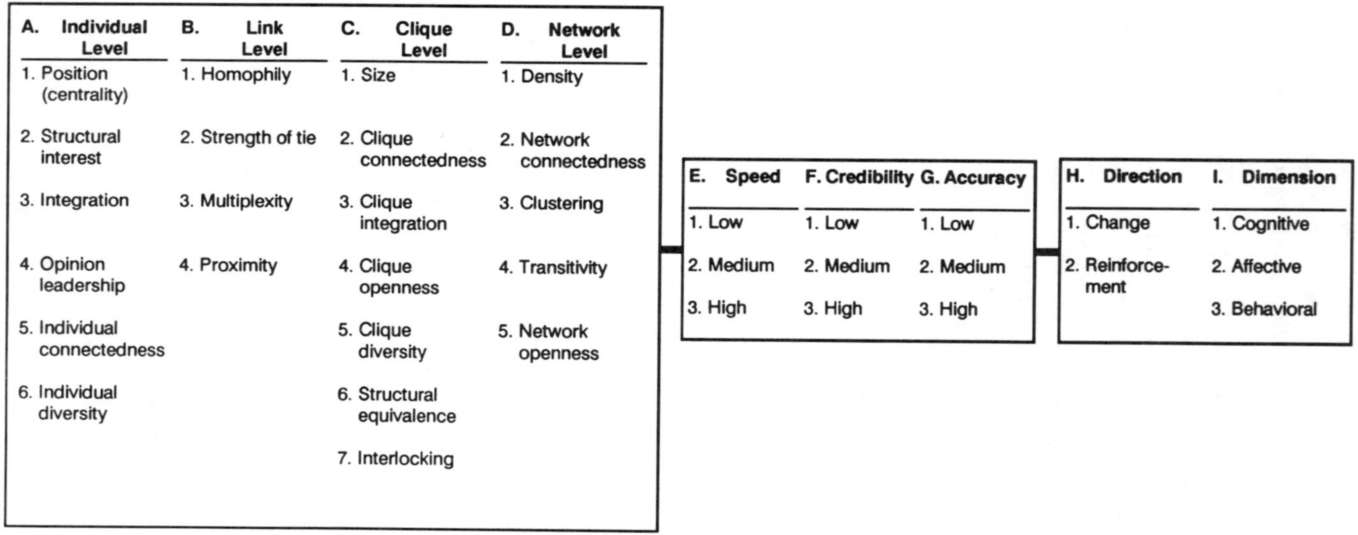

| A. Individual Level | B. Link Level | C. Clique Level | D. Network Level |
|---|---|---|---|
| 1. Position (centrality) | 1. Homophily | 1. Size | 1. Density |
| 2. Structural interest | 2. Strength of tie | 2. Clique connectedness | 2. Network connectedness |
| 3. Integration | 3. Multiplexity | 3. Clique integration | 3. Clustering |
| 4. Opinion leadership | 4. Proximity | 4. Clique openness | 4. Transitivity |
| 5. Individual connectedness | | 5. Clique diversity | 5. Network openness |
| 6. Individual diversity | | 6. Structural equivalence | |
| | | 7. Interlocking | |

| E. Speed | F. Credibility | G. Accuracy |
|---|---|---|
| 1. Low | 1. Low | 1. Low |
| 2. Medium | 2. Medium | 2. Medium |
| 3. High | 3. High | 3. High |

| H. Direction | I. Dimension |
|---|---|
| 1. Change | 1. Cognitive |
| 2. Reinforcement | 2. Affective |
| | 3. Behavioral |

**FIGURE 8.1.** A Model for Cross-Level Communication Network Analysis

combinations. Each of these combinations can be coded by the facets' codes. Thus, for example, what is the combined effect of a central position with multiplex ties in small cliques and a dense network (A1, B3, C1, D1) on the speed, credibility, and accuracy of the communicative act? Moreover, assuming that this flow was, for example, fast, credible, and accurate, what is the effect of this combination (A1, B1, C1, D1, E3, F3, G3) on change or reinforcement (H1 or H2) of knowledge, opinion, or perception (I1); emotion and sentiments (I2); and behavior (I3)?

Each of the 136,080 combinations can serve as a hypothesis, while controlling for some of the facets may reveal the net impact of a specific factor as a specific combination of factors. Thus, for example, a comparison between the communicative functioning of individuals with the same level of integration, in the same network, and in the same clique, yet who differ in the type of tie they activate to communicate (for example, they may differ in the link's strength or multiplexity), may reveal the net impact of the tie strength or multiplexity on the efficiency of the flow or its effects.

The model presented here does not call for studying all possible permutations of the facets and their categories. Rather, it is a systematic mapping of a cross-level network analysis and as such it should serve as an analytical framework to guide future research.

It should be clear that many of the combinations are in fact redundant. This is due to intercorrelations between various network characteristics (e.g., strength of tie and transitivity as demonstrated by Weimann 1982, 1983) and the futility of some combinations.

The choice and formulation of hypotheses for a cross-level network analysis must be based on theoretical considerations. This leads us to the second challenge for future network studies: the bridging of the "theory gap."

### Challenge 2: The Theory Gap

More than a decade ago, one of the participants in the 1975 Symposium on Social Networks dared to challenge the conference with what he called "one nagging question":

> Where is the theoretical underpinning for all these models and analyses? I will argue here, that most network models are constructed in a theoretical vacuum, each on its own items, and without reference to a broader or common framework. Despite continuing progress, therefore, the point of diminishing returns is approaching, and will rapidly overtake us, unless we pay more attention to what I call the "theory-gap" in network studies. (Granovetter, 1979, p. 501)

Despite Granovetter's intriguing argument, not much progress has been achieved in establishing a theoretical framework for network analysis. No wonder that ten years after Granovetter pointed to the "Theory Gap" the same argument was presented: "The problem does not lie with the variety of conceptual and empirical usages. . . . Rather, the problem lies in not having a general framework within which the techniques can be classified and terminological confusion resolved" (Paulson, 1985, p. 106). The lack of such a theoretical framework has led to considerable semantic confusion. Paulson (1985) demonstrates that there are numerous, and often conflicting, operational definitions of key variables in network analysis. One of the examples for this definitional confusion is the variety of conceptualizations of "network," which includes clusters of similar elements (Pennings, 1980); clusters of interacting elements (Rogers, 1979); clusters of similar elements expected to interact (Levine & Roy, 1979); clusters of elements interacting in similar ways (White et al., 1976), and no a priori conceptualization being given at all (Rapoport, 1979). The same confusion is illustrated by Paulson with regard to "distance" and its definition. The absence of a theoretical basis yields not only semantic confusion but also methodological problems. Granovetter (1979) used the principles of network sampling and random-baseline models to illustrate their underlying assumptions: "My point is simply that conditioning procedure expressed an implicit theoretical prejudice that ought to be made explicit and ought to be considered as part of the theoretical backdrop of this model" (Granovetter, 1979, p. 507).

The theory gap in network analysis led several scholars to regard the formulation of a theoretical framework as a precondition for any significant development in this field. Thus the current state of network analysis may be regarded as a "way station" to more comprehensive theoretical development (Wellman, 1983). In this "way station" most of the studies proceed on an ad hoc basis. In fact, Mitchell (1974), after having reviewed the literature, notes that "there is no writer among those using social network theory to analyze field data who does postulate a formal network theory." Mitchell's criticism is valid to this very day. The theory gap is still present and serves as a challenge for future research. Some attempts have been made to suggest a basis for a network theory. Pouche (1979), for example, suggested two basic elements of such a theory: typology of networks and network constraints; considering the aim of the relationships, three different sets of networks can be distinguished— sentiment networks, interest networks, and power networks. These types or their intermixtures, with their distinct action logics, are suggested as basic elements for constituting a more general framework.

An alternative way of facing the theory gap is by trying to apply sociological, psychological, or political theory to network analysis. A successful attempt to carry out such an application is the way "balance theory," originating from social psychology, was applied to network analysis. The potential of this theory was demonstrated by several studies that based their predictions on the guiding assumptions of the balance theory. Moreover, such predictions have yielded empirically validated notions on the individual level, the link level, the clique level, and the network level. The balance theory provided network analysts with a theoretical framework, a working definition, methodological tools, statistical measures, and, finally, a conceptual tradition that enables comparisons of findings and their generalizations.

This is not to suggest that the theory gap is to be bridged by one, leading theory. The possibility that competing theories can be tested and compared by an empirical examination of their predictions appears to be more realistic and promising. The answers to the challenges facing future network analysis, namely, the use of cross-dimensional analysis and the bridging of the "theory gap," however, will determine the applicability of network analysis and its potential for the study of various social phenomena including intercultural communication.

## REFERENCES

Alba, R. D., & Kadushin, C. (1976). The introduction of social circles: A new measure of social proximity in networks. *Sociological Methods and Research, 5,* 77-102.

Barnes, J. A. (1979). Network analysis. In P. Holland & S. Leinhardt (Eds.), *Perspectives on social network research* (pp. 403-423). New York: Academic Press.

Bernard, R. H., & Killworth, P. D. (1978). A review of the small world literature. *Connections, 2,* 15-24.

Bochner, S., Bucker, E. A., & McLeod, B. M. (1976). Communication patterns in an international student dormitory: A modification of the small world method. *Journal of Applied Social Psychology, 6,* 275-290.

Blau, P., & Schwartz, J. (1984). *Cross-cutting social circles.* New York: Academic Press.

Boissevain, J. (1974). *Friends of friends: Networks, manipulators and coalitions.* New York: St. Martin's.

Burstein, P. (1976). Social networks and voting: Some Israeli data. *Social Forces, 54,* 833-847.

Burt, R. S. (1968). Innovation as a structural interest: Rethinking the impact of network position on innovation adoption. *Social Networks, 2,* 327-355.

Burt, R. S. (1976). Positions in networks. *Social Forces, 55,* 93-122.

Coleman, J., Katz, E., & Menzel, H. (1966). *Medical innovation: A diffusion study.* New York: Bobbs-Merrill.

Davis, J. A. (1963). Structural balance, mechanical solidarity and interpersonal relation. *American Journal of Sociology, 62,* 444-462.

Davis, J. A. (1963). Clustering and hierarchy in interpersonal relations: testing two graph theoretical models on 742 sociomatrices. *American Sociological Review, 35,* 843-851.

Fennema, M., & Schijf, H. (1979). Analyzing interlocking directorates: Theory and methods. *Social Networks, 1,* 297-332.

Freeman, L. C. (1979). Centrality in social networks: Conceptual clarification. *Social Networks, 1*, 215-239.

Gluckman, M. (1967). *The judicial process among the Barotse of Northern Rhodesia.* Manchester: Manchester University Press.

Granovetter, M. S. (1973). The strength of weak ties. *American Journal of Sociology, 78,* 1360-1380.

Granovetter, M. S. (1974). *Getting a job: A study of contacts and careers.* Cambridge, MA: Harvard University Press.

Granovetter, M. S. (1979). The theory gap in social network analysis. In P. Holland & S. Leinhardt (Eds.), *Perspectives on social network research.* New York: Academic Press.

Granovetter, M. S. (1983). The strength of weak ties: A network theory revisited. In R. Collins (Ed.), *Sociological theory* (pp. 201-233). San Francisco: Jossey-Bass.

Gudykunst, W. B., & Kim, Y. Y. (1984). *Communicating with strangers.* Reading, MA: Addison-Wesley.

Heider, F. (1958). *The Psychology of Interpersonal Relations.* New York: Wiley.

Holland, P. and Leinhardt, S. (1970). A method for detecting structure in sociometric data. *American Journal of Sociology, 76,* 492-513.

Holland, P. and Leinhardt, S. (1971). Transitivity in structural models of small groups. *Comparative Group Studies, 2,* 107-124.

Holland, P. and Leinhardt, S. (1972). Some evidence on the transitivity of positive interpersonal sentiment. *American Journal of Sociology, 77,* 1205-1209.

Holland, P., & Leinhardt, S. (1977). Transitivity in structural models of small groups. In S. Leinhardt (Ed.), *Social networks* (pp. 49-66). New York: Academic Press.

Homans, G. C. (1950). *The Human Group.* New York: Haracourt, Brace and World.

Katz, E., & Lazarsfeld, P. (1955). *Personal influence.* New York: Free Press.

Kim, Y. Y. (1986). Understanding the social context of intergroup communication: A personal network approach. In W. B. Gudykunst (Ed.), *Intergroup communication* (pp. 86-95). Baltimore: Edward Arnold.

Korte, C., & Milgram, S. (1970). Acquaintance networks between racial groups: Application of the small world method. *Journal of Personality and Social Psychology, 15,* 101-108.

Laumann, E. O. (1973). *The bonds of pluralism: The form and substance of urban social networks.* New York: John Wiley.

Laumann, E. O. (1979). Network analysis in large social systems: Some theoretical and methodological problems. In. P. Holland & S. Leinhardt (Eds.), *Perspectives on social network research* (pp. 379-402). New York: Academic Press.

Lazarsfeld, P. et al. (1948). *The people's choice.* New York: Duell, Sloan and Pearce.

Leavitt, H. (1951). Some effects of communication patterns on group performances. *Journal of Abnormal Social Psychology, 46,* 38-50.

Lee, N. H. (1969). *The search for an abortionist.* Chicago: University of Chicago Press.

Levine, J., & Roy, W. (1979). A study of interlocking directorates. In P Holland & S. Leinhardt (Eds.), *Perspectives on social network research.* New York: Academic Press.

Lin, N., Dayton, P., & Greenwald, P. (1978). Analyzing the industrial use of relations in the context of social structure. *Sociological Methods and Research, 7,* 149-166.

Lundberg, C. C. (1975). Patterns of acquaintanceship in society and complex organizations: A comparative study of the small world problem. *Pacific Sociological Review, 18,* 206-222.

Mears, P. (1974). Structuring communication in working groups. *Journal of Communication, 24*(1), 71-79.

Milgram, S. (1967, May). The small world problem. *Psychology Today,* pp. 61-67.

Mitchell, J. C. (Ed.). (1969). *Social networks in urban situations.* Manchester: Manchester University Press.

Mitchell, J. C. (1974). Social networks. *Annual Review of Anthropology, 3,* 279-299.

Mitchell, J. C. (1979). Networks, algorithms and analysis. In P. Holland & S. Leinhardt (Eds.), *Perspectives on social network research* (pp. 425-451). New York: Academic Press.

Moreno, J. L. (1934). *Who Shall Surive*. Washington, D.C.: Nervous and Mental Disease Publishing.

Newcomb, T. (1961). *The Acquaintance Process*. New York: Holt, Rinehart and Winston.

Paulson, S. K. (1985). A paradigm for the analysis of interorganizational networks. *Social Networks, 7*, 105-126.

Pennings, J. M. (1980) *Interlocking directorates*. San Francisco: Jossey-Bass.

Pool, I. de Sola, & Kochen, M. (1978). Contacts and influence. *Social Networks, 1*, 5-51.

Pouche, W. W. (1979). Network constraints on social action: Preliminaries for a network theory. *Social Networks, 2*, 181-190.

Rapoport, A. (1979). Some problems relating to randomly constructed biased networks. In P. Holland & S. Leinhardt (Eds.), *Perspectives on social network research*. New York: Academic Press.

Rogers, E. (1979). Network analysis of the diffusion of innovations. In P. Holland & S. Leinhardt (Eds.), *Perspectives on social network research*. New York: Academic Press.

Rogers, E., & Kincaid, D. L. (1981). *Communication networks*. New York: Free Press.

Rogers, E., & Shoemaker, F. (1971). *Communication of innovations: A cross-cultural approach*. New York: Free Press.

Sarbaugh, L. E. (1979) *Intercultural communication*. Rochelle Park, NJ: Hayden.

Simard, L. M. (1981). Cross-cultural interaction: Potential invisible barriers. *Journal of Social Psychology, 113*, 171-192.

Travers, J., & Milgram, S. (1969). An experimental study of the small world problems. *Sociometry, 32*, 425-443.

Weimann, G. (1982). On the importance of marginality: One more step into the two-step flow of communication. *American Sociological Review, 47*, 764-773.

Weimann, G. (1983a). The not-so-small world: Ethnicity and acquaintance networks in Israel. *Social Networks, 5*, 289-302.

Weimann, G. (1983b). The strength of weak conversational ties in the flow of information and influence. *Social Networks, 5*, 245-267.

Wellman, B. (1983). Network analysis: Some basic principles. In R. Collins (Ed.), *Sociological theory*. San Francisco: Jossey-Bass.

White, H., Boorman, S., & Brieger, R. (1976). Social structure from multiple networks. *American Journal of Sociology, 81*, 730-780.

Wolfe, A. W. (1978). The rise of network thinking in anthropology. *Social Networks, 1*, 53-64.

# 9 Social Cognition and Intergroup Communication

**William B. Gudykunst**
**Lauren I. Gumbs**

Social cognition refers to the ways in which knowledge about people is acquired and processed (Forgas, 1983) or "how people think about people" (Wegner & Vallacher, 1977, p. viii). Social cognitive processes play an important role in intercultural communication. Categorizing others as members of an ingroup (e.g., from the same culture) or an outgroup (e.g., from another culture), for example, determines, at least in part, whether an encounter is viewed as intracultural or intercultural. Social categorization influences which social schemata, including self-schemata (i.e., the self-concept, which includes cultural/ethnic identity) and role schemata (the content of which is composed of stereotypes), are salient. The way others are categorized and the social schemata that are activated, in turn, affect attributional processes (including uncertainty reduction, a communication-based attributional process).

There is extensive research and theorizing on social cognitive processes in intergroup interactions. There is, however, very little research on social cognition that focuses specifically on intercultural communication. The research on intergroup behavior, nevertheless, is applicable directly to intercultural communication because intercultural communication is a special case of intergroup communication (e.g., the case where group membership is based upon culture; see Gudykunst & Lim, 1986, for a complete rationale for this position). Our analysis, therefore, focuses upon theory and research on social cognitive processes in intergroup encounters. This position is consistent with at least two recent theories developed to explain intercultural communication: Gudykunst's (1988) theory, which focuses on uncertainty and anxiety; and Gallois, Franklyn-

AUTHORS' NOTE: Stella Ting-Toomey provided valuable comments and suggestions on an earlier version of the chapter.

Stokes, Giles, and Coupland's (1988) theory, which focuses on communication accommodation (see Gudykunst & Nishida's chapter in this volume for summaries of these and alternative theories).

## SOCIAL COGNITIVE PROCESSES IN INTERGROUP ENCOUNTERS

Group memberships play an important role in shaping social behavior (Turner, 1987). Two or more people who perceive themselves as members of the same social category constitute a social group (Turner, 1982). Social group membership is based upon, but not limited to, culture, race, gender, minority or majority status, language or dialect spoken, and belonging to stable or changing societies (Triandis, 1986). The major determinant of behavior in intergroup interaction is the interactants' group memberships (Hewstone, 1985; Sherif, 1966; Triandis, 1986). In an intergroup encounter, individuals interact based on a higher level of abstraction and inclusiveness than when they interact as distinct individuals.

Both interpersonal and intergroup factors are relevant in every encounter between individuals (Gudykunst & Lim, 1986). Interpersonal factors may predominate in some encounters (e.g., communication between two lovers), but intergroup factors are still relevant. Similarly, intergroup factors predominate in some encounters (e.g., the first meeting between members of different racial groups); nevertheless, interpersonal factors also affect the interaction. Our focus is on those encounters where the intergroup factors predominate (i.e., intergroup factors are high in salience). While we do not discuss the interpersonal factors (e.g., interpersonal attraction, intimacy of relationships) that influence intergroup communication at length (see Ting-Toomey's chapter in this volume for a discussion of these factors), they ultimately must be included in theories that are developed.

### Social Categorization

The fundamental social cognitive process operative in intergroup interaction is social categorization. Social categorization, according to Tajfel (1978, p. 61), is "the ordering of the social environment in terms of groupings of persons in a manner which makes sense to the individual." This process is influenced by values, culture, and social representations (Tajfel & Forgas, 1981). Tajfel and Forgas (1981) point out that once categories are established, they have a "biasing and filtering effect" on people's perceptions. People tend to be predisposed toward confirming their beliefs about the social world.

There are several consequences of the social categorization process for intergroup communication. Social categorization results in a positive bias toward the ingroup and a negative bias toward outgroups (Doise & Sinclair, 1973). Ingroup bias, according to Brewer (1979), is based on the perception of the ingroup as better than the outgroup, although the outgroup is not necessarily devalued. Ingroup bias occurs when negative interpersonal attraction is associated with category membership (Turner, Shaver, & Hogg, 1983). It occurs even when category membership is arbitrary or when a member of the outgroup is a close personal friend (Vaughan, Tajfel, & Williams, 1981). Ingroup bias is reduced when membership in social groups is "crossed," that is, situations where others are members of an outgroup on one criterion and members of an ingroup on another criterion (Deschamps & Doise, 1978).

Social categorization reduces perceived within-group variability and exaggerates perceived between-groups variability (Fiske & Taylor, 1984; Park & Rothbart, 1982). Individuals, therefore, tend to make more intracategory errors than intercategory errors in the encoding and retrieval processes (Taylor, 1981). Individuals may, for example, confuse Mexicans with one another, but they are less likely to confuse Mexicans with Anglos. Further, what is remembered about a person is influenced by the category into which he or she is placed (Rothbart, Fulero, Jensen, Howard, & Birrell, 1978). To illustrate, a White may not remember which particular traits apply to a "typical" individual Black, but will assume that all traits of the category "Black" are relevant to the individual involved. In addition, expectations about individuals are formed based on knowledge of the category into which an individual is placed, and individuals tend to behave in a manner that is consistent with their expectations (Detweiler, 1986). Word, Zanna, and Cooper's (1974) research supports this conclusion. They found that Whites interacting with Blacks in an interview setting perform nonverbal behaviors consistent with negative expectations of Blacks and Blacks reciprocate these behaviors, thus confirming Whites' negative expectations.

Before proceeding, it is important to point out that there are individual differences in the categorization process. One basis for individual differences is category width (Detweiler, 1986). Category width refers to "the range of instances included in a cognitive category" (Pettigrew, 1982, p. 200). Narrow categorizers tend to place discrepant stimuli in different categories, while wide categorizers tend to place discrepant stimuli in the same category (Pettigrew, 1982). Pettigrew (1982) contends that broad categorizers have expansive views of similarity and perform better on tasks that require holistic strategies, while narrow categorizers have rigid definitions of reality and are successful on tasks that require an emphasis on detail or analytic processing. In intergroup communication, narrow categorizers tend to make more negative attributions about outgroup members' behavior than do wide categorizers (Detweiler, 1980). Other personality factors such as self-monitoring (Snyder, 1974) and public/ private self-consciousness (Fenigstein, Scheier, & Buss, 1975) may also affect self- and other-categorization.

## Social Schemata

Social categorization affects the social schemata individuals apply in a particular intergroup encounter; it places a person, object, or event as a member of a particular category. Social schemata provide the content of the categories and delimit the effects of the categorization process on future perceptions, memory, and inferences (Fiske & Taylor, 1984).

Fiske and Taylor (1984) identify five types of schemata that are used in social cognition: person schemata, event schemata, content free or procedural schemata, self-schemata, and role schemata. Person schemata involve understanding the traits and goals that influence typical and specific individuals. Event schemata include shared knowledge of what generally takes place on particular occasions, such as holidays. Content free schemata operate as processing rules or procedures for specifying links among informational items, but they do not contain much informational content. Of particular importance to the present analysis are self-schemata and role schemata.

Self-schemata contain information about one's own psychological state that guides information processing about the self. The self can be viewed as a superordinate schema that contains "an abstract representation of past experience with personal data" (Rogers, Kuiper, & Kirker, 1977, p. 677). In essence, the self serves as a framework in which incoming stimuli interact with individuals' past experiences and are interpreted (Markus, 1977).

The self-concept is a relatively lasting, multifaceted cognitive structure that "mediates under appropriate circumstances between the social environment and social behavior" (Turner, 1982, p. 19). There are two components of the self-concept: social and personal identity. Social identity involves the individual's knowledge of belonging to a particular group along with the emotional and value significance of membership in that group (Tajfel, 1978). Social identity consists of such factors as sex, nationality, race, ethnicity, and political affiliation, to name only a few (Hofman, 1985). Personal identity consists of such factors as competence, bodily attributes, ways of relating to others, and psycholinguistic features (Turner, 1982). When social identity predominates over personal identity, intergroup communication occurs.

Social identity becomes salient and influences individuals' behavior when they compare their groups with other relevant social groups along various valued dimensions (Tajfel, 1978). When the ingroup is evaluated as superior to the relevant outgroup on a particular dimension, a positive social identity emerges. When an unsatisfactory comparison is made, individuals strive to regain a positive social identity (Tajfel & Turner, 1979). A positive social identity can be achieved either by leaving the existing group for one that provides a more positive identity, or by making the existing group more positively distinct by reinterpreting the comparison (e.g., focusing on other valued dimensions or by direct competition).

Giles and Johnson (1981) argue that language is a vital aspect of the identity of members of ethnic groups. This contention is supported by recent research. Leclézio, Louw-Potgieter, and Souchon (1986), for example, found that spoken language is the most salient feature of the social identity of Mauritian immigrants in South Africa. Drawing together research on ethnolinguistic vitality, group boundaries, interethnic comparisons, status, and social identity, Giles and Johnson (1981, p. 240) conclude:

> Individuals are more likely to define an encounter with an outgroup person in interethnic terms and to adopt strategies for positive linguistic distinctiveness when they:
>
> 1 identify with their ethnic group which considers language an important dimension of its identity;
>
> 2 make insecure interethnic comparisons (for example, are aware of cognitive alternatives to their own group's status position);
>
> 3 perceive their ingroup to have high ethnolinguistic vitality;
>
> 4 perceive their ingroup boundaries to be hard and closed;
>
> 5 identify strongly with few other social categories;
>
> 6 perceive little overlap with the outgroup person in terms of other social category memberships;
>
> 7 consider that the social identities derived from other social category memberships are relatively inadequate;
>
> 8 perceive their status with the ethnic group to be higher than their intragroup status in their other social category memberships. (italics omitted)

Giles and Johnson (1981) originally outlined the theory, but Beebe and Giles (1984) were the first to use the label ethnolinguistic identity theory. More recently, Giles and Johnson (1987) elaborated the theory and Gallois, Franklyn-Stokes, Giles, and Coupland (1988) linked the theory to communication accommodation. (Space does not permit a more elaborate discussion here. Gallois et al.'s theory is summarized in Gudykunst and Nishida's chapter in this volume.)

In addition to self-schemata, role schemata also affect intergroup communication. Role schemata are linked directly to social stereotypes. Because individuals cannot process all of the information they receive from other people, they structure their perceptions of and responses to others through the use of abstract social categories (Turner, 1982). Stereotypes are the contents of the categories that involve people (Hewstone & Giles, 1986). Stereotypes, therefore, can be viewed as "particular types of role schema that organize one's prior knowledge and expectations about other people who fall into certain socially defined categories" (Fiske & Taylor, 1984, p. 160). Role schemata can be based on such factors as age, race, sex, or occupation, to name only a few.

Social stereotyping occurs "when a set of traits, roles, emotions, abilities, and interests is attributed to individuals who have been categorized on the basis of easily identified characteristics" (Hewstone & Giles, 1986, p. 11). The individuals belonging to the stereotyped group are assumed to be similar to each other and different from other groups on a set of attributes. Social stereotypes and related dispositional attributes are activated in social situations where group membership is salient (Tajfel, 1981).

Social stereotypes are associated most closely with individuals who are perceived as typical of a particular group (Hewstone & Giles, 1986). Positive feelings toward an outgroup are generated from intergroup interaction involving a member of an outgroup who is perceived as typical of his or her group, rather than from interaction involving a member of an outgroup who is perceived as atypical (Hewstone & Brown, 1986). Further, Gudykunst and Hammer (in press) found that respondents' social identities are not a salient feature in intergroup interaction when an outgroup member is perceived as atypical. When the outgroup member is perceived as typical, in contrast, respondents' social identities are a salient feature in intergroup interaction. Prejudices and discrimination, however, can be maintained despite the interpersonal relationships that develop with members of an outgroup perceived as typical because outgroup friends and acquaintances generally are viewed as "exceptions to the rule" (Wilder, 1981).

Closely related to social stereotyping is the notion of the illusory correlation, a false inference about the degree of association between two events based on an overestimation of the co-occurrence of two infrequent events (Sonbanmatsu, Sherman, & Hamilton, 1987). Social behaviors that co-occur infrequently are more salient than social behaviors that co-occur frequently (Rothbart et al., 1978). In intergroup interaction between majority and minority groups, the majority group often views the interaction as infrequent and, therefore, highly salient. Additionally, undesirable events are highly salient because of the infrequency of their occurrence. The greater attention that a negative behavior performed by an outgroup member receives makes the co-occurrence more accessible than other events when judgments are prompted (Rothbart et al., 1978; Sonbanmatsu et al., 1987).

Rothbart and his associates (1978) argue that those instances in a class of events that are most available for retrieval serve as a cue for judging the frequency of their occurrence. Negative behaviors performed by minority group members, consequently, are likely to be overrepresented in memory and judgment. Drawing on memory for examples of group characteristics, individuals access individually accurate, but collectively unrepresentative action (Hamilton, 1981). This tendency to create unwarranted associations between highly salient groups and highly salient behavior can lead to unjustified negative stereotypes of outgroup members (Sonbanmatsu et al., 1987).

## Attributional Processes

Social categorization, social stereotyping, and social identity are linked closely to the social attribution process. In intergroup communication, social attributions are based not only on the individual characteristics of the target, but also on the groups or social categories to which the target and the observer belong (Hewstone & Jaspars, 1982).

Attributional processes involve linking an event to its causes. There are two primary types of attributions. Dispositional attributions are based on personality structures, attitudes, needs, beliefs, and social institutions, while situational attributions are based on the context in which an interaction occurs. Observers, however, do not give the "proper weight to situational factors in explaining others' behavior"; that is, they tend to underestimate its influence. In intergroup interactions, Pettigrew (1978) claims this is the "ultimate attribution error."

Jaspars and Hewstone (1982) suggest the tendency is to attribute positive behavior of ingroup members to dispositional factors and positive behavior from an outgroup member to situational factors. Negative behavior by ingroup members, in contrast, is attributed to situational factors, while outgroup members' negative behavior is attributed to dispositional factors. They go on to point out that in intergroup encounters unexpected behaviors from the perspective of one's own culture lead to person attribution and are linked to perceived group differences because social categorization is highly salient. Also, the same behavior that would be attributed to the situation because of its uniqueness in ingroup settings is perceived as person-centered in intergroup encounters. Even when interpersonal contact that contradicts negative stereotypes occurs, individuals may not change previous intergroup attributions or stereotypes. Jaspars and Hewstone (1982) argue that the discounting and augmenting principles provide plausible explanations for these differences in the attribution process. Both principles allow the attributer to view an individual as an "exception to the rule" and, therefore, any incongruities between the individuals and the stereotype can be explained.

Detweiler (1975) highlights the complexity of the attribution process in intergroup interactions when he notes that attributions are based on the assumption of relatively shared meanings. In a situation where individuals from different groups interact, the inference process is influenced by how culturally similar or dissimilar the participants are. As indicated earlier, Detweiler (1975, 1978) draws a distinction between broad and narrow categorizers, with narrow categorizers being less able to accept discrepant interpretations of behavior, seeing dissimilar actors as responsible and intending negative outcomes, and holding more rigidly to stereotypes. Broad categorizers are likely to hold open stereotypes that allow for multiple interpretations.

**Attributional Confidence**

There is extensive research on attributional confidence (the inverse of uncertainty reduction, a communication-based attributional process) in intergroup and intercultural encounters (for a definition and overview of uncertainty reduction, see Gudykunst & Nishida's chapter in this volume). One line of research focuses on the role of cultural similarity on uncertainty reduction. Gudykunst, Chua, and Gray's (1987) research, for example, revealed significant interaction effects between dissimilarities on all of Hofstede's (1980) dimensions of cultural variability (discussed later in this chapter) and stage of relationship development. The data suggest that, as relationships become more intimate, cultural dissimilarities have less effect on uncertainty reduction processes.

Gudykunst, Sodetani, and Sonoda's (1987) research supported extensions of ethnolinguistic identity theory (Beebe & Giles, 1984; Giles & Johnson, 1987) to interethnic uncertainty reduction processes. Recent work by Gudykunst and Hammer (in press) extended this earlier study. Gudykunst and Hammer's study demonstrated that social identity is related to uncertainty reduction processes in general and that it is related positively to interethnic attributional confidence. While inconsistent with the initial version of Giles's (e.g., Giles & Byrne, 1982) intergroup theory of second-language acquisition, this finding is consistent with a recent revision (Garrett, Giles, & Coupland, in press). Gudykunst and Hammer's finding also is compatible with Hall and Gudykunst's (1986) results, which indicated that the stronger the ingroup identification, the greater the perceived competence in the outgroup language. Moreover, Gudykunst and Hammer's results are consistent with Lambert, Mermigis, and Taylor's (1986) study, which suggests that the more secure and positive members of a group feel about their identity, the more tolerant they are of members of other groups. Gudykunst and Hammer's study further revealed that social identity influences uncertainty reduction processes only when members of the outgroup are perceived as typical of their group. When members of the outgroup are perceived as atypical, social identity does not affect uncertainty reduction processes in interethnic relationships. Finally, Gudykunst and Hammer also found that social identity influences uncertainty reduction only when ethnic status is activated.

Gudykunst, Nishida, and Chua's (1986) research revealed that members of high-intimacy intercultural dyads have greater attributional confidence than members of low-intimacy dyads based on the analysis of summation scores. These findings are consistent with Gudykunst, Sodetani, and Sonoda's (1987) study of Japanese-Caucasian interethnic communication in Hawaii. The results from the analysis of the dispersion scores revealed that high-intimacy dyads are more consistent in the degree of attributional confidence they have about each other than are members of low-intimacy dyads.

## CROSS-CULTURAL VARIABILITY

In the previous section we examined the major social cognitive processes affecting intergroup communication. The purpose of this section is to provide an overview of the cross-cultural variability in these processes (for a more complete review of cross-cultural variability in social cognitive processes, see Gudykunst & Ting-Toomey, 1988). We assume that for cross-cultural differences to be theoretically explained they must be linked to underlying dimensions of cultural variability (see Gudykunst & Ting-Toomey, 1988, for a full statement of this position). Foschi and Hales (1979, p. 246) succinctly outline the issues involved in treating cultural differences as a theoretical variable: "A culture X and a culture Y serve to operationally define a characteristic $a$, which the two cultures exhibit to different degrees." Hofstede (1980) isolated four dimensions of culture: individualism, uncertainty avoidance, masculinity, and power distance. Differences along these dimensions can be used to operationalize cultural variability in order to examine its effect on social cognitive processes.

Individualism-collectivism is the major dimension of cultural variability isolated by theorists across disciplines (e.g., see Hofstede, 1980; Triandis, 1986, for reviews). Individualistic cultures emphasize individual goals, while collectivistic cultures stress that group goals have precedence. Triandis (1986) sees the key distinction between individualistic and collectivistic cultures as the focus on the ingroup in collectivistic cultures. Collectivistic cultures emphasize goals, needs, and views of the ingroup over those of the individual; the social norms of the ingroup, rather than individual pleasure; shared ingroup beliefs, rather than unique individual beliefs; and a value on cooperation with ingroup members, rather than maximizing individual outcomes. Triandis also argues that the number of ingroups, the extent of influence for each ingroup, and the depth of the influence must be taken into consideration in the analysis of individualism-collectivism. He contends that the larger the number of ingroups, the narrower the influence and the less the depth of influence. Because individualistic cultures have many specific ingroups, they exert less influence on individuals than ingroups do in collectivistic cultures.

Uncertainty avoidance is "the extent to which people feel threatened by ambiguous situations and have created beliefs and institutions that try to avoid these" (Hofstede & Bond, 1984, p. 419). Members of high-uncertainty-avoidance cultures try to avoid uncertainty, but, at the same time, show their emotions more than members of low-uncertainty-avoidance cultures. Masculinity predominates in countries where the dominant values "are success, money, and things," while femininity predominates where "caring for others and quality of life" are predominant values (Hofstede & Bond, 1984, pp. 419-420). Cultures high in masculinity differentiate sex roles clearly, while cultures low in masculinity (high in femininity) tend to have fluid sex roles. Hofstede's (1980) final dimension is power distance, "the extent to which less powerful members of institutions and organizations accept that power is distributed unequally" (Hofstede & Bond, 1984, p. 418). Members of high-power-distance cultures see power as a basic part of life and believe there is latent conflict between powerful and powerless, while members of low-power-distance cultures think that power should be used only when it is legitimate and that there is latent harmony between the powerful and powerless.

## Social Categorization

Wetherell (1982) found that both Europeans (individualistic) and Polynesians (collectivistic) in New Zealand display bias in the minimal group situation, but Polynesians moderate their discrimination and show greater generosity to outgroup members (i.e., maximize joint profit) compared to Europeans. One interpretation of this study is that members of collectivistic cultures moderate their discrimination toward outgroups more than members of individualistic cultures. Triandis (personal communication, February 4, 1987) disagrees with this conclusion. He suggests, in contrast, that there is no difference between individualistic and collectivistic cultures in the way they deal with outgroups. Rather, the strength of the distinction between ingroup and outgroup is different. The distinction between family and neighbors, for example, in collectivistic cultures is large, but it is small in individualistic cultures. He, therefore, suggests the alternative hypothesis that "there is more trust toward neighbors in individualistic than in collectivistic cultures" (p. 2).

The Wetherell (1982) findings, however, are compatible with Bond and Hewstone's (1986) research, which revealed that British high school students in Hong Kong endorse more intergroup differentiation than do Chinese students. Wetherell's results likewise appear to be consistent with Triandis, Vassiliou, and Nassiakou's (1968) study of role perception in ingroups and outgroups in Greece and the United States, as well as Feldman's (1968) field study in Paris, Boston, and Athens. Feldman found that outgroup members were "treated better" in Athens (the most collectivistic) than in Boston and Paris (both individualistic). Feldman's results, however, may be unique to Greece, where foreigners and guests are perceived as potential members of the ingroup. Strangers in other collectivistic cultures generally are not viewed as potential members of the ingroup (Triandis, 1986). Bond, Hewstone, Wan, and Chiu's (1985) study further suggests that group-serving attributions are maintained in the presence of an audience in individualistic cultures, but not in collectivistic cultures. They argue that this is due to collectivistic socialization for maintaining harmony by suppressing open conflict compared to individualistic socialization for developing harmony by resolving conflict openly in public.

### Social/Ethnolinguistic Identity

While there is little, if any, research theoretically linking culture and social or ethnolinguistic identity, there are several studies that have been conducted in cultures other than where the theories originated. Majeed and Ghosh (1982), for example, examined social identity in three ethnic groups in India discovering differential evaluations of self, ingroup, and outgroups in High Caste Hindus, Muslims, and Scheduled Castes. Their research also indicated that the more common attributes shared, the less differentiation between ingroups and outgroups. Ghosh and Huq (1985) found similar results for Hindu and Muslim evaluations of self and ingroup in India and Bangladesh. Brewer and Campbell's (1976) study of ingroup-outgroup evaluations in Africa and Peabody's (1985) research in Europe support these findings. Bond and Hewstone (1986) found that British high school students in Hong Kong perceived social identity and intergroup differentiation to be more important than Chinese high school students. The British students also perceived group membership to be more important, and had a more positive image of the ingroup, than the Chinese.

Closely related to work on social identity theory is research on ethnolinguistic identity, in general, and ethnolinguistic vitality, in particular. Giles,

Bourhis, and Taylor (1977) argued that ethnolinguistic vitality influences the degree to which individuals will act as members of a group in intergroup situations. Several studies comparing different ethnic groups' perceptions of ethnolinguistic vitality within cultures have been conducted (e.g., Bourhis & Sachdev, 1984; Giles, Rosenthal, & Young, 1985; Young, Pierson, & Giles, in press). Bourhis and Sachdev (1984), for example, examined Italian and English Canadians in both majority and equal situations. They found that both groups had more realistic perceptions in the majority than the equal setting. English Canadians, however, were more biased against the Italian language in the equal setting than in the minority-majority setting.

Gudykunst (in press) examined cross-cultural variability in the ethnolinguistic identity of sojourners in the United States. This "pilot" study isolated nine hypotheses for future research; that is, members of high-uncertainty-avoidance cultures make less secure intergroup comparisons than members of low-uncertainty-avoidance cultures. The hypotheses specify potential relationships between dimensions of cultural variability and dimensions of ethnolinguistic identity isolated by Giles and Johnson (1981). Gudykunst points out, however, that the dimensions of cultural variability may interact to influence ethnolinguistic identity. Future research may reveal, for example, that individualism and masculinity interact to influence ingroup identification.

## Attributional Processes

Cultural variations are among the factors that influence social attributions. Gudykunst and Ting-Toomey (1988) maintain that there are differences between individualistic cultures (e.g., the United States) and collectivistic cultures (e.g., Japan) in the selection of attributes to explain the behavior of outgroup members. Miller (1984) found that individuals in the United States focus on dispositional factors, particularly personality traits, in making attributions of others' behavior, while individuals in India (collectivistic) rely on contextual factors. Bond and Forgas (1984) found that individuals from Hong Kong (collectivistic) rely on conscientiousness as one measure of someone's trustworthiness, while Australians (individualistic) rely on extroversion and emotional stability.

Cultural variations in the conception of the person also influence the attribution process. Miller (1984) contends that in many non-Western cultures (i.e., collectivistic cultures) the individual is conceptualized in a holistic manner. The individual is seen as involved in a relationship of interdependence with the environment; consequently, deviance is viewed as "resulting from some disequilibrium in the agent's relations with the environment" (p. 963). The non-Western view of the person, then, is one cause of the greater use of contextual factors in making attributions in non-Western cultures than in Western cultures. The Western view (i.e., individualistic cultures) of the person, in contrast, separates the individual from the environment. The individual is seen as autonomous and responsible for his or her behavior; consequently, deviance is seen as "arising from dispositional factors within the agent" (p. 963). The Western view of the self, then, is one cause of the greater use of dispositional factors in making attributions in Western cultures than in non-Western cultures.

Detweiler (1978) found that culture influences category width, which in turn influences attributional processes. Specifically, his research on Truck Islanders (collectivistic) and individuals from the United States (individualistic) indicated that Truck Islanders use narrower categories than individuals from the United States.

Ehrenhaus (1983, p. 263) extended earlier work on culture and attribution processes by linking attributions to variations in context. He argued that members of high-context cultures "are attributionally sensitive and predisposed toward situational features and situationally based explanations," and members of low-context cultures "are attributionally sensitive to and predisposed toward dispositional characteristics and dispositionally based explanations."

### Attributional Confidence

Cross-cultural differences in uncertainty reduction processes appear to be related to Hall's (1976) distinction between low- and high-context communication, as well as Hofstede's (1980) individualism-collectivism dimension. Gudykunst and Nishida (1984) found that culture influences attributional confidence. As would be predicted from Hall's (1976) theory, the Japanese respondents displayed a higher level of attributional confidence about strangers' behavior than respondents in the United States.

Gudykunst and Nishida (1986) argue that two types of attributional confidence can be isolated across cultures. These correspond to patterns of low- and high-context communication and, accordingly, are labeled low- and high-context attributional confidence. They expanded Clatterbuck's (1979) earlier work and developed a two-factor measure of attributional confidence. Each factor emphasizes sources of information that are more important in one type of culture. Members of low-context cultures *focus* on information that is specific to the individuals with whom they are communicating, which increases accuracy in direct forms of communication. Members of high-context cultures, in contrast, *focus* on information that increases accuracy in indirect, nonverbal forms of communication. Both types of cultures, however, attune to the information upon which the other culture focuses. Members of high-context cultures utilize information on individual's attitudes, values, feelings, and empathy to predict other's behavior, but this information appears to be secondary to the information used to reduce uncertainty due to the indirect forms of communication that predominate in the culture. Similarly, people in low-context cultures use information regarding whether or not the others understand their feelings, make allowances for them when they communicate, and the degree to which they understand the other person, but these sources of information appear to be secondary to those isolated by Clatterbuck (1979). This is consistent with Hall's (1976) contention that both low- and high-context communication are used in every culture, but one tends to predominate.

Finally, recent research by Gudykunst, Nishida, and Schmidt (1988) indicates that individualism-collectivism influences uncertainty reduction processes in ingroup and outgroup relationships. Specifically, this study found differences in ingroup and outgroup relationships (e.g., more attributional confidence in ingroup than in outgroup) in collectivistic cultures, but not in individualistic cultures. This finding is consistent with Triandis's (1986) conceptualization of ingroup and outgroup in individualistic and collectivistic cultures. Gudykunst, Nishida, and Schmidt also observed that there are differences in same- and opposite-sex relationships (e.g., more attributional confidence in same- than in opposite-sex relationships) in masculine cultures, but not in feminine cultures, consistent with predictions derived from Hofstede's (1980) theory of cultural variability.

## CONCLUSION

To summarize an argument, intergroup encounters activate different social cognitive processes than interpersonal encounters. Figure 9.1 presents an outline of our position. Any encounter begins with social categorization, but the outcome may be either that the social categories are perceived as salient to the encounter (in which case, mainly intergroup behavior will occur) or that the social categories are not perceived as salient to the encounter (in which case, mainly interpersonal behavior occurs). This contention is consistent with most recent analyses of interpersonal/intergroup behavior (see Hewstone & Brown, 1986, for a review). If the social categories are perceived as salient, social identity is the self-schemata that is activated and role-schemata (e.g., stereotyping) become relevant. Social identity and stereotypes, in turn, affect social (i.e., category-based) attributions and attributional confidence. When social categories are not perceived as salient, personal, not social, identity is the self-schemata activated. Role-schemata are not relevant when social categories are not salient. The major interpersonal processes that appear to operate in place of role-schemata involve the perceived similarity of beliefs and similarity-attraction interaction (Hewstone & Brown, 1986).

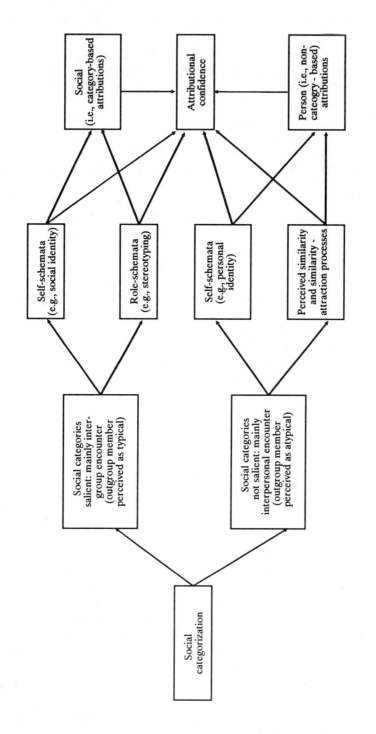

FIGURE 9.1. A Tentative Model of Social Cognitive Processes in Intergroup and Interpersonal Encounters

Personal identity and similarity influence person (i.e., non-category-based) attribution and attributional confidence.

While our "model" summarizes current research and theory, there is a need for additional theoretical development and future research on social cognitive processes in intergroup encounters in general and intercultural encounters in particular. Theoretically, an integration of the interpersonal and intergroup perspectives is needed. The model in Figure 9.1 suggests that the initial social categorization of others determines the degree to which an encounter is interpersonal or intergroup. It obviously is not this simple. How others are categorized can change during an encounter or between encounters due to new information (e.g., learning of other group memberships) or specific behaviors observed. Beginning attempts to address this issue are being made (e.g., see Ting-Toomey's chapter in this volume), but a concerted effort to articulate (Doise, 1986) the interpersonal and intergroup levels of analysis is necessary.

Most of the research on social cognitive processes in intergroup encounters is based on social (e.g., Tajfel, 1978; Turner, 1987) and/or ethnolinguistic (e.g., Giles & Johnson, 1987) identity theory. Beginning attempts have been made to integrate these theories with communication processes (e.g., Gallois et al., 1988; Gudykunst, 1988). The majority of research on social cognitive processes in intergroup relations, however, has been conducted outside of the field of communication. We contend that there is a need for communication research on social cognitive processes in intergroup encounters. The research that is conducted should, of course, be based on sound theory. As indicated earlier, several theories used to explain intercultural communication (see Gudykunst & Nishida's chapter in this volume for an overview of these theories) have incorporated social cognitive processes. Gudykunst's (1988) theory includes ethnolinguistic identity and expectations as independent variables and attributional confidence as one of the two major dependent variables (the other is anxiety). An alternative is Gallois et al.'s (1988) theory, which is based on ethnolinguistic identity and communication accommodation theories. Both of these theories offer numerous hypotheses for future research that focus on specific communication variables.

There are several specific issues that need to be addressed in future research and theorizing. Following Fiske and Taylor (1984), future research should focus on the goals that individuals have in intergroup interaction. Individuals' goals mediate the specific social cognitive processes that become salient; for example, if the goal is to become friends with a member of an outgroup, non-category-based processes take precedence over category-based processes. Studying the "plans" individuals develop to reach their goals in intergroup encounters also is a fertile area for future research (e.g., Berger's, 1988, work on interpersonal relationships can be extended to intergroup relationships). How do the plans individuals have for intergroup encounters differ from those used in interpersonal encounters? Does the sophistication of individuals' plans influence the levels of uncertainty or anxiety they experience in intergroup encounters?

In addition to taking goals and plans into consideration, future research must examine the effects of different types of group memberships on social cognitive processes in intergroup encounters. Which group memberships, for example, are salient in specific encounters? What factors affect the salience of specific group memberships? How does the social identity that is activated influence the plans individuals develop for intergroup encounters?

The relationship of social cognitive processes to affective processes in intergroup encounters also needs to be investigated. Initial attempts to incorporate affective (e.g., anxiety) components into social cognitive theories (e.g., uncertainty reduction theory; Gudykunst, 1988) have been made. No work, however, has been conducted on the effect of different social/ethnolinguistic identities on affective reactions such as intergroup anxiety. The influence of affective processes on how others are categorized and/or the social attributions made also needs to be investigated. Ulti- mately, the role of social cognitive and affective processes in inter- group/interpersonal encounters must be integrated into one coherent theo- retical framework.

Finally, the effect of cultural variability on social cognitive processes warrants further research. Most of the research that has been conducted to date is atheoretical. Recent work (e.g., Gudykunst & Ting-Toomey, 1988; Hofstede, 1980; Triandis, 1986), however, provides the foundation for theoretical predictions regarding cross-cultural differences in social cog- nitive processes. Future cross-cultural research should examine not only the effect of dimensions of cultural variability on specific social cognitive processes (e.g., social categorization, social attributions), it also should investigate how dimensions of cultural variability influence the relation- ships among the social cognitive processes that operate in intergroup/ interpersonal encounters. Is the effect of social identity on social attribu- tions, for example, the same in individualistic and collectivistic cultures? Does perceived similarity of beliefs lead to person attributions in both individualistic and collectivistic cultures? Addressing questions such as these is necessary for the cultural level of analysis to be articulated (Doise, 1986) with the intergroup and interpersonal levels of analysis. To articu- late the intrapersonal level of analysis, personality factors (e.g., locus of control, self-monitoring, category width) can be incorporated into future research (see Bond, 1983, for a statement of the rationale for including personality). Articulation of the four levels of analysis (intrapersonal, interpersonal, intergroup, cultural) vis-à-vis social cognitive and affective processes must occur for a comprehensive theory of communication to be developed.

## REFERENCES

Beebe, L. M., & Giles, H. (1984). Speech accommodation theories: A discussion in terms of second-language acquisition. *International Journal of the Sociology of Language, 46,* 5-32.

Berger, C. R. (1986). Social cognition in intergroup communication. In W. B. Gudykunst (Ed.), *Intergroup communication.* London: Edward Arnold.

Berger, C. R. (1988). Planning, affect, and social action generation. In L. Donohew, H. Sypher, & E. Higgins (Eds.), *Communication, social cognition, and affect.* Hillsdale, NJ: Lawrence Erlbaum.

Bond, M. (1983). A proposal for cross-cultural studies in attribution. In M. Hewstone (Ed.), *Attribution theory.* Oxford: Basil Blackwell.

Bond, M., & Forgas, J. (1984). Linking person perception to behavior intention across cultures: The role of cultural collectivism. *Journal of Cross-Cultural Psychology, 15,* 337-353.

Bond, M., & Hewstone, M. (1986). *Social identity theory and the perception of intergroup relations in Hong Kong.* Unpublished manuscript, Chinese University of Hong Kong.

Bond, M., Hewstone, M., Wan. K.-C., & Chiu, C.-K. (1985). Group-serving attributions across intergroup contexts: Cultural differences in the explanation of sex-typed behaviours. *European Journal of Social Psychology, 15,* 435-451.

Bourhis, R., & Sachdev, I. (1984). Subjective vitality perceptions and language attitudes: Some Canadian data. *Journal of Social Psychology, 3,* 97-126.

Brewer, M. (1979). In-group bias in the minimal group situation. *Psychological Bulletin, 56,* 307-324.

Brewer, M., & Campbell, D. (1976). *Ethnocentrism and intergroup attitudes.* New York: John Wiley.

Catrambone, R., & Markus, H. (1987). The role of self-schemas in going beyond the information given. *Social Cognition, 5,* 349-368.

Clatterbuck, G. (1979). Attributional confidence and uncertainty in initial interactions. *Human Communication Research, 5,* 147-157.

Deschamps, J.-C., & Doise, W. (1978). Crossed category memberships in intergroup relations. In H. Tajfel (Ed.), *Differentiation between social groups.* London: Academic Press.

Detweiler, R. (1975). On inferring the intentions of a person from another culture. *Journal of Personality, 43,* 591-611.

Detweiler, R. (1978). Culture, category width, and attributions. *Journal of Cross-Cultural Psychology, 9,* 259-284.

Detweiler, R. (1980). Intercultural interaction and the categorization process: A conceptual analysis and behavioral outcome. *International Journal of Intercultural Relations, 4,* 275-293.

Detweiler, R. (1986). Categorization, attribution, and intergroup communication. In W. Gudykunst (Ed.), *Intergroup communication.* London: Edward Arnold.

Doise, W. (1986). *Levels of explanation in social psychology.* Cambridge: Cambridge University Press.

Doise, W., & Sinclair, A. (1973). The categorization process in intergroup relations. *European Journal of Social Psychology, 3,* 145-157.

Ehrenhaus, P. (1983). Culture and the attribution process. In W. Gudykunst (Ed.), *Intercultural communication theory*. Beverly Hills, CA: Sage.

Feldman, R. E. (1968). Response to compatriot and foreigner who seek assistance. *Journal of Personality and Social Psychology, 10*, 202-214.

Fenigstein, A., Scheier, M., & Buss, A. (1975). Public and private self-consciousness: Assessment and theory. *Journal of Consulting and Clinical Psychology, 43*, 522-527.

Fiske, S., & Taylor, S. (1984). *Social cognition*. Reading, MA: Addison-Wesley.

Forgas, J. (1983). What is social about social cognition? *British Journal of Social Psychology, 22*, 129-144.

Foschi, M., & Hales, W. H. (1979). The theoretical role of cross-cultural comparisons in experimental social psychology. In. L. H. Eckensberger, W. J. Lonner, & Y. H. Poortinga (Eds.), *Cross-cultural contributions to psychology*. Lisse: Swets & Zeitlinger.

Gallois, C., Franklyn-Stokes, A., Giles, H., & Coupland, N. (1988). Communication accommodation in intercultural encounters. In Y. Y. Kim & W. B. Gudykunst (Eds.), *Theories in intercultural communication*. Newbury Park, CA: Sage.

Garrett, P., Giles, H., & Coupland, N. (in press). The contexts of language: Extending the intergroup model of second language. In S. Ting-Toomey & F. Korzenny (Eds.), *Language, communication, and culture*. Newbury Park, CA: Sage.

Ghosh, E., & Huq, M. (1985). A study of social identity in two ethnic groups in India and Bangladesh. *Journal of Multilingual and Multicultural Development, 6*, 239-251.

Giles, H., Bourhis, R., & Taylor, D. M. (1977). Towards a theory of language in ethnic group relations. In H. Giles (Ed.), *Language, ethnicity and intergroup relations*. London: Academic Press.

Giles, H., & Byrne, J. (1982). An intergroup approach to second language acquisition. *Journal of Multilingual and Multicultural Development, 3*, 17-40.

Giles, H., & Johnson, P. (1981). The role of language in ethnic group relations. In J. Turner & H. Giles (Eds.), *Intergroup behavior*. Chicago: University of Chicago Press.

Giles, H., & Johnson, P. (1987). Ethnolinguistic identity theory. *International Journal of the Sociology Language, 68*, 690-699.

Giles, H., Rosenthal, D., & Young, L. (1985). Perceived ethnolinguistic vitality: The Anglo- and Greek-Australian setting. *Journal of Multilingual and Multicultural Development, 6*, 253-269.

Gudykunst, W. B. (1988). Uncertainty and anxiety. In Y. Kim & W. Gudykunst (Eds.), *Theories in intercultural communication*. Newbury Park, CA: Sage.

Gudykunst, W. B. (in press). Cultural variability in ethnolinguistic identity. In S. Ting-Toomey & F. Korzenny (Eds.), *Language, communication, and culture*. Newbury Park, CA: Sage.

Gudykunst, W., Chua, E., & Gray, A. (1987). Cultural dissimilarities and uncertainty reduction processes. In M. McLaughlin (Ed.), *Communication yearbook* (Vol. 10). Newbury Park, CA: Sage.

Gudykunst, W. B., & Hammer, M. R. (in press). The influence of social identity and intimacy of interethnic relationships on uncertainty reduction processes. *Human Communication Research*.

Gudykunst, W. B., & Lim, T. S. (1986). A perspective for the study of intergroup communication. In W. Gudykunst (Ed.), *Intergroup communication*. London: Edward Arnold.

Gudykunst, W. B., & Nishida, T. (1984). Individual and cultural influences on uncertainty reduction. *Communication Monographs, 51*, 23-36.

Gudykunst, W. B., & Nishida, T. (1986). Attributional confidence in low- and high-context cultures. *Human Communication Research, 12*, 525-549.

Gudykunst, W. B., Nishida, T., & Chua, E. (1986). Uncertainty reduction in Japanese-North American dyads. *Communication Research Reports, 3*, 39-46.

Gudykunst, W. B., Nishida, T., & Schmidt, K. L. (1988). *The influence of cultural variability on uncertainty reduction in ingroup vs. outgroup and same- vs. opposite-sex relationships.* Paper presented at the International Communication Association Convention, New Orleans.

Gudykunst, W. B., Sodetani, L., & Sonoda, K. (1987). Uncertainty reduction in Japanese-American-Caucasian relationships in Hawaii. *Western Journal of Speech Communication, 51,* 256-278.

Gudykunst, W. B., & Ting-Toomey, S., with Chua, E. (1988). *Culture and interpersonal communication.* Newbury Park, CA: Sage.

Hall, B. J., & Gudykunst, W. B. (1986). The intergroup theory of second language ability. *Journal of Language and Social Psychology, 5,* 291-302.

Hall, E. T. (1976). *Beyond culture.* New York: Doubleday.

Hamilton, D. (1981). Stereotyping and intergroup behavior: Some thoughts on the cognitive approach. In D. Hamilton (Ed.), *Cognitive processes in stereotyping and intergroup behavior.* Hillsdale, NJ: Lawrence Erlbaum.

Hamilton, D., & Gifford, R. (1976). Illusory correlations in interpersonal perception. *Journal of Experimental Social Psychology, 12,* 392-407.

Hewstone, M. (1985). Social psychology and intergroup relations: Cross-cultural perspectives. *Journal of Multilingual and Multicultural Development, 6,* 209-215.

Hewstone, M., & Brown, R. (1986). Contact is not enough. In M. Hewstone & R. Brown (Eds.), *Contact and conflict in intergroup encounters.* Oxford: Basil Blackwell.

Hewstone, M., & Giles, H. (1986). Social groups and social stereotypes in intergroup communication. In W. Gudykunst (Ed.), *Intergroup communication.* London: Edward Arnold.

Hewstone, M., & Jaspars, J. (1982). Intergroup relations and attributional processes. In H. Tajfel (Ed.), *Social identity and intergroup relations.* London: Cambridge University Press.

Hofman, T. E. (1985). Arabs and Jews, Blacks and Whites: Identity and group relations. *Journal of Multilingual and Multicultural Development, 6,* 217-237.

Hofstede, G. (1980). *Cultures consequences.* Beverly Hills, CA: Sage.

Hofstede, G., & Bond, M. (1984). Hofstede's culture dimensions. *Journal of Cross-Cultural Psychology, 15,* 417-433.

Jaspars, J., & Hewstone, M. (1982). Cross-cultural interaction, social attribution, and intergroup relations. In S. Bochner (Ed.), *Cultures in contact.* Elmsford, NY: Pergamon.

Lambert, W. E., Mermigis, L., & Taylor, M. D. (1986). Greek Canadians' attitudes toward own group and other Canadian ethnic groups. *Canadian Journal of Behavioural Sciences, 18,* 35-51.

Leclézio, M., Louw-Potgieter, J., & Souchon, M. (1986). The social identity of Mauritian immigrants in South Africa. *Journal of Social Psychology, 126,* 61-69.

Lewicki, P., & Hill, T. (1987). Unconscious processes as explanations of behavior in cognitive, personality, and social psychology. *Personality and Social Psychology Bulletin, 13*(3), 355-362.

Majeed, A., & Ghosh, E. S. K. (1982). A study of social identity in three ethnic groups in India. *International Journal of Psychology, 17,* 455-463.

Markus, H. (1977). Self-schemata and processing information about the self. *Journal of Personality and Social Psychology,* 63-78.

Miller, J. G. (1984). Culture and the development of everyday social explanations. *Journal of Personality and Social Psychology, 46,* 961-978.

Park, B., & Rothbart, M. (1982). Perception of out-group homogeneity and levels of social categorization. *Journal of Personality and Social Psychology, 42,* 1051-1065.

Peabody, D. (1985). *National characteristics.* Cambridge: Cambridge University Press.

Pettigrew, T. (1978). Three issues in ethnicity. In J. Yinger & S. Cutler (Eds.), *Major social issues*. New York: Free Press.

Pettigrew, T. (1982). Cognitive style and social behavior: A review of category width. In L. Wheeler (Ed.), *Review of personality and social psychology* (Vol. 3). Beverly Hills, CA: Sage.

Rogers, T., Kuiper, N., & Kirker, W. (1977). Self-reference and the encoding of personal information. *Journal of Personality and Social Psychology, 35*(9), 677-688.

Rothbart, M., Fulero, S., Jensen, C., Howard, J., & Birrell, P. (1978). From individual to group perspectives. *Journal of Experimental Social Psychology, 14*, 237-255.

Sherif, M. (1966). *Group conflict and cooperation*. London: Routledge & Kegan Paul.

Snyder, M. (1974). Self-monitoring of expressive behavior. *Journal of Personality and Social Psychology, 30*, 526-537.

Sonbanmatsu, D., Sherman, S., & Hamilton, D. (1987). Illusory correlation in the perception of individuals and groups. *Social Cognition, 5*, 1-25.

Tajfel, H. (1978). Social categorization, social identity, and social comparison. In H. Tajfel (Ed.), *Differentiation between social groups*. London: Academic Press.

Tajfel, H. (1981). Social stereotypes and social groups. In J. Turner & H. Giles (Eds.), *Intergroup behavior*. Chicago: University of Chicago Press.

Tajfel, H. (Ed.). (1982). *Social identity and intergroup relations*. Cambridge: Cambridge University Press.

Tajfel, H., & Forgas, J. (1981). Social categorization: Cognitions, values, and groups. In J. Forgas (Ed.), *Social cognition*. New York: Academic Press.

Tajfel, H., & Turner, J. C. (1979). An integrative theory of intergroup conflict. In W. Austin & S. Worchel (Eds.), *The social psychology of intergroup relations*. Monterey, CA: Brooks/Cole.

Taylor, S. (1981). A categorization approach to stereotyping. In D. Hamilton (Ed.), *Cognitive processes in stereotyping and intergroup behavior*. Hillsdale, NJ: Lawrence Erlbaum.

Triandis, H. C. (1985). Collectivism vs. individualism. In C. Bagley & G. Verma (Eds.), *Personality, cognition, and values: Cross-cultural perspectives of childhood and adolescence*. London: Macmillan.

Triandis, H., Vassiliou, V., & Nassiakou, M. (1968). Three cross-cultural studies of subjective cultures. *Journal of Personality and Social Psychology, 8*(Monograph Supp. no. 4), 1-42.

Turner, J. (1982). Towards a cognitive redefinition of the social group. In H. Tajfel (Ed.), *Social identity and intergroup relations*. Cambridge: Cambridge University Press.

Turner, J. C. (1987). *Rediscovering the social group: A self-categorization theory*. London: Basil Blackwell.

Turner, J. C., Shaver, I., & Hogg, M. A. (1983). Social categorization, interpersonal attraction and group formation. *British Journal of Social Psychology, 22*, 227-239.

Vaughan, G. M., Tajfel, H., & Williams, J. (1981). Bias in reward allocation in an intergroup and an interpersonal context. *Social Psychology Quarterly, 44*, 37-42.

Wegner, D., & Vallacher, P. (1977). *Implicit psychology*. New York: Oxford University Press.

Wetherell, M. (1982). Cross-cultural studies of minimal groups. In H. Tajfel (Ed.), *Social identity and intergroup relations*. Cambridge: Cambridge University Press.

Wilder, D. (1981). Perceiving persons as a group. In D. Hamilton (Ed.), *Cognitive processes in stereotyping and intergroup behavior*. Hillsdale, NJ: Lawrence Erlbaum.

Word, C., Zanna, M., & Cooper, J. (1974). The nonverbal mediation of self-fulfilling prophecies in interracial interaction. *Journal of Experimental Social Psychology, 10*, 109-120.

Young, L., Pierson, H., & Giles, H. (in press). The effects of language and academic specialization on perceived group vitalities. *Linguistic Berichte*.

# 10 Emotions in Intercultural Communication

**David Matsumoto**
**Harald G. Wallbott**
**Klaus R. Scherer**

Emotions are not only markers of special episodes in subjective individual experience, they are also motivators and regulators of social interaction. Research on the emotions, especially in the cross-cultural realm, is becoming increasingly abundant. They are a particularly fascinating topic for intercultural study, because their antecedents, reactions, display, perception, and roles, in terms of both individual experience and social/motivational phenomena, can differ substantially across cultures.

Most studies to date have investigated the communication of emotion through facial expressions. But research on other aspects of emotion is also becoming popular. All of the research aims to elucidate cultural similarities and differences in the experience, expression, perception, and consequences of emotion, in the hopes of clarifying the nature and function of emotion in different cultures.

Below we review two major programs of cross-cultural research on emotions. The first is a continuation of a line of studies examining the expression and perception of facial expressions of emotion across cultures. The second represents recent attempts at investigating the subjective evaluation of the antecedents of and reactions to emotions across cultures. For both, we present a brief background of that line of research, review its most recent findings, and outline several issues we feel are most pertinent to future study. We conclude this chapter with a consideration of culture as a variable, and the types of meaningful dimensions that may differentiate among cultures. We hope this discussion will be useful to researchers and theoreticians alike.

## CROSS-CULTURAL STUDIES OF
## FACIAL EXPRESSIONS

### Background

For more than 100 years scientists argued about whether facial expressions are universal or specific to each culture. Until recently, the prevalent view in psychology was that facial expressions were culture-specific, learned differently across cultures, like language. Research from the past twenty years, however, has provided evidence for both universal *and* culture-specific aspects of facial expressions of emotion.

Three different types of cross-cultural studies have documented the universality of (at least) six different emotions (anger, disgust, fear, happiness, sadness, and surprise). In one type, members of one culture were asked to show how their face would look if they were the person in each of a number of different situations designed to elicit certain emotions (e.g. "you feel sad because your child died"—see Ekman & Friesen, 1971). Universality was demonstrated when observers in another culture did far better than chance in identifying which emotional contexts the expressions were intended to portray. This study had unusual import because the persons displaying the expressions were members of a visually isolated culture in New Guinea, and the observers were Americans who had had no previous exposure to New Guineans.

In a second type of experiment, the spontaneous facial expressions shown by Japanese and Americans while they watched stress-inducing (bodily mutilation) and neutral films (nature scenes) were measured (Ekman, 1972). Universality was demonstrated when virtually the same facial responses were emitted by members of both cultures, as the subjects in each culture watched the films alone, unaware of a hidden camera.

In a third type of experiment, photographs of facial expressions were shown to observers in a number of different cultures (Ekman, 1972, 1973; Ekman & Friesen, 1971; Ekman, Sorenson, & Friesen, 1969; Izard, 1971). This set of studies was different from others in that a large number of cultures and a full range of emotional expressions were tested. Universality in expression was documented because very high agreement was found across twelve literate cultures in the specific emotions attributed to facial expressions. Unlike the first two types of studies, this line of research has been repeated in different cultures, with different researchers, using different photographs of facial expression.

Cultural differences in the *display* of emotion have also been documented in the study described above concerning the spontaneous expressions of Japanese and American subjects as they viewed stress-inducing films. When a scientist was present while the subjects watched the films a second time, the Japanese more than the Americans masked negative expressions with smiles (Friesen, 1972). This study was the first to show how cultural differences in the management of facial expressions can mask universal emotions. Ekman and Friesen called these "display rules" (Ekman, 1972, 1973; Ekman & Friesen, 1969).

## Recent Findings

Cross-cultural research on facial expressions continues to generate new information about cultural similarities and differences, particularly in regard to the perception of emotion. Here we present the most recent findings from a new series of cross-cultural studies.

*A possible seventh universal facial expression: Contempt.* Two studies from a total of 11 cultures (Ekman & Friesen, 1986; Ekman & Heider, in press) have reported evidence from a study involving 10 cultures and two judgment tasks suggesting the universality of a contempt expression: a unilateral smile. This finding was totally unexpected, as several different expressions thought to portray contempt were tested. These were originally included in the study to document the existence of culture-specific emotions.

*Cultures agree on the most salient emotion portrayed when judgments are made with intensity ratings.* Findings from two recent studies (Ekman et al., 1987; Matsumoto & Ekman, in press) have indicated that cultures agree on the most salient emotion portrayed in the universal expressions, even when judgments are made using intensity ratings. In these studies, observers were allowed to register multiple emotion judgments for seven different emotion categories, using multiscalar intensity ratings. The findings provided were the first evidence of cross-cultural agreement about the most intense emotion when observers were able to choose more than one emotion.

*Cultures agree on the second most salient emotion portrayed.* Analysis of the multiscalar intensity ratings described above from Ekman et al.'s (1987) study indicated that a majority of subjects in each of the 10 cultures tested agreed about the second most salient emotion. For example, contempt was the second strongest emotion judged by every culture for every disgust expression. Surprise was the second strongest in fear expressions. By contrast, happy and sad expressions did not have discernible second emotions. This finding provides stronger evidence in favor of the notion of universal aspects of emotion recognition.

*Cultures agree on the relative intensity of emotion portrayed.* Ekman et al. (1987) also reported that there was high agreement across cultures concerning which expression of two of the same emotion was the more intense. This provides an even stronger test of the notion of universality in recognition of these emotions, as not only did the cultures have to agree on which emotion was the most intense in each of the expressions separately, but they also had to agree on which expression was more intense.

*Cultures agree on the universal expressions of emotion when portrayed by members of another culture.* High cultural agreement concerning the judgment of the most salient emotion has been reported in a recent study comparing American and Japanese observers viewing Caucasian and Oriental posers portraying the universal expressions (Matsumoto, 1986; Matsumoto & Ekman, in press). While this study was not the first to document this finding (see "American Judgments of New Guinean Faces"—Ekman, 1972), it was the first to use expressions of posers of two different cultures in obtaining judgments of members of both cultures.

*Cultures disagree on how intensely they perceive the emotions.* Findings from several studies have shown that cultures differ in their intensity ratings of the universal expressions (Ekman et al., 1987; Matsumoto, 1986; Matsumoto & Ekman, in press). These studies indicate that the cultural differences exist regardless of whether judgments are made of someone of the same or of a visibly different culture, and regardless of possible differences in the affect lexicons of the cultures. Matsumoto and Ekman (in press) expanded on the concept of display rules (Ekman, 1972; Ekman & Friesen, 1969; Friesen, 1972) for emotional expression in explaining these differences in the perception of emotion.

### Unanswered Questions Concerning
### Culture and Facial Expressions

*Uncovering the bases for universal ambiguities in emotion decoding.* In most cross-cultural studies conducted to date, high agreement has been difficult to obtain for fear expressions. For example, in the study where American observers judged expressions of New Guineans (reported in Ekman, 1972), the American observers could not distinguish the New Guinean portrayals of fear and surprise. Other judgment studies (e.g., Ekman, 1972, 1973; Ekman & Friesen, 1971; Ekman et al., 1987; Izard, 1971; Matsumoto, 1986; Matsumoto & Ekman, in press) have also reported that judges do less well in discriminating fear expressions from surprise.

Future research will address the bases of such ambiguities. One possibility, for example, may be that ambiguities among the emotions may be due to semantic overlap in the terms used to denote emotion, or in actual conceptual overlap between the emotions. For example, ambiguities between fear and surprise may be related to the notion that surprise is included in the sequential patterning of the antecedents to fear (see Scherer, 1984, 1986). Alternatively, ambiguity among emotions may be due to the fact that some emotional expressions are more similar to each other (see scaling approaches like Plutchik, 1980; Russell, 1980;

Schlosberg, 1954). Or ambiguity may indicate that observers do not judge emotional expressions in a categorical fashion, but instead produce "sets of probabilities" for different emotions, which may possibly be inferred from one facial expression (Wallbott, 1988). Ambiguity in judgments of emotional expression may also result from defects in the facial stimuli used; it is possible that other stimuli, corrected for these defects, will result in higher agreement.

*Testing other visually isolated or Third World cultures.* Ekman and Friesen's study of New Guineans still remains the only study to examine cultural differences in the interpretation of universal expressions of emotion in a preliterate non-Western culture. Future research attempts should not overlook the importance of testing other similar cultures that are visually isolated from the Western world.

*Testing the universality of contempt.* Despite the findings reported by Ekman and Friesen (1986), we have no conclusive evidence yet that this finding may not be due to stereotypes that result from such expressions as the unilateral smile used by actors in U.S. TV dramas broadcast world-wide. At least one cross-cultural study (employing subjects from the United States and Italy—Ricci-Bitti, Boggi-Cavallo & Brighetti, 1984) indicates that the expression of contempt is somewhat different in these two cultures and that contempt expressions are recognized better by members of one's own culture.

Izard (Izard & Maynes, 1988) has suggested that the contempt expression is actually a signal of several different expressions related to contempt (e.g., scorn, disdain), and that high agreement across the cultures was obtained simply because there was only one response alternative. Ekman and Friesen (1988) have replied that the single-choice judgment strategy bypasses the ambiguity created by using more than one word to define an emotional state, with the cost that observers may not know what is meant by that word, potentially deflating the level of agreement. Future research needs to explore whether contempt alone is expressed and recognized universally, or whether the contempt expression considered universal is actually an expression signaling several different emotions related to contempt. Studies using several different contempt-related expressions employing several different contempt-related response choices are necessary to resolve the debate.

*Cultural differences concerning the perception of expression intensity.* The most recent work concerning cultural differences in the perception of emotion intensity has included respondents from three very disparate cultures: the United States, Japan, and Sumatra. The findings from these studies, as reviewed above, suggest that intensity differences occur regardless of the culture of the expresser, and regardless of the possible influences of cultural differences in the affect lexicons of the cultures studied.

We do not know, however, whether cultural differences in perception of emotion intensity are particular to making judgments of facial expressions (as opposed to other types of emotional expressions), to making judgments concerning emotion (as opposed to other types of personal attributes), or to a generalized response tendency on the part of the respondents. Future research incorporating a variety of stimuli, emotional and nonemotional, facial and nonfacial, is necessary to resolve this debate.

*Testing a full range of spontaneous expressions of emotion.* Ekman and Friesen's study examining judgments of the spontaneous expressions of Japanese and Americans remains the only cross-cultural judgment study using spontaneous displays of emotion. Because the emotion stimuli used in that study included only scenes of bodily mutilation, only spontaneous expressions of disgust and fear were studied. There is a need to test the degree of cultural agreement or disagreement concerning a wider range of spontaneous expressions, including each of the six (or seven, or even more, including emotional states thus far not considered to be universal) expressions of primary emotion. Of course, such studies are tremendously difficult to conduct, given logistic problems. Such studies should go beyond the serendipitous comparison of just two country samples available by chance due to researchers' connections, and should include not only a multitude of emotions, but also a multitude of countries. Other problems include the difficulty in inducing specific emotions or getting access to naturally occurring emotions (Wallbott & Scherer, 1985).

*The boundaries and limits of the display rule concept.* The notion of cultural control of emotional expression is very old (see the well-argued description in Wundt, 1905, p. 285). While the documentation of the existence of display rules in not a new finding, we believe renewed interest in studies of the display rule concept is of paramount importance to addressing basic questions concerning cultural differences in emotional display that have been left unanswered for years. Since the original display rule study was conducted, few studies have tested the boundaries and limits of the display rule concept. For example, we do not know whether the display rule concept is the same for males and females in any culture, and, if different, whether the differences are quantitative or qualitative. We don't know whether the display rule effect would be the same for female experimenters, and for interactants of the same or of different status. We do not know how display rules differ for different types of emotions, especially positive ones. We do not know how and when during development display rules begin to shape and transform expressions (the exceptions being some developmental studies like Mood, Johnson, & Shantz, 1978, or Saarni, 1979, but these were not conducted cross-culturally), and we do not know how the process of acculturation affects previously learned display rules. Future research on any of these questions is necessary to complete our understanding of display rules begun almost twenty years ago.

*Other behavioral channels of emotional expression.* Until now, we have focused on studies of facial expression, as cross-cultural research on this channel has been most abundant. Unfortunately, only very few cross-cultural studies have been conducted in other areas, such as speech and body posture. Several writers have suggested that specific body postures are associated with certain emotional states (Riskind, 1984; Weisfeld & Beresford, 1982), and that cultural differences exist in the perception of emotion from bodily cues (Giovannini & Ricci-Bitti, 1981; Kudoh & Matsumoto, 1985; Matsumoto & Kudoh, 1987).

The voice is also a promising field of research. There is ample evidence to suggest that the voice may indicate emotional states just as precisely as facial expression (Scherer, 1981, 1986; Wallbott & Scherer, 1986b). A few studies have demonstrated that vocally expressed emotions can be decoded at better than chance accuracy by members of other cultures and language groups than those of the encoders, albeit with a certain loss of accuracy (see Brown, 1980; McCluskey, Albas, Niemi, & Cuevas, 1975; van Bezooijen, 1984). Scherer and his collaborators have started a program of research examining whether vocal expressions are universal, as facial expressions. Preliminary studies indicate that attributions of emotion based on voice samples may be fairly stable across cultures.

## CROSS-CULTURAL STUDIES ON THE ANTECEDENTS OF AND REACTIONS TO EMOTIONS

### Background

Emotional expression is one facet of a whole gamut of complex emotional processes that play important roles in everyday functioning and interpersonal communication. Other aspects of emotional processes include the antecedents of emotions; the evaluation of antecedent events; verbal and nonfacial nonverbal reactions, and perceived physiological symptoms and sensations; the subjective experience of the emotions; and the conscious regulation or control of emotions. In recent years, our laboratories have engaged in several large cross-cultural research programs focused on these processes, for both theoretical and practical reasons. Theoretically, these studies investigate whether aspects of emotion other than facial expressions are universal, and give us ideas concerning the possible impact of innate biological or culture-specific learning processes in emotion. Pragmatically, this line of research offers us insight into the cultural similarities and differences in emotion elicitation and experience. These, in turn, have direct relevance to our actual interactions with people of different cultures.

To this date Scherer and his colleagues have completed a series of questionnaire studies in which participants of different cultures were asked to report situations eliciting several basic emotions, their evaluations of the emotional antecedents, their verbal and nonverbal reactions, their perceived physiological symptoms, their self-control attempts, as well as other aspects of their experience. The first set of studies was conducted in eight different European countries involving a total of 1415 respondents. This study used an open-ended format to assess participants' experiences concerning four emotions: joy, sadness, anger, and fear. We call this set of studies the ESI (Emotion in Social Interaction) project (Scherer, Summerfield, & Wallbott, 1983; Scherer, Wallbott, & Summerfield, 1986).

The second set of studies was conducted in more than 30 countries on all five continents, involving over 2600 respondents. More data from additional countries continue to come in. In these studies, a closed-format questionnaire was used to assess participants' experiences concerning seven different emotions: joy, sadness, anger, fear, disgust, shame, and guilt (Wallbott & Scherer, 1986, in press). This program of research is labeled the International Study of Emotion Antecedents and Reactions (ISEAR).

Below we provide a summary of the major findings of both sets of studies. As the data have indicated many cultural similarities in the emotions, we first report findings concerning universal aspects of emotional experience. In addition, three reports analyzing cultural differences are available. The findings from these studies serve as a basis for making interpretations concerning cultural differences in emotional experience, and are presented below.

### Findings Implicating Universal
### Aspects of Emotional Experience

*The antecedents of emotional experience.* Just as there was debate concerning the origin of facial expressions of emotion, similar controversies existed concerning the nature of emotion antecedents. On one hand, previous work by Osgood and his colleagues concerning universals of affective meaning suggested universals across cultures in the ways antecedent events are interpreted (see Osgood, May, & Miron, 1975). On the other hand, the documentation of possible cultural differences in emotional expression through display rules and the neurocultural model of expression suggests that antecedent events to specific emotions may be specific to culture (see Ekman, 1972).

Research concerning the antecedents of emotional experience within cultures was sparse, and cross-cultural research on this topic was even rarer. Those few who attempted to examine antecedents of emotion across cultures were limited in their sampling of either cultures or emotions. Boucher, for example, did obtain cross-cultural agreement concerning the judgment of antecedent events to six emotions (Boucher & Brandt, 1981). But only two cultures were surveyed in this study (Malay and the United States).

The antecedent situations reported in the ESI study (but not ISEAR as of yet) have been analyzed, and provide us with interesting information concerning the possible universality in antecedents. Because of the large number of responses obtained in the ESI studies, a coding scheme was developed for these antecedent situations. Broad categories of descriptions were used, as an attempt was made to code themes applicable to all four emotions (e.g., "relations with friends" or "achievement-related situations"). Of course, some categories specific only to one or two emotions had to be included. Detailed information concerning the codes and their development can be found in Ellgring and Baenninger-Huber (1986).

In the European sample, we found that there was surprisingly strong agreement across cultures concerning the types of antecedent situations that were major elicitors of each of the four emotions tested. For example, cultural pleasures, birth of new family members, body-centered "basic pleasures," and achievement-related situations were frequent antecedents of joy. Sadness was elicited by death of family members or friends, relationship problems, and world news. Fear was elicited most frequently by traffic, strangers, novel situations, achievement-situations, and risky situations. Finally, anger was elicited most frequently by relationship problems, injustice, and strangers.

*Characteristics of emotional experience.* Participants were asked to report for each of the emotions how long ago the event occurred, how long and intensely they felt the emotion, and the degree to which they made a conscious effort to control or regulate their reactions to the situation. Their responses to how long ago the event occurred were considered to be indicative of the frequency of the occurrence of that emotion, because emotions that are reported to have happened further in the past may be experienced less frequently.

Emotion effects are consistently strong concerning the characteristics of emotion (Table 10.1). Situations eliciting anger and disgust occur most frequently, while situations eliciting fear occur least frequently. Situations eliciting sadness are experienced most intensely, while situations eliciting shame and guilt are experienced least intensely. Also, situations eliciting sadness and joy are experienced for the longest duration, while disgust and fear are experienced for the shortest duration. Finally, shame and guilt

**TABLE 10.1** Findings Concerning Universality of the Characteristics of Emotion

| Characteristics of Emotional Experience | Scherer et al. (in press) | Wallbott & Scherer (1986) |
|---|---|---|
| Frequency | AN = JO > FE = SA | AN > DI > GU = JO > SH = SA > FE |
| Intensity | JO = SA > FE = AN | SA > JO = FE > AN > DI > SH = GU |
| Duration | SA = JO > AN > FE | SA > JO > GU > AN > SH > DI = FE |
| Control | AN = SA = FE > JO | SH > GU > SA = FE > DI > AN > JO |

NOTE: AN = anger, DI = disgust, FE = fear, GU = guilt, JO = joy, SA = sadness, SH = shame.

experiences require the greatest degree of control and regulation of reactions, while experiences eliciting joy require the least.

*Cognitive evaluation of the emotions.* In the ISEAR project, respondents were asked a series of closed-ended questions concerning their cognitive evaluations of the antecedent situations they described. The selection of the questions was guided by Scherer's (1984, 1986) theory of emotion elicitation, which postulates different stimulus appraisals or evaluation checks for the antecedents of emotion. For each of the emotions, subjects were asked to rate how *expected* and *pleasant* the situations were, the degree to which *plans* were hindered as a result of these situations, how *fair* they thought the situations were, who or what was *responsible* for the situations, how they *coped* with the situations, how *moral* or *immoral* the situations were, how one's *self-image* was affected by the situations, and how one's *relations* with others were affected.

Each of the emotions were differentiated according to the respondents' evaluations of the antecedent situations of that emotion. For example, joy-producing situations were the most expected and pleasant. Joy also produced the most positive self-image changes, while guilt and shame produced the least positive changes in self-image. Joy also had positive influence on relationships with others, while anger and disgust produced the least positive influence on relations. Anger and sadness produced the most hindrances to plans, and anger was also judged as most unfair. Disgust experiences were most immoral (see Gehm & Scherer, 1988).

There were also strong and consistent emotion effects concerning attributions of responsibility for the situations, and the evaluation of one's coping potentials. For responsibility, respondents were most likely to attribute responsibility for anger, disgust, and fear-producing situations to others, and to oneself second. Guilt, joy, and shame-producing experiences, however, were attributed mostly to the self. Sadness-producing experiences were attributed mostly to fate. Again, though these differences between emotions were very significant, Wallbott and Scherer (in press) reported some interesting cross-cultural differences, which we will discuss below.

For coping, respondents indicated that no action was necessary for disgust and joy experiences, and that they felt powerless for fear and sad experiences. It is interesting that the modal response for guilt, shame, and anger was that respondents felt they could have a positive influence on the situation through their actions.

*Verbal and nonverbal reactions, and physiological symptoms.* Emotions were also differentiated by verbal and nonverbal reactions to them and physiological symptoms. Table 10.2 presents those reactions and symptoms most characteristic of each of the emotions sampled.

Responses to fear resulted in the most predominant pattern of *physiological symptoms*, which clearly differentiates it from the other emotions. Participants reported a higher incidence of breathing symptoms, stomach symptoms, feelings of cold, heartbeat changes, perspiration, and tensing of the muscles. Joy was also characterized by a distinctive pattern of physiological symptoms, which included, on one hand, feelings of warmth and muscle relaxation, and on the other hand, an absence of such symptoms as a "lump in the throat," stomach problems, feelings of coldness, and tensed muscles.

Temperature symptoms, or symptoms having to do with feelings of being hot, warm, or cold, also distinguished the emotions. Joy was the only emotion experienced as warm. Fear and, to a lesser degree, sadness were experienced as cold emotions, while anger and especially shame were experienced as hot emotions. Differences in blood flow changes for each of these emotions may account for these sensation differences. This finding corroborates experimental data for differences in skin temperature between emotions (Ekman, Levenson, & Friesen, 1983).

Participants' *nonverbal* reactions, such as changes in facial expressions (e.g., laughing, crying), also differentiated the emotions. Joy and shame, for example, were characterized by laughing or smiling, while sadness, as one might expect, was characterized by crying. Other changes in facial expressions were found for all negative emotions, especially anger and disgust. *Voice changes* of all different types accompanied all emotions, and were especially predominant in sadness, anger, and fear. Anger and fear were also characterized by screaming. Different types of *movements* also differentiated the emotions: "moving toward" other people was typical of joy, "moving against" others was typical of anger, and withdrawing was typical of all other negative emotions.

The overall number of nonverbal reactions also differentiated the emotions. Participants reported the most nonverbal reactions for anger and joy, and the least for fear, disgust, shame, and guilt. These findings suggest

**TABLE 10.2.** Major Emotion-Specific Verbal, Nonverbal, and Physiological Reactions

| Joy | Sadness | Fear | Anger | Disgust | Shame | Guilt |
|---|---|---|---|---|---|---|
| **Nonverbal reactions** | | | | | | |
| laugh | crying | screaming | facial expression | facial expression | laugh | |
| moving toward | voice change | abrupt movement | screaming | moving against | with-drawing | |
| | with-drawing | moving toward | voice change | | | |
| | | | gesture change | | | |
| | | | abrupt movement | | | |
| | | | moving against | | | |
| **Verbal behavior** | | | | | | |
| lengthy utterance | silence | short utterance | lengthy utterance | short utterance | | |
| speech melody change | | speech disturbance | speech melody change | | speech disturbance | |
| speech tempo change | | | speech tempo change | | | |
| | | | speech disturbance | | | |
| **Physiological symptoms** | | | | | | |
| feeling warm | lump in throat | lump in throat | change in breathing | | feeling hot | |
| muscles relaxing | feeling cold | change in breathing | feeling hot | | perspiring | |
| | muscles relaxing | stomach troubles | heartbeat faster | | | |
| | | feeling cold | muscles tensing | | | |
| | | heartbeat faster | | | | |
| | | muscles tensing | | | | |
| | | perspiring | | | | |

that anger and joy are more "active" in terms of the nonverbal behaviors and reactions produced in these situations.

While *verbal reactions* did not differentiate among the emotions, they do add to distinctions already made by nonverbal reactions and physiological symptoms. For example, lengthy utterances characterized joy and anger, and are congruent with the findings above concerning the high number of nonverbal reactions reported for these emotions. These findings suggest that not only are anger and joy the most active emotions, they are the most socially based emotions. Speech melody and tempo changes were also especially predominant for anger and joy.

A final set of analyses suggest how emotions may be differentiated by the degree to which subjective experience is internalized or externalized. In order to examine this possibility, a ratio of the number of motor expressive reactions reported to the number of physiological symptoms reported was computed. If this ratio is > 1, then the experience is predominantly external, because the number of reactions is greater than the number of symptoms. If the ratio is < 1, then the experience is predominantly internal, as the number of symptoms reported is greater than the number of reactions (Wallbott & Scherer, 1986). Using this index of internalization/externalization, we found that joy and anger are more externalized than the other emotions, while shame, guilt, and fear were internalized.

### Findings Suggesting Cultural
### Differences in Emotional Experience

In the research reported above, significant cultural effects were often found, although they were generally smaller than the emotion effects. The culture effects indicate that cultures differ to some degree in the experience or evaluation of emotion. Three studies have formally examined culture effects to this date, one comparing a U.S., Japanese, and European sample using the ESI data (Scherer, Matsumoto, Wallbott, & Kudoh, 1988), a second comparing the U.S. and Japan using the ISEAR data (Matsumoto, Kudoh, Scherer, & Wallbott, 1988), and a third comparing the "ISEAR" country samples on an a posteriori basis (Wallbott & Scherer, in press). Below we report the findings, aggregated across studies, concerning cultural differences in the antecedents of emotional experience, the characteristics of emotion, the verbal and nonverbal reactions, and the physiological symptoms.

*Antecedents of emotional experience.* Cultural differences in the antecedents of emotion were studied only in our first comparison study. We had no hypotheses concerning cultural differences in the antecedents because our previous work with European countries did not yield any major cross-cultural differences and we expected that the antecedents that were

238 PROCESSES AND EFFECTS

frequent elicitors of the emotions in Europe would also be frequent elicitors of the emotions in the United States and Japan. While this was generally true, there were antecedent categories that produced significant cultural differences, particularly contrasting the Japanese sample with the American and European samples.

For example, cultural pleasures, birth of a new family member, body-centered basic pleasures, and achievement-related situations were important antecedents of joy in the United States and Europe. In Japan, however, they are less frequently elicitors of joy. For sadness, world news, temporary and permanent separations, and death were more frequent elicitors of sadness in the United States and European samples than in Japan. Relationships, however, was a more frequent elicitor of sadness in Japan than in the other two cultures.

Fear of strangers and risky situations elicited fear more frequently in the United States and Europe than in Japan. But relationships elicited fear more frequently in Japan than in the other two cultures.

The pattern of results for anger was interesting. On one hand, the Japanese were angered less frequently by relationships and situations of injustice than the Europeans or Americans. On the other hand, situations involving strangers elicited anger more frequently in the Japanese than in the Europeans and Americans.

*Characteristics of emotion.* Above we reported that anger and disgust experiences were reported as having occurred most recently, with fear experiences reported as occurring least frequently. The data from our first comparison study suggested that across joy, sadness, fear, and anger, the Japanese reported that their experiences occurred more recently than the Americans or the Europeans. When the cultures were compared on the intensity and duration of emotion in the first study, we found that the American respondents in general reported feeling their emotions more intensely and for longer periods of time than their European or Japanese counterparts. Finally, contrary to our expectations, no cultural differences were found concerning control or regulation of emotion.

*Cognitive evaluation of the emotion-eliciting situations.* In order to examine possible cultural differences in the cognitive evaluation of the antecedents to emotion, the American and Japanese responses on each of the evaluation dimensions from the ISEAR study were compared. The two cultures did not differ on the expectation or pleasantness of the event, the degree to which the experiences facilitated goals, the unfairness of the event, on their judgments of the immorality of the event, or in their judgments of the events' effects on their relationships.

There were, however, provocative cultural differences in the effects of the events on self-esteem, attributions of responsibility, and evaluation of one's coping potential. The cultural effects on self-esteem indicated that

American participants in general reported greater positive self-esteem and self-confidence for the emotion-eliciting events than did the Japanese participants. For attributions of responsibility, the only cultural difference was found for sadness: American respondents attributed their sadness-producing experiences to others or to fate, whereas the Japanese respondents attributed the cause of the event mostly to themselves. Analysis of the respondents' unwillingness to attribute responsibility also produced an interesting cultural difference: A significantly larger percentage of Japanese respondents compared to their American counterparts did not make any attribution of responsibility.

Finally, culture effects on respondents' evaluations of their coping potential indicated a consistent finding across most emotions: More Japanese respondents believed that no action was necessary than American respondents, even for strong negative emotions. This finding is consistent with the findings above concerning the attribution of responsibility of the event: If one is reluctant to make an attribution of responsibility, or attributes the responsibility of the event to others, then coping is indeed limited, and is reflected in the belief that no action would be necessary.

*Verbal and nonverbal reactions, and physiological symptoms.* In our first set of studies, we made a gross differentiation according to the channel of the reaction (voice, face, whole body, and so on), without further specifying the nature of these changes. This was necessary because the open-ended format allowed for a varied range of responses that would have rendered specific categories meaningless. In the second study based on the ISEAR data, analyses were conducted on specific categories given to the respondents. These categories were based on the most frequently occurring open-ended responses given in the first set of studies. The findings indicate a consistent cultural difference between the Japanese and the Americans: Americans reported significantly more verbal and nonverbal reactions to each of the seven emotions than did their Japanese counterparts.

Grossly defined categories, such as pleasant arousal, feelings of warmth or cold, and perspiration, were also used to categorize the types of physiological sensations participants reported in the first set of studies. As we found with verbal and nonverbal reactions, Japanese reported fewer physiological symptoms and sensations on a number of different categories. More specifically, the Japanese reported less stomach troubles and muscle symptoms for all four emotions; less blood pressure changes for joy, fear, and anger; less pleasant arousal and pleasant rest for joy; less unpleasant arousal for sadness and fear; less feelings of cold for fear; and less feelings of warmth for anger. This pattern was repeated when we collapsed across specific precoded categories in the second study as well: American subjects reported significantly more symptoms and sensations than did the

Japanese respondents. This may be related to the finding reported above that Japanese subjects in general judge emotional expressions as being of lower intensity than other cultures do. Because these differences were not predicted, only post hoc explanations based on stereotypical notions concerning the respective cultures could be offered at this point. A first attempt at the development of hypotheses based on these findings can be found in Matsumoto et al. (in press).

## Future Directions Concerning Cross-Cultural Studies on the Antecedents of and Reactions to Emotions

*The need for more behavioral research.* The questionnaire studies described above suggest specific hypotheses to be tested in more refined laboratory or experimental research. We look for future endeavors to include self-report data concerning the characteristics and cognitive evaluations of emotion in combination with measurement of actual verbal and nonverbal behaviors and physiological activity. For example, research examining possible cultural differences in the physiological response to emotion-eliciting situations may address the age-old debate concerning the role of physiology in the arousal of emotion (see Ax, 1953; Duffy, 1941; Ekman, Levenson, & Friesen, 1983; Schachter, 1964).

*Emotion experience and evaluation in development.* The above findings also suggest that we begin to look at the development of emotional experience, in order to examine when in development the constellation of responses to each of the emotions occur. Developmental studies will also be crucial to our understanding of the relative contribution of innate biological processes and learning processes in the development of these aspects of emotion. As it stands now, it is impossible to disentangle the relative contributions of culture and biology in the elicitation and experience of emotion.

*Attitudes toward emotions.* One line of research that we did not address concerns cultural differences in attitudes concerning the emotions. Izard (1971) made a first attempt at examining such differences, and reported provocative findings suggesting possible bases with which cultures can differ. But no studies were conducted to follow up on that line of research. We suggest that, given our recent findings on the evaluation and experience of the emotions across cultures, it is most appropriate now to renew our cross-cultural study of emotion attitudes. These, in turn, may provide us with important and interesting information concerning dimensions underlying cultural differences in the emotion process.

*Examining cultural differences.* As we reported above, we have to date conducted only three studies examining possible cultural differences in the evaluation and experience of emotion, based on our questionnaire studies.

The data set that we have clearly indicates that cultural differences need to be examined. But the large number of cultures, combined with a lack of detailed hypotheses concerning the selection of cultures to compare, has prohibited us from designing an analysis plan with the logic to test cultures on meaningful dimensions. Below we review one previous attempt at classifying and categorizing cultures according to meaningful dimensions, in the hope that it provides us and other cross-cultural researchers with a more refined model with which to understand and study cultures.

## A MODEL OF CULTURE

In most cross-cultural studies of emotion, two or more cultures are compared, either on the basis of anecdotal or impressionistic differences concerning the emotions, or because of convenience. Interpretations of cultural differences, when documented, are often relegated to stereotypes concerning the cultures. This strategy was not problematic in the older cross-cultural studies of facial expressions, because findings generally indicated high agreement rather than disagreement across cultures. With increasing documentation of cultural differences, there is increasing need to incorporate cultural models of classification and categorization according to a series of meaningful and stable dimensions that differentiate cultures. Analysis and interpretation (or reinterpretation) of already existing data can then follow more detailed guidelines established a priori. Also, more meaningful selection of cultures for future cross-cultural comparisons can occur.

The importance of the use of meaningful cultural models in the study of emotion differences is implied by a recent study by Wallbott and Scherer (in press). These researchers performed an a posteriori cluster analysis of the reports on emotion obtained in the ISEAR study, and provided evidence that (most) country samples clustered either with respect to geographical closeness or with respect to language similarity. Also, the relative wealth of the countries (operationalized using the average gross national product per inhabitant) accounted for some variance in the data. Subjects from "wealthy" nations reported more recent emotional experiences, being of less intensity, shorter duration, and being accompanied by fewer physiological symptoms and behavioral reactions, compared to subjects from "poor" countries. Subjects from poor countries attributed the cause of their experiences more often to fate and other people; subjects from wealthy countries saw their emotional experiences as much more often caused by themselves. Such results provide us with interesting leads concerning the basis for cultural differences in emotion.

Hofstede (1980, 1983) has provided an interesting model of cultural variation that may be applicable to studies of emotion. On the basis of a large-scale (40-country) value survey, Hofstede suggests that there are four dimensions along which cultures may vary: *power distance, uncertainty avoidance, individualism,* and *masculinity*. Power distance reflects the way in which interpersonal relationships form and develop when differences in power are perceived. Uncertainty avoidance reflects the degree to which people in a culture feel threatened by ambiguous situations and have created beliefs and institutions that help to avoid them. Individualism is a major dimension of cultural variability postulated by other theorists as well (Kluckhohn & Strodtbeck, 1961; Marsella, DeVos, & Hsu, 1985; Parsons & Shils, 1951; Triandis, 1986). Individual cultures emphasize individual goals and independence, while collectivistic cultures stress collective goals and dependence on groups. Masculinity reflects the degree to which cultures delineate sex roles, with masculine cultures making clearer differentiations between genders.

Two attempts have been made at using these dimensions of cultural variability in accounting for cultural differences with respect to emotion. The first was conducted by Gudykunst and Ting-Toomey (1988). These researchers reanalyzed the data concerning antecedents and nonverbal reactions reported from eight cultures in the ESI study (Scherer, Wallbott, & Summerfield, 1986), coding each of the eight cultures in terms of Hofstede's dimensions. These were then correlated with the percentage of respondents from each culture giving the three most frequent antecedents for the four emotions surveyed. Several significant correlations were found, each of which provided a dimension with which to understand and interpret cultural differences in the percentage of antecedents reported by each culture for the emotions. For example, power distance was negatively correlated with injustice as an antecedent to anger. In high-power-distance cultures, inequality and injustice are expected and taken for granted, while they are not expected or acceptable in low-power-distance cultures. Thus a negative correlation would be predicted between power distance and injustice as an antecedent to anger.

Gudykunst and Ting-Toomey (1988) also computed correlations between the four dimensions and the percentage of respondents in each culture reporting a specific type of verbal reaction. Significant correlations were again found, each of which was interpretable according to the Hofstede (1980, 1983) dimensions. For example, nonvocal reactions and verbalization were positively correlated with individualism. Individualistic cultures place greater emphasis on the verbal dimension of communication, including directness of expression, whereas the verbal dimension is often not trusted in collectivistic cultures, and communication is indirect.

A recent study by Matsumoto (in press) represents a second attempt at using Hofstede's dimensions to account for cultural variability and emotion. This researcher examined each of the cultures sampled in previous cross-cultural studies of the perception of facial expression of emotion. Two correlational analyses were computed. One examined the relationship between the cultural dimensions and the percentage of respondents making correct judgments concerning the universal emotions. The second analysis examined the relationship between the cultural dimensions and cultural variation in intensity ratings of the universal expressions.

Results from the first set of analyses produced no more significant correlations than would be expected by chance. This finding indicated that the cultural differences in the percentage of respondents making correct judgments concerning the universal emotions was not related to the four cultural dimensions. This result suggests that the basic perception and judgment of *which* emotion is portrayed in the universal expressions may be related to more innate processing perceptual abilities not influenced by culture. The results from the second set of analyses, however, did indicate some degree of relationship between the cultural dimensions and perceptions of intensity. For example, more intense ratings of contempt were given by cultures that scored high on power distance and low on individualism. More intense ratings of fear and sadness, however, were associated with cultures that scored less on power distance and higher on individualism.

We cite these studies because they present a possible model of understanding cultures that can be meaningfully used in future research examining the emotions. Our future endeavors, both empirical and theoretical, may be aided greatly by incorporating such models.

## CONCLUSIONS

The near future of cross-cultural research on the emotions promises some of the most interesting findings concerning culture and emotions in the last two decades. The questions we outline above, both concerning facial expressions of emotion and the subjective experience and evaluation of the emotions, provide the basis for much of the impetus for directions in future research that will inform us more about how cultures are similar or different concerning these aspects of emotion. Incorporating models of culture that delineate stable and meaningful dimensions of cultural variability promises researchers and theoreticians alike a useful tool, regardless of the particular aspect of emotion on which they focus. With the knowledge we have already uncovered concerning culture and emotion, the most recent developments, and their future directions, will have further implications for the role of emotion in intercultural communication.


## REFERENCES

Ax, A. F. (1953). The physiological differentiation between fear and anger in humans. *Psychosomatic Medicine, 15*, 433-442.

Boucher, J. D., & Brandt, M. E. (1981). Judgment of emotion: American and Malay antecedents. *Journal of Cross-Cultural Psychology, 12*, 272-283.

Brown, B. L. (1980). The detection of emotion in vocal qualities. In H. Giles, P. W. Robinson, & P. Smith (Eds.), *Language: Social psychological perspectives*. Oxford: Pergamon.

Darwin, C. (1965). *The expression of the emotions in man and animals*. Chicago: University of Chicago Press. (Reprinted from London: Murray, 1872).

Duffy, E. (1941). An explanation of "emotional" phenomena without the use of the concept "emotion." *Journal of General Psychology, 25*, 283-293.

Ekman, P. (1972). Universal and cultural differences in facial expression of emotion. In J. R. Cole (Ed.), *Nebraska Symposium on Motivation* (pp. 207-283). Lincoln: University of Nebraska Press.

Ekman, P. (1973). Darwin and cross-cultural studies of facial expression. In P. Ekman (Ed.), *Darwin and facial expression* (pp. 1-83). New York: Academic Press.

Ekman, P., & Friesen, W. V. (1969). Nonverbal leakage and clues to deception. *Psychiatry, 32*, 88-106.

Ekman, P., & Friesen, W. V. (1971). Constants across cultures in the face and emotion. *Journal of Personality and Social Psychology, 17*, 124-129.

Ekman, P., & Friesen, W. V. (1986). A new pancultural expression of emotion. *Motivation and Emotion, 10*, 159-168.

Ekman, P., & Friesen, W. V. (1988). Who knows what about contempt? A reply to Izard and Maynes. *Motivation and Emotion, 12*, 17-22.

Ekman, P., Friesen, W. V., O'Sullivan, M. O., Chan, A., Diacoyanni-Tarlatzis, I., Heider, K., Krause, R., LeCompte, W. A., Pitcairn, T., Ricci-Bitti, P. E., Scherer, K., Tomita, M., & Tzavaras, A. (1987). Universals and cultural differences in the judgments of facial expressions of emotion. *Journal of Personality and Social Psychology, 53*, 712-717.

Ekman, P., & Heider, K. (in press). The universality of a contempt expression: A replication. *Motivation and Emotion*.

Ekman, P., Levenson, R. W., & Friesen, W. V. (1983). Autonomic nervous system activity distinguishes between emotions. *Science, 221*, 1208-1210.

Ekman, P., Sorenson, E. R., & Friesen, W. V. (1969). Pancultural elements in facial displays of emotion. *Science, 164*, 86-88.

Ellgring, H., & Baenninger-Huber, E. (1986). The coding of reported emotional experiences: Antecedents and reactions. In K. R. Scherer, H. G. Wallbott, & A. B. Summerfield (Eds.), *Experiencing emotion: A cross-cultural study* (pp. 39-49). Cambridge: Cambridge University Press.

Friesen, W. V. (1972). *Cultural differences in facial expressions in a social situation: An experimental test of the concept of display rules*. Unpublished doctoral dissertation, University of California, San Francisco.

Gehm, T., & Scherer, K. R. (1988). Relating situation evaluation to emotion differentiation: Nonmetric analyses of cross-cultural questionnaire data. In K. R. Scherer (Ed.), *Facets of emotion*. Hillsdale, NJ: Lawrence Erlbaum.

Giovannini, D., & Ricci-Bitti, P. E. (1981). Culture and sex effect in recognizing emotions by facial and gestural cues. *Italian Journal of Psychology, 8*, 95-102.

Gudykunst, W. B., & Ting-Toomey, S. (1988). Culture and affective communication. *American Behavioral Scientist, 31*, 384-400.

Hofstede, G. (1980). *Cultures consequences.* Beverly Hills, CA: Sage.

Hofstede, G. (1983). Dimensions of natural cultures in fifty countries and three regions. In J. Deregowski, S. Dziurawiec, & R. Annis (Eds.), *Expiscations in cross-cultural psychology.* Lisse: Swets & Zeitlinger.

Izard, C. E. (1971). *The face of emotion.* New York: Appleton-Century-Crofts.

Izard, C. E., & Maynes, O. M. (1988). On the form and universality of the contempt expression: A correction for Ekman and Friesen's claim for discovery. *Motivation and Emotion, 12*, 1-16.

Kluckhohn, F., & Strodtbeck, F. (1961). *Variations in value orientations.* New York: Row & Peterson.

Kudoh, T., & Matsumoto, D. (1985). A cross cultural examination of the semantic dimensions of body postures. *Journal of Personality and Social Psychology, 48*, 1440-1446.

Marsella, A. J., DeVos, G., & Hsu, F. L. K. (Eds.). (1985). *Culture and self: Asian and Western perspectives.* New York: Tavistock.

Matsumoto, D. (1986). *Cross-cultural communication of emotion.* Unpublished doctoral dissertation, University of California, Berkeley.

Matsumoto, D. (in press). Cultural influences on the perception of emotion. *Journal of Cross-Cultural Psychology.*

Matsumoto, D., & Ekman, P. (in press). American-Japanese cultural differences in intensity ratings of facial expressions of emotion. *Motivation and Emotion.*

Matsumoto, D., & Kudoh, T. (1987). Cultural similarities and differences in the semantic dimensions of body postures. *Journal of Nonverbal Behavior, 11*, 166-179.

Matsumoto, D., Kudoh, T., Scherer, K. R., & Wallbott, H. G. (1988). Antecedents of and reactions to emotions in the US and Japan. *Journal of Cross-Cultural Psychology, 19*, 267-286.

McCluskey, K. W., Albas, D. C., Niemi, R. R., & Cuevas, D. (1975). Cross-cultural differences in the perception of the emotional content of speech: A study of the development of sensitivity in Canadian and Mexican children. *Developmental Psychology, 11*, 551-555.

Mood, D. W., Johnson, J. E., & Shantz, C. U. (1978). Social comprehension and affect-matching in young children. *Merril-Palmer Quarterly, 24*, 63-66.

Osgood, C. E., May, W. H., & Miron, M. S. (1975). *Cross-cultural universals of affective meaning.* Urbana: University of Illinois Press.

Parsons, T., & Shills, E. A. (1951). *Toward a general theory of action.* Cambridge, MA: Harvard University Press.

Plutchik, R. (1980). *Emotion: A psychoevolutionary synthesis.* New York: Harper.

Ricci-Bitti, P. E., Boggi-Cavallo, P., & Brighetti, G. (1984). *Universals and facial expressions of emotion: The case of contempt.* Paper presented at the 8th International Congress of Psychology, Acapulco.

Riskind, J. H. (1984). They stoop to conquer: Guiding and self-regulatory functions of physical posture after success and failure. *Journal of Personality and Social Psychology, 47*, 479-493.

Russell, J. A. (1980). A circumplex model of affect. *Journal of Personality and Social Psychology, 39*, 1161-1178.

Saarni, C. (1979). Children's understanding of display rules for expressive behavior. *Developmental Psychology, 15*, 424-429.

Schachter, S. (1964). The interaction of cognitive and physiological determinants of emotional state. In L. Berkowitz (Ed.), *Advances in experimental social psychology* (Vol. 1, pp. 49-81). New York: Academic Press.

Scherer, K. R. (1981). Speech and emotional states. In J. Darby (Ed.), *Speech evaluation in psychiatry* (pp. 189-220). New York: Grune & Stratton.

Scherer, K. R. (1984). On the nature and function of emotion: A component process approach. In K. R. Scherer & P. Ekman (Eds.), *Approaches to emotion* (pp. 293-318). Hillsdale, NJ: Lawrence Erlbaum.

Scherer, K. R. (1986). Vocal affect expression: A review and a model for future research. *Psychological Bulletin, 99*, 143-165.

Scherer, K. R., & Ekman, P. (Eds.). (1984). *Approaches to emotion*. Hillsdale, NJ: Lawrence Erlbaum.

Scherer, K. R., Matsumoto, D., Wallbott, H. G., & Kudoh, T. (1988). Emotional experience in cultural context: A comparison between Europe, Japan, and the USA. In K. R. Scherer (Ed.), *Facets of emotion*. Hillsdale, NJ: Lawrence Erlbaum.

Scherer, K. R., Summerfield, A. B., & Wallbott, H. G. (1983). Cross-national research on antecedents and components of emotion: A progress report. *Social Science Information, 3*, 355-385.

Scherer, K. R., Wallbott, H. G., & Summerfield, A. B. (Eds.). (1986). *Experiencing emotion: A cross-cultural study*. Cambridge: Cambridge University Press.

Schlosberg, H. A. (1954). Three dimensions of emotion. *Psychological Review, 61*, 81-88.

Triandis, H. C. (1986). Collectivism vs. individualism: A reconceptualization of a basic concept in cross-cultural psychology. In C. Bagley & G. Verma (Eds.), *Personality, cognition, and values: Cross-cultural perspectives of childhood and adolescence*. London: Macmillan.

van Bezooijen, R. (1984). *The characteristics and recognizability of vocal expressions of emotion*. Dortrecht: Foris.

Wallbott, H. G. (1988). Faces in context: The relative importance of facial expression and context information in determining emotion attributions. In K. R. Scherer (Ed.), *Facets of emotion*. Hillsdale, NJ: Lawrence Erlbaum.

Wallbott, H. G., & Scherer, K. R. (1985). Differentielle situations: und Reaktionscharakteristika in Emotionserinnerungen: Ein neuer Forschungsansatz. *Psychologische Rundschau, 36*, 83-101.

Wallbott, H. G., & Scherer, K. R. (1986a). How universal and specific is emotional experience? Evidence from 27 countries on five continents. *Social Science Information, 25*, 763-796.

Wallbott, H. G., & Scherer, K. R. (1986b). Cues and channels in emotion recognition. *Journal of Personality and Social Psychology, 51*, 690-699.

Wallbott, H. G., & Scherer, K. R. (in press). Emotion and economic development: Data and speculations concerning the relationship between emotional experience and socioeconomic factors. *European Journal of Social Psychology*.

Weisfeld, G. E., & Beresford, J. M. (1982). Erectness of posture as an indicator of dominance or success in humans. *Motivation and Emotion, 6*, 113-131.

Wundt, W. (1905). *Grundzuege der physiologischen Psychologie* (Vol. 3). Leipzig: Wilhelm Engelmann.

# 11 Intercultural Communication Competence

## Mitchell R. Hammer

Communication competence has been examined by scholars from a variety of academic disciplines under such diverse linguistic umbrellas as interpersonal effectiveness, social competence, fundamental competence, rhetorical competence, and linguistic competence (see reviews by Bostrom, 1984; Diez, 1984; Larson, Backlund, Redmond, & Barbour, 1978; Parks, 1985; Spitzberg & Cupach, 1984). In addition, communication competence has been investigated in a variety of intracultural milieus (e.g., mental health, educational, occupational; Spitzberg & Cupach, 1984) and intercultural contexts (e.g., sojourner adjustment, immigrant acculturation, intergroup contact, culture shock, transfer of technology, international management, cross-cultural training, tourist travel, interracial/interethnic relations; Benson, 1978; Brein & David, 1971; Brislin, 1981; Dinges, 1983; Dinges & Duffy, 1979; Gudykunst, 1978; Kealey & Ruben, 1983; Landis & Brislin, 1983a, 1983b, 1983c; Ruben, Askling, & Kealey, 1977; Stening, 1979).

Consensus has not been reached concerning the definition and conceptualization of the communication competence construct in either the intracultural or the intercultural contexts. Recently, however, Spitzberg and Cupach (1984) developed a theoretical framework that permits integration of research findings in these two contexts. Thus one purpose in this chapter is briefly to discuss Spitzberg and Cupach's (1984) notion of communication competence and its applicability to the study of intercultural communication competence. One aspect of communicative competence generally posited as integral includes those communication skills that "are instrumental in providing smooth and successful interaction" (Cupach & Spitzberg, 1983, p. 565). A second purpose of this chapter, therefore, is to review research that has examined communication skills within both the intercultural and the intracultural contexts. A general research agenda for future research concerning the nature of the communication competence construct and its relationship to intercultural communication skills also is presented.

## THE NATURE OF
## COMMUNICATION COMPETENCE

Communication competence involves interactants making social judgments concerning the "goodness" of self and others' communicative performances (Spitzberg & Cupach, 1984). According to Spitzberg and Cupach, both appropriateness and effectiveness are dimensions that people use to base their judgments of a communicative performance. Behavior is appropriate when it meets contextual and relational standards or expectations and effective when it is functional in achieving desirable ends or goals or satisfying interactants' needs.

While communication competence refers to the social judgments about behavior, the notion of communication skills refers to interactants' verbal and nonverbal behavior. While communication skills are not themselves competence, they provide the basis for interactants' judgments of self and others' communicative competence. Further, Spitzberg and Cupach (1987, p. 8) suggest that "it seems reasonable to conjecture that certain behaviors *generally* are seen as competent," based on the view that there is "substantial correspondence between actor behaviors and others' perception of that behavior."

The notion of communication competence as a social attribution coupled with the view that some communication behaviors may generally be seen as competent lies at the heart of what is referred to in the intercultural literature as the culture-general versus culture-specific controversy (for a more empirical discussion of this, see Gudykunst & Hammer, 1984; Wiseman & Abe, 1984). The culture-specific approach assumes that an individual's communication competence can best be conceptualized as the degree to which they learn the culture-specific communication rules, rituals, and skills of verbal and nonverbal expression and reception that are practiced by host country nationals. The culture-specific approach views the nature of intercultural communication competence in terms of the degree to which individuals adopt the communication patterns and practices of the host country national.

The culture-general approach assumes that the intercultural transactions are different from intracultural transactions and, because of the differences, additional aspects of communication competence must be included. Ellingsworth (1983, p. 198), for instance, suggests that interactants make particular communicative adaptations "based on their estimates of the foreignness of the other." The culture-general approach tends to investigate those dimensions of communication competence that can best generalize to intercultural interactions, regardless of the specific cultures involved.

While the culture-general versus culture-specific approaches are conceptually important because of their different characterizations of the nature of intercultural communication competence and intercultural communication skills, the question of the ultimate utility of either perspective can only be assessed through empirical investigation. In this respect, Ruben's (1976) behavioral approach represents one method for assessing intercultural communication competency and communication skills. Ruben argues that "it is likely that, in terms of prediction, what one *does* is the best indicant of what one *will do* at some future time or place" (p. 345). Ruben integrates both the culture-specific and the culture-general perspectives contending that, while universal communication skills may exist, the specific behaviors that reflect those skills may vary across cultural contexts:

> While one can argue that the importance of communication behaviors such as empathy, respect, non-judgmentalness, etc., transcends cultural boundaries, the way these are expressed and interpreted may vary substantially from one culture (or one sub-culture) to another. (Ruben, 1976, p. 344)

Further, this approach is consistent with the notion of communication competence as a social judgment; it permits communication skill assessments to be undertaken from both self and other perspectives. Finally, the behavioral observation methodology has been found to be a valid and reliable measurement approach for assessing intercultural communication competence skills using Canadian technical advisers (Ruben, 1976; Ruben & Kealey, 1979), as well as Japanese (Nishida, 1985) and North American (Hammer, 1984) students.

Intercultural research has identified communication skills as important to both cross-cultural adaptation and intercultural effectiveness. In a series of studies, Hammer, Gudykunst, and Wiseman (1978) and Hammer (1987) found that communication skills are one of three central dimensions viewed as important to an individual's effective functioning in a foreign culture (the other two dimensions are the ability to deal with intercultural stress and the ability to establish interpersonal relationships). Further, Hammer, Nishida, and Jezek (in press) confirmed that these three dimensions also are viewed similarly by North Americans in terms of their effective functioning with fellow North Americans in the United States.

Another series of studies also have examined intercultural communication skills and overseas success. In one study, Ruben (1976) identified seven behavioral dimensions (i.e., skills) of intercultural communication competence: (a) display of respect—"the ability to express respect and positive high regard for another person"(p. 339); (b) interaction posture—the ability to respond to others in a nonjudgmental descriptive manner; (c) orientation to knowledge—the ability to recognize that what we know is individual in nature; (d) empathy—the ability to see the world through another person's eyes; (e) self-oriented role behavior—the ability to function in both problem-solving roles and relationship-building roles; (f) interaction management—the ability to take "turns in discussion and initiating and terminating interaction based on a reasonably accurate assessment of the needs and desires of others" (p. 341); and (g) tolerance for ambiguity—the ability to adjust quickly, with little discomfort to new and ambiguous situations. In another study, Ruben and Kealey (1979) examined the relationship among these seven intercultural communication skills and patterns of success or failure in cross-cultural adaptation. For each dimension, the intercultural communication behavioral observation indices developed by Ruben (1976) were used to assess trainees' communication competence following a week-long predeparture training program. One year later, a follow-up field study was conducted to measure culture shock, adjustment, and vocational and interactional effectiveness. While results were not conclusive, the data did suggest that "various behavioral patterns observed during training in Canada did predict with varying degrees of certainty to outcomes in the field, one year hence" (p. 40). Nishida (1985) examined the communication of Japanese individuals who traveled to the United States in terms of their listening and speaking ability, their structure in written expression, and their vocabulary and reading comprehension skills. At the end of their stay in the United States, the outcome dimensions of culture shock, psychological adjustment, and interaction effectiveness were examined. Analysis of pre- and post-test measures suggest that tolerance of ambiguity was correlated significantly with culture shock ($r = .56$, $p \leq .01$) and speaking and listening skills were correlated to effectiveness ($r = .78$, $p \leq .01$; $r = .72$, $p \leq .01$, respectively).

In one of the most comprehensive field research projects conducted to date, Hawes and Kealey (1979, 1981) examined the adaptation and effectiveness of technical personnel and their families working in six countries for the Canadian International Development Agency (CIDA). Over 100 variables were assessed through standardized rating scales and opinions obtained from 250 Canadians and 90 nationals. Overall, results indicated that the concept of overseas effectiveness was composed of three dimensions: intercultural interaction and training of nationals, professional effectiveness, and personal/family adjustment and satisfaction. Further, this study revealed that "interpersonal communication skills" were predictive of satisfaction, intercultural interaction and training of nationals, job performance, and overall effectiveness (as rated by host country nationals). These communication skills included (a) flexibility toward ideas of others; (b) respect toward others; (c) listening and accurate perception of the needs of others; (d) trust, friendliness, and cooperation with others; (e) calm and self-control when confronted by obstacles; and (f) sensitivity to cultural differences (Hawes & Kealey, 1979).

Finally, Hammer and Clarke (1987) replicated portions of the Hawes and Kealey (1981) study with Japanese and North American managers. They examined the influence of three personal characteristics (personal expectations, initiative/self-confidence, and family communication) and two communication skill factors (interpersonal communication skills and self-assertion skills) on four dimensions of intercultural managerial success: actual in-company performance rating, job effectiveness (trainer ratings, other-culture plant manager ratings), personal/family adjustment (trainer ratings), and quality of intercultural interactions (trainer ratings, other-culture plant manager ratings). The results of this study indicated that interpersonal communication skills were the primary predictor of five of the six measures of overseas managerial success.

Results obtained from studies conducted from a behavioral orientation suggest that communication skills are important to overseas success and are significant predictors of various intercultural adaptation and effectiveness outcomes. Intercultural research, however, has not examined specifically the relationship of communication skills to specific judgments interactants make about self and others' communicative competence. Yet it is this notion of communication competence that provides the theoretical framework for determining which communication skills are most important in achieving what outcomes in specific contexts. It is not the communication skill per se that contributes to the various adaptation and/or effectiveness outcomes previously discussed. Rather, it is the individual interactants' judgments of self and other competence based upon the communication performances engaged in that influence the individuals' success in achieving cross-cultural adaptation (e.g., managing culture shock, attitudinal satisfaction with living in a foreign culture) and intercultural effectiveness (e.g., job/task performance, degree of social interaction with host nationals, transfer of technology) outcomes. While research has not examined the relationship between communication skills and social judgments of communication competence within the intercultural context (nor, it should be added, the relationship of communication competence judgments to adaptation and/or intercultural effectiveness outcomes), a number of studies conducted within the intracultural milieu are relevant to this concern. These studies will be discussed in the next section.

## THE APPLICABILITY OF COMMUNICATION
## SKILLS TO THE INTERCULTURAL CONTEXT

A number of communication skills deemed essential to competent communication in the United States have been posited, including self-

disclosure, behavioral flexibility, descriptiveness, understanding, expressiveness, openness, listening, negotiation, social relaxation, interaction
management, attentiveness, interaction involvement, and adaptability (Argyris, 1965; Bochner & Kelly, 1974; Brandt, 1979; Cegala, 1981; Cegala,
Savage, Brunner, & Conrad, 1982; Cushman & Craig, 1976; Duran, 1983;
Duran & Wheeless, 1982; Foote & Cottrell, 1955; Macklin & Rossiter,
1976) along with such personal skills as the ability to initiate interaction
and the ability to establish interpersonal and role-related (e.g., work)
relationships with others (Holland & Baird, 1968). The ability to assume
the perspective or point of view of another—variously termed *other orientation* (Spitzberg & Hecht, 1984), *decentering* (Dance & Larson, 1976),
*social perspective taking* or *role taking* (Flavel, Botkin, Fry, Wright, &
Jarvis, 1968; Hale & Delia, 1976), *empathy* (Allen & Brown, 1976;
Larson, Backlund, Redmond, & Barbour, 1978; Wiemann & Backlund,
1980), and *altercentrism* (Feingold, 1977)—also has been suggested as a
fundamental dimension of communication competence.

Wiemann (1977), summarizing a large body of work on communication
competence, suggests that empathy, affiliation/support, social relaxation,
behavioral flexibility, and interaction management are central communication skills. Spitzberg and Hecht (1984) and Spitzberg and Cupach
(1984), after an exhaustive review of a number of empirically based
(i.e., factor analytic) studies, identify a similar set of communication
skills: immediacy (approach/affiliation orientation), interaction management (conversational turn-taking and episodic punctuation patterns),
social relaxation (anxiety management), expressiveness (degree of involvement in conversation), and altercentrism (other orientation, which
includes attentiveness, interest, and adaptability to the other interactant).

Recently, Coker and Burgoon (1987) identified specific verbal and
nonverbal behaviors that interactants (in the United States) employ for
each of the five skills identified by Spitzberg and Hecht (1984). Their
findings indicate that (a) high immediacy is evidenced by more direct
facial and body orientation and eye gaze, closer proxemics, and more
smiling, head nods, and other positive reinforcers; (b) high expressiveness
is communicated by more facial animation, laughter, and vocal variety;
(c) high conversation management is manifested by fewer silences, greater
body coordination, and better speech coordination; (d) high altercentrism
is communicated through more kinesic and proxemic behavior and vocal
characteristics, which create impressions of interest, involvement, attentiveness, and warmth; and (e) low social anxiety is evidenced by more
nonverbal composure, fewer self-adaptors, and more vocal relaxation and
attentiveness.

As stated earlier, intercultural research has not specifically investigated
the influence of these five (intraculturally derived) communication skills

on impressions of intercultural communication competence. Further, intercultural research has not undertaken an analysis of which (molecular) behaviors are associated with these five skills in intercultural interactions. Nevertheless, these five communication skills appear to be remarkably similar to communication skills discussed in the intercultural literature. Interaction management (Ruben, 1976) and immediacy (approach/affiliation orientation) skills (e.g., friendliness and cooperation with others; Benson, 1978; Hawes & Kealey, 1979, 1981; Mumford, 1975); cultural interaction (Harris, 1973); the ability to establish meaningful interpersonal relationships (Hammer, 1987; Hammer et al., 1978); the ability to establish friendships (Center for Research & Education, 1973); and intimate social relations (Furnham & Bochner, 1982; Selltiz et al., 1963), for example, have been identified as important skills related to intercultural effectiveness and cultural adjustment. Further, social relaxation skills including (a) an ability to deal with depression and loneliness (Hautaluoma & Kaman, 1975); (b) calm and self-control when confronted by obstacles (Hawes & Kealey, 1979, 1981); (c) composure in the face of criticism (Mumford, 1975); (d) the ability to deal with psychological stress (Hammer, 1987; Hammer et al., 1978); and (e) the ability to tolerate inconveniences (Guthrie & Zektick, 1967) have been posited to influence sojourners' effective functioning in a foreign culture. In addition, tolerance of ambiguity (i.e., the ability to adjust quickly with little discomfort to new and ambiguous situations; Ruben, 1976) has been discussed by a number of authors (Dodd, 1987; Gudykunst & Kim, 1984; Hautaluoma & Kaman, 1975; Nishida, 1985; Ruben, 1976) as an important predictor of adjustment and overseas success. Expressiveness skills appear in the intercultural literature predominately in terms of language skills (Barna, 1972; Benson, 1978; Hautaluoma & Kaman, 1975; Mumford, 1975). The ability to express respect toward host country nationals also has been cited widely as an important intercultural skill (Arensberg & Niehoff, 1971; Hawes & Kealey, 1979; Ruben, 1976; Ruben & Kealey, 1979). Finally, altercentrism (other orientation) has been considered an essential intercultural skill. This concept has been discussed under such conceptual labels as empathy (Dodd, 1987; Gudykunst & Kim, 1984; Hwang, Chase, & Kelly, 1980; Ruben, 1976), listening/accurate perception of others' needs and concerns (Hawes & Kealey, 1979, 1981), open-mindedness (Dodd, 1987; Gudykunst, Wiseman, & Hammer, 1977; Maretzki, 1965), and allocentrism (Heath, 1977). In addition to these five skills, task orientation (Brislin, 1981; Ruben, 1976), innovativeness (Dodd, 1987), teaching skill (Harris, 1973), and problem-solving skills (Brislin, 1981; Ruben, 1976) also have been identified as related to intercultural success.

## DIRECTIONS FOR FUTURE RESEARCH

The notion of communication competence as a social impression represents a theoretically important "mediating" variable in research that investigates the relationship of communication skills to various adaptation and intercultural effectiveness outcomes. Multivariate research designs must be used to examine systematically the relationships among communication skills, judgments of self and others' communicative competence, and specific adaptational and effectiveness outcomes.

The culture-general versus culture-specific controversy is an important issue that must be addressed directly in future research efforts. In this regard, the behavioral assessment approach used by Ruben and his associates represents a promising method for integrating the culture-general and culture-specific theoretical concerns in the multivariate study of intercultural communication competence and communication skills.

Much of the previous intercultural research findings in this area have been based on self-report data from subjects. While this information is necessary, it is not sufficient. Communication competence assessment must also include competence judgments from significant others. These may include, for instance, the host country national who is a sojourner's boss in a multinational organization; the host country national with whom the tourist-sojourner typically interacts on a regular basis; and teachers or dormitory counselors of foreign student-sojourners.

While the view of communication competence as a social impression emphasizes its communication basis, other facets of the intercultural competence phenomena must also be examined. For instance, a number of writers suggest that the ability to understand another is a basic element of communication competence. Powers and Lowery (1984, p. 58) define communication competence, which they term *basic communication fidelity,* as the "degree of congruence between the cognitions of two or more individuals following a communication event." Similarly, Littlejohn and Jabusch (1982, p. 30) identify process understanding—"the cognitive ability to comprehend the elements and dynamics of a communication event"—as one basic characteristic of communication competence. Within the intercultural domain, Gudykunst and Kim (1984, p. 191) define communication effectiveness as "minimizing misunderstanding." Further, it can be argued that the notion of interpersonal understanding is conceptually different than social impression formation. To illustrate, it is quite possible for person A to have a social impression of person B as appropriate and effective following a communication episode, yet substantially misunderstand what person B communicated.

Intercultural research that examines communication skills must begin to determine precisely the degree to which identified communication skills and their behavioral expression are generalizable across cultures. That is, intercultural communication competence research must examine the behavioral dynamics that take place when people from different cultures interact with one another. Recent intracultural work by Coker and Burgoon (1987) and intercultural studies by Ruben and Kealey (1979) and Hawes and Kealey (1981) suggest promising directions in this regard.

The central role the appropriateness criterion plays in the formation of communication competence impressions demands that situational expectations be adequately investigated. Further, recent conceptualizations (e.g., Bowers, 1973; Brislin, 1981; Cody & McLaughlin, 1985; Mischel, 1973) argue that variation in human behavior can be accounted for by examining the interaction of individual-level variables and situational factors. Within the United States, Marwell and Hage (1970) identified the following three situational factors as important in 100 role relationships: intimacy, visibility, and regulation. Work by Wish, Deutsch, and Kaplan (1976) identified four situational factors: (a) competitive and hostile/cooperative and friendly; (b) equal power/unequal power; (c) intense/superficial; and (d) socioemotional and formal/task-oriented and formal. A follow-up study by Wish and Kaplan (1977) confirmed the first three dimensions, but divided the final factor into (a) formal and cautious/informal and open, and (b) task oriented/non-task oriented. Cantor et al. (1982) suggest four general categories: (a) ideological situations, (b) social situations, (c) stressful situations, and (d) cultural situations. Pervin's (1976) investigation of "everyday life situations" that respondents viewed as important revealed friendly/unfriendly, tense/calm, interesting/dull, and constrained/free as salient situational characteristics. Finally, Forgas (1978) characterized perceptions of group situations in terms of involvement, evaluation (e.g., pleasant/unpleasant), socioemotional/task oriented, and anxiety.

Clearly, a wide variety of situational factors have been identified. Cody and McLaughlin (1985, p. 287), nevertheless, argue that six dimensions "should provide a minimally adequate account of the structure of situation perception generally": intimacy, friendliness, pleasantness (evaluation), apprehension, involvement, and dominance (equal verses unequal power). Cody and McLaughin's six situational dimensions have been identified as salient influences on intercultural interactions and sojourner adjustment (Brislin, 1981; Detweiler et al., 1983; Triandis, 1972). In addition, intercultural research has identified situational factors such as physical environment, time constraints, feelings of individuation/anonymity, overworked/underworked, presence/absence of a niche, and degree of structure present in the situation (Brislin, 1981; Detweiler et al., 1983) as important influences on intercultural effectiveness and intercultural communication competence. Future intercultural communication competence research must systematically examine the influence of these situational factors on interactants' judgments of self and other communication competence. Only in this way can the relative contribution of appropriateness and effectiveness as subjective competence criteria be ascertained in interactants' formulation of competence impressions.

Early research on the topic of intercultural communication competence was based on a practical and applied observation: communication difficulties arise when people from different cultures meet, live, and/or work together that can lead to misunderstanding, hostility, and sometimes physical confrontation. In developing theory and testing theory through empirical investigation, future research must be grounded substantively in the view that the theories proposed and the studies designed should be both practical and useful. It is through constant attention to this mission that understanding of intercultural communication competence will be advanced and contributions to the study of such intercultural contexts as cross-cultural adaptation and intercultural effectiveness valued. Unless this mission remains uppermost in the minds of researchers interested in intercultural communication competence, integration of research findings in this area will likely remain minimal; and our understanding of this important subject area will continue to resemble more a patchwork quilt of bits and pieces of information than an organized body of knowledge.

## REFERENCES

Allen, R. R., & Brown, K. L. (Eds.). (1976). *Developing communication competence in children*. Skokie, IL: National Textbook.

Arensberg, C. M., & Niehoff, A. H. (1971). *Introducing social change: A manual for community development* (2nd ed.). Chicago: Aldine-Atherton.

Argyris, C. (1965). Explorations in interpersonal competency—I. *Journal of Applied Behavioral Science, 1*, 58-83.

Barna, L. M. (1972). Stumbling blocks to intercultural communication. In L. A. Samovar & R. E. Porter (Eds.), *Intercultural communication: A reader* (pp. 241-245). Belmont, CA: Wadsworth.

Benson, P. G. (1978). Measuring cross-cultural adjustment: The problem of criteria. *International Journal of Intercultural Relations, 2*, 21-37.

Bochner, A. P., & Kelly, C. W. (1974). Interpersonal competence: Rationale, philosophy, and implementation of a conceptual framework. *Speech Teacher, 23*, 279-301.

Bostrom, R. N. (Ed.). (1984). *Competence in communication*. Beverly Hills, CA: Sage.

Bowers, K. (1973). Situationalism in psychology: An analysis and critique. *Psychological Review, 80*, 307-336.

Brandt, D. R. (1979). On linking social performance with social competence: Some relations between communicative style and attributions of interpersonal effectiveness. *Human Communication Research, 5*, 223, 237.

Brein, M., & David, K. (1971). Intercultural communication and the adjustment of the sojourner. *Psychological Bulletin, 76*, 215-230.

Brislin, R. (1981). *Cross-cultural encounters: Face-to-face interaction.* New York: Pergamon.

Cantor, M., Mischel, W., & Schwartz, J. (1982). A prototype analysis of psychological situations. *Cognitive Psychology, 14,* 45-77.

Cegala, D. (1981). Interaction involvement: A cognitive dimension of communication competence. *Communication Education, 30,* 109-121.

Cegala, D. J., Savage G. T., Brunner, C. C., & Conrad, A. B. (1982). An elaboration of the meaning of interaction involvement: Toward the development of a theoretical concept. *Communication Monographs, 49,* 229-248.

Center for Research and Education. (1973). *Improving cross-cultural training and measurement of cross-cultural learning* (Report of supplemental activities conducted under ACTION contract PC-72-42043, Vol. 1). Denver, CO: Author.

Cody, M. J., & McLaughlin, M. L. (1985). The situation as a construct in interpersonal communication research. In M. L. Knapp & G. R. Miller (Eds.), *Handbook of interpersonal communication* (pp. 263-312). Beverly Hills, CA: Sage.

Coker, D. A., & Burgoon, J. K. (1987). The nature of conversational involvement and nonverbal encoding patterns. *Human Communication Research, 13,* 463-494.

Cupach, W. R., & Spitzberg, B. H. (1983). Trait versus state: A comparison of dispositional and situational measures of interpersonal communication competence. *Western Journal of Speech Communication, 47,* 364-379.

Cushman, D. P., & Craig, R. T. (1976). Communication systems: Interpersonal implications. In G. R. Miller (Ed.), *Explorations in interpersonal communication* (pp. 37-58). Beverly Hills, CA: Sage.

Dance, F. E. X., & Larson, C. (1976). *The functions of human communication.* New York: Holt, Rinehart & Winston.

Detweiler, R. A., Brislin, R. W., & McCormack, W. (1983). Situational analysis. In D. Landis & R. W. Brislin (Eds.), *Handbook of intercultural training: Vol. 2. Issues in training methodology* (pp. 100-123). New York: Pergamon.

Diez, M. E. (1984). Communicative competence: An interactive approach. In R. N. Bostrom (Ed.), *Communication yearbook* (Vol. 8, pp. 56-79). Beverly Hills, CA: Sage.

Dinges, N. (1983). Intercultural competence. In D. Landis & R. Brislin (Eds.), *Handbook of intercultural training: Vol. 1. Issues in theory and design* (pp. 176-202). New York: Pergamon.

Dinges, N., & Duffy, L. (1979). Culture and competence. In A. J. Marsella, R. G. Tharp, & T. J. Ciborowski (Eds.), *Perspectives on cross-cultural psychology* (pp. 209-232). New York: Academic Press.

Dodd, C. H. (1987). *Dynamics of intercultural communication.* Dubuque, IA: William C. Brown.

Duran, R. L. (1983). Communicative adaptability: A measure of social communicative competence. *Communication Quarterly, 31,* 320-326.

Duran, R. L., & Wheeless, V. (1982). Social management: Toward a theory based operationalization of communication competence. *Southern Speech Communication Journal, 48,* 51-64.

Ellingsworth, H. W. (1983). Adaptive intercultural communication. In W. B. Gudykunst (Ed.), *Intercultural communication theory: Current perspectives* (pp. 195-204). Beverly Hills, CA: Sage.

Feingold, P. C. (1977). Toward a paradigm of effective communication. *Dissertation Abstracts International, 37,* 4697A-4698A.

Flavel, J. H., Botkin, P. T., Fry, C. L., Wright, J. W., & Jarvis, P. E. (1968). *The development of role taking and communication skills in children.* New York: John Wiley.

Foote, N., & Cottrell, L. (1955). *Identity and interpersonal competence.* Chicago: University of Chicago Press.

258                                                    PROCESSES AND EFFECTS

Forgas, J. P. (1978). Social episodes and social structure in an academic setting: The social
    environment of an intact group. *Journal of Experimental Social Psychology, 14*, 434-448.
Furnham, A., & Bochner, S. (1982). Social difficulty in a foreign culture: An empirical
    analysis of culture shock. In S. Bochner (Ed.), *Cultures in contact* (pp. 161-198). New
    York: Pergamon.
Gudykunst, W. B. (1978). Intercultural contact and attitude change: A review of literature
    and suggestions for future research. In N. Jain (Ed.), *International and intercultural
    communication annual* (Vol. 4, pp. 1-16). Falls Church, VA: Speech Communication
    Association.
Gudykunst, W. B., & Hammer, M. R. (1984). Dimensions of intercultural effectiveness:
    Culture specific or culture general? *International Journal of Intercultural Relations, 8*,
    1-10.
Gudykunst, W. B., & Kim, Y. Y. (1984). *Communicating with strangers: An approach to
    intercultural communication.* New York: Random House.
Gudykunst, W. B., Wiseman, R. L., & Hammer, M. R. (1977). Determinants of a sojourner's
    attitudinal satisfaction: A path model. In B. Ruben (Ed.), *Communication yearbook*
    (Vol. 1, pp. 415-425). New Brunswick, NJ: Transaction.
Guthrie, G. M., & Zektick, I. N. (1967). Predicting performance in the Peace Corps. *Journal
    of Social Psychology, 71*, 11-21.
Hale, C. L., & Delia, J. C. (1976). Cognitive complexity and social perspective-taking.
    *Communication Monographs, 47*, 304-311.
Hammer, M. R. (1984). The effects of an intercultural communication workshop on partici-
    pants' intercultural communication competence. *Communication Quarterly, 32*, 252-262.
Hammer, M. R. (1987). Behavioral dimensions of intercultural effectiveness: A replication
    and extension. *International Journal of Intercultural Relations, 11*, 65-88.
Hammer, M. R., & Clarke, C. (1987, May). *Predictors of Japanese and American managers'
    job success, personal adjustment, and intercultural interaction effectiveness.* Paper pre-
    sented at the SIETAR Annual Congress, Montreal, Canada.
Hammer, M. R., Gudykunst, W. B., & Wiseman, R. L. (1978). Dimensions of intercultural
    effectiveness: An exploratory study. *International Journal of Intercultural Relations, 2*,
    382-392.
Hammer, M. R., Nishida, H., & Jezek, L. (in press). A cross-cultural comparison of intercul-
    tural effectiveness: Japan, Mexico and the United States. *World Communication.*
Harris, J. (1973). A science of the South Pacific: An analysis of the character structure of the
    Peace Corp Volunteer. *American Psychologist, 28*, 232-247.
Hautaluoma, J. E., & Kaman, V. (1975). Description of Peace Corps volunteer's experience
    in Afghanistan. In R. Brislin (Ed.), *Topics in culture learning* (Vol. 3, pp. 79-96). Hon-
    olulu, HI: East-West Center.
Hawes, F., & Kealey, D. J. (1979). *Canadians in development: An empirical study of
    adaptation and effectiveness on overseas assignment.* Ottawa: Canadian International
    Development Agency, Communication Branch Briefing Center.
Hawes, F., & Kealey, D. J. (1981). An empirical study of Canadian technical assistance.
    *International Journal of Intercultural Relations, 5*, 239-258.
Heath, D. H. (1977). *Maturity and competence.* New York: Gardner.
Holland, J., & Baird, L. (1968). An interpersonal competency scale. *Educational Psychologi-
    cal Measurement, 28*, 503-510.
Hwang, J., Chase, L. J., & Kelly, C. W. (1980). An intercultural examination of communica-
    tion competence. *Communication, 9*, 70-79.
Kealey, D. J., & Ruben, B. D. (1983). Cross-cultural personnel selection criteria, issues, and
    methods. In D. Landis & R. W. Brislin (Eds.), *Handbook of intercultural training: Vol. 1.
    Issues in theory and design* (pp. 155-175). New York: Pergamon.

Landis, D., & Brislin, R. W. (Eds.). (1983a). *Handbook of intercultural training: Vol. 1. Issues in theory and design.* New York: Pergamon.

Landis, D., & Brislin, R. W. (Eds.). (1983b). *Handbook of intercultural training: Vol. 2. Issues in training methodology.* New York: Pergamon.

Landis, D., & Brislin, R. W. (Eds.). (1983c). *Handbook of intercultural training: Vol. 3. Area studies in intercultural training.* New York: Pergamon.

Larson, C., Backlund, P., Redmond, M., & Barbour, A. (1978). *Assessing functional communication.* Falls Church, VA: Speech Communication Association.

Littlejohn, S. W., & Jabusch, D. M. (1982). Communication competence: Model and application. *Journal of Applied Communication Research, 10,* 29-37.

Macklin, T. J., & Rossiter, C. M. (1976). Interpersonal communication and self-actualization. *Communication Quarterly, 24*(4), 45-50.

Maretzki, T. W. (1965). Transition training: A theoretical approach. *Human Organization, 24,* 128-134.

Marwell, G., & Hage, J. (1970). The organization of role relationships: A systematic description. *American Sociological Review, 35,* 884-900.

Mischel, W. (1973). Toward a cognitive social learning reconceptualization of personality. *Psychological Review, 80,* 252-283.

Mischel, W. (1979). On the interface of cognition and personality: Beyond the person-situation debate. *American Psychologist, 34,* 740-754.

Mumford, S. J. (1975). *Overseas adjustment as measured by a mixed scale.* Paper presented at the meeting of the Western Psychological Association, Sacramento, CA.

Nishida, H. (1985). Japanese intercultural communication competence and cross-cultural adjustment. *International Journal of Intercultural Relations, 9,* 247-269.

Parks, M. R. (1985). Interpersonal communication and the quest for personal competence. In M. L. Knapp & G. R. Miller (Eds.), *Handbook of interpersonal communication* (pp. 171-204). Beverly Hills, CA: Sage.

Pervin, L. A. (1976). A free-response approach to the analysis of person-situation interaction. *Journal of Personality and Social Psychology, 34,* 456-474.

Powers, W. G., & Lowery, D. N. (1984). Basic communication fidelity: A fundamental approach. In R. N. Bostrom (Ed.), *Competence in communication* (pp. 57-74). Beverly Hills, CA: Sage.

Ruben, B. (1976). Assessing communication competency for intercultural adaptation. *Group and Organizational Studies, 1,* 334-354.

Ruben, B. D., Askling, L. R., & Kealey, D. J. (1977). Cross-cultural effectiveness. In D. S. Hoopes, P. B. Pedersen, & G. W. Renwick (Eds.), *Overview of intercultural education, training and research: Vol. 1. Theory* (pp. 92-105). Washington, DC: Society for Intercultural Education, Training, and Research.

Ruben, B. D., & Kealey, D. J. (1979). Behavioral assessment of communication competency and the prediction of cross-cultural adaptation. *International Journal of Intercultural Relations, 3,* 15-48.

Selltiz, C., Christ, J. R., Havel, J., & Cook, S. W. (1963). *Attitudes and social relations of foreign students in the United States.* Minneapolis: University of Minnesota Press.

Spitzberg, B. H., & Cupach, W. R. (1984). *Interpersonal communication competence.* Beverly Hills, CA: Sage.

Spitzberg, B. H., & Cupach, W. R. (1987). *The model of relational competence: A review of assumptions and evidence.* Paper presented at the Speech Communication Association Convention.

Spitzberg, B. H., & Hecht, M. L. (1984). A component model of relational competence. *Human Communication Research, 10,* 575-600.

Stening, B. W. (1979). Problems in cross-cultural contact: A literature review. *International Journal of Intercultural Relations, 3,* 269-313.

Triandis, H. (1972). *The analysis of subjective culture*. New York: John Wiley.

Wiemann, J. M. (1977). Explication and test of a model of communicative competence. *Human Communication Research, 3*, 195-213.

Wiemann, J. M., & Backlund, P. (1980). Current theory and research in communicative competence. *Review of Educational Research, 50*, 185-199.

Wiseman, R. L., & Abe, H. (1984). Finding and explaining differences: A reply to Gudykunst and Hammer. *International Journal of Intercultural Relations, 8*, 11-16.

Wish, M., Deutsch, M., & Kaplan, S. (1976). Perceived dimensions of interpersonal relations. *Journal of Personality and Social Psychology, 33*, 409-420.

Wish, M., & Kaplan, S. (1977). Toward an implicit theory of interpersonal communication. *Sociometry, 40*, 234-246.

# 12 Interpersonal Power and Influence in Intercultural Communication

## Dorthy L. Pennington

But Jackson's world view, in some of its particulars, is refreshingly uncon-
ventional. Thus the hunch here is that the same provocative, gadfly way that
Jackson's candidacy may influence and enliven the Democratic Party's contest
for the presidency on domestic issues, so he may have some measurable effect
on international issues as well. (Geyelin, 1983, p. A17)

This chapter explores how the phenomenon of interpersonal power and
influence operates across cultural lines. Power, here, is defined as the
ability to influence the behavior of others, both with and against their will.
In providing this basic definition, it is important to indicate that, in the
social sciences, the terms, *power, authority,* and *leadership* are closely
associated, so that the type of power that one exercises is often defined in
terms of types of authority or leadership. Weber (1971) makes this association and provides a typology of power/authority/leadership. The types are
(a) traditional, (b) rational-legal, and (c) charismatic. Traditional authority
is bound to precedents handed down from the past and is oriented to rules.
Kings and monarchs are examples of this type of authority. Rational-legal
authority, which is synonymous with what is referred to as bureaucratic,
is based on a process of judicial decision making in which there are formal
rules and precedent. Under this type of authority, there is an appropriation
of official powers on the basis of social privilege and there are established
administrative organs. The presidency of the United States is based on this
type of authority and power. Charismatic authority, on the other hand, is
based on the quality of an individual's personality. Its possessor is believed
to be endowed with exceptional qualities that set him or her apart from
ordinary people. The qualities are thought to be of a divine origin and the
leader assumes power on the basis of a "call," rather than on the basis of
heredity or a bureaucratic election. In charismatic authority, there is no
such thing as a definite sphere of authority or competence, although there

may be territorial or functional limits to this type of power (Weber). Iran is an example of a country that practices charismatic leadership.

This chapter uses a case report to demonstrate how different types of power are effective in different cultural settings. The power types contrasted here are the rational-legal and the charismatic. Because, however, social behavior is a manifestation of an undergirding worldview, the worldviews that are shown to be the basis for the types of power illustrated here are also discussed. Those worldviews may best be conceptualized as mechanical-temporal versus organic-spiritual.

## CASE REPORT

In December 1983, two American servicemen were shot down as they flew a bombing mission over Syrian positions. One of the servicemen was killed and the surviving one, Navy Lieutenant Robert Goodman, a Black flier, was captured and held by the Syrians as a prisoner of war. The need to intensify efforts to gain his release from Syrian captivity became pronounced when it was learned that special Middle East envoy, Donald Rumsfeld, had visited Syria during the time that Goodman was being held but had not mentioned the issue of his release during discussions with Syrian officials.

Jesse Jackson, Democratic presidential candidate at that time, sent a telegram to the Syrian government seeking permission to lead an ecumenical delegation to Syria to aid in Goodman's release ("Jackson Is Invited," 1983). The Syrian government responded positively by inviting Jackson and a delegation selected by him to come to Syria to "discuss Middle East issues and the specific question of your concern for the release of a captured American flier" ("Jackson Is Invited," 1983, p. A13).

Before making his final decision about traveling to Syria, Jackson sought the endorsement of President Reagan and U.S. government officials. He, in fact, made his trip to Syria contingent on winning their approval. The Reagan administration's endorsement was not forthcoming, however. Jackson repeatedly failed in his attempts to reach Reagan by telephone ("Jackson Debates," 1983).

The refusal to endorse Jackson's trip stemmed from its being placed in a political vein by those in power. The Logan Act was the articulated basis for the refusal. In brief, this act, adopted in 1799, prohibits private citizens from negotiating on behalf of the U.S. government. This act is named for George Logan, a wealthy Philadelphia Quaker and U.S. senator, who, after the United States and France severed relations in 1798, traveled to France on his own to meet with French leaders. He returned with a proposed basis of mutual agreement. Although Logan had obtained letters from Thomas

Jefferson and the governor of Pennsylvania, Congress took exception to Logan's self-appointed role as negotiator and enacted a law prohibiting such travel by private citizens ("Jackson Is Invited," 1983).

Presumably, based on this act, the fact that objections to Jackson's trip came as a result of its being placed in a political vein was readily apparent. For example, one journalist, echoing the opinions expressed in numerous American newspapers, held that "Mr. Jackson's sudden offer to visit Syria is typical of his campaign, which has moved with the nimbleness of light infantry from one attention-getting issue to another" ("Jackson Wins," 1983, p. A18). Sol M. Linowitz, U.S. envoy to the Middle East under President Jimmy Carter, warned that Jackson's trip to Syria could "muddy up" ("Linowitz Warns," 1983, p. A12) diplomatic moves to free Goodman. Speaking further on his perception of Jackson's lack of authority, Linowitz said, "We ought to be working through a duly established governmental authority and Jesse Jackson's in the political race . . . I am a little afraid that this does very easily become politicized and the Syrians [could] use it for further delay or for trying to negotiate a deal which our government would not countenance" ("Linowitz Warns," 1983).

Furthermore, not only was there the perception of political motivation underlying Jackson's proposed trip, but the perception of political manipulation, as well: "No matter how sincere Jackson may be about his mission," opined one editor, "there is a sharp overtone of political maneuvering, and there is always the prospect that the flamboyant presidential hopeful will do more harm than good, as the lieutenant's father has warned" ("Jackson Decides," 1983, p. 4). The reference to Goodman's father's objection to Jackson's trip was based on the perception by the senior Goodman that Jackson's trip might harm foreign policy and that he "should be held responsible" ("Jackson Decides," 1983, p. 2) if the effort prolonged the younger Goodman's detention.

When Reagan finally reacted publicly to Jackson's proposed trip, he said that private efforts to secure Goodman's release, such as Jackson's, could be "counterproductive" ("Jackson Debates," 1983, p. 2) and could impair the administration's own efforts to win the flier's freedom. Reagan, however, stopped short of issuing a direct appeal to Jackson to call off his mission. He said that he wanted a "better understanding" ("Jackson Debates," 1983) of Jackson's efforts.

Lacking official endorsement, nonetheless, Jackson felt compelled by a larger, transcendent sense of moral mission, which is best described as messianism. He answered the opposition through reassurance and through justification, showing that his motive was moral and spiritual, rather than political. Responding to criticism that his trip could have political overtones that could embarrass the American government, Jackson remarked that "a political force can engage in a moral act, just as a moral force can engage in political acts" ("Flier New," 1983, p. 2). Jackson stated further that his concern was "not to embarrass our government but to use the credibility we have in that part of the world to try to do something to break the loggerjam" ("Flier New," 1983). Promising to "operate clearly within the law and within protocol" ("Jackson Set," 1983, p. A24), Jackson made it clear that he viewed the trip to Syria as a "humanitarian mission," based on "moral imperative" ("Jackson Decides," 1983). Using language appropriate to the then Christmas season and placing his trip in a clear spiritual vein, Jackson iterated that "we have high hopes this visit will be able to bring forth our message of peace" ("Jackson 'Hopeful,'" 1983, p. 2). He called for "prayers and fasting" by well-wishers, saying that he would be fasting "substantially so, himself" ("Jackson Begins," 1983, p. A25).

The spiritual vein in which Jackson viewed his trip was further evidenced by two facts. First, he decided to make the trip on faith ("Jackson Begins," 1983), lacking either a sign of approval from Reagan or an assurance from the Syrian government that it would release Goodman. Neither did he know with whom in the Syrian government he would be meeting. Yet, he felt compelled to make the trip on moral grounds. Second, Jackson's delegation was largely composed of ministers, including Louis Farrakhan, Wyatt T. Walker, and William Howard, as opposed to politicians ("Jackson Is Off," 1983).

Once in Damascus, Syria, Jackson and his delegation were met by U.S. Ambassador, Robert P. Paganelli, and Syrian Deputy Foreign Minister, Isam Annayet. Within hours after their arrival, Jackson was told that meetings had been arranged with Syrian religious leaders ("Jackson Sees," 1984), with Foreign Minister Abdel Halim Khaddam, with Lieutenant Goodman, and, later, with Syrian President, Hafez al-Assad, himself ("Jackson, in," 1983). During his hour-long meeting with Lieutenant Goodman, the flier revealed to Jackson that he had been well treated by the Syrians and needed only a "plane ticket home" ("Jackson, Captured," 1984, p. 2A). When Jackson met with Khaddam, this Syrian official said that his mind was receptive to what Jackson had to say, but that "there [was] a strong body of opinion in this country (Syria) that he (Goodman) should not go until the flights stop because Syria feels threatened and in a sense insulted" ("Jackson 'Hopeful,'" 1983) by them. Although he received no guarantee of Goodman's release at this meeting with Khaddam, Jackson viewed the time spent as being fruitful.

The epitome of the trip to Damascus was Jackson's eventual meeting with Syrian President Assad. Upon their meeting one another, Assad "warmly embraced Jackson and listened to his plea for Goodman's release" ("Jackson Talks," 1984, p. A10). At the meeting, however, Assad gave no indication of whether he would release Goodman.

Within five days after Jackson's arrival and within two days after his meeting with President Assad, however, the Syrian government released Lieutenant Goodman and allowed him to return to the United States with Jackson.

## JACKSON'S POWER AND INFLUENCE IN AMERICA AND IN SYRIA: A COMPARISON

It is clear from the facts found in the case story that Jackson's power and influence operated differently in the Syrian culture than in America. It is important to ascertain why this was true. Why, for instance, did the Syrians perceive Jackson and his mission differently than American government officials?

From the case it is clear that power, authority, and influence in American politics were derived through a rational-legal system wherein politics and religion were viewed as separate, discrete entities and that, of these two, political bureaucratic power took precedence in international affairs. That is, while Jackson was known as a charismatic religious leader in America, this, in the minds of his detractors, did not qualify him to be an ambassador in foreign affairs. He was not perceived to have what one authority on power, Raven, calls legitimate power or influence. Raven (1965, p. 375) indicates that there are "broad, general norms about the behaviors, beliefs, opinions, and attitudes that are appropriate in a given situation" and that these may come from tradition, internalized values, or from present expectations of others. These determinations give rise to a set of role prescriptions for behavior in terms of "oughtness," "legitimacy," and non-legitimate behaviors. He explains further how legitimate power operates:

> Legitimate behaviors may differ according to a person's position in a social structure. . . . Included in these "role prescriptions" is the expectation that a person in one position may legitimately determine behaviors or beliefs of one in another position. . . . Legitimate influence, then, is based on the influencee's acceptance of a relationship in the power structure such that the agent is permitted or obliged to prescribe behaviors for him and the influencee is legitimately required to accept such influence. (Raven, 1965, p. 375)

In the American view, Jackson's position in the social structure was not one that authorized his going to Syria to seek the release of the captured flier. Such authority was reserved for elected or appointed officials. Reagan, therefore, never allowed himself to become the influencee in the power relationship between him and Jackson. Their interpersonal relationship was governed and constrained by the rational-legal system of American politics, wherein the belief in the rightness of the law is the basis of legitimacy and wherein the leader holds his or her position and power as a result of legal procedures, such as an election or an appointment (Brantley, 1979). In indicting Jackson's efforts and inferring his "non-legitimacy" due to his lack of elective achievement, columnist George Will viewed Jackson as "someone determined to start at the top of American politics, someone who has never held public office and is vulnerable to the suspicion that he considers no chair except Lincoln's large enough to accommodate him" (Will, 1984, p. 5A).

For the Syrians, on the other hand, Jackson's ability to influence them was based on their seeing him in a different light. He was able to exercise influence over them because they allowed themselves to become the influencees. For them, Jackson's legitimacy was not based on an elective status, but on the organic interaction among many factors that can best be conceptualized as charisma. As indicated in a preceding section, charisma, or charismatic power, is based on qualities seen in an individual. Four of the factors contributing to Jackson's charisma were (a) the Syrians' perception of his sincerity, (b) their perception of his interest in their welfare, (c) his religious pathos and their ability to identify with it, and (d) his demonstrated ability to trust them at a critical moment.

Beginning with Jackson's landing in Damascus, U.S. Ambassador Paganelli stated that his presence at the airport indicated "our very deep respect for Reverend Jackson" ("Jackson, in," 1983, p. A4). He further stated that he welcomed Jackson's efforts on "humanitarian grounds" ("Jackson, in," 1983). This perception of Jackson's sincerity in the stated humanitarian purpose of his trip was in direct contrast to Americans' doubt of his stated motivation. For example, Will (1984) termed as "silly" Jackson's argument for going to Syria on humanitarian grounds and referred to Jackson as a "political harlequin."

Jackson's perceived sincerity, coupled with his interest in the welfare of Syria, was evinced by Foreign Minister Khaddam's statement made after Jackson's arrival in Syria. He assured Jackson that "we're following your activities closely and we know you're interested in development in the region. We hope this visit will allow you to have a better understanding" ("Jackson Sees," 1984, p. A12). Jackson impressed the Syrians as someone who was genuine, without affectation, and who exercised resonant, intense listening. In intercultural communication, Smith (1973) concludes that genuineness and a lack of hidden agenda on the part of communicators facilitates normalization and understanding. If normalization and understanding were the goal of the interpersonal relationship between American government officials and Jackson and between Syrian government officials and Jackson, the leaders of the two governments set about achieving it in very different ways. Both Reagan and Khaddam expressed the need to have a "better understanding" with Jackson. Yet,

Reagan refused to grant Jackson an audience, wherein such an understanding could have been derived, contrasted with the Syrians, who arranged a face-to-face meeting with Jackson primarily to achieve a better understanding. In Syria, Jackson's perceived earnestness, as a personality trait, transcended any civil, governmental constraints that might have affected the interaction.

Jackson displayed religious pathos and a concern with morality in his meetings with both Khaddam and President Assad. As earlier indicated, Khaddam had failed to give Jackson an idea of whether Goodman would be released. The pathos characterizing Jackson's appeal was clear, however. Seated a few feet from Khaddam at their meeting, Jackson listened as Khaddam spoke:

> We respect your humanitarian gesture . . . but we are in a state of war alert. How can we let this young man go and keep our army morally prepared to fight a war if necessary to defend our land? What effect would it have on the morale of our troops? After all, we made no aggressions against America. They were flying reconnaissance missions over our positions. (Cheers, 1984, p. 158)

As a hush fell over the room, Jackson responded with an oration, delivered in sermonic style, "as if God had jumped into his mouth":

> I didn't come here on a mission seeking justice. I didn't come here because America is morally correct. I came on a mission of mercy. I don't argue the righteousness or wrongness of Goodman. I am seeking mercy and the lowering of the temperature of war so that peace may come. (Cheers, 1984, p. 158)

Khaddam's allusion to the moral preparation of the Syrian army showed that the communication climate was ripe for the moral appeal made by Jackson. He was on solid ground in making this kind of an appeal, because morality and humanitarianism were subjects with which the Syrians could identify. Establishing this kind of context virtually prescribed the Syrians' need to respond in kind. By showing mercy, rather than meting out justice, the Syrians could show themselves to be leaders in humanitarianism. This image would fare them well in world opinion wherein establishing peace was an international, transcendent objective.

Later, during his long-awaited meeting with Syrian President Assad, Jackson's use of pathos in his appeal was even more pronounced. He pleaded with Assad not to

> send me home empty-handed. If I go back empty-handed, people are able to see clearly that a humanitarian appeal does not work with you, but I think it does. It is important that you take the leap of faith and break the cycle of pain

and return that boy to his parents and leave a good taste in the mouth of the American people. (Cheers, 1984, p. 161)

Coupled with using vivid imagery, such as "cycle of pain," Jackson placed the burden of proof on Assad by putting humanitarianism to its ultimate test. Could the Syrians, as humanitarians, reconcile in their minds the thought of breaking up a family—the Goodmans—by holding one of its members in captivity? Only time would tell. Although Assad listened intently to Jackson, he did not give an immediate answer about his willingness to release Goodman. At the same time, Assad indicated that he would hold a meeting with Syrian officials to have the case of Goodman "reconsidered" (Cheers, 1984). The overture to reconsider suggests that, before Jackson's appeal, the case of Goodman's being held indefinitely had been a closed matter. Any doubt about the validity of such an inference was dispelled the following morning when it was learned that Jackson's intervention had been the decisive factor. Meeting with Jackson, Khaddam relayed Assad's verdict: "Mr. Jackson . . . President Assad has asked me to inform you that he has decided on the basis of your moral appeal to release Lieutenant Goodman" (Cheers, 1984). With the Syrians, Jackson's moral, humanitarian appeal was successful.

Jackson showed trust of the Syrians, as well as sincerity. His trust was demonstrated at a critical point in the negotiation process. After seeing Assad, Jackson gave up American Secret Service protection for a time "in respect for the sovereignty of Syria and having confidence in their ability to secure us" ("Jackson, Sees," 1984, p. A12). His ability to trust, as well as to be trusted, contributed to his credibility and charisma with the Syrians. Jackson's charisma was enhanced by their personalizing his power.

What was allowed to emerge as personal power for Jackson in Syria failed to materialize as personal power among American governmental officials. In addition to being accounted for by the actualization of a charismatic form of power versus a rational-legal one, the difference in the reaction to Jackson's trip on the part of the Americans and the Syrians can be further explained by examining personal power as a construct. Minton (1972) identifies four aspects of personal power: (a) motivational, (b) manifest, (c) subjective, and (d) potential. Motivational power is the desire to obtain social compliance; manifest power is the actual implementation of intentions; subjective power refers to one's subjective evaluation of effectiveness in implementing personal intentions; and potential power refers to previously demonstrated instances in which intentions have been attained, thus allowing for predictions about a person's power in future situations (Minton).

In the Jackson-Reagan situation, it can be assumed that both men held as a goal the gaining of Goodman's release. Jackson wanted to embark on a personal mission of mercy to accomplish this goal. Reagan, on the other hand, wanted to leave such a mission to elected or appointed officials. Analyzing the transaction from Jackson's point of view, we can assume that he was motivated to obtain Reagan's compliance. Indeed, as the case report shows, Jackson persistently sought Reagan's endorsement for the trip. Jackson's desire to obtain social compliance was an example of power motivation. He was motivated to carry out his intention of going to Syria to rescue Goodman, thereby overcoming Reagan's objections. Had Reagan endorsed the trip, then Jackson would have exercised his power motivation. Jackson's ability to carry out his intentions, therefore, would have been an example of manifest power. Viewed from the Burkean perspective of considering the alternatives available to Jackson, his motivation to seek Reagan's approval should have been taken as an indication of his integrity and concern with morality, that is, with doing the right thing. After all, Jackson could have chosen the alternative of going to Syria as a roving messiah on a mission of mercy, without having sought Reagan's endorsement. He, instead, tried to operate within the recognized channels. Reagan, undoubtedly, recognized that to have granted Jackson approval would have, by implication, allowed Jackson manifest power. By refusing to endorse Jackson's mission, however, Reagan deferred facing the reality that would soon come back to haunt him: that, in some contexts, power is as power does. Thus after Jackson had won Goodman's release, Reagan made the predictable remark that "you don't quarrel with success" ("Flier Release," 1984, p. 1).

Although Assad's statement left no doubt that Jackson's appeal was the reason for his decision to release Goodman, some American sources expressed doubt about Jackson's charismatic power in Syria. The editor of the *Portland Oregonian* wrote that "undoubtably there was more to Assad's change of heart than Democratic presidential candidate Jesse Jackson's recognized power of persuasion. Perhaps Assad wished to embarrass Reagan" ("Editorials Discuss," 1984, p. 28). Similarly, the Orange County, California, *Register* preferred: "It is unlikely that Goodman was released because President Assad of Syria found himself impelled by feelings of humanitarian concern after discussing the matter with Rev. Jackson" ("Editorials Discuss," 1984). These journalists, the "gatekeepers" of public opinion, could not phantom, even in the face of incontrovertible evidence, the possibility that Assad made his decision to release Goodman on the basis of Jackson's humanitarian appeal and persuasive power. Thus, although Reagan granted Jackson subjective power after the fact, the journalists made no such concession. For Reagan, Jackson could have potential power in future situations, due to his demonstrated effectiveness in the Syrian negotiations. For the journalists, however, Jackson was denied even potential power; they were uncompromising in their unwillingness to ascribe to him power. The Syrians, on the other hand, allowed Jackson legitimate, motivational, manifest, subjective, and potential power.

The fact that American governmental officials and those in "gatekeeper" positions doubted Jackson, his motivation, and his ability is suggestive of a more fundamental problem, as far as interpersonal power and influence in intercultural communication are concerned. A deeper probe into the matter can be directed by taking linguistic references from their planted contexts and examining them in order to obtain a more comprehensive view. The fundamental problem reflected here was a difference in worldviews, as far as power and influence were concerned.

The different worldviews were implied in the reference to, and judgment of, Jackson's moves as "gadfly," found in the introductory quotation, on the one hand, and in the term, "leap of faith," on the other. Jackson appealed to Syrian President Assad to take a "leap of faith."

## POWER AND WORLDVIEW IN
## INTERCULTURAL COMMUNICATION

The mechanical-temporal worldview of Reagan and the Americans who criticized or were confounded by Jackson's actions is formally referred to as *mechanism*. The root metaphor of mechanism is a machine, with each part having a specified location and specified function (Pepper, 1942). The machine's parts are modular in that a new unit can be inserted to replace a defective one, thus allowing the system to continue functioning. There are laws that hold among the parts of the machine, with each part remaining discrete. Without such complete systematization, frustration is the likely result. Any perceivably unregulated behavior, therefore, is held in tact by the checks and balances of the system, the machine. For mechanists, that is, those whose worldview is Mechanism, objects must exist in time and space in order to be real; they do not want to believe in anything that is not on the ground.

In applying this worldview's root metaphor to human behavior as shown in the case study, the theme of modularity is seen in the fact that, in the American system of government, it is believed that one human can replace another in the same position, with little disruption to the system. Here, the power lies in the position, rather than in the personality of its holder. When judged from the perspective of the mechanistic worldview, Jackson's actions were both inappropriate and anomalous. Jackson was viewed as having no power or right to engage in negotiations with a foreign head of state unless elected or unless appointed by the American president. After all, power in the mechanistic system lies in the position rather than in the charismatic personality of an individual. Because Jackson confounded the need of the mechanistic structure of the American government for systematization, frustration resulted—hence the behavioral description of "gadfly." And the fact that mechanists do not want to believe in anything that is not on the ground explains, in part, why Reagan was unwilling to operate in the vein of faith, as far as granting approval for Jackson to visit Syria was concerned. Jackson had made it clear that he was making the trip on faith, a fact that seemed to have confounded Reagan, who, admittedly, wanted to have a better understanding of Jackson's efforts. Reagan's reaction was predictable, given his mechanist worldview and his being a part of a rational-legal system of power that he was bound, by oath, to uphold.

In contrast to the mechanist worldview of Reagan, Jackson's organic-spiritualist worldview can be formally labeled as *organicism*. According to Pepper (1942), the root metaphor of organicism is integration among parts, with the integration being achieved through flexible, spontaneous, and dynamic action and interaction. Organicists believe that what may appear as fragments of experience are actually pieces whose nexuses or connections to other pieces or to the whole are waiting to be discovered. While conflicts or contradictions may arise, such difficulties are resolved by transcending to a higher level of integration and coherency, thus achieving organic wholeness among parts. Progress toward the goal of organic wholeness exhibits the criteria of inclusiveness, determinateness, and organicity. In the organicist view, as one progresses toward organic wholeness, it becomes clear that any action or fragment finds its completeness in the whole; more and more fragments are brought together toward integration. As integration takes place, one begins to see the whole picture thus steadily increasing the view of determinateness, that is, knowing what is necessary to complete the whole. This is analogous to completing a jigsaw puzzle. Pieces, which at first are only fragments, all have a place on the board. The possibilities for completing the puzzle are suggested by shapes and sizes. While the player initially fails to recognize how the puzzle will come together, there is a sense of faith that the pieces of the puzzle will fit together to create the whole. As the puzzle nears completion, the few spaces remaining suggest the correct pieces to be used, thus creating a sense of determinateness. When organicity is achieved, therefore, every element within the system implies every other and an alteration in any part of the system affects the whole. The limits or parameters of the system are defined by the series:

It is the all-inclusive, completely determinate system of mutually implicative or causally interdependent data. At the limit, implication and causality would coalesce, for logical necessity would become identified with ultimate fact. (Pepper, 1942, p. 301)

From the organicist perspective, Jackson did not view his trip to Syria as being anti-Reagan or as an attempt to embarrass Reagan. His vision was more spiritual. He viewed his trip as a mission that was based on a sense of cosmic compulsion. The cosmic compulsion for the trip prompted the logical necessity that became identified with ultimate fact, that is, with the success of his trip. Knowing in advance how his mission would turn out was not important to Jackson. As an organicist, he could operate on faith, due to a sense of divine determinateness of that which is good. It was consistent for Jackson to believe, therefore, that with divine determinateness, all action that had a positive, spiritualist motivation would come to a good end. To use the puzzle analogy, Jackson, as a player, did not know how the pieces would fit together, but he had faith in the puzzle's creator, who had made the pieces to fit together. The ultimate fact was that Jackson's mission was a success. While in the opinion of some, his success could be attributable to luck or to coincidence, organicists would not share this view. To them, all good things come together, determinately, to create an organic whole. As an organicist, Jackson's desire was to bring all fragments—both human ones and culturally compartmentalized ones—into harmonic integration. As is true in organicism, achieving ultimate integration often requires rising to a higher level of transcendence. Unfortunately for Jackson, the boundaries transcended were those that were subject to national, civil control; his vision was much larger. His organicist view, which required a leap of faith, was better understood in Syria because President Assad and other Syrian leaders leaned toward organicism in their willingness to be flexible and to participate in the process of arriving at the "truth."

For many Americans, as demonstrated in this case study, there was a clear separation between the spheres of religion and politics, inter alia. Jackson, although a religious leader, was disallowed power by Americans as an official negotiator in foreign affairs. As a result, interpersonal relations between him and American officials were held at bay. In his worldview, on the other hand, religion and politics were connected, not only in their operationalization, but also through the transcendent metaphor, morality, which holistically linked all the parts. From the American perspective, power was derived from authorization and legitimacy of right, through a mechanical, bureaucratic, rational-legal process. Here, power lay in the structure, the position. From Jackson's perspective and that of the Syrians, power was derived through charisma, through an organic process in which a variety of factors interacted dynamically. Here power lay in the quality of the individual's personality. After all, "charismatic authority is specifically irrational in the sense of being foreign to all rules" (Weber, 1971, p. 232). In intercultural communication, therefore, worldview plays a part in determining one's interpersonal power and influence.

## CONCLUSION

Based on this investigation, it is clear that interpersonal power and influence can inhere from more than one source, depending on the culture and on the context. Power and influence are, therefore, culture-and-context-specific, culture-and-context-functional. In intercultural communication, it is best to conceptualize power and influence as being multidimensional. This recognition has two implications. First, the variables that translate to one's having power and influence may differ in quantity, quality, form, and process from culture to culture. Second, if the differences in the way by which power is derived are not recognized or acknowledged, dogmatism can result. Even more tragic is the fact that dogmatism can occur from cultural myopia, wherein one is unaware of the possibility of differences. Failure to recognize other derivatives of power is tantamount to denying their existence. The lesson derived from this investigation is that those who view power as being multidimensional seem to be more tolerant of other perspectives than are those who view power in highly structured, unilinear ways. For example, the Syrians were more open to views other than their own than were the Americans. The challenge for intercultural communication is to determine what kinds of compromises are obtainable when different forms of power are in competition with one another.

## REFERENCES

Brantley, D. (1979). *The charismatic political leader: A study in political authority and leadership.* Unpublished doctoral dissertation, Howard University, Washington.

Cheers, M. (1984, March). Lt. Robert Goodman, the story behind his rescue. *Ebony,* pp. 158-161.

Editorials discuss Jackson's success. (1984, January 5). *Lawrence Daily Journal World,* p. 28.

Flier new priority, Jackson says. (1983, December 27). *Lawrence Daily Journal World,* p. 2.

Flier release is praised by Reagan. (1984, January 3). *Lawrence Daily Journal World,* p. 1.

Geyelin, P. (1983, December 29). Jesse Jackson's world. *Washington Post,* p. A17.

Jackson begins "pilgrimage" to Syria. (1983, December 30). *Washington Post,* pp. A1, A25.

Jackson, captured flier meet. (1984, January 1). *Lawrence Daily Journal World,* pp. 2A, 5A.

Jackson debates canceling Syrian trip. (1983, December 28). *Lawrence Daily Journal World,* p. 2.

Jackson decides in favor of Syria trip. (1983, December 30). *Lawrence Daily Journal World,* p. 2.

Jackson "hopeful" on airman's release. (1983, December 31) *Lawrence Daily Journal World,* p. 2.

Jackson, in Syria, sets up 3 meetings. (1983, December 31). *New York Times*, p. A4.

Jackson is invited to Syria for talks. (1983, December 26). *New York Times*, p. A13.

Jackson is off to Syria to seek flier's release. (1983, December 30). *New York Times*, p. A8.

Jackson sees airman in Syrian compound; does not meet Assad. (1984, January 1). *Washington Post*, p. A12.

Jackson set to visit Syria to urge airman's release. (1983, December 26). *Washington Post*, p. A24.

Jackson wins attention but strength is unclear. (1983, December 28). *New York Times*, p. A18.

Linowitz warns on Jackson trip. (1983, December 27). *Washington Post*, p. A12.

Minton, H. L. (1972). Power and personality. In J. T. Tedeschi (Ed.), *The social influence processes*. Chicago: Aldine-Atherton.

Pepper, S. C. (1942). *World hypotheses*. Berkeley: University of California Press.

Raven, B. (1965). Social influence and power. In I. D. Steiner & M. Fishbein (Eds.), *Current studies in social psychology*. New York: Holt, Rinehart & Winston.

Smith A. L. (1973). *Transracial communication*. Englewood Cliffs, NJ: Prentice-Hall.

Weber, M. (1971). *The interpretation of social reality*. New York: Scribner.

Will, G. (1984, January 1). Jackson risks identity as political harlequin. *Lawrence Daily Journal World*, p. 5A.

# 13 Intercultural Adaptation

## Young Yun Kim

Imagine the countless immigrants and refugees all over the world. Think, also, of diplomats, missionaries, students, researchers, Peace Corps volunteers, employees of multinational corporations, and numerous others, who, at this very moment, are going through the process of adapting. Through continuous new learning, trial and error, and more learning, they are finding ways to carry out their life activities with increasing ease, confidence, and proficiency. For new immigrants and refugees who have resettled on a permanent basis, the necessity for adaptation is often comprehensive and all-consuming. Their survival and livelihood are largely dependent on their ability to acquire new learning and to perform according to the standards and practices of the host society.

Social scientists have been far from homogeneous in approaching the process of intercultural adaptation. Traditionally, scholars in anthropology and sociology have approached the field mainly on the level of immigrant (or ethnic) groups rather than on the level of individuals. Anthropological studies have been interested primarily in describing the dynamics of cultural change in various societies (primarily "primitive" cultures) resulting from continuous contact with another culture (primarily technically advanced cultures). Sociological studies have attempted to explain the socioeconomic and political dynamics between and among immigrant/ethnic and dominant groups within societies.

Due to limited space, the focus of this chapter is primarily on studies of individual-level adaptation. The adaptation experiences of individuals have been investigated primarily by researchers in social psychology, cultural anthropology, communication, and psychiatry, in the major countries receiving immigrants and sojourners, such as the United States, Great Britain, Canada, and Australia. Special attention will be given to parallels in studies of long-term immigrant adaptation and short-term sojourner adaptation. Several conceptual and methodological issues will be addressed along with suggestions for dealing with them in future studies.

Reference citations in this chapter are not intended to provide a thorough literature review, but to highlight this writer's assessments of the field. (Readers interested in a more extensive literature review may consult Kim, 1988.) The term *adaptation* is employed here broadly to serve as a concept that represents various other terms such as *assimilation, acculturation, integration,* and *adjustment.* The term *intercultural adaptation* is used exchangeably with *cross-cultural adaptation.*

## SOJOURNER ADAPTATION

Studies of sojourners and their relatively short-term intercultural adaptation were stimulated by the post-World War II boom in student exchanges, military stationing overseas, governmental and intergovernmental technical assistance programs, the Peace Corps movement, and the increase in multinational trade in the 1960s. Extensive literature describes the "problems" of psychological well-being in encountering unfamiliar environmental demands particularly during the initial phase of the sojourn.

By and large, these practical concerns appear to have influenced the focal issues and approaches of many sojourner adaptation studies. Terms often used for intercultural adaptation include *psychological adjustment* or *adjustment,* and four research issues tend to have dominated the area: "culture shock," or psychological responses of sojourners to an unfamiliar culture; factors that contribute to sojourn effectiveness; adaptive changes in sojourners' psychological responses over time; and personal development as a consequence of such changes.

### Culture Shock

The issue concerning the psychological difficulties facing sojourners in an alien culture has been extensively discussed and investigated focusing on the concept of "culture shock." Because encounters with alien cultural environments present surprises and uncertainties, the idea that entering a new culture is potentially a confusing and disorienting experience has been amply discussed, written about, and researched. Oberg (1960, p. 177) first defined culture shock as the "anxiety that results from losing all of our familiar signs and symbols of social intercourse."

Since Oberg, the concept has been employed by many in various ways. Taft (1977), for instance, identified a number of common reactions to cultural dislocation: "cultural fatigue" as manifested by irritability, insomnia, and other psychosomatic disorders; a sense of loss arising from being uprooted from one's familiar surroundings; rejection by the individual of members of the new society; and a feeling of impotence from being unable to deal competently with the environmental unfamiliarity. Bennett (1977) expanded the meaning of this term and regarded it as a part of the general "transition shock," a natural consequence of the state of a human organism's inability to interact with the new and changed environment in an effective manner. According to Bennett (1977, p. 45), transition shock occurs when individuals encounter "the loss of a partner in death or divorce; change of life-style related to passages; loss of a familiar frame of reference in an intercultural encounter; or, change of values associated with rapid social innovation." (See Furnham & Bochner, 1986, for a recent review of literature on culture shock.)

The concept "culture shock" has been extended further recently to include "reentry shock," the emotional and physiological difficulties an individual may experience on returning home from overseas. Gullahorn and Gullahorn (1963) have suggested that reentry difficulties are likely to be more severe a short time after return than immediately on return to the home culture. (See Martin, 1984, for a discussion of reentry shock.)

## Effectiveness

Alongside the issue of culture shock, studies have often attempted to identify factors that promote sojourners' overseas effectiveness. Different researchers, however, have focused on different factors as promoting effectiveness ranging from personality characteristics (such as patience and honesty), and technical skills, to communication behavior characteristics (such as interaction management and listening skills). (See Kealey & Ruben, 1983, for a recent review.) For the most part, selection of overseas effectiveness factors in these studies tended to be based on specific practical interests pertinent to specific situations of cross-cultural adaptation, not on rigorous theoretical reasoning.

Relatedly, Coelho (1958), in a study of Indian students in the United States, investigated how they perceived Americans and how these images affected their interactions with Americans. The Indian students' perception of Americans was found to be closely related to the extent to which they associated with Americans. Further, the students' perceptual patterns increased in complexity and refinement the longer the students stayed in the United States. Also, Selltiz, Christ, Havel, and Cook (1963) investigated the attitudes and social relations of foreign students in the United States. They found that certain characteristics that the students had brought with them, along with certain conditions of their stay, strongly influenced the extent and nature of their association with citizens of the host country (p. 253).

Although varied, sojourn effectiveness generally has been assessed based on the sojourner's psychological reactions to the sojourn experience and to the host society. Klineberg and Hull (1979), in their 11-country study of university exchange students, focused on the level of *satisfaction* as the indicator of adaptation. They concluded that prior foreign experiences and social contact with people local to the host culture are the two most important factors that enhanced the students' adjustment. Similarly, Torbiorn (1982), in presenting a psychological model of "subjective adjustment," paid particular attention to the way individual sojourners are likely to respond to their surroundings and to their opportunities for achieving satisfaction in their new settings. Gudykunst, Wiseman, and Hammer (1977) similarly assessed subjective ratings of comfort and satisfaction with life in the host culture as indicators of overseas effectiveness.

A somewhat different approach was taken by Hawes and Kealey (1981), who, in studying Canadian technical assistance personnel working in developing countries, defined overseas effectiveness as personal/family adjustment, intercultural interaction, and task accomplishment. Based on this definition, Hawes and Kealey observed that interpersonal skills, identity, and realistic predeparture effectiveness were the best predictors of overseas effectiveness. On the other hand, Collett (1971) relied on ratings by host culture members of the acceptability or competence of the visitors. In Peace Corps studies, ratings by the field supervisors of an individual's effectiveness at the job have been often used (see Argyle, 1982).

### Adaptive Change

Many sojourner adaptation studies also have attempted to understand what adaptive experiences follow the initial shock experience and, thereby, to identify the "stages" of adaptation. Oberg (1960), for instance, described four stages: a "honeymoon" stage characterized by fascination, elation, and optimism; a stage of hostility and emotionally stereotyped attitudes toward the host society and increased association with fellow sojourners; a recovery stage characterized by increased language knowledge and ability to get around in the new cultural environment; and a final stage in which adjustment is about as complete as possible, anxiety is largely gone, and new customs are accepted and enjoyed.

These and other similar adjustment stages often have been described in "curves." These curves indicate the patterns of change over time in the degree of satisfaction in living in the alien environment or of positive attitude toward the environment. Some empirical support has been found for what has been described as a U-curve of psychological adaptation. The U-curve depicts the initial optimism and elation in the host culture, the subsequent dip in the level of adaptation, followed by a gradual recovery to higher levels (see Deutsch & Won, 1963; Lysgaard, 1955). This popularized observation and prediction of the sojourner adaptation process has been further extended to the "W-Curve" of adjustment (Gullahorn & Gullahorn, 1963; Trifonovitch, 1977) by adding the reentry (or return-home) phase of the sojourn experience when the sojourner's feelings and attitudes regain strength. (See Figure 13.1.)

The U-curve and W-curve patterns of change, however, have not always been observed consistently in empirical research. As Church (1982) noted in his review of literature, support for the U-curve hypothesis is weak, inconclusive, and overgeneralized. Not all studies, for instance, have reported that sojourners begin their cross-cultural experiences with a period of elation and optimism (Klineberg & Hull, 1979). Even those supporting the hypothesis have shown marked differences in the time parameters of the curve, making the U-curve description too variable to be useful.

## Personal Development

Writers on the three issues in sojourn adaptation reviewed thus far—culture shock, sojourn effectiveness, and adaptive change—have tended to view intercultural adaptation experiences of sojourners as mainly problematic or undesirable, and thus to be minimized. Countering this view, an alternative approach was proposed by Adler (1972/1987). Adler placed culture shock in a broader context, in which culture shock is regarded as a profound learning experience that leads to greater self-awareness and personal growth. Thus culture shock is viewed not as a "disease for which adaptation is the cure, but is at the very heart of the cross-cultural learning experience, self-understanding, and change" (Adler, 1972/1987, p. 29).

Similarly, Ruben (1983) questioned the problem-oriented conventional perspectives on cross-cultural adaptation as he discussed the results of a study of Canadian technical advisers and their spouses on two-year assignments in Kenya (Ruben & Kealey, 1979). In this study, the intensity and directionality of culture shock was found to be unrelated to patterns of psychological adjustment at the end of the first year in the alien culture. Of still greater interest was the finding that, in some instances, the magnitude of culture shock was related positively to social and professional effectiveness within the new environment. These findings suggest implications that directly contradict the mainly problem-oriented perspective on the nature of a sojourn.

In the perspectives of Adler and Ruben, then, culture shock experiences are the core or essence, though not necessarily the totality, of the sojourn experience. Experiencing culture shock is regarded as fundamental in that individuals must somehow confront the physiological, psychological, social, and philosophical discrepancies they find between their own internalized cultural dispositions and those of the host culture. The sojourn experience, accordingly, is viewed in large part as a transitional experience reflecting a "movement from a state of low self- and cultural awareness to a state of high self- and cultural awareness" (Adler, 1972/1987, p. 15).

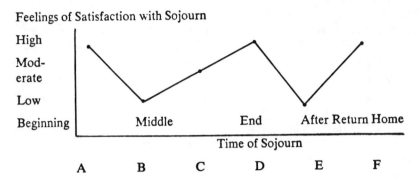

**FIGURE 13.1.** The U-Curve and W-Curve Adaptive Change of Sojourners

## IMMIGRANT ADAPTATION

Immigrant adaptation has been approached for the past several decades by focusing mainly on the subjective experiences of individuals and their social interaction patterns. Varied terms have been used in this area including *acculturation, assimilation, adjustment,* and *integration,* each of which emphasizes somewhat different aspects of adaptation from the others.

Common themes, however, emerge from the various approaches to intercultural adaptation experiences of immigrants (see Nagata, 1969). First, most scholars agree, implicitly or explicitly, that change inevitably occurs in individuals whose primary learning has been in one culture as they acquire traits from another culture. Second, immigrant adaptation is commonly viewed as a continuous process, in which individuals differ in their adaptation rate over the same period of time. Given these general agreements, the present analysis focuses on three issues that are considered to be most basic to understanding the process of adaptation: how the adaptation process should be described; what factors influence the adaptation rate (or degree, level); and what adaptive changes result from cumulative experiences in dealing with the host environment.

### Conceptualizing the Adaptation Process

Aside from the general agreements that adaptation is a process and that individuals show differential rates of adaptation, there exists some divergence in views on the directionality of the adaptation process. The predominant view has been that adaptation occurs cumulatively and progressively, that is, immigrants become increasingly better adapted as they continue to interact and deal with the host environment. Extensive empirical data have been reported in support of this view. For example, Nagata (1969) demonstrated a clear trend toward increasing levels of cultural integration across three successive generations of Japanese Americans. In this study, adaptation was assessed by the overall increase in the degree that Japanese Americans participated in the communication activities of the American society and the corresponding decrease in their ethnic communication activities.

Similarly, the cumulative-progressive adaptation process has been observed in Kim's (1977, 1978a, 1978b, 1980) study of several immigrant groups in the Chicago area. Based on cross-sectional comparisons of the immigrants according to their length of residence in the United States, Kim reported a gradual and incremental adaptation trend in intrapersonal (cognitive, affective, and behavioral), interpersonal, and mass communication patterns, even though the progressive trend tended to slow down after more than 10 years in the United States. More recent empirical support has been provided by Hurh and K. Kim (1988), who observed an increasing life satisfaction level among Korean immigrants in the Chicago area over time.

A theoretical explanation for this cumulative-progressive nature of the adaptation process has been proposed by Kim (1988). Kim argues that adaptation inevitably takes place in all individuals as long as they are functionally dependent on, and continue to communicate with, the host environment. Based on systems-theoretic principles of human behavior vis-à-vis the environment, Kim proposes the "stress-adaptation-growth" dynamics as the central "mover" of each individual along the passage of a "draw-back" and "leap-forward-upward" spiral pattern. (See Figure 13.2.)

Although the cumulative-progressive view of adaptation has been accepted widely, a number of researchers have proposed a contrasting view that can be labeled as "pluralistic-typological." This view opposes the notion of the single directionality of the cumulative-progressive view. It emphasizes, instead, at least several possible adaptation "types" for different individuals. This pluralistic view reflects an ideological concern for the "marginality" of immigrant status and for the maintenance of immigrants' original cultural identity.

For example, Stonequist (1964) viewed the process of cross-cultural adaptation of individual immigrants as following one of three major directions: assimilation into the dominant group, assimilation into the subordinate group, or some form of accommodation between the two societies. Similarly, Chang's (1972) work, based a study of Korean immigrants in Los Angeles, identified three types that correspond to Stonequist's "cultural assimilation group," "nativistic group," and "bicultural group," based on the degrees of change in the original cultural values. A

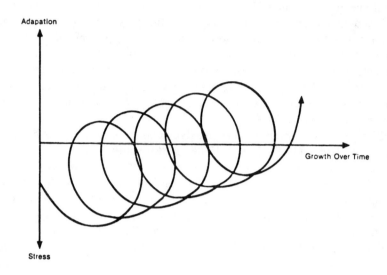

**FIGURE 13.2.** Stresss-Adaptation-Growth Dynamics

further refinement of the typological view has been presented by Berry (1980). In discerning adaptation types, Berry relies on two key questions: "Are [ethnic] cultural identity and customs of value to be retained?" "Are positive relations with the larger society of value, and to be sought?" By combining the responses (yes, no) to these two questions, Berry identifies four types of adaptation: "integration," "assimilation," "rejection," and "deculturation" (see Figure 13.3).

The pluralistic-typological approach as a whole argues that, for some immigrants, adaptive experiences can make them become even more "ethnic" than they had been prior to being exposed to the host culture. This is a clear departure from the linear-progressive view which assumes no "regressive" change once the adaptation process is set in motion.

### Factors Influencing the Adaptation Rate

Attempts to identify factors that help explain an immigrant's adaptation rate (or level) have been made mostly by those who follow the cumulative-progressive view. Few studies based on the pluralistic-typological view have attempted to specify a set of factors to explain individual adaptation rates. This is understandable because the pluralistic view focuses on discerning different adaptation types, and not assuming a single continuum of minimum-maximum adaptation (see Berry, U. Kim, & Boski, 1988).

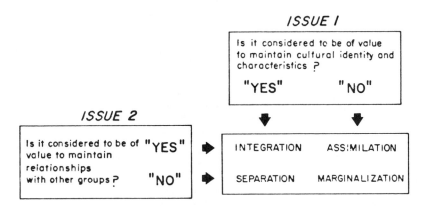

**FIGURE 13.3.** Four Types of Adaptation

Within the research tradition of the cumulative-progressive view, factors that have often been included in assessing individual adaptation rates include knowledge of the host language, motivation for adaptation, positive attitude toward the host society, participation in interpersonal networks of the host society, and use of the host mass media (see Kim, 1988; Nagata, 1969, for reviews). A somewhat different approach has been proposed by Gudykunst and Hammer (1988), who theorize that reduced uncertainty and decreased experiences of anxiety are directly responsible for increased adaptation.

A comprehensive theoretical explanation of the different individual adaptation rates has been presented in the interactive, multidimensional model of intercultural adaptation by Kim (1988). In this model, Kim proposes theoretical linkages among an immigrant's adaptive predisposition and conditions of the host environment. She further proposes that these two dimensions together influence the immigrant's host communication competence and social participation in interpersonal and mass communication activities within and outside his or her ethnic community. These communication dimensions, in turn, are viewed in this model as influencing the immigrant's adaptation level at a given time (see Figure 13.4).

## Adaptive Changes

A related key issue that has received considerable research attention asks: What changes occur in individuals as they adapt to the host society? One of the consequences of adaptation often considered in immigrant

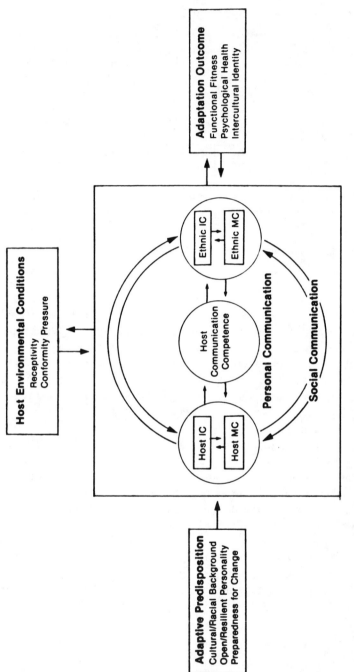

**FIGURE 13.4.** An interactive, Multidimensional Model of Intercultural Adaptation

NOTE: IC = interpersonal communication, MC = mass communication.

SOURCE: Kim (1988, p. 79).

adaptation studies is psychological or mental health (as in culture shock phenomena in sojourner adaptation studies). Inquiries on mental health of immigrants have emphasized the extent to which the adaptation experiences challenge the individual with stressful psychosocial demands. Aside from experiencing psychological distress, immigrants at least initially are considered to be prone to behavior impairment in social productivity. Such psychological health issues have been studied mainly as empirical "problems" that some immigrants experience, but have not been integrated into the conceptual scheme of the adaptation process itself until recently. As such, many investigations have been made to assess different immigrant groups' mental health status or to present specific clinical cases of mental illness and counseling (see Dyal & Dyal, 1981, for a review).

A number of attempts, however, have been made recently to integrate psychological health into the overall theoretical explanation of the adaptation process. Hurh and K. Kim (1988), for example, conceptualize mental health as reflected in the overall "life satisfaction" of immigrants as directly linked to their psychological, social, and economic adaptation. Berry and his associates (1986, 1988) explain "stress" as a consequence of five groups of factors: the nature of the host society; the type of adapting group; the type of adaptation being experienced (i.e., integration, assimilation, separation, and marginalization); demographic, psychological, and social characteristics of individual immigrants; and interactions among these sets of factors.

In addition, Kim (1988) theorizes that increased psychological health is an important consequence of cumulative adaptive experiences over time. In this model, psychological health is viewed as a progressive adaptive change that occurs along with increased "functional fitness" and "intercultural identity" (or the gradual transformation of an individual's cognitive, affective, and behavioral tendencies beyond both the host and the ethnic cultural boundaries).

## TOWARD SYNTHESIS

The foregoing analysis of sojourner and immigrant adaptation studies reveals a lack of cohesiveness and consensus among the existing approaches. Different concepts and conceptualizations are offered to describe what the adaptation process is, what factors must be examined to understand the rate of individual adaptation, and what significant changes occur in individuals as they participate in the adaptation process. This general failure to share a set of common terms and conceptualizations of adaptation is symptomatic of, and at least partially responsible for, the current lack of cross-fertilization within and across individual studies.

On the whole, however, scientific knowledge and insight into the adaptation process is becoming increasingly comprehensive and integrated, a trend reflected in the latest theoretical and research developments presented by Kim (1988), and by several others in the anthology edited by Kim and Gudykunst (1988). Many challenges still lie ahead for the field to move forward toward a fuller integration, without which various efforts to describe and explain the adaptation process cannot effectively account for the complex and dynamic process with sufficient theoretical "power" and "precision." The varied theoretical approaches need to be fully debated and tested against the reality of the experiences of sojourners and immigrants.

It is in this regard for continued theoretical dialogues and advancement of research that a number of suggestions are made below. These suggestions focus on what this writer considers to be some of the major stumbling blocks to be overcome before an advancement of the field.

## Studies of Immigrants and
## Sojourners Must Be Integrated

The two groups' adaptation experiences are, of course, not identical. The immigrants (or refugees) who must depend on the host sociocultural system for their livelihood for a long, indefinite period are likely to go through a more extensive adaptive change. Sojourners, on the other hand, are generally less dependent on the host environment than immigrants in their relatively short stay and, therefore, are less likely to experience extensive adaptive change. Indeed, no two immigrants or sojourners share exactly the same experiences, even if they live in the same neighborhood for the same length of time.

That everyone's adaptation experiences are unique, however, does not deny the existence of common "patterns" of adaptation that all immigrants and sojourners follow. In both short-term and long-term situations, common patterns can be isolated and explained by investigators in the form of theory. Both groups of studies have commonly emphasized the importance of understanding the nature of the adaptation process, and factors that influence the process, as well as some of the changes (or reactions) that occur in individuals as the result of adaptation experiences.

Recently, a number of serious attempts have been made to push for theoretical integration so that the adaptive process can explain all cultural strangers including immigrants and sojourners. Gudykunst and Hammer (1988), for example, integrate the two groups in their theory, which focuses on the psychological process of reducing uncertainty and anxiety as directly responsible for increased adaptation. Kim's interactive, multidimensional model of adaptation does so by dealing with an individual's residence status (immigrant or sojourner) in terms of theoretical constructs, such as the individual's "preparedness for change" and "conformity pressure" in the host environment. A further extension of this theory is presented by Kim and Ruben (1988). Their theory of "intercultural transformation" focuses on that aspect of intercultural adaptation in which an individual's original cultural identity is becoming more *inter*cultural and less rigidly culture-bound. In this theory, individuals are predicted to demonstrate at least a minimum psychic movement toward a greater interculturalness in their psychological state, as they experience intercultural adaptation for a prolonged period.

These theoretical ideas are as yet in their early stages of development and thus are subject to further conceptual refinement and empirical validation. Yet, they offer an encouraging sign for the field to move ahead toward greater cohesiveness and integration. Through integration, the activities of individual researchers become more helpful by informing one another and thereby facilitating the collective discovery of the intercultural adaptation principles that are truly complete and useful.

## The Cumulative-Progressive View and the Pluralistic-Typological View of Adaptation Must Be Reconciled

The cumulative-progressive view "accepts" adaptation as a natural, inevitable phenomenon that at least minimally occurs in all individuals to the extent that they communicate with the host environment and are in some way functionally dependent on the host environment in carrying out daily life activities. Ample empirical evidence supports this view. Almost all research studies, regardless of how adaptation was assessed, have shown an overall forward-upward developmental trend in individual adaptation levels over time.

Curiously, however, this cumulative-progressive view has been held widely by many researchers alongside the pluralistic-typological view even though the latter view not only rejects the former view but also argues for the existence of "regressive" change in individuals toward the original culture (Berry, 1980). These two seemingly contradictory and opposing views have not been sufficiently debated, and their underlying assumptions have not been examined with intensity and seriousness.

Only recently, Kim (1988) has attempted to locate an ideological basis for the apparent inconsistency in conceptualizing the adaptation process. Continued scrutiny is called for if we are to push forward the field of intercultural adaptation toward greater integration.

**More Investigations Need to Explore the
Influences of Environmental Conditions and
Premigration Attributes on Adaptations**

At any given time, the state of strangers' psychological and social adaptation is influenced by the forces of their environment and by the conditions that they had individually brought with them to the new environment. It is the host environment that serves as the "foreground" or sociocultural context in which strangers mobilize their resources and to which they strive to adapt. At the same time, it is the cultural strangers' own disposition that serves as the "background" from which their adaptive responses are mobilized. Together, the environmental and predispositional conditions help set the parameters within which each individual finds a uniquely personalized passage of adaptation.

Studies of both sojourner adaptation and immigrant adaptation have been approached primarily from the social psychological and communication perspectives. There has been a general lack of close examination of the way each stranger's premigration characteristics influence the way he or she adapts to the host environment. Nor has it been extensively examined as to the influences of the characteristics of the specific host environment on the adaptation process. This almost exclusive emphasis on the individual's intrapsychic patterns has tended to lead researchers to neglect the environmental-intrapsychic interdynamics that operate in the adaptation process (see Mechanic, 1974, p. 32).

This means that research in intercultural adaptation needs to be expanded to incorporate the traditionally sociological and anthropological considerations such as institutional or structural factors of the original society, the host society, and the ethnic community of which the individual is a member. Such an integration can be realized in an approach that views intercultural adaptation as an interactive, multidimensional process (see Berry, 1980; Kim, 1979, 1988), in which the individual and the host environment are viewed as coinfluencing the adaptation process. For example, the theoretical model of Kim (1979, 1988), described earlier in Figure 13.4, causally links an individual's predispositional conditions (cultural/racial background, personality attributes, and preparedness for change) and the host environmental conditions (receptivity and conformity pressure), to his or her communication activities within and outside the ethnic community.

Such predispositional and environmental factors need to be examined and elaborated further. Partial evidence has been made available for some of the predispositional factors proposed by Kim (1988). Yet very few environmental conditions have been directly assessed in relation to individual adaptation. This existing gap must be filled through systematic inclusion in research of environmental considerations.

## Research Needs to Be
## Integrated with a Theory

An unfortunate pattern in the traditions of sojourner and immigrant adaptation research has been that of "variable-orientation." Narrow conceptualizations have been generated by placing a number of variables into a regression equation without careful prior theoretical reasoning. Indeed, many studies appear to have been aimed primarily at developing measurement devices, rather than constructing or testing theoretical explanations of the adaptation process.

A probable consequence of this limited conceptual correspondence to theory is a fragmented view of the cross-cultural adaptation phenomenon, the opposite of the direction in which the field must move. This "ad hoc" nature of research must be at least partly responsible for the many varied and inconsistent "models," "indexes," and "scales." Proponents of a variety of limited perspectives often disregard or "argue past one another" with mention of the relations that may exist between alternative measures of the same concepts. The variables in one scientific model thus cannot necessarily add up, or bear coherent relationships to, the variables of any other model.

For these reasons, an integrative approach is advocated here as *ideally* suited for intercultural adaptation research (see Kim, 1988). The integrative approach refers to a research approach designed to maximize the conceptual correspondence with the theory as well as the methodological fit in relation to the nature of the reality that is theorized. This approach can be applied to all phases of the research process, including the conceptual scheme that underlies research, the operationalization of constructs, the modes of observation (or assessment), and appropriate statistical methods to link the data.

Designing integrative research presents a challenge of dealing not with one or two links at a time but with all the links simultaneously as conceptualized in even a moderately complex theory. Yet we need to do the best we can to make a research design *follow* a theory (or at least a thorough theoretical reasoning). This is not to say that atheoretical, limited-scale studies cannot serve any useful purpose: They can, indeed, be vital in exploring the areas of adaptation issues insufficiently known to researchers. Yet, it is only through a sound theoretical reasoning that a researcher can better avoid errors of neglecting to include crucial factors or making inflated claims for research findings.

## "Compromise Plans" Need to
## Be Developed for Research

Researchers, of course, are well aware of the numerous difficulties inherent in designing and implementing integrative research, based on a fully developed, comprehensive theory. Additional difficulties stem from the usually limited time and financial resources, allowing only short-term research efforts. Further, the specialized intellectual backgrounds, interests, and perspectives across disciplines present additional constraints on testing a theory that incorporates elements from several disciplines. (See Blalock, 1984, for an elaboration of this point.)

We must, nonetheless, consider the elements required in ideal research for developing and testing a theory, so that the limitations imposed on a given study may be more readily recognized. Once we recognize such limitations, we will be able to articulate the extent to which the research findings adequately or inadequately compare to the overall theoretical structure and attributes. Such articulation of limitations of a given study will, in turn, help us to develop creative "compromise plans" in which the integrity of the theory and the challenges of the research reality may be maximally balanced.

For example, the research may control the excluded causal variables through sampling; develop a multiphased design testing the entire theory in equivalent samples over time; or develop a multifaceted design testing the entire theory simultaneously in multiple equivalent samples—the overall conceptual integrity of the research is thus likely to be preserved maximally. By maintaining the systematic coherence in conceptualization, samples, assessment methods, data analysis, and interpretation of findings, these "compromise" research plans will allow us to test the entire theory and at the same time help make the research process more manageable (see Kim, 1988).

## Multiple Indicators and
## Measurements Need to Be Used

Improvement is also needed in designing methods of observation. In many studies of intercultural adaptation, concepts have been assessed based on less than sufficiently justifiable measurement instruments and limited numbers of indicators per variable. Typically, researchers rely on asking questions about respondents' opinions and perceptions, or utilizing "paper-and-pencil" measurement scales to assess variables indirectly. This obviously popular method has intrinsic limitations. The information obtainable by this method is admittedly inadequate in mirroring the depth, richness, subtleties, and complexities of the real world of intercultural adaptation. For example, a statistically revealed positive relationship between "host language skills" and "psychological health" fails to describe in detail how these two variables are related in concrete ways as experienced by individual immigrants and sojourners.

The limitations of quantitative data based on subjective responses and the statistical analyses thereof can be compensated for by using qualitative, naturalistic case studies employing assessment methods of participant observation and intensive interviewing to generate detailed "idiographic" verbal accounts with additional nonverbal behavioral accounts of how things operate in reality. Individual participation in ethnic communication networks can be assessed by combining the quantitative measurements of the size of ethnic relational ties, the frequency of interactions, and the subjective rank-ordering of the intimacy level of each relational tie (see Kim, 1987; Yum, 1988). Additional data may be obtained qualitatively by observing the individual communication behaviors. Also, all parties involved in such relationships may be interviewed for detailed accounts of the various ways they relate to their partners.

An increasing recognition of the value of multiple indicators and assessment methods has been made by social scientists. Cook and Campbell (1979) discussed the value of qualitative work in psychological research, and developed a number of specific ways such work can be done through "quasi-experimental designs." Alderfer (1967) observed data showing that interviews and questionnaires may profitably be used in conjunction with one another. Additional innovative methods of assessments have been developed in recent years, particularly ways to combine complex observational and interview data with elaborate statistical analyses (see Moos, 1974, for a review). Techniques described by Moos include the Q-technique used in interviews allowing factor analysis; focused semistructured interviews allowing rank-order data for statistical analysis; and the use of diaries, autobiographic essays, sentence-completion, and responses to short story and problem situations analyzed statistically through content analysis or factor analysis.

These methods are some of the more promising forms of utilizing multiple indicators and assessments, integrating the relatively efficient quantitative methods and the involving feature of qualitative methods. The goal of maximizing the benefits of both approaches can be achieved by conducting a large-scale quantitative assessment of variables, followed by smaller-scale in-depth interviews and participant observation of individuals selected from the original sample. The sequence may be reversed: One may begin with smaller-scale in-depth interviews and then proceed with a large-scale quantitative assessment.

## CONCLUSION

Academic interests in intercultural adaptation continue to grow, clearly reflecting the ever-increasing intercultural predicaments of our time. The theoretical and research issues that have been discussed in this chapter should be viable for years to come. The present analysis, then, concludes with an emphatic assertion for integration—both in theorizing and in researching. Integration is a central task that must be carried out diligently, so that the field of intercultural adaptation may realize a significant leap toward a greater unison. It is through integration that its collective scientific wisdom serves the countless immigrants, sojourners, and all others involved. It may yet reach many more who find themselves in the midst of rapidly changing cultural, technological, and other life circumstances. As Morrow (1985, p. 25) has put it, "everyone is an immigrant in time, voyaging into the future."

## REFERENCES

Adler, P. S. (1987). Culture shock and the cross-cultural learning experience. In L. F. Luce & E. C. Smith (Eds.), *Toward internationalism* (pp. 14-35). Cambridge, MA: Newbury. (Original work published 1972)

Alderfer, C. (1967). Convergent and discriminant validation of satisfaction and desire measures by interviews and questionnaires. *Journal of Applied Psychology, 51*, 509-520.

Argyle, M. (1982). Inter-cultural communication. In S. Bochner (Ed.), *Cultures in contact: Studies in cross-cultural communication* (pp. 61-79). New York: Pergamon.

Bennett, J. (1977). Transition shock: Putting culture shock in perspective. In N. Jain (Ed.), *International and intercultural communication annual* (Vol. 4, pp. 45-52). Annandale, VA: Speech Communication Association.

Berry, J. W. (1980). Acculturation as varieties of adaptation. In A. M. Padilla (Ed.), *Acculturation: Theory, models and some new findings* (pp. 9-25). Washington, DC: Westview.

Berry, J. W., & Kim, U. (1986). Acculturation and mental health: A review. P. Dasen, J. W. Berry, & N. Satorius (Eds.), *Applications of cross-cultural psychology to healthy human development*. London: Sage.

Berry, J. W., Kim, U., & Boski, P. (1988). Psychological acculturation of immigrants. In Y. Y. Kim & W. B. Gudykunst (Eds.), *Cross-cultural adaptation: Current approaches* (pp. 62-89). Newbury Park, CA: Sage.

Blalock, H. M., Jr. (1984). *Basic dilemmas in the social sciences*. Beverly Hills, CA: Sage.

Chang, W. H. (1972). *Communication and acculturation: A case study of Korean ethnic groups in Los Angeles*. Unpublished doctoral dissertation, University of Iowa, Iowa City.

Church, A. T. (1982). Sojourner adjustment. *Psychological Bulletin, 91*, 540-572.

Coelho, G. V. (1958). *Changing images of America: A study of Indian students perceptions*. New York: Free Press.

Collett, P. (1971). Training Englishmen in the non-verbal behavior of Arabs. *International Journal of Psychology, 6*, 209-215.

Cook, T. D., & Campbell, D. T. (1979). *Quasi-experimentation: Design and analysis for field settings*. Chicago: Rand McNally.

Deutsch, S. E., & Won, G. Y. M. (1963). Some factors in the adjustment of foreign nationals in the United States. *Journal of Social Issues, 19*(3), 115-122.

Dyal, J. A., & Dyal, R. T. (1981). Acculturation, stress and coping. *International Journal of Intercultural Relations, 5*, 301-328.

Furnham, A., & Bochner, S. (1986). *Culture shock: Psychological reactions to unfamiliar environments.* London: Methuen.

Gudykunst, W. B., & Hammer, M. R. (1988). Strangers and hosts: An uncertainty reduction based theory of intercultural adaptation. In Y. Y. Kim & W. B. Gudykunst (Eds.), *Cross-cultural adaptation: Current approaches* (pp. 106-139). Newbury Park, CA: Sage.

Gudykunst, W. B., Wiseman, R. L., & Hammer, M. R. (1977). Determinants of the sojourner's attitudinal satisfaction: A path model. In B. D. Ruben (Ed.), *Communication yearbook* (Vol. 1, pp. 415-425). New Brunswick, NJ: Transaction.

Gullahorn, J. T., & Gullahorn, J. E. (1963). And extension of the U-curve hypothesis. *Journal of Social Issues, 19*(3), 33-47.

Hawes, F., & Kealey, D. J. (1981). An empirical study of Canadian technical assistance. *International Journal of Intercultural Relations, 5*(3), 239-258.

Hurh, W. M., & Kim, K. C. (1988). *Uprooting and adjustment: A sociological study of Korean immigrants' mental health* (Project report submitted to the National Institute of Mental Health). Washington, DC: Department of Health & Human Services.

Kealey, D. J., & Ruben, B. D. (1983). Cross-cultural personnel selection criteria, issues and methods. In D. Landis & R. W. Brislin (Eds.), *Handbook of intercultural training* (Vol. 1, pp. 155-175). New York: Pergamon.

Kim, Y. Y. (1976). *Communication patterns of foreign immigrants in the process of acculturation: A survey among the Korean population in Chicago.* Unpublished doctoral dissertation, Northwestern University, Evanston, IL.

Kim, Y. Y. (1977). Inter-ethnic and intra-ethnic communication: A study of Korean immigrants in Chicago. In N. Jain (Ed.), *International and intercultural communication annual,* (Vol 4, pp. 55-68). Annandale, VA: Speech Communication Association.

Kim, Y. Y. (1978a). A communication approach to acculturation processes: Korean immigrants in Chicago. *International Journal of Intercultural Relations, 2,* 197-224.

Kim, Y. Y. (1978b). *Acculturation and patterns of interpersonal communication relationships: A study of Japanese, Mexican, and Korean communities in the Chicago area.* Paper presented at the Speech Communication Association Conference, Minneapolis, MN.

Kim, Y. Y. (1979). Toward an interactive theory of communication-acculturation. In B. D. Ruben (Ed.), *Communication yearbook* (Vol. 3, pp. 435-453). New Brunswick, NJ: Transaction.

Kim, Y. Y. (1980). *Indochinese refugees in Illinois: Vol. 4. Psychological, social and cultural adjustment of Indochinese refugees* (Project report submitted to the Department of Health, Education and Welfare, Region V). Chicago: Travelers Aid Society.

Kim, Y. Y. (1987). Facilitating immigrant adaptation: The role of communication. In T. C. Albrecht, M. B. Adelman et al. (Eds.), *Communication social support* (pp. 192-211). Newbury Park, CA: Sage.

Kim, Y. Y. (1988). *Communication and cross-cultural adaptation: An integrative theory.* Avon, England: Multilingual Matters.

Kim, Y. Y., & Gudykunst, W. B. (Eds.). (1988). *Cross-cultural adaptation: Current approaches.* Newbury Park, CA: Sage.

Kim, Y. Y., & Ruben, B. D. (1988). Intercultural transformation. In Y. Y. Kim & W. B. Gudykunst (Eds.), *Theories in intercultural communication.* Newbury Park, CA: Sage.

Klineberg, O., & Hull, W. F., IV. (1979), *At a foreign university: An international study of adaptation and coping.* New York: Praeger.

Lysgaard, S. (1955). Adjustment in a foreign society: Norwegian Fulbright grantees visiting the United States. *International Social Science Bulletin, 7*(2), 131-148.

Martin, J. N. (1984). The intercultural reentry: Conceptualization and directions for future research. *International Journal of Intercultural Relations, 8*, 115-134.

Mechanic, D. (1974). Social structure and personal adaptation: Some neglected dimensions. In G. V. Coelho, D. A. Hamburg, & J. E. Adams (Eds.), *Coping and adaptation* (pp. 32-44). New York: Basic Books.

Moos, R. H. (1974). Psychological techniques in the assessment of adaptive behavior. In G. V. Coelho, D. A. Hamburg, & J. E. Adams (Eds.), *Coping and adaptation* (pp. 334-399). New York: Basic Books.

Morrow, L. (1985, July 8). Immigrants. *Time*, p. 25.

Nagata, G. (1969). *A statistical approach to the study of acculturation of an ethnic group based on communication oriented variables: The case of Japanese Americans in Chicago.* Unpublished doctoral dissertation, University of Illinois, Urbana.

Oberg, K. (1960). Culture shock: Adjustment to new cultural environments. *Practical Anthropology, 7*, 170-179.

Ruben, B. D. (1983). A system-theoretic view. In W. B. Gudykunst (Ed.), *Intercultural communication theory* (pp. 131-145). Beverly Hills, CA: Sage.

Ruben, B. D., & Kealey, D. J. (1979). Behavioral assessment of communication competency and the prediction of cross-cultural adaptation. *International Journal of Intercultural Relations, 3*, 15-47.

Selltiz, C., Christ, J. R., Havel, J., & Cook, S. W. (1963). *Attitudes and social relations of foreign students in the United States.* Minneapolis: University of Minnesota Press.

Stonequist, E. V. (1964). The marginal man: A study in personality and culture conflict. In E. W. Burgess & D. J. Bogue (Eds.), *Contributions to urban sociology.* Chicago: University of Chicago Press.

Taft, R. (1977). Coping with unfamiliar cultures. In N. Warren (Ed.), *Studies in cross-cultural psychology* (Vol. 1, pp. 121-153). London: Academic Press.

Torbiorn, I. (1982). *Living abroad: Personal adjustment and personnel policy in the overseas setting.* New York: John Wiley.

Trifonovitch, G. (1977). Culture learning/culture teaching. *Educational Perspectives, 16*, 18-22.

Yum, J. O. (1988). Network theory in intercultural communication. In Y. Y. Kim & W. B. Gudykunst (Eds.), *Theories in intercultural communication.* Newbury Park, CA: Sage.

# 14 Electronic Mass Media Effects Across Cultures

Peter Yaple
Felipe Korzenny

This chapter will provide an overall framework for identifying and understanding the issues involved in the study of mass media effects across cultures. While focusing on broadcast media—television and radio—studies of the effects of all media that channel information across cultural boundaries could be framed by this discussion. We see a continuum of technological innovation beginning with the earliest use of tools and signs. Therefore, Neolithic *bulla* (clay tokens) and the electronic-based technologies, beginning with the telegraph and continuing with the multifaceted, computer-based information exchange systems, are seen as part of the same trajectory of human adaptation through use of mediational tools.

Underlying the study of media effects across cultures is the problem posed by the burgeoning new technologies of satellite broadcast and networked computer information systems. For decades, scholars and politicians have argued over the merits of an open system of information and cultural exchange. On one side are those who see that fragile cultures of emerging nations need protection, both for their self-identity, values, and beliefs, and for their own cultural production. On the other are those who believe that human lifeways must operate within an open system, that to do otherwise is to invite entropy (disorder). Settlement of such a question must not rest on the rhetoric of political debate alone—there must be a common understanding of the actual mechanisms at work.

Perhaps more important than settlement of this essentially political question is the question of the effects themselves. Regardless of our inclinations on the freedom to communicate and exchange information, the simple fact is that intercultural contact through electronic communication continues to grow. Short of some cataclysmic reversal of current trends, our ability to communicate and our desire to do so will only increase. What are the intentions of the senders? How are the messages decoded—what is the mediation and remediation (interpretation) of the message? Answers to such questions offer clues to both the sociocultural and the cognitive development of the human species.

After over a half century of investigation, a central question remains: Does the mass media as the cultural production of one society influence another, and, if so, how? Some scholars believe that our world is in a continuous state of homogenization; traditional lifeways are breaking down, their memberships forming an atomized mass—not a romanticized *gemeinschaft*, but a collection of alienated individuals—susceptible to the influence of a dominant culture. Others believe that our lives are structured by information coming from an array of channels, interpersonal as well as mass. They suggest that cultures (and individuals) will retain their differentiation in the face of a dominant hegemonic force. Thus a primary task for communication research is to describe the principles of mediation and remediation and to measure the intervening influence of cultural diversity.

In the struggle to achieve a universally workable set of principles—those that could be operative in a wide range of paradigms—it is most important to understand the conceptual parameters that have framed previous studies. To do this, we must incorporate an understanding of the observer's location. While the observer can never be ideologically free, the bias that is brought to a study may be identified thereby minimizing its "noise." The location of the observer is not only important for our own studies, but for understanding the context of past findings—the body of literature upon which we will build future investigations.

## THE QUESTION OF INFLUENCE

What is so essential about the role of mass communication that we need worry about the effect of *Dallas* on a family watching in Israel (Katz & Liebes, 1984)? Are they inundated by a wave of crass, commodity-based values that reorder their lives and belief systems? Or do they remediate the message to conform to their own needs and understandings of the world? To answer these important questions we first must address the social role of communication.

Jürgen Habermas (1986, p. 397)—converging the thoughts of scholars as seemingly diverse as Marx and Mead—suggests that our species "maintains itself through the socially coordinated activities of its members and that this coordination is established through communication." From this it can be argued that communication forms the basic infrastructure of all human activity. The intrusion of one lifeway's cultural product—a set of values, traditions, signs—upon another is a matter of deep concern. Values pertinent to one social environment are no longer constrained to their origin. The power of satellite-beamed broadcasts can now bring values, hopes, and dreams that may be totally inappropriate in the recipient society. For example, the casual reference to alcohol and sex in a North American dramatic series might be highly disturbing to an audience in Saudi Arabia. Traditional barriers that have protected cultural diversity are potentially vulnerable to an influx of alien information made possible through the foreign mass media.

## IN SEARCH OF A WORLD VIEW

Historically there have been a number of approaches to understanding how a mass medium affects its audience. We suggest that all of these can be categorized *roughly* as belonging to two major conceptual "streams": (a) mass society, closely allied to a Marxist influenced understanding of society; and (b) plural society, a tradition that, while born in Europe, has flowered in the multifaceted social environment that constitutes the North American experience.

The first of these, under a sobriquet of "structuralism" or "social conflict theory," which includes—in a communication-specific context—critical, dependency, cultivation, and technological determinist approaches, is dominated by a class-conflict socioeconomic paradigm. Basically these scholars view their role as *critics* of a mass media that seeks to control an *atomized* audience through the agency of a *hegemonic* force directed by an elite class. Some scholars (Mattelart, 1983; Schiller, 1969) working from within this paradigm have been criticized for accepting at face value the exaggerated assertions of power of the mass media made by advertising and media executives—those whose financial interests are tied to the promotion of such a conceptualization. In creating models such as cultural imperialism or enculturation, they have in the main ignored the limited effects claims made by exponents of the functionalist perspective (Ravault, 1985).

This latter approach, the "functionalist," "empiricist," "positivist," or the "administrative" school, seeks to study communication processes of public influence by empirical means. Through empirical studies, its advocates have found that the power of the media is limited (De Fleur & Ball-Rokeach, 1975; Klapper, 1960). They have been attacked by the critical school as being apologists for the elite—obscuring the true role of mass media and providing information as to how the elite may better control a dominated society. The functionalists, on the other hand, view the difference as one of focus: the "conflict" or "critical" examining the dysfunctions of the mass media; and the "functionalist" scientifically studying the role of mass media in the creation and maintenance of social order.

Another approach, more phenomenologically oriented, is that of the symbolic interactionists who work from the basic premise authored by Mead (1934). They assert that an individual's perception of reality is a function of communication interaction with society. Further, they believe that a collective reality can be achieved from a summation of individual realities. As Mead represents a synthesis of Hegelian dialectic with a distinctly American experiential perspective, it is in such an approach that a path to convergence may lie.

## Mass Perspective

The label "mass perspective" is used because of the assumption that relatively undifferentiated masses are affected globally by the media of a society. Class conflict is the motor of the grand theories at the core of this orientation. Grand theories of social change emphasizing conflict have endorsed the idea that change is endemic to all social organisms. Marx clearly pointed out that conflicts are not random but a systematic product of the structure of society itself (Appelbaum, 1970).

Max Weber (1968) attempted to reconcile the emancipatory theory of Marx with the emerging realities of the nascent industrial-bureaucratic social orders of the twentieth century. In his restructuring of the principles of social conflict, Weber stressed that the evolving industrial-bureaucratic base was a "rationality" that emphasized "means-ends." Optimally, this produced a more equitable relation of power, which in turn decreased the potential for conflict—while at the same time creating an environment where the system and its goals of production superseded the human society that it was meant to serve.

The Frankfurt School originated in Germany in 1923, at a time during which the political "Left" was dominated by the rise of Stalinism and the "Right" by Fascism. Led by individuals like Lukács, Horkheimer, and Adorno (Ewen, 1983; Rosengren, 1983), they attempted to carry forward Marx's emphasis on praxis, that is, theory-based action, employing it for the emancipation of society from class domination.

Out of the mass tradition, a "critical" movement emerged in the 1970s. This perspective directly and decisively confronted the neoevolutionary/diffusionist perspective. One of the initial communication manifestations of this conflict paradigm was found by communication scholars in the work of Paolo Freire (1970, p. 101), who argued for the *conscientização* of people, a "deepening of the attitude of awareness characteristic of all emergence." At the center of Freire's thinking is the idea that one cannot simply deposit ideas in people's minds, but that people become actors in the creation of their knowledge when they are aware of their role in society and history.

A growing group of communication scholars have contributed a vision of communication structures, means of communication, and latent meaning as the crucial issues in communication across cultures. Ownership of the media, and analysis of covert cultural messages, are to be more revealing of social change than more obvious, quantitative measures. This "critical" approach can be traced directly to the Frankfurt School. Critical scholarship has focused on the experience of underdevelopment and the role of mass media institutions in that process.

The critical perspective appears to support the proposition that the combination of economic and media dependency leads to highly complex social, psychological, and economic/political effects when countries are developmentally dissimilar. Further, within this tradition, it is argued that traditional empirical research methodologies bear little relevance to the national conditions of less developed nations, and are more appropriate to the needs of outside forces. Suspicion exists regarding an insidious link between traditional economics, metropolitan media, and traditional research methodologies. Stripping media research in less developed countries of the international context creates research that is insensitive to the real issues that underlie the historical, sociological, and economic context of underdevelopment, and the role the mass media play in that process. It is in such reductionism, they argue, that cultural imperialism is perpetuated through the research tools of empiricism.

It is not only in the message and the institutions that dominate its production that media may control a mass society. The technology itself has been seen as the determining mechanism. McLuhan (1962) was strong in his belief in technology, or, perhaps more essentially, tool use, as the driving mechanism behind culture change (as distinct from cultural advance). He posited that new communications media create an "interiorization (stockpiling)" (1962, p. 174) of technology, and its effect is the shaping of a new humankind: for example, Whitehead's "invention of the invention," which McLuhan (1962, p. 275) ascribes to "the Gutenberg method of homogeneous segmentation, for which centuries of phonetic literacy had prepared the psychological ground." This sixteenth-century European "invention" of the printing press (the "Gutenberg Galaxy)— which brought to prominence the visual sense at the expense of the aural and tactile, and the sense of human independence—was, according to McLuhan (1962, p. 253), "theoretically dissolved in 1905 with the discovery of curved space (relativity)."

In its midst, through a process of gradual transformation, has come the electronic galaxy and with it a resurgence of an oral, tribally structured humankind. As the waxing and waning galaxies commingle, it is difficult to locate self, to become aware of the impact of the technology on self, both individually and collectively. McLuhan suggests that this is because the new technology arouses dormant senses, thereby hypnotizing society. Yet it may be at such moments of juncture that the ideal moment of observation occurs. If one views culture as a trajectory of relationships, and wishes to locate a material object of such a trajectory (e.g., self, a group, or a society), then the opportunity for "triangulation" on the two galaxies seems promising.

In a more empirically grounded discussion of technological determinism, Head and Gordon (1976) proposed that broadcasting possesses an intrinsic continuity that flows through time in a analogic fashion unlike other more discrete forms of mass media, such as newspaper, book, or film, which in informational terms have the characteristics of Zeno's "at-at" concept of motion through time. It was Head and Gordon's assertion that audiences exposed to such an information continuum develop a more limited attention span for more discrete media forms.

James Day (1978) explained how American commercial television has conditioned viewers in the United States and abroad to accept more readily those programs that are the least demanding. Day suggested that it is the business of American television to deliver audiences to eager advertisers who calculate success on a scale known as "cost per thousand." To this end, "Hollywood" has concentrated on form, raising it to a level of high art. American commercial television has developed a "visual grammar," a way of seeing that is unique to American television—fast-paced, and action-oriented, substituting movement for substance. This has created a medium whose content need not be watched to be enjoyed. The audience is in effect narcotized and thus placed in an ideal mode for the reception of the advertiser's message. Therefore, the dilemma: If the world is to be saved from a slow process of cultural homogenization, the flow of cultural production must be made to move in more than one direction—foreign cultural products must have the opportunity to share the highly lucrative American market (and the markets that have been patterned on the American model). But to enter the market successfully, the foreign product must conform to the technological standards and "visual grammar" of the American system of broadcasting and the purpose it serves.

Technological determinism is seen as being naive by some scholars. De Fleur and Ball-Rokeach (1975, pp. 199-217) feel that "technology alone determined neither how people encounter and respond to mass media." They believe that McLuhanist explanations of the media flow are likely to be devoid of (a) the social intention of those who developed the media technology; (b) the international power stratification; and (c) the media tradition and social system of the recipient nations. This view concurs with studies of polysemy in the work of the more empirically based critical scholars (Fiske, 1986; Hall, 1973; Radway, 1984). It is their contention that, while there is hegemonic construction of a dominant ideology in the message, the structures of the cultural product and the recipient society allow for the negotiation of meaning. Thus, in addition to the dominant intent, there can be an oppositional and alternative reading. As Ravault (1985) suggests, there can also be an oppositional use of an alien media system. He offers the example of the Iranian manipulation of the U.S. mass-media during the 1979-1980 "hostage crisis."

There is no reason to believe that the technological know-how could have prevented an utterly different medium from being devised, but the cultural inputs dictated otherwise. Williams (1976, p. 25) states: "It is not only that the supply of broadcasting facilities preceded the demand; it is that the means of communication preceded their content." It has been argued that television content requires "certain" standard practices in mass production and consequently has to exhibit a "certain" kind of program. The fact that television sets in China, as Tunstall (1977) implies, are displayed in public places for ideological indoctrination undercuts the explanatory power of technological-cultural determinism. Finally, the spread of low-cost mass media technologies poses an excellent case for the potential diversity of technological adaptation or "reinvention" (Rogers, 1983).

## Plural Perspective

In relative contrast to mass/structural perspectives, plural, functional, or empirical paradigms have differed in their approach to social change. The label "plural perspective" is used here as being associated most closely with functionalism and empiricism because it is based on the empirical finding of diversity and highly conditional media effects. The "empirical functionalism" of Robert K. Merton (1949) was an attempt to create a researchable (middle-range) theory as opposed to the grand theory of Talcott Parsons. Merton's goal was to create a testable foundation for a total system theory, which he felt that Parsons, in particular, and sociology, as a whole, had neglected. Key to our understanding of Merton's functionalism—for the development of a plural approach—is his concept of "Net Functional Balance Analysis," which considered from a positivist stance both the psychological and the social structural levels.

Within his analytical framework, Merton (1949) provided a theoretical and methodological paradigm with which communication research could test growing assertions of the mass media's overpowering control of an atomized audience. With Lazarsfeld (1948), he focused on specific research issues for the study of mass communication effects that examined social implications for both a single society and comparatively across cultural and social boundaries. Much of this work has been attacked by critical scholars as it sought to understand stimulus-response mechanisms that then might be employed in efforts at social engineering. From empirically based investigations of these issues, they concluded that mass media has the ability both to confer status and to set agendas or, in their words, "canalizing preexisting behavior patterns or attitudes" (Lazarsfeld & Merton, 1948, p. 114). Charles Wright (1986), a student of Lazarsfeld and Merton, sees that by participating in a process of mass communication the individual becomes a functioning member of society.

Despite Merton's attempt to ground theory in empirical fact, grand theories of social change persist. Selected scholars have taken more deterministic and global views that have incorporated Darwinian mechanisms of evolution into schemas of social change. A central theme for this approach is that cultures around the world tend to modernize as they evolve (Appelbaum, 1970). Modernization has been seen as a desirable end state. Lerner (1958) spoke of the need for a more rational and positivistic spirit in less developed nations, seeing *modernity* as an "interactive behavioral system." Here it should be noted that the term *modern* has often been equated with that which is contemporary in the West. Much research has been premised on the assumption that the Western model was of a higher order to which all societies must aspire. It is only in recent years that it has been recognized that modernity is defined by the frame of reference of each culture's trajectory.

Neoevolutionary theorists (Sahlins & Service, 1960) have argued that cultures may borrow from each other without recapitulating stages of development in order to achieve a state of "modernity." This borrowing, then, becomes the core of the well-known perspective called "diffusion of innovations" (Rogers, 1983). The paradigm of diffusion of innovations across cultures originated in the work of those who saw less developed nations as lacking an advantage. Clearly, such a perspective endorses a value system highly aligned with Western values. It was not until recently, however, that the tendency toward modernization has been acknowledged as a Western bias. It took thirty years for communication scholars—and not all of them—to acknowledge that Western-style modernization is not necessarily the end state—or even a desirable stage—of civilization.

Scholars with neoevolutionary perspectives have left a clear stamp on the way in which we look at effects of the media across cultures. It has been suggested (Deutch, 1953) that dependent nations, and other entities who share a worldview, must participate in the growing market of information. This is necessary not only for nations to remain competitive in the international marketplace, but to prevent the possible creation of cul de sacs of cognitive development—not in any genetic sense but in the alienation of a specific culture group from potentially enriching technological innovations such as the computer. In the language of information science, the introduction of external information will prevent entropy from taking over (Attali, 1975).

Daniel Lerner (1958)—perhaps coming himself from what we consider here to be a "mass perspective"—conceptualized four stages in the modernization process: urbanization, literacy, media participation, and political participation. Changes in the psychological makeup of people were seen as central to the modernization process. The values of modern society were seen as being the subject of fast and efficient transmission through literacy and media involvement. For Lerner, the media could play a crucial role in accelerating the takeoff point of societies toward development through his hypothesis of the "revolution of rising frustrations" (Lerner, 1958, p. 331). He argued that the media have the potential for increasing the *want/get ratio* through the promotion of alternative life-styles. The motivating force of such potential imbalance could then serve as the motor of change.

Wilbur Schramm (1964) saw the potential of the mass media as great multiplier agents that could assist nations, particularly rural areas in those nations, to enter the modern world. Inkeles and Smith (1974), in their extensive study of the modernization process in Argentina, Chile, Israel, Nigeria, India, and Bangladesh, found that, after education, mass media exposure was a strong predictor of modernity. Ithiel de Sola Pool (1977) had advocated for a long time that a free flow of information would eventually be of benefit to all nations. He argued that nations benefit from mutual learning processes, and that the emotional attachment to the preservation of culture is a natural but passing affective state that will give way to a widespread cultural interplay. With all the optimism that neo-evolutionary perspectives infused, the assumption was that eventually, through mass education and mass media across cultures, all countries, and all peoples, would finally become modern. Poverty would be averted, starvation would be thing of the past. Modernity would make us all rational and forward-looking human beings.

While the diffusion of culture "across cultures" had not been explicitly stated until recently (Rogers, 1986), little consideration was given to the fact that commercial structures would be prevalent as to the content that "media-rich" nations would export to others. It has to be acknowledged that Schramm (1964) did anticipate that the export of entertainment materials could seriously hurt the role of the media in development. Generally speaking, the media technologies available became so closely associated with the content of the exporting nations that it can be said the medium became the message in the sense intended by McLuhan (McLuhan & Fiore, 1967), and also in the sense that the technology package would have a life and demands of its own.

## Symbolic Interactionism

Pragmatism, a philosophical antecedent to symbolic interactionism, was an outgrowth of "functionalism." It espoused the bourgeois hope that progress, hence salvation from the more tumultuous alternatives offered by Marx, could be found in the integration of science and technology. Yet, perhaps, deeper roots of symbolic interactionism can be found in the same mind that sparked Marxist thought. Hegel saw that there must be an object for there to be a subject, in a process of dialogue the human animal must interact with other human animals. Such a process produces society and in this production can be found the origin of self, mind, and communication.

One of the leaders of the American pragmatist movement (along with John Dewey) was the social psychologist Mead (1934). In the development of his seminal contribution to interactionist theory, Mead was influenced by the Hegelian tradition encountered during his studies in Germany. It was there that he came to understand that communication is a social process whose origins can be traced to the coming together of individual humans to solve problems of survival, such as the procurement of food, defense, and propagation of the species.

The linchpin of Mead's (1934) conceptual orientation is the genesis of self, the image one has of the entity of which the individual feels him- or herself to be in at least some physical control (or at least that which we feel we should control). We can only see ourselves in relation to the norms of that social entity to which we belong. We may not subscribe to the norms, but we are nevertheless enmeshed in them and we can only view ourselves by relating to them—orienting our position on the map of reality through the coordinates of our society's norms. The process of establishing position is as continuous as the radar sweep of the modern mariner. It is in this process that lies the true sense of communication. It functions through myriad known and unknown sensory channels. We can "locate" ourselves only through the perceived reflection of self in the other—and this process requires that communication be entered into between self and society. It is out of this communication that the self is realized.

Modern interpretations of Mead's thought have tempered his extreme social determinism. With some divergence, Herbert Blumer (1969) and Manford Kuhn (1964) have been this paradigm's greatest proponents. Blumer defines symbolic interaction as the formation of behavior of an individual within the social relationship. These behaviors are responses to perceived meanings of intentional gesture—the gesture takes on a shared meaning or symbolism—which Mead (1934) termed the "significant symbol." It is through the construction of a symbolic consciousness that we develop as sense of self and of other creating a sense of commonality.

The weakness of this approach is its vagueness in describing the actual linkage between interactionist mechanisms and process, and the structure of society itself. To bring such linkage into a more concrete conceptual frame, more involved schema have evolved. These are a range of ideas commonly grouped together under "Role Theory"—both in its "structuralism" (Faber, 1966) and "process" (Turner, 1962)—and "Ethnomethodology" (Birdwhistell, 1971; Garfinkel, 1967; Goffman, 1959). It is probably ethnomethodology that holds the greatest potential for an innovative contribution to the understanding of phenomena of cross-cultural mass media effects.

Interactionists focus on the social environment of emerging definitions, norms, or values in order to reveal the organization of a society. Ethnomethodology, from a slightly different perspective, is the study of methods used by people to create a sense of order in situations in which they interact. Ethnomethodologists are concerned with the process individuals undertake to reach agreement on the *impression* of how rules, definitions, and values come to exist—how those being studied maintain or change their belief that there is, in reality, a social order.

Remembering the origins of interactionism in Hegelian thought, it is interesting to consider a possible convergence with another descendent tradition that emerged from a Marxist-Leninist perspective—the sociohistorical approach (Cole, in press). The principal framers, Vygotsky (1962, 1978), Luria (1976), and Leontiev (1981) are just now entering the mainstream of Western thought. A marriage of empiricism and sociohistoricism has produced studies (Scribner & Cole, 1981) on the cognitive affect of literacy across cultures.

It is the belief of this approach that the study of technology—more precisely tool-sign use—must be examined in the context of its historical development. This requires that studies be framed within the contextual totality of human experience. While the empirical data may be drawn from contemporary activities, they must not be isolated from a trajectory that extends back in time to the earliest use of mediational symbols. In an age of dazzling technological advances, it is easy to loose sight of the fact that what seems so impressive may in historical perspective be insignificant—for example, when compared to the transformation of a writing system from iconic to alphabetic representation.

Perhaps even further in expanding such a "holistic" conceptualization is hermeneutics. In this approach it is not only the analysis of the symbolic system that is the focus of the study, but also the investigator's frame of reference. Thus in the current trend of research the possibilities for a frame of understanding continue to expand. We need to put aside the study of an effect in isolation and work toward the construction of increasingly more complex models that capture the complexities of cross-cultural relationships.

## ARGUMENTS AND FINDINGS

Here, theoretical standpoints have been classified in terms of "mass" and "plural" perspectives. In the light of ethnomethodology and symbolic interactionism, and also taking into consideration the unit of observation, to categorize studies and methods in which these paradigms have been applied requires additional axes. We, therefore, suggest a three-dimensional space composed of a *mass/plural* axis; a *social/cultural* axis, that is, the human dimension of the study; and a *macro/micro* axis, the level of the unit of observation, which may or may not coincide with the level of the unit of analysis (see Figure 14.1). The *social* end considers political, economic, class, and technological phenomena, primarily from a *macro* approach, and from a *mass* perspective. The *cultural* pole addresses variables that affect worldview, both individually and collectively, as cultural entities—these might be races, nations, or ethnic minorities—groups of individuals who themselves perceive and are perceived to share common elements of culture, that is, language, belief systems, traditions. The primary unit of observation of this cultural approach is most likely to be *micro,* focused on individuals, and plural in its view.

Approaches framed from within the symbolic interaction or sociohistorical perspectives, in that they attempt to integrate the traditionally discrete forms of individual, social, and cultural analysis, tend to be located closer to the convergence of the three axes than to their poles. It is at this point of convergence that the "ideal" study might be found.

### Social Effects: The Macro View

Much of the work generated by this approach has focused on the international debate over the rights of nations and their citizenry to transmit and receive information—"New International Information Order (NIIO)" (McBride, 1980). [Editors' Note: See Chapter 4, Nordenstreng & Kleinwächter, in this volume for a discussion NIIO.] Those arguing for a "free flow" of information (Pool, 1977; Stanton, 1972; Stevenson, 1984) have attempted to rationalize in "natural" market forces a perceived American dominance in the production and international distribution of mass culture and information. This view is countered by those whose argument suggests that "free flow" is but the guise for a potentially destructive force of alien ideas whose aim is to destroy fragile, emergent national identities and their embryonic mass media "culture industries" (Hamelink, 1983; Mowlana, 1986; Nordenstreng & Varis, 1974; Schiller, 1969).

Yet all of this debate centers on the unresolved question of the existence of a globally dominant mass media. Can powerful nations, or transnational corporations, control the world's cultural production, and what would be

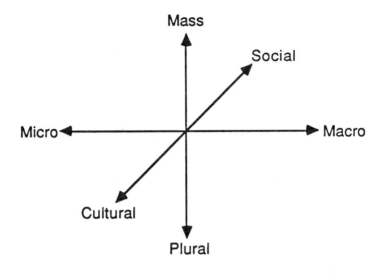

**FIGURE 14.1** A Three-Dimensional Model of Axes of Approach to the Study of Mass Media Effects Across Cultures

the impact on the myriad lifeways of humankind. To explore this question, we will examine work that considers the institutions of the so-called dominant elite: the *senders;* the audience: the *receivers;* and the technologies of mass communication: the *channels.*

Herbert Schiller (1969) posits that there is a "cultural imperialism" that is fostered today by the U.S. military-industrial complex in its efforts to spread American *hegemony* around the globe. He has based his analysis on the sponsors, producers, and transmitters of the dominant cultural production, the multinational or transnational corporations. Schiller is particularly interested in the motivation of these transnationals in supporting their brand of NIIO. From a political/economic perspective, he looks at media impact as being related very closely to the social structures that produce the media and the content associated with it. Further, Schiller (1986) views communication, particularly high-technology communication, as a support system for the operations of transnational corporations. He argues that, under the guise of democracy, Western governments subsidize the development of new communication technologies that then are exploited by transnational giants. Both Schiller and Pronk (1978) posit that the international communication order (superstructure) is intimately tied to the economic order (base). Thus communication patterns are directly tied to economic relationships.

Murdock and Golding (1979, p. 33), in a criticism of the "cultural imperialism" model, see two areas of failure. The first lies in "assuming a simple relationship between economic structures and relationships and the nature of the culture produced by the mass media in a capitalist society." The second is in the critical examination of the cultural product—that is, the attempt to read the "intentions and deliberations of the producers" from the text. Murdock and Golding suggest that future studies should inter-relate cultural production to the material interests that underlie their existence. Most studies have failed to address the impact of ideology on the construction of the message and to understand the totality of patron/audience interrelationship in which the producer/product is mediator.

The need for audience forces the producer to focus on materials com-patible to the audience needs. These needs are located in the cultural matrix underpinning the society. They are not solely dictated by an elite (unless that elite does, in fact, constitute the system) but rather rise in response to the system's intrinsic needs for equilibrium and survival. In short, the system takes on a "life" of its own and its survival mechanism can be seen in *hegemony*.

Raymond Williams (1980, p. 38; based on Gramsci, 1971) has defined hegemony as

> a set of meanings and values which are experienced as practices and expecta-tions; our assignments of energy, our ordinary understanding of the nature of man and the world . . . which as they are experienced as practices become *reciprocally confirming*.

It is argued that hegemony saturates the consciousness of a people, structuring their belief systems, setting their agendas, ordering every aspect of their lives. It is at this level that a system sustains its own momentum creating a "dominant" myth structure known as "tradition"—a composite set of beliefs that facilitate the continuance of a lifeway.

The relationship between sender/receiver is not "mirrorlike." Stuart Hall (1973) presents a model of meaning transformation in which he shifts the analysis from behavior to semiotics. To underscore this, he points to George Gerbner et al.'s (1970) comment that "violence on TV is not violence but messages about violence." When encoder and decoder share the same set of interpretational rules then, as in the case of the "genre" (the good/bad dualism of the "western" offering the obvious example), the amount of noise or misunderstanding will be minimized. But in the cross-cultural situation, where there is little convergence in interpretational rules, then it becomes *polysemic*, in that its meaning is dependent on the full range of context of both the message and the environment of its mediation. The reader should notice that this line of argumentation, para-doxically, opens the conceptual possibility for great variance in inter-pretation, instead of uniformity.

In considering the role of a dominant culture in the international arena of mass media exchange, it is important to describe the nature of its dominant myth, the hegemonic intention of its message system. At the same time, it is equally important to perceive the transformation in meaning that takes place when the message is exported from one hegemonic environment to another. Hall (1973) has demonstrated the barriers to the intracultural mediation of meaning. It is obvious that even greater obstacles lie in such an exchange between cultures. Yet despite the high level of distortion, some effect must take place.

Again we return to a central question. Does the mass media construct hegemony, maintain hegemony, or more simply require it for the construction of a shared system of meaning? Does it impact, effect, or affect? To explore this question further we will turn to an examination of the technology itself.

In examining the impact of technology, Mowlana (1983) presents an integrative theory. He calls for a shift in emphasis in the analysis of mass communication systems, from "source and content of messages to analysis of the message-distribution process." Parameters of mass communication systems are formed by "actions more or less directly related to the formation and distribution of its messages in a society" (p. 158). Further Mowlana (1983, p. 163) sees that an act of communication at the level of a society, nation, or world can be explained by "(1) who produces and (2) who distributes (3) what to (4) whom in which (5) channel under what (6) conditions (values), with what (7) intention (purpose) under what (8) political economy and with what (9) effect?" Therefore, any mass media system striving to integrate itself into a national cultural system must have its policies clear in regard to the following areas: cultural heritage, human rights, development policy and spread of culture, cultural exchange, cultural pluralism, cost-effective selection of communication technology (especially in regard to its hardware aspect), and the media.

Hamelink (1983), in resonance with Schiller and Mowlana, argues that cultural autonomy is fundamental for the survival of human beings who have developed particular cultures for their unique adaptation to the environment. Hamelink argues for international dissociation in which self-reliant development is encouraged along with cooperation among developing nations. He hypothesizes with dismay that the great variety of the world's cultural contexts is disappearing due to a process of "cultural synchronization": facilitating a conscientious effort toward "synchronic transnationalization," which will allow multinational corporations to create a uniform global marketplace for their products. While Hamelink recognizes that the concept of authentic culture is questionable, he endorses the idea of "diachronic" flow of information, in which diversity, independence, and decentralization are given preference.

## Cultural Effects: The Micro View

These types of studies are scarce, perhaps because of the difficulties involved in the empirical investigation of effects across cultures. Part of the work in this area has been conducted intranationally with the effects of dominant culture mass media on nondominant ethnic groups being measured. It is our feeling, along with Howell (1986), that such minorities constitute a "Fourth World." These communities act as microcosms of larger entities and may provide the ideal environment to study cultural mass media effects—effects that may then be seem to exist across national boundaries.

Identifying the basis of cultural effects within the symbolic interactionist perspective, Noble (1975) asserts that television can become for some "the Other," creating a socially interactive process through which a symbolic consciousness arises. It serves the functions of a village (which could become a global village), providing a system of symbolic events that establish, or at least reinforce, existing norms. In essence this paradigm is a micro application of the Gerbner and Gross (1976, p. 175) "cultivation" thesis: "We begin with the assumption that television is the central arm of American society . . . its function, in a word, is enculturation." The "cultivation" thesis posits that television has become the major avenue of social interaction, shaping and reifying the dominant culture's symbolic consciousness. Further, specifically addressing the effect of television on the collective political consciousness, it suggests that "the 'television mainstream' may be the true twentieth-century melting pot of the American people" (Gerbner et al., 1982, p. 126). This ability of television to shape various aspects of social consciousness was noted by Dembo and McCron (1976), who felt that television research must explore cultural, rather than psychological, significance.

The character of Canada and the United States, in that they are nations composed almost entirely of immigrant populations, created an early interest in the phenomena of acculturation/assimilation. This interest has traditionally been focused on the process of adaptation to a new dominant culture. As the myth of the "melting pot" has given way to that of the "salad bowl," more attention has been paid to understanding how the use of dominant and ethnic mass media effect the retention of a traditional ethnic identity (pluralism). Ethnic identity is created out of race, national origin, and culture as determinants of ethnicity. The categories of race and national origin are seen as determining classification, that is, to what ethnic group does the individual belong. The degree of such identification is determined by a more careful study of cultural factors, such as language, religion, communication patterns, and social structures.

Two major models have emerged from studies of communication and ethnicity—demonstrating how mass media can work to facilitate both cultural homogeneity or diversity. The first has been called (Subervi-Velez, 1986) the "assimilationist" and the later "pluralist." The former focuses on how communication patterns affect what is seen as a positive, and inevitable, evolutionary trajectory of, first, acculturation and, then, in some cases, assimilation. The later model or pluralistic point of view reflects the adoption by certain communication scholars of an alternative to the more traditional acculturation/assimilation paradigm. They "seek mostly to explain the processes by which such ethnics maintain some of their ethnic culture by way of identification and behaviors" (Subervi-Velez, 1986). This plural model suggests that often embedded within the nondominant culture is a communicational infrastructure capable of withstanding the inroads of a dominant society—a society, such as in the American setting, whose most salient tool for eventual assimilation may be its media.

In an effort to understand the effects of mass media on the acculturation/assimilation, Young Yun Kim (1984) examined the effect of television and other mass media on "foreign immigrants," particularly on how these media contribute or retard their acculturation. Kim borrows Marden and Meyer's (1968, p. 36) definition of acculturation as "the change in individuals whose primary learning has been in one culture and takes over the traits of another culture." Kim, from an assimilationist position, believes that the increased use of "host mass media" will facilitate acculturation, and ultimately assimilation, while immigrants relying on "ethnic media" maintain their cultural identity. This is based on the research of Robert Park (1922), who found that ethnic media, specifically newspapers, slowed the process of assimilation. Goldlust and Richmond (1974) reasserted this hypothesis in their finding that Chinese immigrants in Canada who relied on ethnic media were less acculturated than those who did not, even when education and length of residence were constant.

Kim (1984, p. 366) proposes several preimmigration variables that affect the acculturation process:

> (1) similarity between the original and the host culture; (2) age at the time of immigration; (3) educational background; (4) various personality characteristics such as gregariousness and tolerance for ambiguity; and (5) familiarity with the host culture before immigration.

Also, in the post-immigration stage, it is important to note the effects of social status and geographic location.

While Kim approached the study from an acculturation bias, there is a growing body of research that does not assume that acculturation/assimilation is a necessarily positive or inevitable goal. Goldlust and Richmond (1974) found evidence to suggest that, in the case of immigrants to Canada, those who received their information solely from ethnic media were less likely to reach the levels of acculturation achieved by fellow immigrants who used Canadian media—even though the level of education and length of residence were held constant.

Jeffres and Hur (1981) conducted a series of studies that focused on European ethnics in the Cleveland, Ohio, area. They found, using a multivariate approach, that "ethnic media use is directly linked to maintenance or strengthening of ethnic identification" (Jeffres & Hur, 1981, p. 130); and "mass and interpersonal communication variables fill mediating positions between social status and ethnic cultural behaviors" (Jeffres, 1982, p. 17). The point is that rather than seeing ethnic media in the negative—a barrier to a "desired" inevitable acculturation—Jeffres and Hur see it as a positive function in a normative desire for ethnic identity. Jeffres (1983) concluded that ethnic media consumption is related to other measures of media uses and that "clearly, ethnic media use is directly linked to maintenance or strengthening of ethnic identification."

A study by Yaple (1987) on the impact of the VCR on a Philadelphia Vietnamese community found that as a user-defined medium—that is, programming choice was to an extent in the hands of the consumer—it was the individual cultural identification that dictated programming choice. Thus young Vietnamese, who through education and work more fully participated in the dominant culture, favored dominant cultural products. Recent arrivals and elderly members of this community retained a preference for ethnic materials. Language, while, of course, a factor, was not the sole criterion. Chinese-language programming, though unintelligible, was preferred to Western productions: similarity in cultural and racial features were offered as prime reasons.

Studies of Western Canadian media effects on inhabitants of the far north have also shown that the cultural background, context, modal personality, and prevalent social issues seem to be crucial in determining message interpretation (Granzberg, 1985; Lonner, Thorndike, Forbes, & Ashworth, 1985). Gavriel Salomon (1985, p. 388) questions:

but is television always the *determinant* of changes? To what extent can culture affect television use, thereby determining its nature and "effects"? . . . we continuously influence the "situations" of our lives as well as being affected by them in a mutual organic interaction.

This symbolic interactionist perspective is appealing and consistent with the type of research we believe should now be advocated, as it appears to be the reciprocal impact of cultural elements that need to be addressed in a holistic fashion. Studies across nations have been conducted (Barnett & McPhail, 1980; Katz & Liebes, 1984; Korzenny & Neuendorf, 1983; Payne, 1978; Payne & Caron, 1982; Penacchioni, 1984; Pingree & Hawkins, 1981; Skinner, 1984; Sparkes, 1977; Tan, Tan, & Tan, 1987) that have concluded that media effects across national cultural groups are detectable but relatively small in magnitude, and that emphasize that the environment, cultural situation, and context affect selectivity and the interpretation of content. Salomon's (1985) model of reciprocal relations argues against simplistic technological determinism. The model looks at the mutual interactions between media, media experiences, behaviors, personality and cognition, and environment and culture. This model better fits a symbolic interactionist perspective, which ultimately prevents us from making definite predictions of what media effects across cultures will be in a simplistic fashion. Actually, this model and the evidence referred to here seem to open the door for cultural diversity over time at the expense of hegemonic thought.

## FUTURE DIRECTIONS

The key to understanding effects is that the mass media are an activity remediated by many diverse environmental factors. Whether the effect of the extracultural production results in an interpretation that is (in the terminology of Raymond Williams, 1980) *oppositional, alternative,* or approximates the *dominant* intent depends on a complex matrix of socio-cultural factors forming the *gestalt* that is the audience's worldview. As the Katz and Liebes (1984) study suggests, we cannot currently see that effects of media go directly from a dominant producer, unremediated to the foreign audience. At each level of cultural identity, national, ethnic community, region, and so on, remediation takes place.

We believe that the lack of a consensus on the mechanisms of media effects lies not in a basic conflict of findings. Rather it is that the principal energy of communication research has focused on discrete phenomena with little attempt at integration. What is needed is a multidimensional approach (incorporating the gamut of directions we have considered) that seeks to describe specific relationships emicly, yet is tied to a more abstract theoretical frame capable of placing in an etic matrix a range of such relationships. Thus from such an inductive method a more universal theory could be constructed. It is absurd to think that the mechanics of mass media effects could work in the same fashion in all cultural environments. To assert this would be to deny the existence of cultural diversity, not to mention the effects of history.

To describe actual phenomena of cross-cultural contact, and thus a useful standing point for the growth of knowledge, requires an empirically based science of culture—imbued with *reliability* and *validity*. In addition, the observation must be framed from within the system of communication, which in the case of cross-cultural communication includes the cultures both as entities and as a relationship. Essentially, we are examining a phenomena of human activity. Each culture has a unique set of rules, traditions, and beliefs that frame activity—put it into context. Unless this context is understood, both as historical and as contemporary fact, then ruminations on the effect of a discrete representation of a behavior—such as violence—are meaningless. For what is "violence?" Is it the same in Beirut and Kansas City?

We suggest the construction of series of descriptive models of culture-specific decoding and recoding (mediation and remediation) infrastructures. While, of course, the range of variation is great, a more pragmatic approach must devise several broad categories and then look to these as representational of the entire range. In other words, a study of cross-cultural effects must be built on an understanding of the disparities in meaning systems between two or more cultures.

Such an understanding is crucial when the media are used for development purposes, that is, in the promotion of health, agricultural practices, nutrition, education, and the like. In these endeavors we are confronted with questions that are different from the questions derived from the flow of entertainment or news content across cultural lines. Incidental effects can be expected from both perspectives; however, the media materials produced have clear objectives at the source that cannot be neglected.

It is our contention that neither the plural nor the mass perspectives reviewed here have a monopoly on the truth. What does seem to be true is that communication, as Habermas and others have posited (and we continue to suggest), is the coordinator of society. As a specific channel comes to dominate this process of coordination, it may dominate the structuring of worldview—it may become a prevalent perceptual framework.

If we wish to understand the evolution of national or cultural world-views and how these are, or might be, interrelated, we must attempt to analyze the nature of their communication (symbolic interaction) trajectory. This must be done as an analysis of intraspecies communication concerning the creation of a planetary culture growing out of a planetary system of communication. Whether this is a process of one lifetime or ten, it is inevitable for the survival of humankind.

The question, we believe, is not of whether a planetary culture will eventually emerge. But what shape, from what sources, and who will control it? The principal task for communication scholars is not to decry the perceived momentary status, but to understand the processes that have led to current conditions, what those conditions are, and where they might lead, in the context of reciprocal relations.

## REFERENCES

Appelbaum, R. P. (1970). *Theories of social change*. Chicago: Markham.

Attali, J. (1975). *La parole et l'outil*. Paris: University of Paris Press.

Barnett, G. A., & McPhail, T. L. (1980). An examination of the relationship of United States television and Canadian identity. *International Journal of Intercultural Relations, 4*, 219-232.

Birdwhistell, R. L. (1971). *Kinesics and context*. Philadelphia: University of Pennsylvania Press.

Blumer, H. (1969). *Symbolic interactionism: Perspective and method*. Englewood Cliffs, NJ: Prentice-Hall.

Cole, M. (in press). Cross-cultural research in the sociohistorical tradition. *Human Development, 604*.

Day, J. (1978). Visual grammar as a barrier to international program exchange. *Rockefeller Foundation*, pp. 12-15.

De Fleur, M., & Ball-Rokeach, S. (1975). *Theories of mass communication*. New York: Longman.

Dembo, R., & McCron, R. (1976). Social factors in media use. In R. Brown (Ed.), *Children and television*. Beverly Hills, CA: Sage.

Deutch, K. (1953). *Communication and social integration*. Cambridge: MIT Press.

Ewen, S. (1983). The implications of empiricism. *Journal of Communication, 33*, 219-236.

Faber, B. (1966). A research model: Family crisis and games strategy. In B. Faber (Ed.), *Kinship and family organization*. New York: John Wiley.

Fiske, J. (1986). Television: Polysemy and popularity. *Critical Studies in Mass Communication, 3*, 391-408.

Freire, P. (1970). *The pedagogy of the oppressed*. New York: Herder and Herder.

Garfinkel, H. (1967). *Studies in ethnomethodology*. Englewood Cliffs, NJ: Prentice-Hall.

Gerbner, G., & Gross, L. (1976). Living with television: the violence profile. *Journal of Communication, 26*(1), 173-199.

Gerbner, G., Morgan, M., & Signorielli, N. (1982). Charting the mainstream: Television's contributions to political orientations. *Journal of Communication, 32*, 100-127.

Gerbner, G. et al. (1970). *Violence in TV drama: A study of trends & symbolic functions*. Philadelphia: University of Pennsylvania, Annenberg School.

Goffman, I. (1959). *The presentation of self in everyday life*. Garden City, NY: Anchor.

Goldlust, J., & Richmond, A. (1974). A multivariate model of immigrant adaptation. *International Migration Review, 8*, 193-225.

Gramsci, A. (1971). *Prison notebooks*. New York: International.

Granzberg, G. (1985). Television and self-concept formation in developing areas: The central Canadian Algonkian experience. *Journal of Cross-Cultural Psychology, 16*, 313-328.

Gross, L. (1975). How true is television's message. In *Getting the message across*. Paris: UNESCO.

Habermas, J. (1986). *The theory of communicative action: Reason and the rationalization of society* (Vol. 1). Boston: Beacon.

Hall, S. (1973). The structured communication of events. In *Obstacles to communication symposium*. Paris: UNESCO.

Hamelink, C. (1983). *Cultural autonomy in global communications: Planning national information policy*. New York: Longman.

Head, S., & Gordon, T. (1976). The structure of world broadcast programming: some tentative hypothesis. *Gazette, 22*(2), 121-129.

Howell, W. J. (1986). *World broadcasting in the age of the satellites: Comparative systems, policies and issues in mass telecommunication*. Norwood, NJ: Ablex.

Inkeles, A., & Smith, D. H. (1974). *Becoming modern: Individual change in six developing countries*. Cambridge, MA: Harvard University Press.

Jeffres, L. (1982). Communication, *"class" and culture*. Paper presented at the Association for Education in Journalism Convention, Athens, OH.

Jeffres, L. (1983). Media use for personal identification: Linking uses and gratifications to culturally significant goals. *Mass Communication Review, 10*, 6-12.

Jeffres, L., & Hur, K. K. (1979). *Communication channels and information flow among ethnics.* Paper presented at the International Communication Association Convention, Philadelphia.

Jeffres, L., & Hur, K. K. (1981). Communication channels within ethnic groups. *International Journal of Intercultural Relations, 5*, 115-132.

Katz, E., & Liebes, T. (1984). Once upon a time in Dallas. *Intermedia 12*(3), 28-32.

Kim, Y. Y. (1976). *Communication patterns of foreign immigrants in the process of acculturation: A survey among the Korean population in Chicago.* Unpublished doctoral dissertation, Northwestern University, Evanston, IL.

Kim, Y. Y. (1984). Searching for creative integration. In W. B. Gudykunst & Y. Y. Kim (Eds.), *Methods for intercultural communication research.* Beverly Hills, CA: Sage.

Klapper, J. T. (1960). *The effects of mass communication.* New York: Free Press.

Korzenny, F., & Neuendorf, K. (1983). The perceived reality of television and aggressive predispositions among children in Mexico. *International Journal of Intercultural Relations, 7*, 33-51.

Kuhn, M. (1964). Major trends in symbolic interaction theory in the past twenty-five years. *Sociological Quarterly, 5*, 61-84.

Lazarsfeld, P. F., & Merton, R. K. (1948). Mass communication, popular taste and organized social action. In L. Bryson (Ed.), *The communication of ideas.* New York: Harper.

Leontiev, A. N. (1981). *Problems in the development of mind.* Moscow: Progress.

Lerner, D. (1958). *The passing of traditional society: Modernizing the Middle East.* New York: Free Press.

Lonner, W. J., Thorndike, R. M., Forbes, N. E., & Ashworth, C. (1985). The influence of television on measured cognitive abilities: A study with Native Alaskan Children. *Journal of Cross-Cultural Psychology, 16*, 355-380.

Luria, A. R. (1976). *Cognitive development.* Cambridge, MA: Harvard University Press.

Marden, C. F., & Meyer, G. (1968). *Minorities in American Society* (3rd ed.). New York: Van Nostrand.

Mattelart, A. (1983). *Transnationals and the Third World: The struggle for culture.* Boston: Bergen & Garvey.

McBride, S. (1980) *Many voices, one world.* Paris: UNESCO.

McLuhan, M. (1962) *The Gutenberg galaxy.* Toronto: University of Toronto Press.

McLuhan, M., & Fiore, Q. (1967). *The medium is the message: An inventory of effects.* New York: Bantam.

Mead, G. H. (1934). *Mind, self, and society.* Chicago: University of Chicago Press.

Merton, R. K. (1949). *Social theory and social structure.* Glencoe, IL: Free Press.

Mowlana, H. (1983). Mass media and culture: Toward an integrated theory. In W. Gudykunst (Ed.), *Intercultural communication theory.* Beverly Hills, CA: Sage.

Mowlana, H. (1986). *Global information and world communication.* New York: Longman.

Murdock, G., & Golding, P. (1979). Capitalism, communication and class relations. In J. Curran (Ed.), *Mass communication and society.* Beverly Hills, CA: Sage.

Noble, G. (1975). *Children in front of the small screen.* Beverly Hills, CA: Sage.

Nordenstreng, K., & Varis, T. (1974). Television traffic: A one way street? *Reports and Papers on Mass Communications*, no. 70. (Paris: UNESCO)

Park, R. (1922). *The immigrant press and its control.* New York: Harper.

Payne, D. (1978). Cross-national diffusion: The effects of Canadian TV on rural Minnesota viewers. *American Sociological Review, 43*, 740-756.

Payne, D., & Caron, A. H. (1982). Anglophone Canadian and American mass media: Use and effects on Québecois adults. *Communication Research, 9*, 113-144.

Penacchioni, I. (1984). The reception of popular television in Northeast Brazil. *Media, Culture and Society, 6*, 337-341.

Pingree, S., & Hawkins, R. (1981). U.S. programs on Australian television: The cultivation effect. *Journal of Communication, 31,* 97-105.

Pool, I. de S. (1977). The changing flow of television. *Journal of Communication, 27,* 139-149.

Pronk, J. (1978). *Some remarks on the relation between the New International Economic Order and the New International Information Order* (Document no. 35). Paris: UNESCO, International Commission for the Study of Communication Problems.

Radway, J. (1984). *Reading the romance: Feminism and the representation of women in popular culture.* Chapel Hill: University of North Carolina Press.

Ravault, R. J. (1985). Resisting media imperialism by coerseduction. *Intermedia, 13*(3).

Rogers, E. (1983). *Diffusion of innovations* (3rd ed.). New York: Free Press.

Rogers, E. (1986). *Communication technology: The new media in society.* New York: Free Press.

Rosengren, K. E. (1983). Communication research: One paradigm, or four? *Journal of Communication, 33*(3), 185-207.

Sahlins, M. D., & Service, E. R. (Eds.). (1960). *Evolution and culture.* Ann Arbor: University of Michigan Press.

Salomon, G. (1985). The study of television in a cross-cultural context. *Journal of Cross-Cultural Psychology, 16,* 381-397.

Schiller, H. (1969). *Mass communication and the American empire.* New York: Kelly.

Schiller, H. (1978). *Communication Accompanies Capitol Flows.* (Document no. 47). UNESCO, International Commission for the Study of Communication Problems.

Schiller, H. (1986). *Information and the crisis economy.* New York: Oxford University Press.

Schramm, W. (1964). *Mass media and national development.* Stanford, CA: Stanford University Press.

Scribner, S., & Cole, M. (1981). *The psychology of literacy.* Cambridge, MA: Harvard University Press.

Skinner, E. C. (1984). *Foreign TV program viewing and dependency: A case study of U.S. television viewing in Trinidad and Tobago.* Unpublished doctoral dissertation, Michigan State University, East Lansing.

Sparkes, V. (1977). TV across the Canadian border: Does it matter? *Journal of Communication, 27,* 40-47.

Stanton, F. (1972, October 22). Will they stop our satellites? *New York Times,* pp. 23, 29.

Stevenson, R. (1984). The "world news" study: pseudo debate. *Journal of Communication, 34*(1), 134-138.

Subervi-Velez, F. (1986). The mass media and ethnic assimilation and pluralism. *Communication Research, 13,* 71-96.

Tan, A. S., Tan, G. K., & Tan, A. S. (1987). American TV in the Philippines: A test of cultural impact. *Journalism Quarterly, 64,* 65-79.

Tunstall, J. (1977). *The media are American.* London: Constable.

Turner, R. H. (1962). Role-taking: Process versus conformity. In A. Rose (Ed.), *Human behavior and social processes* (pp. 20-40). Boston: Houghton Mifflin.

Vygotsky, L. S. (1978). *Mind in Society.* Cambridge, MA: Harvard University Press.

Vygotsky, L. S. (1962). *Thought and Language.* Cambridge: MIT Press.

Weber, M. (1968). *Economy and society.* New York: Badminster.

Williams, R. (1976). *Keyword: A vocabulary of culture and society.* New York: Oxford University Press.

Williams, R. (1980). *Problems in materialism and culture.* London: Verso.

Wright, C. R. (1986). *Mass communication: A sociological perspective* (3rd ed.). New York: Random House.

Yaple, P. (1987). *The role of the VCR in a polycultural society: Patterns of video use by twenty Vietnamese families in Philadelphia.* Unpublished master's thesis, University of Pennsylvania, Annenberg School of Communications.

# 15 Television and Social Perceptions Among African Americans and Hispanics

**Oscar H. Gandy, Jr.**
**Paula W. Matabane**

Stimulated by the civil rights movement, the women's movement, and the rise in urban violence, social scientists took on the challenge of investigating the impact of television on viewers' values, belief systems, and perceptions of social reality. The application of energies to the experiences of minorities, however, was sparse and problematic. Generally, the study of minorities focused on television's impact on racial attitudes, self-esteem, and, to a lesser extent, self-concept (Graves, 1975; Stroman, 1984, 1986). The broader implications of social learning by a subordinate group through the cultural apparatus of the dominant group was usually not made an explicit part of the theoretical perspectives utilized in these studies. Very often researchers considered the integrative role of television as a positive achievement of its social function of providing "the ethos of the social order" in which it operates. The assimilation of subordinate groups has been viewed as a desirable process in the forging of "civil society."

Influences on viewers have been characterized as having direct and indirect effects. Modes for theorizing and testing propositions about the nature of these effects have raised as many questions as they have answered. It is our goal to bring together many of the insights from these often contradictory studies in a way that helps to frame the questions that must be pursued in the future. We have organized this review in terms of what we believe to be the principal components of a comprehensive approach to studying the impact of mass media.

Stephen Resnick and Richard Wolff (1987) argue forcefully for the indeterminacy of an essential cause. Each process and relationship within

AUTHORS' NOTE: We would like to acknowledge the generous comments and suggestions offered by George Gerbner and Federico Subervi-Velez, and the valuable assistance of Michael A. Williams of the Center for Communications Research at Howard University.

a social system is in some way linked, influencing, and being influenced by those links. The task of theorists is to be as comprehensive as possible in describing those relationships. This task begins with identifying conceptual points of entry. From our perspective, no theory of media effects can ignore the economic and political environment that is involved in regulating the production and distribution of media images. At the same time, exposure to and interpretation of those images are conditioned and regulated by the cultural, subcultural, and personal experiences that forge the differences between us. Thus in the pages that follow we will discuss the representations of Blacks and Hispanics in the context of the changing media environments that produce them. We will examine the evidence of media effects in the context of socially generated individual and group differences. And we will suggest areas where we believe additional research is warranted.

## POLITICAL ECONOMY OF THE MASS MEDIA

Sandra Ball-Rokeach (1985) offers a sociological perspective that focuses on the micro- and macro-level determinants of media dependencies, which may provide some insight into the social origins of the particular patterns and orientations we find within Black and Hispanic populations. Her study is unique among mainstream analyses in that it includes historical patterns and structural relationships between mass media and other social systems in which Blacks and Hispanics organize their lives. Thus Ball-Rokeach argues that individuals are dependent upon the mass media as their basic link to the economic and political system. It is important, therefore, to examine the political and economic structure of the mass media environment in order to develop some insights into the ways Hispanic and Black dependencies develop and change in time.

### Hegemony

The theory of hegemony has been identified with Antonio Gramsci's (1983) attempt to explain the conformity of the Italian working class to the ideology of the dominant classes. Critical researchers in the United States have borrowed from Gramsci's concept to argue that television is the primary vehicle through which subordinate groups are taught dominant values and philosophy (Gitlin, 1979; Tuchman, 1978). Hall (1979) maintains that the mass media have colonized the cultural and ideological sphere of society. The main purpose of the mass media, from Hall's perspective, is to provide the audience with the raw materials from which they may construct an image of the "lives, meanings, practices and values of other groups and classes" (p. 140). The media rank and arrange these images as preferred meanings and interpretations that reproduce and extend the dominant ideology.

Gitlin (1979) focuses our attention on television as the primary instrument of cultural hegemony that does not in his view *create* ideology, but instead selects, reproduces, processes, and packages it in ways that are accepted as normal or natural. For Gitlin, hegemony is "leaky," constantly changing in order to remain hegemonic. Hegemony is seen as a dynamic process that grows and changes and maintains its power through its domestication and absorption of oppositional elements of subordinate cultures. Thus Gitlin argues that Black television sitcoms become available when there is a market-driven recognition of a growing Black consuming class, at the same time that such programs remain acceptable as comedy to the White mainstream.

Not all hegemony theorists accept the notion of ruling-class domination of the cultural sphere as is implied in Gitlin's (1979) analysis of television. Kellner (1982) argues that within the television text there remains the possibility for differential individual decoding of the message, at the same time suggesting that, because of their overall concern with profitability, capitalist media managers will broadcast oppositional messages if there are sufficiently large audiences for them. Such an emancipatory outcome is unlikely, however, as in reality, messages that directly challenge the core beliefs about good and evil in society would be rejected by the mainstream audience as abnormal, radical "fringe" television.

## The Market

Félix Gutiérrez has been a vital source in the conceptualization of the nature of Spanish-language media, and he, as well as Schement (1976), explicated a model of internal colonialism to describe that environment. Later, Gutiérrez (1980) provided an overview of the Latino-media relationship in the United States, which reveals similarities and differences in the media histories of Hispanics and Blacks. The mainstream media are seen to provide a similar variety of negative, stereotyped images for both Latinos and Blacks, and they tend to present Latino reality in the news from a middle-class, Anglo perspective. Like the Black press, there is a long history of Spanish-language newspapers dating back to the early 1800s. Unlike the Black experience in broadcasting, however, where White owners of Black-oriented stations hired Blacks as personalities, the White owners of Spanish-language stations depended upon Latin American professionals rather than upon local Latinos, and much of the recorded music was imported from Latin America as well. Gutiérrez notes that the Spanish International Network (SIN) was controlled by a Mexican corporation (Televisa), and served as a lucrative mechanism to tap the television export market in the United States.

Because of the growth, in terms both of size and of wealth, of the Spanish-speaking population, the competition for access to that audience has become fierce (Besas, 1987; Fitch, 1987; Spadoni, 1987; Walley, 1987). Wilson and Gutiérrez (1985) call our attention to the emergence of audience segmentation and targeting, which parallels the growth in the size and importance of Black and Hispanic populations.

## Protests and Ethnic Group Activism

While the economic interests of advertisers and investors are the dominant forces determining the structure and content of mainstream- and ethnic-targeted media, there is some evidence that organized social protest, by threatening the economic well-being of media outlets, has also been influential in changing the portrayals of Hispanics and Blacks.

Published studies of ethnic group activism are relatively rare within the literature. Schement et al. (1977) provided a critical case history of Chicano involvement in challenges of television station licenses in the early 1970s, as a special case of the more comprehensive study of the Chicano movement by Francesco Lewels. Wilson and Gutiérrez (1985) provide an informative chapter on the history of Black, Hispanic, Asian, and other ethnic group advocacy for improved treatment in the media in the United States.

Because of the substantial limits on the ability of African Americans and Hispanics to avoid their dependence upon mainstream advertising, one may wonder, along with Muriel Cantor (1978), whether it really makes any difference if Blacks and Hispanics own or control broadcast media outlets. This question has been addressed by very few studies (Fife, 1986; Singleton, 1981). Singleton seems to feel that providing specialized programming is a responsibility that racial or ethnic group broadcasters should not be expected to bear to any greater extent than do majority group broadcasters. Singleton ignores much broadcasting history in that special allocations of frequencies to educational broadcasters did come with the expectation that they would provide an alternative or ancillary service. A similar logic might apply with regard to those Blacks or Hispanics who received broadcast properties at a special discount, although the rules of the marketplace would still mean that they would be condemned to a marginal economic existence.

Fife's (1986) work is exemplary in that it demonstrates significant differences between African American, Hispanic, and mainstream broadcasters, and suggests further that, because of the nature of competition in urban markets, racial or ethnic group broadcasters may serve as positive role models for other broadcasters, thereby increasing/improving racial or ethnic group treatment in the news.

## The Future of African American and
## Hispanic Representations

With the multiplication of media channels available in any household through broadcast, cable, disc, and tape distribution systems, there is an expectation that audiences for particular programs may become increasingly homogeneous. Shoemaker et al. (1985) report that where Spanish-language television is available to them, less than 40% of the Hispanics surveyed indicate that they do not view it. And while there are clearly income barriers that keep many Blacks and Hispanics from enjoying the abundance of the new media, race itself does not appear to be a predictor of which families are likely to adopt the newer information technologies (Oates, Ghorpade, & Brown, 1986).

Valdez (1985) reflects the same kind of optimism about the potential benefits of emerging information technology, which Webster and Robins (1986) describe as having captured the spirits of futurists of the Right and the Left. For Valdez (1985, p. 11), the only question is whether or not "Latino entrepreneurs recognize the opportunities in this industry" for innovation, investment, and the creation of a viable Latino market. It is Gutiérrez (1985, p. 112) who calls for caution, suggesting that "the obvious applications [of technology] are quickly appropriated and tested by the giants. To the extent that Latinos participate in these efforts they will either be employees or consumers." The role that Hispanics will play in controlling the production of racial or ethnic group images in the future is as yet unclear.

### TELEVISION CONTENT:
### THE STIMULUS EXPLORED

Television content, as the product of the media system, and the presumed determinant of social perceptions, is the principal focus of research and writing on minorities and media. Social scientists and activists have long expressed a concern that the pervasive nature of racism in television content may influence the way that viewers organize their thoughts and behavior regarding race and ethnicity. Berry (1982, p. 225) expressed that concern: "The continued transmission of faulty racial attitudes and ideas can only reinforce the racist legacy and cause our institutions to maintain their retardative force on the humane growth and development of all of its citizens." Thus we find that concern about Black images and later about those of other minorities in television derived not from aesthetic considerations of form, genre, and style, but from social and political concerns that the medium would contribute to the further entrenchment of social inequality and discrimination. This has influenced the way minority images have been studied.

We examined some of the major theoretical assumptions and beliefs about Black and Hispanic content within the context of three methodological approaches. These include empirical content analysis, the popular culture, or literary critique and critical qualitative analysis. We focused our study on the images of the 1980s because these contemporary representations demonstrate a significant shift in the demography, social structuring, and, ultimately, the ideological impact of that content (MacDonald, 1983). Our focus on stars, or leading roles, unfortunately ignores the potential for identifying meaningful differences between foreground and background representations of Black and Hispanic reality. Readers may acquire a more complete history of Black and Hispanic television images in some of the following: Barcus (1983), MacDonald (1983), U.S. Civil Rights Commission (1977), Gerbner and Signorielli (1978), Signorielli (1981), and Greenberg and Baptista-Fernandez (1980).

## Quantitative Content Analysis

Who are the Blacks and Hispanics who populate the world of commercial television in the 1980s? African Americans very often are found in the reruns of series from an earlier decade such as *The Jeffersons, What's Happening, Different Strokes*, among others. These programs have been dubbed "the New Minstrelsy" by MacDonald (1983), but they remain popular with Black audiences, and are presented in comedy strips five times weekly, in a way that supports the habitual viewing by the fringe audiences of independent stations. The new programs developed in the 1980s featured the successful middle class: *The Cosby Show, 227, Amen, Webster, Benson, Frank's Place*, among others, as well as several Black supporting actors in the *Facts of Life, Head of the Class, Rags to Riches, Miami Vice, Night Court*, among others.

Quantitative content analyses in the past focused on demography, behavior and interactions, linguistic styles, dress, violence, social status, and settings as indicators of Black and Hispanic existence and progress. Nearly all of these studies were published by 1982 (Greenberg, 1986), perhaps representing an end of an era of researcher interest, financial support, or journal receptiveness to head counts unsupported by any deeper theoretical insight.

Analyses of minority images frequently begins with comparisons of television demography with that of the reality captured in official statistics. The demand for inclusion of minorities in a manner proportionate to their share of the population has been expressed politically by media activists, as well as by minority actors and other media professionals. Hispanics may note that, while Blacks nearly achieved representational parity at around 10% in 1980, Hispanic representation in the television world lagged far behind. Although the Hispanic population is expected to exceed that of African Americans by the end of this century, there are few signs to suggest that their presence will be reflected on television. Presumed barriers of language, divergent cultural history, and social experience may retard the growth of the Hispanic population in the world of mainstream television.

Greenberg and Fernandez-Collado (1979) identified 53 Hispanic characters on network television during 1975 to 1978. The Latina had a minuscule presence, outnumbered by males, five to one. *Fantasy Island* and *CHIPS* featured Latino male stars, but were not primarily about Hispanic life, *a.k.a. Pablo*, a controversial series that did present a version of Hispanic life, was set in a Los Angeles barrio, but enjoyed a very short run, as did *Condo*, a Latino version of *The Jeffersons*.

In the 1980s, identifiable Hispanic characters are few and far between (Barcus, 1983; Wilson & Gutiérrez, 1985), and frequently involve negative roles as criminals involved in the drug trade or recall the traditional stereotype of the Latin lover. While one might applaud *L.A. Law* for casting one Hispanic character as a successful attorney, and *I Married Dora* for costarring a Latina (as a maid who marries her boss), the rest of the television landscape in the fall 1987 season was the familiar territory of drugs and crime (Stewart, 1987). Unless there is a dramatic change in the way Hispanics are portrayed by mainstream television, Latinos may be better off without parity. Very few Hispanic characters have had vehicles that survived from one season to the next. This is in sharp contrast to the vehicles in which Black actors played roles in the most popular shows of their season. The limited success of Hispanic characters may provide some insight into the kind of location Hispanics and Latin culture shares in mainstream popular culture.

Signorielli (1981) states that it is from aggregate patterns of casting, characterization, and fate that meaning is derived from television programs. Values are distributed among characters hierarchically according to social status and power. She defined underrepresentation more broadly to include "restricted scope of action, stereotyped roles, diminished life chances, and undervaluation" (Signorielli, 1981, p. 99). In the past, minorities were very much underrepresented in the sense of lacking a proportionate share of representation. At the same time, the characters that were presented were unidimensional, therefore, lacking a proportionate representation of their human qualities. Black representations have changed through increased portrayal of middle-class life-styles, but this has meant a decline in portrayals of the full range of Black social locations. Quantitative analysts must be challenged to link the demographic comparisons to indices of ethnic and racial authenticity.

## The Popular Culture Critique

Popular culture researchers view television as a "cultural force" (Newcomb & Hirsh, 1987), and resist its categorization as an instrument of class and cultural hegemony (Kaminsky & Mahan, 1985). Indeed, the popular culture approach usually avoids political issues, including racism, generally concluding that such analyses are irrelevant to the study of cultural forms (Seiter, 1986). From their perspective, television serves the cultural function of storytelling in society. It is art, myth, and ritual constructed from familiar content, contexts, and themes, and is structured to generate a popular discourse acceptable to a mass audience. The popular culture critique is employed to provide a meaningful approach for understanding the "vast majority of television content and its durability as a form of entertainment" (Kaminsky & Mahan, 1985). Unfortunately, the popular cultural approach has not been applied in any systematic way to the study of Black and Hispanic images. The *Humanities Index* identifies precious few studies from 1980 to 1987 about Blacks, and none about Hispanics, in prime-time U.S. television.

Reeves (1987) offers one attempt to link a Black fictional character (Mr. T) to the Black subculture. He attributes Mr. T's great popularity among Black audiences to his similarity to Muhammad Ali, a familiar cultural hero. The two men share the same "cultural space" with a contradictory discourse that is sometimes radical, sometimes mainstream. And while on the one hand, Mr. T. seems to resurrect the discredited "ethnic fool" with his wild hairstyle and slave chains, his phenomenal mechanical skills and physical strength elevate him to the level of a hero. Reeves argues that if you look beyond Mr. T's outlandish appearance, he is very much like the respectable characters portrayed by Bill Cosby in *I Spy* and Greg Morrison in *Mission Impossible*. Both were cast as highly talented specialists, accepted as equals within all-White teams prone to violent heroic action.

Reeve's critique offers some useful insights into one type of television character, but not all Black (or Latino) characters are heroic. The issue of racism largely is ignored, as Greenberg and Baptista-Fernandez (1980) observed. Black characters on television rarely discuss racism or race relations. Setting may account for some of the blindness with regard to racial interactions. Blacks historically have been excluded from television programs situated in the South, with the notable exception of miniseries such as *Roots* and *Roots II*. Until the fall 1987 season, and the scheduling of *A Different World* and *Frank's Place*, most series featuring Blacks were set in northern cities or Los Angeles. In the cultural mythology of television, the South was a trivialized setting full of bumbling but lovable "good old boys" as in the *Dukes of Hazzard*, or the *Andy Griffith Show*. The presence and history of African Americans in the South has been annihilated symbolically, leaving the issue of race as a dimension solely of urbanized urban ghetto life.

Intercultural relations were addressed somewhat more directly with regard to the interactions between Latinos and Anglos in the West. In *Condo*, another of the short-lived series featuring Latino characters, the question of assimilation was addressed directly. A condominium serves as the setting where a Latino family, moving up the economic ladder, becomes neighbors to an Anglo family recently faced with economic hard times. Subervi-Velez (1987, p. 14) suggests that the "program carried a general message that Latinos can be upwardly mobile, relate to Anglo neighbors, and still retain aspects of their own culture."

## Critical Qualitative Analysis

Critical researchers have focused on the analysis of dominant political meanings and symbols in minority television content. This emphasis reflects their general critique of television as a corporate, commercial enterprise that serves both the financial and the ideological interests of its owners (Shoemaker, 1987). Consistent with this analysis is the assumption that television content is developed primarily for consumption by Whites. Thus Gray (1986, p. 223) quotes NBC executive Perry Lafferty as saying, "I think the mass audience likes to see Blacks in roles that are not threatening." The mass audience, despite the fact that Blacks spend more time in that role than do Whites, is composed primarily of White consumers. In the past, as Wilson and Gutiérrez (1985, p. 65) remind us, "Movie producers capitalized on audience insecurities by using minority stereotypes to bolster their [White viewers'] self-esteem and reinforce racial attitudes" such that "virtually every minority characterization was designed to reinforce the attitude of White superiority." Too often, critical researchers approach contemporary media decision making about minority images on the basis of similar assumptions about symbolic functions.

Gerbner and Signorielli (1978), Matabane (1982), and others have argued that television content changes in accordance with broader dominant political agendas. In his analysis of the various stages minority images have gone through, Clark (1969) theorized that Black images would pass through a law enforcement phase into an era of racially transparent roles. He did not mean the return of "Pinky" and other light-skinned Blacks trying to "pass for White," but as Greenberg and Fernandez-Collado (1979, p. 3) have suggested, the blending of minority roles into "the fabric of media messages in both minority-related and non-minority contexts and situations. The characters develop broader dimensions and are not as differentiated from the roles given to majority ethnics."

The recent proliferation of programs featuring minorities in integrated settings validates these predictions. And, in that light, we would argue that the symbolic function of the images of racial and ethnic groups described by Wilson and Gutiérrez (1985) has been modified in the 1980s. Bill Cosby's Dr. Huxtable cannot easily meet the needs of racists in search of self-esteem.

Gray (1986, p. 229) suggests that the Black characters cast in professional roles and in upscale White settings express "preferred and acceptable white upper middle class definitions of racial interaction." For Gray, the competence, articulateness, and attractiveness of these characters make them models of assimilation. Their Blackness is muted behind professionalism and racial invisibility. Other circumstances of Black life are not presented in these scenarios.

Mark Miller (1986) suggests that there is another commercial purpose behind the integration of Blacks into prime time. Miller argues that television programs are commercial vehicles for the consumer mentality, in the background, context, and the story lines of the programs just as much as, if not more than, in the commercial minutes themselves. With *The Cosby Show* as the ultimate commercial vehicle, Miller (1986, p. 210) notes: "Cliff Huxtable and his dependents are not only fashionably comfortable and mild, but also noticeably black. Cliff's blackness serves an affirmative purpose within the ad that is *The Cosby Show*. At the center of this ample tableau, Cliff is himself an ad, implicitly proclaiming the fairness of the American system: "Look!" he shows us. "Even *I* can have all this!"

Miller (1986, p. 214) sees Cosby's character along with the nonthreatening Blacks of *Strokes* and *Webster* as playing a necessary reassuring role for White Americans: "By and large, American whites need such reassurance because they are now further removed than ever, both spatially and psychologically, from the masses of the black poor." Miller's latter assertion, however, needs greater specification as to which sectors of White America are so thoroughly alienated from Black America. Is is also necessary to understand if alienated middle-class African Americans may also feel isolated from poor Blacks and thus these programs may serve similar symbolic functions for them.

## THE IMPACT OF MINORITY PORTRAYALS

The research community consistently has sought to raise questions about the impact of negative images of Blacks and Hispanics on the aspirations, expectations, and beliefs of minorities (Stroman, 1984). Implicit in this concern is the belief that members of racial and ethnic minorities exposed repeatedly to such portrayals will develop negative self-images, and will underestimate their life chances in society, and, as a result, will lower their aspirations and expectations thereby guaranteeing their own continued oppression.

## Behavioral Evidence

From a behavioral perspective, we arrive at such an effect through a complex chain of personal choices involving exposure to particular stimuli or content. It is differences in the content, and the context, of exposure that account for the observed differences between people where other individual differences have been controlled through randomization or statistical partition. The primary weaknesses of the behavioral paradigm are twofold. First, under tightly controlled experimental conditions, we may have great confidence in our causal analyses of the single case, but may know very little about the generation of these effects in the natural environment.

Second, in the case of ex post facto investigational or other non-experimental designs, our confidence in the causal interpretation is weakened critically by a lack of random assignment to comparable exposures to content. This is revealed most graphically in the virtual impossibility of analysts determining whether the social perceptions influenced the exposure to television fare, or whether the exposure to television produced the social perceptions. Attempts to remove social experience statistically from the relationship between viewing and social perceptions frequently reduce the strength of the primary correlation to a nonsignificant level. And, because the estimates of explained variance (R-squared) in most studies are so low, it is clear that the empirical models are poorly specified, and include only a small proportion of the relevant influences.

McLeod and Reeves (1981) provide a detailed review of the complex of competing and complementary influences upon which media effects depend. It is a rare study that recognizes, let alone attempts to measure or control for, the multiple sources of variance in audience response. This is not meant to be a blanket criticism of behavioral research, but a recognition of the seemingly insurmountable epistemological barriers such an approach sets in its own path. McLeod and Reeves (1981, p. 255) argue that, in order to develop a scientific understanding of mass media impact, we need "knowledge of the stimulus material, control of its application, assessment of effect, and an understanding of the mechanism or process underlying the effects"; and in order to accomplish this, we must meet the following requirements.

First, we must specify the media *content*, or stimulus. It is not always clear that the content as perceived by the analyst is the same as the content perceived by the audience. Gunter (1987) suggests that this is the essential weakness in the work of the Gerbner's Cultural Indicators team. The objective description of manifest content that is produced by trained coders may bear only a marginal relationship to the content that different (untrained) audiences might perceive. In addition, the manifest, surface content that is more easily specified may also be unrelated to the more essentially ideological content that serves to frame media representations of Black and Hispanic realities, and may operate more powerfully in structuring their social perceptions.

Second, we must control the *exposure* of the audience to the content. In the laboratory, control of exposure is relatively less troublesome than in the natural environment, where individuals exercise greater choice based on their tastes and preferences for different media content. Because of this, we have little confidence that exposure to the stimulus is at all comparable within or between nonexperimental studies. "Television viewing" itself has been recognized as a complex theoretical construct that has been operationalized in numerous ways, with considerable measurement error. A variety of personal and contextual factors will influence the amount of attention viewers pay to the content of television. Garramone (1985) demonstrates that individual's motivations regarding political information will influence their attention to different editorial formats within the general category of television news. Many of those factors also influence how much of the content is actually understood, or received. In their study of what White children learn from exposure to Black portrayals on television, Atkin, Greenberg, and McDermott (1983) determined that what mattered was not the portrayals the youngsters were exposed to, but what they *thought* they had seen. And what they thought they were shown might have been influenced by what they brought with them to the screen, or what might have occurred in the context of their exposure. Most of these influences are beyond the direct control of behavioral researchers.

Third, we must specify, and then measure or *assess the effect* of, exposure to media content. Again the problems are both conceptual and methodological. Effects that are conceived of as being group, cultural, or aggregate are too often measured at the individual level. Because effects at the interpersonal and institutional/societal levels are too difficult to measure, they tend to be ignored. Complex relational understandings, or the products of "sense making" by active audiences, are frequently limited by opinion survey instrumentation to positions along agree/disagree continua, or worse, to yes or no responses (Morley, 1980).

Fourth, and perhaps most important, we must "elaborate the *conditional processes* that help interpret and specify the relationship" (Morley, 1980, p. 256). Here, we are concerned with those "third variables" that intervene in the theoretical path between exposure and effect. The conditional processes together form the Achilles' heel of behavioral social science, which is rarely shielded by the cloaking magical incantation "ceteris paribus."


## DIFFERENCES IN EXPOSURE

### Subcultural Experience and Social
### Location as Sources of Differentiation

The impact of unique or repeated exposure to television portrayals is conditioned in part by the orientations that individuals bring to the experience. David Morley (1980), in an attempt to find a workable compromise between the search for media effects and the search for the meanings of media content, sought to discover the role that concrete, but shared social experience plays in determining how one decodes a message with ideologically "preferred readings" imposed upon it. In his analysis, it becomes important to identify what are the "structural conditions which generate different cultural and ideological competencies" (Morley, 1980, p. 19). Although he studied Blacks in Britain who were primarily from the West Indies, the observed differences in their decoding of television's preferred message underscored the importance of subcultural, as well as class influences, on message processing.

What people choose to view, and how well they attend to its message is conditioned in part by the confidence they have in the source. McLeod and O'Keefe (1972) studied audience preferences and credibility assessments as the products of a socialization process. Over time people learn which media they like and trust, and for the media they prefer, they come to know which formats, programs, or personalities are more likely to meet their needs for information or entertainment. These orientations develop and change in response to changes in a person's "life cycle" or age, which operate in addition to the generally more influential social and structural constraints of race and class. Unfortunately, much recent research in this area tends to utilize race and class as social categories, rather than as purposefully selected indexes of particular shared socializing experiences, thus we have little more than speculation about the conditions that contribute to the development of different media orientations.

Ball-Rokeach (1985) argues that one's location in the social structure is likely to influence one's media orientations or dependencies, and such differences mediate the impact of any media exposure. For her, structural location "includes all the conventional stratification variables, such as class, status, and power," but she suggests further that we should not "limit our concerns to structural locations that bear on political and economic matters" (Ball-Rokeach, 1985, p. 505). Our needs for, and structural limitations upon our access to, alternatives for play or recreation also influence our media dependencies. A number of studies have sought to describe how race, sex, and class are related to different media orientations and patterns of media dependency of Hispanics and African Americans.

Richard Allen (1981) argues that the reported differences between Blacks and others in the relationship between television viewing and class is largely due to problems of measurement and design. Where other studies reported that the relationship between viewing and class was not inverse for Blacks as it was for Whites, Allen finds no such differences. He cites an earlier study (Allen & Bielby, 1979), which found viewing to decline as one moved up the class ladder. In this study, however, Allen and Bielby utilized a measure of perceived social class, rather than the traditional indices of education and employment. We note as well that Gerbner et al. (1982) suggest that television viewing *itself* may produce distortions in personal assessments of class location. Among Whites studied, heavy television users who were objectively members of the lower class were more likely to identify themselves as members of the middle class. Of course, it is not clear that such patterns would be repeated in a Black sample.

Age, education, and income were used to examine differences in African Americans' assessments of the performance and credibility of local Black and White television newscasters. Elizabeth Johnson (1984) reports that Blacks tended to see Black reporters as more attractive, and more believable, than the Whites presented to them, although Whites were more likely to be seen as "better performers." In this study, demographic factors were associated only with differences in attractiveness ratings.

Education as a predictor of media use patterns continues to be revealed in studies focused primarily on effects rather than on patterns of use. Allen and Hatchett (1986) report that Blacks who are younger, have less education, and who report parental training specifically related to race were more likely to view Black-oriented television. When comparing Blacks, Whites, and Jews, Gandy and ElWaylly (1985) reported that Blacks were more dependent on television as a source of information about the Middle Eastern conflict, and they suggested that dependence upon television was conditioned by the lower levels of education that Black respondents had acquired.

A comprehensive review of the literature on Blacks and television was provided by Poindexter and Stroman (1981). They offered a number of summary propositions about the nature of Black uses, tastes, and preferences in television fare. Constrained perhaps by what was available in the contemporary literature, they avoided any explicit discussion of social structural factors that might explain patterns of media behavior among Blacks. Indeed, they recommended the elimination of traditional demographic variables in favor of social psychological variables as a way of discovering "what is it about being black or young or poor which makes the television experience unique" (Poindexter & Stroman, 1981, p. 120).

Valenzuela (1981) provides a review of Latino television use in the context of a study of Latinos and public television, and concludes the evidence is mixed about whether Latinos view more television than the general population. O'Guinn, Faber, and Meyer (1985) reported that the differences between Mexican Americans who preferred Spanish-language television and those who preferred English can largely be reduced to indices of social class and degree of acculturation.

The most comprehensive study of Latino media orientations was produced to assist the Gannett corporation in their attempt to reach the large and growing Latino population. This study (Greenberg et al., 1983) focused on Mexican Americans as the largest subgroup of Hispanics in the United States. Again, we find discussion of the substantial cross-generational differences in media use patterns among Latinos, where the older groups were more likely to identify themselves as Mexicans, and to prefer Spanish-language media, and youngsters who viewed Spanish-language television reportedly did so because their family was watching, rather than as a matter of personal choice. Television is seen to provide for the same "open window," or social learning needs, of Latinos as it provides for Blacks and others who have limited options as a result of poverty or racism. Hispanics in this study tended to be more satisfied with all of their media than Anglos, and were more likely to see television portrayals as realistic.

Allen and Clarke (1980, p. 23) argued that little research into the media behaviors of different ethnic groups "focused on the historical, cultural, and political antecedents that may distinguish these groups." Suberu-Velez (1986) addresses this problem as well in his discussion of ethnicity.

Francisco Lewels (1981) examined Mexican American attitudes toward the mass media. This analysis differs from much of the research, which seeks to compare racial and ethnic groups, in that it sought to understand the role that background differences might play in the development of the various perspectives that Mexican Americans hold toward media. This study utilized a Q-analysis of responses from 36 respondents, 12 of whom were media professionals. Five person-types are identified and discussed in a way that reveals considerable diversity among Mexican Americans. Socialization as media professionals appears to have played a significant role in producing similar views among those respondents with mass media linkages. Lewels (1981, p. 27) suggests that, while there are important differences, there is a critical thread that runs through each of the identifiable attitude segments—"a deep-seated distrust of the media (particularly large corporations) and a suspicion that racial or ethnic interests are not their prime concern."

## Ethnic Identification as a
## Source of Differentiation

Pamela Shoemaker (1985) questions what communication researchers really have in mind when they study "ethnicity." She suggests that all too often they have conceived of ethnicity in terms of deviance or difference from the patterns of the White, or dominant, culture. Keefe and Padilla (1987) pursued the construct in a study of Chicanos in Southern California. Ethnicity was seen to have objective and subjective dimensions. Factor analysis of the subjective aspects of ethnicity identified distinct components identified as "cultural awareness" and "ethnic loyalty," and these factors were differentially associated with objective indicators such as generation, education, barrio residence, occupation, and rural background.

Berry and Mitchell-Kernan (1982, p. 8) suggest that "ethnic identity is associated with patterns of experience that exhibit significant common denominators from the perspective of socialization. These shape the manner in which the socialization potential of television is realized." The difficulty in establishing a causal relationship between cultural or ethnic identity and media orientations is based on the recognition that the relationship is nonrecursive. While ethnic identification can influence media choice, media exposure will also potentially influence ethnic identification. Allen and Hatchett (1986) offered three measures of Black self-identification—mainstream, nonmainstream, and Black separatist. All were positively correlated with exposure to Black-oriented television, although the strongest correlation was with mainstream Black group identification. The theoretical posture of the researchers, however, was that these racial orientations were the *products* rather than the causes of television exposure.

Kimberly Neuendorf (1982) examined the relationships between self-designations for Anglos and Hispanic youngsters, and media exposure, preference, and evaluation variables. Hispanics could identify themselves as being Latino, Cuban, Puerto Rican, Chicano, Mexican, Spanish American, or Mexican American. The "hyphenated" Hispanics were expected to be more assimilated, or Americanized, than other Hispanics. In this study of five southwestern U.S. cities, among Hispanic youngsters choosing a single label for themselves, "Mexican-American" was the most popular (41%), followed by "Spanish-American" (20%), "Chicano" (19%), and "Mexican" (18%). While self-designated Chicanos and Mexican Americans were similar in their media tastes and preferences, Spanish Americans were nearly indistinguishable from non-Hispanics in terms of their tastes. There was also substantial support for the hypothesis that the selection of an Americanized self-identification would be linked with avoidance of ethnic media. Here again, there is evidence of more demonstrably "ethnic" audiences using the media for social learning or advice.

## Racial Attitudes as a Factor

Jannette Dates (1980) examined viewing, evaluation, and identification with Black television characters by Black and White teenagers. Television characters were evaluated with an index reflecting mean ratings of semantic differential scales. Racial attitudes were measured with an index derived from the Multifactor Racial Attitude Inventory (MRAI). Consistent with earlier findings (Frank & Greenberg, 1980), Black viewing levels for programs with Black characters were higher than those of Whites, and there were no significant differences for the general-audience programs. Similarly, Blacks evaluated Black characters more positively, were more likely to identify with them, and were more likely to rate them as realistic than were their White classmates. Racial attitudes were found to be less reliable predictors of attitudes toward television characters. Dates's discussion includes the possibility that those with negative attitudes toward African Americans might avoid many of those programs with Black characters, and thereby have less strongly developed impressions of them.

Racial attitudes were found to be reliable predictors in another study, however. Debora Heflin (1981) utilized a continuous measure of ethnicity, or racial orientation (the Developmental Inventory of Black Consciousness), to explain differences in evaluations of television commercials. Black subjects gave the highest ratings and exhibited greater recall for commercials with Black models, but those with the lowest level of Black consciousness were likely to give more favorable ratings of the White commercials than were those with higher levels of Black consciousness. It should be noted, however, that the distribution of scores on the Black consciousness inventory were not independent of age, education, or marital status, which suggests that life stage factors may be substantially involved in both consciousness and orientations to media content. In a recent, unpublished study, Allen, Dawson, and Johnson (1987) offer a general model of "black racial identity," and identify several antecedents to the development of those beliefs. Location in the social structure and religious activity are important influences on this belief system. Television is again identified as an influence on racial beliefs, which are themselves components of a person's racial identity.

## Perspectives on Selectivity

From the functionalist perspective of "uses and gratifications," Lee and Browne (1981) explored the behavior of Black children, teenagers, and adults, primarily to identify the motivations that guide their media activity.

Utilizing the data set developed by Frank and Greenberg (1980), Willis Smith (1985) sought to determine if differences in needs for personal identification, learning, or diversion might be useful in predicting Black preferences for television program types. Contrary to his expectations, he found that the traditional demographic indicators of sex, age, education, and occupation were more important predictors of tastes in television program fare.

Fairchild, Stockard, and Bowman (1986) offered a reanalysis of a 1981 survey of African Americans that asked respondents to recall viewing *Roots*, their reasons for viewing, and their impressions of the series. The overwhelming majority of Blacks surveyed viewed some of the series, and nearly all were pleased with it. Where the differences emerged were in the things they liked most about the series. The somewhat circular reasoning of the uses and gratifications perspective (Elliot, 1974), and some contemporary studies of television viewers (Barwise & Ehrenberg, 1987), would suggest that there are strong correlations between what viewers say they found and what they initially sought in the program.

Ronald Simmons (1987), utilizing an educational cognitive style inventory, successfully predicted the preferences of Black college students for a variety of popular television programs. The selection of particular cognitive styles was based on the assumption that individuals preferred programs that provided content with attributes that they found easier, or more enjoyable, to process.

Federico Subervi-Velez (1986) has provided a recent review of the literature on Hispanics, with a particular focus on the role of the media in the assimilation of Hispanics into mainstream American culture. He notes that ethnic media may serve as "shields" against the acculturating/ assimilationist influence of mainstream media, at the same time that they might provide guidance to newcomers that aids their immersion into a new culture. Presuming the operation of conscious and purposive choice of media, the overwhelming conclusion to be drawn about the use of ethnic media is that it is used to maintain or even strengthen ones' ethnic identification, thereby tempering the influence of other forces of acculturation.

Pia Nicolini (1986) examined Puerto Rican leaders' perceptions of Spanish-language media. This study of media available in Philadelphia found general satisfaction with the news coverage provided by the Spanish International Network (SIN) station, especially coverage of Latin America. Because the SIN station is a network outlet, with no local production capability, however, it did not represent an alternative to local television as a source of information, or as a way for leaders to reach local audiences.

Numerous studies have examined racial or ethnic use of media for public affairs information. Active participation in political activities is thought to stimulate use of mass media. Tan (1981) argued that political participation predicts media use for both Blacks and Mexican Americans. He suggested that political activists may believe that others expect them to be well informed, and this expectation serves as a motivation for media exposure. The reported data support that argument, although they do not falsify the alternative that media exposure produces interest and involvement. Tan also notes that the model is stronger for Whites than for either Mexican Americans or Blacks. In a later analysis of this data, Tan (1983) divided his ethnic populations into two groups on the basis of their educational attainment, and utilized political participation as the criterion variable in a regression model. In this analysis, media use was unrelated to political participation for Blacks or Mexican Americans once other predictors were in the equation.

Correlations reported by St. George and Robinson-Weber (1983) suggest that political participation is more strongly associated with the desire to view political content on television for Blacks than for Whites. Gandy and Coleman (1986) reported that Black college students felt that the news media treated Jesse Jackson unfairly, and their dissatisfaction with media coverage grew throughout the life of the campaign. Somewhat paradoxically, their reported use of television also increased over the same period. Gandy and Coleman offer as a possible explanation for this contradiction the suggestion that students used television selectively, relying more on Jackson's unmediated performance in the debates than upon journalists' interpretations of what Jackson had done. In a later study, Matabane, Gandy, and Omachonu (1987) report that Black college students generally viewed television news more frequently than they read newspapers, and felt that television was the most useful source of information about the South African conflict. Students who were more involved in issues tended to rely more on newspapers than on television for information about the conflict.

In 1976, Blacks were no more or less likely to have viewed public television than was the total population (National Analysts, 1981). Because they expected greater Black interest in Africa, however, Matabane and Gandy (in press) believed that Blacks would be more likely to have viewed the controversial PBS series, *The Africans* than Whites. The data from their small sample of supporters of a Black PBS affiliate suggested that Blacks were somewhat more likely than Whites to have viewed any segment of the series, but being Black was unrelated to the number of episodes viewed.

## Summary

When we examine the literature of Hispanic and African American orientations to mass media in general, and to television in particular, we are forced to conclude that we have only a partial inventory of differences, and a bare minimum of understanding about those factors that produce them.

Hispanics may be drawn to Spanish-language television because they are more familiar with and comfortable decoding messages in Spanish. This interpretation would also explain the marked age differences in revealed preferences for Spanish-language media where older Hispanics might be less comfortable with English. With the increased immigration of Latinos from Mexico and Central America, however, the relationship between age and preference for Spanish may be weakened.

Several studies underscore the importance of cultural differences within Black and Hispanic populations. Country of origin explains some of the differences in tastes and preferences of Hispanics, while demographic or social location variables are more useful in explaining differences in Black consciousness, which is reflected in different orientations toward media.

Despite the criticisms of activists and intellectuals, Black and Hispanic viewers are heavy users of television, and they tend to ascribe substantial credibility to it as a source of information about economic and political matters. Because of the nonlocal production base of the industry, however, Spanish-language television is seen as less useful than mainstream media for information about day-to-day influences on the lives of Hispanics, which thereby increases their dependence upon Anglo media. Berry (1982, p. 53) suggests that "systematic research is needed to identify why there seems to be this apparent acceptance of inaccurate or negative portrayals, and how this audience acceptance may function as a creative source for certain portrayals."

## DIFFERENCES IN OUTCOMES

As Greenberg (1986) has indicated, the number of studies that attempt to apply the behavioral science model to the study of media effects on minorities is distressingly small. The kinds of outcomes that might be explored include media orientations, knowledge, attitudes and behavior, evaluations of themselves in comparison with others, and evaluations of the social and economic system in which they live. While Greenberg cites not a single study, Poindexter and Stroman's (1981) 30-year retrospective was able to cite several studies of what social roles and behaviors Black children learned from television. They noted as well the major contribution of Stuart Surlin's studies of learning from the Norman Lear television series, and from *Roots* (which stimulated the greatest surge of interest in media and race to date).

It is surprising that the historic presidential campaign of Jesse Jackson produced only a handful of effects-oriented studies (Gandy & Coleman, 1986). With regard to learning from television, Gandy and ElWaylly (1985) and Gandy, Matabane, and Omachonu (1987) suggest that Blacks are handicapped by their reliance on television for public affairs information. To the extent that studies of the relationships between media use and knowledge can be conceived as a societal-level effect, although measured at the level of the individual, Gandy and ElWaylly (1985) demonstrate that reliance on television contributes to the substantial gap between Blacks and others in terms of public affairs knowledge.

Gandy and Coleman (1986) determined that television news exposure was more important than newspaper use in predicting Black student perceptions of the Jesse Jackson campaign, especially with regard to aspects of candidate character and style, although not with regard to knowledge of a candidate's stance on issues.

Surette (1985) examines the link between media use and preferences for social policy. If the mass media generate a sense of a mean world, overrun with violent criminals, it should follow that an acceptance of a more punitive criminal justice policy would be cultivated among the heavier users of television. Although race is dichotomized as White or non-White, it is likely that this Dade County Florida sample had a majority of Blacks and Hispanics in the non-White category. Surette reports that Whites, especially those who favor crime-oriented television drama, were more supportive of a more punitive policy. Indeed, race was the most reliable discriminator between supporters of liberal or punitive policies. Amount of exposure to television in general was not a significant discriminator.

The majority of the effects studies reported that link any outcomes to Hispanic media use are those studies that evaluate the learning gains of children associated with viewing specialized public television series, some of which had specific social learning goals (Greenberg et al., 1983; LaRose & Eisenstock, 1981). A few studies, such as Gombeski et al. (1980), evaluated the effectiveness of televised Spanish-language public service announcements in informing and motivating Hispanics to modify their health behavior.

### The Cultivation Hypothesis

The Cultivation Hypothesis associated with George Gerbner and his associates relates the common and recurring patterns of events and outcomes in television content to the social perceptions of individuals. As a television-specific formulation of social learning theory, the cultivation hypothesis simply argues that the more one is exposed to a particular construction of reality, the more one will come to perceive that reality in similar terms. Through message system (content) analysis, Gerbner and his associates (1980) have identified stable, recurring patterns of violence, with classifications of minorities and women as violents and victims, respectively, with different opportunities, resources, and outcomes. Exposure to this content is thought to cultivate the "dominant tendencies of our culture's beliefs, ideologies and world views" (Gerbner et al., 1980, p. 14). Cultivation is said to produce an indirect effect on viewers that develops cumulatively through repeated exposure, rather than in response to exposure to any particular program.

The Cultivation Perspective has several simplifying assumptions that have been subject to repeated criticism and empirical challenge (Good, 1984; Hawkins & Pingree, 1982; Rubin et al., 1987). The first is that the television message is largely invariant with regard to the underlying cultural message. Thus the second assumption emerges that it matters not what you view, only how much you view. The third, which serves to reinforce the prior two, suggests that audiences are relatively nonselective about what they view, such that even if there were differences in television content across genre, heavy viewers would see more of everything.

The Cultivation Hypothesis has been tested empirically in a number of studies, including 48 reviewed by Hawkins and Pingree (1982), and more recent critiques by Potter (1986) and Perse (1986). Mainstream criticisms of cultivation have focused on the hegemonic perspective underlying it and the basic methodological weakness in its use of cross-sectional survey data to measure indirect, cumulative effects (Hirsh, 1981; Hughes, 1980; Newcomb, 1978).

The Cultivation Hypothesis rarely has been concerned with the effect of television use by Blacks or Hispanics, except when their responses have proven to be contrary to theoretical expectations. Richard Allen, however, who has been a primary source of studies of Black media use, has offered a sophisticated test of television effects (Allen & Hatchett, 1986) that further extends the reach of cultivation analysis to Blacks. Allen and Hatchett suggest that background and social structural variables play a more powerful role in the development of social perceptions among Blacks, but exposure to Black-oriented television programs affected each of their dependent measures of social reality. Matabane (1985) differs from Allen and Hatchett in that the mainstreaming design she employs explicitly assumes an influence of objective social experience, whereas they include social reality as an equal partner in the prediction model. The two studies are not directly comparable because of markedly different operationalizations of social experience and exposure to Black-oriented programming.

## Mainstreaming

Mainstreaming means the process through which we find "the sharing of the commonality among heavy viewers in those demographic groups whose light viewers hold divergent views" (Gerbner et al., 1980, p. 15). Television plays a vital role in the forging of social consensus through mainstreaming. Groups that are out of the mainstream, by virtue of their holding extreme positions reflective of their objective social experiences, are brought inside, through their repeated exposure to televisions' constant messages. The incremental effect of television may be quite subtle as members of racial and ethnic minority groups may hold a mixture of social values, some dominant, some representing negotiated positions, and some representing radical, oppositional views (Parkin, 1971). While African Americans and Hispanics clearly share many dominant values about certain aspects of contemporary society, on many other dimensions, there are clearly identifiable differences between Blacks and Whites (Rokeach, 1973). Matabane (1985) offers an explicit test of mainstreaming among Blacks and finds strong support for the hypothesis that socially determined differences in social perception are eliminated through common exposure to television.

## THE ROAD AHEAD

It is not enough to say that there is a need for more research on all the fronts we have explored in our search for insight. We seek to understand the place of television, the most pervasive of all communication media, in the lives of its Black and Hispanic audiences, because we are concerned with the role communication plays in shaping their understanding of the world. Understanding the world, both the threats and the opportunities that present themselves, is an essential part of communication competence (Gandy, 1987). It is only when we understand the world, from our own perspectives and from the perspectives of others, that we are able to act in our own interests to change that world.

It is clear that a variety of factors combine to ensure that many Hispanics and African Americans are severely constrained in their efforts to construct genuinely useful, comprehensive images of social reality. A market-dominated communication and information system undersupplies content that meets the needs of minority subcultures. Like left-handers who are always forced to adapt to a right-handed world, members of racial and ethnic subcultures have come to rely on information systems that are always awkward to use, but must be used anyway because there are no readily available alternatives. Thus we find that older and newly immigrated Hispanics who rely on Spanish-language television actually consume exports from the larger markets of Mexico, Brazil, and Puerto Rico, and find very little television content that speaks in their own language about their present circumstances.

We have noted that the media marketplace is changing, in part in response to dramatic changes in the demography of the nation's urban areas. Wilson and Gutiérrez (1985) have suggested that we are moving toward an end of mass media, toward diversified, narrowly targeted media channels. What they have not concluded is whether or not African Americans and Hispanics will be any better off as that occurs. Gandy and Simmons (1986), on the other hand, offer a critical, less sanguine view of the future of isolated, homogeneous audiences. They suggest that narrow-casting increases the potential for more efficient, purposeful manipulation of social consciousness.

We are certain of the power of television. We are not dissuaded by the inherent weakness of behavioral research, or the narrow vision of its practitioners, which somehow misapprehends its essence. We are challenged by its complexity and dynamism, and we are committed to following its twists and turns in order to describe it as it changes shape and form.

While we have matured sufficiently in our perspective to recognize that the power of television is realized through the differential filters of concrete social experience, we cannot forget that much of that experience is structurally conditioned, and flows through the conduits of race and class. As Camarillo (1984, p. 1) suggests, "Given the parallels that exist between the urban experiences of blacks and Chicanos, it is important that scholars study these two groups in comparative perspective. Any analysis of the history of race relations as well as class relations cannot be fully explained without equal attention paid to both groups." Insight into the nature of shared experiences of urban segregation, employment discrimination, and educational abandonment will assist our analysis of Black and Hispanic media dependency.

## REFERENCES

Allen, R. L. (1981). Communication research on Black Americans. In H. Myrick & C. Keegan (Eds.), *In search of diversity*. Washington, DC: Corporation for Public Broadcasting.

Allen, R. L., & Bielby, W. (1979). Blacks attitudes and behavior toward television. *Communication Research, 6*, 437-462.

Allen, R. L., & Clarke, D. (1980). Ethnicity and mass media behavior: A study of Blacks and Latinos. *Journal of Broadcasting, 24*, 23-34.

Allen, R. L., Dawson, M., & Johnson, R. (1987). *Introduction: African American beliefs, and belief systems*. Unpublished paper, University of Michigan, Ann Arbor.

Allen, R. L., & Hatchett, S. (1986). The media and social reality effects: Self and system orientations of Blacks. *Communication Research, 13*, 97-123.

Atkin, C., Greenberg, B., & McDermott, S. (1983). Television and race role socialization. *Journalism Quarterly, 60*, 407-414.

Ball-Rokeach, S. (1985). The origins of individual media-system dependency: A sociological framework. *Communication Research, 12*, 485-510.

Baptista-Fernandez, P., & Greenberg, B. S. (1980). The context, characteristics, and communication behaviors of Blacks on television. In B. S. Greenberg (Ed.), *Life on television*. Norwood, NJ: Ablex.

Barcus, F. E. (1983). *Images of life on children's television*. New York: Praeger.

Barwise, T., & Ehrenberg, A. S. C. (1987). *Television and its audience*. Newbury Park, CA: Sage.

Berry, G. (1982). Research perspectives on the portrayal of Afro-American families on television. In A. Jackson (Ed.), *Black families and the medium of television*. Ann Arbor: University of Michigan, Bush Program in Child Development and Social Policy.

Berry, G., & Mitchell-Kernan, C. (Eds.). (1982). *Television and the socialization of the minority child*. New York: Academic Press.

Besas, P. (1987, March 25). Hispanic TV giants slug it out. *Variety*, pp. 1, 150.

Blumler, J., & Katz, E. (Eds.). (1974). *The uses of mass communications*. Beverly Hills, CA: Sage.

Brown, J., & Campbell, K. (1986). Race and gender in music videos: The same beat but a different drummer. *Journal of Communication, 36*, 94-106.

Camarillo, A. (1984). *Blacks and Hispanics in urban America: Some comparative historical perspectives* (Working paper no. 3). Stanford, CA: Stanford Center for Chicano Research.

Cantor, M. (1978). *Will more women make a difference: A sociological perspective on employment and portrayal in television*. Paper presented at the 6th Annual Telecommunications Policy Research Conference, Airlie, VA.

Cherry, D. (1987). Tv's missing mate: Whatever happened to Billy Dee Williams? In O. H. Gandy, Jr., & M. Carter-Williams (Eds.), *Developing leadership and power through communications: Selected proceedings from the 16th annual communications conference*. Washington, DC: Howard University, Center for Communications Research.

Clark, C. (1969). Television and social controls: Some observations on the portrayals of ethnic minorities. *Television Quarterly, 8*, 18-22.

Comstock, G. et al. (1978). *Television and human behavior.* New York: Columbia University Press.

Cook, D. A. (1981). *History of narrative film*. New York: Norton.

Curran, J., Gurevitch, M., & Woolacott, J. (1982). The study of the media: Theoretical approaches. In M. Gurevitch et al., *Culture society and media*. New York: Methuen.

Dates, J. L. (1979). *The relationship of demographic variables and racial attitudes to adolescent perceptions of Black television characters*. Unpublished doctoral dissertation, University of Maryland.

Dates, J. L. (1980). Race, racial attitudes and adolescent perceptions of Black television characters. *Journal of Broadcasting, 24*, 549-560.

Deutsch, K. (1966). *Nationalism and social communication*. Cambridge: MIT Press.

De Fleur, M., & Ball-Rokeach, S. (1984). *Theories of mass communication*. New York: Longman.

Doob, A., & MacDonald, F. (1977). Television viewing and fear of victimization: Is the relationship casual? *Journal of Personality and Social Psychology, 37*, 287-302.

Eastman, H., & Liss, M. (1980). Ethnicity and children's tv preferences. *Journalism Quarterly, 57*, 277-280.

Elliot, P. (1974). Uses and gratifications research: A critique and a sociological alternative. In J. Blumler & E. Katz (Eds.), *The uses of mass communication*. Beverly Hills, CA: Sage.

Fairchild, H., Stockard, R., & Bowman, P. (1986). Impact of Roots: Evidence from the National Survey of Black Americans. *Journal of Black Studies, 16*, 307-318.

Fife, M. (1981). The missing minority in mass communication research. In H. Myrick & C. Keegan (Eds.), *In search of diversity*. Washington, DC: Corporation for Public Broadcasting.

Fife, M. (1986). The impact of minority ownership on minority images in local news. In Oscar H. Gandy, Jr. (Ed.), *Communications: A key to economic and political change*. Washington DC: Howard University, Center for Communications Research.

Fitch, E. (1987, February 9). Buying power bursts poverty-stricken image. *Advertising Age*, pp. S1 ff.

Frank, R., & Greenberg, M. (1980). *The public's use of television*. Beverly Hills, CA: Sage.

Freeman, L. (1984, November 19). New magazines deliver professional niche. *Advertising Age*, p. 45.

Gandy, O. H., Jr. (1981). Toward the production of minority audience characteristics. In H. Myrick & C. Keegan (Eds.), *In search of diversity*. Washington, DC: Corporation for Public Broadcasting.

Gandy, O. H., Jr. (1987). The political economy of communications competence. In V. Mosco & J. Wasko (Eds.), *The political economy of information*. Madison: University of Wisconsin Press.

Gandy, O. H., Jr., & Coleman, L. G. (1986). The Jackson campaign: Mass media and black student perceptions. *Journalism Quarterly, 63*, 138-143.

Gandy, O. H., Jr., & ElWaylly, M. (1985). The knowledge gap and foreign affairs: The Palestinian-Israeli conflict. *Journalism Quarterly, 62*, 777-783.

Gandy, O. H., Jr., Matabane, P., & Omachonu, J. (1987). Media use, reliance and active participation: Exploring student awareness of the South African conflict. *Communication Research, 14*, 644-663.

Gandy, O. H., Jr., & Simmons, C. (1986). Technology, privacy and the democratic process. *Critical Studies in Mass Communication, 3*(2), 155-168.

Garramone, G. (1985). Motivation and selective attention to political information formats. *Journalism Quarterly, 62*, 37-44.

Gaziano, C. (1982). *The knowledge gap: An analytical review of media effects*. Paper presented at the meeting of the Association for Education in Journalism, Athens, OH.

Gaziano, C., & McGrath, K. (1986). Measuring the concept of credibility. *Journalism Quarterly, 63*, 451-462.

Gerbner, G., Gross, L., Morgan, M., & Signorielli, N. (1986). Living with television: The dynamics of the cultivation process. In J. Bryant & D. Zillman (Eds.), *Perspectives on media effects*. Hillsdale, NJ: Lawrence Erlbaum.

Gerbner, G., & Signorielli, N. (1978). The dynamics of cultural resistance. In G. Tuchman et al. (Eds.), *Hearth and home: Images of women in the mass media*. New York: Oxford University Press.

Gerbner, G., & Signorielli, N. (1979). *Women and minorities in television drama, 1969-1978*. Unpublished paper. Philadelphia: University of Pennsylvania.

Gerbner, G. et al. (1977). TV violence profile No. 8. *Journal of Communication, 27*(2), 171-180.

Gerbner, G. et al. (1980). The mainstreaming of America: Violence profile No. 11. *Journal of Communication, 30*(2), 10-29.

Gerbner, G. et al. (1982). Charting the mainstream: TV's contributions to political orientations. *Journal of Communication, 32*, 100-126.

Gitlin, T. (1979). Prime time TV: The hegemonic process in tv entertainment. *Social Problems, 26*, 251-266.

Good, L. T. (1984). *Cultivation theory: A critical reconsideration of George Gerbner's theoretical position*. Paper presented at the International Communication Association Conference, San Francisco.

Gombeski, W. et al. (1980). *Television public service announcements: Are they an effective channel for communicating health information to urban Mexican-Americans?* Paper for the American Public Health Association Meeting, Detroit.

Gramsci, A. (1983). *Selections from prison notebooks.* New York: International.

Gray, H. (1986). Television and the new Black man: Black male images in prime time situation comedy. *Media Culture and Society, 8,* 223-242.

Greenberg, B. S. (1986). Minorities and the mass media. In J. Bryant & D. Zillman (Eds.), *Perspectives on media effects.* Hillsdale, NJ: Lawrence Erlbaum.

Greenberg, B. S., & Baptista-Fernandez, P. (1980). Hispanic-Americans: The new minority on television. In B. S. Greenberg (Ed.), *Life on television.* Norwood, NJ: Ablex.

Greenberg, B. S., Burgoon, M., Burgoon, J., & Korzenny, F. (1983). *Mexican Americans and the mass media.* Norwood, NJ: Ablex.

Greenberg, B. S., & Dominick, J. R. (1969). Racial and social class differences in teen-agers' use of television. *Journal of Broadcasting, 13,* 331-344.

Greenberg, B. S., & Fernandez-Collado, P. (1979). *Hispanic-Americans: The new minority on television* (Report no. 12, Project CASTLE). East Lansing: Michigan State University.

Greenberg, B. S., & Nuendorf, K. A. (1980). Black family interactions on television. In B. S. Greenberg (Ed.), *Life on television.* Norwood, NJ: Ablex.

Gunter, B. (1987). *Television and the fear of crime.* London: John Libbey.

Gutiérrez, F. (1980). *Latinos and the media in the United States: An overview.* Paper presented at the conference of the International Communication Association, Acapulco.

Gutiérrez, F. (1985). Latino telecommunications employment and ownership. In A. Valdez (Ed.), *Telecommunications and Latinos.* Stanford, CA: Stanford Center for Chicano Research.

Gutiérrez, F. (1987). *Racial inclusiveness: Journalism education's second chance.* Paper presented at the Institute for Journalism Education's Conference on Racial Diversity, Washington, DC.

Hall, S. (1979). Culture, the media and the "ideological effect." In J. Curran et al. (Eds.), *Mass communication and society.* Beverly Hills, CA: Sage.

Hartman, P., & Husband, C. (1972). Mass media and racial conflict. In D. McQuail (Ed.), *Sociology of mass communication.* Harmondsworth, England: Penguin.

Hawkins, R., & Pingree, S. (1982a). Television's influence on social reality. In D. Pearl (Ed.), *Television and behavior: Ten years of scientific progress and implications for the eighties* (Vol. 2). Rockville, MD: U.S. Department of Health and Human Services.

Hawkins, R., & Pingree, S. (1982b). Uniform messages and habitual viewing: Unnecessary assumptions in social reality effects. *Human Communication Research, 7,* 291-301.

Heflin, D. (1981). *The acceptance of television commercials among Black consumers.* Paper presented at the meeting of the American Psychological Association, Los Angeles.

Hirsh, P. (1981). On not learning from one's mistakes: A reanalysis of Gerbner et al.'s findings on cultivation analysis. Fart II. *Communication Research, 8,* 3-37.

Hughes, M. (1980). The fruits of cultivation analysis: A re-examination of the effects of TV watching on fear of victimization, alienation and the approval of violence. *Public Opinion Quarterly, 44,* 287-302.

Hunter-Lattany, K. (1984). Who shot Buckwheat? *Melus, 2*(3), 79-85.

Johnson, E. (1984). Credibility of Black and White newscasters to a Black audience. *Journal of Broadcasting, 28,* 365-368.

Kaminsky, S., & Mahan, J. (1985). *American television genres.* Chicago: Nelson-Hall.

Keefe, S. E., & Padilla, A. M. (1987). *Chicano ethnicity.* Albuquerque: University of New Mexico Press.

Kellner, D. (1982). TV, ideology, and emancipatory popular culture. In H. Newcomb (Ed.), *Television: The critical view* (3rd ed.). New York: Oxford University Press. (Reprinted from *Socialist Review,* 1979, *45*)

Kilson, M. (1977). Generational change among Black Americans. In R. Samuels (Ed.), *Political generations and political development*. Lexington, MA: Lexington.

LaRose, R., & Eisenstock, B. (1981). *Techniques for testing the effectiveness of minority portrayals in multi-cultural children's programming*. Paper for the International Communication Association Conference, Minneapolis.

Leckenby, J., & Surlin, S. (1976). Incidental learning and viewer race. "All in the Family" and "Sanford and Son." *Journal of Broadcasting, 20*, 481-494.

Lee, E. B., & Browne, L. A. (1981). Television uses and gratifications among Black children, teenagers, and adults. *Journal of Broadcasting, 26*, 203-208.

Levine, L. (1977). *Black culture and Black consciousness*. New York: Oxford University Press.

Lewels, F. J. (1981). An indicator of Mexican-American attitudes toward the mass media. *Mass Communication Review, 8*(3), 19-27, 18.

Loughlin, M., Donohue, T., & Gudykunst, W. (1980). Puerto Rican children's perceptions of favorite television characters as behavioral models. *Journal of Broadcasting, 24*(2), 159-171.

Lowery, S., & DeFleur, M. (1983). *Milestones in mass communication research*. New York: Longman.

MacDonald, J. F. (1983). *Blacks and White TV: Afro-Americans in television since 1948*. Chicago: Nelson-Hall.

MacDonald, J. F. (1984, November 19). Stereotypes fall in tv ad portrayals. *Advertising Age*, p. 44.

Matabane, P. (1982). Black women on America's commercial television. *Western Journal of Black Studies, 6*, 22-25.

Matabane, P. (1985a). *Mainstreaming the Black audience*. Unpublished paper, Howard University, Washington, DC.

Matabane, P. (1985b). *The relationship between experience, television viewing and selected perceptions of social reality: A study of the Black audience*. Unpublished doctoral dissertation, Howard University.

Matabane, P., & Gandy, O. H., Jr. (in press). Through the prism of race and controversy: Did viewers learn anything from *The Africans? Journal of Black Studies*.

Matabane, P., Gandy, O. H., Jr., & Omachonu, J. O. (1987). Understanding social conflict: Media and student perspectives on the struggle in South Africa. In O. H. Gandy, Jr. (Ed.), *Communications: A key to economic and political change* (pp. 61-76). Washington, DC: Howard University, Center for Communications Research.

McGee, M. (1983). Prime time Dixie: Television's view of a "simple south." *Journal of American Culture*, pp. 100-109.

McLeod, J., & O'Keefe, G. (1972). The socialization perspective and communication behavior. In F. G. Kline & P. J. Tichenor (Eds.), *Current perspectives in mass communication research*. Beverly Hills, CA: Sage.

McLeod, J., & Reeves, B. (1981). On the nature of mass media effects. In G. C. Wilhoit & H. deBock (Eds.), *Mass communication review yearbook* (Vol. 2). Beverly Hills, CA: Sage.

McQuail, D. (1983). *Mass communication theory*. Beverly Hills, CA: Sage.

Miller, M. C. (1986). Deride and conquer. In T. Gitlin (Ed.), *Watching television*. New York: Pantheon.

Morley, D. (1980). *The nationwide audience: Structure and decoding*. London: British Film Institute.

National Analysts. (1981). *Attracting minority audiences to public television*. Washington, DC: Corporation for Public Broadcasting.

Neuendorf, K. A. (1982). *Hispanic youth's cultural identities: Predictions from media use and perceptions.* Paper for the International Communication Association Conference, Boston.

Newcomb, H. (1978). Assessing the violence profile of Gerbner and Gross: A humanistic critique and suggestions. *Communication Research, 5,* 264-282.

Newcomb, H., & Hirsh, P. (1987). Television as a cultural forum. In H. Newcomb (Ed.), *Television: The critical view.* New York: Oxford University Press.

Nicolini, P. (1986). Philadelphia Puerto Rican community leaders' perceptions of Spanish-language media. *Mass Communication Review, 13,* 11-17.

Oates, W., Ghorpade, S., & Brown, J. (1986). *Media technology consumers: Demographics and psychographics of "Taffies."* Paper presented at the meeting of the Association for Education in Journalism and Mass Communication, Norman, OK.

O'Guinn, T. C., Faber, R., & Meyer, T. (1985). Ethnic segmentation and Spanish-language television. *Journal of Advertising, 14*(3), 63-66.

Parkin, F. (1971). *Class inequality and political order.* London: Granada.

Perse, E. (1986). Soap opera viewing patterns of college students and cultivation. *Journal of Broadcasting, 30,* 159-174.

Peterson, T., Jensen, J., & Rivers, W. (1985). *The mass media and modern society.* New York: Holt, Rinehart & Winston.

Peterson-Lewis, S., & Chennault, S. (1986). Black artists music videos: Three success strategies. *Journal of Communication, 36*(1), 107-114.

Poindexter, P., & Stroman, C. (1981). Blacks and television: A review of the research literature. *Journal of Broadcasting, 25*(2), 103-122.

Potter, W. J. (1986). Perceived reality and the cultivation hypothesis. *Journal of Broadcasting, 30*(1).

Rayburn, J. D., II, & Palmgreen, P. (1984). Merging uses and gratifications and expectancy-value theory. *Communication Research, 1,* 537-562.

Reeves, J. (1987). Television stars: The case of Mr. T. In H. Newcomb (Ed.), *Television: The critical view.* New York: Oxford University Press.

Resnick, S., & Wolff, R. (1987). *Knowledge and class.* Chicago: University of Chicago Press.

Rokeach, M. (1973). *The nature of human values.* New York: Free Press.

Rubin, A. M. (1986). Uses, gratifications, and media effects research. In J. Bryant & D. Zillman (Eds.), *Perspectives on media effects.* Hillsdale, NJ: Lawrence Erlbaum.

Rubin, A. M., Perse, E., Hahn, M., & Taylor, D. (1987). *A methodological investigation of cultivation.* Paper presented at the meeting of the Association for Education in Journalism and Mass Communication, San Antonio, TX.

St. George, A., & Robinson-Weber, S. (1983). The mass media, political attitudes and behavior. *Communication Research, 10,* 487-508.

Schement, J. R. (1976). *Primary Spanish language radio as a function of internal colonialism: Patterns of ownership and control.* Unpublished doctoral dissertation, Stanford University, Stanford, CA.

Schement, J. R. et al. (1977). The anatomy of a license challenge. *Journal of Communication,* 89-94.

Seggar, J. et al. (1981). Television's portrayals of minorities and women in drama and comedy drama, 1971-1980. *Journal of Broadcasting, 26,* 277-287.

Seiter, E. (1986). Stereotypes and the media: A re-evaluation. *Journal of Communication, 36*(2), 14-26.

Shoemaker, P. (1985). What do communication researchers mean by "ethnicity"? *Mass Communication Review, 11*(3), 12-17.

Shoemaker, P., with Mayfield, E. (1987). Building a theory of news content. *Journalism Monograph,* no. 103.

Shoemaker, P. et al. (1985). *Media in ethnic context: Communication and language in Texas.* Austin: College of Communication, University of Texas.

Signorielli, N. (1981). Content analysis: More than just counting minorities. In H. Myrick & C. Keegan (Eds.), *In search of diversity.* Washington, DC: Corporation for Public Broadcasting.

Simmons, R. (1987). *The relationship between cognitive style and television preferences among African-American college students.* Unpublished doctoral dissertation, Howard University, Washington, DC.

Singleton, L. A. (1981). FCC minority ownership policy and non-entertainment programming in Black-oriented radio stations. *Journal of Broadcasting, 25,* 195-201.

Smith, W. (1985). *Black television audience heterogeneity: A uses and gratifications approach.* Paper presented at the Association for Education in Journalism and Mass Communications Conference, Memphis, TN.

Spadoni, M. (1987, February 9). Mom and Pops out of TV ownership picture. *Advertising Age,* pp. S8 ff.

Stewart, A. S. (1987, October, 9-11). Hollywood's latest Latin look. *USA Weekend,* pp. 1, 4-5.

Stroman, C. (1984). The socialization influence of television on Black children. *Journal of Black Studies, 15,* 79-100.

Stroman, C. (1986). Television viewing and self-concept among Black children. *Journal of Broadcasting, 30,* 87-93.

Subervi-Velez, F. (1984). *Hispanics, the mass media, and politics: Assimilation vs pluralism.* Unpublished doctoral dissertation, University of Wisconsin-Madison.

Subervi-Velez, F. (1986). The mass media and ethnic assimilation and pluralism. *Communication Research, 13,* 71-96.

Subervi-Velez, F. (1987). *Interactions between Latinos and Anglos on prime time television: A case study of* Condo. Unpublished paper, University of California, Santa Barbara.

Surette, R. (1985). Television viewing and support of punitive criminal justice policy. *Journalism Quarterly, 62,* 373-377.

Surlin, S. (1974). Bigotry on air and in life: The "Archie Bunker case." *Public Telecommunications Review, 2,* 34-41.

Surlin, S. (1976). *Race and selective exposure/perception of racial integration in tv entertainment programming.* Paper presented at the Speech Communication Association Meeting, San Francisco.

Surlin, S. (1977). Race, education and fatalism: Predictors of involvement in radio programming. *Journal of Broadcasting, 21,* 413-426.

Tan, A. (1980). Mass media use, issue knowledge and political involvement. *Public Opinion Quarterly, 44,* 241-248.

Tan, A. (1981). Political participation, diffuse support and perceptions of political efficacy as predictors of mass media use. *Communication Monographs, 48,* 133-145.

Tan, A. (1983). Media use and political orientations of ethnic groups. *Journalism Quarterly, 60,* 126-132.

Tan, A., & Tan, G. (1979). Television use and self-esteem of Blacks. *Journal of Communication, 29*(1), 129-135.

Thomas, C. W. (1985). Social science research and some implications for Afro-American scholars. *Journal of Black Studies, 15,* 325-338.

Thorburn, D. (1987). Television as an aesthetic medium. *Critical Studies in Mass Communication, 4,* 161-174.

Trayes, E. J. (1987). *Minorities and mass media careers: Pipeline problems of the 1980s.* Paper presented at the Invitational Conference on Minorities and Communications, Washington, DC.

Tuchman, G. (1978). Introduction: The symbolic annihilation of women by the mass media. In G. Tuchman et al. (Eds.), *Hearth and home: Images of women in the mass media*. New York: Oxford University Press.

U.S. Civil Rights Commission. (1977). *Window dressing on the set: Women and minorities in television*. Washington, DC: Author.

Valdez, A. (Ed.). (1985). *Telecommunications and Latinos: An assessment of issues and opportunities*. Stanford, CA: Stanford Center for Chicano Research.

Valenzuela, N. (1981). Latinos in public broadcasting: Developing a research agenda. In H. Myrick & C. Keegan (Eds.), *In search of diversity*. Washington, DC: Corporation for Public Broadcasting.

Vidmar, N., & Rokeach, M. (1974). Archie Bunker's bigotry: A study in selective perception and exposure. *Journal of Communication, 24*, 36-47.

Walley, W. (1987, March 21). Spanish-dubbing new Hollywood trend. *Advertising Age*, p. 12.

Booker T. Washington Foundation, Cablecommunications Resource Center-West. (1977). *How Blacks use television for entertainment and information*. Washington, DC: Booker T. Washington Foundation.

Webster, F., & Robins, K. (1986). *Information technology: A Luddite analysis*. Norwood, NJ: Ablex.

Williams, R. (1973). Base and superstructure in Marxist cultural theory. *New Left Review, 82*, 3-16.

Wilson, C. C., II, & Gutiérrez, F. (1985). *Minorities and media: Diversity and the end of mass communication*. Beverly Hills, CA: Sage.

# Part III
Contexts

# 16 Identity and Interpersonal Bonding

## Stella Ting-Toomey

The linking between self-conceptions and the intergroup-interpersonal bonding process is the focus of this chapter. Identity is viewed as the key vehicle that facilitates the ebbs and flows of dyadic relationship development. Cultural variability shapes the structure and the content of the identity, and the "self" or "identity" is refined and modified through the process of dyadic verbal and nonverbal negotiation.

The objectives of this chapter are to integrate two strands of research in the area of identity management and communication accommodation and to apply the convergent approach to the study of identity and relational bonding processes. Identity is defined as (a) the meaning a person attributes to the self as an object in a social situation or a social role, (b) relational, (c) reflexive, and (d) a source of motivation (Burke, 1980, p. 18). Relational bonding refers to "the process of forming individualized relationships—affinities that are close, deep, personal, and intimate" (Bochner, 1984, p. 544). Identity presentation and management is viewed as the motivational force for the initiation and transformation of the relational bonding process.

The chapter is developed in three sections. The first section presents two contemporary perspectives that link cross-cultural variability in identity to communication, and intergroup identity to communication. In the second section, the implications of the convergent approach to the intergroup-interpersonal bonding process are drawn out. The third section contains a discussion of the future directions that the study of identity and relational bonding processes should take.

## IDENTITY PERSPECTIVES

There are many diverse perspectives (Gergen & Davis, 1985; Marsella, DeVos, & Hsu, 1985; McCall, 1987; Shweder & Bourne, 1984; Yardley & Honess, 1987) in the study of identity maintenance and human interaction.

Two lines of research have accumulated a systematic body of research. One focuses on cross-cultural variations in identity, while the other focuses on intergroup identity within cultures. Most studies under the cultural variability perspective have focused on identity formation and interpersonal relationship development across cultures. The studies under the rubric of ethnolinguistic identity perspective have focused on linguistic identity formation and intergroup relationship accommodation within cultures.

### Cultural Variability Perspective

The cultural variability perspective is concerned primarily with how definable dimensions of a culture affect identity conceptions and relationship development. Dimensions of cultural variability influence the underlying social structures and norms of a situation, and the social norms, in turn, influence how one should or should not behave in a certain manner (Gudykunst & Ting-Toomey, 1988). The identity salience dimension, which is defined as the "degree to which an individual's relationships to particular others depended upon his or her being a given kind of person . . . playing a particular role, and having a particular identity" (Stryker, 1987, p. 97), depends heavily on the cultural context in which the encounter takes place. How one constructs and presents a "self" in a relationship is, to a large degree, situationally-dependent and culturally-dependent.

On a more specific level, when one examines the cultural variability dimensions that have been isolated by theorists in different disciplines, the one cross-cultural dimension that appears to have strong etic endorsement is individualism-collectivism (Gudykunst, 1987; Hofstede, 1980; Hofstede & Bond, 1984; Hui, 1988; Hui & Triandis, 1986; Ting-Toomey, 1988a; Triandis, Bontempo, & Betancourt et al., 1986; Triandis, Bontempo, Villareal, Asai, & Lucca, 1988). Individualism-collectivism refers to the culturally grounded "cluster of attitudes, beliefs, and behaviors toward a wide variety of people" (Hui & Triandis, 1986, p. 240). In an etic analysis of the dimension in nine cultures (Chile, Costa Rica, France, Greece, Hong Kong, India, Indonesia, the Netherlands, and three ethnic samples in the United States), Triandis et al. (1986) uncovered four stable etic factors: Individualism has two factors (*separation from ingroups* and *self-reliance with hedonism*) and collectivism has two factors (*family integrity* and *interdependability with sociability*).

Overall, members of the individualistic cultures (such as Australia and the United States) tend to place a high emphasis on the "I" identity over the "we" identity, the "I" assertion over the group assertion, and tend to maintain a considerable social distance between the "I" identity and ingroup social influences. Conversely, members of the collectivistic cultures (such as China and Japan) tend to place a high premium on the "we" identity over the "I" identity, the group assertion over the individualistic assertion, and tend to be more susceptible to ingroup influences than members in the individualistic cultures. Triandis (1986) argued that there are two types of collectivism: "simple" collectivism and "contextual" collectivism. "Simple" collectivism allows members to choose how to behave when multiple ingroups are relevant, while "contextual" collectivism designates an ingroup influence that is specific. In addition, while the boundary conditions between ingroups and outgroups are fairly diffused and loosely structured in individualistic cultures, the boundary conditions between ingroups and outgroups, and also between memberships in various ingroups (e.g., kin, coworkers, neighbors), are more sharply defined and tightly structured in collectivistic cultures (Triandis et al., 1986).

In a recent study, for example, Triandis et al. (1988) found that individualism in the United States is reflected in (a) *self-reliance with competition*, (b) *low concerns for ingroups*, and (c) *distance from ingroups*. In addition, a higher-order factor analysis suggests that *subordination of ingroup goals to personal goals* may be the most important aspect of individualism in the United States. In comparison, samples from two collectivistic cultures (Japan and Puerto Rico) indicate that "which ingroup is present, in what context . . ., and what behavior (e.g., paying attention to the views of others, feelings similar to others, competing with others)" are critical to role enactment and performance (Triandis et al., 1988, p. 336). Furthermore, the psychological dimension of idiocentrism-allocentrism (e.g., the personality dimension equivalent to individualism and collectivism, respectively) also asserts influence on individuals' behavior within cultures. Overall, allocentric individuals reported more social support and perceived a better quality of such support than idiocentric individuals, while idiocentric individuals reported being more lonely. Related research by Gudykunst and Nishida (1986) and Gudykunst, Yoon, and Nishida (1987) obtained results similar to Triandis et al.'s study (1986). For example, Gudykunst, Yoon, and Nishida (1987) found that members of collectivistic cultures (Japan and Korea) perceive greater social penetration (personalization and synchronization) in their ingroup relationships than do members of individualistic cultures (United States). Their data further revealed that perceived outgroup relationships in collectivistic cultures are influenced by either "simple" collectivism or "contextual" collectivism. Overall, the Korean culture exhibits "simple" collectivistic patterns, while the Japanese exhibits "contextual" collectivistic patterns.

In the cross-cultural interpersonal conflict literature, Chua and Gudykunst (1987), Leung (1988), and Ting-Toomey (1985) observed that members of individualistic cultures tend to use a direct conflict communication style and a solution-orientation style, and members of collectivistic cultures tend to use an indirect conflict communication style and a conflict-avoidance style. In addition, collectivists tend to use the equality norm (the equal distribution norm) with ingroup members and use the equity norm (the deservingness norm) with outgroup members more than individualists (Leung & Bond, 1984; Leung & Iwawaki, 1988). Collectivists also display stronger preference for conflict mediation and bargaining procedure than individualists (Leung, 1987). Preferences for a direct conflict style, for the use of the equity norm, and for the direct settlement of disputes reflect the salience of the "I" identity in individualistic cultures; while preferences for an indirect conflict style, for the use of the equality norm, and for the use of mediation procedures reflect the salience of the "we" identity in the collectivistic cultures.

Ting-Toomey (1985, 1988a) developed a theory of face-negotiation and cross-cultural conflict styles. Conflict is viewed as an identity-bound concept in which the "faces" or the "situated identities" of the conflict interactants are called into question. Based on the two dimensions of self-concern focus versus other-concern focus and positive-face need (inclusion need) versus negative-face need (autonomy need), twelve theoretical propositions were developed to account for the relationship between cultural variability and conflict style. The first four propositions, for example, were as follows:

(1) Members of individualistic cultures would tend to express a greater degree of self-face maintenance in a conflict situation than would members of collectivistic cultures.

(2) Members of collectivistic cultures would tend to express a greater degree of mutual-face or other-face maintenance than would members of individualistic cultures.

(3) Members of individualistic cultures would tend to use more autonomy-preserving strategies (negative-face need) in managing conflict than would members of collectivistic cultures.

(4) Members of collectivistic cultures would tend to use more inclusion-seeking strategies (positive-face need) in managing conflict than would members of individualistic cultures.

In sum, under the domain of cultural variability perspective, a body of theoretical and empirical literature has been systematically accumulated in the past ten years. Explicitly or implicitly, the concept of identity has been tied to the study of social relationships, to interpersonal relationship development, and to conflict communication processes across cultures. Most cultural variability studies employ survey or experimental methods of data collection. Alternative theoretical efforts on the study of cross-cultural identity and communication can be found in Carbaugh's (1988) and Philipsen's (in press) work on personhood and communication, in Cushman and Cahn's (1985) work on self-concept and cultural communication, and in Cronen, Pearce, and Tomm's (1985) work on CMM (coordinated management of meaning) identity and dialectical patterns in communication.

## Ethnolinguistic Identity Perspective

The ethnolinguistic identity perspective (Beebe & Giles, 1984) is concerned mainly with group membership influences on identity salience vis-à-vis the critical role of language. Giles and Johnson (1981), for example, argue that language plays a critical role in shaping the ethnic/ cultural identity salience dimension for individuals. Giles, Bourhis, and Taylor (1977) contend that perceived ethnolinguistic vitality influences the degree to which individuals will act as an ethnic/cultural group member in an intergroup encounter situation. Perceived high ethnolinguistic vitality means individuals perceive their own ingroup language as assuming a high-status position and as receiving wide-based institutional support from the language community. Perceived low ethnolinguistic vitality means individuals perceive their own ingroup language as assuming a low-status position and as receiving narrow-based institutional support from the government, education, industry, and the mass media (for a detailed review on ethnolinguistic identity, see Chapter 5, Franklyn-Stokes & Giles, in this volume; Gudykunst, in press; Chapter 9, Gudykunst & Gumbs, in this volume).

In addition to the issue of ethnic/cultural identity salience dimension, Tajfel's (1978) and Turner's (1987) social identity theory argues for the critical role of social identity salience in the formation of an individual's self-concept. Tajfel (1978, p. 63) states: "Social identity is that *part* of an individual's self-concept which derives from his [or her] knowledge of his [or her] membership in a social group (or groups) together with the value and emotional significance attached to that membership." Incorporating the main ideas in ethnolinguistic identity theory and social identity theory, Gudykunst (in press) identifies five factors that influence ethnolinguistic identity development: (a) the strength of ingroup identification, (b) the salience and overlaps of multiple group memberships, (c) the valence of intergroup comparisons, (d) the permeability of ingroup/outgroup boundaries, and (e) the perceived vitality of ingroup language. According to Gudykunst (1988), the more secure and positive members of a group feel about their identity, the more positive the intergroup comparisons, the more tolerant and receptive they are toward members of other groups. He further theorizes that an increase in the strength of strangers' ethnolinguistic identities will produce an increase in their attributional confidence regarding the behaviors of other groups' members. He contends that secure ethnolinguistic identity, positive expectations, perceived group similarity, shared intergroup networks, interpersonal salience, second-language competence, and personality factors affect the reduction of uncertainty and anxiety in intergroup encounter processes. Reducing uncertainty and anxiety, in turn, influences intergroup-interpersonal adaptation and effectiveness. Identity security, in short, brings about confidence in oneself to initiate the exploration of the world of a stranger, and the exploration, in turn, brings about greater knowledge and understanding of the stranger's background and normative culture.

Members who are secure in their ethnolinguistic identities will have an overall sense of positive self-concept. They will be likely to take risks in strangers' interaction. They will also be likely to explore and cultivate deeper levels of intergroup relationship with outgroup members, and will be more receptive to move the relationship to different bonding stages such as close friendship, romantic relationship, or marital relationship than members with insecure ethnolinguistic identities. There exists, of course, an optimal level of the ethnolinguistic identification process. Members who are at the extreme far ends of the continuum of identification will have either extreme marginal identities or extreme ethnocentric identities. Secure ethnolinguistic identification in this chapter means a healthy, optimal level of cultural role identities and social role identities that constitute the integral part of an individual's positive sense of "self."

More recently, an alternative perspective, namely, Collier and Thomas' (1988) cultural identity theory, has been developed to explain how members of two ethnic or cultural groups manage meanings, interpretations, and identities through the intercultural discourse process. From a process-emergent orientation, they theorize that "the more the consistency in each individual's ascription of the other's cultural identity matching the other's avowed cultural identity, the higher the intercultural competence" and "the higher the degree of intercultural competence, the higher the likelihood that the relationship will be developed or maintained." The mutual identity validation process is critical to forming intergroup-interpersonal ties in their theory.

In sum, this section has presented two contemporary perspectives on the study of identity and relational development processes: cultural variability perspective and ethnolinguistic identity perspective. The cultural variability perspective focuses on cross-cultural comparisons of "self" concerning the communication processes within and between individualistic cultures and collectivistic cultures. The ethnolinguistic identity perspective focuses on identity salience and the intergroup encounter process and emphasizes the paramount importance of secure identity comparisons as an anchoring point to the rest of the intergroup-interpersonal relationship bonding process. For the next section, the implications of a convergent approach of cultural variability theory and ethnolinguistic identity theory to the study of intergroup-interpersonal bonding phenomenon are explained.

## INTERGROUP-INTERPERSONAL BONDING PROCESS

### A Convergent Approach

Bochner (1984, p. 583), in discussing the functions of human communication in interpersonal bonding, proposes five specific functions of relational communication: "(1) to foster favorable impressions; (2) to organize the relationship; (3) to construct and validate a conjoint world view; (4) to express feelings and thoughts; and (5) to protect vulnerabilities." As intercultural communication researchers, however, we cannot discuss the interpersonal bonding process adequately unless the dynamics of intergroup factors are taken into consideration. The factors of language, ethnolinguistic identity salience, preconceived expectations of outgroup members, and the boundary conditions between ingroup and outgroup members are critical to the development of the evolving, long-term relationships of the intergroup-interpersonal dyad.

In order to examine the bonding ties between members of two ethnic or cultural communities, we have to make some basic assumptions. For example, the intergroup members have a common means (i.e., a common language) to communicate with one another. They are in close proximity with one another, they have the opportunities to communicate, and they have a sense of reciprocal awareness of the other's presence (Ting-Toomey, 1981, 1986a). The first intergroup bonding question asks: What are the conditions that promote the initiation of intergroup-interpersonal encounters?

The theories and research based on ethnolinguistic identity theory can provide initial observations to answer this question. Under the conditions that intergroup comparisons are positive, ethnolinguistic identities are strong, and group boundaries are permeable, members of culture X are more likely to venture out to initiate contact with members of culture Y, and vice versa. As Axiom 1 in Gudykunst's (1988) intergroup uncertainty reduction theory indicates: Strangers' positive ethnolinguistic identities are more likely to increase attributional confidence regarding outgroup members' behavior and decrease initial anxiety they experience with outgroup members' contact. The axiom, however, *only* holds when members of the outgroup are perceived as "typical" and when ethnic status is activated.

Nevertheless, while ethnolinguistic identities serve as a critical factor during the initial intergroup contact phase, it does not assume equal values and equal statuses during actual interactions in all cultures. In some cultures, personal identity salience outweighs the importance of role identity salience. In other cultures, cultural role and social role identities are of paramount importance to one's sense of "self" and personhood construction. Explaining these differences is where the cultural variability perspective can facilitate our understanding of the intergroup-interpersonal bonding process.

Applying the individualism-collectivism theoretical dimension, we can state the basic assumption that members of individualistic cultures will place a greater emphasis on the salience of personal identities over role identities, while members of collectivistic cultures will place a greater emphasis on the salience of role identities over personal identities during the intergroup encounter process. For example, members of individualistic cultures will emphasize personal identity factors such as personal ideals or achievements during initial attraction stages, while members of collectivistic cultures will emphasize role identity factors such as educational or occupational background during initial intergroup encounters. This basic assumption, in turn, influences how intergroup members attune to different aspects of the encounter—to foster favorable impressions, to validate a conjoint worldview, to organize the relationship, to express feelings and thoughts, and to protect relational vulnerabilities (Bochner, 1984).

### Fostering Impressions

Impression management is critical to the cultivation of intergroup-interpersonal ties. Both the cultural norms of the encounter situation and the identity negotiation process between the two individuals will have a profound influence on the further development of the relationship. If the intergroup encounter takes place in a heterogeneous, individualistic culture, norms and rules will assert relatively less pressures on the dyad than if the intergroup encounter takes place in a homogeneous, collectivistic culture like Japan. Beyond the contextual setting of the encounter, the identity negotiation process between the two individuals will be critical to the further evolution of the relationship. While interpersonal attraction variables such as physical attraction, personality attraction, perceived attitudinal similarity, and close proximity may be necessary conditions for the intergroup-interpersonal bonding process to occur, identity negotiation and reciprocal support are the vital conditions that propel the intergroup relationship forward, moving toward an individualized relationship that is "close, deep, personal and intimate" (Bochner, 1984, p. 544; Cushman & Cahn, 1985; Ting-Toomey, 1986a).

In attempting to foster a favorable impression, especially during actual initial encounters, the intergroup dyad has to grapple with two sets of problems: self-presentation versus other-validation. This section focuses on the self-presentation dimension, while the next section contains a discussion of the other-validation dimension.

In terms of self-presentation acts, there are four possible intergroup impression presentation options: (a) member categorizes or identifies self as a typical cultural member, and behaves typically; (b) member categorizes or identifies self as an atypical cultural member, and behaves atypically; (c) member categorizes or identifies self as a typical cultural member, but acts atypically; and (d) member categorizes or identifies self as an atypical cultural member, but acts typically. All four options probably are influenced more by the dyadic partner's perceptions and interpretations than by the member's projected sense of self in the encounter. The partner's knowledge of the culture, the degree of favorableness toward the outgroup, the levels of expectations of the role enactment from outgroup member, and the degree of tolerance of ambiguity will create either a positive or a negative climate for the initial intergroup contact. Past intergroup literature (Hewstone & Brown, 1986) has indicated that positive feelings toward outgroup members as a whole are more likely to be generated from intergroup interaction involving an outgroup member who is perceived as typical of his or her group rather than from interaction involving an outgroup member who is perceived as atypical. We may want to qualify this finding, however, by adding on the variables of degree of favorable outgroup attitude and the valence of typical/atypical outgroup member's behavior. A favorable outgroup attitude, in conjunction with desirable typical/atypical outgroup member's behavior, will promote further intergroup-interpersonal relationship development, while an unfavorable outgroup attitude, with undesirable typical/atypical outgroup member's behavior, will impede further relationship progress.

Dimensions of cultural variability may help us explain the possible intergroup relationship outcomes in the mixed categories such as favorable outgroup attitude but perceived negative outgroup member's behavior or unfavorable outgroup attitude but perceived positive outgroup member's behavior. Previous research (Triandis et al., 1986) indicates that members of individualistic cultures are less susceptible to ingroup influence than members of collectivistic cultures. Members of individualistic cultures tend to separate the cultural levels of attraction with the personal identity salience levels, while members of collectivistic cultures tend to integrate the two levels. In addition, while members of individualistic cultures will focus more on personal identities' impression negotiation, members of collectivistic cultures will focus more on the role identities' negotiation especially during the initial relationship formation process. Members of individualistic cultures will be predisposed to desirable personal attributes displayed by outgroup members above and beyond cultural role categories or social role categories, whereas members of collectivistic cultures will be predisposed to desirable role attributes rather than individualized, personal attributes in initial encounter phase.

The construction of personhood in individualistic cultures is based on intrinsic qualities and characteristics, while the construction of person-hood in collectivistic cultures is tied closely to the sociocultural webs of the system. As Shweder and Bourne (1984, pp. 191-192) summarize, in the individualistic cultures, "each person is conceived of as . . . a monadic replica of general humanity. A kind of sacred personalized self is developed and the individual qua individual is seen as inviolate, a supreme value in and of itself. The 'self' becomes an object of interest *per se*," whereas in collectivistic cultures, the "context-dependent, occasion-bound concept of the person" is expressed through "(a) no attempt to distinguish the individual from the status s(he) occupies; (b) the view that obligations and rights are differentially apportioned by role, group, etc.; (c) a disinclination to ascribe intrinsic moral worth to persons merely because they are persons."

Taken together, the cultural variability perspective and ethnolinguistic identity perspective unveil the following three observations:

(1)   Persons with secure ethnolinguistic identities will be more likely to initiate intergroup-interpersonal bonding ties than persons with insecure ethnolin-guistic identities.

(2)   Persons from individualistic cultures will be more likely to be attracted to outgroup members with desirable personal attributes, while persons from collectivistic cultures will be more likely to be attracted to outgroup mem-bers with desirable cultural or social role attributes.

(3)   Persons from individualistic cultures will tend to foster favorable impres-sions through emphasis on positive "I" identity presentation, while persons from collectivistic cultures will tend to foster favorable impressions through emphasis on positive "role" identity presentation.

## Validating the Other

Accurate coorientation and reciprocal, mutual support of identities occur in conjunction with fostering favorable impressions. Mutual vali-dation and confirmation is vital to further relational growth and progress (Ting-Toomey, 1986a). Three issues (identity validation, the content of validation, and the means of validation) are of central concern in the intergroup-interpersonal validation process.

As mentioned in the previous section, identity presentation can come in different forms. Likewise, identity validation can take on different shapes. To validate someone's identities, we have to obtain the following identity information about the other group members: (a) the extent to which he or she identifies with cultural role categories, social role categories, or personal identity categories; (b) the salience (important-unimportant) and the valence (positive-negative) in which he or she identifies with different role types; and (c) the consistency and frequency distributions in which he or she enacts each role category. Beyond obtaining the basic relational knowledge, the members have to possess a certain degree of attributional confidence in themselves to infer whether the obtained information is accurate or inaccurate.

Ethnolinguistic identity theory suggests some initial predictions. Members who are secure about their ethnolinguistic identities are more confident in their predictions of the outgroup members' behavior, while members who are insecure about their ethnolinguistic identities are probably less confident in their predictions of outgroup members' behavior. Members who are secure in their own identities possess a sense of awareness, knowledge, and acceptance of their own self and behavior. Members who are self-aware are also likely to be alert and aware of their outer environment. Self-awareness leads to other-awareness, self-knowledge leads to other-knowledge, and self-acceptance leads to other-acceptance and tolerance. Members who have strong ethnolinguistic identities will be more ready to engage in an active information-seeking process concerning strangers' behavior than members who have weak ethnolinguistic identities. Members who are secure in their identities are not afraid of losing their "selves" in the searching process, while members who are insecure in their identities will have a high apprehension level in losing their "selves" in interactions with dissimilar strangers.

Cross-cultural studies of uncertainty reduction (Gudykunst & Nishida, 1984, 1986) indicate that the individualism-collectivism dimension influences uncertainty reduction content and uncertainty reduction modes of intergroup-interpersonal communication. Members of individualistic cultures tend to reduce uncertainty in the personal identity salience area, while members of collectivistic cultures tend to reduce uncertainty in the role identity salience area. Personal identity salience means a set of self-definitional personal identities that are derived from unique, idiosyncratic individual characteristics (e.g., active-passive, fast-slow). Role identity salience is conceptualized as a set of self-definitional role identities that are derived from cultural and/or social membership categories (Ting-Toomey, 1986a).

Applying the results of cross-cultural studies of uncertainty reduction to the intergroup-interpersonal validation process, the findings suggest that members of individualistic cultures are more likely to validate an outgroup member's personal identity salience, while members of collectivistic cultures are likely to validate an outgroup member's role identity salience. Furthermore, previous work (Hall, 1983; Okabe, 1983; Ting-Toomey, 1985, 1988a) reveals that members of individualistic cultures tend to use a direct, verbal mode of communication to reduce relational uncertainty, while members of collectivistic cultures tend to use an indirect, nonverbal mode of communication to reduce uncertainty. Individualistic cultures are low-context cultures and collectivistic cultures are high-context cultures (Hall, 1983). Low-context cultures emphasize direct verbal assertion, explicit meanings, and personal identity interactions, and high-context cultures value indirect verbal assertion, implicit meanings, and role identity interaction. In terms of intergroup modes of validation, members of low-context, individualistic cultures are likely to engage in a direct, explicit verbal mode of identity validation, while members of high-context, collectivistic cultures are likely to engage in an indirect, implicit nonverbal mode of identity validation.

Finally, social networks play a critical role in the intergroup-interpersonal identity validation process. According to Triandis et al. (1988, p. 325), in collectivist cultures, "the ingroup's influence on behavior is broad, profound, and diffuse; in the individualist [cultures] it is narrow, superficial, and specific." In individualistic cultures, identity validation is a private, dyadic affair, while in the collectivistic cultures, identity validation is embedded within the approval of family and social networks. Identity validation is an intensive affair in individualistic cultures, while identity validation is a diffused activity in collectivistic cultures.

In sum, three observations on the identity validation process are posited:

(1) Persons with secure ethnolinguistic identities will have a higher degree of attributional confidence in intergroup-interpersonal identity validation process than persons with insecure ethnolinguistic identities.

(2) Persons from individualistic cultures will tend to validate outgroup members' personal identity salience dimension, while persons from collectivistic cultures will tend to validate outgroup members' role identity salience dimension.

(3) Persons from individualistic cultures will rely more on a direct verbal mode of identity validation, while persons from collectivistic cultures will rely more on an indirect, nonverbal mode of identity validation.

## Organizing the Relationship

Organizing the relationship refers to how the intergroup couple establishes rules for the relationship, and the rules "constitute the *definition of the relationship* and form the organizational basis for controlling *what* actions will take place in the relationship, as well as *how* thoughts and feelings may be expressed" (Bochner, 1984, p. 591; Duck, 1985). Different levels of rules concerning how a relationship should be conducted are reflective of basic cultural ideologies and themes surrounding the structure, content, and meanings of a relationship. According to Bochner

(1984), there are four types of bonding rules: (a) common consent rules, (b) idiosyncratic rules, (c) explicit or implicit rules, and (d) metarules. *Common consent rules* are rules that are learned during primary socialization process via family interaction (i.e., are determined culturally). *Idiosyncratic rules* are rules that reflect the private beliefs concerning what is fair and just in the relationship by the involved parties. *Explicit* or *implicit rules* are prior agreement rules that are either publicly acknowledged or publicly denied to a third party outside the relationship. Finally, *metarules* are rules about who may set the rules, and also about rules against seeing or knowing about certain rules in the relationship (Bochner, 1984, pp. 591-592).

Common consent rules are rules with high normative cultural forces. They constitute the cultural "scripts" of what it means to be a "good" friend, what it means to be a "dating" couple, or what it means to be a "harmonious" family. Argyle (1986), in a series of studies testing 33 common rules in four cultures (Britain, Hong Kong, Italy, and Japan), found that respect for privacy is a basic rule regulating all relationships across cultures. In addition, there are more rules about obedience, avoiding loss of face, maintaining harmonious relations in groups, and restraining emotional expression in the collectivistic cultures than in the individualistic cultures.

The issue of privacy-regulation is related directly to identity respect and the identity validation process. With respect to the influence of cultural variability on privacy negotiation, we can predict that members of individualistic cultures probably display a higher privacy need in interpersonal relationships than members of collectivistic cultures. Members of individualistic cultures treasure autonomy and freedom in a relationship, while members of collectivistic cultures value mutual interdependence and restraint. While the dialectic of freedom and restraint is present simultaneously in all intimate relationships, cultural variability will influence members' preference for one end of the dialectic over another. In addition, members of individualistic cultures will be likely to articulate their need for privacy or privacy respect, while members of collectivistic cultures will be subdued about it. Privacy respect is a reflection of respect extended to the personhood of "I"; whereas privacy regulation, in the context of the collectivistic cultures, may mean dyadic privacy away from kinship network and social network influences, but may not necessarily mean the separate, autonomous privacy between the "you" and the "I."

Idiosyncratic rules are private beliefs concerning what constitutes "fairness" in a relationship. According to Leung and Iwawaki (1988), collectivists typically follow the "equality norm" in reward allocation, while individualists typically follow the "equity norm" in reward distribution. The equality norm requires an equal allocation of a reward among the participants regardless of their input to the obtaining of the reward, while the equity norm requires that reward distribution should be proportional to participants' input (Leung & Iwawaki, 1988, p. 36). In the initial intergroup-interpersonal attraction phase, members of individualistic cultures will probably practice the equity norm of self-deservingness, while members of collectivistic cultures will probably practice the equality norm for the sake of preserving relational harmony and solidarity. In addition, there are differences in the reciprocity norm in intergroup relationship development across cultures. The reciprocity norm in individualistic cultures means *individualized* responsibilities and exchange obligations, whereas in collectivistic cultures, it means *role* responsibilities and exchange obligations (Ting-Toomey, 1986a). To be attracted to a member of a collectivistic culture means to take on additional responsibilities and obligations toward the member's social networks. In terms of the *explicit-implicit rules*, while violation of relational rules in the public may be acknowledged explicitly in individualistic, low-context cultures, violation of relational rules will be noticed but may not be acknowledged explicitly in collectivistic, high-context cultures. To acknowledge relational rules' breakdowns in public will bring on enormous "loss of face" to members of the collectivistic cultures.

Finally, Bochner's (1984) *metarules* category refers to role prescriptions and decision-making power behavior and about purposeful masking of perceptions concerning relational rules. In individualistic, low-power-distance cultures like the United States, rules may be defined conjointly and negotiated actively by both participants involved in the relationship. In collectivistic, high-power-distance cultures like Japan, rules are set by the member with the higher status or the higher prescribed role position in the relationship. In addition, while accurate perception is necessary to ascertain whether certain relational rules are enforced or violated in the individualistic cultures, the masking of perception may be practiced occasionally by members of collectivistic cultures, in order to "give face" to the relational partner and, in turn, not to cause oneself to "lose face" even in the context of an intimate relationship.

Three observations can be drawn from this section:

(1) Persons from individualistic cultures will display a higher privacy need in relationships than persons from collectivistic cultures.

(2) Persons from individualistic cultures will use the equity norm to evaluate the level of "fairness" in a relationship, while persons from collectivistic cultures will use the equality norm to assess the level of "justice" in a relationship.

(3) Persons from individualistic, low power distance cultures will be more likely to practice symmetrical decision-making power patterns, while per-

sons from collectivistic, high power distance cultures will be more likely to practice asymmetrical decision-making power patterns.

## Expressing Thoughts and Feelings

According to Bochner (1984, p. 600), *expressive communication* refers to "messages that signify emotive and subjective experiences such as feelings, private sentiments, and personal qualities." Beyond normative rules of the culture, second-language competence is critical to expressive communication in intergroup encounters. The normative rules of individualistic, low-context cultures stress verbal expressive communication, while the normative rules of collectivistic, high-context cultures emphasize nonverbal affiliative expressiveness (Gudykunst & Nishida, 1984; Okabe, 1983; Ting-Toomey, 1985). Second-language competence is critical for collectivists who are attracted to individualists, especially when the intergroup encounter takes place in individualistic, low-context cultures. On the other hand, nonverbal affiliative expressiveness is of paramount importance for individualists who are attracted to collectivists, and, particularly when the intergroup encounter takes place in collectivistic, high-context cultures. As Gudykunst, Nishida, and Chua's (1987) study indicates, perceived second-language competence for the Japanese in the United States is correlated positively with the social penetration process of greater perceived personalization, greater perceived synchronization, and less perceived difficulty with U.S. members. The cultural context of expressive communication asserts strong influence over the critical role of second-language competence. While relational commitment will be expressed through verbal forms of communication in individualistic, low-context cultures, relational commitment will be expressed through subtle forms of nonverbal communication in collectivistic, high-context cultures.

The perceived ethnolinguistic identity dimension is also linked positively with second-language competence. The more secure and positive individuals feel about their identities, the greater the perceived competence in the outgroup language, and also the more receptive they are of members of other groups (Hall & Gudykunst, 1986). Members with secure ethnolinguistic identities tend to take more risks with cultivating second-language competence and intergroup relationship competence. Successes in both areas probably act as a feedback loop to reinforce the security of the group members' identities.

Expressive communication or relational openness, however, does not follow a unidirectional trajectory in the development of intergroup-interpersonal relationships. As Bochner (1984, p. 610) comments, "the dialectical qualities of interpersonal communication make it obvious that things are not always what they seem; yet interactants sometimes are pressured to act as if things are. . . . Talk may inhibit what it exhibits—expressiveness mandating protectiveness, revealing necessitating concealing, openness petitioning discretion, weakness used to dominate, freedom as a constraint."

Individuals who are involved in an interdependent intergroup-interpersonal relationship have to face many relational paradoxes, dilemmas, and mixed emotions throughout their relationship development process. From the choice of language usage (if both are bilinguals), to the negotiation of cultural role identities and personal idiosyncratic identities, the timing of relational validation and expression has to be synchronized, and the dialectics of openness versus protectiveness, revealment versus concealment, and freedom versus constraint have to be delicately balanced. Individuals who are secure in their ethnolinguistic identities are probably more skillful in dealing with their relational dilemmas and paradoxes than individuals who feel insecure about their identities. Individuals with secure ethnolinguistic identities will possess a high degree of attributional confidence, and this sense of confidence will spill over to the management of relational paradoxes and double binds. Conversely, individuals with insecure ethnolinguistic identities will possess a low degree of attributional confidence, and this lower sense of confidence will produce a "halo effect" for the overall self-concept of the individuals. Individuals who have a negative self-concept will probably not function as effectively or as competently as individuals who have a positive self-concept in managing various relational issues.

Three implications can be drawn from this section:

(1) Persons from individualistic cultures will be more likely to practice verbal expressive communication, while persons from collectivistic cultures will be more likely to practice nonverbal expressive communication.

(2) Second-language competence is critical to intergroup-interpersonal encounters in individualistic, low-context cultures, and less critical in collectivistic, high-context cultures.

(3) Persons with secure ethnolinguistic identities will be more competent in managing relational dilemmas and paradoxes than persons with insecure ethnolinguistic identities.

## Protecting Vulnerabilities

The sense of the "self" is the most vulnerable and the most sacred in any type of intimate relationships. In the individualistic cultures, the "I" identity is most vulnerable to attack and to relational hurts. In the collectivistic cultures, the "face" identity is most sensitive to hurts and violations. To hurt someone's "I" identity in individualistic cultures means direct violation of the other person's sense of personal privacy, the betrayal of private information to a third person, or the bringing up of deeply personal taboo topics that hurt the other person's ego. To hurt someone's "face" identity in the collectivistic cultures means verbally assaulting the other person's face in front of a third party, separating the other person's connection with family and kinship network ties, or bringing up taboo topics that deal with ingroups' ineffectiveness or inadequacy.

Respecting and protecting relational vulnerabilities requires high role-taking ability. High rhetorically sensitive persons (Hart, Carlson, & Eadie, 1980; Ting-Toomey, 1988), high self-monitoring persons (Snyder, 1987), or allocentric personality types (Triandis et al., 1988) probably possess a higher role-taking ability than low rhetorically sensitive persons, low self-monitoring persons, or idiocentric personality types. Members who are secure in their ethnolinguistic identities are also good role-takers because their sense of identity security will push them to take relational risks more easily than members with insecure ethnolinguistic identities. Members with ambivalent or insecure ethnolinguistic identities will have a harder time taking on the perspective of the other person because they have to spend time and energy struggling with their own identity problems and definitions. In addition, members of collectivistic cultures are probably better role-takers than members of individualistic cultures because members in collectivistic cultures have been socialized in cultural systems that emphasize a high other-orientation rather than a high I-orientation. Anticipating the other person's need, empathizing with the other's response, and learning the discretion and sensitivity of when to speak and when to remain silent are some of the fundamental training that collectivists receive early on in their family socialization process (Clancy, 1986).

Finally, we also can predict that people with secure ethnolinguistic identities have few relational taboo topics, while people with insecure ethnolinguistic identities will have many relational taboo topics. If individuals do not feel secure about their ethnolinguistic identities, then conversations surrounding both the role identity salience dimension and the personal identity salience dimension will oftentimes becomes strained and awkward. Taboo topics and vulnerable feelings along these two dimensions will also accumulate.

Three final observations that can be summarized from this section are as follows:

(1) Persons with secure ethnolinguistic identities will tend to be more sensitive to the vulnerable spots of the relational partners than persons with insecure ethnolinguistic identities.

(2) Persons from collectivistic cultures will tend to be more sensitive to the vulnerable areas of the relational partners than persons from individualistic cultures.

(3) Persons with insecure ethnolinguistic identities will hold more personal taboo topics in their relationships than persons with secure ethnolinguistic identities.

## FUTURE DIRECTIONS

The skills of fostering positive impressions, validating the other person's point of view, rules negotiation, appropriate expressive communication, and protecting relational vulnerabilities constitute the beginning of bonding competence. Bonding competence is a "communicative accomplishment requiring considerable perceptual and behavioral skill" (Bochner, 1984, p. 611, 1985; Parks, 1985).

Cultural variability factors and intergroup interaction factors are probably more critical at the initial stages of the intergroup-interpersonal bonding process than at the later intimate stages. The degree of cultural similarity/dissimilarity along the individualism-collectivism continuum, and the valence of various intergroup attitudinal factors, will influence the start-up process of intergroup-interpersonal contacts. At the later intimate stages of relatedness, members have achieved "mutuality, their actions and attitudes have become significantly influenced by each other. Their lives have 'intersected,' meaning that each bears a burden of responsibility for the quality of the other's experience" (Bochner, 1984, p. 575).

To summarize briefly, intergroup-interpersonal bonding competence requires both the perceptual and the behavioral skills of members being sensitive to (a) the extent of cultural variability influence on the partner's behavior; (b) the degree of ethnolinguistic identification of the partner with his or her ingroup culture; (c) the context in which the encounter takes place; (d) the changing stages of the relationship; and (e) the preferred modes of relational negotiation in different cultures.

Future directions of research on the intergroup-interpersonal bonding process should focus on investigating the conjoint effect of the cultural variability dimension and the ethnolinguistic identity dimension on context, relational change, and relational negotiation.

Context has been viewed as a critical variable for the initiation, maintenance, and termination of the intergroup-interpersonal bonding process. Context consists of three components: relational context, situational context, and cultural context. Relational context refers to the influence of family networks or friendship networks on the intergroup bonding pair. Situational context refers to both the psychological and the physical characteristics of the setting. Psychological characteristics can be defined via Forgas's (1988) "social episode" construct, which means "consensual cognitive representations about recurring interaction sequence." Dimensions such as degree of (a) friendliness, (b) intimacy, (c) activity, and (d) positive or negative evaluation about each encounter have been used to tap at the cultural variability influence on perceived social episodes. Physical characteristics refer to the actual physical nonverbal arrangements of the setting. Finally, cultural context refers to whether the intergroup encounter takes place in a heterogeneous, low-context culture, or a homogeneous, high-context culture. If the intergroup-interpersonal encounter takes place in a highly heterogeneous, individualistic culture, deviation from normative behavior is tolerated. If the encounter takes place in a highly homogeneous, collectivistic culture, conformity of behavior is expected. All these contextual factors will interact and influence relational change and development in the intergroup dyadic pair.

The second direction for future research is to examine the critical turning points of the intergroup-interpersonal bonding process from a developmental perspective (Ting-Toomey, 1988b). Relational change takes on different forms and trajectories in intergroup-interpersonal relationships. The intergroup-interpersonal relationship process will swing back and forth on a continuum between stability and change, openness and closedness, progression and regression. Relationship movements are only made possible, however, by such oscillating and fluctuating actions and events. A "process" approach to the study of intergroup-interpersonal bonding development should focus on the dialectical management process of cultural identity on one hand, and personal identity on another. In addition, the bonding competence of managing stability and change, openness and closedness, and intimacy and privacy is critical to the further development of intergroup-interpersonal ties. Altman, Vinsel, and Brown (1981,pp. 139, 140) recommend that researchers can examine the relationship between openness-closedness and stability-change through the dimensions of:

> (1) the *frequency* with which participants shift from openness to closedness . . ., (2) the *amplitude*, or absolute amount of openness-closedness, (3) the *regularity*, or redundancy with which given cyclical patterns recur, and (4) the *relative duration*, or proportion of time openness and closedness appear in a given culture. Finally, stability-change patterns may differ in various content areas and modalities.

To understand intergroup-interpersonal developmental process from a dialectical orientation, we have to track the tensions and the patterns, the pacing, and the rhythms in which the intergroup-interpersonal bonding process spirals or regresses.

Finally, intergroup members are not passive recipients who are subjected to the binding pressures of cultural norms and rules. As relationships progress to the intimate areas of the bonding process, the facilitating dimension of communication takes on central importance. Individuals will use active verbal and nonverbal negotiation strategies to redefine the rules of their relationship, and to transcend the trappings of their respective cultures. More research is needed to study the different verbal and nonverbal strategies that two strangers use to foster personal versus cultural impressions, to validate personal versus cultural identities, to transcend versus to abide by the relational rules, and to express and protect relational vulnerabilities simultaneously. We need research that deals with the use of second-language competence and language code-switching patterns at different developmental stages of the intergroup-interpersonal bonding process. We also need to understand the role of nonverbal communication synchrony in the development of intergroup-interpersonal ties. Finally, we need multimethod studies to explain and understand the interpretive level, the affective level, the behavioral level, and the ideological level of intergroup-interpersonal bonding competence (Ting-Toomey, 1984).

Identity conceptions and development are viewed as a critical vehicle to the various facets of the intergroup-interpersonal bonding relationship. The convergent approaches of the cultural variability perspective and the ethnolinguistic identity perspective are a beginning effort to examine the ties that bind two culturally opposing, dissimilar strangers together.

## REFERENCES

Altman, I., Vinsel, A., & Brown, B. (1981). Dialectical conceptions in social psychology: An application to social penetration and privacy regulation. In L. Berkowitz (Ed.), *Advances in experimental social psychology*. New York: Academic Press.

Argyle, M. (1986). Rules for social relationships in four cultures. *Australian Journal of Psychology, 38*, 309-318.

Beebe, L. M., & Giles, H. (1984). Speech accommodation theories: A discussion in terms of second-language acquisition. *International Journal of the Sociology of Language, 46*, 5-32.

Bochner, A. (1984). The functions of human communication in interpersonal bonding. In C. Arnold & J. Bower (Eds.), *Handbook of rhetorical and communication theory*. Boston: Allyn & Bacon.

Bochner, A. (1985). Perspectives on inquiry: Representation, conversation, and reflection. In M. Knapp & G. Miller (Eds.), *Handbook of interpersonal communication*. Beverly Hills, CA: Sage.

Burke, P. (1980). Measurement requirements from an interactionist perspective. *Social Psychology Quarterly, 43*, 18-29.

Carbaugh, D. (1988). *Talking American: Cultural discourses on Donohue*. Norwood, NJ: Ablex.

Chua, E., & Gudykunst, W. (1987). Conflict resolution style in low- and high-context cultures. *Communication Research Reports, 4*, 32-37.

Clancy, P. (1986). The acquisition of communicative style in Japanese. In B. Schieffelin & E. Ochs (Eds.), *Language socialization across cultures*. Cambridge: Cambridge University Press.

Collier, M., & Thomas, M. (1988). Cultural identity: An interpretive perspective. In Y. Kim & W. Gudykunst (Eds.), *Theories in intercultural communication*. Newbury Park, CA: Sage.

Cronen, V., Pearce, B., & Tomm, K. (1985). A dialectical view of personal change. In K. Gergen & K. Davis (Eds.), *The social construction of the person*. New York: Springer-Verlag.

Cushman, D., & Cahn, D. (1985). *Communication in interpersonal relationships*. Albany: State University of New York Press.

Duck, S. (1985). Social and personal relationships. In M. Knapp & G. Miller (Eds.), *Handbook of interpersonal communication*. Beverly Hills, CA: Sage.

Forgas, J. (1988). Episode representations in intercultural communication. In Y. Kim & W. Gudykunst (Eds.), *Theories in intercultural communication*. Newbury Park, CA: Sage.

Gergen, K., & Davis, K. (Eds.). (1985). *The social construction of the person*. New York: Springer-Verlag.

Giles, H., Bourhis, R., & Taylor, D. (1977). Towards a theory of language in ethnic group relations. In H. Giles (Ed.), *Language, ethnicity and intergroup relations*. London: Academic Press.

Giles, H., & Johnson, P. (1981). The role of language in ethnic group relations. In J. Turner & H. Giles (Eds.), *Intergroup behavior*. Chicago: University of Chicago Press.

Gudykunst, W. (1987). Cross-cultural comparisons. In C. Berger & S. Chaffee (Eds.), *Handbook of communication science*. Newbury Park, CA: Sage.

Gudykunst, W. B. (1988). Uncertainty and anxiety. In Y. Y. Kim & W. B. Gudykunst (Eds.), *Theories in intercultural communication*. Newbury Park, CA: Sage.

Gudykunst, W. B. (in press). Cultural variability in ethnolinguistic identity. In S. Ting-Toomey & F. Korzenny (Eds.), *Language, communication, and culture: Current directions*. Newbury Park, CA: Sage.

Gudykunst, W. B., & Nishida, T. (1984). Individual and cultural influences on uncertainty reduction. *Communication Monographs, 51*, 23-36.

Gudykunst, W. B., & Nishida, T. (1986). Attributional confidence in low- and high-context cultures. *Human Communication Research, 12*, 525-549.

Gudykunst, W. B., Nishida, T., & Chua, E. (1987). Perceptions of social penetration in Japanese-North American dyads. *International Journal of Intercultural Relations, 51*, 256-278.

Gudykunst, W. B., & Ting-Toomey, S., with Chua, E. (1988). *Culture and interpersonal communication*. Newbury Park, CA: Sage.

Gudykunst, W. B., Yoon, Y. C., & Nishida, T. (1987). The influence of individualism-collectivism on perceptions of communication in ingroup and outgroup relationships. *Communication Monographs, 54*, 295-306.

Hall, B. J., & Gudykunst, W. B. (1986). The intergroup theory of second language ability. *Journal of Language and Social Psychology, 5*, 291-302.

Hall, E. (1983). *The dance of life*. New York: Doubleday.

Hart, R., Carlson, R., & Eadie, W. (1980). Attitudes toward communication and the assessment of rhetorical sensitivity. *Communication Monographs, 47*, 1-20.

Hewstone, M., & Brown, R. (1986). Contact is not enough: An intergroup perspective on the "contact hypothesis." In M. Hewstone & R. Brown (Eds.), *Contact and conflict in intergroup encounters*. London: Basil Blackwell.

Hofstede, G. (1980). *Culture's consequences: International differences in work-related values*. Beverly Hills, CA: Sage.

Hofstede, G., & Bond, M. (1984). Hofstede's culture dimensions: An independent validation using Rokeach's value survey. *Journal of Cross-Cultural Psychology, 15*, 417-433.

Hui, C. (1988). Measurement of individualism-collectivism. *Journal of Research in Personality, 22*, 17-36.

Hui, C., & Triandis, H. (1986). Individualism-collectivism: A study of cross-cultural researchers. *Journal of Cross-Cultural Psychology, 17*, 225-248.

Leung, K. (1987). Some determinants of reactions to procedural models for conflict resolution: A cross-national study. *Journal of Personality and Social Psychology, 53*, 898-908.

Leung, K. (1988). Some determinants of conflict avoidance. *Journal of Cross-Cultural Psychology, 19*, 125-136.

Leung, K., & Bond, M. (1984). The impact of cultural collectivism on reward allocation. *Journal of Personality and Social Psychology, 47*, 793-804.

Leung, K., & Iwawaki, S. (1988). Cultural collectivism and distributive behavior. *Journal of Cross-Cultural Psychology, 19*, 35-49.

Marsella, A., DeVos, G., & Hsu, F. (Eds.). (1985). *Culture and self: Asian and Western perspectives.* New York: Tavistock.

McCall, G. (1987). The structure, content, and dynamics of self: Continuities in the study of role identities. In K. Yardley & T. Honess (Eds.), *Self and identity: Psychosocial perspectives.* Chichester, England: John Wiley.

Okabe, R. (1983). Cultural assumptions of East and West: Japan and the United States. In W. Gudykunst (Ed.), *Intercultural communication theory: Current perspectives.* Beverly Hills, CA: Sage.

Parks, M. (1985). Interpersonal communication and the quest for personal competence. In M. Knapp & G. Miller (Eds.), *Handbook of interpersonal communication.* Beverly Hills, CA: Sage.

Philipsen, G. (in press). Speech and the communal function in four cultures. In S. Ting-Toomey & F. Korzenny (Eds.), *Language, communication, and culture: Current directions.* Newbury Park, CA: Sage.

Shweder, R., & Bourne, E. (1984). Does the concept of the person vary cross-culturally? In R. Shweder & R. LeVine (Eds.), *Culture theory: Essays on mind, self, and emotion.* Cambridge: Cambridge University Press.

Snyder, M. (1987). *Public appearances, private realities.* New York: Friedman.

Stryker, S. (1987). Identity theory: Development and extentions. In K. Yardley & T. Honess (Eds.), *Self and identity: Psychosocial perspective.* Chichester, England: John Wiley.

Tajfel, H. (1978). Social categorization, social identity, and social comparison. In H. Tajfel (Ed.), *Differentiation between social groups.* London: Academic Press.

Ting-Toomey, S. (1981). Ethnic identity and close friendship in Chinese-American college students. *International Journal of Intercultural Relations, 5*, 383-406.

Ting-Toomey, S. (1984). Qualitative methods: An overview. In W. Gudykunst & Y. Kim (Eds.), *Methods for intercultural communication research.* Beverly Hills, CA: Sage.

Ting-Toomey, S. (1985). Toward a theory of conflict and culture. In W. Gudykunst, L. Stewart, & S. Ting-Toomey (Eds.), *Communication, culture, and organizational processes.* Beverly Hills, CA: Sage.

Ting-Toomey, S. (1986a). Interpersonal ties in intergroup communication. In W. Gudykunst (Ed.), *Intergroup communication.* London: Edward Arnold.

Ting-Toomey, S. (1986b). Japanese communication patterns: Insider versus the outsider perspective. *World Communication, 15*, 113-126.

Ting-Toomey, S. (1988a). Intercultural conflicts: A face-negotiation theory. In Y. Kim & W. Gudykunst (Eds.), *Theories in intercultural communication.* Newbury Park, CA: Sage.

Ting-Toomey, S. (1988b). Culture and interpersonal relationship development: Some conceptual issues. In J. Andersen (Ed.), *Communication yearbook* (Vol. 12). Newbury Park, CA: Sage.

Ting-Toomey, S. (1988c). Rhetorical sensitivity style in three cultures: France, Japan, and the United States. *Central States Speech Communication Journal, 38*, 28-36.

Triandis, H. C. (1986). Collectivism vs. individualism: A reconceptualization of a basic concept in cross-cultural psychology. In C. Bagley & G. Verma (Eds.), *Personality, cog-*

*nition, and values: Cross-cultural perspectives of childhood and adolescence.* London: Macmillan.

Triandis, H., Bontempo, R., Betancourt, L., Bond, M., Leung, K., Brenes, A., Georgas, J., Hui, H., Marin, G., Setiadi, B., Sinha, J., Verma, J., Spangenberg, J., Touzard, H., & Montmollin, G. (1986). The measurement of the etic aspects of individualism and collectivism across cultures. *Australian Journal of Psychology, 38*, 257-267.

Triandis, H., Bontempo, R., Villareal, M., Asai, M., & Lucca, N. (1988). Individualism and collectivism: Cross-cultural perspectives on self-ingroup relationships. *Journal of Personality and Social Psychology, 54*, 323-338.

Turner, J. C. (1987). *Rediscovering the social group.* London: Basil Blackwell.

Yardley, K., & Honess, T. (Eds.). (1987). *Self and identity: Psychosocial-perspectives.* Chichester, England: John Wiley.

# 17 Encounters in the Interracial Workplace

**Molefi Kete Asante**
**Alice Davis**

Human encounters occur in a wide assortment of places. Each encounter and each place constitute the nexus for achieving an understanding of how we adapt to cultural diversity. Encounters in the interracial workplace, particularly in the United States, can be intercultural as well as interracial. Of course, we recognize the possibility of divergence in terms of race and culture but in the case of communication between Blacks and Whites in the workplace in the United States, race and culture often converge, therefore, we seek to examine the manifold dimensions and implications of such communicative encounters.

Communication between people in the workplace constitutes a primary area of intercultural communication. Although literature in this area remains scarce in the sense of employer/employee relationships, there is evidence of growing numbers of studies in intercultural communication generally. While it is possible that a predisposition against research in this area has existed because of the lack of theoretical work, this hardly seems to be a reason for the dearth in the field, especially because significant advances have been made in other disciplinary areas cognate to inter-cultural communication in the workplace. Specifically, the work of Koch-man (1983) on language styles of Blacks and Whites, Folb (1980) on the nature of language of Black teenagers, Daniel and Smitherman (1976) on the characteristics of the deep structure of African American language, and Asante and Atwater (1986) on the nature of the rhetorical structure of intercultural communication contribute to the corpus of work that is perspective-driven in relationship to intercultural and interracial communication.

Kochman (1983) advances an ethnographic position in the study of Black and White cultural styles that adds to the theoretical literature on intercultural communication possibilities in general and is applicable specifically to studies of the workplace. In effect, Kochman argues that Blacks and Whites tend to assign dissimilar meanings to verbal and nonverbal behaviors. The result of this divergence in assignation creates numerous misunderstandings when Blacks and Whites communicate in the workplace. It is his contention that "cultural differences play a covert role in the communication process" (Kochman, 1983, p. 7).

Because we understand how cultural differences may impinge upon what might be an ordinary communicative event, we suggest certain interactive frames that might help to categorize aspects of the international communication encounter in the workplace.

## INTERACTIVE FRAMES

What we mean by an interactive frame is a venue of the human communicative encounter within the boundaries of a given organized area of activity, such as workplace, church, or baseball diamond. When we consider the work of a number of scholars such as Rich (1974; Asante, Newmark, & Blake, 1979; Gudykunst & Kim, 1984), we can see the development of an intercultural perspective based on the study of organized areas of activity. Yet this is only one dimension of the intercultural field, and certainly not the only emphasis in the studies and essays by these scholars. It is in the work of Kochman, however, that the concept of assignation emerges to cross areas and to provide a way to describe what happens when the cultural styles of Blacks and Whites interfere with communication. According to Kochman, the student of intercultural communication must assume that when Blacks and Whites interact in public meetings the interactants believe that "the meanings they are assigning to all of these matters are the same, and therefore, that the motives they are ascribing to each other—based on this assumption—are justified" (Kochman, 1983).

This type of assignation can lead to communicative and, therefore, interpretative difficulty. In the workplace or anywhere else the communication happens to be taking place, the possibility that humans will "miss" each other is heightened by any false sense of what is in the other's mind. Linguistic and semantic distinctions must be accepted and understood; behaviors that are derivative from cultural and societal sources must be appreciated and learned if we are to become successful in communication. The African American expression "I'm fixner go" cannot be translated "I am getting ready to go" as is often done by some scholars. The verb "fixner" carries with it the idea of completion; thus the person is not getting ready to go, but has completed the getting ready and is irrevocably going. This completive nuance suggests how cultural usages can often lead to misunderstanding. But we cannot be too quick to make this type of interpretation, particularly if we do not account for culture and class differences as well as race. Indeed, we have seen that race may play a decreasing role in communication between people of similar socio-economic backgrounds. This is certainly not to say that race is negligible in a communicative situation, particularly because it is very much a part of the American psychosocial and historical setting and as such has informed a large part of how human beings relate to each other within this society. Stereotypes and predispositions derived from family, school, television, movies, books, and important and respected others, such as politicians, rabbis, preachers, commentators, and editors, have a profound impact on how we relate to people of other races during communication. The workplace as a venue of communication simply changes the location of the interaction, not the predispositions and stereotypes that human beings bring to the situation.

Situational modalities converge with cultural modalities to create either understanding or misunderstanding in the workplace among culturally dissimilar employees and employers. Actually, the same holds true in cases where the persons of different cultural backgrounds are of the same class, such as partners in a company, executive managers, or employees. Thus intragroup as well as intergroup communicative situations among those in the workplace reveal the same potentialities and problems because they are embedded in the same social realities.

The workplace provides a fruitful setting for examining how Blacks and Whites communicate with each other despite the embedded predispositions. In our analysis we have simply looked at the employers/employees dichotomy along all possible cultural/racial variations of the workplace situation involving Black and White persons. Thus in situations where there are Black employers and White employees or vice versa we have applied the same analysis to the communicative event because for us as communicationists the relevant quality of this interaction is the communication between the persons. As in other fields, however, not enough work has been done on cross-cultural relationships involving characteristics of White and Black workers.

Triandis (1976) did attempt to establish characteristics of this group of workers in a pioneering work. In fact, Triandis identified five characteristics that may have value for analyzing how Black and White workers communicate. Because Triandis's work dealt with perceptions of workers, it gives us some guidelines about how such workers communicate with these perceptions at the core of their actions. According to Triandis there were five major characteristics that emerged in his research into the nature of the cross-cultural workplace. Although there were some other characteristics discovered in his research, we have found these five characteristics appropriate for our work:

(1) Blacks see good jobs as opportunities to move to better houses; Whites see good jobs as a means to status.

(2) Blacks see Black job foremen as less lazy and more aggressive than Whites see them.

(3) Black and White females see Black job foremen as less lazy and more aggressive than White males see them.

(4) White males see Black job foremen as much more lazy than White females, Black males, and Black females see them.

(5) Blacks are most likely to respect Black job foremen; Whites are most likely to criticize Black job foremen.

The differences observed by Triandis point to the enormity of the communication problem within the workplace. Affected by the general social climate of the society, the workplace itself bears the marks of the attitudes and predispositions about race and culture that we find in the American society at large. Although this analysis was essentially concerned with race, the gender issue would have revealed a similar array of perceptions. This opens the possibility for future communication analysis based on race, gender, and class in the workplace. For the purposes of our chapter, we have chosen to establish generic modalities of *situation*, *culture*, and *interaction* in the workplace in order to organize our analysis within the context of interactive frames.

The outcome of the convergence of the situational and cultural modalities is the expressiveness of the intercultural communicators. In effect, because the Black person and White person bring their cultural backgrounds to a communicative situation, the results will reflect the diversity of their experiences. We know, of course, that homogeneity and heterogeneity have been principal categories for examining attraction (Rich, 1974). Beier et al. (1961) and Broxton (1963) took similar positions on attraction. And more recently Kang, Pearse, and Stanback (1983) have shown how intercultural communication has made contributions in a similar way to communication theory in general. From these works and others we know that attraction and communication are not the same thing. Furthermore, what may be true of intercultural attraction is not necessarily true of intercultural communication. It is generally accepted that attraction can be either negative or positive. Communication, on the other hand, is considered a positive activity even though the communicators may find the information conveyed negative in some ways. That means that people of different cultural backgrounds who may not like each other as individuals can communicate. We believe that the modalities operating in the White employer/Black employee or vice versa situation are extremely varied and for this reason have posited three interlocking meshes that constitute the context for studying the intercultural communication between Whites and Blacks in an employer-employee relationship.

## MODALITIES OF SITUATION

Modalities of situations are grounded in the structural nature of the interaction setting. One could speak of certain stabilized social and economic relationships deriving from the character of institutions. Indeed both Marxists and radical theorists have used this formulation in defining race relations within the United States. Structural analysis in the socioeconomic field has meant that social scientists have emphasized the difficulty of changing relationships without changing economic realities. Willhelm (1983) claims that racism is endemic among White Americans and the economic structure of the society reflects discriminatory practices. His is fundamentally an analysis with sociological consequences; others have taken a linguistic view, believing that the nature of communication forms dictates the types of relationships to which people adhere (Goldschlager, 1982). What this means is that the structure of a situation determines to a large degree how people communicate within the limits of that structure. In this respect, the communication between Black and White persons is "caught" in much of the symbolic assignation of our society. Therefore, it is impossible to speak of the communication relationships without referring to the modalities of situations that occur in workplaces.

The modalities of situations are based in the structural nature of interaction situations, but there is more to be said on the subject. For purposes of our discussion, modalities of situations refers to those behavioral conditions that exist because of the structural constraints of the interaction setting. Behavioral conditions are mainly verbal or physical expressions that are interpreted as communicative in the workplace. An interaction setting may be the office of the chief of personnel, director of public operations, executive vice president, or president of a company. Such venues have built-in constraints on the communication event regardless of the cultural or racial backgrounds of the communicators. Add to this, however, the racial and cultural factors and we have another mesh in the interactive situation. We are aware of the fact that employers are free to choose any appropriate venue for communicative interaction with employees, such as restaurants, bars, hotel lobbies, or company clubhouses. What normally happens, of course, even in these settings, if they are objectively workplace related, is that the conversation is about the job or the company. The use of the expression "free to choose" is deliberate on our part because it underscores the power that inheres in the position of employer within our society. There is a structural significance to the position of the employer within the interaction setting. He or she may "choose" the place for the interaction whereas the employee is not usually granted such choices. Nothing inherent in the person of the employer suggests this power; it is merely the function of the office with whatever personality he or she brings to it to differentiate his or her office from the identical position, more or less, of his or her counterpart at similar companies or organizations.

## Hierarchy

Hierarchy refers to the system of ranking by position. It is a principal factor in modalities of situations because office serves as a basis for authority. In the employer/employee relationship the hierarchical structure is built into every conversation, every passage of information, and every command. In effect, the employee knows some things about the situation by virtue of company hierarchical arrangements. And to be an effective employee the person must know who "the boss" is. This may even be contrary to the wishes of the employer as some employers practice several behaviors that are meant to break down the barriers that exist between them and their workers. Thus they leave their doors open and profess an open-door policy, or they leave the chairs at their desk when talking to subordinates and sit beside the subordinates in an effort to show collegiality and a degree of egalitarianism. Yet the idea that the "boss" can give the impression of openness to the employees by moving away from the desk has some basis in the research done by some scholars. Mehrabian (1971) reported that the desk sometimes makes persons less at ease in communication because they become uncomfortably aware of covert stresses on status differences. We suggest that the venue itself, the office, for example, is the principal structure factor in designating the difference in hierarchy.

A discussion of communication between Blacks and Whites in the workplace, whether they are variously employers or employees, must always take into consideration the hierarchy created by the social, political, economic, and cultural factors that are maintained by a governing Marcusean one-dimensionality. In many ways this hierarchy is programmed into much of the speech and conversation between Whites and Blacks in the workplaces in the United States. Furthermore, evidence of this programmed hierarchy often appears in the real expressions of power such as choosing workers, promoting workers, and providing merit to workers. Real shifts in attitudes have been infrequent even though there is now more interaction. What usually happens with the interaction is that Whites define the interaction within their own structural system. Thus because of what we call the power variable in communicative relationships Black people are often accepted but not on intercultural terms. The terms are dictated by the White value system that is itself already constrained by the principles inherent in the denial of pluralism. Governing the conversations and other communications that may occur between the communicators is the overarching structural constraint system that determines hierarchy in the first place. Inescapably the relationship of Blacks and Whites in the workplace is historically linked to the fact that Africans were brought to the United States as chattel. This is the principal difference in communication between Whites and other racial or ethnic groups and communication between Whites and Blacks. Consequently, the process of demystifying the intercultural encounter based upon the elimination of racial prejudice is assisted when hierarchy is properly understood. Much communication between people in the workplace will continue to be clouded by ethnocentric prejudices until communicators learn to overcome the structural constraints imposed by history. Stella Ting-Toomey (1985, p. 75) makes an exceptional point in her chapter "Toward a Theory of Conflict and Culture" when she says that "it is the patterned ways of thinking, acting, feeling, and interpreting that constitute the fundamental webs of a culture. Conflict, as a form of intense, antagonistic communicative experience, is bounded by the cultural demands and constraints of a particular situation." Although she does not establish the role of economics in the process of constraints as we have done, she nevertheless recognizes the extent to which communication is dictated by a set of demands and constraints beyond the control of the communicators. Only through a concerted effort to operate within these constraints as free and willful human beings can we ever succeed in establishing normal communication in the workplace or any other venue. In America, such an open challenge to human communication in the workplace cannot be achieved without a recognition of the role of racism in the structural constraints.

Racism is essentially articulated when people possess the power to enforce their attitudes and ideas based on racial preference. The workplace, perhaps more than any other setting, creates opportunities for the communicative encounter between Blacks and Whites to be distorted by interpretative complexes based on race.

Because understanding only signals the possibility of effectiveness in a communicative situation, we suggest a law of understanding that says that when persons of different racial or cultural backgrounds interact they will be able to produce the appropriate linguistic and symbolic codes necessary for interpretation once they have achieved affective understanding. Affective understanding is an attitude toward the culturally different communicator that demonstrates the willingness to communicate; humility before the other's culture, which says "I do not know all I need to know but am willing to learn about this person's culture"; and the ability to speak a language intelligible to the other (Smith, 1973).

Due to the intervening nature of society's racial and cultural perceptions, human beings often surprise themselves with how much they have understood when a fellow worker says something. We are often able to repeat the expression in our own words though we may not have understood everything. On the other hand, when we think we have understood, a repeat of the situation often means that we have only understood a linguistic segment. And in the workplace this could be disastrous for workers who misperceive a communication because of understanding only a portion of what was said.

## Status

Status is related to hierarchy inasmuch as hierarchy determines status. Any ranking system that allots to some persons, positions or postures of privilege based upon birth, merit, race, religion, or custom confers status. We have discussed hierarchy in connection with the structural constraints imposed by the society. Here we discuss status as it relates to individuals within the system communicating with each other. The underlying metaphor is one associated with power. Generally people behave in a more ritualized manner when there is status difference, perceived or real.

Given the fact that interaction occurs within the setting of work, the relevant questions have to do with the position of the communicators. Quite frankly, communicative efficacy depends upon the subject narrative as well as the position of the communicators. A reasonable assumption is that people will interact more favorably, that is, with greater freedom and less apprehension, with people of similar positions on subjects and themes of common interests than with people not of equal position. This is why it is often said that the White and Black persons in South Africa, for example, cannot communicate effectively; they have, by law, different positions of status within the society.

It is fair to assume, given the status situation as well as the hierarchical condition within the American society, that a Black employee will normally experience some psychological stress around communication with a White employer if sufficient groundwork in intercultural interaction has not been achieved either from experience or training. Status difference complicates the communicative situation because the Black worker never knows when a comment, a racial slur, an off-color joke, or an allusion might occur that will test the worker's ability to interact with the White employer. Similar conditions hold true when the Black worker interacts with White workers of the same professional or technical status; that condition is more aptly a part of the interpretative complexes occurring in the area of hierarchy. But in the situation in which you have a Black worker and a White supervisor, manager, or employer, the communicative situation has a different twist to it in the interactive setting. The White employer being the person of higher status may increase immediacy and informality by reducing a ritualized setting to one of personal diplomacy. The employer can do this by sitting close to the employee or by suggesting the reciprocal use of first names as is often done in the United States. The White person may not be assumed to be of higher status by virtue of race if the Black person is the employer or is a peer or supervisor. The factor of race is significant in enough status-different situations, however, that in the workplace it will probably be no different than in the society at large. Whites tend to be thought of as managers, supervisors, employers; and Blacks, as workers and employees. This is in fact the economic reality of the society.

## Space

There are two types of spaces for our workplace analysis: (a) interior space, inside a building; and (b) exterior space, outside a building. As the modalities of situations posit that all human communication, even that between White employer and Black employee, takes place within some space, the type of space establishes certain physical constraints on the communication. Take an office, for example, normally used for interviews, discussions, and conversations between the employer and his or her employee. The arrangement of furniture, size of office, and lighting can affect the reaction of the communicators. In fact, if a Black employee considers a White employer to be "cold," it could very well be as much a problem of the space arrangement as the personality of the employer.

Space can convey power and in this way participate in the total metaphor of power that is involved in modalities of situation. One can find oneself immersed in the proxemics debate simply by asking how much distance should be maintained between a White employer and a Black employee. Is the distance different from the distance maintained by communicators of the same race?

One mode of behavior manifest itself in how we use space. Personal space is always used within the context of interior or exterior spaces; in other words, our personal space is always encapsulated within a larger context. Therefore, when we speak of personal space we are talking about the type of space one uses during an interaction with another person. Given a certain set of factors, one's use of personal space may vary. For example, speaking to a friend in a bar is different from speaking to an employer at a seminar. This example is extreme only to make the point that all personal space varies according to the communicative situation. In the workplace the idea of personal space is usually defined by the position of the worker.

We shall not dwell on the use of exterior space by White employer and Black employee or vice versa for the simple reason that most communication around work takes place in the locality of the job and, therefore, inside a building. If it takes place outside a building, then it is normally the employer who makes the arrangements. An employee is seldom in the position of deciding where the communication will take place.

This is not to minimize those workstations that exist outdoors such as of athletics, recreational services, and road construction. What is necessary for us to remember is that, if the same perceptions exist, it does not matter whether the activity takes place outside or inside. Indeed, in most jobs, even those where the activity is largely out of doors, the real communication takes place inside an office building or factory. In view of the optimism we express about the future of interracial/intercultural communication when human beings are open to all possibilities of understanding, and the apparent concurrence with this view in the literature, we are tempted to advance the idea that status may not be as significant a factor as we contend. There are several cautions that must be imposed, however. Because we know that status plays a role in human perception of power and because we appreciate the structural constraints imposed on communicative situations by virtue of power relationships, we cannot underestimate status as a factor in the interracial workplace.

## Gender

A number of studies have been conducted on intercultural or interracial communication across the sexes. Chidester (1986) studied the pseudo-interracial dyad paradigm, Kanter (1977) looked at men and women in the corporation, Hall (1984) explored nonverbal sex differences, Fernandez wrote on racism and sexism in corporate life, and Shuter (1982) did a study of the initial interaction of American Blacks and Whites in interracial and intraracial dyads. In addition to these works, the studies of Mayo and Henley (1981) have shown the close correlation in some instances between gender and communication styles.

Kochman (1983) discusses how White males interact with Black females and Black males. He does not spend significant space to discuss Black males and Black females interacting with White females. This appears to be a judgment made on the basis of the amount of interaction that occurs between Whites in power positions and Blacks. Normally, among Whites it is the male who occupies the power position. The same holds true for the workplace situation. We know, of course, that women and men have different communication styles. This research is important in that it can be used as a guide in discussing the communication interaction between Whites and Blacks on the job. What we do not know yet is to what degree the cultural variable influences the communication between the sexes of different races. Based on the work with which we are familiar, for example, the fact that Hall (1984) demonstrates through a review of studies that women are more apt to attend to nonverbal cues than

men, we believe that gender plays a major role in how employers and
employees react to each other


## MODALITIES OF CULTURE

Modalities of culture are characterized by a group's total experience and
its consequent behaviors and attitudes based upon that experience. In that
respect culture is an action as well as an attitude. In an employer-employee
relationship certain behaviors are assumed primarily, as we have discussed, because of the modality of the situation; but in addition to whatever behaviors are assumed in that regard, others are assumed based upon
the cultures of individuals involved in the interaction.

A generally accepted tenet of most behavioral research is that people
approach liked things and avoid disliked things. There is an acceptance in
communication literature of the importance of hemophily in explaining
attraction and efficacy in human interaction. Of course, heterophilous
situations give us an opportunity to explore the limits of human ability to
adapt to different cultural styles.

The White employer typically has little understanding of the African
American culture that is everywhere present in most urban American
areas. In fact, the White employer might only see Black behaviors as
"deviant," "abnormal," and "subcultural." These terms are used where
"White" behavior is given the position of being considered regular and
normal. Such is the power of the racial and cultural ethic in the media of
the society that often African Americans, Mexican Americans, and Asian
Americans participate in the abnormality (Smith, 1973). They become, in
effect, players in the arena of a Eurocentric view that often places them in
opposition to their own traditional behaviors and culture. In other cases,
African Americans have objected to the imposition of European cultural
characteristics in the workplace. The case against AVIS rental car in
Philadelphia, which was won by two Black female employees who had
been ordered to "straighten" their hair in order to maintain their jobs, is
an instance in point. Kariamu Welsh wrote a brief for the plaintiffs that
showed that the hairstyle "cornrows" worn by the women had been used
by African women for more than 5000 years. The case was one more
example of how employers might attempt to force employees to conform
to behaviors that are antithetical to their own cultures.

As a mesh for understanding the relationship between Black-
White/employer-employee communication, the modality of culture must
be seen in connection with the modalities of situation and interaction.
Consequently, it is necessary for us to discuss interaction theory in order
to get a clearer picture of how people communicate in the workplace.

Howell (1979, p. 28) argued that many writers had "pledged allegiance" to process and circularity but continued to observe and describe intercultural communication from a linear perspective.

One of the major problems confronting the analysis of communicative behaviors among people is the Eurocentric manner in which all behavior is assessed. Howell's logic might be extended to say that we not only see intercultural communication described from a linear perspective but Whites in the workplace tend to prefer linear reasoning to any other kind. There is a sort of legitimacy to the efficiency this kind of logic brings to the enhancement of the work situation that is not found in more indirect kinds of reasoning. In the end, we assume, that the dominant culture of the workplace asserts itself as White, male, and European, regardless of the composition of the work force. Therefore, the understanding of the process occurs but does not make itself felt in the way human beings in this sort of situation carry on conversations unless, of course, there is also a modification of the power relationship.

## MODALITIES OF INTERACTION

By "modalities of interaction," we mean those verbal and nonverbal behaviors that characterize interaction between persons. Our contention is that "communication is a social act" (Howell, 1979, p. 29) and as such must be seen as representing episodes of interaction between dyads, the fundamental unit of social interaction.

### Episodes

In developing our conception of communication between Black and White people in the workplace, we utilize the episodic perspective where each communication is localized in time and space. Such episodes are assigned a beginning and an end. One advantage of this view of communication is that it helps us to account for the fact that few intercultural communicators operating within dyads have the time consciously to analyze the other communicator. The appropriate response appears, at times, to be automatic, not consciously directed (Howell, 1979).

### Hyperexplanation

An explanation functions to clarify previously stated information. Hyperexplanation, following Erickson (1976), functions so that one repeats oneself while explaining. In a study of counseling dyads, Erickson found that in White/Black dyads White counselors tended to repeat themselves more often than when they counseled White clients. Two intersubstitutable forms of hyperexplanation exist: (a) talking down to a listener repeatedly (lowering the level of abstraction in successive clauses that repeat the same point being explained) and (b) giving reasons repeatedly, each successive reason justifying the initial point (Erickson, 1976). Erickson discusses the fact that "a white speaker may persist at a speaking point more with black listeners than with white simply because the white speaker thinks the black listeners are likely to be less bright" (Erickson, 1976, p. 62). In the workplace this behavior could have disastrous consequences because the Black worker is usually sensitive enough to sense the unusual behavior of the White speaker in explaining to the Black workers as opposed to White workers. This "prejudice theory" is one of the areas in which the modality of culture impinges upon the modality of interaction.

Although it is generally acceded that Blacks are more likely to possess "bicultural competence," that is, knowledge of both the Black and the White patterns of doing things, little research has been done on the effect of the lack of such bicultural competence on the part of White employers, supervisors, and managers has on intercultural and interracial communication. Bowser and Hunt (1981), however, made an excellent study of the impact racism had on the thinking of Whites, albeit with limited information on the impact of racism on White interaction styles and nothing on the effect the lack of bicultural competence had on communication. It is probably correct as Erickson (1976, p. 65) points out that "things are more likely to go wrong interculturally and interracially, and people are not usually consciously aware of what it is interactionally that is going wrong."

This is why we have contended all along that a true picture of the interracial encounter in the workplace cannot be separated from all the other aspects of society. If we are talking about communication between people of different cultural and racial backgrounds, we are also talking about historical, functional, and structural differences in the way they approach interaction. Thus an integrated rather than a compartmentalized approach to the study of language must be added to the study of intercultural interaction. Furthermore, because Blacks and Whites increasingly live in proximity to each other in the large cities of the United States, the issue of diffusionary communicative symbols and styles becomes important in any true understanding of the workplace. Although the workplace may pose problems of cultural different styles of communication, cultural similarity might also be present. This is not to say, however, that cultural similarity will always result in effective communication where the race of the communicators differ. Such a condition cannot even be guaranteed where communicators are of the same racial background.

## Eyes

Research in intercultural communication has centered mainly on verbal interactions, and the implications of difference in language codes have been extensively discussed (Labov, 1965; Shuy, 1964; Smith, 1973). Although LaFrance and Mayo (1976) and Johnson (1971) have given some attention to the differences in visual interaction between Blacks and Whites, few studies have been made of visual interaction. Because the studies have shown that Blacks are often reluctant to look another person directly in the eyes when talking, especially if the person is perceived to occupy a position of authority, Blacks would have more difficulty in communication with Whites in positions of authority if communication were defined simply by how a person appeared visually. This is where the work of Kechman becomes significant in that it deals with the intricacies of the interpersonal interactions between Blacks and Whites. Among Whites the maintenance of eye contact is desirable in face-to-face communication. Johnson (1971) maintains that within Black culture the failure to avoid eye contact with a person of higher status is a sign of disrespect. Obviously this means that there is an enormous area for misunderstanding in a case where a Black employer is discussing a controversial issue with a White employee who constantly looks the Black employer in the eye. It is not considered normal behavior by the Black employer that an employee would dare challenge the employer. On the contrary, if a White employer cannot get a Black employee to look at him or her in the eye, the employer is likely to conclude that the employee has something to conceal. In neither case is the employee wrong; he or she is merely operating out of a different cultural context.

Rules governing eye contact among Whites state that a person's trustworthiness, masculinity, sincerity, and directness are communicated by maintaining eye contact. Thus, to a White in the workplace, a Black who does not maintain eye contact in a conversation on responsibility or about a task may seem to be "shifty." On the other hand, in White culture, a "higher percentage of eye contact between communicators is typically associated with more positive attitudes between the communicators" (Merabian, 1969, p. 369). As Kochman (1983) has discovered in the area of Black and White interaction, what passes for guilt and innocence in the culture may appear to be the opposite in another. Thus, to the Black employer/employee, the White person who maintains eye contact may be doing so in order to "put something over" on someone.

## Nods

Related to visual interaction is the nodding behavior of Blacks and Whites. In a situation where a White worker is talking with a Black worker, there may be considerable rolling forward of the head by the Black person as the White person talks. Rules for this type of nodding behavior seem to be different from the rules in Black culture. Such nodding does not indicate either agreement, acceptance, or understanding; it merely serves to acknowledge that a speaker in a dyadic situation is saying something. It would be a mistake for an employer to assume that because the person responded with what would be an affirmative nod that the person agreed with position stated. Of course, the Black person does use the nod affirmatively. This nod is usually accented with greater emphasis and less continuous motion. The accented nod is usually accompanied by a verbal response. The point is that the Black listener may use the unaccented form of the nod and not mean what a White listener might mean with an accented nod.

### Verbal response

We have seen some support for the view that Blacks do not use the same listening response patterns as Whites. Hall (1976) contends that, in the Black culture system, mere copresence is enough to signal attention. Hall says that when a Black listener is in a room with a Black speaker, there exists an understanding that the social space is sufficient for attention. Therefore, it is neither gaze involvement nor kinesic or vocal back-channel that is necessary for a Black listener to give attention to a Black speaker. Showing attention for the Black listener, according to Hall, is different than for Whites. If this is the case, as we believe it is, the White speaker/ employer might underestimate the amount of listening going on with the Black listener and start to hyperexplain. Actually, the most frequent listening response mode of the Black listener is verbal, a pattern almost never seen among Whites. Erickson (1976) observes that among Black/ Black dyads, the verbal-alone response was more than twice as frequent for listening response as the nonverbal-alone, for example, nodding, applause. Consequently, we can see the implications to an employer/ employee situation where the Black person, particularly male, sits in an office and says periodically "yes," "right or," "got'cha," "dig," and so on in response to a White colleague's conversation.

Because the three interconnecting modalities—situation, culture, and interaction—all play a role in influencing behavior, it is important to emphasize how the employer-employee relationship in communication can be directed toward implementing a task. There are five principal ways of influencing behavior through communication. We derive these modes of influence in the workplace from both linear and nonlinear approaches to communication: (a) to demand, (b) to request, (c) to persuade, (d) to suggest, and (e) to demonstrate. In the first mode the communicator asks with authority; in the second, a person asks as a courtesy; in the third, one urges action; in the fourth, one hints at consideration; and in the fifth, one makes evident. The impact of these modes of influence on the intercultural workplace depends to a large degree on the type of cultural influences dictating the behavioral modes. For example, a demand in a White cultural style may not be viewed as such in a Black cultural style, if we speculate on the basis of Kochman's theories. On the other hand, authority, a central aspect of the demand, is often acceded to among Whites more quickly than among Blacks. This is probably a function of what constitutes authority for both groups. A White colleague, at a similar level, may say to a Black worker, "You had better operate that machine for another half an hour" and be shocked to receive the reply, "You gon' make me." Although the White person may have assumed that he or she was offering "good advice," this advice was rejected by the Black person as ill-conceived meddling because the person offering the advice was not a supervisor. Black professionals and nonprofessionals have complained about this penchant of White colleagues, even White subordinates, to "demand" that something be done in a certain way, often contrary to the way the Black person wants to do it or is doing it. In effect, the same principles of analysis have been used by feminists who see males often usurping their judgments.

To request usually means to ask for a favor or courtesy or to petition. A request from a Black person to a White person, however, may be construed as a demand if the sufficient intercultural understanding does not exist. It is not the formal language of the request that causes such a reaction but rather the entire communication environment that we have discussed as modalities of situation, culture, and interaction. Whites in America may assume unconsciously that Blacks cannot tell them anything and, consequently, react negatively to the Black communication. The Black worker who makes a request or gives a suggestion often anticipates a negative response from the White person. This self-fulfilling prophecy makes communication in the workplace and any place much more difficult and masks the potentially valuable interaction of workers.

In *Communicating Racism,* Teun A. van Dijk (1986) has said that in Western Europe and North America racism must be taken as a serious sociocultural and political problem. This is why we maintain that future research into the dilemmas facing intercultural and interracial communication might profit from additional work on the generic modalities of situation, culture, and interaction as they are affected by socioeconomic realities.

# REFERENCES

Asante, M. K., & Atwater, D. (1986). Rhetorical condition as symbolic discourse. *Communication Quarterly, 34,* 1-8.

Asante, M. K., Newmark, E., & Blake, C. (Eds.). (1979). *Handbook of intercultural communication.* Beverly Hills, CA: Sage.

Beier, E. G., Rossi, A. M., & Garland, R. L. (1961). Similarity plus dissimilarity of personality basis for friendship. *Psychological Reports, 8,* 3-8.

Bowser, B., & Hunt, R. (1981). *Impact of racism on whites.* Beverly Hills, CA: Sage.

Broxton, J. A. (1963). A test of interpersonal attraction predictions derived from balance theory. *Journal of Abnormal Social Psychology, 63,* 394-398.

Chidester, T. (1986). Problems in the study of interracial interaction: Pseudo-interracial dyad paradigm. *Journal of Personality and Social Psychology, 50,* 74-78.

Daniel, J., & Smitherman, G. (1976). How I got ovah: Communication dynamics in the Black community. *Quarterly Journal of Speech, 62,* 1.

Deutsch, K. (1952). On communication models in the social sciences. *Public Opinion Quarterly, 16,* 356-380.

Erickson, F. (1976). *Talking down and giving reasons: Hyper-explanation and listening behavior in interracial interviews.* International Conference on Non-verbal Behavior, Ontario Institute for Studies in Education, Toronto, Canada.

Fernandez, J. (1982). *Racism and sexism in corporate life.* Lexington, MA: Lexington.

Folb, E. (1980). *Runnin' down some lines.* Cambridge, MA: Harvard University Press.

Goldschlager, A. (1982). Toward a semiotic of authoritarian discourse. *Poetics Today, 3,* 1.

Gudykunst, W. B., & Kim, Y. Y. (Eds.). (1984). *Methods for intercultural communication research.* Beverly Hills, CA.: Sage.

Hall, E. (1976). *Beyond culture.* Garden City, NY: Doubleday.

Hall, J. (1984). *Nonverbal sex differences.* Baltimore: Johns Hopkins University Press.

Howell, W. (1979). Theoretical directions in intercultural communication. In M. Asante et al. (Eds.), *Handbook of intercultural communication.* Beverly Hills, CA: Sage.

Johnson, D. (1971). Black kinesics: Some non-verbal communication patterns in Black culture. *Florida FL Reporter, 9,* 1-2.

Kang, K., Pearce, W., & Stanback, M. (1983). Some contributions of intercultural communication for communication theory. In S. Thomas (Ed.), *Studies in communication theory and interpersonal interaction.* New York: Ablex.

Kanter, R. M. (1977). *Men and women of the corporation.* New York: Basic Books.

Kochman, T. (1983). *Black and White: Styles in conflict.* Urbana: University of Illinois Press.

Labov, W. (1965). Linguistic research on non-standard English of Negro children. In A. Dorr (Ed.), *Problems and practices in New York City schools.* New York: New York Society for the Experimental Study of Education.

LaFrance, M., & Mayo, C. (1976). Racial differences in gaze behavior during conversation. *Journal of Personality and Social Psychology, 33,* 547-552.

Mayo, C., & Henley, N. (Eds.). (1981). *Gender and non-verbal behavior.* New York: Springer-Verlag.

Mehrabian, A. (1969). Significance of posture and position in the communication attitude and status relationship. *Psychological Bulletin, 71,* 359-372.

Mehrabian, A. (1971). *Silent messages.* Belmont, CA: Wadsworth.

Rich, A. (1974). *Interracial communication.* New York: Harper & Row.

Shuter, R. (1982). Initial interaction of American Blacks and Whites in interracial and intraracial dyads. *Journal of Social Psychology, 117,* 45-52.

Shuy, R. (1964). Social dialects and language learning. *Proceedings of the Bloomington, Indiana Conference, National Council of the Teacher of English.*

Sitaram, K. S., & Cogdell, R. (1976). *Foundation of intercultural communication*. Columbus, OH: Charles E. Merrill.

Smith, A. [Asante, M.] (1973). *Transracial communication*. Englewood Cliffs, NJ: Prentice-Hall.

Ting-Toomey, S. (1985). Toward a theory of conflict and culture. In W. B. Gudykunst, L. Stewart, & S. Ting-Toomey (Eds.), *Communication, culture, and organizational processes*. Beverly Hills, CA: Sage.

Triandis, H. (1976). *Variations in Black and White perceptions of the social environment*. Urbana: University of Illinois Press.

van Dijk, T. (1986). *Communicating racism*. Newbury Park, CA: Sage.

Willhelm, S. (1983). *Black in a White America*. Cambridge, MA: Schenkman.

# 18 The International Marketplace

## Robert Shuter

Japan's stellar performance in international trade can be traced to many economic, political, and social factors, most notably Japan's emphasis on producing quality products that fit the needs and tastes of consumers. Despite Japan's long history of cultural and geographic isolation, the country's international success is founded on understanding each market and its people, and then adapting products and communication to local needs. Japan has demonstrated that success in the international marketplace is influenced dramatically by cultural understanding and effective communication.

With Japan's ascendancy in international trade, corporate executives and university researchers in North and South America, Europe, Asia, and Africa have devoted increasingly more attention to the cultural and communicative dimensions of international trade. Cross-cultural management studies tend to be the most plentiful, with researchers like Adler (1984), Hofstede (1983), and Tung (1984) leading the way in cross-cultural management studies. Recently, researchers have turned their attention to additional international organizational communication issues like headquarter/foreign subsidiary communication, electronic global communication, and country variations in corporate culture (Cushman & King, 1985; Shuter, 1985a, 1985b; Stewart, 1985). Finally, investigators have also explored marketing communication across cultures, but studies are not as abundant as would be expected in this critical international area (Crespy, 1986; Diaz, 1985; Korey, 1986; Shuter, 1984).

This chapter has two objectives: to review critical research on the relationship between culture, communication, and the international marketplace, and to describe an original framework for analyzing the relationship between communication, culture, and the international marketplace.

## RESEARCH ON THE
## INTERNATIONAL MARKETPLACE

### Cross-Cultural Management Research

Numerous studies have been conducted on management issues across cultures (Adler, 1983a, 1983b). Adler (1983b) identified six types of cross-cultural management research: (a) parochial research, (b) ethnocentric research, (c) polycentric research, (d) comparative research, (e) geocentric research, and (f) synergistic research. Parochial research consists of single-culture studies, and it is founded on the assumption that findings generated from one society are applicable to many societies. Management research is often parochial in nature; that is, there is an assumed similarity between societies because most management research is conducted with American subjects in U.S. corporations. These findings are often converted into management theory without questioning whether the results need to be tested in other countries to determine their generalizability.

Unlike parochial studies, ethnocentric research searches for similarities rather than assuming similarities in management behavior across cultures. This type of research flows from a central management question: Can we use home country theories abroad? Ethnocentric research questions the universality of management behavior; parochial research assumes universality across cultures.

Polycentric research denies the universality of management behavior and searches for differences in management practices and protocols. Studies that flow from this research orientation focus on management approaches in specific national cultures, and dispense with home country theories and models, emphasizing descriptive approaches to understanding organizational patterns. Polycentric studies are scarce because most management research emerges from either a parochial or an ethnocentric base.

Comparative research searches for similarities and differences in management behavior by conducting comparative organizational investigations in several societies. This type of research attempts to determine whether management behavior and theory are similar or different across cultures. As a result, comparative research does not deny universality but assumes that there are similarities and differences in organizational patterns across cultures.

Geocentric research focuses almost exclusively on multinational organizations and corporate cultural issues that affect effective management behavior. This type of research ignores national culture—the society in which the organization is located—and instead examines organizational and management practices as though they are unaffected by national culture. Management behavior is considered just another dimension of organizational life, regardless of the cultural backgrounds of the employees. Ironically, this type of research is characterized as international management investigations.

Adler's major contribution to management research is her sixth and last category: synergistic investigations. This type of research examines intercultural interaction within work settings, and rather than pointing out similarities and differences within organizations, she asks: How can the intercultural interaction within a domestic or international organization be managed? How can organizations create structures and processes that will be effective for members of all cultures? As a result, Adler's research seems to strike a balance between specific and universal processes within an organization. She classifies this research as intercultural management studies, and she tries to identify organizational structures that enhance cultural similarities and differences within a multinational organization.

Management literature seems to be weighted heavily toward geocentric and parochial research, and the studies are conducted predominantly in North America and Western Europe (Adler, 1983a). There are few comparative studies available, and even fewer polycentric investigations. As a result, management research is a rich resource of information on multinational management patterns in Western society, but it provides little insight into comparative management approaches or single-culture management behavior.

Intercultural communication plays a minor role in most management studies. Because geocentric research predominates in management studies, communication is considered just another organizational behavior uninfluenced by national culture. Hence, the cultural backgrounds of managers and employees are not considered significant factors in the communication process.

One of the most ambitious cross-cultural management studies of a comparative nature is Geert Hofstede's (1983) analysis of the impact of national culture on organizational behavior. This study examined cultural values in 50 countries through questionnaires administered to over 116,000 company employees. Hofstede's investigation essentially examined four dimensions of national culture: individualism versus collectivism, large or small power distance, strong or weak uncertainty avoidance, and masculinity versus femininity. His goal was to investigate the relationship between national cultural values and management behavior. The study is a model of comparative management analysis with a strong polycentric thrust.

Even Hofstede's research does not examine the role of intercultural communication within organizations. That is, the four dimensions of national culture that he tested are psychological dimensions and, as a result, are distanced from issues of language, nonverbal behavior, decision making, communication style, and other communicative factors. While Hofstede's dimensions may certainly influence communication, his research did not examine *how* these dimensions affect message development, media selection, and message reception—the heart of communication. Research like Hofstede's is critically important, but it is not communication research.

Ironically, there is not a study in the management or communication literature on the order of Hofstede's analysis that examines any dimension of intercultural communication on a global basis. As a result, there is a gap in the literature on how national culture affects management communication across societies.

## Organizational Development and Communication Across Cultures

Studies on organizational development across cultures come in three varieties: (a) complex organizational studies, (b) corporate cultural analysis, and (c) international human resource management. Complex organizational studies are generally conducted in multinational companies and are founded on the assumption that organizational processes are the same the world over. For example, Vladimir Pucik (1986) argues that multinational corporations must coordinate global activities to gain a global competitive advantage. He proposes a series of control systems to coordinate global operations and ultimately argues for flexibility of action.

Similarly, Yves Doz and C. K. Prahalad (1986) write that the main challenge confronting multinational corporations is controlling the variety of different operations under their purview. Doz and Prahalad identify three areas of variety in need of control: (a) subsidiaries in the company, (b) interbusiness differences, and (c) differences in types of ownerships and relationships. Arguing for local control of subsidiaries, the authors articulate the fundamental organizational challenge of multinational companies: balancing global priorities and corporate needs with local options and economic participation.

Some research on international organizational development recommends specific management systems to better coordinate global operations of multinational companies. Thomas Naylon (1985), for example, describes an organizational strategy for multinational companies that includes strategic planning and matrix management. Strategic planning involves formulating corporate goals and objectives in terms of multiple predictors of business conditions. Matrix management is a decentralized management system where decision making is pushed lower into an organization and employees usually report to more than one manager to coordinate rather than control activities in several company departments.

The matrix approach, according to Naylon, increases teamwork, cooperation, and flexibility—key factors in successful coordination of multinational companies.

Although numerous international studies have been conducted on complex organizations, few of them examine organizational communication.
This type of research generally focuses on the development of models,
paradigms, and strategies for maintaining control of multinational subsidiaries and activities rather than examining communication processes
within a multinational company. As a result, communication factors like
organizational decision making, vertical and horizontal communication,
and interdepartmental communication are traditionally absent from international complex organizational research.

While organizational communication researchers have turned their attention recently to the international arena, the data are neither rich
nor varied. In fact, an examination of organizational communication research conducted since 1974 uncovered only 16 published studies on
non-American organizations, and most of this research was executed in
the 1980s appearing in Volumes 9 and 10 of *Organizational Communication: Abstracts, Analysis, and Overview* (Falcione et al., 1983-1984).

The second type of international organizational development research
is corporate cultural studies. Most of this research is conducted as though
corporate culture were not a product of national culture; however, there
are few international studies that describe the linkage between corporate
culture and national culture, providing insight into the organizational
behavior of companies located in specific countries and world regions
(Cushman & King, 1985; Shuter, 1985; Stewart, 1985).

International corporate culture research has been conducted more on the
Japanese than any other national culture (Bowman, 1986; Kume, 1985;
Takamiya, 1981). These studies frequently charted the relationship between Japanese culture and organizational behavior. For example, anec-
dotes about Japanese group decision making and worker loyalty are le-
gion: Corporate cultural studies trace these organizational dynamics and
values to the national culture (Takamiya, 1981). That is, because Japanese
society embraces *Amae*—Japanese for debts and obligations—it is not
surprising that Japanese workers and employers share a keen sense of
reciprocal obligation. Similarly, understanding the Japanese concept of
group and its preeminence in the larger society leads naturally and inevitably to a collective approach to organizational decision making referred to as *ringisho* in Japan.

Japanese corporate culture research is particularly helpful in explaining
why overseas Japanese subsidiaries sometimes experience organizational
conflicts particularly with non-Japanese personnel. Amano (1979), for
example, documents corporate culture problems in U.S.-based Japanese

firms, and describes how some of these companies attempt to bridge the gap between U.S. and Japanese personnel. Similarly, Tsurumi (1978) sites seven cultural mismatches between Japanese and American organizations, which include (a) differences in leadership style, (b) formal versus informal organizational communication, (c) verbal versus written communication, (d) lifetime versus mercenary employment, (e) avoidance of conflict versus adversarial communication, (f) the management and rank-and-file dichotomy, and (g) organizational size differences and accommodation versus conflict strategies. Japanese companies that succeed in the United States, according to Tsurumi, attempt to understand the national and management cultures in the United States and adapt their organizations to local conditions.

Turning to Europe, there are few reported international organizational studies that link national and corporate cultures (Edstrom & Lorange, 1984; Shetty, 1979; Welge, 1981). Cushman and King (1985) describe Yugoslavian organizational culture and its linkage to Yugoslavian values and customs. Shuter (1987) examines Swedish organizational communication within the context of Swedish national culture. Scattered research of this nature is also reported for South Asia and the Middle East (Gemmel, 1986; Yousef, 1974).

In an era of global acquisitions and mergers, international corporate culture research is particularly important. For one, it is generally descriptive and ideographic, detailing the communication rules, values, customs, and rituals of selected organizations within a particular society. This type of information is useful in predicting communication problems between corporate cultures located in different countries. For example, corporate cultural analysis of Swedish and U.S. organizations has isolated several communication areas that produce misunderstanding and friction between Swedish and U.S. employees (Edstrom & Lorange, 1984; Shuter, 1987). As indicated earlier, studies on Japanese corporate culture have also isolated many communication areas where Japanese and American organizations collide due to different values, customs and communication patterns. Despite the potential value of this research, it is traditionally done within U.S. companies and it rarely is linked to national cultural values.

The third area in organizational development is international human resource management, which includes the selection, development, and management of personnel who relocate internationally as well as the formulation and execution of international personnel policy including compensation and benefits (Laurent, 1986). The data in this area grow exponentially because it has significant impact on the success or failure of multinational companies in the international marketplace.

Rosalie Tung (1984) argues that international human resource planning in most U.S. multinational companies is either weak or nonexistent.

Absent from international human resource policy are such factors as (a) adequate cultural training for employees and family members who are relocating abroad, (b) sufficient examination of employee interpersonal skills in international interactions, (c) systematic evaluation of expatriate success overseas, and (d) carefully planned durations of employee assignments—which are too short, according to Tung.

Similarly, Philip Harris (1986) adds that multinational companies do not provide sufficient on-site support of international personnel or reentry counseling. On-site support includes cultural training during and after an employee's first year abroad in such areas as language communication skills and living problems. Reentry counseling helps employees and family members readjust to their country of origin when returning from an extended overseas assignment.

Tung and Harris represent the personnel training faction of the international human resource field, which consists of numerous other business researchers as well (Adler, 1983a, 1984; Doz & Prahalad, 1986; Harvey, 1985; Pucik, 1986). This area has considerable implications for intercultural communication and, it is not surprising, has attracted more attention from communication researchers than any other issue in the international marketplace (Bennett, 1977; Casse, 1979; Church, 1982; Martin, 1986). Nevertheless, communication research in this area has been surprisingly narrow, with intercultural communication effectiveness receiving considerable attention (Abe & Wiseman, 1983; Gudykunst & Hammer, 1984; Ruben, 1977; Ruben, Askling, & Kealey, 1977). Communication researchers virtually have ignored many other communication issues that directly influence international family relocation, on-site employee support programs, reentry counseling, personnel selection and evaluation, and organizational adjustment.

Ruben's (1977) initial research on cross-cultural effectiveness spawned numerous investigations on the communicative behaviors that inspire effective and successful intercultural exchanges. While intercultural effectiveness is certainly worthy of investigation, the studies tend to be redundant, focusing either on the behavioral characteristics of the effective or competent intercultural communicator or on whether effectiveness makes a difference in intercultural exchanges. Not only is the research on effectiveness only tangentially related to international business, but it is just one of many communication variables that intercultural communication researchers ought to be investigating in human resource management.

Organizational adjustment, for example, is one area within human resource management where intercultural communication researchers can make a significant contribution. This area refers to the factors that determine employee success on international job assignments and has traditionally been associated with cultural orientation training for employees and their families. Curiously, no reported intercultural communication studies have correlated employee awareness of corporate cultural communication rules with organizational adjustment on international assignments. For example, would American employees experience more success on assignment in France if they were aware of the communication rules of French organizations? The available data suggest that the answer is most likely affirmative, and yet few communication researchers have examined organizational rules in countries outside the United States (Moran, 1984).

Another human resource issue that intercultural communication researchers could examine productively is what Harvey (1985) calls the "repatriation dilemma" of international personnel. Repatriation refers to employees returning to their country of origin after an extended international assignment. While expatriation education of employees is generally weak, repatriation training is virtually nonexistent; returning employees too often discover that there is no place in the organization for them. Harvey argues that the employee is often professionally and personally isolated from U.S. headquarters while abroad, and, as a result, has lost touch with the corporate culture and its people. If Harvey and others are accurate, there is compelling need for systematic communication training that "reconnects" an international employee with the country and organization of origin before and after repatriation. There is no available communication data on the dynamics of repatriation despite its obvious relationship to both intercultural and organizational communication.

## International Marketing Communication

International marketing communication is concerned with packaging, pricing, promoting, and advertising products globally. Until 1983, a decentralized philosophy of international marketing dominated academia and business: Multinational companies were supposed to customize products, packaging, and advertising for individual markets (Boddewyn, 1986; Korey, 1986). With the publication of Theodore Leavitt's (1988) article on global marketing in the *Harvard Business Review*, the semantics of marketing shifted dramatically. Global marketing replaced international marketing as the new strategy, and it referred to selling the same product in the same way all over the world. Leavitt argued that because market tastes and product needs are becoming so similar worldwide, global companies can successfully produce standardized, low-cost products for global distribution, packaging and promoting them in exactly the same way regardless of national culture.

While the academic and business communities have been attracted to Leavitt's theory, several researchers wonder whether products can be uniformly manufactured and sold worldwide despite converging consumer tastes and product needs (Hammel & Prahalad, 1985). John Quelch and

Edward Hoff (1986) argue, for example, that products and promotion must be customized to local market needs. Too much centralization and uniformity—key dimensions of global marketing—can frustrate foreign subsidiary managers and eliminate products needed for specific local markets. Moreover, global marketing ignores national cultures, homogenizing people and their tastes, which can be dangerous, according to Walters (1986). Parker Pen learned the hazards of global marketing when it decided in 1984 to standardize its products and advertising—the most ambitious global marketing plan to date—and failed miserably (Winski & Wentz, 1986).

International marketing, be it a global approach or more decentralized strategies, has dramatic implications for intercultural communication. In particular, public relations and advertising are rich communication activities that could be insightfully examined by intercultural communication researchers, who have not, to date, published any research in this area. Curiously, the business literature on international advertising and public relations is also limited, and the focus tends to be on legal matters (regulations worldwide), selection of advertising agencies, and translation issues (Diaz, 1985; Dugas, 1984; Lynch, 1984). Few advertising studies have systematically examined the influence of national culture on the development and transmission of international advertising and public relations messages.

International advertising is also a potentially rich area for rhetorical analysis. The selection of argument—its efficacy and reception—is a critical component of international advertising, and it lends itself to culturally sensitive rhetorical analysis. Even pictorial elements of an advertisement, from selection of pictures to how people/artifacts are posed, can be rhetorically examined to determine cultural appropriateness and potential persuasive success.

Intercultural communication researchers have neglected to examine international marketing, along with human resource management, international management, and organizational development. This neglect—albeit benign—has kept the field at a distance from the international marketplace. The next section attempts to close that gap by providing an intercultural communication framework for examining the international marketplace.

## INTERCULTURAL ORGANIZATIONAL COMMUNICATION: A CONCEPTUAL FRAMEWORK

Intercultural communication plays a dramatic role in the international marketplace and affects all dimensions of organizational life, especially corporate culture, international management, human resource management, and international marketing—the areas examined in the preceding section of this essay. Because these areas are the marrow of organizational life, they are generally examined within the framework of organizational communication. For the purpose of this chapter, these areas are subsumed under a new category of organizational communication that is called intercultural organizational communication.

Intercultural organizational communication is defined as communication that occurs within or between organizations that have one or more of these characteristics:

(1) communicates on a regular basis across national borders;

(2) is composed of personnel from more than one national cultural or domestic coculture (i.e., Black American/Hispanic American); and

(3) is located geographically in one culture but is controlled either partly or wholly by a parent company in a different national culture (e.g., parent company/foreign subsidiary relationship).

With this definition, there are many possible intercultural transactions that can occur within or between organizations—which is referred to as internal intercultural organizational communication (within an organization) and external intercultural organizational communication (between organizations; see Table 18.1).

Internal intercultural transactions include the following: (a) organizational structure and communication, (b) role performance in an organizational culture, and (c) human resource communication. External intercultural organizational communication refers to transactions between organizations across national borders and includes (a) communication between parent organization and foreign subsidiaries, and (b) marketing communication across cultures.

## Internal Intercultural
## Organizational Communication

Organizational structure refers to the nature of the hierarchy within which actors enact roles. It includes the following components: type of chain of command and its communication rules; type of organizational department and departmental communication; type of organizational roles and interrole communication; and the nature of organizational decision making. The type of chain of command refers to the number and complexity of organizational levels and the rules for communicating between organizational levels. Departmental communication consists of the number and type of departments within a company, their status within an organization, and the rules of departmental communication. Finally,

**TABLE 18.1.** Intercultural Organization Communication

---

Internal intercultural organizational communication

   I. Organizational structure and communication

      A. chain of command and communication

      B. departmental communication

      C. organizational decision making

   II. Role performance in an organizational culture

      A. communication style (i.e., management style)

      B. role to role communication in the hierarchy (i.e., supervisor/subordinate communication)

  III. International human resource communication

      A. interpersonal communication between personnel (i.e., greeting patterns, small talk expectations)

      B. expatriate/repatriate communication

External intercultural organizational communication

   I. Communication between corporate headquarters and foreign subsidiaries

      A. interorganizational communication pathways (*who* to contact, *where* to send a message, *what* to say, and how [media] to send it)

   II. Marketing communication across cultures

      A. message development/message transmission (i.e., media choice) and message reception of international advertising

---

organizational decision making is the type of decision-making model used predominantly in an organization and it ranges from consensus paradigms to more autocratic frameworks.

Role performance in an organizational culture refers to the array of communication rules that influence the performance of organizational roles. Role performance is the behavioral component of an organizational role and includes the following: an agent's communication style in performing a role, and an agent's communication with other role players in the hierarchy. Traditional areas within this category include management style, employee communication with supervisors, communication of top managers, and secretarial communication patterns.

International human resource communication includes interpersonal communication between personnel in an organization as well as expatriate/repatriate communication. Interpersonal exchanges include horizontal or vertical communication conducted face to face, in written form, or through electronic media. Numerous verbal and nonverbal variables make up any interpersonal encounter including initial interaction, polite expressions, communicating style, and conflict approaches.

Expatriate and repatriate communication is composed of intercultural communication training and support communication for employees who transfer internationally (expatriates), and personnel returning to their country of origin at the conclusion of an international assignment (repatriates). Intercultural training can include pre-/postdeparture business and cultural training for expatriates and/or their families. Support communication refers to the nature, frequency, and duration of communication between home office and expatriates/repatriates and can include written updates for expatriates on headquarter corporate changes, assisting expatriates' adjustment to their new national culture, and providing repatriates with a personnel plan several months before returning to their country of origin.

### External Intercultural
### Organizational Communication

Interorganizational communication pathways refers to the appropriate communication pathways for initiating interorganizational contacts. These communication pathways are a by-product of the communication rules that influence organizational structure and role performance. As a result, these interorganizational communication pathways are generally identified after intraorganizational rules are discovered with respect to chain of command, departmental communication, organizational decision making, and role performance. This category focuses on such issues as who should send and receive an interorganizational message, where the message should be sent (e.g., which department), what is the proper content of the message, and how the message should be sent (e.g., type of medium).

The focus of international marketing communication is being limited to advertising, be it broadcast or print. Components of international marketing that have communicative implications are message development, message transmission, and message reception. Message development includes the identification and utilization of culturally appropriate content. Message transmission refers to the selection of media to optimize message impact. Finally, message reception consists of listener interpretation and attendant behavioral responses.

It is argued that internal and external organizational communication is significantly influenced by national culture. That is, the structure of an organization and its communication rules, role performance of organizational personnel, communication to human resources, and marketing communication reflect the values and traditions of the country in which the organization is situated. Certainly Geert Hofstede's (1983) research demonstrates how management style and personnel communication are a reflection of national cultural values. Similarly, Shuter's (1985a, 1985b,

1987) studies on Scandinavian companies and Ouchi's (1981) work on Japanese organizations reveal the tight relationship between corporate hierarchy, communication rules, and a country's values and traditions.

It is posited that organizations existing within a particular country—the United States, for example—would share distinct similarities in areas like organizational structure and attendant communication rules, human resource communication, and role performance issues like management style. This assumption does not deny corporate cultural differences between organizations within a country; on the contrary, it affirms and expands the notion of organizational diversity by providing an intercultural framework for investigating differences between organizational cultures situated in distinct societies.

## CONCLUSION

After reviewing seminal literature on communication and the international marketplace, this essay introduced a new term, *intercultural organizational communication,* and a conceptual framework for conducting this type of analysis and research. The term and framework are offered as an alternative to past research on communication and the international marketplace, which tends to be about neither communication nor national culture, as demonstrated in the preceding literature review. Intercultural organizational communication as described in this chapter focuses research questions and analysis on communication and national culture within an organizational setting, which consists of specific internal and external communication factors.

With the framework presented in this chapter, comparative intercultural analysis can be readily conducted between two or more international organizations. Similarly, this framework will simplify intraorganizational communication analysis of corporate cultural patterns within companies located in different societies. Finally, the framework can also be used to shape future communication research projects on the international marketplace by providing investigators with a communication paradigm for developing intercultural hypotheses on selected dimensions of organizational life.

## REFERENCES

Abe, H., & Wiseman, R. (1983). Cross-cultural confirmation of the dimensions of intercultural effectiveness. *International Journal of Intercultural Relations, 7,* 53-67.

Adler, N. (1983a). Cross-cultural management: Issues to be faced. *International Studies of Management and Organization, 13,* 7-45.

Adler, N. (1983b). A typology of management studies involving culture. *Journal of International Business Studies, 14*, 29-47.

Adler, N. (1984). Expecting international success: Female managers overseas. *Columbia Journal of World Business, 19*, 79-85.

Amano, M. (1979). Organizational changes of a Japanese firm in America. *California Management Review, 2*, 51-59.

Bennett, J. (1977). Transition shock: Putting culture shock in perspective. *International and Intercultural Communication Annual, 4*, 45-52.

Boddewyn, J. (1986). Standardization in international marketing: Is Ted Leavitt right? *Business Horizons, 29*, 69-75.

Bowman, J. (1986). The rising sun in America. *Personnel Administration, 3*, 63-77.

Casse, P. (1979). *Training for the multicultural manager.* Washington, DC: Society for Intercultural Education, Training, and Research.

Church, A. (1982). Sojourner adjustments. *Psychological Bulletin, 91*, 540-592.

Crespy, C. (1986). Global marketing is the new public relations challenge. *Public Relations Quarterly, 3*, 5-12.

Cushman, D., & King, S. (1985). National and organizational cultures in conflict resolution: Japan, the U.S., and Yugoslavia. In W. Gudykunst, L. Stewart, & S. Ting-Toomey (Eds.), *Communication, culture, and organizational processes* (pp. 115-133). Beverly Hills, CA: Sage.

Diaz, R. (1985). Advertising effectively in foreign markets. *Advanced Management Journal, 50*, 12-20.

Doz, Y., & Prahalad, C. K. (1986). Controlled variety: A challenge for human resource management in the MNC. *Human Resource Management, 25*, 55-71.

Dugas, C. (1984). Global marketing: Will one sales pitch work worldwide? *Ad Forum, 5*, 20-27.

Edstrom, A., & Lorange, P. (1984). Matching strategy and human resources in multinational corporations. *Journal of International Business Studies, 15*, 125-137.

Falcione, J., Greenbaum, P., & Hellwig, D. (Eds.). (1983-1984). *Organizational communication: Abstracts, analysis, and overview* (Vols. 9, 10). Beverly Hills, CA: Sage.

Gemmel, A. (1986). Management in a cross-cultural environment: The best of both worlds. *Management Solutions, 3*, 28-33.

Gudykunst, W., & Hammer, M. (1984). Dimensions of intercultural effectiveness: Culture specific or culture general? *International Journal of Intercultural Relations, 8*, 1-10.

Hofstede, G. (1983). The cultural relativity of organizational practices and theories. *Journal of International Business Studies, 14*, 75-89.

Hammel, G., & Prahalad, C. (1985). Do you really have a global strategy? *Harvard Business Review, 63*, 139-148.

Harris, P. (1986). Employee abroad: Maintain the corporate connection. *Personnel Journal, 65*, 107-110.

Harvey, M. (1985). The other side of foreign assignments: Dealing with the repatriation dilemma. *Columbia Journal of World Business, 17*, 53-59.

Korey, G. (1986). Multilateral perspectives in international marketing dynamics. *European Journal of Marketing, 20*, 34-42.

Kume, T. (1985). Managerial attitudes toward decision-making: North America and Japan. In W. Gudykunst, L. Stewart, & S. Ting-Toomey (Eds.), *Communication, culture, and organizational processes* (pp. 231-252). Beverly Hills, CA: Sage.

Laurent, A. (1986). The cross-cultural puzzle of international human resource management. *Human Resource Management, 25*, 91-102.

Leavitt, T. (1983). The globalization of markets. *Harvard Business Review, 61*, 92-103.

Lynch, M. (1984). Harvard's Leavitt called global marketing guru. *Advertising Age, 55*, 49-50.

Martin, J. (1986). Training issues in cross-cultural orientation. *International Journal of Intercultural Relations, 10*, 103-116.

Moran, R. (1984). *Getting your yens worth: How to negotiate with the Japanese*. Houston: Gulf.

Naylon, T. (1985). The international strategy matrix. *Columbia Journal of World Business, 20*, 11-19.

Ouchi, W. (1981). *Theory Z*. New York: Avon.

Pucik, V. (1986). Information, control, and human resource management in multinational firms. *Human Resource Management, 25*, 121-132.

Quelch, J., & Hoff, E. (1986). Customizing global marketing. *Harvard Business Review, 64*, 59-68.

Ruben, B. (1977). Human communication and cross-cultural effectiveness. *International and Intercultural Communication Annual, 4*, 98-105.

Ruben, B., Askling, L., & Kealey, D. (1977). Cross-cultural effectiveness. In D. Hoopes, P. Pedersen, & G. Renwick (Eds.), *Overview of intercultural education, training, and research* (pp. 92-105). Washington, DC: Society for Intercultural Education, Training, and Research.

Shetty, Y. (1979). Managing the multinational corporation: European and American styles. *Management International Review (Germany), 19*, 39-48.

Shuter, R. (1984, September 2). Know the local rules of the game. *New York Times*, pp. 86-87.

Shuter, R. (1985a, September). Assignment America: Foreign managers beware. *International Management*, pp. 93-97.

Shuter, R. (1985b, November 22). When the manager is a stranger in a familiar land. *Wall Street Journal*, p. 55.

Shuter, R. (1987). *Linking organizational culture and national culture: A study of Swedish multinational organizations*. Paper presented at the Conference on Communication and Society, Dubrovnik, Yugoslavia.

Stewart, L. (1985). Subjective culture and organizational decision-making. In W. Gudykunst, L. Stewart, & S. Ting-Toomey (Eds.), *Communication, culture, and organizational processes* (pp. 212-250). Beverly Hills, CA: Sage.

Takamiya, M. (1981). Japanese multinationals in Europe: Internal operations and their public policy implications. *Columbia Journal of World Business, 16*, 5-17.

Tsurumi, Y. (1978). The best of times and the worst of times: Japanese management in America. *Columbia Journal of World Business, 13*, 56-61.

Tung, R. (1984). Strategic management of human resources in the multinational enterprise. *Human Resource Management, 23*, 129-143.

Walters, P. (1986). International marketing policy: A discussion of the standardization construct and its relevance for corporate policy. *International Business Policy, 16*, 55-69.

Welge, M. (1981). A comparison of managerial structures in German subsidiaries in France, India, and the U.S. *Management International Review, 19*, 24-37.

Winski, J., & Wentz, L. (1986). Parker Pen: What went wrong? *Advertising Age, 57*, 60-61.

Yousef, F. (1974). Cross-cultural communication: Aspects of contrasting social values between North Americans and Middle Easterners. *Human Organization, 4*, 383-387.

# 19 Diplomacy

## Glen Fisher

Rather obviously, international diplomacy is always, in part at least, an exercise in intercultural communication. With profound consequences often turning on the quality of diplomatic communication, it is appropriate to consider the degree that the intercultural component of the diplomatic process is understood and managed. The potential for dissimilar perceptions of issues, for misperception of events, and for misattribution of motive is great enough in any kind of negotiation or problem solving. When the intercultural dimension is added, that potential increases enormously.

"Diplomacy" is a wide-ranging subject. People engage in diplomacy on many levels of international interaction and negotiation. Aside from conducting traditional governmental business, there is now a substantial level of international business diplomacy. There is diplomacy conducted within international organizations, in development and technical assistance programs, and in the international activities of many private institutions. While the central focus here will be on diplomacy in government-to-government relations, much of what follows could be directed toward these other concerns as well.

Many aspects of the intercultural communication field apply to the conduct of diplomacy in one way or another. Complications derive from contrasting forms of nonverbal behavior, from interpreting role behavior, and from trying to mesh cognitive gears. Diplomats like others experience "cultural shock" and even "reentry shock." Indeed, most of our concerns in the intercultural field can be applied to diplomats and to diplomatic endeavors in the same way that they would be relevant to others working cross-culturally. In diplomatic practice, however, certain conditions and circumstances stand out to make the diplomat's intercultural communication task somewhat unique. This chapter will concentrate on that with emphasis on special aspects of the diplomat's mission and working environment, on factors that affect competence, and on the agenda for increasing effectiveness.

In setting this out, I will draw heavily on my own experience as a sociologist/cultural anthropologist turned Foreign Service Officer and, therefore, on something of a participant observer's conclusions as intercultural communication considerations have presented themselves in field situations abroad, in Washington, in the United Nations, and in designing programs at the State Department's Foreign Service Institute.

There is relatively little literature to draw upon that *directly* addresses the intercultural communication aspect of diplomacy, a rather surprising condition given diplomacy's long existence as a specialized field. Part of the explanation is that, through a long history of Western-centered international relations, diplomacy was considered an arena unto itself with its own culture; the advice contained in books like Sir Harold Nicolson's (1939/1950) *Diplomacy* was read by aspiring diplomats from all countries. As the Western-centered orientation became less relevant, Robert Rossow's (1962) article titled "The Professionalization of the New Diplomacy" suggested new times and new needs to take the intercultural factor into account. Still, such increased attention as was given to the endeavor was contained in lectures and seminars rather than in additions to the literature of either diplomacy or the intercultural relations field.

There has, however, been important work in psychological factors in international affairs, in decision making, and in conflict resolution (for example, George, 1980; Jervis, 1976; Kelman, 1965; White, 1984). Concepts such as "cognitive mapping" and "operational codes" are germane to diplomacy, and enjoy a growing literature (reviewed in Cottam, 1986; Hermann, 1986). Our problem with these is that culture's specific significance generally is not treated.

The importance of "national character"—never a very precise concept—receives occasional attention since its more salient impact when Ruth Benedict (1946) wrote about Japanese cultural factors in her classic World War II era *The Chrysanthemum and the Sword*. A more recent if less penetrating example that relates cultural factors to European Economic Community affairs is Luigi Barzini's (1983) *The Europeans*.

Currently, international negotiation is a prime subject of attention (Binnendijk, 1987, is a sample), with the American-Japanese case most explored. But again, intercultural communication aspects are more often presented in seminars than in available literature. The pertinence of culturally molded patterns of reasoning and styles of debate to diplomacy has been an occasional theme (Glenn, 1981), and will be referred to later. Further citations will be made in our discussion as appropriate, including my own attempts to fill in the intercultural gap, which have been directed toward factors in public perceptions, negotiation, and the role of mind-sets in international relations (Fisher, 1972, 1980, 1988).

## THE DIPLOMAT'S MISSION AND
## WORKING ENVIRONMENT

The first factor that tends to make the diplomats' intercultural communication task unique is that by being assigned abroad to represent their government *they become brokers bridging cultural gaps.* On one hand, they must be interculturally effective in foreign environments as they work with their local staffs, observe and analyze local developments, or try to be persuasive with the local press or Foreign Office. On the other hand, they have to try to interpret the foreign scene to people at home who operate essentially within the perspectives and enthnocentrism of domestic affairs. Thus diplomats have intercultural communication problems going in both directions, with as much difficulty in communicating the meaning of a successful exchange with their "foreign" counterparts back to their home-based decision-making bureaucracies as they had in communicating with the host society in the first place. This constitutes a core quality in the diplomat's professionalism.

Diplomats, then, are the go-betweens. Their normal concern is mindsets that are out of synchronization across national boundaries, with mental computers operating on differing floppy discs (Fisher, 1988). Especially under a democratic system such as that found in the United States, domestic decision makers are often people who have moved into their positions socialized out of awareness in the cultural rationale that underlies their society's political processes. This becomes the common sense of politicians and bureaucrats, and skill in using it has made them successful. They, therefore, have a built-in difficulty in using the diplomat's information and advice when they get it because that advice necessarily reflects the diplomat's understanding of some contrasting "common sense" as it has been generated by the culture and circumstances of the nation of assignment. Diplomatic reporting and counsel often does not seem reasonable; diplomats become suspect as the source of alien information, as people who may have "gone native."

This may be the worst case scenario, but Alexander George (1980) has noted in studying presidential use of information and advice that, as decision makers try to maintain cognitive consistency, they tend to reject unprocessable information. Therefore, calculated steps have to be taken to be sure that relevant out-of-the-ordinary information is given full attention in the decision-making process. This would apply especially to information that has a cross-cultural quality. This fundamental of communication is a constant challenge to professionalism in diplomatic service communities, and a fact of life that tends to unite diplomats of all countries in a sense of common mission.

Hence, it is well to recognize that the intercultural objective in diplomacy is a compounded one. Diplomats are the people assigned to live in foreign areas; they are expected to speak local languages and experience local day-to-day concerns. To be effective, they have to become adept in empathizing and in absorbing the fuller meaning of issues as seen by local governments and their officials. Ideally, they will be able to anticipate the habits of perception that will be directed toward them and their activities, and to the issues that need to be addressed cross-nationally. If they are successful, their chances of accuracy in making judgments in their foreign environment and in establishing the meaning and nuance of positions taken are enhanced. And this empathy also helps them anticipate the ways in which their own actions and positions may be misunderstood cross-culturally.

In sum, the task of the diplomat is not simply to be cross-culturally "sensitive," but to be a manager of a complex intercultural communication process. Therefore, in determining the prospects for diplomacy profiting from achievements in the intercultural field, it is not just a matter of transferring a practitioner's art and technique for being culturally sensitive and adapting in a foreign place, but of providing the behavioral science theories and concepts that apply to understanding the intercultural communication process itself. While diplomats, like others working abroad, have to cope personally with the experiential reality of intercultural communication problems, they also have to be practical diagnosticians of the process. In application, this is an intellectual demand of a high order, and one that promoters in the intercultural field have to appreciate.

The next circumstance that stands out is the fact that *diplomatic functions are most typically carried out in highly cosmopolitan environments where elements of a growing international culture are often reflected*, at least superficially. The international community of diplomats itself was an early leader in creating a transnational cultural base by defining norms for addressing issues, by adopting customs for protocol, and by setting standard operating procedures. They have formed something of an international society of diplomats with its own ethics and standards. There is even an international language: English has become the de facto common language of diplomacy, having overtaken French in recent decades.

But growth of an international culture has gone far beyond traditional diplomatic circles. As the web of international interaction has grown through commerce and finance, through an explosive media and information system, travel, multinational organizations, and the sheer mixing of peoples conducting their affairs on a transnational basis, a true body of "culture" that is not nation-specific has, in the sense of learned, shared, and transmitted norms of thinking and behaving, been pragmatically adopted. Happily for Americans and Europeans, this globalized culture tends to be cast in the American and West European mold.

On the surface, this would make it appear that there is much less of an intercultural communication problem. Diplomats mix easily. By their experience, they are not really thrown off by strange gestures, unusual dress, cuisine, or varied forms of polite behavior. And, in fact, diplomats tend not to be impressed with much that is presented routinely as advice or prescriptions by intercultural communication enthusiasts. They know that their Japanese colleagues bow and use intricate forms of polite address at home—but, after all, the Japanese shake hands in cosmopolitan settings. Or they know that, while in the Muslim world, women tend to be covered and segregated, the ones they have to deal with directly usually are world-travelled people frequently attired in Paris fashions.

Nonetheless, it is precisely because of this surface urbanity that diplomats face special problems in intercultural communication, for they are constantly dealing with people with bi- or multicultural personalities, with people who speak more than one language, and, therefore, with people who go back and forth in their thought processes and perception habits as they communicate about international events and issues. Americans may have to judge when their English-speaking counterparts are speaking English and thinking English thoughts, and when they are speaking English and thinking Japanese or Indian or Thai thoughts.

Being bicultural does not necessarily mean breaking away entirely from the mold of one's native culture. Understanding the behavior of bicultural people still requires a comprehension of base cultural roots as that cultural orientation may be the *operative* one even in cosmopolitan situations. For example, diplomats in Pakistan might have had occasion to understand the thinking of people like opposition leader Benazir Butto, who, as a woman active in politics, agreed to have an arranged marriage. This hardly would have been the expectation given her Harvard and Oxford education, and the groom's own enculturation at the London School of Economics, in modern business, and in polo as a sport. Yet she was the unusual woman politician in a Muslim society, and reflected a bicultural personality prepared to make a deeply personal decision in accord with the Muslim society side of her cultural amalgam. Therefore, to understand "where she was coming from," one had to understand both the reality of a bicultural personality, and the Pakistani cultural background from which the less familiar elements derived.

Diplomats often need to anticipate which set of understandings or perceptions are to be expected in a given situation, or which will determine future behavior or compliance with an agreement. The actual outcome of diplomatic interaction will depend on this often overlooked aspect of modern international behavior, especially overlooked in a situation in which one's own cultural programming is not challenged and the full significance of other patterns of perceiving and reasoning lacks a sense of immediacy.

The immediacy returns quickly, of course, when institutional decision makers not schooled in intercultural diplomacy bypass their diplomats, as when presidents meet with other chiefs of state, congressional delegations go abroad, or specialized negotiating teams meet. At this point, diplomats are hard-pressed to manage intercultural factors (Cohen, 1987).

The third aspect of diplomatic communication that needs to be emphasized is the fact that *the subjects that diplomats communicate about are typically abstract*: policies, laws, institutions and their functions, trends, agreements, governmental processes, finance at a macro level, and so on. These are subject matters that are not visualized readily in one time and place. They are complexities that have reality over periods of time and in the behavior of many people fulfilling varied roles.

In general, the more abstract an issue, the more one must draw on the computer banks of the mind to supply meaning. One must draw on stored knowledge about the subject, on images, on beliefs, and on habits of logic and reasoning for putting the parts together. It follows that the more abstract the subject, the more one depends on the programming supplied by the culture.

This calls for a special order of intercultural communication analysis in that it demands that one go beyond descriptions of behavior to explore explanations for the perceiving and reasoning behind the behavior. For example, it is one thing to read a law and compare it with the prescriptions of another country. It is another to understand that law as a function of beliefs about social relations, morality, or the proper function of government. This is not to dismiss the importance of studying contrasts in behavior that can be directly observed and described. But across a range in which one can apply intercultural communication analysis either to very concrete patterns of behavior on the one end, or to more abstract aspects of information processing that supply the meaning for communicating about abstract and complex subject matter on the other, diplomacy is much concerned with the abstract end of the range.

Among intercultural communication specialists, various people have been concerned with the relationship between culture and modes of thinking and reasoning. The late Edmund Glenn, a former State Department interpreter, was acutely aware of the way that cultural factors complicated his task of interpreting for presidents Truman, Eisenhower, Kennedy, and Johnson, and for Secretaries of State Acheson, Dulles, Herter, and Rusk. His book *Man and Mankind: Conflict and Communication Between Cultures* (1981, Glenn) summarizes his theories and their applications. Edward Stewart (1972) saw this level of analysis as essential when he worked with technical assistance trainees, and produced the study familiar to many readers, *American Cultural Patterns: A Cross-Cultural Perspective*. More recently, he has been concerned with this level of inquiry as directed to international business and managerial applications.

The importance of this dimension for diplomacy is illustrated by recalling the frustrations that Edmund Glenn used to report from his role as interpreter in private meetings between heads of state. He noted that he often felt that the two principals were talking past each other, in effect not even talking about the same subject. Although one of the most skilled interpreters using English, French, Polish, and Russian, *there was nothing he could do about these mismatched meanings* short of going into a seminar about the subjective meaning of words, the relationship between language and thought, and the differences in the way that cultures lead people to order their reasoning processes. And, of course, that was not possible in such a situation.

The fourth consideration in the diplomat's working environment is that *diplomatic communication proceeds against a backdrop of public-to-public intercultural communication, especially via the media.* In effect, media intensifies intrusion of intercultural factors into the diplomatic process. It goes very far in establishing the public's knowledge and attitude base and, therefore, public perceptions both at home and abroad as it selects its subject matter, categorizes and defines events and issues, and transmits images and rhetoric often cut off from context. Diplomats have to cope with this; sometimes they try to manage it. Use of the term *public diplomacy* at least indicates that how publics understand and react to issues is part of the diplomatic formula. The problem for diplomats is not what actually happens or what the reality of an issue is, but what publics *think* happened or is at stake.

The point here is that, in applying intercultural communication analysis to diplomacy, one needs to extend the inquiry to include the communication role performed by the journalists, news copy translators, and the TV and newspaper editors who have to select and assign meaning to the news items that will cross their gatekeeper thresholds. And on a deeper level, the longer-range intercultural exposure carried via literature, entertainment programming in movies and television, travelers and tourists, and so forth all contribute to public images held of the counterpart country, its peoples, and its intentions. For the United States this makes the U.S. Information Agency a direct part of the larger diplomatic process, although the total stream of American communication is so great that USIA's efforts are much diluted as far as the consequences of its efforts are concerned. Other nations also address this public dimension of their diplomatic fortunes.

There is considerable logic in including the intercultural factor in news flow in the context of diplomacy and in raising parallel questions regarding the *intercultural* sophistication of journalists and reporters. We often fail to recognize that the international reporter has a fundamentally different function to fulfill as compared with a domestic colleague. When the media transmits news *within* one society, meaning and context are understood; they are more or less the same for reporter as for readers and listeners, as all are programmed by the same culture. But international reporters face the need to transmit both the news and the meaning of the news as it crosses cultural boundaries. This is a different mission, one that is rarely taken into account either in training international journalists or in evaluating their professionalism and performance.

## HOW INTERCULTURALLY COMPETENT
## DO DIPLOMATS BECOME?

In assessing the prospects for extending the intercultural communication inquiry to diplomatic practice, things become muddled as one considers the wide range of people who conduct "diplomacy" in one form or another. On one hand, nations have diplomatic services made up of professionals whose career missions are to deal with other societies and "communicate" with them. On the other, people become diplomats by the nature of their specialties—aviation regulation, finance, expertise in a technical field, military command, concern with agricultural commodities, or whatever. But they become diplomats on something of a case-by-case basis and as occasion demands. They may find themselves representing their governments or organizations in negotiating with foreign counterparts, but this is not what they do on a career basis. The number of people thus involved in a nation's total diplomatic activity increases enormously as the world becomes more interdependent and more and more aspects of national affairs assume an international dimension. By the same trend, career diplomatic generalists play a decreasing role, and such competence as they have as intercultural brokers in the national interest is diluted.

Even within embassy staffs, "diplomat" is not easily defined, particularly in American embassies. Typically, less than 30% of American personnel in an embassy is made up of State Department Foreign Service personnel, and even among those, one finds much variation in the degree of involvement in the substance of diplomatic interaction. Officers in the political affairs and economic "cones" of the Service do the large part of the basic reporting, analysis, negotiating, and advising; they engage in most of the substantive communication with host country governments. Consular officers basically administer American laws and regulations. Foreign Service Officers in the administrative specialty may have occasion to negotiate cross-culturally on administrative matters, but they are mostly engaged in making the embassy work as they concentrate on personnel, security, communications facilities, budgets, motor pools, office space, and importation of equipment. They would not be "diplomats" in the tradition of international diplomacy. All these officers have intercultural communication demands placed on them, but these demands differ widely.

The other 70% of American Embassy personnel is made up of a bewildering array of people representing other agencies of the United States government, agencies that have some special international role to play. Thus one finds Cultural Affairs Officers, commercial and military attachés, Marine security guards, Foreign Agricultural Service Officers, Treasury officers, Agency for International Development advisers, Central Intelligence officers, Drug Enforcements agents ("diplomats" who like to carry guns)—the list is extensive. Obviously, a need to communicate interculturally cuts across this range too, but in seeking a strategy for enhancing their competence consideration has to be given to the differences in previous intercultural experience that this spread of personnel brings with it, and the kinds of communication that is to be conducted.

So we see that there are career diplomats, and there are ad hoc diplomats. In the latter category must be added people on temporary assignment or special missions, often people with no previous international experience whatsoever, people with only an ethnocentric view of the subject matter with which they deal and of foreigners. This may include political appointee ambassadors, potential disasters as intercultural communicators. They speak no foreign languages; they use interpreters or work with counterparts who speak English. When the Foreign Service is criticized for lack of intercultural sophistication or language abilities, the complaint may well be prompted more by this larger embassy crowd that visitors encounter than by those more correctly designated as the diplomats to which this chapter primarily is directed.

This is not to say that all career diplomatic officers are competent intercultural communicators, or that they could not be better with appropriate effort and training. How good they are is not easily judged; there are no measurements or data to provide a competence profile, although language achievement is recorded (Department of State, 1987). There have been suggestions made around the Foreign Service Institute that officers be rated for their specific area and country study achievement as they are in foreign-language speaking and reading achievement. Thus officers might be rated "A-3" in Thai area studies in the same way as they might be rated S-3 and R-3 in Thai language. This idea has not prospered, however. And in any case, rating knowledge about an area might not indicate an equivalent communicating adeptness.

In following officer careers and performance, however, it seems safe to make a few generalizations. Officers who come into the Service after having lived abroad in situations in which they have had to cope on their own, and who speak a foreign language, seem to make cultural transitions more easily. Former Peace Corps participants would be an example; they have lived abroad outside cosmopolitan environments and have confronted foreign culture at its ordinary everyday base, often in rural areas. This is an experience that is not likely to be duplicated in most diplomatic assignments. Further, officers who have spent part of their careers in areas with highly contrasting culture, who have learned these languages, and have been given specialized area study either in university programs or along with language training seem to be the ones most tuned to look for cultural factors in their analysis and reporting, and most likely to feel at ease in any intercultural communication situation. Thus Foreign Service Officers known as Japanese, or Chinese, or Arabic language Officers give the impression of having greater depth in their comprehension of the relationship between culture and mind-sets, and are more likely to seek the cultural roots for explaining behavior at the institutional level as well as at the personal.

Conversely, officers who have delayed their introduction to language training, whose assignments have been to easy-to-adjust-to Western capitals, and especially officers who deal in commercial, economic, military, or technological affairs fields, seem to be less aware of the full significance of culture in their international interaction, and less able to see the uniqueness of their own cultural programming as Americans. In conducting interviews with a variety of officials with international negotiating experience in connection with a study regarding cultural factors in negotiation, the trend seemed to be that officers who did not speak a foreign language and who had dealt only with European counterparts (e.g., French) were the most likely to insist that culture posed no problem. Interestingly, officials who did speak French and who knew the French scene rather well were most insistent that cultural hurdles in negotiating with the French were very significant (Fisher, 1980).

One of the subtle impediments to moving more forthrightly to address intercultural competence is the tendency in the State Department to consider an officer an expert by the fact of language competence and having served for a number of years in an area. The Latin American expert, for example. And, indeed, such experience often does lead to real intercultural competence even without specific cross-cultural or extended area training. Sensitive and observant officers do absorb local cultures, often very well. But speaking a language is only one facet of communicating, and ten years' experience may in fact be one year's experience repeated ten times. Further, there is a tendency to carry what one has learned by naive experience in one foreign place to apply it uncritically in a second culture. For example, after extended experience in Latin America, one might see Philippine behavior as a variation of Latin American life and culture.

The Foreign Service Institute (FSI) is an in-service training arm of the State Department. It is there that most diplomats, both those in the career Foreign Service and other government personnel sent abroad on shorter assignments, are most likely to encounter an emphasis on intercultural communication skills. FSI has been concerned with this since the early 1950s, starting especially when large numbers of advisers were being sent out on first assignments in technical assistance and development programs. This was the era when Edward T. Hall was on the FSI staff, when he along with other anthropologists and linguistic scientists were making early efforts to apply their disciplines to intercultural training. (From this, Hall went on to write *The Silent Language*—1959—the book that first established his name in the intercultural field.) The fortunes of intercultural training at FSI have varied considerably over the years. How best to do it remains today a subject of debate within the FSI staff and in the Foreign Service.

The problem is that diplomatic practitioners are not sure what is meant or intended in intercultural training, and, in turn, those who are called in to advise typically are not well tuned to the needs and experience of the variety of people who pass through FSI. Adult training for self-assured professionals is not easily promoted, especially when training to "communicate" seems to imply a shortcoming in a skill that such professionals firmly believe they already have. To be sent back to school to learn to be interculturally sensitive is not something to boast about among one's colleagues. To be sent for language study is a much more acceptable prospect as a new language skill is seen to augment one's resources for applying the professional competence in which one is already proud and confident.

What has been attempted in intercultural communication at FSI has varied widely. Much of what has been offered has catered to the novice who wants easy answers; it has been "briefing" for living overseas, mixed in with discussions of how to ship household effects and place children in overseas schools. Sometimes that which has passed as intercultural training simply involved description of a country's institutions and typical customs. Sometimes it has been an exercise in sensitization to cultural difference, which may have proved useful for those who had never thought about it before, but also often tended to be patronizing to those who either knew, or thought they knew, a lot about cultural differences. Less frequently, intercultural communication has been presented at the more abstract level of application, as, for example, in looking at the way that national character influences philosophy and law, or becomes part of the psychological dimension of foreign affairs.

Extended programs in area or country study accompanying language courses have probably been the most effective context for presenting cultural factors in communication, especially in programs dealing with the "hard" languages (e.g., Chinese, Arabic, or similar longer courses). Here the role of values and the relationship of culture to personality becomes a logical extension of established diplomatic training.

In sum, the intercultural dimension enjoys an uncertain image among those involved in diplomatic affairs. For some, the impression is left that when you know how to bargain in a Moroccan market and feel good about it, or know not to "blow your cool" when your Latin American appointment arrives late, you know about intercultural communication. For those who do recognize more profound implications as reflected in negotiation or in patterns of implicit assumption by which laws and regulations operate, the precise relationship to culture is still hard to define and articulate. And it is difficult to distill out of all the multidisciplinary resources that could be directed to the field a consistent direction of inquiry that can be applied across the board to widely scattered subject matter and cultures.

To many diplomats, then, the intercultural communication field appears to offer most where they think they need it least, that is, at the sensitizing and experiential or descriptive level. In turn, it is vague and poorly prepared to offer intellectually challenging approaches for attacking the problems that diplomats face most urgently—communicating interculturally about abstract, value-laden subjects, where comprehension depends on interpreting the style and social meaning of communication, and appreciating the implicit assumptions and habits of perceiving and reasoning that go with culture's conditioning. For diplomats, "sensitization" needs to start at the more abstract level, or at least move quickly to emphasize the way that culture affects thinking about the substance of foreign affairs concerns and establishes the rationale for the way that people attack problems in complex organizations related to abstract issues.

Further, for diplomats the skill objective is to become one's own field diagnostician of factors that affect the intercultural communication process. This is different from simply receiving help to adjust to differing cultures. As was noted earlier, diplomats have to manage the process. Therefore, the intercultural communication field has to be able to supply a set of effective conceptual tools so that diplomats are prepared to ask the right questions more efficiently, to order their observations, to use local counsel and advice, and to organize the evidence of intercultural considerations into workable estimates of what is going on interculturally and of what can be done to address the problems identified.

This is not the kind of application that can be provided in a "briefing," or in abbreviated programs, even though these appeal to administrators who do not want officers to be away from their desks too long, or who do not want delays in arrival on new assignments—short-sighted as that might be. Unfortunately, it is probable that intercultural specialists have been too willing to accommodate to such imposed constraints, too willing to present the half-day seminar or provide the quick experiential exercise that will leave the client with a strong impression in a short time, but with not much increased intellectual ability to go further in cross-cultural analysis on their own.

## THE AGENDA FOR ADDRESSING
## INTERCULTURAL EFFECTIVENESS

Both diplomats and leaders in the intercultural field have a vested interest in considering where we go from here. So does the public, given the role that the diplomatic process plays in problem solving in today's world.

Perhaps the first consideration is to take further steps to establish the bona fides of the intercultural communication field as grounded in social science theory and research, and as a practical applied social science. Diplomats have to be convinced that the field offers a tested approach and a set of insights, usable by non-social scientists, that go beyond their own more habitually used body of knowledge derived from such disciplines as political science, economics, international relations, and area studies. This is a challenge then to intercultural specialists to be sure that they do in fact present a new amalgam of applied social science that, while probably borrowing heavily from existing fields such as communication theory, social psychology, social anthropology, and comparative sociology, does represent a disciplined and orderly contribution to knowledge in the tradition of scientific inquiry and application.

I recall some years ago being asked to talk to the Anthropological Society of Washington (D.C.) about the role of anthropology in international relations. As it happened, the well-known anthropologist Margaret Mead was resident in Washington that winter, and was asked to be the discussant—which drew a large audience. In her discussion time, someone complained that the government never asked anthropologists for their advice. Mead, who was impatient with the tendency at that time for anthropologists to concentrate at length on technical details of cultures rather than on application to larger contemporary problems, was scathing in her answer: "Suppose the government *did* ask you for advice. What would you have to tell them? *Kinship patterns?*" This may apply somewhat to the current state of the art in intercultural communication. Suppose the diplomats did ask for advice. Would there be any coherence in what intercultural specialists would tell them?[1]

This may pose the problem too starkly, especially as it implies a gulf between specialist and client that may not be warranted. The field is maturing as an applied social science, especially as it can draw the attention and contribution of behavioral scientists who address culture and the communication process. And diplomats have to take their share of responsibility in seeking out the resources that will help them cope with the cross-cultural nature of their endeavors. In any event, to summarize and propose an agenda for moving ahead in applying intercultural communication resources to diplomacy, the following four considerations are proposed:

*(1) Shift the balance in emphasis in the intercultural communication field toward culture's impact on value orientations, social priorities, thought processes, ideas, implicit assumptions, and styles of reasoning and debate.* That is, address the problem of communicating about abstract ideas and the subjects that command attention at the institutional level as compared with the person-to-person end of the range. At the same time, while trying to introduce or sensitize clients to culture's role, stress application to communicating about abstract matters. This would lead to a more serious image for the intercultural communication field, and more likely invite cooperation in the inquiry from professionals in the diplomatic field.

*(2) Focus more clearly on conceptual tools that can be passed on to diplomats whose competence will need to be that of diagnosticians able to transfer their analytical approach from one country to another.* This is difficult as the field is inherently so interdisciplinary, and so much borrowing is in order from related behavioral science disciplines. The objective, however, is to achieve a much more coherent and transferable sense of scientific discipline for the intercultural communication field.

*(3) Give more attention to the full intercultural communication significance of language learning.* Diplomats are prepared to learn languages, and would be even more so if the effort were seen as part of the larger objective of achieving reliable communication—of which language is only a part. Diplomats know this in an imprecise way, but they find little consistent help in exploring techniques by which language learning becomes an entry into the thought processes of another culture. At a time when language translation is being trivialized by turning to computer technology to make it all easier, the intercultural communication field can contribute to effective diplomacy by stressing the nonmechanical aspects of what is going on as communication crosses language barriers. The need is to place more emphasis on the relationship between culture and sub-

jective meaning, and on reexamining the implications carried in the Whor-fian hypothesis (Whorf, 1964) that states that differing languages present differing worlds of experience and thought; in effect, that they present differing mind-sets by which speakers of a language view the world and its events. The significance for diplomacy could hardly be overestimated.

*(4) Seek more effective linkage between the intercultural communication inquiry and area studies.* Diplomats are reasonably convinced of the need to do their homework in dealing with societies foreign to them. But they tend to see the objective of area study as simply accumulating descriptive fact and data useful as background rather than more purpose-fully comprehending the mind-sets that can be expected when people are enculturated in the kind of society studied. Trying to understand patterns of perception and reasoning can supply a rationale for area study and lend the sense of coherence and discipline to the effort that is now often lacking. Such an approach would also be useful for intercultural training as it would become easier to be culture-specific, a shortcoming that the clients often see in their intercultural communication advisers.

In conclusion, diplomacy is an example of a field in which intercultural communication consists most essentially of crossing cultural boundaries by which people in institutional settings are programmed to think and perceive differently about abstract institution-related subjects. This fact perhaps goes the furthest in defining priorities for both diplomats and intercultural communication specialists.

## EDITOR'S NOTE

1. I think the answer to this question is yes. Chapter 1 (Gudykunst & Nishida) in this volume presents the major theories used to explain intercultural communication. Many of these theories can be applied directly to diplomacy [WBG].

## REFERENCES

Barzini, L. (1983). *The Europeans.* New York: Simon & Schuster.
Benedict, R. (1946). *The chrysanthemum and the sword: Patterns of Japanese culture.* Boston: Houghton Mifflin.
Binnendijk, H. (Ed.). (1987). *National negotiating styles.* Washington, DC: Department of State, Foreign Service Institute.
Cohen, R. (1987). Problems of intercultural communication in Egyptian-American relations. *International Journal of Intercultural Relations, 11,* 29-47.
Cottam, M. L. (1986). *Foreign policy decision making: The influence of cognition.* Boulder, CO: Westview.
Department of State. (1987, January 2-14). Report on language training. *State Newsletter.* (Washington, DC)

Fisher, G. (1972). *Public diplomacy and the behavioral sciences*. Bloomington: Indiana University Press.

Fisher, G. (1980). *International negotiation: A cross-cultural perspective*. Yarmouth, ME: Intercultural Press.

Fisher, G. (1988). *Mindsets: The role of culture and perception in international relations*. Yarmouth, ME: Intercultural Press.

George, A. (1980). *Presidential decisionmaking in foreign policy: The effective use of information and advice*. Boulder, CO: Westview.

Glenn, E. S. (1981). *Man and mankind: Conflict and communication between cultures*. Norwood, NJ: Ablex.

Hall, E. T. (1959). *The silent language*. New York: Doubleday.

Hermann, M. G. (Ed.). (1986). *Political psychology: Contemporary problems and issues*. San Francisco: Jossey-Bass.

Jervis, R. (1976). *Perception and misperception in international politics*. Princeton, NJ: Princeton University Press.

Kelman, H. C. (1965). *International behavior: A social-psychological analysis*. New York: Holt.

Nicolson, H. (1950). *Diplomacy*. London: Oxford University Press. (Original work published 1939)

Rossow, R. (1962). The professionalization of the new diplomacy. *World Politics, 14*, 561-575.

Stewart, E. C. (1972). *American cultural patterns: A cross-cultural perspective*. Yarmouth, ME: Intercultural Press.

White, R. (1984). *Fearful warriors: A psychological profile of U.S.-Soviet relations*. New York: Free Press.

Whorf, B. L. (1964). *Language, thought and reality*. Cambridge: MIT Press.

# 20 National Development

## Njoku E. Awa

If the eighteenth was the century of the industrial revolution in Western Europe and North America and the nineteenth that of mass production and the birth of the consumer society in the West, then the twentieth is the century of decolonization and development in the Third World. The term *Third World,* which has supplanted the disparaging *underdeveloped,* refers to the countries of Africa, Asia, and Latin America, where many aspects of human activity and human institutions are currently being transformed. In the West, the transformation of social and economic institutions—that is, the adaptation of existing institutions to changing functions—occurred gradually, sometimes over several centuries, and change was evolutionary, occurring mostly by autonomous diffusion. In current Third World countries, by contrast, change is rapid, sometimes abrupt; it is induced deliberately by the "modernizing elite" or change agents, and most if not all of the new ideas and practices that people are exhorted to adopt are of foreign origin (Black, 1966; Esman, 1969).

The challenge facing the Third World is how to accomplish in a few years what it took Western Europe and North America several centuries to do. This challenge raises questions often ignored in social science research and in the analysis of Third World accomplishments. Is there a practical, as opposed to a psychological, need to catch up with those countries that started earlier in the development process? If some societies are developed and others are developing, how do we determine the latter's position on the development continuum when the former have not stopped developing? Is it possible for development experts—domestic and foreign—to understand the social and cultural needs of farmers without listening to the farmers? Should development culminate in what Hamelink (1983, p. 26) calls "transnational cultural synchronization"?

What might happen to peasants who have yet to develop the mental flexibility necessary to process dissonant information, such as the slogan based on Western economic rationality and used in family planning campaigns: "Small families are happy families"? The majority of Third World cultures hold that large families are happy families, because of the value of children as part of the labor force in subsistence farming and their function as a sort of retirement annuity when their parents are old and senile. Western cultures encourage individualism and prize individualized self-fulfillment; and as Phillips and Metzger (1976, p. 78) note, "we are each to have our own drummer, and each to march in our own parade." In contrast, most Third World cultures encourage communal feeling and collective action. They value the extended kinship patterns that interweave individuals and groups in deference and respect to form the very fabric of society (Awa, 1980).

These various questions address widely different aspects of social and economic life in societies at different points on the development continuum. What holds them together is their common basis in an understanding of the idea of development. This chapter explores the concept of development, its dimensions and foci, and examines three critical issues— planning, decentralization, and participation—in national development.

## THE CONCEPT OF DEVELOPMENT

Several terms have been used to describe the process by which social change occurs in society. Some of these candidates (as Frey, 1973, p. 340, calls them)—*growth, industrialization, modernization, Europeanization, Westernization, sociocultural evolution,* and even *Christianization*—have won adherents. Although they may be useful in understanding the historical adaptation of organisms to changing situations, they are inappropriate for describing and measuring the phenomena of interest in national development. Some, *growth* for example, are too broad, whereas others, such as *industrialization*, are too narrow. Still others, *Westernization* and *modernization*, for example, are ambiguously parochial, highly ethnocentric, and teleologically problematic (Elliott & Golding, 1973; Frey, 1973). These last terms assume a rigid wall, a dichotomy between modernity and tradition.

A traditional society generally is thought of as static, rural, and ascriptive, and modern society is seen as dynamic, industrialized, urbanized, and rational. Such notions have a kernel of truth, but as generalizations they mask behaviors and values that are *etic* in nature. In fact, all societies incorporate both traditional and modern values: consider the rituals associated with the coronation in Britain and libation ceremonies performed by even the most Westernized of the African elite.

*Modernization* is hard to conceptualize or measure because different scholars offer different definitions. Black (1966, p. 7), for example, defines modernization as "the process by which historically evolved institutions are adapted to the rapidly changing functions that reflect the unprecedented increase in man's knowledge, permitting control over his environment, that accompanied the scientific revolution." But Rogers (1969, p. 14) sees it as "the process by which individuals change from a traditional way of life to a more complex, technologically advanced, and rapidly changing style of life." According to Rogers, "modernization at the individual level corresponds to development at the societal level." So what Black sees as a macro-level process, Rogers sees as a micro-level one. These definitions are intellectually inadequate because they call attention to units of analysis that are sometimes mutually exclusive. Moreover, they are vague about the source of innovations. The term *modernization*—and even *development*, for that matter—neglects the impact of less industrialized societies on Western development and civilization: "It is easy to forget that India, China, Persia, and Egypt were old, old centers of civilization, and that their rich cultures had in fact provided the basis for contemporary Western cultures" (Rogers, 1986, p. 4). Yet as Black (1966, p. 9) asserts, even "the most advanced countries are still modernizing, and it is only by an effort of the imagination that one can conjecture" which of their characteristics are likely to be *emic* and which are purely *etic*.

More recently, development experts have begun to conceive of development in operational terms and to demand that it be measurable. Two approaches, basic needs and human development, bear examination. The *basic needs approach* to development places priority on meeting the basic needs for food, clothing, shelter, education, water, and sanitation of all citizens so as to prevent illness, undernourishment, and the misery that is the concomitant of hunger and homelessness (Streeten et al., 1981). That these needs are met is evidence of a developed society. At the same time, adequate nutrition, housing, water supply, and universal education are prerequisites for further development and social change. The main drawback of this approach is its limited attention to physical needs, but, as advocates argue, the approach has the merit that "it provides a powerful basis for organizing analysis and policymaking" (Streeten et al., 1981, p. 23).

What about measurement? Streeten and his associates (1981, p. 69) suggest four broad approaches to measurement. The first is "adjustments to the GNP measure." They recognize the inherent deficiencies of orthodox indicators of social change and development, such as gross national product per capita, and suggest ways to capture some of the human welfare aspects of development and methods to improve transnational comparability of data. The second is the well-known *social indicators approach*, which seeks to define "nonmonetary measures of social progress." Related to this idea is the third of the approaches proposed by Streeten and his associates: social accounting systems, which provide "an organizing framework for some of the social indicators." The fourth approach is the development of composite indexes, using various social indicators to generate a single index of human and social development or of the "quality of life" in a given society. A fifth method is still rudimentary: to interview a sample of people and have each one place him- or herself on a basic needs scale (0 to 10), indicating whether his or her basic needs were being met more adequately than they were at some specified date in the past. These approaches can be adapted, *mutatis mutandis,* to measure human and social development in any given culture.

Similar are the tenets of the *human development group,* which emphasizes the development of people. The human development school argues that although development can be measured in "economic aggregates or technological and physical achievements," human development is the only "dimension of intrinsic worth" in national development. This school consists of development experts, practitioners, and scholars from both the North and the South. It emphasizes the development of human resources in terms of (a) education, including training in basic sciences in Third World countries, because technology cannot flourish in societies where illiteracy reigns supreme; (b) nutrition and health, which require simultaneous action in several sectors—agriculture, public health (immunization and diarrhea disease control), basic health education, and mass media support in spreading information and helping to mobilize nationwide action; (c) enhancement of the position of women through the liberalization of educational opportunities for women and the promotion of women's involvement in decisions affecting their lives, families, and communities; and (d) the new scientific and technological revolutions taking place in such disparate areas as informatics, biotechnology, materials, and energy. These technologies, the human development school says, can be harnessed to the central purpose of development, that is, the human factor in national development (Haq & Kirdar, 1986). In the human development perspective, the problem of measurement has not been adequately addressed, but advocates explicitly support a central role for women in development and allude to measurement in terms of indicators "measuring the physical health and well-being of people—such as life expectancy, infant mortality rates, rates of morbidity, levels of nutrition and literacy rates—as well as nonphysical indicators to measure achievement in employment (in quantity and quality), social cohesions and stability, and political liberty" (Haq & Kirdar, 1986, p. 3).

## DIMENSIONS OF DEVELOPMENT

Problems of conceptualization arise when scholars see their own discipline as the sole or primary engine of change in a society. A competition for disciplinary primacy among scholars in the development field results in different emphases on economic development, educational development, political development, media development, and so forth.

Initially economic growth was seen as the primary goal of national development. Affluence was, axiomatically, the measure of happiness. But affluence, as one astute commentator on economic development asserts, does not translate into happiness, or Americans would be the happiest people in the world:

> Comparison on a happiness scale with non-Western peoples is difficult, but among Western peoples Americans are probably the most anxious, that is, the least happy. The simple evidence is that in addition to tranquilizers, sleeping pills, pep pills, pills to relieve headaches, and potions to relieve stomach distress that Americans can buy across the drugstore counter without a prescription and in addition to the illicit drugs to which a number of Americans resort, almost one half of American adults must relieve the anxiety of their lives or mitigate their state of depression by taking tranquilizers, soporics, or antidepressant medications so dangerous that they can be obtained legally only through prescription by a physician. Historical accounts of American colonial life do not leave one sure that Americans of the 20th century are happier than were their colonial forebears at a time when per capita income was perhaps $250 or $300 per year. The contrary seems more likely. (Hagen, 1980, p. 10)

If early development policies and decisions had been informed by Hagen's observations, development planning might not have been premised on the argument that the ascent of a country to affluence increases its happiness and earns for it the respect of other, equally affluent societies. Nevertheless, it is certainly true that economic growth is a vital component of national development. Economic growth must, however, be seen in perspective—how it influences and is influenced by growth in other sectors.

Rostow's stage-analytic model of economic development postulates an initial stage of traditional, predominantly agricultural society with a small market sector "whose penetration by market-orientated forces is essential to the developmental process" (Frey, 1973, p. 369). Especially at the "takeoff" stage, characterized by "the existence or quick emergence of a political, social and institutional framework which exploits the impulses to expansion in the modern sector and the potential external effect of the take-off and gives to growth an on-going character," Rostow assumes a corps of educated entrepreneurs and the availability of communication and information systems and technologies to facilitate interaction among development agencies (see Rostow, 1960, p. 38). Communication is an inevitable tool in promoting the objectives of the fifth stage of the Rostowian model—mass consumption. But Rostow and other economists writing about economic growth often pay only lip service to the contribution of noneconomic factors to national development. Hagen (1962, p. 37, n. 2) cites two eminent economists who have acknowledged the role of social attitudes, risk-taking behavior, and political climate in accelerating economic development but concludes that "virtually without exception, the economists who make such acknowledgements in passing then proceed to present economic theories of growth as if they were the full and sufficient explanations."

The same is true of the scholars who wrote about the value of education in the development enterprise and the political scientists who saw political development as the key to understanding the dynamics of change in the postindependence era. The field of communication, whose potential to catalyze rapid change was not initially apparent in the Third World, later made its appearance on the development scene and carved a niche for itself as a potent engine of change and national development. Lerner's (1958) study of modernization in the Middle East, Iran, and Turkey showed how participation in the network of public communication especially helped transitionals to gain awareness of events occurring in remote places, thereby widening their horizons and familiarizing them with a range of opinions and beliefs held by other people. In this way, that is, through vicarious experience, transitionals developed empathy, "the basic communication skill required of modern men" (Lerner, 1958, p. 412). Lerner's book, *The Passing of Traditional Society*, was the culmination of a ten-year study of the dynamics of change and of the comparative effectiveness of oral versus modern media channels in fostering psychic mobility. His findings, most of which are incontrovertible, showed that the media spread mobility more efficiently than oral tradition among those who have "achieved in some measure the antecedent conditions of geographic and social mobility" (p. 55). Of greater significance to our discussion is Lerner's proclamation, "No modern society functions efficiently without a developed system of mass media." This statement was taken literally by development agencies and Third World leaders. As a result, Third World countries built impressive media houses and infrastructures, and foreign aid policies changed dramatically toward the use of modern communication channels in the service of national development.

The idea that mass communication could of itself cause or influence social change may, in retrospect, seem overly optimistic. But most of the arguments advanced by the principal actors in the development communication drama—Lerner, Rogers, Schramm, and Ithiel de Sola Pool—

sounded plausible at the time. Moreover, the theoretical position on mass communication posited by Lerner was itself consistent with the central paradigm of diffusion research championed by Rogers. Rogers's research on the diffusion of new ideas and practices, especially in agriculture, demonstrated the value of communication in agricultural and economic development and helped the field of communication establish the hegemony it has enjoyed in the development enterprise since the mid-1960s. And as time went on, communication indicators became the predominant measures of media, and by extension, national development. The minimum standards of media development established by UNESCO in the post-independence period were as follows:

100 copies of daily newspapers per 1,000 population
50 radio receivers per 1,000 population
20 cinema seats per 1,000 population
20 television receivers per 1,000 population

General agreement on the pressing need for a mass communication network, and the value of such a network in effecting rapid and radical change, concealed crucial disadvantages (Awa, 1982, pp. 9-11). Perhaps the most important was that no feedback mechanism was incorporated into the media network—indeed, no attempt was made to design such mechanisms. Development communication moved in only one direction, downward from the designers and executors of development programs, and change agents received from their clients no clues on the effectiveness, or even the acceptability, of new programs.

Message treatment, the adaptation of change-oriented messages to the specific needs and aspirations of different segments of the population, also was largely ignored. Innovations were accepted or rejected at different rates by different peoples in different regions. Inequalities sprang up: Those (usually rich) clients who accepted the process received higher returns, and received them earlier, than those (usually poor) clients who accepted them later and less willingly. Because of this variation, the rich were able to acquire additional resources while the social and economic values of those resources were still relatively low. The rich became richer as these disparities became entrenched. Gain multiplied gain, and the gap between the haves and the have-nots grew ever wider.

Another disadvantage, as Tunstall (1977, pp. 210-211) notes with regard to Schramm, is that "Schramm's book urged the developing nations to move towards a full-scale modern media system" without mentioning the choices that must be confronted in operating complex and highly sophisticated media systems. Consequently, "there are no real policy recommendations—just that more and more media are a good thing, because they speed up modernization as Lerner . . . had shown." In practice, however, there is a policy vacuum in many Third World nations. The majority of Third World countries have a fuzzy notion of press freedom, and some have shown active interest in the debate on a New World Information and Communication Order without telling the world what their domestic policies are. As Ekwelie (1985, p. 29) notes, "instead of turning world forums into 'Wailing Walls', each country should endeavour to solve its own internal information-sharing problems." According to Ekwelie, there has been no change in the pattern of development introduced in Africa in the mid-1960s: The media are still based in urban areas, making it difficult for them to fulfill the functions envisaged by Lerner in rural communities; government monopoly of the broadcast media has not changed, so these media are largely devoted to government "propaganda." Ironically, government-owned media, including radio, television, and newspapers, have no clear mandate to make development communication a top priority.

Several conferences have been convened by UNESCO to examine the ideological context of communication policy, especially the "role of the state in the formulation of a national, coherent and corrective policy" (UNESCO, 1974, p. 6). The Bogotá meeting of international experts in the early 1970s defined communication policy as "a set of prescriptions and norms laid down to guide the behavior of communication institutions in a country" and stressed the importance of linking national development policy with communication policy. The conferees felt it was necessary "to link the concept of development with that of social change and public participation so that the vast majority of the population would be integrated in this fundamental process of mass communication" (p. 7). But as we hear from Ekwelie (1985, p. 28), the system established by foreign communication experts in the Third World has become entrenched: "All in all, infrastructural deprivation, cultural impediments, political intolerance, lack of media skill and professionalism, official [penchants] for excessive secrecy, poverty and the lack of will to try new methods of communication or adjust the old to local conditions—have contributed to making the mass media a poor servant of development." Ekwelie recapitulates the consequences of urging Third World countries to move toward a full-scale modern media system without considering media policies and the need to adapt media content and format to the cultural norms and tendencies of a given country.

Lack of explicit policy for the media in Third World countries has added a new dimension to the historical impediments to communication planning in national development programs. These impediments, according to Hancock (1983), include the following:

(a) "The relative low status and priority attached to communication"—despite the exaggerated promise of the Lerner paradigm and the inordinate power he assigned to communication in the service of national development, most government agencies have little faith in the ability of mass communication to transform their societies. The result, in many cases, is that communication is seldom integrated into national development plans. Usually, it is appended to a blueprint when obstacles to program implementation reveal deficiencies in communication strategies developed ad hoc by program implementers.

(b) "The professional interests of communicators themselves"—which are seldom developmental. Third World journalists and film producers, who received their training in Western Europe and North America saw little about development in their textbooks.

(c) "The identification of communication, in general, with activities which are commonly financed or assessed on profitability grounds"—initially, Third World leaders were unconvinced about the role of communication in catalyzing rapid change. They expected tangible benefits from programs that involved massive media—radio, film, and television—campaigns. Unfortunately, such campaigns did not always produce tangible benefits, as measured, for example, by the number of people who adopted a particular innovation as a direct result of a media campaign. Perhaps if Third World leaders had been told early in the development decade of the 1960s about the power and limitations of mass communication in changing attitudes and behaviors, they might have developed a more pragmatic orientation toward communication and change.

(d) "The traditional reticence of communication research"—which often seeks respectability and scientism. In development communication research, vigorous manipulation of statistical data is sometimes unnecessary but the researcher's need to publish in reputable journals often results in the identification of problems already studied in the West, which lend themselves to established quantitative techniques. The problem, however, is that variables derived from Western theories are sometimes hard to generate in their pure forms in non-Western cultures.

The optimism of early communication experts seems in retrospect to have created a "revolution of rising expectations" about the power of the media to accelerate the pace of social change. Because of the cluster of factors discussed above, the mass media have been unable to achieve the miracles Third World leaders were led to expect. There has been, in consequence, a counterrevolution of "rising frustrations" both on the part of Third World leaders, who expect media professionals to do "something" to make their (the leaders') development dreams come true, and on the part of media professionals whose training in the West causes them to relegate development communication and related activities to the background.

## CRITICAL ISSUES IN
## NATIONAL DEVELOPMENT

Development is a multifactorial phenomenon that defies universal precepts and the myth of unidirectionality. There are, nevertheless, lessons of experience that people in the development enterprise cannot ignore. One of these is development planning, which includes program implementation and evaluation, decentralization, and participation.

### Development Planning

Planning has been defined by Waterston (1969, p. 8) as "an organized, intelligent attempt to select the best available alternatives to achieve specific goals." Planning represents

> the rational application of human knowledge to the process of reaching decisions which are to serve as the basis of human action. The central core of the meaning remains the establishment of relationships between means and ends with the object of achieving the latter by the most efficient use of the former. (Sociedad Inter Americana de Planificacion, quoted in Waterston, 1969)

Planning is thus the application of intelligence to the analysis of current situations and the search for strategies to solve specific problems in a town, region, or nation. In Africa, Asia, and Latin America, development requires social, cultural, and political change, as well as economic growth.

Development planning emphasizes growth, progress, or movement from a less desirable to a more desirable state. It is predicated on two related assumptions. First, problems exist—lack of pipe-borne water supply, lack of electricity and basic agricultural infrastructure, and lack of health delivery systems. Second, these problems and the harms they cause to society cannot be eliminated under current institutional and other arrangements. As a result, a plan needs to be formulated to select the most feasible strategy to tackle them. Planning helps a society translate development dreams into realities.

To be effective, development plans must have goals and objectives (Foote, 1985). Goals are broad (often abstract) statements of desired states; objectives are narrow and operational statements specifying the end-states of intervention programs. Good planning begins with analysis of existing problems and the identification of what ought to be. The types of data needed for planning are often dictated by the nature of the plan, but all development plans require data on human and natural resources. Thus, as Waterston (1969, p. 173) asserts:

> Planning for enlarging the . . . output of agriculture requires knowledge about the nature of soils and the current and potential uses of land. For the development of mining or petroleum industries, data on incidence, extent, and location of mineral deposits are necessary. For planning irrigation or other waterworks, hydroelectric power projects and the development of river basins, facts about the supply, and the rate and periodicity of water flows are needed.

Planning is no stranger to Third World countries. There is not a single nation that does not engage in periodic planning. But most countries make plans that are either difficult to implement (because plans are seldom accompanied by implementation plans) or discarded after a year or two (because of a military coup or even a nonviolent overthrow of an existing regime). One major impediment to development planning in the Third World is the absence of good, reliable data. Even in those countries where agriculture is the most important sector, reliable information on soil characteristics and land resources is generally lacking. Because Third World leaders hoard information, and sometimes manipulate information to promote their own interests or those of the party in power, good data are hard to come by. Sometimes data supplied by national governments are fabricated and development plans based on such data do more harm than good to the countries concerned. It is necessary, therefore, to pay adequate attention to factors that affect development planning so as to improve the quality of development plans and planning data.

## Implementation

Development plans in and of themselves do not ensure that action will be taken and progress made. In Third World countries, program implementation is often hampered by politics, ethnic cleavages, and poor communication. Political instability often causes a program designed by a deposed leader, no matter how good it may seem, to be scrapped by his successor. Military takeovers, after all, are often justified by charges about corruption and ineptitude of the erstwhile regime, so it would make little sense for a revolutionary leader to adopt the program and policies of a discredited regime.

Ethnicity also has a profound impact on program implementation. Like many countries in the industrialized West, Third World nations are characterized by ethnic pluralism. Unlike in the former, however, the loyalty of the majority of Third World leaders is first to the tribe and only then to the nation. So program implementation, including the speed with which it is executed, is determined by a number of ethnically related factors: What tribe benefits most from the program? Where is the new program located, in which part of the country? Who is the director of the program?

Poor communication is unplanned communication strategy. Until recently, programs across the Third World were implemented without a communication plan to guide the actions of the principal implementing agency and its relationships with agencies or organizations that shared its objectives. The situation is now changing. Development agencies no longer pay mere lip service to the need to formulate communication plans to guide their actions in program implementation.

## Evaluation

Development is a continuous process. Without periodic evaluation, deviation from project goals will be detected only after mistakes have been made. Lack of accurate and timely reports often hampers attempts at evaluation. Waterston (1969, p. 356) laments that, in Third World countries, information provided is often

> too vague and sketchy for a central planning agency to be able to assess the progress made. Progress may be reported in percentage terms without adequate criteria for determining whether the progress made is better, worse or equal to what had been expected. Many operating agencies do not establish physical and financial criteria against which to measure programs, nor do they maintain up-to-date records on the physical and financial progress of their projects. They, therefore cannot furnish accurate and meaningful information on the status of their projects or programs.

These problems are exacerbated by the general inadequacy and tardiness of reports prepared for central planners by program implementation personnel. Finally, in some countries the forms used for submitting progress reports are cumbersome, and junior officials find them difficult to complete (Haq, 1963).

Experience has taught us that evaluation implies much more than program assessment in terms of input-output analysis. Evaluation is blossoming into a science in its own right, with its unique language, methods, and metaphors. Rossi, Freeman, and Wright (1979, p. 32) identify four types of evaluations: research for development or program planning, program monitoring, impact assessment, and research on project efficiency. The primary value of evaluation research in development planning and implementation is that it allows change agencies to estimate with relative accuracy the resources (human, financial, and technological) needed to implement a program and the extent to which a program meets the need it was designed to serve. Also, evaluation helps program designers detect unanticipated obstacles to program implementation and allows them to take corrective action before it is too late.

## Decentralization

Studies from several parts of the Third World show that while decentralization has resulted in administrative efficiency, especially from the point of view of program implementation, it is not an unmitigated blessing. According to Cheema and Rondinelli (1983, p. 295), decentralization has meant different things to different countries. In India, the Sudan, and Tanzania, for example, it has meant delegating decision-making authority to local governments; in Argentina, Brazil, Mexico, and Venezuela, it has involved assigning specific planning and administrative functions to "semiautonomous organizations." In other regions of the Third World, North Africa and Southeast and South Asia, for example, governments have delegated specific development functions to district or provincial administrative units. And in a few, decentralization has meant debureaucratization as functions previously performed by governments have been transferred to voluntary organizations or the private sector.

Motivations vary for decentralizing planning and management. Among factors frustrating the implementation of decentralization are sociocultural traditions in North Africa, "traditional deference to authority, reluctance of lower-level officials to disagree openly with superiors, . . . and vestiges of colonial behaviors in East Africa" (Cheema & Rondinelli, 1983, p. 308). In Asia, an inegalitarian power structure, "which gives a dominant position to the rural elite," prevented a large number of the rural poor from participating in voluntary organizations. But in many instances the overwhelming impediment was resource scarcity. Cheema and Rondinelli say that more studies are needed on factors affecting the design and implementation of decentralization policies in the Third World: Decentralization provides a rich and rewarding research agenda through which development scholars, policy analysts, and practitioners can help refine and improve the implementation of decentralization policies in developing countries.

### Participation

The meanings of words change frequently and from discipline to discipline. Changes occur through generalization, as when meaning is relaxed to embrace a broader concept; specialization, as when meaning is narrowed to give the word a specific or delicate nuance; elevation, as when a word rises in prestige; and degradation, as when changes occur in denotative meaning, from neutral to pejorative (Lodwig & Barrett, 1973). *Participation* has come to mean different things to different people. In communication and allied fields, the word is used almost interchangeably with *talking*—thus, for instance, "in learning and discussion groups we ask facilitators to encourage participation, to find ingenious ways to motivate the reticent to participate" (Awa, 1986, p. 1). In this sense, *participation* means not just being present but being actively involved. Describing the characteristics of a good participant in group meetings, Bormann (1975, p. 338), a group dynamicist, illuminated the similarity in meaning between *participation* and *talking*: "A participant contributes to the program with his full ability. His comments are short and to the point. He gears his contribution exactly to the topic and develops only one point at a time." Sometimes, however, the term is used euphemistically to elevate the social importance of a behavior. In *The Passing of Traditional*

*Society*, for example, Lerner (1958/1966) refers to voting as "political participation" and to TV viewing, radio listening, newspaper and magazine reading, and the like as "media participation."

In the field of organizational behavior, *participation* has a slightly different meaning. The word is used chiefly to describe a particular type of leadership style, management approach, and decision-making strategy. Likert (1961), an advocate of participative management, classifies management systems in a fourfold typology: (a) exploitative-authoritative, (b) benevolent-authoritative, (c) consultative, and (d) participative-group. The first two categories reflect the assumptions of classical organizational theory, which holds that it is legitimate for a leader to make unilateral decisions and to assume major responsibility for directing, coordinating, and evaluating the performance of workers. Authoritative systems treat workers not as individuals but as objects to be manipulated by management: They are rewarded when they meet management's expectations or perform above par, punished when they perform below par. The third category, the consultative, straddles the divide between authoritative and participative styles. Such management systems encourage upward communication and cooperation between managers and workers, yet managers have little "confidence in workers' ability to make adequate organizational decisions" (Kreps, 1986, p. 93).

The fourth system enlists workers as full participants in different facets of organizational activity—goal setting, decision making, and policy implementation. It fosters trust and builds highly cohesive work groups in an organization. According to Likert, participative-group management makes for high productivity, because workers attracted to the organization presumably want it to succeed and "so work harder to achieve the goals of the organization" (Shaw, 1981, p. 222).

Shaw's assertion reflects an underlying hypothesis about organizational behavior: the more cohesive the group, the higher its productivity. This hypothesis has been tested in laboratory and field experiments and found to be generally valid. The evidence is likely to be equivocal, however, if we study groups working toward a goal set by external agencies without input from group members. Where outside agencies set goals, in other words, the result is an attenuation of the effect of cohesiveness on productivity. Rural development projects all too frequently fit this description: They are planned by outside agencies, some of them domestic, and operating from capital cities, others international, but all perceived by local people as remote and foreign.

One can look at participation in rural development from two perspectives: that of classical theory, which emphasizes organizational structure and control, and that of the human relations theory of organization, which sees human beings as the essence of human organization and the proper object of study in psychology. Humanistic psychology arose in revolt against the positivistic epistemology of behaviorism and the associationism of classical psychoanalysis. Behavioral psychology suggests that "people's actions are determined by the external environment" (Crider et al., 1983, p. 23); psychoanalysis, on the other hand, suggests that human behavior is regulated by unconscious, internal motivations or drives. Humanistic psychology rejects both the external explanation of behaviorism and the internal explanation of psychoanalysis. Instead, humanistic psychologists present human beings as inherently good, making social pressures and social constraints responsible for the inability of some people to realize their full potential.

Abraham Maslow and Carl Rogers, two leading figures in humanistic psychology, think psychologists need to place more emphasis on "what a person is like as an adult, how people perceive the world around them, how they feel, how they understand their own behavior, and how they grow and develop their full capacities" (quoted in Crider et al., 1983, p. 412). The self-actualization model proposed by human relations theorists (e.g., Maslow, 1954) repudiates the tenets of the classical theory of organization, one of which is that human beings prefer to be directed, wish to avoid responsibility, have "relatively little ambition," and want "security above all" (see McGregor, 1960, p. 34). As Kreps (1986, p. 91) observes, human relations theorists "identify human beings as mature, responsible individuals who will participate actively in organizational activities [including decision making and goal setting] if given proper opportunity and personal reinforcement (self-actualization)."

Humanistic psychology and the human relations school constitute the moving force behind a theory of participation in rural development. A useful working definition is offered by Davis (1977, p. 140): Participation is the "mental and emotional involvement of persons in group situations that encourage them to contribute to group goals and share responsibility for them." Three important ideas emerge from this definition: participation requires (a) mental and emotional involvement, not just mere physical presence; (b) a motivation to contribute, which requires creative thinking and initiative; and (c) an acceptance of responsibility, which involves seeing organizational problems as corporate problems—"ours," not "theirs" (see Awa, 1986, pp. 4-5).

This understanding of the active, involved nature of participation carries important implications for the successes and failures of rural development programs. Participation in rural development will be effective, we may hypothesize, if the following conditions are met:

– The subject of participation is relevant to the needs, wants, and aspirations of local people.

- The participants have the ability—knowledge, intelligence, and group problem-solving skills—to contribute ideas and opinions and to ask pertinent
questions related to goal clarity and goal-path clarity. Davis (1977, p. 143)
observes that "it is hardly advisable . . . to ask janitors in a pharmaceutical
laboratory to participate in deciding which of five chemical formulas deserves
research priority." The example is a powerful one, implying strongly that local
leaders and potential participants in rural development planning and project
evaluation need to be trained in the principles of group dynamics and group
problem-solving techniques.
- The participants are able to talk each other's language.
- Development experts and local groups interact in a climate devoid of threat.
Human beings, we assume, want to be treated with respect and empathy.
Recently, one major research institution in New York started housing students
in townhouses rather than in institutionlike dormitories, on the assumption that
students, when treated like mature and responsible adults, will behave less like
students. Preliminary results show students in the townhouse behaving much
more responsibly than those in crowded dormitories.

Adherence to some of the principles of the human relations school of
organizational theory and humanistic psychology will, through participative management of rural development programs, produce results more
beneficial than those likely from following the authoritative and paternalistic doctrine of classical theory. Currently, most intervention agencies use the consultative system of management, which is characterized
by moderate interaction with subordinate groups and a reasonable amount
of confidence and trust. Obviously, the consultative system is better than
the authoritative, father-knows-best approach, but it still allows those in
a superior position (development agencies) to define development priorities and to determine when and to what extent those in subordinate
positions (the clientele) can participate. This is at best a truncated version of participation. It assumes complementarity (a "one-up" and "one-
down" relationship) in interactions between development agencies and
rural communities. It is the antithesis of the participative-group system,
which involves input—knowledge, intuition, expectations, and aspirations—from both parties.


## CONCLUSION

What needs to be stressed is that national development is a complex
process that defies the myth of unidirectionality as reflected in some of
the early terms used in defining the concept. At first emphasis was on
economic growth, but later it was discovered that national development is
a total process involving not only economic change but also social, politi-

cal, and agricultural transformation of a given society. Consequently, emphasis has shifted from a preoccupation with single elements of the development process to a holistic view. And, contrary to the old paternalistic development paradigm, the emerging paradigm "stresses the importance of local considerations in the formulation of development policies and programs" (Hope, 1984, p. 11). In addition to participation, indigenous knowledge has also come to play an important role in both rural and national development.

## REFERENCES

Awa, N. E. (1980). *Continuity and change in traditional and modern communication systems in Africa.* Paper presented at the annual conference of the International Communication Association, Acapulco, Mexico.

Awa, N. E. (1982). Mass communication and change in Africa: Implications for the Commonwealth Caribbean. *Journal of Black Studies, 13,* 1-10.

Awa, N. E. (1986). *The concept of participation in national development.* Paper presented at the annual conference of the International Communication Association, Chicago.

Awa, N. E. (1987). Bringing indigenous knowledge into planning. *Media Development, 34,* 22-24.

Black, C. E. (1966). *The dynamics of modernization.* New York: Harper & Row.

Bormann, E. G. (1975). *Discussion and group methods: Theory and practice* (2nd ed.). New York: Harper & Row.

Cheema, S. G., & Rondinelli, D. A. (Eds.). (1983). *Decentralization and development: Policy implementation in developing countries.* Beverly Hills, CA: Sage.

Crider, A. B., Goethals, G. R., Kavanough, R. D., & Solomon, P. R. (1983). *Psychology.* Glenview, IL: Scott, Foresman.

Davis, K. (1977). *Human behavior at work: Organizational behavior* (5th ed.). New York: McGraw-Hill.

Ekwelie, S. A. (1985). African nations must redirect information flow. *Media Development, 32,* 5.

Elliott, P., & Golding, P. (1973). Mass communication and social change. In E. Kadt & G. Williams (Eds.), *Society and development.* London: Tavistock.

Esman, M. J. (1969). Institution building as a guide to action. In D. Thomas & J. G. Fender (Eds.), *Proceedings: Conference on institution building.* Washington, DC: Agency for International Development.

Foote, J. S. (1985). *Communication planning.* Unpublished paper, Cornell University, Department of Communication, Communication Planning and Strategy Workshop, Ithaca, NY.

Frey, F. W. (1973). Communication and development. In I. S. Pool et al. (Eds.), *Handbook of communication.* Chicago: Rand McNally.

Hagen, E. M. (1962). *On the theory of social change.* Homewood, IL: Dorsey.

Hagen, E. M. (1980). *The economics of development.* Homewood, IL: Irwin.

Hamelink, C. J. (1983). *Cultural autonomy in global communications: Planning national information policy.* New York: Longman.

Hancock, A. (1983). *A communication planning scenario.* Unpublished manuscript, UNESCO, Paris.

Haq, M. U. (1963). *Strategy of economic planning: A case study of Pakistan.* Karachi: Oxford University Press.

Haq, K., & Kirdar, U. (Eds.). (1986). *Human development: The neglected dimension* (Papers prepared for the Istanbul Round Table, September 2-4, 1985). Islamabad, Pakistan: North South Round Table.

Hope, K. R. (1984). *The dynamics of development and development administration.* Westport, CT: Greenwood.

Kreps, G. L. (1986). *Organizational communication.* New York: Longman.

Lerner, D. (1958). *The passing of traditional society: Modernizing the Middle East.* New York: Free Press. (Reprinted 1966)

Likert, R. (1961). *New patterns of management.* New York: McGraw-Hill.

Lodwig, R. R., & Barrett, E. F. (1973). *Words, words, words: Vocabularies and dictionaries.* Rochelle Park, NJ: Hayden.

Maslow, A. H. (1954). *Motivation and personality.* New York: Harper & Row.

McGregor, D. (1960). *The human side of enterprise.* New York: McGraw-Hill.

Phillips, G. M., & Metzger, N. J. (1976). *Intimate communication.* Boston: Allyn & Bacon.

Pye, L. W. (1963). *Communication and political development.* Princeton, NJ: Princeton University Press.

Rogers, E. M. (1969). *Modernization among peasants; The impact of communication.* New York: Holt, Rinehart & Winston.

Rogers, E. M. (1986). *Perspectives on development communication.* Paper presented at the workshop, Communication Development, Pune University, Pune, India.

Rossi, P. H., Freeman, H. E., & Wright, S. R. (1979). *Evaluation: A systematic approach.* Beverly Hills, CA: Sage.

Rostow, W. W. (1960). The stage of economic growth. New York: Cambridge University Press.

Shaw, M. E. (1981). *Group dynamics: The psychology of small group behavior* (3rd ed.). New York: McGraw-Hill.

Streeten, P., with Burki, S. J., Haq, M. U., Hicks, N., & Stewart, S. (1981). *First things first: Meeting basic human needs in the developing countries.* London: Oxford University Press.

Tunstall, J. (1977). *The media are American: Anglo-American media in the world.* New York: Columbia University Press.

Ugboajah, F. O. (1985). "Oramedia" in Africa. In F. O. Ugboajah (Ed.), *Mass communication, culture and society in West Africa.* München: Hans Zell.

UNESCO. (1974). *Report of the meeting of experts on communication policies in Latin America.* Paris: Author.

Waterston, A. (1969). *Development planning: Lessons of experience.* Baltimore, MD: Johns Hopkins University Press.

Wilson, D. E. (1981). *From the gong to electronics: A survey of Trado-modern mass communication techniques in the Cross River State of Nigeria.* Unpublished master's thesis, University of Ibadan, Nigeria.

# 21 Intercultural Communication Training

## Richard W. Brislin

Intercultural communication training, also called intercultural or cross-cultural training, refers to planned efforts to assist adjustment when people are to live and work in cultures other than their own. Training can take place when people are to live in another country, or when they are to interact extensively with members of different cultures within their own nation. Common goals include reducing the stress and anxiety associated with the adjustment of both the individual and family members, assisting effective communication with culturally different others, giving guidelines for such work-related concepts as negotiation styles and management practices, and suggesting ways to develop support groups. More generally, intercultural training attempts to develop the qualities of effectiveness identified by scholars interested in adjustment to other cultures (Brislin, 1981; Dinges, 1983; Hammer, Chapter 11, this volume; Hammer, Gudykunst, & Wiseman, 1978; Chapter 13, Kim, this volume).

Intercultural training programs are marked by a number of factors. They are planned efforts scheduled for specific times. Programs have a budget and one or more staff members responsible for program content, administration, and support services. They take place in settings ideally that facilitate learning and interaction among participants and staff members. Programs can range in length from one hour to four months. The former would occur when an intercultural specialist has a limited amount of time with trainees who are receiving many other types of information. For instance, businesspersons might find themselves in a two-week program where economic, marketing, and finance in Asia are covered. They may receive only one hour of material that could be considered intercultural, such as differences in manager-to-subordinate communications in Asia compared to the United States. Such a time period, of course, is inadequate for any sort of serious effort, but such a time allotment is part of the status quo, which will hopefully change in the future.

Four-month programs can take place when administrators have a serious commitment to cross-cultural effectiveness and when extensive language training is part of the training package. Peace Corps personnel assigned to India, for instance, have participated in programs that lasted as long as four months.

## EFFECTS, AND, CONSEQUENTLY, REALISTIC GOALS, OF TRAINING

Several book-length treatments and collections present the assumptions, goals, methods, and outcomes of intercultural training in great detail (Brislin & Pedersen, 1976; Landis & Brislin, 1983; Martin, 1986; Paige, 1986). One way to examine the *goals* of training is to review research studies that have documented the *effects* of good programs. A list of documented effects provides a good set of realistic goals toward which others can aim in their new programs. The following list was begun by Brislin, Landis, and Brandt (1983) and has been updated based on recent research (e.g., Albert, 1986; Cushner & Broaddus, 1988; Lefley, 1985; Sharma & Jung, 1985). "Hosts" in the following paragraphs refer to people in the society where the trainees will eventually live and work.

### Cognitions

Training's impact on a person's thinking or cognitions includes greater understanding of hosts from *their* point of view. Trained individuals can be less willing to use negative, pejorative stereotypes and can be more willing to look beyond stereotypes and to consider individuals and their differences. Their thinking about other cultures can become more complex, and they can learn facts about other cultures that hosts themselves think are important. Trained individuals can identify the source of problems in a variety of intercultural encounters. In longer programs (approximately ten weeks), people can become more cosmopolitan, more world-minded, and more interested in international affairs.

### Affect

Changes in emotions, feelings, or affect include greater enjoyment while interacting with hosts. There can also be the more global feeling that people are enjoying their overseas stay or their extensive interaction with culturally different others in their own country. Such a feeling can be matched by hosts who observe that trained sojourners are indeed interacting effectively and are enjoying their assignments. Trained people have more self-insight into puzzling intercultural difficulties in their own lives. They can also learn to cope with the anxiety that inevitably accompanies intercultural interaction. The comfort stemming from successful interaction leads to fewer prejudicial attitudes in which physically different others are automatically given less attention and respect. Trained individuals can accept the viewpoint, perhaps on an emotional as well as a cognitive basis, that people in other cultures have different ways of accomplishing important goals, but that difference does not mean deficiency.

## Behavior

Behavioral effects include better working relations in multicultural groups working together on the same task. There is better coping with the stresses and strains of cross-cultural adjustment (e.g., less time needed to settle into one's work or to establish support groups) and a more realistic sense of goal setting for both the work and the social aspects of one's stay in another country. When aspects of visible behavior have a cultural component that can be addressed in training, there can be behavioral change indicative of better job performance. For instance, Lefley (1985) found that training could improve a therapist's problem-solving skills during counseling sessions with members of different cultural groups. Further, trained counselors were more effective problem solvers with clients from the lower socioeconomic classes within their society. The issue of increased job performance is delicate because clients would naturally like to see such changes, but intercultural trainers should not overpromise their potential contributions. The key point is whether or not the job performance has a cultural component that can be addressed effectively during training. O'Brien, Fiedler, and Hewett (1971) documented such a case among young health workers assigned to Honduras. Trained individuals were able to combine the culturally sensitive behavior of respect for elders with their task of hands-on health care (e.g., giving inoculations in a culture where young people do not have as much status as older people). With their newly gained knowledge of how to interact in a respectful way with elders, trained medical personnel were able to engage in more health delivery activities than untrained colleagues.

## THE CONTENT OF TRAINING

The positive effects of training just reviewed, of course, are dependent upon the content of a program. Long descriptions of possible content are available in a number of sources (Brislin & Pedersen, 1976; Gudykunst, Hammer, & Wiseman, 1977; Landis & Brislin, 1983; Martin, 1986; Paige, 1986; various issues of the *International Journal of Intercultural Relations*, 1977 to present). One way to summarize program content is to discuss combinations of three levels of trainee involvement crossed with three targets of training. The three involvement levels refer to the degree of trainee participation, and it ranges from passive reception of knowledge through very active collaboration with the trainers. The three targets of training refer to the three aspects of the cross-cultural experience already introduced: people's thinking or cognitions, their emotions or affect, and their behavior. A summary of the resulting three-by-three matrix is pictured in Table 21.1, which also summarizes examples of training methods that will now be discussed. This framework is designed to organize approaches to training rather than to create hard and fast categories. The way given trainers approach a certain method can place it in various cells, and some methods can address various aspects of the cross-cultural experience. For instance, very charismatic lecturers can engage people's emotions as well as their thinking, and they can also model desirable behaviors. The more typical use of the lecture will be covered here.

### Low Involvement Aimed at Cognitions

Trainees are often placed in the role of audience members who listen to facts delivered in a lecture format. The lectures are meant to increase trainee sophistication by giving them important information about the host culture or about the nature of cross-cultural adjustment. While sometimes dismissed in a cavalier manner by cross-cultural training specialists, lectures will probably always be a good method to employ in select circumstances. Time demands often work against the use of other techniques. A good lecturer, who can skillfully integrate visual aids, intriguing examples, and an enthusiastic tone, can often convey a great deal of information in a short time period. Further, a good lecturer can introduce basic concepts such as culture shock or culturally influenced decision-making styles that can be further examined through methods that demand more trainee involvement. Another technique that falls under this heading is assigned readings. Trainees might prepare for a group discussion by reading selected materials, provided by the trainer, the day before their more active involvement. The danger of these approaches is that too many facts are presented to trainees. Further, there are too many challenges to their memories and to their tolerance for fatigue. In addition, and in everyday language, too many lectures and assigned readings can lead to a dull program.

### Low Involvement Aimed at Affect

A variety of methods can be employed to increase the emotional involvement of trainees without incorporating their direct participation. These are useful, again, when there is limited time and when the training group is so large that division into small working groups is impossible.

**TABLE 21.1** Approaches to Cross-Cultural Training

| Amount of Trainee Involvement | Target of Training | | |
|---|---|---|---|
| | *Cognitions* | *Affect* | *Behavior* |
| Low* | lectures from experts; assigned readings | lectures from "old hands"; films; viewing cultural presentations, such as folk music or dance | presenting trainees with models who demonstrate appropriate behaviors |
| Moderate | attribution training; analysis of critical incidents | self-awareness; group discussions of prejudice, racism, values; participation in guided encounters such as restaurant visits | cognitive/behavioral training; field trip assignments that demand new behaviors |
| High | applying sophisticated concepts from the behavioral and social sciences (e.g., rules, labels, individualism-collectivism) | role-playing; simulations of real-life demands, such as negotiation with culturally different others | extended experiential encounters with another culture or complex approximations of another culture; guided practice of newly learned behaviors |

*Note that low involvement places trainees in the role of audience members.

The goal of these methods is to address the participants' emotions, such as interest in and enthusiasm about their upcoming intercultural experiences. Examples include lectures from "old hands" who have lived in the same culture and who have dealt with the same problems as those facing the trainees. Experience has shown that skillful old hands with at least minimal public speaking skills can be valuable additions to the training staff. Because trainees see the old hands as having made the necessary adjustment, they are often given more credence than the principal trainer. Recently returned sojourners often convey positive emotions about their experiences that are hard to convey through other means. A caveat is that "old hands" can sometimes relate all kinds of war stories that add up to no clear set of conclusions. A trainer will want to work closely with recent returnees to make sure that their stories and advice fit into the total program design. Of course, the returnees should be carefully selected because not all people who have lived and worked in other culture are good models for the next generation of sojourners.

The use of films can also be a good way of addressing affect. All readers of this chapter will be able to identify certain films that have engaged their emotions. Ideally, the emotional impact of a film (e.g., there are several concerned with doing business in Japan) can stimulate interest in a topic such that follow-up activities are received with increased trainee attention. The Society for Intercultural Education, Training, and Research (1505 22nd St., NW, Washington, D.C. 20037) can give guidance on the current availability of films and videotapes. Members of this organization can also give guidance on what films or tapes work best in different types of programs. Viewing artistic presentations from different cultures can also stimulate interest in a very different way than that possible through books and lectures.

## Low Involvement Aimed at Behavior

Trainers can stage-manage skits and demonstrations so that audience members can be exposed to behavior that is appropriate in other cultures. The suggested behaviors can be modeled by the trainer, assistants, old hands, actors playing the roles with which the training is concerned (e.g., businesspersons, diplomats), and members of the target culture. Possible behaviors for coverage include methods people use to greet each other (in general, proper nonverbal behaviors); the distance they stand from one another while conversing, as well as the angle formed by their bodies; and typical leisure time group activities in which outsiders have a difficult time participating. As an example of the type of demonstration, three or four American graduate students might sit at a table and engage in behaviors typical of Friday afternoon gatherings. They would tell jokes, complain about their professors (especially the statistics teacher), and discuss what they will do the rest of the weekend. Foreign students studying in the United States have difficulty integrating themselves in such groups because they do not understand the referents of the jokes, are unaccustomed to criticizing professors in public, and do not know if they are being purposely excluded from the others' discussions of weekend plans. A further aspect of the demonstration might involve foreign students who integrate themselves adequately into the group discussion. The word *adequately* is important. Research (Meichenbaum, 1977) suggests that the models should *not* be extraordinarily graceful and proficient in their behavior. If they are overly skillful, audience members may dismiss themselves by saying, "I'll never be that good." Rather, models should be just competent enough to demonstrate acceptable behaviors. They should make enough mistakes to show that they are like most audience members and readers of this chapter: We all stumble sometimes. Further, if models demonstrate mistakes, they can also demonstrate adequate recovery skills to follow up one's social blunders.

## Moderate Involvement Aimed at Cognitions

Training aimed at cognitions has the goal of expanding people's thinking about another culture or about the cross-cultural experience. Moderate involvement means that trainees participate in exercises under the watchful eye of an experienced staff. The exercises used are "tried and true" in the sense that they can engage trainees' interest without frustrating them because of their difficulty, emotional content, or behavioral skills not yet possessed.

The most researched approach is called "attribution training" (Albert, 1986) and it encourages trainees to analyze problems from the viewpoint of people in the host culture. Or, if the goal is to encourage more trainee sophistication about the nature of cross-cultural experiences, then the goal is to analyze problems from the viewpoint of the most knowledgeable researchers and practitioners in the field. The assumption is that if trainees learn to analyze problems according to other viewpoints, they will be more likely to adjust successfully. They will not be as likely to impose their own limited culture-bound viewpoint learned during their own socialization. In turn, hosts will be pleased that they are not being judged from an ethnocentric viewpoint and will be more likely to seek out sojourners and to assist in their adjustment.

The new learning can include conceptual tools for the analysis of problems such as "cultural relativity"; new scripts for appropriate behavior, such as how to criticize constructively according to a culture's norms; and new categories. New learning about the limitations of stereotypes is an example of category enlargement because stereotypes are a type of category that summarizes information about a specific group of people. A major goal of good training is that people must learn to *look behind* stereotypes and to admit individual differences. Further, adjustment is threatened if sojourners treat people like stereotypes. A good exercise (often blending with affective goals of training) is to ask trainees to think of a time in their lives when they were treated like a stereotype. How did they feel? Did they maintain a relationship with the person doing the stereotyping? Trainees can share their examples with others in a group discussion format.

A set of materials exist for increasing the sophistication of trainee thinking. Brislin, Cushner, Cherrie, and Yong (1986) have prepared 100 critical incidents as well as 18 essays that integrate points made in the 100 incidents. The incidents and essays deal with problems that are regularly faced by sojourners regardless of the cultures in which they will live. The incidents can also be used in culture-specific training because each deals with interactions among hosts and sojourners in a specific country. Here is one of the incidents:

Learning the Ropes

Helen Connor had been working in a Japanese Company involved in marketing cameras. She had been there for two years and was well-respected by her
colleagues. In fact, she was so respected that she often was asked to work with
new employees of the firm as these younger employees "learned the ropes."
One recent and young employee, Hideo Tanaka, was assigned to develop a
marketing scheme for a new model of camera. He worked quite hard on it, but
the scheme was not accepted by his superiors because of industry-wide
economic conditions. Helen Connor and Hideo Tanaka happened to be working at nearby desks when the news of the nonacceptance was transmitted from
company executives. Hideo Tanaka said very little at that point. That evening,
however, Helen and Hideo happened to be at the same bar. Hideo had been
drinking and vigorously criticized his superiors at work. Helen concluded that
Hideo was a very aggressive Japanese male and that she would have difficulty
working with him again in the future.

Which alternative provides an accurate statement about Helen's conclusion?

Readers then chose *one or more* of the following explanations.

1. Helen was making an inappropriate judgement about Hideo's traits based
on behavior that she observed.

2. Since, in Japan, decorum in public is highly valued, Helen reasonably
concluded that Hideo's vigorous criticism in the bar marks him as a difficult
coworker.

3. Company executives had failed to tell Helen and Hideo about economic
conditions, and consequently Helen should be upset with the executives, not
Hideo.

4. Helen felt that Hideo was attacking her personally.

Explanations for each of the alternatives are provided, and the points
made can be later reviewed in the 18 thematic essays that provide a
conceptual framework for the understanding and analysis of cross-cultural
interaction.

The incident will obviously be helpful for people adjusting to Japan. In
addition, it makes general points useful to all sojourners. Alternative one
is correct: There is a strong tendency to overinterpret colorful behaviors
and to make permanent conclusions. This is especially true in cross-
cultural interactions because a person has little knowledge about the host
culture and about what might be acceptable "time-out" behavior that
allows stress reduction. The point of widespread usefulness is that colorful
events should not be overinterpreted. People should consciously seek

additional information and should postpone making final judgments. Another alternative also has merit: alternative four. In cross-cultural interactions, there is the temptation to infer that nonstereotypical behavior somehow is due to the presence of sojourners. Again, quick conclusions of this sort are often wrong.

These materials have been used extensively in programs held all over the world (all continents except Antarctica). A caveat is that, because the 100 incidents are all written with the same interest-generating style involving well-meaning people trying to make sense out of a confusing world, trainees identify quickly with the issues addressed. They may want to discuss any one incident for such a long time that the trainer will sometimes feel dogmatic in suggesting that the group move on to other issues.

## Moderate Involvement Aimed at Affect

Cross-cultural interactions have a major impact on people's feelings and emotions. For instance, such interactions increase people's anxiety level above and beyond the level they experience while interacting with familiar others in their own culture. The anxiety can have somatic consequences such as headaches, difficulty sleeping, diarrhea, increased blood pressure, muscle tension, and queasiness in the stomach. One goal of training is to address such feelings without causing debilitating anxiety *during* training.

Techniques incorporating moderate participation allow the examination of emotions in a secure training setting. Exercises can include group discussions emphasizing self-awareness during which people can discuss cultural values in their own backgrounds that influence their current behavior. Typically, Americans discuss individualism, freedom, equality, access to the legal system for the redress of grievances, opportunities to rise above one's status at birth, and the pursuit of happiness. People from many of the Asian countries are likely to discuss the value placed on loyalty to a collective, the importance of hard work, and the role of education, moderation, thrift, and individual achievement so as not to burden one's ingroup (see Hui & Triandis, 1986; Chinese Culture Connection, 1987, for treatments of values suitable for group discussions). Trainers can also introduce the emotional confrontation brought on when these values, taken for granted in one's own culture, come under challenge when people live in a culture other than their own.

Other topics for group discussion include prejudice, racism, sexism, and discrimination. Most people will be able to give an example of these concepts in their own lives. The trainer can then guide the discussion toward such topics as (a) the sojourner as target of discrimination; (b) the tendency for sojourners to discriminate against hosts as one consequence of culture shock; and (c) the roles that women can comfortably play in the host culture. Material introduced during training becomes more meaningful as links are made between what people have already experienced and their probable interactions in the host culture. The materials discussed in the previous section (Brislin et al., 1986) can also be used to encourage discussions of affect because each of the 100 incidents has an *element* that people have undoubtedly experienced. In the incident already reviewed, almost everyone has been in a situation in their own culture where someone became unexpectedly angry. Trainers can then guide the discussion of the incident to such topics as appropriate outlets for anger, the danger of overinterpreting angry outbursts, and the need to understand both the antecedents and the consequences of emotional expression.

## Moderate Involvement Aimed at Behavior

Trainees can practice new behaviors under the supportive guidance of the training staff. One way is to have trainees list the behaviors that they find reinforcing or pleasurable, and those that they find punishing or unpleasant, in their own culture. Then, they can examine the host culture to find which reinforcing behaviors they can maintain and which they will have to eliminate given societal demands. Further, they can analyze which unpleasant behaviors they will have to accept. Women, for instance, might list that they enjoy taking long walks by themselves. This is impossible in some Arab countries where severe restrictions are placed on the movement of women. Some men might list that they enjoy doing all the cooking for the family. This will be difficult in some countries where hosts expect sojourners to hire servants. Sojourners cannot easily appeal to the value of equality in their refusal to hire servants. Many developing countries have a high unemployment rate that will go unchanged if sojourners remain comfortable with their distrust of the employer-servant relationship. Not all treatments of the list will point to problems. Many trainers recommend that people bring their hobbies with them, if at all possible, because spending time on enjoyable activities is a good buffer against stress.

Field trip assignments can also allow the introduction of new behaviors. In large cities, visits to ethnic restaurants can be arranged. Such activities may seem unimportant, but experienced trainers agree that engaging people in any sort of out-of-session activity can provide a tremendous boost to subsequent group discussion and general involvement in the program.

Stress reduction methods (see Meichenbaum, 1977, for guidance) can be introduced. For aspects of the host culture that are irritating but cannot be changed, trainees can be introduced to new cognitions that can lessen tension. Thoughts such as the following, which people say to themselves when faced with stress, are usable in many settings:

(a) "Is this really worth being upset about, with resulting damage to my body?"

(b) "At least this will make a good story someday."

(c) "Let me tote up the positive aspects of what seems to be a difficulty here."

(d) "I wonder if there is another piece of information that, if I had it, would help me interpret what is going on?"

Such self-thoughts can be a very effective intervention and can actually lessen the symptoms of stress.

## High Involvement Aimed at Cognitions

Trainers can challenge future sojourners to think hard about their upcoming experience and to learn concepts at the cutting edge of knowledge. If people comment that they are tired (as distinguished from bored) after working with a set of challenging materials, trainers have evidence that they have encouraged high involvement. The concepts can be very practical. Argyle (1986) has studied the rules of social interaction, or the behaviors that most members of a culture feel should or should not take place within a given relationship (e.g., boss-subordinate; male-female date). He argues that rules in the following areas lead to the most difficulties when people move across cultures because the rules are unknown, confusing, or impossible to follow: "bribery, nepotism, gifts, buying and selling, eating and drinking, punctuality" and relations with members of the opposite sex (Argyle, 1986, p. 310). Confusions often arise when behaviors that are perfectly appropriate in one culture are seen as boorish in another. For example, good-natured teasing may be a sign that people are becoming close in one culture, but it can be seen as rejecting and rude in another.

Generally, any theoretical concept that has a relation to cross-cultural interactions can be covered. The best trainees will be those who are well versed in theory within the behavioral/social sciences. Well-read trainees will be able to choose among many theoretical concepts to best meet the needs of a specific training program. Of course, the trainer will want to be confident that attention has been given to careful choices among concepts and that trainees will not be overburdened with details. Brislin (1981; see also Brislin et al., 1986) has suggested large numbers of concepts for possible inclusion that are based on recent research. The overinterpretation of colorful events has already been reviewed. Others include the fact that sojourners interpret colorful host behaviors as being due to their traits, but sojourners interpret the same behaviors performed by themselves as due to the situational pressures of the moment. Another is that once a person has been assigned a label (e.g., Black, Japanese American, pushy female), all the information from the corresponding category can be called upon during interactions with the person. This increases the chances of a problematic encounter because people do not enjoy being treated like stereotypes. Triandis, Brislin, and Hui (in press; see also Triandis, Bontempo, Villareal, Asai, & Lucca, 1988) presented a detailed set of concepts for training that stem from people's socialization in an individualist in contrast to a collectivist culture. Suggestions are made for individualists moving to a collectivist culture, and vice versa. For instance, individualists in collectivist societies often meet their needs by calling upon a few long-term relationships that they have carefully developed. Collectivists in individualist societies have to learn to meet needs by calling upon a wide variety of short-term relationships, often referred to as one's "network" of acquaintances.

## High Involvement Aimed at Affect

Trainees can actively engage in simulated interactions with either hosts or staff members who role-play hosts. They can either participate in a carefully scripted role-play that they help write, or they can engage in interactions without knowing exactly what will happen. The Contrast-American technique (Stewart, 1966) is an example of this second type. An American trainee participates in a role-played negotiation with a carefully prepared staff member who acts out the opposite of typical American values. Assume that the negotiations are concerned with the start of a construction project. When the American wants to get down to business, the hosts want to chat. When the American discusses the qualifications of the staff to be hired, the host mentions the names of relatives who could be put on the payroll. When the American asks for schedules indicating the delivery dates for building materials, the host points to the many factors that make scheduling impossible. A possible addition to this method involves videotaping the interactions, playing the tape back at a later session, and soliciting commentary from the active participants and the other trainees.

While often a very good method for encouraging trainees to think about the importance of value differences and the emotional nature of cross-cultural disagreements, trainers must exercise great care and must be aware of risks. Such role-plays are extremely involving and participants often become very emotionally aroused. Because, in many role-plays, the exact directions the interactions will take is unknown, one trainee may bring up topics with which another person is very uncomfortable. The second person then becomes distraught and the program comes to a halt. The most seemingly innocuous remarks can cause such reactions: Playful male-female banter can remind the female of a rape attempt in her past.

My advice is that trainers new to the field should apprentice themselves to their seniors who have experience with the method. Role-plays should be used late in long-term programs (e.g., the fourth day of a five-day program), after people are very comfortable with each other. Role-plays can be scripted by encouraging trainees to go off into separate areas and to write key elements of the scenario. All dialogue is not written. Rather, the highlights are planned and key pieces of dialogue are rehearsed: "When I introduce the new concept of quality control, then you attempt to change the subject, and then we close with the meeting breaking up in a clumsy manner." Such meetings to plan role-play scenarios (which are themselves to last five to ten minutes) take about one-half hour. The rule for the role-plays becomes "no surprises." People should accept the group norm that no unrehearsed matters will be brought up during the role-plays, because the trainer has pointed out that these can trigger unpleasant memories.

## High Involvement Aimed at Behavior

In long and well-budgeted programs, simulations of host cultures can be created in which trainees can engage in the actual behaviors necessary for long-term adjustment. Trifonovitch (1977) developed programs for Peace Corps volunteers and contract teachers about to live in Pacific Island cultures. He supervised the creation of simulated Pacific villages in rural parts of Oahu and Molokai in the Hawaiian Islands. There, trainees lived like islanders surviving in a subsistence economy. They gathered and cooked their own food; made their own entertainment; learned to tell time by the position of the sun, moon, and tides; interacted with hosts according to island norms; experienced a lack of privacy; and carried out their jobs with a shortage of materials compared to their previous positions. In addition to Trifonovitch's work, this approach has been used when training takes place *in country.* This term refers to training that takes place at a site within the country where sojourners will assume their eventual assignments. Obvious advantages include the ability to integrate hosts into the training program.

A positive feature of this approach is that it can approximate life in another culture in a more realistic manner than other methods. The disadvantages, however, are many. The programs are expensive, emotionally draining on staff members, and can lead to trainee dropout and subsequent return home. This latter point can be looked upon as an advantage, because people might realize during the realistic program that the overseas assignment is not for them. But the emotional stress felt by the trainee falls upon the training staff, and the subsequent staff-trainee interactions are rarely pleasant. If trainees don't actually leave, they will often argue that they were unprepared and were "set up" for an unnecessarily intense program. After several such programs and reactions from trainees, staff members can easily "burn out" and seek careers elsewhere.

These intense methods can be successfully used by only a limited number of trainers. These select people must actually enjoy the give-and-take of emotional confrontations with resistant and angry trainees. They must enjoy the challenge of interacting with trainees who feel that these intense methods are unwise, damaging, and indicative of incompetence. Not all trainers will fit this description, and such a state of affairs is not evidence that they should leave the field. Rather, it means that many trainers will want to choose other methods with which they are more comfortable. This point about the match between trainer characteristics and various methods brings up the more general area of how best to administer programs, and this is the next topic for coverage.

## ADVICE FROM EXPERIENCED TRAINERS

Good programs, of course, are dependent upon qualified trainers who are well prepared and knowledgeable. But even trainers who possess most of the qualities previously reviewed will sometimes make grave mistakes. There are pieces of advice for the organization of successful programs that come from "the school of hard knocks." I have gathered the following pieces of advice by asking experienced and successful trainers such questions as "What do you know now that you wish you knew when you started out in the field?"

Trainees should always be allowed to individuate themselves at the start of a program. Self-introductions, or exercises in which people interview and then introduce each other, are a must. The time invested in introductions pays great dividends later. Frequently, trainees become resistant, feisty, and unpleasant even in those programs called "low or moderate involvement." The exact reason is not known. One possibility is that in a good program trainees learn, for the first time, that *their* culture has had a major influence on their behavior. Further, their behavior has an impact on their communication with culturally different others and with adjustment to other societies. This new set of realizations leads to anxiety and to clumsy coping mechanisms such as feistiness. Good trainers prepare for such occurrences, perhaps by assigning one staff member with counseling skills to be on the lookout for such reactions and to intervene quickly. Trainers should always solicit feedback from trainees and should not withdraw during breaks and lunch periods. They should clearly send the message that they are available for informal discussions.

No matter how long a program, trainees become fatigued at the midpoint. If the program runs three days, a low point occurs during the afternoon of the second day; if five days, then the point is reached late the third day. Trainers deal with this reaction by scheduling exercises that are especially exciting and interesting. But the exact exercises to be scheduled at this point, or any other, will differ across trainers. Confidence in, and comfort with, a given technique is paramount. Trainers should learn to differentiate between techniques that admired colleagues use from techniques that they themselves can use. They should be enthusiastic about their final choices. Enthusiasm and confidence are quickly communicated to trainees.

Trainers should develop a range of short presentations that make key points and that can be inserted at different points during training. The more such minipresentations at their disposal, the more flexible trainers can be. Such presentations can last thirty seconds, sixty seconds, two minutes, five minutes, fifteen minutes, and so forth. Such presentations can also summarize key points during explanations of one's work to potential clients. I have seen contracts lost because a trainer had two minutes to give some key ideas about his program, but he declined to speak. He argued that he needed at least thirty minutes to make his presentation. While perhaps true, he lost the opportunity to make the thirty-minute presentation at a later date because of his inability to be impressive in the allotted two-minute period.

Many benefits stem from developing close relationships with colleagues: new ideas, referrals, reciprocal relationship, joint ventures when a large training staff is needed, and opportunities to discuss difficult problems with sympathetic people. There is a downside: There is as much territoriality in cross-cultural training as in any specialty. Some trainers will not share their methods, calling their contributions "proprietary." Some trainers become quite adept with one or two methods and then cease considering any other approaches. This can lead to a lack of intellectual growth and eventual dullness. Both of these negative outcomes can be communicated to trainees.

## CONCLUSIONS

A variety of cross-cultural orientation methods have been reviewed, and references have been suggested where longer discussions can be found. Using the language of Table 21.1, my recommendation is that programs start with low-involvement activities that give trainees key information and that begin to generate interest. The low-involvement activities allow trainees to become comfortable with the program staff. Then, moderate-involvement approaches can be added. Approaches aimed at cognitions, affect, and behavior can be integrated into a program, which will both excite and challenge trainees. Whenever possible, trainers should encourage hands-on behaviors: interacting with hosts, role-plays of cross-cultural encounters, field trips, and analysis of critical incidents such as those that will be encountered in the actual cross-cultural assignment. With all hands-on activities, the distinction between moderate and high involvement should be kept in mind. High-involvement activities should be used only by the most experienced trainers who have thought through and have prepared for negative trainee reactions. Trainers should be flexible and should be able to draw upon many sources of knowledge and many methods as trainee needs become clear during the actual program.

## REFERENCES

Albert, R. (1986). Conceptual framework for the development and evaluation of cross-cultural orientation programs. *International Journal of Intercultural Relations, 10*, 197-213.

Argyle, M. (1986). Rules for social relationships in four cultures. *Australian Journal of Psychology, 38*, 309-318.

Brislin, R. (1981). *Cross-cultural encounters: Face-to-face interaction*. Elmsford, NY: Pergamon.

Brislin, R., Cushner, K., Cherrie, C., & Yong, M. (1986). *Intercultural interactions: A practical guide*. Newbury Park, CA: Sage.

Brislin, R., Landis, D., & Brandt, M. (1983). Conceptualization of intercultural behavior and training. In D. Landis & R. Brislin (Eds.), *Handbook of intercultural training: Vol. 1. Issues in theory and design* (pp. 176-202). Elmsford, NY: Pergamon.

Brislin, R., & Pedersen, P. (1976). *Cross-cultural orientation programs*. New York: Pergamon.

Chinese Culture Connection. (1987). Chinese values and the search for culture-free dimensions of culture. *Journal of Cross-Cultural Psychology, 18*, 143-164.

Cushner, K., & Broaddus, D. (1988). *Empirical tests of the culture general assimilator in cross-cultural orientation programs*. Manuscript submitted for publication.

Dinges, N. (1983). Intercultural competence. In D. Landis & R. Brislin (Eds.), *Handbook of intercultural training: Vol. 1. Issues in theory and design* (pp. 176-202). Elmsford, NY: Pergamon.

Gudykunst, W., Hammer, M., & Wiseman, R. (1977). An analysis of an integrated approach to cross-cultural training. *International Journal of Intercultural Relation, 1*(2), 99-110.

Hammer, M., Gudykunst, W., & Wiseman, R. (1978). Dimensions of intercultural effectiveness: An exploratory study. *International Journal of Intercultural Relations, 2*, 382-393.

Hui, C. H., & Triandis, H. (1986). Individualism-collectivism: A study of cross-cultural researchers. *Journal of Cross-Cultural Psychology, 17*, 225-248.

Landis, D., & Brislin, R. (Eds.). (1983). *Handbook of intercultural training* (3 vols.). Elmsford, NY: Pergamon.

Lefley, H. (1985). Impact of cross-cultural training on Black and White mental health professionals. *International Journal of Intercultural Relations, 9*, 305-318.

Martin, J. (Ed.). (1986). Theories and methods in cross-cultural orientation [Special issue]. *International Journal of Intercultural Relations, 10*(2).

Meichenbaum, D. (1977). *Cognitive-behavior modification: An integrative approach*. New York: Plenum.

O'Brien, G., Fiedler, D., & Hewett, T. (1971). The effects of programmed culture training upon the performance of volunteer medical teams in Central America. *Human Relations, 24*, 209-231.

Paige, R. M. (Ed.). (1986). *Cross-cultural orientation: New conceptualizations and applications*. Lanham, MD: University Press of America.

Sharma, M., & Jung, L. (1985). How cross-cultural social participation affects the international attitudes of U.S. students. *International Journal of Intercultural Relations, 9*, 377-387.

Stewart, E. (1966). The simulation of cultural differences. *Journal of Communication, 16*, 291-304.

Triandis, H., Bontempo, R., Villareal, M., Asai, M., & Lucca, N. (1988). Individualism and collectivism: Cross-cultural perspectives on self-ingroup behavior. *Journal of Personality and Social Psychology, 54*, 323-338.

Triandis, H., Brislin, R., & Hui, C. H. (in press). Cross-cultural training across the individualism-collectivism divide. *International Journal of Intercultural Relations, 12*.

Trifonovitch, G. (1977). On cross-cultural orientation techniques. In R. Brislin (Ed.), *Culture learning: Concepts, applications and research* (pp. 213-222). Honolulu: University Press of Hawaii.

# Part IV

Research Issues

# 22 Problems in Intercultural Research

## J. David Johnson
## Frank Tuttle

There are problems in all social science research, whether it is done in one society or in many. This chapter focuses on those problems that are most salient to research whose aim is to discover the nature of communication between different cultures. We will focus on research that investigates communication between people of different cultures, rather than on how communication may differ within or across cultures (Gudykunst, 1985; Gudykunst & Wright, 1980). Many of the problems that arise in conducting intercultural research are also the very areas that our theories attempt to address. Thus intercultural research can and should be a case of applied intercultural communication theory. As such it takes on some of the dimensions of an art form, as well as a rigorously defined set of procedures.

Perhaps the best metaphor to use in this regard is research as a craft (Daft, 1983). Research is a set of skills and attitudes applied to problems. The traditional view of craft involves applying manual skills to materials, something not necessarily characteristic of social science research. In most other particulars, however, the role of the social scientist is very much that of a craftsperson—"the craftsmen as participant in a specific craft tradition, wherein he practises *artisanry,* by means of his mental and manual acumen aided by an assortment of tools" (Schlereth, 1980, p. 41).

The skills of a craftsperson are his or her most valuable possession, setting him or her apart from the more specialized focus of the conventional laborer or technician. Typically, one or a few individuals, often apprentices to a more senior researcher, carry on the process of production from the gathering of raw material (data), through analysis, to the production of a final research report. This wholeness of enterprise gives the researcher a sense of aesthetic satisfaction not available to specialists in other fields.

In its highest form a craftsperson's labors take on the aspects of a calling, becoming an expression of values. The work itself becomes a form of sacrament. Thus a craftsperson must "start with a total dedication to the craft, fascination with all its aspects, and an enjoyment of it" (Massey, 1981, p. 11). But these qualities alone are not sufficient: "The craftsman needs many other things: self-discipline, good critical judgment, patience, perseverance in the face of difficulties, respect for and sensitivity to materials, mastery of technique, and above all, an ability to work" (Massey, 1981, p. 11).

Another essential quality that a craftsperson must possess is the recognition that his or her craft is never perfected, that the attainment of one plateau is just a preparation for the next higher one. Working on the craft always contains an element of self-discovery, and a recognition that who one is is intimately bound up in the work one accomplishes. To accomplish this work a craftsperson needs tools. Without good tools, work becomes frustrating and barriers become insurmountable. This chapter is partially about a researcher's tools, but it is also about judgment.

One of the key elements that characterizes research as a craft is the notion of judgment calls (McGrath, Martin, & Kulka, 1982). Judgment calls are crucial decisions made without the benefit of hard-and-fast "objective" rules and often even without the benefit of rules of thumb (McGrath, 1982). Sarbaugh (1984) has noted that often, without thinking about it, we make a large number of yes-no decisions in intercultural communication research. The cumulative results of these judgment calls determine research outcomes (McGrath, 1982). The most troubling aspects of these judgments is that they are often really dilemmas. You can only maximize one research value at the expense of another. For example, maximizing the generalizability of research findings often involves selection of populations by means that diminish the precision in the control and measurement of variables (Blalock, 1982). Thus experimental studies, while typically employing the most rigorous methods, have the least generalizability (McGrath, 1982).

The goal of this chapter is to overview the issues that are central to the pursuit of intercultural research—making the research process more effective and making better judgments. As such we are not going to critique existing research, except insofar as a discussion of problems in this research illustrate in a meaningful way the issues of concern. It must be recognized that judgment calls are often choices between two "bad" alternatives, and that when research is criticized the reviewer has a responsibility to point out specifically how an alternative approach would have improved the research.

The general focus of this chapter will be on intercultural research as a craft in which judgment calls determine the ultimate quality of the research. It will also focus on the problems of a Western researcher doing intercultural research. While the focus of this chapter is primarily on quantitative research, many of the dilemmas discussed here are also central to qualitative intercultural research. This chapter will not focus on the following issues, some of which are covered in other chapters of this handbook: comparative cross-cultural research, specific step-by-step guidelines for doing research, detailed criticisms of existing research, substantive theoretical issues, ethics, or translation problems.

This chapter will be organized by the major sections of a traditional report of research. In each section, major problems, dilemmas, and questions involved in conducting intercultural research will be systematically discussed. The reader, however, should be aware that following this overall framework gives an impression of a rational, linear process that does not necessarily reflect research as it happens (Martin, 1982).

## THEORETICAL PROBLEMS

Fundamentally, intercultural communication research is a special case of applied intercultural communication theory. Both inform each other and, at a meta level, theory serves to guide research and to help avoid critical pitfalls, because the research enterprise is also an intercultural experience. One of the first ways this becomes evident is in the presence of a large number of exogenous variables relating to cultural and societal differences that form the contexts in which relationships between variables explicitly are specified in a theory.

Communication often has been described as a contextually determined process (Hall, 1976). At the most general level, different cultures represent different contexts for the study of communication. Through the socialization process a group's culture is programmed into its members such that they attend to different stimuli and interpret these stimuli according to the norms of their social group. According to Hall (1976), the "contexting" of culture affects all the messages that constitute social interaction, including verbal and nonverbal expressions, the physical setting, and social circumstances. As social scientists doing research in cultures other than the ones into which we have been socialized, we run the risk of wrongly interpreting the process of communication and the variables that determine the outcomes of these activities.

Linking the individual to culture is the social system (Parsons, 1968). The social system is less general than culture and provides a variety of contexts for studying communication behaviors. Parsons (1951) further divides the social system into four subsystems or contexts—the economic, through which an individual's social status is often determined; the political; the educational; and the religious. There are also others, such as the family and the media. These institutional contexts should be explored when conducting research in other social systems because members of these groups may bring different meanings to the communication process.

Status is perhaps the most frequently overlooked of these variables for U.S. researchers, because our culture fosters a view that it is relatively unimportant. But as the classic work of Bennet and McKnight (1958) makes clear it is a factor that permeates intercultural relations. Whomever U.S. citizens interact with are more likely to have well-defined intra-cultural status differences that affect all of their relationships. Citizens of the United States are not likely to be sensitive to how differences in status affect social relationships. For example, young, female U.S. executives are likely to encounter many difficulties related to status when they attempt to do business overseas.

The overall status differences between the cultures of which the participants are members may also color interpersonal relationships between members of different cultures (Bennett & McKnight, 1966). These status differentials may erroneously lead to attributions about the level of introversion and assertiveness characteristic of members of a culture. These perceived characteristics do not reflect uniform intracultural differences, but rather reflect perceived status differentials between the cultures.

Political systems also have profound impacts on intercultural communication variables. The general bias in U.S. interpersonal research to promoting openness in communication relationships is a case in point (Parks, 1982). Openness in relationships is often taken as a sign of health. This value is directly linked with our political system, which promotes freedom of expression. But in a traditional or totalitarian society, openness can be viewed as destructive at a societal level and literally fatal for individuals. Any research into the flow of communication between individuals needs to take these societal variables into account, because they will profoundly affect the factors that can lead to and promote open communication relationships.

Further, they will affect the process of communication research. Consider interviewing in this context. We assume that when asked a question an individual will give an honest answer, rather than one his or her government wishes us to hear. Also, our political system has led to our expectation that everyone has an opinion about the issue of the day. After all, how can an individual participate in a democracy without an opinion upon which to base his or her vote? Consider, however, an example from research on communication and national development conducted in a democracy, Turkey, in the 1950s (Frey, 1966). When villagers were asked their opinion on political issues, their response was that they had no opinion, and that if the interviewer wanted an answer, he should ask the headman of the village. When the voting decision was discussed, the villager said he would vote as told by his headman. Clearly, there is a discrepancy between our interpretation of the theory and practice of democracy.

The United States generally is regarded as a secular society. Religion plays a less significant role in contexting communication behavior than the other subsystems of society. Further, the pluralistic nature of the religion in the United States has contributed to what Hall (1976) regards as a "low-context" society. There are many societies that are homogeneous in terms of religion, however. This has facilitated the development of a "high-context" society. Religion is often the dominant factor in shaping everyday life. Consider the communication activities within Islamic societies, such as Saudi Arabia or Iran. In these societies, the teachings of Muhammad determine many aspects of social interaction, including at which time and under what circumstances people may communicate, nonverbal communication, greeting and leave-taking rituals, and how one communicates with strangers.

One of the social goals of the United States is a literate populous. As such, people have a right to a free, publicly financed education and the vast majority of the population is literate. This allows the American people access to a variety of written mass media, including printed materials and such interpersonal media as letters and computer-based messages. Thus, when studying the process of communication, American scholars assume that these channels are available and used by respondents. Further, they help form the context for communication. This has led Marshall McLuhan (1964) to suggest that Americans, and indeed members of all literate societies, process information in a linear fashion, a requisite for written media.

In societies with lower levels of literacy, researchers cannot assume that the written media have contexting effects on the population. These societies often must rely on broadcast media or print that relies primarily on pictures or icons, as well as interpersonal communication. For example, a population-planning campaign in India made use of a poster without words. It contained two large people, one male and one female, and two smaller ones—children. All of the characters were smiling, implying that two children resulted in a happy family.

The education subsystem performs other functions aside from the creation of a literate populous. It is a socializing mechanism for society. In this context, children are taught the culture of society, including its values, history, and civic responsibilities, as well as being prepared for future occupations. The educational system helps determine how members of society view themselves and the manner in which they communicate. For example, because public education in the United States must by law be secular, members of society tend to take an objective or scientific view of the world. Reality rather than illusion is communicated. While education is universal in modern societies, the socialization function may be performed by other institutions in traditional societies. It is often performed by religious institutions. Thus their universe operates according to a higher order, rather than a scientific one.

There are additional contextualizing factors that affect the process of communication, the most important of which is a society's level of technology and its infrastructure. For example, it is absurd to study the cross-cultural effects of mass media in societies without reliable electricity. A society's level of development and its technological infrastructure should be considered when conducting intercultural research. As a guide, there are many models that describe communication's role in the national development process (Frey, 1973; Rogers, 1983). Typically, they discuss the relationship among literacy, urbanization, mass media exposure, and political and economic participation (Alker, 1966; Lerner, 1985; Lerner & Schramm, 1967; McCrone & Cnudde, 1967; Winham, 1970). While critical of these models, Rogers (1983) discusses the role of interpersonal and mass communication in the process of diffusion of innovations.

Finally, the very diversity of U.S. society sets it apart from almost every other country in the world. The presence of numerous subcultures spread across a continent gives a scope and range to the U.S. experience that is atypical. Just as each additional individual in a small group increases almost exponentially the number of possible relationships, so does the presence of numerous subcultures increase the individual's possibilities of creating linkages to different cultures that "custom fit" their needs. Thus our own intracultural experience carries within it many of the characteristics of intercultural ones.

As a result of these numerous subcultures, someone could stereotypically describe U.S. society as low in context for its members and primarily oriented toward individuals. These factors also make our society more changeable; that is, individuals can make their own decisions and do not need to worry about the impact of them on a large number of other cultural factors. Thus our society is more dynamic than others. This can be linked with the fascination within our field with process (Berlo, 1977). One of our fundamental assumptions is that communication is a process, and understanding process is crucial to understanding communication. In fact, one of the most frequently lamented criticisms of our research is that our theoretical assumptions are processually based, while our research methods are static (Monge, 1982).

In other societies, however, static communication, ritually oriented communication, may be the critical form, with scripts operative to a greater extent than our own. These other societies also have timeframes that are much longer than our own, so that intercultural encounters that

U.S. cultural members consider failures because of the lack of immediate results may be proceeding quite nicely in the view of cultural members who have a different temporal frame of reference.

One question scholars doing research in other societies should keep in mind at all times is this: "Do theoretical relationships have the same meaning across different societies?" Much of the discussion above revolved around the observation that a society's different subsystems contextualize communication in a unique manner for that society. For example, we expect the process of communication to occur somewhat differently in modern than in traditional societies. In a related example, Gudykunst and Nishida (Gudykunst, 1983; Gudykunst & Nishida, 1983, 1984, 1986) in a series of studies found systematic differences in interpersonal communication between societies that Hall (1976) characterized as high-and low-context societies.

Other cross-cultural communication research has found that the relations among the variables vary among cultures. Barnett et al. (1981) evaluated perceptions of the media in seven different countries and found that, while respondents used the same three dimensions to evaluate media in society, the proportion of variance attributable to these dimensions ranges from 59% to 81%. These differences among societies were primarily attributable to language and level of development. Johnson and his colleagues (Johnson, 1983, 1984a, 1984b, 1987; Johnson & Oliveira, 1987) have tested a model of media evaluation in a variety of different societies and found that the coefficients varied. Likewise, Osgood (1974) has evaluated affective meaning in 27 different societies using the semantic differential. He found that affective meaning could be characterized along the same three dimensions—activity, potency, and evaluation—in all societies, but there was considerable variance in the coefficients for translated equivalents. In other words, the symbols had different meanings depending upon culture.

Hofstede's (1980) work on multinational organizations in particular points to a number of problems in generalizing well-founded social science research results from one society to another. He found the traditional individualistic orientation of the United States to result in a calculative form of involvement among employees of U.S. firms. This has led to a number of management expectancy theories of motivation that have received research support in U.S. firms. Because the U.S. was one of the most individualistic societies studied, these theories tend to be useful in explaining behavior within U.S. firms. In societies with more collectivist orientations, however, the linkage between individuals and organizations tends to be much more moral. These contrasting perspectives pose great difficulties in intercultural relations within multinationals for members of these diverse cultures and they create considerable problems for management theories that are exported to different cultures.

Similarly, definitions for key concepts may differ markedly cross-culturally. Words for which we have taken-for-granted meanings often have radically different meanings in other cultures, a problem that is at the heart of many of the controversies surrounding the New World Information Order. Western societies tend to view the free flow of information as a societal right to be protected by our political systems, while other societies view the press as a means of accomplishing larger societal goals, particularly economic ones. If the press operates in the often adversarial Western tradition, then in the view of Marxist and Third World countries, it might detract from the achievement of economic advancement. Thus, to promote societal values, the press needs to be controlled.

At the root of this controversy are two contrasting definitions of the central political concept of democracy. Westerners tend to define democracy in terms of equal protection of legal and political (e.g., voting) rights. On the other hand, other perspectives, particularly Marxist ones, tend to define democracy by equality of economic outcomes. Thus egalitarianism in economic resources becomes central in determining democracy—a factor that is revealed in the linkage of the New World Information Order to the New World Economic Order. Therefore, the orientation of different cultures to the key concept of democracy reveals more about the differences between these societies than their commonalities.

These differences in underlying meanings for key concepts also are associated with another key factor we must consider: Do concepts have the same importance across societies? For example, one of the proposals made by Third World countries is that journalists should be licensed in order to operate in different countries. This is a perfectly logical extension of their view that the news media should serve the interests of the state. Thus this proposal is not seen as controversial. On the other hand, Western journalists saw this proposal as the first step to government suppression of the free flow of news. It became a symbolic rallying cry that alienated Western media organizations to many other complaints of the Third World to which they may have been more sympathetic. This became a classic case of the deterioration of intercultural relations arising from a misunderstanding of the relative importance of factors cross-culturally and their differential meanings.

Knowledge of these factors is important to specifying correctly relationships between intercultural variables. Thus one of the problems encountered in intercultural research is the lack of relevant information about these factors. Unlike other areas of the social sciences, it is hard to point to any one research area where there is a wealth of information. With the possible exception of Japan, it is also difficult to say that we have comprehensive information about intercultural communication with any one particular culture. Thus the researcher typically only encounters the above problems when trying to explain the results of an already completed study.

There are at least three strategies that a researcher can pursue in trying to address this problem. The first is to conduct preliminary studies and/or extensive pretests, a topic we will come back to later in the chapter. The second is to cast the net more widely for relevant source materials, perhaps consulting libraries and academic journals within the other society, something that is not done frequently enough (Gudykunst, 1985). The third is to engage in collaborative research with a member of the culture that is the focus of the intercultural research.

Collaborative research is essential to overcoming problems in intercultural research, a theme we will come back to again and again in the course of this chapter. Given our lack of formal intercultural knowledge, our next best source is key informants who represent the cultural groups that are going to be studied. They can provide the "visiting" researcher with information about the society's history and culture and contextualizing sectors of the social system. They can describe how communication operates within that culture. Further, they can identify problems in their society that can be ameliorated through a well-designed and implemented communication campaign. They may have developed an indigenous communication theory, perhaps without Western, positivist, or capitalist biases, and have ideas about how to examine the phenomenon in question in their society. Also, they may suggest outlets to publish in their society so that the host society may benefit from the products of the research. The researcher needs to weigh their reports, however, because of a tendency of indigenous social scientists to overgeneralize about the presence of phenomenon within their own society (Carter, 1966).

These issues can also help the researcher to address the problem of whether they are indeed conducting intercultural research, rather than international or comparative cross-cultural research. This is an issue that should always be addressed before one proceeds with any study. Just because research is conducted on a population from a different society does not mean it is intercultural. The researcher should carefully apply some perspective such as Sarbaugh's (1979) to determine if he or she is indeed conducting intercultural research. The researcher should also be aware that all communication has a cultural component (Ellingsworth, 1977), so that the question is really a matter of degree, rather than of differences in kind.

Given our lack of comprehensive understanding of intercultural communication research processes, perhaps the best strategy is to focus on a few central concepts, such as homophily (Rogers & Bhowmik, 1971), that can be expected to have great explanatory power and to be present in a wide array of intercultural situations. Although this is somewhat at odds with discovering as much about the situation as possible, a good strategy given the state of intercultural research at the present would be to design research as a poem (Daft, 1983). Daft suggests that the researcher examine the interrelationships among a few variables that hang together as a meaning unit. This meaning unit must also have depth, and be rich in its heuristic implications. Daft characterizes many fundamental organizational theories, such as Theory X and the Theory Y, as having these properties.

Somewhat related is the notion that we should strive for elegance in our research, examining relationships that are fundamental. There are so many possible exogenous variables and possible interactions between variables that trying to explain everything is a hopeless task. In fact, a case could be made for the thesis that for every additional endogenous or central variable added to our models, the less we ultimately will come to know about the phenomenon.

Given the welter of variables, and judgments concerning whether they should be included and at what level, a guide and sense of direction are needed in intercultural research. Nothing substitutes for a good theory. Generally the more linkages that can be made to existing theory, the fewer the problems that are going to be encountered further down the road (Selltiz et al., 1959). This theory and the related choice of the problem should inform every other choice made in a study, because those problems that are most fruitful are the ones that examine theory-based relationships (Sarbaugh, 1984).

Intercultural research is the ultimate test of a theory because the greater the range of contexts examined offers the greatest potential for understanding communication in general (Sarbaugh, 1984) and for perhaps uncovering universals of human communication (Gudykunst, 1985; Gudykunst & Kim, 1984). Thus theory leads to research that modifies theories in a cyclical, iterative process (Korzenny & Korzenny, 1984). Without the test of theories in intercultural settings, with all the difficulties involved, we are at the end going to be left with an ethnocentric social science, which is temporally, spatially, and, most important, culturally bound.

## METHODOLOGICAL PROBLEMS

Except in those rare cases of well-tested intercultural propositions, the researcher should structure his or her methods in a flexible manner to compensate for the possibility of error and surprise (Daft, 1983). Error is always possible given that our preconceived notions of another culture may be flawed. Surprise is part of any intercultural experience, where the unexpected or the unknown is always a possibility. For example, because of the novelty of social research in much of the world, it is much more vulnerable to outside events (Kulka, 1982). That is, threats to the internal validity of the research are perhaps more problematic in unfamiliar settings. The researcher should pay special attention to the effects of history, maturation, and instrumentation (Cook & Campbell, 1979).

The first step in preparing for error and surprise is consciously building them into the research process by conducting it in iterative steps. Initially the researcher should structure the enterprise to discover more about the intercultural context by conducting preliminary qualitative research, especially if the literature in a given area is sparse. This research could take on many forms: unstructured interviews and ethnography, for example. The researcher should find out more about the cultural context using methods that do not allow him or her to approach the situation with blinders. He or she could ask the following questions: What is everyday life like in this cultural setting? What meanings do its members give events both daily and ceremonial? This qualitative research may reveal unanticipated factors that require a modification of the researcher's thinking about the phenomenon and about what should be measured in a more structured way.

Once the qualitative data has been accumulated and compared to the theoretical framework, and the result has generated a more structured research design, then a pretest becomes a necessity. While the significance of a pretest is well known in domestic intracultural research, it takes on paramount importance in intercultural research, because all of the components of the research (e.g., language and scaling) may produce unknown reactions in the populations of interest. The proper interpretation of the results of the initial qualitative data collection and pretests requires collaboration with members of a host culture. This is especially important in dealing with unanticipated, undocumented problems and in preparing strategies for overcoming them. Procedures to guarantee quality in translation are beyond the scope of this chapter; for a complete discussion, see Brislin et al. (1973).

Another, somewhat unrelated, way of coping with error and surprise is to be flexible in the research design by employing multiple strategies for collecting data. For example, the researcher may decide that a high level of redundancy is necessary and include multiple operationalizations of central variables. This is important not only because the dimensionality of constructs may be different cross-culturally, but also because if unanticipated problems are encountered they can be dealt with by focusing on those aspects of the design and measurement that "worked" rather than including flawed variables in the study—a strategy adopted by Johnson,

Oliveira, and Barnett (1987) in their study of communication factors affecting the desire for closer ties in Belize.

One area of concern for intercultural researchers is what population to examine. In the United States, researchers typically want to generalize to the population as a whole, although there is considerable research that focuses upon particular ethnic or demographic groups. Because of the relative mobility of U.S. citizens and the lack of clearly defined status and group differences, at least when compared to other societies, the question of which populations should be examined is treated as rather obvious and not subject to much consideration. In other societies, however, this question may become paramount. Thus when conducting intercultural research we should ask the question: "Are we interested in the population as a whole or in some particular group, such as the Westernized elite?"

For example, the U.S. Information Agency, in its quantitatively oriented evaluation research, has long concentrated on elite groups on the assumption that they will be the real decision makers in any society. In the mid-1970s their evaluation research in Iran focused on Westernized elites, slighting more traditional cultural groups, which were felt to be no longer relevant. This research focus produced a distorted image of the society, with grave implications for later decision making and intercultural relations between the United States and Iran.

Once the population of interest is defined, however, then the researcher must deal with problems of how particular groups can be accessed. The most accessible groups within societies are bound to be the ones most similar to the researcher, perhaps representing a third culture (Ellingsworth, 1977). These groups will be the most Westernized within a society and often trained in Western educational traditions (Ellingsworth, 1977). There may, in fact, be less difference between them and Western researchers than there is between them and other members of their own country. While these groups may provide very interesting insight into international communication processes, one must question how much information they truly provide on intercultural communication processes.

Those groups that are the most different from the researcher are often the least accessible and also the least sympathetic with the researcher's goals. They may be "protected" from contact with Western researchers by other members of the society, such as the case of traditional Arabic women, or alternatively, they may shun contact with the representatives of such a foreign perspective. If a researcher is to attain access to these groups, as in any intercultural experience, he or she may have to engage in self-censorship. He or she may feel a need to consciously limit the areas to be explored, which limits the range of possible research questions.

Inherent in the very notion of sampling are Western assumptions of individual autonomy, egalitarianism, and democracy. In public opinion polls everybody's opinion is equally valued because they are ultimately equal at the ballot box. In non-Western cultures, however, the assumptions underlying sampling may be irrelevant. In these cultures where economic circumstances, elites, and authoritarian power structures run counter to sampling's underlying assumptions, the unquestioned use of random sampling will produce a very distorted picture of the society and how it will relate to others. In these situations, the use of alternative means of selecting respondents may be appropriate, even the use of techniques, like quota sampling, which have been severely criticized in Western settings. For example, in examining the question of what communication factors promote closer ties between countries, Johnson and Tims (1985), recognizing that the oligarchical nature of Mexican elites would largely determine the actual orientation of Mexico, used purposive quota sampling to examine the opinions of eight elite groups.

Given the importance of families and other social groupings in many countries, cluster sampling may also be a better match of research techniques to conceptualizations, with the added benefit of additional precision. In fact, the group will often be the most appropriate unit of analysis in cross-cultural research (Lowry, 1978). Cluster samples, such as intact classes of students or entire villages, might also be used for more pragmatic reasons such as the researcher's lack of mobility due to an underdeveloped transportation infrastructure, difficulty in gaining access to subjects, or a lack of resources to conduct a random sample.

All this raises questions about the appropriateness of different forms of sampling and the generalizability of results. The appropriateness of the sample is partially a function of what use will be made of the results. Are they going to be compared with samples from other cultures? For example, are students from the United States to be compared with students from Japan, or are elites from various countries being studied? While the results from a nonrandom sample may not be generalizable to the society as a whole, this is not to suggest that the research should not be conducted. In fact, Cook and Campbell (1979) recommend conducting research in a variety of different settings rather than conducting the research in a single setting with one large random sample. They suggest that each data collection represents a replication and that by conducting many small replications one gains greater confidence in the results than can be gained from a single trial.

The relationships of operationalizations to their underlying latent constructs can also be quite different in varying societies. For example, status, a crucial variable in most cultures, has many possible components; how they interact to determine someone's ultimate standing can be problematic. Another difficulty related to status is some conditions being necessary, but not sufficient. For example, being born into a noble class may be prerequisite to high status in some societies, but it also may be necessary for individuals within this class to have certain skills and material resources at their command to be considered of specially high status. In pluralistic societies, status may be achieved through a number of pathways, with high scores on any one of these dimensions permitting the classification of an individual as being of high status. It is also possible for numerous combinations of variables to result in a classification of someone as being of high status.

If the researcher is to examine intercultural communications between members of societies with differing definitions of status, then she or he is confronted with a major problem if status is crucial to the process that is to be examined. Which operationalization of status will she or he use, or will she or he have to develop some form of co-orientational framework to assess the various possible interaction effects of different status perspectives? Clearly, choosing one of the status operationalizations will not be an accurate portrayal of the intercultural experience.

The reliability of any research protocol, or established instrument, should be evaluated in each cultural context in which communication research is conducted. There are a number of factors that would render an instrument reliable (and valid) in one country and useless in another. Subjects in the United States are familiar with their role in the process of social research. People from other countries may not be as comfortable or as motivated in their role as subjects. There are idiosyncrasies of local language and differential cultural values (competitiveness, unwillingness to ask questions, the desire to tell people of higher social status what they wish to hear) that may affect subjects' responses. This suggests that one should always conduct a pretest to determine if a study's instrumentation is reliable in that culture. Further, the researcher should not be afraid to modify the original instrumentation to make its scales reliable and valid for that society.

When attempting experimental research in a different cultural setting, the researcher should ask him- or herself if the procedures translate directly into the other culture. For example, participation in an experiment, or for that matter any social research, may be a novel experience for someone from a Third World country. As a result, participation in a "control" group may itself represent a "manipulation" to the subject.

Because the researcher, as a craftsperson, must always construct an experiment to fit the situation, he or she must decide how much variation, if any, there is to be in procedures across cultures. Particularly, does the manipulation have the same meaning or must the researcher develop a new one that is theoretically more appropriate, but at the same time equivalent? Sources of data for determining if the manipulated variable is theoretically equivalent include anthropological reports, results from other cross-cultural investigations and prior research conducted in that setting, discussions with social scientists from the host culture, extensive pretesting, and interviews with the subjects after pretesting (Brislin et al., 1973).

This suggests that the researcher should pay special attention to experimental controls. For example, consider the example from above. If participation in an experiment is a novel experience, news about the event may be disseminated rapidly throughout the research setting. Participation in the study or receiving the manipulation may be perceived as an indicator of social status and, despite the researcher's requests not to disclose what occurred, the social rewards for disclosure might be greater. In this case, the entire population may, for all practical purposes, become part of the experimental group.

## DATA COLLECTION PROBLEMS

When collecting data in either an experimental or a survey situation in a cross-cultural situation, anticipate that any problem that can develop will. Brislin et al. (1973, pp. 117-120) provide 19 principles to guide the administration of tests for people unfamiliar with them. Space prevents us from providing their list here. The essence of their discussion is that nothing, from the handling of pencils to the administer's eye or head movements, should be taken for granted. Test administration conditions vary by culture. Working with a member of the host culture may help the researcher to anticipate potential problems. This information will allow him or her to act proactively and to modify the data collection procedures to increase the probability of gathering valid data.

Conducting surveys in cross-cultural situations provides a series of special data collection problems. The most important of which is who should conduct the survey interviews. After the researcher has taken special care to craft a survey instrument that is valid in that culture, determined and chosen the most appropriate sample to answer the research question, and obtained access to these people, it would be extremely frustrating if he or she obtained biased data due to the interviewer's behavior.

This problem can be avoided through their selection and training. The selected interviewer should be familiar with the culture and have a command of the vernacular used among the people being interviewed. He or she should have a high level of education but should not be a member of the underemployed middle-class common in the Third World. These people tend to have low motivation, feel superior to the research, and tend to interject their own biases into the interview (Brislin et al., 1973).

Ideally, he or she should come from the same racial or ethnic group and be of equivalent social status to the population being interviewed.

The researcher conducting a survey in a foreign culture should pay special attention to training the interviewers. The training session should go through the interview protocol question by question so that the interviewer understands every detail of the interview process, including how much latitude the interviewer has in administration. Training should also include modeling the procedure with trainees watching an experienced interviewer handling a difficult interview. Different forms of potential bias should be demonstrated and properly condemned. They should be made aware of the demand characteristics of the interview situation and taught how to avoid them. Trainees should then practice on each other with feedback from the researcher.

The researcher should verify a sample of the interviews. In order to avoid feelings that the verification process is an insult or expression of distrust, the researcher should provide feedback to the interviewer in the form of discussion about the interviews and his or her interpretation of what the answers mean. Interviewing the interviewer is a valuable source of available data that adds richness to the survey data. Further, it goes a long way to helping ensure the reliability and validity of the survey.

Discussions with the interviewers (or person conducting an experiment or administering a standardized test) also may help reveal the demand characteristics of the research context. The research assistant may be familiar with the subjects. As such, the subjects may wish to please the researcher by giving him or her the responses they perceive the researcher wants to hear. Further, because participation in social research may be a novel experience involving a researcher of higher social status (or a rich American), subjects may be intimidated into socially desirable responses. When the research is conducted by an outsider, polite or evasive responses, common in Arab and Asian cultures, could result. Finally, because the researcher must often gain official access to the subjects, the subjects may perceive that the research is being manipulated by their government. This may lead to a variety of different responses depending on the culture.

## RESEARCH INFRASTRUCTURE PROBLEMS

We have come to assume the existence of certain research facilities when conducting social research in the United States. These include readily available, accurate, and current sampling frames like a population census, telephone books, or city directories. These are not available in much of the world. For example, the junior author was involved in a survey in Mexico City. The absence of an accurate sample frame led the research team to take aerial photographs to identify a population of households from which to sample.

The preparation of written materials is accomplished without difficulty in the United States because of ready access to printing presses, mimeo and ditto machines, and photocopiers. Paper to produce written materials is inexpensive and available. Generally, all we have to do is to walk into our department's supply cabinet and take sufficient paper to copy our research instruments. When we have to alter a questionnaire after a pretest, we think nothing of throwing the old version of the instrument into the garbage and producing hundreds of copies of a revised one. This is not the case in much of the world. Paper and production facilities are not readily available, especially at a moment's notice when an instrument revision is required. Further, the cost of these objects may be considerably more than what we anticipated. Governments frequently tax paper products and printed materials. The cost of information that is for developmental purposes only may restrict our access to paper and printed materials.

We also take for granted readily available electricity to power broadcast receivers, video- and audiotape machines, movie projectors, and other research equipment including computers. This may not be the case throughout the world, especially in rural areas of lesser developed countries. While a plethora of software has been developed for social research, including that for the transcription of ethnographic notes, the lack of a guaranteed source of electricity makes their use problematic (Heise, 1981).

## RESULTS PROBLEMS

Due to the lack of a research infrastructure, the investigator may have difficulty analyzing data in the host society. For example, a Nigerian colleague of ours was in the habit of coming to the United States for data analysis. There were many reasons for this. First, there may be no trained computer personnel to key the coded data or even a computer upon which to conduct the analysis. Second, the computer may frequently and unpredictably go down due to intermittent electricity. Third, the software necessary to analyze the data may not be available in the country where the research is conducted as the cost for common statistical software may be prohibitively high given its infrequent use.

When conducting data analysis in unfamiliar settings, the researcher should pay special attention to error terms in statistical analysis. The residuals may hold the key to variables not explicitly considered by the theoretical model. Systematic variation in the behavior of the residuals

may be unique to the cultural setting and provide insights into understanding the process of communication in that context. For example, the
authors recently examined the pattern of language use among bilinguals
in Belize (Barnett et al., 1987). They found systematic differences in the
pattern of the residuals when the theoretical model was tested in English
and Spanish. This analysis helped us to understand the different ways the
languages were used by this population. Further, failure to carefully
consider possible new factors operative in a different culture can lead to
errors in the specification of the model and an erroneous understanding of
how communication operates in society.

   In addition to the analysis of the residuals, the researcher should examine the variables' variances both within cultures and across cultures.
This may tell more about the cultural process than the differences between
averages of groups. For example, the variance on an attitude measure is
an excellent indicator of the extent of cultural consensus regarding communication norms. If the variance is restricted, then the consensus is great.
If the variance is broad, there is little cultural consensus. Similar interpretations of variances may be made across cultural groups.

   The very nature of statistical analysis raises concerns about its appropriateness within certain cultural contexts. One assumption behind
parametric statistics is multivariate normality—the variables are distributed normally in the population upon which the analysis is to be conducted.
This may be problematic when considering that the samples for much
intercultural research consist of elites who come from the tails of the
distributions of certain variables, particularly income, education, and
media use behaviors. Thus these variables may have restricted variance
that threatens underlying assumptions of certain statistical analyses.


## DISCUSSION PROBLEMS

   Results are often treated as endings rather than as beginnings. They are
really transitions to thinking about the next study in a line of research.
Thus implications and discussions are a way of pausing and noting where
we have been, but, most important, they provide clear directions as to
where we should be going.

   In intercultural research implications are particularly important, because often we will encounter "surprise." That is, our results do not make
sense in the context of what we know. But the results may make perfect
sense in the context of the culture that we only know partially. The
researcher needs to have a prepared mind that can appreciate the unexpected and be ready to take advantage of serendipitous findings. The
researcher must not be subject to the curious form of ethnocentrism that

comes from "hypothesis myopia," the unwillingness to see other things and patterns in research results (Bachrach, 1965). Collaboration with a member of the host culture can substantially aid the research process by interpreting the results in the context of the host culture.

Intercultural research can heighten the awareness of both cultures. Many individuals rightly criticize the arrogance of a researcher who passes judgments on the mores of another society solely based on those of his or her own cultural value systems. In the same breath the argument will typically run that only a member of a culture can really understand it. It is also well understood, however, that all cultures contain within them a "taken-for-granted reality" that is typically not explicitly understood and that serves as the context within which interaction occurs (Berger & Luckmann, 1966). Often an outsider is needed to point to the taken-for-granted assumptions of a culture. The point is not that a single true perspective exists, but that to understand intercultural communication multiple perspectives are required before even an approximation of the truth can be arrived at. To expect that a researcher can have at one in the same time a taken-for-granted understanding of a culture and an ability to stand outside of it is perhaps unrealistic. Here again collaboration between members of two different cultures is critical. Without such collaboration any discussion of the results and implications is likely to be incomplete.

Collaboration is especially important in intercultural research because the researcher needs to understand not only *both* cultures involved but the dynamic interactive effects of relationships between them as well. Research results must be placed in the context of both cultures examined and then the unique *inter*cultural issues must be examined.

Adding to the complications of interpreting intercultural communication research results is the large number of competing hypotheses that might explain the pattern of findings involving the interaction of culture and research methods (Gudykunst, 1985; Gudykunst & Wright, 1980). For example, because methods often have to be changed to make them compatible cross-culturally, we do not know if any changes in results are attributable to differences in method or to true cultural differences.

In discussing results that differ from the expected, or where totally unexpected findings occur, the researcher must always try to grapple with whether or not differences in degree are actually differences in kind. That is, is there a totally unexpected alternative explanation stemming from enmeshment of the variables in nonparallel cultural processes? Somewhat relatedly, we need to be sensitive to the fact that just because we find differences does not mean there are not commonalities as well. We should also be sensitive to presence of intracultural differences that may be even more pronounced than intercultural ones.

## CONCLUSION

In this chapter we have suggested that the process of social research, in general, and intercultural communication research, specifically, may be viewed as a craft. Conducting social research in unfamiliar cultural settings requires the researcher to make judgments about the "best" way to carry out the process. By "best" we are suggesting that the scholar conduct him- or herself in such a manner as to maximize the validity of the research and maximize his or her understanding of the process of communication in the context of the culture in which the research is conducted. Because we view social research as an art as well as a science, we anticipate that mistakes will be made. Not all findings will add to our understanding of culture's role in the process of communication. Unanticipated events will render even the most carefully laid research plans ineffective. When this occurs the scholar learns from his or her mistakes and, with his or her newfound wisdom, should avoid these problems in the future.

It is not possible—in principle—to do an unflawed social science research study (McGrath, 1982). In maximizing crucial research values in any one study (e.g., generalizability), other values are inevitably slighted (e.g., precision of measurement). The researcher's goal then is to ensure in any one study that some research value is preserved. That is, any one study should do at least one thing extremely well. In doing this one thing well the researcher may need—for various reasons, such as costs—puposively to choose to slight another important research value; thus, in Staw's (1982) more colorful language, researchers should jealously guard the central elements of a study by feeding less central ones to predators.

But what is a researcher to do if there are known flaws in his or her study? The answer lies in thinking in broader terms. Science is supposed to be cumulative, with replication as one of the key paths to "truth." Unfortunately, these factors have come to be ignored in communication research generally, with the focus of the researcher on doing disjointed studies on "hot" topics. As a result the primary solution to flawed single studies is not typically apparent. But at the level of the individual study, it has been suggested that individual researchers can strive for "triangulation" of methods to achieve more valid results (Staw, 1982).

The ultimate solution, of course, is to conduct research programs in which separate studies look at the problem in slightly different ways, with different methods, and, as a result, complement each other's strengths and weaknesses (McGrath, 1982); and, we hope, each succeeding study will tackle successive alternative explanations to the central hypothesis. "We should seek not perfection in the single study, but accumulation over studies using diverse means" (McGrath et al., 1982, pp. 107).

Nowhere is the need to do complementary studies more evident than in intercultural research where the complementary approaches may not be just on the level of methods, but also on the level of cultural assumptions and values. Thus complementary studies examining central problems should operate at the conceptual frame of reference as well as at a more technical/methodological one—attempting triangulation of cultural perspectives as well as methods.

Of course, all of this establishes a nearly impossible set of requirements for intercultural research—a level of effort that no one person, or even a small group of persons, is likely to achieve. But, of course, science is itself a cultural enterprise. A craftsperson depends on tradition and operates within it. His or her work enriches the whole, but only in terms of variations on a theme, not the theme itself. Thus, if the craftsperson serves his or her craft and does his or her individual studies well, eventually the whole enterprise moves forward, not through any one individual contribution, but through the work done in concert by many.

## REFERENCES

Alker, H. A. (1966). Causal inference and political analysis. In J. Bernd (Ed.), *Mathematical applications in political science*. Dallas: Southern Methodist University Press.

Bachrach, A. J. (1965). *Psychological research: An introduction*. New York: Random House.

Barnett, G. A., Oliveira, O. S., & Johnson, J. D. (1987). *Multilingual language use and television exposure and preferences: The case of Belize*. Unpublished manuscript, State University of New York, Buffalo, Department of Communication.

Barnett, G. A., Wigand, R. T., Harrison, R. P., Woelfel, J., & Cohen, A. A. (1981). Communication and cultural development. *Human Organization, 40*, 330-337.

Bennett, J. W., & McKnight, R. K. (1966). Social norms, national imagery, and interpersonal relations. In A. G. Smith (Ed.), *Communication and culture: Readings in the codes of human interaction*. New York: Holt, Rinehart & Winston.

Berger, P. L., & Luckmann, T. (1966). *The social construction of reality*. New York: Doubleday.

Berlo, D. K. (1977). Communication as process: Review and commentary. In B. D. Ruben (Ed.), *Communication yearbook* (Vol. 1). New Brunswick, NJ: Transaction.

Blalock, H. M., Jr. (1982). *Conceptualization and measurement in the social sciences*. Beverly Hills, CA: Sage.

Brislin, R. W., Lonner, W. J., & Thorndike, R. M. (1973). *Cross-cultural research methods*. New York: John Wiley.

Carter, R. E. (1966). Some problems and distinctions: Cross-cultured research. *American Behavioral Scientist*, pp. 23-24.

Cook, T. D., & Campbell, D. T. (1979). *Quasi-experimentation: Design and analysis issues for field settings*. Boston: Houghton Mifflin.

Chu, G. C. (1964). Problems of cross-cultural research. *Journalism Quarterly, 47*, 557-562.

Daft, R. L. (1983). Learning the craft of organizational research. *Academy of Management Review, 8*, 539-546.

Ellingsworth, H. W. (1977). Conceptualizing intercultural communication. In B. D. Ruben (Ed.), *Communication yearbook* (Vol. 1). New Brunswick, NJ: Transaction.

Frey, F. W. (1966). *The mass media and rural development in Turkey*. Cambridge: MIT Press.

Frey, F. W. (1973). Communication and development. In I. S. Pool, F. W. Frey, W. Schramm, N. Maccoby, & E. B. Parker (Eds.), *Handbook of communication*. Chicago: Rand McNally.

Gudykunst, W. B. (1983). Uncertainty reduction and predictability of behavior in low- and high context cultures. *Communication Quarterly, 31*, 49-55.

Gudykunst, W. B. (1985). Intercultural communication: Current status and proposed directions. In B. Dervin & M. J. Voight (Eds.), *Progress in communication science* (Vol. 6). Norwood, NJ: Ablex.

Gudykunst, W. B., & Kim, Y. Y. (1984). *Communicating with strangers*. Reading, MA: Addison-Wesley.

Gudykunst, W. B., & Nishida, T. (1983). Social penetration in close friendships in Japan and the United States. In R. Bostrom (Ed.), *Communication yearbook* (Vol. 7). Beverly Hills, CA: Sage.

Gudykunst, W. B., & Nishida, T. (1984). Individual and cultural influences on uncertainty reduction. *Communication Monographs, 51*, 23-36.

Gudykunst, W. B., & Nishida, T. (1986). The influence of cultural variability on perceptions of communication behavior associated with relationship terms. *Human Communication Research, 13*, 147-169.

Gudykunst, W. B., & Wright, J. E. (1980). Methodology in intercultural communication. In N. Asuncion-Lande (Ed.), *Ethical perspectives and critical issues in intercultural communication*. Annandale, VA: Speech Communication Association.

Hall, E. T. (1976). *Beyond culture*. Garden City, NY: Anchor.

Heise, D. R. (1981). *Microcomputers in social research*. Beverly Hills, CA: Sage.

Hofstede, G. (1980). *Culture's consequences: International differences in work-related values*. Beverly Hills, CA: Sage.

Johnson, J. D. (1983). A test of a model of magazine exposure and appraisal in India. *Communication Monographs, 50*, 148-157.

Johnson, J. D. (1984a). International communication media appraisal: Tests in Germany. In R. N. Bostrom (Ed.), *Communication yearbook* (Vol. 8). Beverly Hills, CA: Sage.

Johnson, J. D. (1984b). A test of a model of media exposure and appraisal on two magazines in Nigeria. *Journal of Applied Communication Research, 12*, 63-74.

Johnson, J. D. (1987). A model of international communication media appraisal: Phase IV, generalizing the model to film. *International Journal of Intercultural Relations, 11*, 129-142.

Johnson, J. D., & Oliveira, O. S. (1987). *A model of international communication media appraisal and exposure: A comprehensive test in Belize*. Paper presented at the Speech Communication Association Convention, Boston.

Johnson, J. D., Oliveira, O. S., & Barnett, G. A. (1987). *Communication factors related to closer international ties: An extension of a model in Belize*. Paper presented at the International Communication Association Convention in Montreal, Canada.

Johnson, J. D., & Tims, A. R. (1985). Communication factors related to closer international ties. *Human Communication Research, 12*, 259-273.

Korzenny, F., & Korzenny, B. A. G. (1984). Quantitative approaches: An overview. In W. B. Gudykunst & Y. Y. Kim (Eds.), *Methods for intercultural communication research*. Beverly Hills, CA: Sage.

Kulka, R. A. (1982). Idiosyncrasy and circumstance: Choices and constraints in the research process. In J. E. McGrath, J. Martin, & R. A. Kulka (Eds.), *Judgment calls in research*. Beverly Hills, CA: Sage.

Lerner, D. (1958). *The passing of traditional society*. Glencoe, IL: Free Press.

Lerner, D., & Schramm, W. (1967). *Communication and change in the developing countries*. Honolulu: East-West Center Press.

Lowry, D. T. (1978). *Communication research in less developed countries: Towards appropriate methodology*. Paper presented at the annual convention of the International Communication Association.

Martin, J. (1982). A garbage can model of the research process. In J. E. McGrath, J. Martin, & R. A. Kulka (Eds.), *Judgment calls in research*. Beverly Hills, CA: Sage.

Massey, H. (1981). *The craftsman's way: Canadian expressions*. Toronto: University of Toronto Press.

McCrone, D. J., & Cnudde, C. F. (1967). Towards a communications theory of democratic political development: A causal model. *American Political Science Review, 61*, 72-79.

McGrath, J. E. (1982). Dillematics: The study of research choices and dilemmas. In J. E. McGrath, J. Martin, & R. A. Kulka (Eds.), *Judgment calls in research*. Beverly Hills, CA: Sage.

McGrath, J. E., Martin, J., & Kulka, R. A. (Eds.). (1982). *Judgment calls in research*. Beverly Hills, CA: Sage.

McLuhan, H. M. (1964). *Understanding media: The extensions of man*. New York: McGraw-Hill.

Monge, P. R. (1982). System's theory and research in the study of organizational communication: The correspondence problem. *Human Communication Research, 8*, 245-261.

Osgood, C. E. (1974). Probing subjective culture part 1: Cross-linguistic tool-making. *Journal of Communication, 24*, 21-35.

Parks, M. (1982). Ideology in interpersonal communication: Off the couch and into the world. In M. Burgoon (Ed.), *Communication yearbook* (Vol. 5). New Brunswick, NJ: Transaction.

Parsons, T. (1951). *The social system*. New York: Free Press.

Parsons, T. (1968). Social systems. In D. L. Sills (Ed.), *International encyclopedia of the social sciences* (Vol. 15). New York: Macmillan.

Rogers, E. M. (1983). *The communication of innovation* (3rd ed.). New York: Free Press.

Rogers, E. M., & Bhowmik, D. K. (1971). Homophily-heterophily: Relational concepts for communication research. *Public Opinion Quarterly, 34*, 523-538.

Sarbaugh, L. E. (1979). A systematic framework for analyzing intercultural communication. In N. C. Jain (Ed.), *International and intercultural communication annual* (Vol. 5). Falls Church, VA: Speech Communication Association.

Sarbaugh, L. E. (1984). An overview of selected approaches. In W. B. Gudykunst & Y. Y. Kim (Eds.) *Methods for intercultural communication research*. Beverly Hills, CA: Sage.

Schlereth, T. J. (1984). *Artifacts and the American past*. Nashville, TN: American Association for State and Local History.

Selltiz, C., Jahoda, M., Deutsch, M., & Cook, S. W. (1959). *Research methods in social relations*. New York: Holt, Rinehart & Winston.

Staw, B. M. (1982). Some judgments on the judgment calls approach. In J. E. McGrath, J. Martin, & R. A. Kulka (Eds.), *Judgment calls in research*. Beverly Hills, CA: Sage.

Winham, G. R. (1970). Political development and Lerner's theory: Further test of a causal model. *American Political Science Review, 64*, 810-818.

# 23 Translation

## Christiane F. Gonzalez

Communication is often made possible by translation. What reader, however, is aware that, when he or she reads a translation, every word, every punctuation mark, is not the author's, but the translator's? Actually, the reader's impression of important works of literature has been shaped for generations by translations. Throughout the ages, translators and interpreters have acted as mediators between people of different tongues. Since World War II, the rapid increase in global communication and the sharp rise in a worldwide technical and scientific exchange have created a greater demand than ever before for people dedicated to the task of translation. This chapter will present a brief summary of the history of translation and of translation theories, explain basic techniques of translating and interpreting (for the sake of brevity, the examples are mostly taken from English and German), discuss various models for a science of translation and translation theories, and analyze the limits of translatability.

### HISTORY

Translation, defined in its simplest terms as the interpretation of verbal signs by the verbal signs of another language, has been an integral part of intercultural communication for millennia. The biblical story of the tower of Babel exemplifies the biblical and mythological roots of translation and of the human race's awareness of the need for translation. Oral translation (interpretation) dates back further than written translation; the terms *interpres* in Latin, *hermeneutes* in Greek, or *tolmetze* in Middle High German describe someone who mediates between two languages, but who also comments and explains (e.g., *interpres iuris*).

As early as the sixth century B.C., the Greeks translated papyruses of the classical African civilizations into their language. Numerous Greeks, including Homer, Herodotus, Solon, Plato, Anaximander, and Pythagoras, studied in the African Nile Valley and produced works in Greek from Egypt and Ethiopia (Asante, 1987; Bernal, 1987).

Plutarch mentions an "interpreting school" in Alexander the Great's Greece where 30,000 Persian boys were studying Greek (Koller, 1972). The Romans, however, are considered to be the actual "inventors" of the art of translation; their literature originated with translations from Attic tragedies and comedies, and with Livius Andronicus's "Homer" translation. In the last century B.C., Cicero was presumably the first in a long line of translators to reflect upon methods and theories of his art. His antithesis "ut orator"/"ut interpres" (free translation versus literal translation), still surprisingly modern, sums up what has been a vital aspect of dealing with translation problems to this day: the discussion about "literal" or "free" translation. Martin Luther (Sendbrief vom Dolmetschen, 1530), whose Bible translation marked a new epoch, spoke out for free translation, except in instances of crucial theological importance. Bible translation is a fascinating subject as it goes back more than 2,000 years, involves around 1,400 languages (and cultures), includes literary texts from lyric poetry to theological discourse, and has been a subject of translation theory to this day. It is a prime example of "receptor-oriented" translation, with the "United Bible Societies" aiming at not one, but numerous translations for different purposes: from scientific to church use, from scholars to illiterates.

## PRACTICAL ASPECTS

Every translator must be aware of the fact that words, phrases, and sentence patterns in the target language (the language to be translated into) differ from those in the source language (the language to be translated from) as to form and content. Yet the translator has at his or her disposal innumerable ways of joining together words and phrases in sentences, conveying the meaning of the source language text. A translation should reproduce the meaning and intent of the original text correctly and completely, affect readers the same way the original does, and not sound like a translation; that is, read like an original. Or should it? Decision making is a large part of translation; the translator is confronted with numerous contradicting principles (Koller, 1972, p. 101).

1. A translation must give the words of the original.
   or:
   A translation must give the ideas of the original.
2. A translation should read like an original work.
   or:
   A translation should read like a translation.

3. A translation should reflect the style of the original.
   or:
   A translation should possess the style of the translator.
4. A translation should read as a contemporary of the original.
   or:
   A translation should read as a contemporary of the translator.
5. A translation may add to or omit from the original.
   or:
   A translation may never add to or omit from the original.
6. A translation of verse should be in verse.

The translator has to ask a number of questions, for example: What is the status of the source language text? Which of its components or features must at any cost be expressed in a translation? May the translation violate target language use? Should the text have to be adapted to the needs of the target language reader? Who will the readers be? What purpose does the translation serve? The translator, in a manner that is both subjective—decision depends on ability and intentions—and objective—decision depends on the material at hand—thus decides on certain methods and types of translation. Basically, there are two choices: a source-language-oriented translation, which is a "literal" or "documentary" method of translating, aiming at being close to the original text; or a target-language-oriented translation, which is a method of integrating the source language text into the environment of the target language.

According to Güttinger (1963), one criterion for a good translation is the translator's use of words common in the target, but not in the source, language. This is regarded as proof that the translator knows his own language. For example, there is no English word for the German *leise* (in a low voice, in a whisper, barely audible, and the like), or for *Geschwister* (brother and sister), or for *schweigen* (to say nothing, to keep silent, and the like). In such instances, the good German translator takes the opportunity to shorten the translation and to improve the translation's style.

## ISSUES IN TRANSLATION

### Importance of Mother Tongue

The translator is constantly in danger of neglecting the most vital tool: his or her own native tongue. Any scrupulous translator will strive, if at all possible, to be working only into his or her mother tongue. This may seem obvious and irrefutable, but it is all too often forgotten. Especially in literary translation, the translator's love for his or her own language and its literature is imperative. The translator's extensive-passive-vocabulary in and knowledge of the source language must be complemented by superior-active-command of the target language.

## Dictionaries and Other Aids

Bilingual dictionaries are an indispensable aid for any translator. Their use is more limited—and trickier—than is generally assumed, however. Dictionaries can never take over the job of translating; they cannot tell us which one of the many meanings of a word will fit into a certain context. What they do best is activate the translator's passive vocabulary—one looks up a word one is familiar with, but cannot think of offhand. On the other hand, if a source language word that the translators thinks he or she knows perfectly appears strange in a given context, he or she should not hesitate to look it up. One example (Güttinger, 1963, p. 116): in "Sanctuary" by William Faulkner, a "moccasin" is not an Indian shoe, as surmised in one German translation, but a venomous snake—a good example that translation is so much more than a word-for-word code-switching process. An English one-language encyclopedia or dictionary would have been a much better resource here. Often needed tools of the trade also include a dictionary of synonyms; a dictionary of quotations; legal, technical, and scientific dictionaries; and last but not least the translator's own personal card file, which one expands and works with over the years.

## Differing Word Connotations in
## Source and Target Languages

There are very few words in any two languages with identical emotional value and impact. Classic examples of words considered to be untranslatable are *understatement* and *gentleman* in English, *Gemütlichkeit, Heimat,* or *Wald* in German. Each language instills its words with different values on the emotional ladder, as the following example shows:

One can ask a Russian who knows some English what the Russian word /drúk/ means, and the answer will be "friend." This is roughly true, but the precise social circumstances under which a Russian calls another person /drúk/ are by no means the same as those under which we call someone a friend. The meaning of /drúk/, or of "friend," for a speaker of the language involved, is the result of all his past experiences with that word. Within a single speech community, the differences between the accidents of personal history of different individuals tend to cancel out, so that if the meanings of morphemes never become absolutely identical for different speakers, they are at least sufficiently similar that communication via speech is possible. From one community to another, however, this levelling-out does not occur. Bilingual dictionaries and easy word-by-word translations are inevitably misleading;

the shortcut of asking what a form means must ultimately be supplemented by active participation in the life of the community that speaks the language. This, of course, is one of the major reasons why semantic analysis is so difficult. (Hockett, 1967, p. 141)

One has to keep in mind, however, that words appear in context, and that the translator does not transfer individual words, but thoughts and ideas, and those can very well be conveyed in the other language.

## Realia, Humor, Dialects

Challenges are frequently presented by "realia": words, objects, stereotypes, and historical allusions pertaining to the source language text. The translator has several possibilities of dealing with "realia":

(1) He or she uses the source language term in the target language; *Wunderkind, Angst,* or *Ostpolitik* are used in English texts just as *public relations* or *know-how* are used in German, to name just a very few.

(2) He or she adapts the source language word to the target language; for example, English verbs are often used in German verb forms: *to lease— leasen.*

(3) He or she translates word by word: *data processing—Datenverarbeitung.*

(4) He or she describes or explains the source language word in the text; footnoting is a rather clumsy solution, but in a few cases it cannot be avoided.

(5) He or she replaces the source language "realia" with one from the target language. Thus, when the Bible was translated for the Eskimos, the word *sheep,* which does not exist in their language, was substituted by *seals.*

Puns, word plays, jokes, and humor in general often pose insurmountable problems. If they cannot be reproduced in any way, the translator might attempt a word play in a different place in the target language—a controversial method, because the author put the word play in a certain place with a purpose. Sometimes, rather than risking such chancy operations, the translator will be better off leaving the humor out altogether. If the purpose of the source language text, namely to create laughter, cannot be served, a word-by-word translation, even with an explanation, seems superfluous.

Names must be translated if they are "talking" names, that is, if the author uses the name to describe traits in a character's personality. One famous example of this is "Alice in Wonderland." Dialects can occasionally be replaced by a dialect of the target language when the text to be translated is so old that an association with modern-day circumstances seems unlikely. In modern texts, such as dramas, novels, or film scripts, it has become a generally accepted and common practice not to replace the dialect of the source language with one of the target language. Reasons of style forbid a replacement. Also, different dialects evoke totally different associations. The information content of the original would not be preserved, but falsified. Sometimes a translator will change the syntax in the target language slightly to indicate to the reader that the source language text deviates from standard speech. The one exception where a transfer of dialects seems possible is in the case of big city lower-class dialects, the classical example for this being, of course, "My Fair Lady":

(6-14a)  The rain in Spain stays mainly in the plain.
       [ə raɪn ɪn spaɪn staɪz 'maɪnlɪ ɪn ə plaɪn]
(6-14b)  Es grünt so grün, wenn Spaniens Blüten blün'n.
       [es jriːnt zoː jriːn vɛn 'spaːnjəns bliːtn bliːn] (Diller & Kornelius, 1978,
       p. 117)

The peculiarities of Cockney speech are replaced by those specific to the Berlin dialect.

## Images and Quotations

It is surprising that you will find a word-for-word translation of source language images that make no sense whatsoever in the target language. In reading a German translation of Raymond Chandler's letters, I came across the nonsensical phrase "die Bohnen verschütten." Of course, the person in question had "spilled the beans" in English. This is a good example of the negligent way often underpaid translators treat what they, or their publishers, define as trivial literature. This sort of thing happens on a much more "elevated" style of literature as well; for example, direct or disguised quotations from the Bible are much more frequent in English than in German literature. The phrase "he who runs may read" is derived from the Bible and not easily recognizable as a quote.[1] The translator must develop an "instinct" for detecting things of this nature, and, if possible, find an appropriate image or quote in the target language.

## Grammar and Style

Advocates of the idea that a translation should not read like an original may find the following a good translation from the German: "It is forbidden to cross the railroad lines" (Güttinger, 1963, p. 7). German syntax was taken over into the English. Even though the English-speaking reader will understand this sentence, it is not in keeping with normal English syntax, which would be "Do not cross the tracks" or simply "No crossing." Grammar and style of the source language must be transformed into the grammar and syntax of the target language in order to avoid clumsy, unidiomatic, or even false translation.

Nida's (1964) book *Toward a Science of Translation* was a major milestone in the emergence of a science of translation; at the same time, the title of the book reflected—and still does—the unfinished character of translation science:

> In actual practice, translators rarely if ever pursue their work as though they were guided by only one underlying theory. Most translators are highly eclectic in practice. If they are confronted with a literary text that has a rather special history in the sense that it is derived from various sources and has been subjected to a variety of interpretations, they tend to begin with a philological approach to their work. If, however, a text is nonliterary and the source and receptor languages are relatively similar and represent basically the same cultural milieu, the approach is essentially linguistic. If, however, a translation involves languages that are widely separate in time and represent quite different cultures, and if the text is structurally rather complex and the prospective audience possibly varied, the translator is almost compelled to think of his task in sociolinguistic terms.
>
> What is ultimately needed for translation is a well-formulated, comprehensive theory of translation that can take into account all the related factors. Because translating always involves communication within the context of interpersonal relations, the model for such activity must be a communication model, and the principles must be primarily sociolinguistic in the broad sense of the term. As such, translating becomes a part of the even broader field of anthropological semiotics. Within the structure of a unified theory of translation it would be possible to deal with all the factors that are involved in and influence the nature of translation. These could be assigned their proper roles and their significance for the process of translating could be properly weighted on a number of sliding scales, depending in several cases on the extralinguistic factors involved. (Nida, 1964, p. 97)

## A THEORETICAL OUTLINE

### Historical Development Toward a Science of Translation

Over the centuries, various approaches to translation theory have evolved and coexisted. One, the literary theory, focused on the creative aspects of translating literature, on the status of the source language and target language texts in their respective literary traditions, and on the relation between form and content. One continual theme has been the controversy over literal and free translation. Linguistic aspects—other than this last one—were widely ignored, and it was not acknowledged that not all translation is literary.

In contrast to the literary tradition, linguists and grammarians of different schools defined theory in terms of semantics and grammar and translation as the application of linguistics. The object of their theories was to describe lexical and grammatical language structures both in source and in target language to create a text of equivalent meaning. The fathers of modern linguistics have had a lasting influence on linguistic translation theory. Ferdinand de Saussure revolutionized linguistics. His distinction between *parole* (concrete language expression), *language* (general language competency) and *langue* (language as system) described different aspects of language, which to him was a special form of more general systems of signs. To Saussure, language signs were an arbitrary link between things describing ("signifiant") and described ("signifiée), or between reference and meaning. Saussure in turn influenced major linguists such as Louis Hjelmslev and Leonard Bloomfield.

In the hermeneutic concept, language and its signs were treated as creative energy. The German romantics, like Wilhelm von Humboldt, thought that words—and languages—are not merely an index to a concept, but shape concepts and cultures. This tradition continued into the twentieth century (Martin Heidegger, G. Steiner); like the literary approach, it neglects linguistic and other aspects of translation theory, and does not take into account the fact that not all translation, or language, is creative.

Even though they had and still have their merits, none of these theories was complementary or comprehensive. After World War II, the increase in scientific and technical translation, the rise of linguistics (structuralism, generative transformational grammar), the evolution of sociolinguistics, and a renewed interest in comparative linguistics all contributed to the emergence of numerous models for a science of translation. Some theorists considered translation to be a special "brand" of comparison and, therefore, wanted it to be integrated into the field of comparative descriptive linguistics, or contrastive linguistics, that is, the method for comparing the workings of different languages. The impact of the following theories is evident even today.

### "Stylistique comparée"

Developed in France in the 1950s, "stylistique comparée" constituted a first systematic effort to categorize the interlingual transfer process. "Stylistique comparée" concluded that all translation processes could be summarized in seven main categories, the first three in the area of literal translation ("traduction directe"), the other four in the area of free translation ("traduction oblique"). Using English and German, here is a brief summary of the categories:

1. *emprunt*: taking over intact source language lexemes into the target language;
   E: Know-how; G: know-how.

2. *calque*: loan translation; G: Meisterstück; E: masterpiece.

3. *traduction littérale*: replacing syntactic structures in the source language with corresponding syntactic structures of identical meaning in the target language;
   E: How many fish have you caught?
   G: Wieviele Fische hast du gefangen?

4. *transposition*: reproducing source language text elements by changing patterns of speech while retaining the original content:
   E: There is no truth in his claim.
   G: Seine Behauptung ist unzutreffend.

5-7. *modulation, équivalence, adaptation*: the shifting of semantic structures in source and target language while preserving functional equivalence:
   E: It grows on you.
   G: Man gewöhnt sich daran. (Wilss, 1977, pp. 113-116)

Theorists have discussed these categories in detail and tried to regroup them; Wilss (1977, pp. 117-119) maintains that "emprunt" and "calque" hardly qualify as translation procedures, as they operate on a subsentence level. He also argues that the term *literal* translation must be better defined and differentiated; and that drawing a sharp line between "traduction directe" and "traduction oblique" might not be realistic.

It remains to be seen whether concrete translation procedures can be listed, described, and evaluated in a classification scheme of this nature. Be that as it may—"stylistique comparée," by trying to create a comprehensive taxonomy of translation procedures, played a decisive role in the emergence of a language-pair-related descriptive and a language-pair-related applied science of translation.

## Linguistic Theory

In the 1950s and 1960s, linguistics rose to be an accepted academic science, using proven scientific methods, while the human sciences in general were being challenged for not being "full-fledged" sciences. What could be more logical than to see the analysis of translation procedures as a part of linguistics? These theorists (O. Kade, A. Neubert, G. Jäger) considered translation as an operation performed on languages—a process of substituting a text in one language for a text in another, and they came to the conclusion that translation theory had to be based on a general linguistic theory. From this developed the idea that the texts to be analyzed had to meet standards of scientific description, meaning the exclusion of all texts determined by subjective and coincidental factors, that is, all literary texts. The theorists, influenced by and in turn influencing the recently emerging machine translation, distinguished between two basic types of translating: literary translation (prose and poetry of all kinds; dialectic relation between form and content), and pragmatic translation (priority of content over form).

Despite the severe restrictions of this purely linguistic approach, it is indispensable in the field of language-pair-related research (which in turn is vital to research on machine translation), as it deals with a systematic description of which grammatical and lexical equivalents can be found in any two languages. The yield from this descriptive work—in the context of an applied science of translation—will ideally be the basis for translation dictionaries for the translator's everyday use.

## Translation as Communication

In his book, *Toward a Science of Translation*, Nida (1964) views translation as a complex act of communication. He focuses on semantic problems and integrates modern linguistic approaches (B. L. Whorf; B. Russell, and others) in his analysis of the problem of "meaning":

> Basic to any discussion of principles and procedures in translation is a thorough acquaintance with the manner in which meaning is expressed through language as a communication code. (Nida, 1964; Koller, 1979, p. 84)

For Nida, the term can never be seen in isolation from its communication context; thus "meaning" must be seen in relation to the communication process with its three components—source, message, receptor. Nida analyzes the use of language and argues that

> to suggest that the interlingual communication involved in translating is in some way basically different from intralingual communication is to seriously misjudge the very nature of language use. (Nida, 1976; Koller, 1979, p. 5)

Nida's sociolinguistic concept of the translation process is receptor-oriented; he even replaces the term *target language* with the term *receptor language,* and challenges the idea of one perfect translation, because, in his reasoning, different groups of receptors require different translations.

## COMPONENTS OF A
## SCIENCE OF TRANSLATION

### Text Typology

Translation theorists eventually came to realize that it would be next to impossible to find principles of unqualified validity for all forms of texts;

it became evident that groups of texts and their relevance to translation science had to be analyzed separately, and that a text typology must be developed (Koller, 1979). First came the distinction between literary and pragmatic texts; excelling theorists of literary translation in the framework of translation science were R. Kloepfer and J. Levy, whose work went beyond the analysis of translation procedures and defined literary translation as a subject for scientific research, embracing aspects of literature as well as aspects of aesthetics, style, cultural context, and linguistics.

At about the same time, R. Jumpelt's (1961) book on the translation of scientific and technical texts distinguishes between aesthetic/poetic and pragmatic/factual texts, and develops a theory for the latter. Mounin (1967) in his text classification differentiates between religious, literary, and technical texts; children's books; theater plays; and film synchronization texts. K. Reiss (1971), according to the functions of language, classifies texts in three groups: information-oriented texts (priority of content), expression-oriented texts (priority of form), and imperative texts (command-oriented). It remains doubtful whether all texts or groups of texts will be covered by this classification scheme, or any other. Some texts cannot be limited to one communicative function; sometimes functions overlap. These theorists and others have pointed the way, however, and in the interest of a comprehensive science of translation, it is essential that research into the field of text typology and text linguistics continues.

## Translation Criticism

Translation criticism as it is being practiced today is inadequate; it lacks expertise as well as a theoretical foundation; this becomes evident especially in one- or two-line "appraisals" of translation work in book reviews in magazines or newspapers. Constructive translation criticism in the framework of applied translation science can contribute to a higher quality of translation. Translation criticism as a part of a science of translation is tentatively composed of three parts (Reiss, 1971, p. 58):

1. In text analysis, the source language text is examined for its linguistic function, characteristics of its content, style, form, and pragmatic traits.
2. Text comparison—the comparison of the translation with the original—evaluate if and how these functions are conveyed in the target language, what procedures the translator uses to this end, and why he uses them.
3. Translation evaluation tries to determine whether equivalence has been achieved.

As in most fields of translation science, a lot remains to be done in the field of translation criticism. One problem is that the term *equivalence* is without a solid theoretical base and still awaits a valid definition.

## Equivalence in Translation

All theorists agree that equivalence between original text and translation is one of the key issues of a science of translation, and, incidentally, of a good translation. To this day, however, definitions of the term have been manifold and tentative. Here are just some random examples:

- functional equivalence (Jäger, 1968)
- equivalence in difference (Jakobson, 1966)
- principle of equivalent effect (Jumpelt, 1961)
- preservation of invariance on the content level (Kade, 1968)
- text interchangeability in a given situation (Catford, 1965)
- adequacy of intent, or communicative equivalence (Wilss, 1977)
- the closest natural equivalent (Nida, 1964)
- "formal" (source language-oriented) versus "dynamic" (target language-oriented) equivalence (Nida, 1976).

In the literature of translation science, you find content equivalence; stylistic, formal, functional, textual, communicative, and pragmatic equivalence; as well as equivalence of effect. Koller (1979, pp. 186-189) argues that equivalence postulates a relation between source language and target language text. This relation must be defined by giving the framework and the conditions for equivalence in a given context. The translator must decide on a hierarchy of values to be preserved in a translation; from this decision, he or she can deduct a hierarchy of equivalence from the following five groups of equivalence:

(a) "denotative" equivalence (or invariance of content) refers to the nonlinguistic context of a text;

(b) "connotative" equivalence (or stylistic equivalence) refers to the choice of words determining such things as style level and geographical and social backgrounds;

(c) "text normative" equivalence refers to the text and language norms of certain groups or types of text (for example, the norms of usage for contracts, business letters, and instructions must be reflected in the translation);

(d) "pragmatic" equivalence (or communicative equivalence) refers to receptor-orientation of texts (this implies translating a text for a specific group of readers/receptors); and

(e) "formal" equivalence (or aesthetic equivalence, equivalence of expression) refers to formal and aesthetic traits of texts, for example, in translation of poetry—the importance lies in achieving the source language's aesthetic effect in the target language.

Each of those areas is—as yet—tentatively defined; translation science is a young, insecure science; in its publications, one frequently detects the desire to assert itself as a legitimate science, using scientific methods. Sometimes this results in an exaggerated effort to use an extremely abstract vocabulary, which in turn frightens away many students or even experts (from a practical viewpoint) of translation.

## THE QUESTION OF TRANSLATABILITY

Is translation possible at all? This question is as old as translation theory. From Schleiermacher to Walter Benjamin, philosophers and linguists have argued that language (i.e., the structure, vocabulary, and so on of our mother tongue) determines our view of the world. They have said that the process of thinking depends on the language in which we are thinking; that we think what we think because of the language we speak. Language is regarded here as a giant structural system that not only determines the native speaker's use of language, but also his intellect, his emotions, his whole consciousness. In the twentieth century, this school of thinking was largely influenced by the ethnolinguistic approach of Sapir and Whorf. Benjamin Whorf, basing his work on the ethnolinguistic studies of the father of ethnolinguistics, Edward Sapir, analyzed language structures and thinking patterns between European languages and languages of native Americans, in particular, that of the Hopis. He stated basic differences especially in the perception of time and space. (Whorf called his theory the "linguistic principle of relativity.")

The advocates of this philosophy, from Humboldt to Ortega y Gasset, argue that adequate truthful translation is impossible. They demand that the translator deny his or her own language and try to create a blueprint of the original, making the target language sound awkward while attempting to maintain the structure and syntax of the source language to convey the author's original style and intent. (What self-denial on the part of the translator!) In this concept, translation is but a pale substitute for reading the original, that is, learning the foreign language.

In literary translation, especially in poetry, there is some foundation for this rather sinister view of translation. Apart from the actual content or subject matter, which pose no problems for the translator, the rhythmic structure and the verbal effects ("music" of language; subtleties of style) of a poem, or even certain novels, are close to impossible to translate. The translation of a poem will always remain a paraphrase of the original, or, ideally, a work of art in its own right—but never an identical or equivalent reproduction of the original. In his charming and highly readable book,

Güttinger (1963, p. 37) gives the following example of the "most perfect of all translations":

CHRISTIAN MORGENSTERN

Fisches Nachtgesang                    Night Song of Fish

—                                       —
‿ ‿                                     ‿ ‿
— — —                                   — — —
‿ ‿ ‿ ‿                                 ‿ ‿ ‿ ‿
— — — —                                 — — — —
‿ ‿ ‿ ‿                                 ‿ ‿ ‿ ‿
— — — —                                 — — —
‿ ‿ ‿ ‿                                 ‿ ‿ ‿ ‿
— — —                                   — — —
‿ ‿ ‿ ‿                                 ‿ ‿ ‿ ‿
— — —                                   — — —
‿ ‿                                     ‿ ‿
—                                       —

The upshot of these reflections is that while literary texts are translatable from a purely linguistic point of view, many of them remain untranslatable from a literary or aesthetic viewpoint. Even though the translator can use various procedures to replace them by varying word connotations, he or she will often not be able to reproduce them completely, so many nuances will go untranslated and be lost.

In direct opposition to the approach that questions translatability on principle, one finds the conviction that translation is possible in all instances, a conviction historically rooted in the Age of Enlightenment (Descartes, Leibniz) and based on a mathematical and logical foundation. Every language is seen as a key to a "universal" language inherent in all human beings. In the twentieth century, Hjelmslev went so far as to define language by its translatability; he defined a "natural" language as a language that can serve as a target language. Roman Jakobson claimed that "all cognitive experience and its classification is conveyable in any other language" (Jakobson, 1959, p. 235). Noam Chomsky, in his generative transformational grammar, made the thesis of a deep structure common to all languages an integral part of modern linguistics:

> The deep structure that expresses the meaning is common to all languages, being a simple reflection of the forms of thought. The transformational rules that convert deep to surface structure may differ from language to language. The surface structure resulting from these transformations does not directly express the meaning relations of the words, of course, except in the simplest cases. It is the deep structure underlying the actual utterance, a structure that is purely mental, that conveys the semantic content of the sentence. This deep structure is, nevertheless, related to actual sentences in that each of its component abstract propositions . . . could be directly realized as a simple propositional judgment. (Chomsky, 1966, p. 35)

Nida (1964) pointed out that there are considerable resemblances in the basic structures of languages: All possess something akin to subject-verb and topic-comment constructions; all discern in some form between nouns and verbs. A certain inventory of semantic features is seen here as an inherent trait of all languages and of all people.

Between these two extremes—total untranslatability versus total translatability—it seems essential that a science of translation find a "middle of the road" solution; Koller (1979, p. 94) calls it "relative translatability." While admitting that untranslatability is a "fact of life"—especially so in literary translation—relative translatability holds that most translation problems can be solved by translation methods and procedures. It also maintains that human beings do share the same basic emotions and thoughts, no matter what their language. Translation is not seen as a process that is determined once and for all, but as a process that is subject to varying influences over time.

## INTERPRETATION

Interpretation, as opposed to written translation, is the oral transfer of a spoken text into another language. There are two basic methods of interpreting: simultaneous interpretation, which takes place via an interpreting booth and microphones/earphones; and consecutive interpretation, with the interpreter taking notes and then, after a few sentences or after an interval of up to ten or fifteen minutes, rendering the source language text in the target language.

Though some linguistic aspects overlap—a transfer between two languages is involved in both instances—the basic activity of the interpreter and his or her working conditions differ greatly from those of the translator. The translator has time to muse about the appropriate term to use; the interpreter has but an extremely brief moment (especially in simultaneous interpretation) to grasp the speaker's meaning—and to transform it into the target language. The decisive difference between translating and interpreting is the fact that the interpreter ignores all attempts at finding purely linguistic equivalents; he or she focuses solely on what meaning the speaker conveys, not on which words he chooses. Many people see the interpreter as a sort of walking dictionary on two feet; frequently, interpreters hear the question: "How do you say this in German, or English?" People asking this think of translating as a code-switching operation—one term in the source language is replaced by another in the target language. The interpreter will answer: "What is the context?" or "What exactly do you mean?" (Seleskovitch, 1974). The time pressure in interpreting is enormous, as the interpreter, thinking on his or her feet, is forced to keep up with the normal tempo of human speech; this is especially true in the case of (often unpracticed) speakers "rattling off" prepared speeches (on which the interpreter has never laid eyes) without meaningful intonation. On the other hand, the recipient of the interpreter's work is present and feedback is sometimes possible.

What makes a good interpreter? Being in perfect command of one or more foreign languages is a prerequisite for an interpreter and not necessarily a major object in his or her training. Most established interpreting institutes start from the assumption that the knowledge of foreign languages per se does not make a good interpreter; rather, it is an ability that used to be considered by some to be a unique talent, but that—on the basis of practical experience, and of interpreting theories—can also be taught, at least to a degree. Furthermore, the interpreter needs a solid all-around education and the ability of quickly absorbing and understanding information in highly technical and scientific fields for specific conferences. The latter requires an excellent short-term memory, which is also something that can be trained, and taught. Some of the best interpreting schools will only accept candidates with a university degree in a different field to ascertain that the student has a knowledge of how to acquire knowledge.

While consecutive interpretation has been around longer than written translation, simultaneous interpretation is largely a product of post-World War II technology. Today, conference technology is constantly being improved; certain technical standards are being developed and required for the size, ventilation procedures, and sound insulation of interpreting booths; infrared systems are beginning to replace the old wired microphones and earphones.

Young as simultaneous interpretation is, there have been efforts in the last decades to develop theories of interpretation, to systematize research in the field, and to make the results available for practical use, that is, for teaching interpretation. Actually, interpretation theories start from the very process of interpreting and with questions like "What is involved in the act of interpretation? What happens in the interpreter's mind?" Here are some of the possible answers.

The interpreter looks for the thought behind the word, finds it, and expresses it—the thought, not the word—in his or her own language. (Like the translator, the interpreter should only be working into his mother tongue, though this is not always implemented in practice.) Unlike the translator, he or she uses the spoken, not the written, word; unlike the translator, he or she cannot go back of his or her text but has one single moment to grasp its meaning.

A theory of interpretation must take into account the fact that, in most instances, interpretation transcends the linguistic aspects of the message conveyed; unlike translation theory, it can, therefore, not be concerned with (or, indeed, be part of) descriptive or comparative linguistics. What interpretation is concerned with are not the many possible meanings of

language described in grammars and dictionaries, but with the one meaning the speaker thinks of at a certain point in time, and the conveying of
that meaning: the theory of interpretation deals not with linguistics, but
with speech performance (Seleskovitch, 1974). Normally, the processes of
speech (expression of ideas) and understanding (comprehension of ideas)
are split between two persons; the interpreter uniquely combines both roles
in one person. Thus the interpreting process as such—even though there
are but a few thousand conference interpreters worldwide—might be of
universal interest as it could give us unexpected insight into aspects of the
relation between thought and language that are not obvious in ordinary
communication. For this reason, and also because of the significance of
theory for the didactic of interpretation, it will be interesting to follow the
further development of interpretation theory.

## NOTE

1. Güttinger (p. 74) names Boswell and Gertrude Stein as examples for using the phrase
from prophet Habakuk: "Write the vision and make it plain upon the table/That he may run
who readeth it."

## REFERENCES

Asante, M. K. (1987). *The Afrocentric idea*. Philadelphia: Temple University Press.
Bernal, M. (1987). *Black Athena*. New Brunswick, NJ: Rutgers University Press.
Chomsky, N. (1986). *Cartesian linguistics: A chapter in the history of rationalist thought*.
    New York/London: University Press of America.
Diller, H. J., & Kornelius, J. (1978). *Linguistische Probleme der Übersetzung*. Tübingen:
    Max Niemeyer Verlag.
Güttinger, F. (1963). *Zielsprache: Theorie und Technik des Übersetzens*. Zürich: Manesse
    Verlag.
Hockett, C. (1967). *A course in modern linguistics*. New York: Macmillan.
Jäger,. (1968). Elemente einer Theorie der bilingualen Translation. In. A. Neubert (Ed.),
    Grundfragen Übersetzungswissenschaft: Beihefte zur Zeitschrift Fremdsprachen. Leipzig:
    VEB Enzyklopädie Verlag.
Jakobson, R. (1959). On linguistic aspects of translation. Cambridge: MIT Press.
Jumpelt, R. (1961). *Die Übersetzung naturwisssenschaftlicher und technischer Literatur*.
    Berlin-Schöneberg: Langenscheidt.
Kade, O. (1968). Kommunikationswissenschaftliche Probleme der Translation. In A. Neubert
    (Ed.), *Grundfragen der Übersetzungswissenschaft: Beihefte zur Zeitschrift fremdspra-
    chen*. Leipzig: VEB Enzyklopädie Verlag.
Kapp, V. (1974). *Probleme von Theorie und Praxis in der Ausbildung zum Übersetzer und
    Dolmetscher*. Heidelberg: Quelle & Meyer.
Koller, W. (1972). *Grundprobleme der Übersetzungstheorie: Unter besonderer Berücksich-
    tigung schwedisch-deutscher Übersetzungsfalle*. Bern and München: Stockholmer Ger-
    manistische Forschungen.
Koller, W. (1979). *Einführung in die Übersetzungswissenschaft*. Heidelberg: Quelle &
    Meyer.
Leech, G. N. (1974). Semantics. Harmondsworth: Penguin.

Nida, E. (1964). *Toward a science of translation*. Leiden: E. J. Brill.

Nida, E. (1976). Translation as communication. In G. Nickel (Ed.), *Proceedings of the Fourth International Congress of Applied Linguistics* (Vol. 2). Stuttgart: Hochschulverlag.

Reiss, K. (1971). *Möglichkeit en und Grenzen der Übersetzungskritik*. München: Max Huber Verlag.

Seleskovitch, D. (1974). Zur Theorie des Dolmetschens. In V. Kapp (Ed.), *Probleme von Theorie und Praxis in der Ausbildung zum Übersetzer und Dolmetscher*. Heidelberg: Quelle & Meyer.

Willett, R. (1974). Die Ausbildung zum Konferenzdometscher. In V. Kapp (Ed.), *Probleme von Theorie und Praxis in der Ausbildung zum Ubersetzer und Dolmetscher*. Heidelberg: Quelle & Meyer.

Wilss, W. (1977). *Übersetzungswissenschaft: Probleme und Methoden*. Stuttgart: Ernst Klett Verlag.

# Author Index

502

# Subject Index

# About the Authors

PETER A. ANDERSEN received his Ph.D. in Communication in 1975 from Florida State University and is currently Professor at San Diego State University. His specializations are in interpersonal communication, communication theory, and nonverbal communication. His articles have appeared in *Human Communication Research, Communication Monographs, Communication Quarterly, Western Journal of Speech Communication, Progress in Communication Sciences, Management Communication Quarterly,* and *Journal of Nonverbal Behavior,* among others.

MOLEFI KETE ASANTE is Professor and Chair, Department of African American Studies, Temple University. The first president of SIETAR, he has been active in research on and teaching intercultural communication throughout the world. His latest book, *The Afrocentric Idea,* introduces a new theoretical approach to culture.

NJOKU E. AWA is Professor of Communication at Cornell University. He has been an active participant in international organizations and has been Chairman of the Intercultural and Development Communication Division of the International Communication Association and Treasurer of the Society for Intercultural Education, Training and Research. He has contributed ten chapters to edited books, published numerous articles in professional and technical journals, and edited two proceedings on agricultural development in Africa and development communication in the Third World. He is now completing a book tentatively titled "Communication, Culture, and Bureaucracy in African Development."

RICHARD W. BRISLIN is Research Associate at the Institute of Culture and Communication, East-West Center, in Honolulu, Hawaii. He attended the Pennsylvania State University and received a Ph.D. in psychology in 1969. He coedited a volume of the *Handbook of Cross-Cultural Psychology* (Harry Triandis, senior editor). His other books include *Cross-Cultural Research Methods* (with W. Lonner and R. Thorndike); *Cross-Cultural Orientation Programs* (with P. Pedersen); *Cross-Cultural Encounters: Face to Face Interaction*; the three-volume *Handbook of*

513

*Intercultural Training* (coedited with D. Landis); and *Intercultural Interactions: A Practical Guide*.

ALICE DAVIS is Cooperative Education Coordinator at the University of Tennessee at Chattanooga. She hold an M.A. in Communication from State University of New York at Buffalo and has done research and testing in intercultural communication at SUNY and the University of Tennessee. Her interests are intergroup and intragroup relations.

GLEN FISHER, a sociologist-anthropologist and former U.S. Foreign Service Officer, is currently Professor-Diplomat at the Monterey Institute of International Studies. He has taught at Georgetown University School of Foreign Service and the State Department's Foreign Service Institute (where in his last assignment he was Dean of the Center for Area Studies). His most current book is *Mindsets: The Role of Culture and Perception in International Relations*. Previous books include *Public Diplomacy and the Behavioral Sciences, American Communication in a Global Society*, and *International Negotiation: A Cross-Cultural Perspective*.

ARLENE FRANKLYN-STOKES is currently a postgraduate student, investigating children who are suspended from school, at the Department of Psychology, University of Bristol, England. She is also involved in collaborative studies with Howard Giles, Miles Hewstone, and William B. Gudykunst on various aspects of intercultural and intergroup communication. Her research interests include disruptive behavior in secondary school children, school differences and school effectiveness research, and intercultural, intergenerational, and intergroup communication.

OSCAR H. GANDY, Jr., is Associate Professor of Communication at the Annenberg School of the University of Pennsylvania. He came to Pennsylvania from a position as director of the Center for Communication Research at Howard University. He is the author of *Beyond Agenda Setting: Information Subsidies and Public Policy* (1982), and numerous articles, chapters, and reviews covering a range of topics in mass communication. His recent work focuses on the political economy of information, with a special emphasis on questions of privacy and personal control over information. His doctorate in Public Affairs Communication was awarded by Stanford University in 1976.

HOWARD GILES is currently Professor of Social Psychology and Director of the Center for the Study of Communication and Social Relations at the University of Bristol, England. He is founding editor of the *Journal of Language and Social Psychology*, coeditor of the (forthcoming) *Journal of Pacific Rim Communication*, and general editor of a number of book series including *Intercommunication* and *Monographs in the Social Psychology of Language*. His research interests include ethnic language attitudes, interethnic language strategies, second-language acquisition, miscommunication, and cultural aspects of intergenerational communication as they relate to health.

CHRISTIANE F. GONZALEZ is a graduate of Heidelberg University (Institute for Translating and Interpreting, 1972). She has worked as a freelance interpreter and translator in Germany and Texas. She is currently a mother, rancher, wife, tourist guide, high school German teacher, translator, and interpreter.

WILLIAM B. GUDYKUNST is Professor of Communication at Arizona State University. His research focuses on explaining uncertainty reduction processes across cultures and between members of different groups. His most recent books include *Intergroup Communication* (Edward Arnold) and *Cross-Cultural Adaptation* (coedited with Y. Y. Kim for Sage). He recently completed *Culture and Interpersonal Communication* (with S. Ting-Toomey and E. Chua for Sage) and *Theory in Intercultural Communication* (coedited with Y. Y. Kim for Sage) and currently is working on *Strangeness and Similarity: A Theory of Interpersonal and Intergroup Communication* (with Gao Ge for Multilingual Matters).

LAUREN I. GUMBS is a master's student in Communication at Arizona State University. Her research interests focus on Black-White communication using a social cognitive perspective.

BRADFORD J. HALL is currently working on his Ph.D. at the University of Washington in the Department of Speech Communication. He is interested in the relationship between culture, norms, and communicative conduct; the process of explanation; and organizational communication.

MITCHELL R. HAMMER is a faculty member in the School of International Service at American University. His research interests include intercultural communication effectiveness, and cross-cultural training. His work has appeared in *Human Communication Research, International Journal of Intercultural Relations, Journal of Black Studies*, and *Communication Yearbook*, among others.

MICHAEL L. HECHT received his Ph.D. in Speech Communication from the University of Illinois and is currently Associate Professor of Communication and Director of the Communication Research Consortium at Arizona State University. His research interests include the study of interethnic communication, nonverbal communication, and communication and love. He recently edited a book on nonverbal communication and is beginning a book on Black-White communication patterns. His articles have appeared in a variety of journals, including the *Journal of Social and Personal Relationships, Human Communication Research, Language and Social Psychology*, and *Personality and Social Psychology Bulletin.*

J. DAVID JOHNSON (Ph.D., Michigan State University, 1978) is currently Associate Professor at Michigan State University. His publications have appeared in such journals as *International Journal of Intercultural Relations, Communication Yearbook, Human Communication Research, Communication Monographs, Communications, Journalism Quarterly*, and the *Journal of Social Psychology*. His major research interests focus on organizational communication structures and international communication.

YOUNG YUN KIM (Ph.D., Northwestern) is Professor of Communication at Governors State University (University Park, IL). She has written *Communicating with Strangers* (with W. Gudykunst, Random House, 1984) and *Communication and Cross-Cultural Adaptation: An Integrative Theory* (Multilingual Matters, 1988). Among her edited books are *Interethnic Communication* (Sage, 1985), *Cross-Cultural Adaptation: Current Approaches* (with W. Gudykunst, Sage, 1987), and *Theories in Intercultural Communication* (with W. Gudykunst, Sage, 1988). Her current research interests include intercultural communication competence and interethnic conflict management and relationship building.

WOLFGANG KLEINWÄCHTER is Professor of International Relations at the Institute for International Studies, Karl Marx University, Leipzig (German Democratic Republic). He is Chairman of the Intersectoral Study Group of the Communication Section of the GDR UNESCO Commission, a member of the Commission for Studies, and a member of the Advisory Board of Transnational Data and Communication Report.

FELIPE KORZENNY is Professor of Communication and Coordinator of Graduate Studies at the Department of Speech and Communication Studies, San Francisco State University. He was born in Mexico City and has worked in multiple Latin American countries on development projects dealing with health, nutrition, agriculture, and education. He is coeditor of Volumes 13 through 16 of the *International and Intercultural Communication Annual* of the Speech Communication Association. He has served as Chairperson of the Intercultural and Development Communication Division of the International Communication Association. His recent work includes a book on Mexican Americans and the mass media, and articles and research projects on communication discrimination, communication and drug usage across cultures, effects of international news, ethnicity as a factor in communicating with strangers, and AIDS communication.

PAULA W. MATABANE is graduate Associate Professor in the Department of Radio, TV and Film, School of Communications, Howard University, where she also serves as Television Production Sequence coordinator. Her research interests center on what audiences learn from television, the relationship between subcultural experience and television viewing, and representations of health-related content in the mass media. She has made recent contributions to the *Journal of Communication, Journal of Black Studies, Communication Research*, and *Television and Its Audience: International Perspectives* (British Film Institute, in press).

DAVID MATSUMOTO received his Ph.D. from the University of California, Berkeley, in Clinical Psychology. He is currently Assistant Professor at the Wright Institute, and Visiting Assistant Professor at the University of California, Berkeley. His main research interests include cross-cultural similarities and differences in emotional expression and perception, and the relationship between emotional expression, perception, and experience.

THOMAS L. McPHAIL is Director of the Graduate Program in Communication Studies at the University of Calgary. He is a graduate of McMaster University and holds a Ph.D. in Communication from Purdue University. He is the author of *Electronic Colonialism: The Future of Broadcasting, Telecom 2000*, and he has also coedited *Communication in the 80s* (with Seymour Hamilton) and *Canadian Developments in Telecommunications: An Overview of Significant Contributions* (with David Coll).

TSUKASA NISHIDA is Associate Professor of International Relations at Nihon University in Mishima, Japan. His research interests focus on Japanese-North American communication. He has published research in *Human Communication Research, Communication Monographs, International Journal of Intercultural Relations*, and *Communication Yearbook*, among others.

KAARLE NORDENSTRENG is Professor of Communication at the University of Tampere. His recent work focuses on New International Information and Communication Order.

DORTHY L. PENNINGTON is Associate Professor of Communication Studies and of African and African-American Studies at the University of Kansas. She teaches and publishes in the areas of intercultural communication, rhetoric, and women's studies. Her basic research interest is that of the epistemology of culture. She has contributed editorial service to various journals, including *Communication Education* and the *Journal of Black Studies*. She is a consultant to and educational evaluator for the Department of Defense Equal Opportunity Management Institute in the areas of interracial communication and culture.

SIDNEY A. RIBEAU received his Ph.D. in Speech Communication from the University of Illinois and is currently Dean of Undergraduate Studies at California State University, San Bernardino. His research interests include interracial communication, intercultural communication, and the rhetoric of representative Black spokespersons. His articles appear in the *International Journal of Intercultural Relations, Journal of Black Studies*, and *Journal of Language and Social Psychology.*

EVERETT M. ROGERS has been involved in research and teaching on development communication over the past 25 years in Colombia, India, Nigeria, Brazil, Indonesia, and Korea. Currently, he is investigating the effects of educational soap operas in India and in Spanish-speaking nations, and, with James Dearing, technology transfer in Japan. He is a Walter H. Annenberg Professor, Annenberg School of Communication, at the University of Southern California. He is author of *Diffusion of Innovations* (1983, Free Press) and (with Arvind Singhal) *India's Information Revolution* (in press, Sage).

KLAUS R. SCHERER has been Professor of Psychology at the University of Giessen since 1973. In addition, since 1985 he has been Professor of Psychology of Emotion at the University of Geneva, Switzerland. His major research interests include the psychology of emotion, nonverbal and vocal communication, and applications of the psychology of communication.

KAREN L. SCHMIDT is a doctoral student in the Interdisciplinary Ph.D. program in Communication at Arizona State University. Her research interests include cross-cultural communication, family communication, and the negotiation of developing interpersonal relationships. She has presented papers at the International Communication Association and the Speech Communication Association and published an article in the *Journal of Language and Society*.

ROBERT SHUTER is Chairperson of the Department of Communication and Rhetorical Studies at Marquette University and Director of the Center for Intercultural Communication. He has written three books and over forty academic articles that have appeared in the *Journal of Social Psychology, Journal of Communication, Communication Monographs, Journal of Applied Behavioral Science*, and many others.

STELLA TING-TOOMEY is Associate Professor of Communication at Arizona State University. Her research focuses on cross-cultural conflict styles and face-negotiation in interpersonal relationships. Her most recent books include *Culture and Interpersonal Communication* (with W. Gudykunst and E. Chua) and *Communication, Culture, and Organization Processes* (coedited with W. Gudykunst and L. Stewart). Her publications have appeared in *American Behavioral Scientist, Communication Monographs, Human Communication Research*, and the *International Journal of Intercultural Relations*, among others.

FRANK TUTTLE's research focuses on communication and sociocultural change, the role of the media in national development, bilingualism in multicultural environments, and methods to determine the accuracy of translation.

HARALD G. WALLBOTT is currently Assistant Professor of Social Psychology at the University of Giessen, West Germany. His major research interests include nonverbal communication, person perception, psychology of emotion, and media psychology.

GABRIEL WEIMANN (Ph.D., Hebrew University of Jerusalem, 1980) is the Chairman of the Department of Sociology at Haifa University, Israel. His research interests are media effects, network analysis, and, recently, terrorism and the mass media. His publications include the book *Hate on Trial* and he is now completing a book (*The Theater of Terror*) on modern terrorism and the media.

PETER YAPLE received his M.A. at the Annenberg School of Communication, University of Pennsylvania. Under the diverse mentorships of George Gerbner and R. L. Birdwhistell, he completed a thesis on the role of the VCR in the local South Eastern Asian Communities—the role of communication technology in acculturation/assimilation. Currently, he is pursuing a Ph.D. in communication at the University of California, San Diego. As a student of Michael Cole, his focus is the incorporation into intercultural communication theory of a convergence of Soviet socio-historicism in the tradition of L. S. Bygotsky with American interactionism based on the work of G. H. Mead.